SAT® PREP PLUS

UNLOCKED EDITION
2022

Get cracking.

Copyright 2019-2021 by Egghead Prep.

Published by Kelley Creative, Rowlett, Texas USA. All rights reserved. No portion of this publication may be reproduced in any form without the consent of the publisher. Write to permissions@kelleycreative.design. SAT® is a registered trademark of the College Board, which was not involved in the production of, and does not endorse this book.

SAT® PREP PLUS: UNLOCKED EDITION 2022

Print ISBN 978-1-7331088-5-0
Ebook ISBN 978-1-7331088-3-6

Table of CONTENTS

Preparing for the SAT Reading Test   7

- *Strategy and Test Content: It's All About Evidence!*   8
- *Vocabulary*   8
- *Evidence-Based Conclusions About Main Ideas*   10
- *Questions About Ideas Implied in the Passage*   13

Preparing for the SAT Writing Test   15

- *The SAT Writing Section: Strategy and Content*   16
- *The Logic of Writing, Part One: Word Choices*   16
- *The Logic of Writing, Part Two: Sentence Order, Paragraph Organization*   18
- *Conventions of Standard Written English*   20
- *Conventions Governing Punctuation, Part One: Comma Use*   21
- *Conventions Governing Punctuation, Part Two: Use of Semicolons and Colons*   22
- *Parallel Structure: The Art of Making Lists Readable*   23
- *Conventions Governing the Use of Their/They're/There*   24
- *Conventions Governing the Use of It's/Its*   25
- *Final Thoughts on the SAT Writing Test*   26

Preparing for the SAT Essay Test   27

- *What is the SAT Essay Test?*   28
- *Should I Take the Essay Test?*   28
- *What Kind of Essay Will I Have to Write for the Test?*   29
- *Scoring Categories for the Essay Section*   29
- *Reading*   29
- *Analysis*   30
- *Writing*   30
- *A Brief Example*   31

Preparing for the SAT Math NC Test (No Calculator)   33

- *Computations: What to Expect, What NOT to Expect*   34
- *Algebra and Advanced Algebra*   36
- *Geometry*   37
- *Percents*   38
- *Trigonometry*   38

- *Statistics 39*
- *Probability 39*

Preparing for the SAT Math C Test (Calculator) — 41

- *General Overview of the Math C Section: Strategy & Topics 42*
- *SAT Math C Test Topics, in Detail 43*
- *Statistics 44*
- *Probability 44*

SAT Practice Tests — 47

SAMPLE TEST 1 — 49

- *Section 1: Reading Test 50*
- *Answers, Section 1 67*
- *Section 2: Writing & Language Test 68*
- *Answers, Section 2 83*
- *Section 3: Math Test 84*
- *Answers, Section 3 90*
- *Section 4: Math Test 91*
- *Answers, Section 4 103*
- *Answer Explanations 104*
- *Scoring Conversion 134*

SAMPLE TEST 2 — 137

- *Section 1: Reading Test 138*
- *Answers, Section 1 154*
- *Section 2: Writing & Language Test 155*
- *Answers, Section 2 171*
- *Section 3: Math Test 172*
- *Answers, Section 3 178*
- *Section 4: Math Test 179*
- *Answers, Section 4 191*
- *Answer Explanations 192*
- *Scoring Conversion 223*

SAMPLE TEST 3 — 227

- *Section 1: Reading Test 228*
- *Answers, Section 1 245*
- *Section 2: Writing & Language Test 246*
- *Answers, Section 2 263*
- *Section 3: Math Test 264*
- *Answers, Section 3 270*
- *Section 4: Math Test 271*
- *Answers, Section 4 283*
- *Answer Explanations 284*
- *Scoring Conversion 318*

SAMPLE TEST 4 — 321

- *Section 1: Reading Test 322*
- *Answers, Section 1 340*
- *Section 2: Writing & Language Test 341*
- *Answers, Section 2 357*
- *Section 3: Math Test 358*
- *Answers, Section 3 364*
- *Section 4: Math Test 365*
- *Answers, Section 4 377*
- *Answer Explanations 378*
- *Scoring Conversion 409*

SAMPLE TEST 5 — 413

- *Section 1: Reading Test 414*
- *Answers, Section 1 431*
- *Section 2: Writing & Language Test 432*
- *Answers, Section 2 447*
- *Section 3: Math Test 448*
- *Answers, Section 3 454*
- *Section 4: Math Test 455*

- *Answers, Section 4   466*
- *Answer Explanations   467*
- *Scoring Conversion   501*

Preparing for Your Road to College   505

- *Your Road to College: We'll Help You Map It Out!   505*
- *Welcome to Our Guidance Center for College-Bound Students.   506*
- *What You'll Find Here: Answers, Information, and an Express Lane to the Experts   506*
- *Guide to Our Resource Pages   507*

Resources for the College-Bound Student   509

- *Start at the Guidance Office ... and Possibly Leave Quickly   510*
- *Nearby Colleges and Universities   511*
- *Reliable News Sources for Information   511*
- *Key Resources for First-Generation College Students   511*
- *Financial Aid Resources   512*

Preparing for College: Which Courses Should I Take?   513

- *The Basics: Which Courses Will College Admissions Officers Expect to See on a High School Transcript?   514*
- *Humanities Classes for the College-Bound Student   514*
- *Mathematics Classes for the College-Bound Student   515*
- *Science Classes for the College-Bound Student   515*
- *Seek Additional Advice on Course Selections   515*
- *To STEM or Not to STEM, Or Is That Even the Question?   516*
- *What If I Cannot Complete All the Recommended Courses?   516*

College Admissions Expectations: What Do They Want from Me?   519

- *Tiers and Rankings: What They Mean and What They Don't   520*
- *Some General Notes on Admissions Expectations Based on Tier   520*
- *Tier One: What It Means to Be Elite   521*
- *Tier Two: Schools That Seek Exceptional Students Who May Not Fit the Tier One Mold   521*
- *Tier Three: Good Colleges, Good Students   522*
- *Specific Information for Your Top Choice Schools   522*
- *So, It's All About Test Scores, Right?   522*
- *Teacher Recommendations   523*
- *For Further Reading   523*

Financial Assistance for the College-Bound Student: It Costs HOW Much?!   525

- *If You Are Qualified to Go, You Deserve to Have a Way Get There!   526*
- *Getting the Ball Rolling: What FAFSA Is and Why It's Important   526*
- *Public (Government) Resources Available   527*
- *Resources Available from Private Sources   528*
- *Is It Safe to Accept Loans as Financial Aid?   528*

Preparing for the Gap Year   531

- *What is a "Gap" Year and is it Right for Me?   532*
- *That Sounds Like Me!   532*

- *Advanced Study: The Academic Gap Year* 532
- *Travel and Study Abroad: Bridging the "Gaps" of Culture and Learning* 533
- *Internships and Volunteer Work: Hands-On Gap Years* 533
- *Design It Yourself: A Gap Year of Your Own Making* 534
- *Your Well-Being Matters: Emotional Health Gap Years* 534
- *If I Am Considering a Gap Year, Should I Even Apply to Colleges During My Senior Year of High School?* 535

Preparing for the SAT® Reading Test

Including...

- ▶ *Strategy and Test Content: It's All About Evidence!*
- ▶ *Vocabulary*
- ▶ *Evidence-Based Conclusions About Main Ideas*
- ▶ *Questions About Ideas Implied in the Passage*

Strategy and Test Content: It's All About Evidence!

The full name of the Reading section on the current SAT is the Evidence-Based Reading Test. The vast majority of test questions in the Reading section are intended to evaluate your ability to (a) identify and understand the main ideas presented in a reading passage, and (b) locate within the passage specific statements that articulate those main ideas and/or provide supporting evidence for them.

In addition to the principal questions regarding main themes and supporting evidence, Reading section test questions will also include vocabulary questions and questions about ideas that are implied by the passage but not explicitly stated.

All reading passages will be presented with line numbers in the margins. The line numbers will help you find statements referred to in the questions.

Here is an in-depth look at each type of question to be found in the SAT Reading section.

 ## *Vocabulary*

Vocabulary questions come in two main types.

Vocabulary, type one: "Big words"

These questions test your knowledge of the meanings of words generally associated with a high level of reading and writing proficiency. There are generally only one to three questions of this type among the 52 questions on the Reading Test.

EXAMPLE 1: The passage contains the sentence,

> Mr. Adams castigated young Allen for the boy's actions.

The corresponding test question might read,

> As used in line 1, "castigated" is most similar in meaning to
>
> A) catapulted.
>
> B) congratulated.
>
> C) instigated.
>
> D) reprimanded.

The sentence doesn't provide any obvious clues as to the meaning of "castigated." The word could have either positive or negative connotations and the sentence would still be logical. But even if you had no familiarity with the word "castigated," you would certainly be able to rule out answer (A) if you knew the meaning of "catapulted" (rapidly ascended, as if fired from a catapult). You might also be able to rule out answer (C); since one generally instigates events or actions, not people, the phrase, "Mr. Adams instigated young Allen" would not make sense. To be certain of the correct answer, however, you would need to have prior knowledge that to castigate means to scold vehemently, and that "reprimand" is a synonym for "scold." Therefore, **the correct answer is (D).**

Notice that in the example above, there are answer choices that look and/or sound like the word "castigated" but are incorrect. Sometimes, the correct answer actually does look and sound a lot like the word given in the question. Thus, you should not assume either that lookalike and/or soundalike words are always correct or that they are always decoys. Treat such answer choices as neither more nor less likely to be correct than others.

The best way to prepare for these questions is simply to do a great deal of reading, always pausing to look up the meaning of words with which you are not familiar.

Vocabulary, type two: Common words with contextual clues

Many of the vocabulary-related question on the SAT Reading section deal with familiar, "everyday" words that can have many different meanings. Sometimes, the word will be used in an unconventional manner. In every case, however, the key is to look at the context in which the word appears to determine its meaning.

EXAMPLE 2: The passage contains the sentence,

> Vanessa's future as a member of the production cast rides entirely on whether she successfully memorizes her lines over the next 48 hours.

The corresponding test question might read,

As used in line 1, "rides" is most similar in meaning to

A) sits atop.

B) depends.

C) is carried along as a passenger.

D) teases.

All four answer choices are accepted meanings of the word "rides." However, in the context of the sentence above, only "depends" is a logical substitute for "rides." Notice, then, that answering this question correctly rides on examining the evidence presented by the context of the sentence, not on having memorized a definition. For the SAT Reading section, it is always the evidence clearly apparent in the passage that matters most!

 ### *Evidence-Based Conclusions About Main Ideas*

Main ideas can come in several different forms. In the case of an excerpt from a work of fiction (short story or novel), the main ideas will usually be the central themes (for example, the ways a significant event alters the lives of the characters) and the defining attributes of the characters. The main ideas of an essay or article are generally the conclusions that the author wishes to persuade the reader to accept. In an article reporting on a scientific hypothesis or discovery, the main ideas will typically include descriptions of experimental procedures employed and the conclusions suggested by the data.

You may or may not agree with the main ideas of the passage. You are of course fully entitled to your opinion, but remember that you are being tested on your understanding of the author's ideas, not your own. When asked to locate evidence in support of a main idea, search for statements that support the author's claims or demonstrate your understanding of important themes. DO NOT select answers representing conclusions that you feel are more appropriate than the author's, and DO NOT choose answers that do not highlight clear and explicit evidence supporting the theme or idea in question.

EXAMPLE 3: Suppose the passage contains the following paragraphs.

> A firestorm is brewing over the loss of valuable beachfront property in several Caribbean countries due to rising sea levels. As the affected countries struggle to recover from the losses, officials are far quicker to lay blame than to take meaningful action. Many have zeroed in on the Panama Canal expansion project as the target of their wrath. They claim that the dredging being done to widen the channel has led to the dumping of millions of tons of silt into the Caribbean, causing sea levels to jump by a meter or more. Others direct their anger toward the US, China, Russia, and other large, industrial nations, noting that carbon dioxide emissions have triggered a global warming trend, resulting in melting glaciers and rising sea levels worldwide.
>
> Hydrogeologists, however, have brought forth the disappointing news that the primary culprit is planet Earth itself. Many Caribbean islands lie along a subduction zone—an area where one tectonic plate is gradually sliding underneath another plate with which it has collided. Crustal uplift frequently occurs in subduction zones. In short, in the Caribbean, it is actually the sea floor itself that is rising due to geological forces. The water is just coming along for the ride.

Preparing for the SAT Reading Test

A question accompanying the passage reads,

> To which of the following causes does the author attribute the rise in sea level affecting multiple Caribbean nations?
>
> A) Ocean expansion due to higher levels of carbon dioxide in seawater
>
> B) Glacial melting caused by global warming
>
> C) Tectonic plate subduction, resulting in an uplift of the Earth's crust
>
> D) The expansion of the Panama Canal

Let's examine each answer in detail.

We should immediately recognize that the cause proposed in answer (A), ocean expansion caused by carbon dioxide, is not mentioned anywhere in the passage. **Therefore, even if ocean expansion caused by carbon dioxide were the accepted scientific explanation for rising sea levels in the Caribbean, answer (A) would be INCORRECT,** because it does not correspond to statements made and evidence presented in the passage.

As for answer (B), you are likely aware that there is a very strong scientific consensus that a rise in global temperatures caused by carbon dioxide emissions is occurring, and that the melting of glaciers, with resulting rises in worldwide sea levels, is an observed effect of that rise in temperatures. Furthermore, these phenomena are explicitly mentioned in the passage (lines 7-10). However, in the second paragraph (lines 11-17), the author clearly asserts a belief that the primary cause of the rapid rise in sea levels in the Caribbean is NOT one of the causes discussed in lines 1-10. **Therefore, even though there is a scientific basis for agreeing with the conclusion presented in answer (B), and even though that conclusion is specifically mentioned in the passage, answer (B) would be INCORRECT,** because other evidence in the passage points more strongly to a different conclusion.

The project described in answer (D), the Panama Canal expansion, is also mentioned in the passage, but rejected in the second paragraph (lines 11-17) as an explanation for the rising sea levels in the Caribbean. Once again, you may be aware that there is indeed a Panama Canal expansion project currently underway, and that some experts fear the project will have unintended environmental impacts. Nevertheless, for the same reasons given in the preceding paragraph for answer (B), **answer (D) is incorrect.**

The author explicitly discusses the phenomenon described in answer (C), tectonic plate subduction, in the second paragraph (lines 11-17). Most importantly, lines 15-17 ("In short … ride.") provide an important clue showing that the author accepts this conclusion above all others. Notice that in discussing the possible causes proposed in answers (B) and (D), the author makes clear that he or she is describing opinions expressed by others ("Many have zeroed in…" and "Others direct their wrath…"). But in identifying tectonic plate subduction as the cause of Caribbean sea level

egghedprep.com

rise, the author presents the idea as fact, without attributing the conclusion to someone else. We therefore know that the author believes that the cause proposed in answer (C) is, in fact, the primary cause. Therefore, because it is consistent with a view the author clearly expresses, **answer (C) is CORRECT.**

The author explicitly discusses the phenomenon described in answer (C), tectonic plate subduction, in the second paragraph (lines 11-17). Most importantly, lines 15-17 ("In short ... ride.") provide an important clue showing that the author accepts this conclusion above all others. Notice that in discussing the possible causes proposed in answers (B) and (D), the author makes clear that he or she is describing opinions expressed by others ("Many have zeroed in..." and "Others direct their wrath..."). But in identifying tectonic plate subduction as the cause of Caribbean sea level rise, the author presents the idea as fact, without attributing the conclusion to someone else. We therefore know that the author believes that the cause proposed in answer (C) is, in fact, the primary cause. **Therefore, because it is consistent with a view the author clearly expresses, answer (C) is CORRECT.**

(NOTE: The actual scientific consensus regarding rising sea levels in the Caribbean is, in fact, that crustal uplift is the primary cause, with worldwide sea level rise due to global warming acting as a secondary cause. But again, that information is irrelevant to correctly answering the question!)

The next test question would likely read,

> Which answer choice provides the best evidence in support of the correct answer to the previous question?
>
> A) Lines 2-4 ("As the ... action.")
>
> B) Lines 4-7 ("Many ... more.")
>
> C) Lines 7-10 ("Others ... worldwide.")
>
> D) Lines 14-17 ("Crustal ... ride.")

Obviously, it would be very difficult to answer this question correctly if you answered the previous question incorrectly. There is no getting around that issue; it is one of the challenges posed by the Reading section. Notice, however, that no matter how you answered the previous question, you should still be able to rule out answer (A) here, because the quoted sentence from the passage does not propose any cause at all for rising sea levels in the Caribbean.

Based on the above analysis of the previous question and its answer choices, it is clear **that the correct answer here is (D),** since it refers to the lines in the passage where the author makes his or her case for tectonic plate movement as the primary cause of Caribbean sea level rise. The purpose of questions like this one, then, is to make sure your previous answer was based on evidence explicitly presented in the passage, not on personal opinion or outside knowledge that you carried into the test with you.

Preparing for the SAT Reading Test

 ## *Questions About Ideas Implied in the Passage*

These questions, like "big word" vocabulary questions, make up a small minority of the questions on the SAT Reading Test. They principally occur when the passage is an excerpt from a personal recollection, short story, or novel. For many students, these will be the most challenging questions on the Reading section of the SAT. It is necessary to not only identify evidence in the passage but also deduce what the author believes or intends, even though that belief or intention is never plainly stated. The primary rule to follow in these instances is, **stay as close to the content of the passage as possible.** Do not go drifting off on flights of the imagination that aren't supported by the author's words.

EXAMPLE 4: Suppose the passage contains the following paragraphs.

> Caroline understood that the next decision she made would have far-reaching consequences, not just for her, but for everyone she cared about as well. Yes, she could leave the only town she had ever called home and join her aunt and uncle in California to pursue her acting dreams, but how could she leave her younger brother's side at a time when bullies were tormenting him at every opportunity? She could instead accept the offer to attend business school in Paramount City, just 230 miles away, and thus be assured of a financially secure future, but did she really value security more than artistic achievement? Or, she could stay here and attend the local college, continuing to be a protector for her brother, a community leader that younger girls embraced as a mentor, and a rock of support for her financially struggling mother and father. But what then would become of her own dreams?
>
> As she continued wandering aimlessly in the woods, Caroline saw in the distance a half- fallen tree, precariously balanced on the limbs of three other trees. The slightest disturbance of the ground or air would have sent it crashing to the ground, destroying dozens of promising young seedlings and beautifully aging ferns in its path.

A question accompanying the passage reads,

> Which of the following symbolic interpretations of the half-fallen tree mentioned in line 14 is most reasonable?
>
> A) The half-fallen tree represents the fragility of Caroline's situation and the negative impacts she fears if she makes the wrong decision.
>
> B) The half-fallen tree symbolizes the destructive impacts of human activity on natural environments.

eggheadprep.com

C) The vulnerability of the half-fallen tree to a disturbance of the ground represents Caroline's fears about earthquake activity in California.

D) The fact that the half-fallen tree is balanced upon three other trees symbolizes Caroline's dependence on her mother, father, and brother for support.

There is no doubt that many human activities have destructive environmental impacts. Many authors employ symbolic devices to portray such impacts. However, this passage makes no mention of the environmental impacts of human activity at all. **Answer (B) is therefore far-fetched and incorrect.**

Regarding answer (C), the passage does mention the possibility of Caroline moving to California, but no indication is given that she has any concerns about earthquakes. **Answer (C) is therefore also far- fetched and incorrect.**

Answer (D) is the trickiest answer choice to evaluate. It is very clear from lines 4-6 and 9-11 of the passage that Caroline cares deeply for her younger brother and parents, but those lines also describe her family's dependence on her, not the other way around. That is why **answer (D), even though it is closely related to ideas put forth in the passage, is unreasonable and incorrect.**

Now look back at answer (A). Clearly, this answer must be correct, since we've ruled out the other choices. To see why the interpretation proposed in answer (A) is indeed very reasonable, consider the following:

1. The tree is balancing on three other trees, much as Caroline's future is "hanging in the balance" as she chooses between three possible paths.

2. If the wrong circumstance occurs, the tree will fall, with major consequences, just as Caroline fears the consequences of making the wrong choice.

3. Caroline specifically notices that young seedlings and aging plants will be harmed if the delicate balance is disturbed. We know from the first paragraph of the passage that she most fears the impact of her decision on those younger than her—her brother (lines 5 and 10) and young girls (line 10)—and on her parents (line 11), who are of course significantly older than she is.

For all of these reasons, **(A) is the correct answer.**

The best ways to prepare for these Reading section SAT test questions, and for many similar questions you will encounter in college courses, are to participate actively in all classroom discussions of books, to put your best effort into every literary criticism paper you are required to write for English and literature courses, and to regularly discuss books you're enjoying with your friends and family. Challenge each other to uncover the hidden meanings behind favorite passages.

Preparing for the SAT® Writing Test

Including...

- *The SAT Writing Section: Strategy and Content*
- *The Logic of Writing, Part One: Word Choices*
- *The Logic of Writing, Part Two: Sentence Order, Paragraph Organization*
- *Conventions of Standard Written English*
- *Conventions Governing Punctuation, Part One: Comma Use*
- *Conventions Governing Punctuation, Part Two: Use of Semicolons and Colons*
- *Parallel Structure: The Art of Making Lists Readable*
- *Conventions Governing the Use of Their/They're/There*
- *Conventions Governing the Use of It's/Its*
- *Final Thoughts on the SAT Writing Test*

The SAT Writing Section: Strategy and Content

The Writing section of the SAT is intended to test your understanding of the logic of effective writing and your knowledge of standard written English. The focus of the test is not on ways to make a piece of writing suspenseful or exciting, but rather, on the techniques that ensure clear, efficient communication of ideas. At that, some of the correct answers may strike you as a bit stiff, even boring. The idea behind the test is that if everyone understands how to state ideas clearly, then all writers will have more freedom to develop their own distinctive styles, just as a great musician uses the same scales as a young piano student but sounds like no one else on Earth.

The test will consist of four reading passages, each accompanied by 11 questions. Most of the questions will refer to words or phrases in the passage that are underlined and marked with a number. There will also be 2-3 questions for each passage that deal with the logic and structure of entire paragraphs or even of the passage as a whole.

We will look at many of the common types of questions on the SAT Writing section in detail below.

The Logic of Writing, Part One: Word Choices

A number of questions on the SAT Writing section are intended to test your ability to choose an appropriate word or phrase at a specified point in the passage.

EXAMPLE 1: Suppose a passage contains the following pair of sentences.

> Scientists have known since the early twentieth century that Earth's magnetic field has reversed directions multiple times during the planet's history. **(5)** <u>For example</u>, many people are unaware of this fact.

Question 5 for the passage reads,

5.

    A) NO CHANGE

    B) Consequently

    C) Likewise

    D) Nevertheless

The words "for example" should only be used to introduce a specific instance that illustrates an idea presented, or justifies a conclusion drawn, in the previous sentence(s). In Example 1 above, it would only be appropriate to begin the second sentence with "For example" if that sentence actually detailed a specific case of reversal of Earth's magnetic field. Since the sentence does not do so, a change of wording is required, and answer (A) can be eliminated.

"Consequently" would suggest that either the magnetic field reversals themselves or scientists' knowledge of those reversals has *caused* many people to be ignorant of the field changes. Such a statement is clearly illogical, so answer (B) is also incorrect.

The word "likewise" suggests that a similarity is about to be described. The two sentences in Example 1, however, do not describe a similarity. Rather, they point out the *difference* between what scientists know and what is widely known among the general population. Answer (C), therefore, is incorrect as well.

Answer (D) is the only remaining option, and so would have to be correct by default. There is in fact a clear reason why answer (D) is the best choice. The word "nevertheless" is used to set up a *contrast* between the information or ideas presented in one sentence (or a sequence of sentences) and the information or idea presented in the sentence that follows. Since the sequence of two sentences in Example 1 clearly focuses on the contrast between scientists' knowledge and others' lack of knowledge, **answer (D), "Nevertheless" is the logical choice to replace the underlined words**.

Words commonly found in questions on word choice

Following is a list of some of the words that most often appear in questions on logical word choices (and are most often misused by writers), with notes on their correct use.

For example, for instance, specifically. All of these are used to introduced specific examples or cases that are clearly connected to the ideas or assertions presented in the previous sentence(s).

EXAMPLE 2: Statistics show that there is actually no significant correlation between daylight fluctuation and depression. ***For instance***, the percentage of people who suffer from depression in the country of Funderland, which receives virtually no daylight in winter, is identical to the percentage in Sunderland, which receives approximately twelve hours of daylight every day of the year.

Therefore, consequently, as a result, thus. These are all used to indicate either a cause-and-effect or an evidence-conclusion relationship between two statements. The relationship should be such that it is reasonable to believe that the second statement can be made *specifically because* of the phenomenon, ideas, or logical premises described in the first statement. It would not be considered appropriate to write: *It did not rain the day the Belmont Stakes horse race was run in 2015. Consequently, American Pharoah won.* Both statements are true—it did not rain the day of the race, and American Pharoah was the winner—but it would be ludicrous to believe American Pharoah, an accomplished champion, won specifically because of the lack of rain. (As a matter of fact, he won the Preakness Stakes, an equally competitive race, just three weeks earlier on a rain-soaked track.)

EXAMPLE 3: The committee was deadlocked at 6-6 over the issue of whether to change the criteria for club membership. ***As a result***, the issue was tabled and will be reconsidered at next month's meeting.

EXAMPLE 4: The murder occurred at the paper mill on October 12. Research has shown that all visitors to the paper mill have bits of paper pulp in their hair for 3-5 days afterward. Yet the defendant was tested just two days after the murder, and not a trace of paper pulp was found in his hair. ***Therefore***, he could not have been at the mill when the murder occurred.

However, nonetheless, nevertheless, by contrast, though (when used as a substitute for "however" in the *middle* of a sentence). All of these are used to indicate some sort of distinction, contrast, or apparent contradiction between the ideas presented in a sentence and those presented in the preceding sentence(s).

EXAMPLE 5: Joachim was painfully aware of the risks associated with confronting his father.

Nevertheless, he walked proudly toward their meeting place, showing not a single sign of hesitation.

EXAMPLE 6: Jupiter's mass is over 315 times that of Earth. As impressive as that figure may sound, ***however***, it is a mere fraction of what the ratio of masses would be if Jupiter had a rocky, rather than gaseous, composition: a whopping 1400 to 1!

Similarly, likewise. These words should only be used when there is a high degree of certainty that the ideas or situations being compared are, in fact, alike. It would be inappropriate to write: *A dark, cloudy sky signals rain or snow here on Earth. Similarly, it must rain heavily on Venus, which is continuously shrouded in thick clouds.* (The clouds on Venus are not at all like those on Earth. They are predominantly composed of sulfur, not water vapor, and do not cause precipitation.)

EXAMPLE 7: Athletes and dancers who cross train in a variety of physical disciplines display greater physical agility and quicker reaction times than those who practice only their chosen sport or dance style. ***Likewise***, students who devote substantial time and effort to mastering multiple subjects display greater mental agility and problem-solving speed than those who reserve their best efforts for a single, favorite class.

The Logic of Writing, Part Two: Sentence Order, Paragraph Organization

About 8-10 of the 44 questions in an SAT Writing section will deal specifically with organizing a piece of writing logically. You will be asked about whether it would be appropriate to change the order of

sentences within a paragraph, whether it would be best to delete a particular sentence from the paragraph,

or whether it would be advantageous to add a proposed new sentence.

Keep closely related sentences together!

If two or more sentences function together to present an idea or argument, they should appear one after the other, without unrelated sentences interrupting the flow.

EXAMPLE 8: Imagine that a passage contains the following sequence of three sentences.

> [1] Dutch elm disease has decimated elm populations across North America, stripping many small town boulevards of their former cathedral-like majesty. [2] Emerald ash borer syndrome and oak wilt are now affecting many municipalities as well. [3] The disease is most often spread from one elm tree to another by flying beetles that unknowingly transport infected sap, though it can also spread through root grafts between two trees in close proximity to each other.

Sentence 2 creates the impression that the author is leaving the topic of Dutch elm disease behind and proceeding to examine other tree ailments. Sentence 3 then throws the reader off balance by unexpectedly returning to the subject of Dutch elm disease (as is clear by the mention of a disease spreading "from one elm tree to another"). Since sentence 1 and sentence 3 both specifically address Dutch elm disease, while sentence 2 does not, sentence 3 should follow sentence 1 directly. Sentence 2 should either be moved to a different place in the passage or deleted altogether; which of those possibilities applies would depend on the specific wording of the test question and the answer choices provided.

Each paragraph should have ONE main idea.

One of the major principles all writers are taught is that paragraphing is done for the reader's sake, not the writer's. Paragraphs should both help the reader to organize the ideas presented in a passage in his or her own mind and make it easier for him or her to scan back through the passage to locate a particular detail. Therefore, whenever possible, each paragraph should focus on a single main idea. A shift to a new idea should be signaled by the start of a new paragraph.

EXAMPLE 9: Consider this excerpt from a reading passage:

> [1] Potential negative environmental impacts of building the Pottisquoddy dam are numerous. [2] Flooding of the forested plain upstream of the proposed dam site will jeopardize the survival of multiple plant species found only along the upper Pottisquoddy River. [3] Reduced water flow downstream of the dam will result in dwindling food supplies for native fish like the pickerel and brook trout. [4] The artificially steep drop in the surrounding terrain that the dam will create will impede seasonal migrations of a dozen or more species of reptile. **(27)[5]** In short, everything that makes the Pottisquoddy valley unique may disappear within a decade after the dam's construction.

Question 27 reads,

> At this point, the author is considering inserting the following sentence.
>
> It is anticipated that area residents will save up to $400 per year on their electric bills once dam construction has been completed.
>
> Should the author add this sentence here?
>
> A) Yes, because it provides additional information that supports the paragraph's main idea.
>
> E) Yes, because saving people money is more important than protecting fish, plants, and reptiles.
>
> F) No, because there is no source provided for the information, so the figure of
>
> G) $400 in savings per year cannot be trusted.
>
> H) No, because it blurs the focus of the paragraph by introducing information not related to the paragraph's main idea.

Sentence 1 announces that the paragraph will focus on the effects building the dam would have on the surrounding environment. Sentences 2, 3, and 4 all describe specific environmental impacts the dam may have. Sentence 5 wraps up the paragraph by summing up the information and restating the main idea in more forceful terms. The proposed new sentence, however, has nothing to do with environmental concerns; it details a possible economic benefit of the dam's construction. Even if you agree with the statements made in answer choices (B) and (C), the proposed sentence still doesn't belong in the paragraph shown. It would need to appear in a paragraph that either describes potential *economic* effects of the dam project or presents a general overview of possible benefits of building the dam. **The correct answer choice is (D).**

Conventions of Standard Written English

Most of the questions on the Writing Test that do not fit one of the descriptions above require you to evaluate whether the passage complies with the conventions of standard written English, and make changes where it does not.

What is standard written English?

No one on Earth speaks the language called standard written English. Standard written English is a version of the English language[1] specifically developed to facilitate *written* communication between

---

1   Actually, there are *two* versions of English known as standard written English: one based on US English, the

English speakers, especially between those who speak very different versions of English. It is governed by conventions regarding matters of punctuation, spelling, word choice, and word order. There are thousands of such conventions, but only twenty or so of them are regularly tested on the SAT Writing section.

Conventions are not laws or rules. They are agreements intended to help people work together in harmony. Great writers break from convention regularly and to great effect. Writers of the SAT Writing

Test do not believe that everyone who writes should blindly obey every convention of standard written English all the time. In fact, no one believes that! The aim of the Writing Test is to evaluate your *knowledge* of the conventions of standard written English, not your obedience to those conventions in your own writing. With such knowledge, a writer can "break the rules" knowingly, and for a specific purpose, rather than unwittingly, in a way that confuses the reader.

Depending on where you grew up, the version of English you speak on a daily basis may be quite different from standard written English. As a result, some correct answers will sound weird to you. For the purpose of this test, keep in mind that your mission is to identify the *conventional* answer choice, not the one you personally prefer. And above all, remember that no one is saying there is anything wrong with the way you speak. If everyone spoke English the exact same way, it would be a far less interesting and expressive language than it is. There would have been no Shakespeare, no Toni Morrison, no J. R. R. Tolkien, no JK Rowling.

Conventions Governing Punctuation, Part One: Comma Use

Commas and list organization

In most cases (and all cases on the SAT Writing section), the items in a list should be separated by commas.

EXAMPLE 10: Camila came home from the farmers market with romaine lettuce, carrots, strawberries, acorn squash, and watermelons.

Notice how the placement of the commas helps the reader to identify the items in the list. For example, the fact that there is no comma after "romaine" ensures that the reader will instantly recognize that "romaine lettuce" is a single item. The same is true for the two-word item, "acorn squash."

Notice that there are two places where a comma should NOT appear: after the word "with" and after the word "and." Answer choices with a comma in one or both of those positions may be ruled out immediately.

---

other based on UK English. The SAT is written in the US and follows the conventions of US standard written English. However, the test writers are careful not to include Writing Test questions for which the correct answers would be different if the conventions of UK standard written English were followed.

In Example 10, a comma appears after the next-to-last list item, that is, right before the "and." This comma is called the serial or Oxford comma. Its use is favored, but not absolutely required, in most forms of writing. You will find that the serial comma is commonly used in SAT reading passages, but there are no test questions that specifically address the question of whether it is needed.

Commas and supplemental phrases

A supplemental phrase, or supplemental clause, provides additional information about a person, place, thing, or idea for the benefit of the reader. Consider the following sentence.

EXAMPLE 11: Dr. Melinda Bhattacharya, a professor of genetics at Johns Hopkins University, points out that random mutations are only one of several driving forces behind the variations within a species that make evolution possible.

Notice that if you were to delete the phrase, "a professor of genetics at Johns Hopkins University," the sentence would still be perfectly readable and logical: *Dr. Melinda Bhattacharya points out that random mutations are only one of several driving forces behind the variations within a species that make evolution possible.* Thus, the phrase, "a professor of genetics at Johns Hopkins University," is a *supplemental phrase*. It is not needed for the sentence to be understood, but it is helpful to the reader because it explains who Dr. Bhattacharya is and why her statement is credible.

<u>**Supplemental phrases are ALWAYS set off by commas, at both the beginning and the end of the phrase**</u>, just as has been done in Example 11. Any other punctuation would not comply with the conventions of standard written English.

Conventions Governing Punctuation, Part Two: Use of Semicolons and Colons

Many people have difficulty sorting out the various conventions associated with the use of the semicolon (;) and colon (:). The SAT Writing section focuses on a few very specific conventions about the use of these two punctuation marks.

Semicolons

The most common use of a **semicolon (;)** is to separate two related statements, each of which could stand on its own as a complete sentence. This use of the semicolon provides a cue to the reader that the two statements work together to express a single idea.

EXAMPLE 12: No one had to explain to Emily the devastation that drug abuse can wreak upon a family; she had lived it.

Notice that writing the same passage as two sentences would also be perfectly compliant with the conventions of standard written English: *No one had to explain to Emily the devastation that drug abuse can wreak upon a family. She had lived it.*

Choosing between the two versions (which you would never have to do on the Writing Test) is really a matter of stylistic preference. The first version emphasizes that the statement, "she had lived it," completes the idea expressed in the previous statement. The second version creates a dramatic pause that may heighten the emotional impact of the passage.

In any case, within the context of the SAT Writing section, if a semicolon appears anywhere other than between two closely related statements that both qualify as complete sentences, then that answer choice is almost certainly incorrect.

Colons

The most common uses of a colon are to introduce a list and to introduce a word, phrase, or statement that essentially answers a question raised by the first part of a sentence.

EXAMPLE 13: The causes of heart disease are many: genetic factors, tobacco use, diabetes, alcoholism, unhealthy eating habits, lack of exercise, and more.

In this example, there would be other ways to introduce the list that would also comply with standard written English conventions. For example, *The causes of heart disease are many, and include genetic factors, tobacco use, diabetes, alcoholism, unhealthy eating habits, and lack of exercise.*

Neither version of the sentence is "better" than the other. The important point is that the colon in Example 13 is correctly used. Note that a **semicolon should NEVER be used to introduce a list**.

EXAMPLE 14: Many people blamed the dwindling of the town's population on the unwillingness of young people to work hard, but the mayor knew the sad truth: even if the youth wanted to work, the area had no jobs for them.

Here, the colon signals to the reader that the statement to follow answers the question of what the mayor knows. This use of a colon is rather subtle, but do not be intimidated by it. SAT Writing Test questions on this topic will provide only one sensible answer, with the colon properly positioned. The remaining answers choices will present options that you can eliminate by following the other conventions described above.

 ## *Parallel Structure: The Art of Making Lists Readable*

In standard written English, each item in a list should be presented in a similar way to all the others. This *parallel structure* helps the reader to understand the logic of the list without having to reread it several times.

EXAMPLE 15: Tomas's reasons for missing the meeting included scheduling difficulties, traffic woes, and how he was really tired from working the night shift.

The sentence is perfectly understandable, but most readers would have to do a "stutter step" upon hitting the third item in the list. They may even have to restart reading the sentence from the beginning in order to fit the pieces together.

"Scheduling difficulties" and "traffic woes" are both noun phrases. It would be helpful to the reader if the third item on the list began with a noun or noun phrase as well. Here is a rewrite that would represent a correct answer choice on the SAT Writing section:

Tomas's reasons for missing the meeting included scheduling difficulties, traffic woes, and exhaustion from working the night shift.

Parallel structure can be tricky. Consult a writers' manual or style guide for additional examples to help you get the hang of it.

 ## Conventions Governing the Use of Their/They're/There

This matter crops up at least once on every SAT Writing section. Pay carefully attention to the differences between these three words.

Their

"Their" is a *possessive* pronoun; it is used to indicate that an object, possession, place, or person *belongs to* or *is associated with* them.

EXAMPLE 16: All the employees brought their own lunches to the picnic.

EXAMPLE 17: You should have seen the looks on their faces.

EXAMPLE 18: Parents are welcome to bring their children to the festival.

Notice that in all three cases, the word "their" is used to signal that whatever is being described either belongs to or is associated with the group that would be identified as "them." In Example 16, the employees would be "them," and the lunches *belong* to *them*. In Example 17, we actually don't know who *they* are, but we know the faces described *belong* to *them*. As for Example 18, children don't exactly *belong* to their parents, but they are certainly closely associated with their parents. The parents are *them*, and the children *are associated* with *them*.

<u>**The word "their" should therefore ONLY be used to indicate possession.**</u>

They're

The word "they're" is a contraction of the two words "they are," and therefore should only be used when it would be correct to use those two words instead.

EXAMPLE 19 (*Correct*): The people at the party are running around like maniacs. I have no idea what they're doing.

EXAMPLE 20 (*Incorrect*): People were outside on the sunny day, many washing they're cars.

In Example 19, it's apparent that writing "they are" in place of "they're" would make perfect sense. Therefore, the word "they're" is correctly used in that example. In Example 20, however, replacing "they're" with "they are" would be comically incorrect: *People were outside on the sunny day, many washing they are cars.* Here the cars *belong to* the people (them), and therefore (see above), the correct word choice would be "their." Here is the sentence, correctly revised:

People were outside on the sunny day, many washing their cars.

<u>**Again, only use "they're" when it would be logical to use the two words "they are" in its place.**</u>

There

Unlike "their" and "they're," the word "there" has *many* uses. It can be used to indicate a location ("I was *there* when the riot occurred"), to declare the existence of something ("*There* are numerous species of bears"), and to announce arrival at the conclusion of an argument ("And *there* you have it, undeniable proof"), among many other purposes.

In short, <u>**if the word cannot logically be replaced by "they are" and is not being used to indicate possession, then "there" is almost certainly the correct choice**</u>.

Conventions Governing the Use of It's/Its

These two words cause headaches for English writers everywhere. Be very careful when distinguishing between them on the SAT Writing Test.

It's

The word "it's" is a contraction of the two words, "it is." <u>**Therefore, "it's" should only be used when it can be logically replaced by the two words, "it is."**</u>

EXAMPLE 21 (*Correct*): We should grab an umbrella because it's raining outside.

EXAMPLE 22 (*Incorrect*): Marge's umbrella has a bird's head on it's handle.

In Example 21, it is clear that the sentence would suffer no change in meaning if the word "it's" were replaced by "it is." Therefore, "it's" is used correctly in the sentence. In Example 22, however, replacing "it's" with "it is" would create a nonsensical statement: *Marge's umbrella has a bird's head on it is handle.*

Its

The word "its" (with no apostrophe) is *not* a contraction. Like "their," it is a possessive pronoun, signaling that an item *belongs* to *it*. It may seem strange to indicate possession without using an apostrophe, but this is the standard practice with pronouns. We don't write, "That hat is hi's;" we write, "That hat is his" (no apostrophe!). So the convention is actually the same for all pronouns: **possessive forms of pronouns do NOT have apostrophes.**

EXAMPLE 23 (*Correction of Example 22 above*): Marge's umbrella has a bird's head on its handle.

Since the handle "*belongs to*" the umbrella, the next-to-last word is intended to indicate possession, and so "its" (no apostrophe) is the correct choice.

EXAMPLE 24: The eagle had a large trout in its talons as it ascended to the top of the cliffs above Lake Superior.

The talons *belong to* the eagle (it), and so "its" is the correct word, because it indicates possession.

To reiterate, the word "its" (no apostrophe) should ONLY be used to indicate possession.

Final Thoughts on the SAT Writing Test

The best ways to prepare for the SAT Writing section are to

- complete all writing tasks you are assigned for your current classes at school.
- pay careful attention to your teachers' feedback on your work for those assignments.
- regularly read publications that follow the conventions of standard written English, such as school textbooks, publications of the Smithsonian Institution, newspapers like the New York Times and the Wall Street Journal, etc.

Preparing for the SAT® Essay Test

NOTE: *The practice tests included in this book do NOT include the Essay portion.*

Including...

▶ *What is the SAT Essay Test?*

▶ *Should I Take the Essay Test?*

▶ *What Kind of Essay Will I Have to Write for the Test?*

▶ *Scoring Categories for the Essay Section*

▶ *A Brief Example*

What is the SAT Essay Test?

The Essay section is an optional extension of the SAT. The purpose of the section is to test your ability to analyze an argument put forth by another author, and to present your analysis is clearly and effectively.

You will write the essay by hand. It will be scored by two separate human graders who do not consult with each other. Each grader will score your essay on a scale from 1 to 4 in three categories: Reading, Analysis, and Writing. (See below for more information on the scoring categories.) Your total score will be determined by adding the scores of the two graders.

When you register to take the SAT, you will be given the option to either complete the Essay portion or leave the test facility upon completion of the other four test sections (Reading, Writing, Math No Calculator, Math Calculator). If you choose to take the Essay test, your performance will not affect your 400-1600 "overall" SAT score, which is based only upon the two English language sections (Reading and Writing) and two Math sections (No Calculator and Calculator). Rather, your score on the Essay will be reported separately.

Should I Take the Essay Test?

Some colleges and universities require completion of the SAT Essay section for admission. Contact all the schools to which you are considering applying and ask if they have such a requirement. If so, then you will obviously sign up to take the Essay portion when you register for the SAT.

Otherwise, if you routinely receive high marks on the papers you write for your classes and/or are frequently praised by your instructors for your writing, then taking the Essay Test will afford you the opportunity to showcase your abilities to college admissions officers. If the feedback you have received on your writing has indicated that you are a competent, but not yet excellent, writer, then preparing for the SAT Essay portion may be a great way to improve your skills. Consult with your teachers or any highly skilled writers you may know. Ask them if they would be willing to help you by offering feedback on any writing you do to practice for the test.

The good news is that when it comes to preparation for the SAT Essay Test, there is no such thing as wasted effort! Even if you ultimately choose not to complete the Essay section, any time and effort you devote to preparing for it is guaranteed to make you a better writer. And writing skill is one of the most reliable predictors of college success.

Preparing for the SAT Essay Test

 ## *What Kind of Essay Will I Have to Write for the Test?*

The SAT Essay section focuses on the writing of one specific type of essay, formally known as a *rhetorical analysis.* You will be presented with a reading passage of about 650-750 words. The passage will be a persuasive essay, meaning that the writer will advocate for a particular belief or course of action, bolstering his or her case with evidence, logical arguments, and appeals to emotion. You will be asked to write an original essay in which you present an analysis of the methods the writer employs to convince the reader to accept his or her conclusions.

Notice that your task will be to **summarize and analyze the author's arguments, NOT to present arguments of your own!** At no point in your own essay should you comment on whether you share the author's point of view, or whether you think his or her conclusions are right or wrong. Nor should you introduce new evidence not discussed within the passage in an attempt to justify agreeing or disagreeing with the author. You are of course just as entitled to your own opinion as the author is to his or hers, but the instructions for the SAT Essay section will clearly indicate that you are to **discuss** the author's arguments, **NOT** respond to them.

Therefore, your primary goals in constructing your essay should be to

- point out specific pieces of evidence that the author uses to support his or her claims (for example, results of surveys or scientific studies).

- evaluate whether the author is employing appeals to emotion as a persuasive technique (examples might include sharing personal recollections from childhood, describing the nature of the sorrows endured by people negatively affected by a situation, etc.).

- highlight striking word choices or other stylistic devices employed by the author to strengthen the impact of his or her arguments (for example, "a seemingly harmless act of negligence now could unleash cataclysmic consequences upon future generations").

- demonstrate a keen understanding of the ways in which the author logically connects specific evidence with the general conclusions he or she draws.

 ## *Scoring Categories for the Essay Section*

Each grader will assign a score from 1 to 4 to your essay in three categories.

Reading

Your first task when crafting your essay is to demonstrate that you have read the passage thoroughly and understood the author's arguments. Start your essay with a brief (typically, 1-3 sentence) introduction that summarizes the author's main point and methods of supporting it. For example, you might write, "In his essay, 'A Future on Thin Ice,' Harvey Lazerbach forcefully argues in favor of rules changes in professional hockey to protect players' health. Through the use of evocative language, appeals to emotion, and evidence culled from scientific studies, Lazerbach drives home his point that every momentary delay in implementing such changes puts another young player at risk."

Within the body of your essay, focus on presenting specific evidence from the passage that supports your interpretation of the author's argument. Make use of quotations from the passage, but make sure you provide context for each quotation so that it is clear to the grader that you understand the meaning of the quoted material. Paraphrase excerpts from the passage as well to show that you can restate the author's ideas in your own words. (When paraphrasing, always attribute the statement to the author of the passage, even though you have reworded it. To do otherwise is plagiarism!)

Conclude your essay with another brief paragraph that refers back to the introduction, while adding nuances suggested by your detailed analysis of the author's arguments.

Analysis

To arrive at a score for your essay in the Analysis category, graders will examine the clarity of your reasoning. Have you demonstrated a clear understanding of which sentences in the reading passage were intended to appeal to the emotions rather than the intellect? Have you identified rhetorical devices used by the author, such as rhetorical questions? Is your description of the author's logic both sufficiently accurate

to show that you understand how the claims and evidence work together in support author's main point, and sufficiently original to show that you are not simply parroting the author's words?

Try to infuse your essay with a natural flow, with each idea leading effortlessly into the next. Student essays that bounce between ideas in a haphazard way receive low marks for Analysis.

Writing

When determining your score in the Writing category, graders will focus on the finer points of writing: effective word choices, frequent variations in sentence structures to keep a reader's interest, smooth transitions between paragraphs, etc. Graders will also be examining your mastery of standard written English, but you should not psyche yourself out by trying to be too perfect. Allowances will be made for the fact that you are writing under a strict time limit that does not allow you to make a lot of revisions.

Notice that in theory, your skill as a writer will only account for one-third of your score on the Essay section. In reality, however, writing skill will be the single most significant factor in determining how you perform on the test. After all, in order to evaluate your essay in the Reading and Analysis categories, the graders must first be able to understand what you are saying. Therefore, the single most important way to prepare for the SAT Essay Test is to practice writing clearly and concisely about as many different topics as possible.

For more information on what constitutes standard written English, visit our page on **Preparing for the SAT® Writing Test.**

 ## A Brief Example

Suppose the reading passage is an essay by Sarah Jackson, advocating for a nationalized (sometimes called single-payer) health care system in the US. The following are excerpts from the passage.

> A rather horrific fall during a bike ride three months ago sent me to the emergency room with a badly fractured left arm. Due to the severe separation of the broken bone, I was assigned high priority and spent only about 15 minutes in the waiting room. That was long enough, however, to see the plight of a fear-stricken mother and her ailing son, with his relentless, racking cough, and weak, desperate eyes. …
>
> Politicians who favor a continuation of our current health care system often speak of a "European nightmare," implying that people are far worse off in the many European countries with nationalized health care than we are here. A recent study by the Pew Research Center, however, showed that 83% of Americans who require medical care while in Europe for work or pleasure report that the experience of seeking and receiving appropriate treatment over there is simpler and significantly more pleasant than it is in the United States. Do the words "simpler" and "more pleasant" sound like descriptions of a nightmare? …
>
> Most importantly, over 300,000 physicians, representing all 50 US states plus DC and Puerto Rico, recently signed a petition stating that they would be able to serve their patients better under a nationalized system. Shouldn't the primary objective of any health care system be to empower doctors to do their best work? …
>
> To let the voices of hospital administrators and insurance company executives drown out those of patients and their care providers is indefensible. It is imperative that a new era in American health care begin without further delay. …
>
> Between X-rays, consultation with an orthopedic surgeon, and the bone-setting operation itself, my stay at the ER lasted over seven hours. On my way out, I saw that same frail, exhausted, helplessly coughing boy, his disheveled mother still waiting for his name to be called, his bloodshot eyes still asking in vain when his country will start caring about his fate.

In writing your essay about this passage, you might emphasize

- the way Jackson frames the essay with the story of the suffering young boy to appeal to the reader emotionally.

- Jackson's use of the rhetorical technique of raising a likely objection to her proposal, and then presenting evidence (the Pew study) to discredit that objection.

- Jackson's use of the evidence of the petition to make the case that doctors themselves favor her plan.

- Jackson's use of rhetorical questions ("Do the words 'simpler' and 'more pleasant' sound like descriptions of a nightmare?" and "Shouldn't the primary objective of any health care system be to empower doctors to do their best work?") to persuade the reader that reasoned analysis can only lead to the conclusion she is presenting.

- the logical foundations of Jackson's argument, such as her focus on the experiences of patients and the wishes of doctors as more important considerations than the opinions of others in the health care industry.

- Jackson's use of forceful language, such as "indefensible" and "imperative," to urge the reader to action.

It is also acceptable to point out possible weaknesses in the author's argument or evidence, but remember to do so in a way that keeps the focus squarely on the author's rhetorical techniques and methods of persuasion. Do NOT attempt to point out logical flaws purely as a basis for presenting your own opinion. You might, for example, write, "Jackson cites a recently circulated petition as compelling evidence of physician support for a nationalized system. Although she does not provide details regarding the doctors' specialties or the socioeconomic status of the patients they serve, she effectively references the geographic diversity of the petition signers to bolster her case."

Remember, regardless of whether you ultimately take the SAT Essay Test, any preparation work you do with that end in mind will serve you well throughout your college career.

Preparing for the SAT® Math NC Test (No Calculator)

Including...

▶ *General Overview of the Math NC Section: Strategies & Topics*

▶ *Algebra and Advanced Algebra*

▶ *Geometry*

▶ *Percents*

▶ *Trigonometry*

▶ *Statistics*

▶ *Probability*

Computations: What to Expect, What NOT to Expect

Strategy: don't assume your calculator is always an advantage!

The primary purpose of the NC (No Calculator) Math section of the SAT is to test your ability to reason mathematically. Mathematical reasoning includes computational work, but only to a degree. Some people can perform mental calculations astonishingly quickly; most of us are a little more plodding. However, if you take the right approach to the Math NC section, you will find that your speed at performing computations is almost irrelevant. DO expect to do some old-fashioned, pencil-and-paper arithmetic, but only a small amount of it. Remember, the focus of the test is on your reasoning ability, not your skills as a "human calculator." DO NOT expect to tackle complex arithmetic at any point during this test section. If you find yourself heading down that road, pause and give the problem a second look. There is almost certainly an easier way to solve it.

A couple of tricks of the trade when working with fractions are especially helpful. You may want to brush up on these skills, since you most likely learned them in pre-algebra, which many of you took four or more years ago. First, reduce fractions to lowest terms, or at least lower terms, before beginning computations.

EXAMPLE: Juanita buys 180 greeting cards for $60. If Riley pays the same price per card as Juanita did, how much should she expect to pay for 339 cards?

Solution: The standard method for this problem would be to set up a proportion, as follows.

The standard method for solving a proportion is "cross multiplication," which yields the equation, $180x = 339*60$. That multiplication looks pretty daunting. Notice how much simpler the problem becomes if we first reduce the fraction:

Using the final pair of equal fractions, we cross multiply to get $3x = 339$. Dividing both sides by 3, we end up with $x = 339 \div 3 = 113$. So Riley should expect to pay $113, and we solved the problem with very little computational work.

It is also advantageous when working with fractions to remember that **when fractions are multiplied, it is possible to reduce any numerator with any denominator.**

Preparing for the SAT Math NC Test (No Calculator)

EXAMPLE:

$$\frac{12}{25} \times \frac{45}{14} \times \frac{28}{9}$$ Reduce 12 with 14 and 25 with 45 to get

$$= \frac{6}{5} \times \frac{9}{7} \times \frac{28}{9}$$ Reduce 9 with 9 and 7 with 28 to get

$$= \frac{6}{5} \times \frac{1}{1} \times \frac{4}{1}$$ Multiply straight across to get final answer:

$$= \frac{24}{5}$$

Multiple choice vs. grid-in questions

The majority of questions (15 of 20) on the SAT Math NC Test are multiple choice questions, for which you will choose the best answer from among the options provided. The remaining questions are "grid-in," which means you will write in your answer by hand and also enter it using a special bubble grid. (For our practice tests, you will simply type in your answer using your computer keyboard.) Be sure to read the directions for entering your answers to grid-in questions very carefully. Remember, these questions, just like the multiple choice questions, will be scored by machines that cannot figure out what you meant if your answer entry is unclear. So mind the details, because *if there is doubt, you'll lose out!*

Units and graph scales

Many SAT Math questions, both with and without calculator, require you to convert between different units of measurement. If you struggle with unit conversions, find a friend or other helper to work with as you prepare to take the SAT. Seek help from science teachers as well as math teachers; many students find the unit conversion methods taught in chemistry and physics classes to be easier to apply than those taught in pure math classes.

When evaluating information that appears in graphs or tables on the SAT Math sections, be very thorough in reading graph titles, axes labels, and any other textual information that will help you to correctly interpret the data. Is the vertical axis marked in hundreds, or in thousands, or in percentage points? Or is it indicating frequency (how many times a particular result was observed)? Do the numbers on the horizontal axis represent years since a specified year (for example, years since 2002)? Taking the time to consider these matters is often the difference between correct and incorrect answers for questions based on graphs and tables.

Topics included in the Math NC section

Predominantly, both Math sections on the SAT focus on the following topic areas:

- Algebra, basic and advanced, with a special focus on lines, parabolas, and exponential growth and decay

- Geometry, especially area, volume, surface area, and fundamental properties of angles and triangles

eggheadprep.com

- Percents, including compound interest (formulas are usually provided)
- Trigonometry, both right triangle trig and fundamentals of advanced trig.
- Basic statistics
- Basic probability

Ideally, you will have completed algebra II (also called advanced algebra) and at least some advanced study of trigonometry by the time you take the SAT. However, if you have completed geometry and algebra and have received some basic instruction in statistics and probability, you will be well prepared for most of the problems on the Math NC section.

Following is a more detailed look at the major topic areas covered on the Math NC Test.

Algebra and Advanced Algebra

Some of the major topics from algebra and advanced algebra that are prominent on the SAT Math NC section are listed below. *NOTE: This list does not show every algebra topic covered on the SAT Math sections, only those that are tested most frequently.*

Linear, quadratic and exponential functions

Because so many SAT Math problems are about lines (linear functions), parabolas (quadratic functions), and exponential growth and decay (exponential functions), it is especially important to be very familiar with these three types of graphs and their equations.

The equation of a **linear function (line)** will generally take one of three forms:

- $Ax + By = C$, a form that is often used to solve systems of linear equations, but must be converted to one of the two forms shown below for many other purposes
- $y = mx + b$, in which m represents the slope (also called the *rate of change*) and b represents the y- intercept (also called the *initial value*) of the line/function
- $y = a + bx$, in which a represents the y-intercept (also called the *initial value*) and b represents the slope (also called the *rate of change*) of the line/function

The equation of a **quadratic function (parabola)** will generally take one of these three forms:

- $y = ax^2 + bx + c$, in which c is the y-intercept
- $y = a(x - h)^2 + k$, in which the ordered pair (h, k) is the vertex of the parabola
- $y = a(x - r_1)(x - r_2)$, in which r1 and r_2 are the x-intercepts of the parabola

Preparing for the SAT Math NC Test (No Calculator)

Both **exponential growth** and **exponential decay** (that is, **exponential functions**) can be represented by the equation, $y = ab^x$, where a is the initial value (*y*-intercept) and b is the growth (*b > 1*) or decay (*b < 1*) factor. In the case of compound interest problems (for instance, calculating the amount of money in a bank account after x years), $b = 1 + r$, where r is the interest rate in its decimal form. For example, if an account pays 4.5% interest, compounded annually, then $b = 1 + 0.045 = 1.045$.

Other major topics

- Factoring
- Systems of two (usually linear) equations
- Fraction operations
- The Quadratic Formula (which you **MUST** memorize), as well as the use of the discriminant, $b^2 - 4ac$ to determine the number of real solutions (roots)
- Adding, subtracting, multiplying, and dividing polynomials
- Zeros (*x*-intercepts) of functions, especially polynomial functions
- Operations involving the number $i = $

Geometry

Major geometry topics covered on the SAT Math sections include:

- Area, volume, and surface area of various shapes. The needed formulas are provided for you with the instructions for the test section. However, you will be able to work more efficiently if you **memorize the most frequently used area and volume formulas** before taking the test.

- Length of a circular arc and area of a sector of a circle. **These formulas will NOT be provided on the test and therefore MUST be memorized!**

- Fundamental angle relationships: the sum of the interior angles of any triangle is 180°; adjacent angles that form a straight line have measures with a sum of 180°; vertical angles have equal measures; if two parallel lines are crossed by a transversal, there are many pairs of angles with equal measures (see Figure 1 below)

- The Pythagorean Theorem ($a^2 + b^2 = c^2$) for right triangles

- Proportional side lengths of similar figures, especially similar triangles

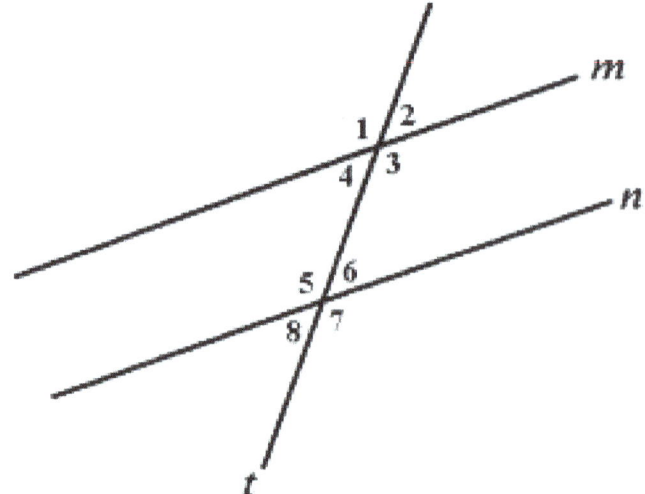

Figure 1: Two parallel lines (lines m and n) are crossed by a transversal (line t). All the odd-numbered angles are equal to each other in measure, as are all the even-numbered angles. Also, ∟1 and ∟2 are adjacent angles that form a straight line, and so have measures with a sum of 180°; ∟1 and ∟3 are vertical angles.

 Percents

By the time you have taken four or five practice SATs, you will have seen examples of almost all the major types of percent problems you have ever solved. However, because percent problems often involve time-consuming computations, they are more often presented within the SAT Math C (calculator) Test.

See our page on **Preparing for the SAT® Math C Test (Calculator)** for more information on this topic.

 Trigonometry

Trigonometry problems are a minor presence on both SAT Math sections, but every SAT has at least one trigonometry problem, usually two (one on each of the Math sections). <u>**Note that although many trigonometry problems require intense calculations, the writers of the SAT focus on trig problems that require very few calculations, if any. Therefore, trig problems are often found on the Math NC Test.**</u> These problems generally take two forms:

Preparing for the SAT Math NC Test (No Calculator)

$$\sin(\angle A) = \frac{\text{leg opposite } \angle A}{\text{hypotenuse}}$$

$$\cos(\angle A) = \frac{\text{leg adjacent to } \angle A}{\text{hypotenuse}}$$

$$\tan(\angle A) = \frac{\text{leg opposite } \angle A}{\text{leg adjacent to } \angle A}$$

Trigonometry type one: right triangle problems

You should be familiar with the right triangle definitions of the sine (sin), cosine (cos), and tangent (tan) functions:

Many students use the memory device SOHCAHTOA to recall these definitions.

Trigonometry type two: fundamentals of advanced trigonometry

If you have taken or are taking a precalculus course, you are familiar with topics from advanced trigonometry: analysis of the unit circle; graphs of sine, cosine, and tangent functions; proving and using trigonometric identities; etc. On the SAT, two particular trigonometric identities are highlighted regularly:

$$\sin(90° - x) = \cos x \text{ and } \cos(90° - x) = \sin x$$

Remembering this formula will earn you a correct answer every time you take an SAT.

Statistics

Problems on topics from statistics are common on both SAT Math sections. We discuss key statistics topics on our **Preparing for the SAT® Math C Test (Calculator)** page.

Probability

Likewise, probability problems are common on both SAT Math sections, but are discussed in detail on our **Preparing for the SAT® Math C Test (Calculator)** page. Please visit that page for more information.

eggheadprep.com

Preparing for the SAT® Math C Test (Calculator)

Including...

- *General Overview of the Math C Section: Strategy & Topics*
- *SAT Math C Test Topics, in Detail*
- *Probability*

General Overview of the Math C Section: Strategy & Topics

Strategy: don't assume your calculator is always an advantage!

Even though the Math C (calculator) section of the SAT allows you to use a calculator, if you employ appropriate methods, you will find that you actually don't use your calculator for the majority of the problems. Just as with the Math NC section, the test writers' primary goal is to test your ability to reason mathematically. They consider your level of skill in exploiting the capabilities of a calculator to be a secondary matter.

It is therefore very important to approach the problems on the SAT Math C Test with the right mindset. **Do not start looking for ways to employ your calculator as soon as you start reading the problem.** Rather, approach each problem the way you would approach any mathematical problem, regardless of whether you have a calculator at your disposal: analyze the given information, then choose an appropriate method from arithmetic, algebra, geometry, or statistics with which to work out a solution. If the steps required to execute your chosen procedure entail extensive computation or quick generation of a detailed graph, then reach for your calculator. This strategy will ensure that you use allotted time, available technology, and your own knowledge all to best advantage while completing the problems on the SAT Math C section.

Test format: multiple choice vs. grid-in

As is true for the Math NC section, the majority of questions (30 of 38) on the SAT Math C Test are multiple choice questions, for which you will choose the best answer from among the options provided. The remaining questions are "grid-in," which means you will write in your answer by hand and also enter it using a special bubble grid. (For our practice tests, you will simply type in your answer using your computer keyboard.) Be sure to read the directions for entering your answer very carefully, especially the instructions on how to enter decimal numbers that do not terminate after three decimal places. Remember, these questions, just like the multiple choice questions, will be scored by machines that cannot figure out what you meant if your answer entry is unclear. So mind the details, because *if there is doubt, you'll lose out!*

Test contents

The main topics covered on the Math C section are the same as those covered on the Math NC section:

- Algebra, basic and advanced, with a special focus on lines, parabolas, and exponential growth and decay

- Basic statistics

- Basic probability

Preparing for the SAT Math C Test (Calculator)

- Percents, including compound interest (needed formulas usually provided)

- Geometry, especially area, volume, surface area, and fundamental properties of angles and triangles

- Trigonometry, both right triangle trig and fundamentals of advanced trig.

You'll find in-depth discussions of most of these topics on our **Preparing for the SAT® Math NC Test (No Calculator)** page. Here, we will focus on a few topics that have a much stronger presence within the Math C section than within the Math NC section.

 SAT Math C Test Topics, in Detail

Percents

Just about every type of percent problem you have ever seen in a math class comes up somewhere on the SAT Math sections. Reviewing all the various techniques for solving percent-related problems should be a central component of your SAT Math preparation. Be especially alert for two notorious pitfalls that claim many victims every time an SAT is administered:

- **Percent increase and percent decrease.** Remember that a percent increase is added to 100% to arrive at the correct percent to use in the problem, whereas a percent decrease is *subtracted from* 100% to arrive at the correct percent to use. For example, if the value of a chest of drawers *increases* by 7.3% per year, you will need to use 100% + 7.3% = 107.3%, or 1.073, in your computations. If the value of a car is *decreasing* by 12% per year, you will need to use 100% − 12% = 88% in your computations.

- **Asymmetry of percent problems.** Consider this question: *Pedro has 30% more marbles than Mustafa. Therefore, Mustafa has _____% fewer marbles than Pedro*. Most people would fill in the blank with "30," since that is the answer suggested by "common sense." Unfortunately, common sense is dead wrong in this case. To see why, imagine that Mustafa has 100 marbles. To say that Pedro has 30% more marbles than Mustafa means that we want to compute a 30% *increase*. We will therefore use the figure, 100% + 30% = 130% = 1.30 to solve the problem (see **Percent increase and percent decrease,** above). We compute the number of marbles Pedro has as, 1.30 * 100 = 130. Now look at the problem from Mustafa's perspective. Mustafa has 100 ÷ 130 = .7692 , or 76.92% of the number of marbles Pedro has. Therefore (see **Percent increase and percent decrease,** above), Mustafa has 100% − 76.92% = 23.08% fewer marbles than Pedro. **The correct answer is 23.08% , completely different from 30%!** Because percent problems are asymmetrical (that is, reversing the direction in which one works alters the answer), <u>it is very important to read percent problems carefully and set them up exactly as instructed.</u>

 *Statistics*

In-depth knowledge of statistics is not in any way required for either SAT Math section. It is critical, however, that you understand the following statistical terms:

- **Mean:** The mean is the <u>average</u> of a set of numbers.

- **Mode:** The mode is the number that occurs <u>most frequently</u> in a set of data.

- **Median:** The median is the middle number in a set of data arranged from least to greatest or greatest to least. If two numbers fall in the middle, they are averaged to find the median.

- **Range:** The range is the difference between the greatest and least values in a data set.

- **Standard deviation:** The standard deviation is a measure of the spread of a data set—how far apart the values are from the mean. It is <u>NOT</u> necessary to know how to compute the standard deviation of a data set for the SAT Math sections. It <u>IS</u> necessary to know that **<u>a larger standard</u> <u>deviation indicates greater spread, while a smaller standard deviation indicates numbers that are more closely grouped around the mean.</u>**

- **Outlier:** An outlier is an extreme value that is very different from the other numbers in a data set. For example, in the data set {7, 12, 14, 14, 17, 19, 19, 20, 20, 20, 23, 25, 98}, the number 98 is an outlier. The presence (or removal) of an outlier significantly affects the *mean, range, and standard deviation. The median* is much less affected by an outlier. In most cases, the *mode isn't affected at all.*

 *Probability*

Most of the probability problems on the SAT Math sections test your knowledge of, and ability to apply, the basic probability principle that

$$\text{Probability of an event} = \frac{\text{Number of outcomes that qualify as event E}}{\text{Total number of possible outcomes}}$$

Be very careful to count outcomes that correspond to the question being asked. Consider, for example, the following table:

Preparing for the SAT Math C Test (Calculator)

Favorite Rides of Middle School Students at the Amusement Park

Grade Level	Roller coaster	Log flume	Bumper cars	Total
6th grade	27	19	43	89
7th grade	35	32	14	81
8th grade	48	34	6	88
Total	110	85	63	258

EXAMPLE 1: If a middle school student is chosen at random at the amusement park, what is the probability his or her favorite ride will be either the log flume or bumper cars?

Solution: Since we are choosing *any* middle school student, the denominator of the probability fraction should be the total number of middle school students, 258. Our event E is, *the student's favorite ride is the log flume OR bumper cars.* Therefore, the numerator of the probability fraction should be the total number of middle school students who chose either of those two rides as their favorite, which is 85 + 63 = 148. The correct probability is **148/258**, which reduces to **74/ 129**, or converts to a decimal as, **148 ÷ 258** ≈ 0.57 = 57%.

EXAMPLE 2: If a middle school student is chosen at random from among those whose favorite ride is the roller coaster, what is the probability the student will be a 6th grader?

Solution: Since we are choosing only from among those students whose favorite ride is the roller coaster, the denominator of the probability fraction should be the total number of students who chose the roller coaster as their favorite, or 110. The numerator of the probability fraction should be the number of *6th graders who chose the roller coaster as their favorite,* or 27. Therefore, the correct probability is **27 / 110,** which converts to a decimal as, **27 ÷ 110** ≈ 0.245 = 24.5%.

Most probability problems on the SAT math sections can be solved quite simply as long as you carefully count appropriate outcomes.

SAT®
Practice Tests

▶ *We are pleased to offer you five full-length, SAT-style practice tests meticulously prepared by top line pros who know the SAT as well as anyone. Five 3,000+ word articles on the five sections of the present-day SAT (Reading, Writing, Math Without Calculator, Math With Calculator, and the optional Essay)*

The SAT® essay section is now optional, but some schools may still require it. This book does not provide a practice section for the essay portion.

INTRODUCTION

In terms of lifelong impact, a college degree remains one of the most valuable possessions a person can obtain. It has been said many times, by everyone from Nobel Prize winning scientists to the great musician B. B. King, that learning is in fact the most precious of all things, because no one can ever take it away from you. Your decision to pursue opportunities in higher education is therefore one of which you should already feel proud. By offering you the opportunity to maximize your scores on standardized tests and providing you with reliable, objective information on a variety of topics of interest to college-bound students, this website will help you move from decision to action to success.

By the time you first sang the alphabet song, you had already begun training your mind to organize information in ways that would later enable you to analyze and solve sophisticated problems. You were taking your first steps toward college readiness, without the least awareness you were doing so.

> "But the upside of painful knowledge is so much greater than the downside of blissful ignorance."
> *- Sheryl Sandberg*

EGGHEAD PREP

SAMPLE TEST 1

Including...

- ▶ SECTION 1: READING TEST   50
- ▶ ANSWERS, SECTION 1   67
- ▶ SECTION 2: WRITING & LANGUAGE TEST   68
- ▶ ANSWERS, SECTION 2   83
- ▶ SECTION 3: MATH TEST   84
- ▶ ANSWERS, SECTION 3   90
- ▶ SECTION 4: MATH TEST   91
- ▶ ANSWERS, SECTION 4   103
- ▶ ANSWER EXPLANATIONS   104
- ▶ SCORING CONVERSION   134

SECTION 1: READING TEST
65 MINUTES, 52 QUESTIONS

DIRECTIONS

Each group of questions below is based on a passage or pair of passages. Read each passage carefully, then choose the best answer to each question based on what is stated in or suggested by the passage(s). The questions may also refer to any graphical displays that accompany the passage(s), such as tables or graphs.

Questions 1-11 are based on the following passage.

    Lindiel knew she was showing a reckless disregard for tradition. To stride right through the central compound and arrive here, at the doorstep of the Chieftain's home, without seeking out an elder to
5 escort her and advocate for her, was to act with no consideration of her place in society. Few who crossed such lines lived to tell about it.
    Certain that one more act of rebellion would obliterate any slight chance she had of receiving a fair
10 hearing, she refrained from announcing her presence. She knew that even those of her own rank considered such an announcement an intolerable intrusion except in the direst emergency. The Chieftain's wrath at such a transgression would be beyond her imagination. She
15 therefore stood in silence, waiting, knowing that the wait might last for hours, possibly even all through the long, cold night to come.
    Just as the first stars began flickering to life directly above her—a sign that the ancestors were
20 watching over her journey, her mother had taught her—Lindiel heard the shuffling of feet on the other side of the thin, thatched door. She stepped back to yield the way to anyone who might be rushing out on an errand, when suddenly, the door was pushed aside
25 and she found herself face to face with Arandala, the Chieftain herself.
    Lindiel lowered her gaze immediately, knowing she had done violence to protocol yet again by meeting the Chieftain eye to eye. Although she hoped
30 that her gasp of surprise had assured Arandala that the offense was unintentional, Lindiel's feet tensed. She was poised to run away from the village forever if her intentions had been misunderstood.
    "Frightened girl, have you lost your way in the
35 darkness?" asked Arandala, her voice gently melodic.
    "Great Chieftain, no, thank you," said Lindiel, struggling to find the air to support her words. "I would ask the gift of a moment of your time."
    "Who represents you?" came the reply, much
40 sterner in tone.
    "Begging your forgiveness, Leader, time did not permit me the opportunity to seek an elder to assist me. The knowledge I wish to share demanded to reach your ears without delay."
45   Arandala's face darkened. She slowly stepped outside, closing the door behind her. Suddenly uncomfortable with her own height, Lindiel instinctively bowed to keep her head below the Chieftain's. With a regal flourish, Arandala turned
50 her back to the girl.
    "You may speak," she declared. "But know that if I should turn to you, it will be to show the full force of my anger. In that case, I hope your feet can carry you beyond the village before my
55 eyes fall upon you. If not, you will no longer need to lower your head, for it will be removed."
    "Thank you, Great One," Lindiel began. "I have over the last week journeyed to the farthest northern reaches, beyond our hunting grounds."
60   "Well, what a fine adventure," Arandala said with a laugh. "And you have decided this feat was worthy of keeping the Chieftain from her bed?" she asked, her tone icy. Secretly, Arandala found the innocent enthusiasm of children inspiring, but
65 a Chieftain could not display such feelings for others to see.
    "It is not the journey I wish to speak of, Chieftain, but what I saw there. The Great River of the North has run dry." Lindiel paused,

70 watching the Chieftain's back intently, wondering if she had already said too much.

"It is to be expected. Have you not struggled against the dry dirt in our growing fields like everyone else this season?"

75 "Of course, Chieftain, my family has suffered greatly," Lindiel conceded. "But you see, the river has always blocked our passage to the distant valley of the trees. We could make the journey now in safety."

80 Arandala considered wheeling on the insistent girl at that moment. Surely, the child wasn't suggesting that the village should be abandoned—she wouldn't dare—but what else could she mean? Finally, with a deliberate calm, the Chieftain said,

85 "My child, this homeland was given to us by many generations of ancestors. You cannot suppose we would simply leave."

"But Chieftain, our enemies surround us here and block all our trade routes," Lindiel protested,

90 bracing to set her feet into flight. "We have little food and barely any clothing. We cannot survive here. We could make the journey in two weeks. Then the snow on the mountains will melt, the river will rise again, and we will be safe from our

95 enemies."

"Never!" cried the Chieftain, clenching her fists in the air. "Fly, foolish girl, and take your family with you! Run like the coward you are!" She reached for the door as Lindiel disappeared

100 with the speed of the wind.

Arandala shook her head in wonder, allowing herself a slight laugh. What state of affairs was this, when a child would question a Chieftain, and the people would consider abandoning their

105 homes? Still, she knew that her people would understand the wisdom of their leader's ways, that they would obey her, stay, and fight their enemies, even at the cost of their lives.

She pulled back the door, expecting to give her

110 husband and children a moment of mirth by sharing the story of the misguided young girl. Instead, she found them readying for a journey.

Excerpted from "The Girl, the River, and the Night," by B. Siems, ©2016.

1. Which choice offers the best description of what takes place in the passage?

   A) Two characters disagree about the best route to take for a journey.
   B) One character remembers the fun of being a child and exploring the world.
   C) One character tells another about an impending environmental disaster and the need to protect the people of the village.
   D) One character challenges another character's authority by suggesting a new course of action.

2. Which choice best describes the primary development of the passage?

   A) A detailed account of a conversation
   B) An in-depth look at a specific cultural tradition
   C) A humorous look at a case of mistaken identity
   D) The posing of a number of questions, followed by a series of responses

3. As used in line 12, the word "intolerable" most nearly means:

   A) pleasant.
   B) surprising.
   C) unacceptable.
   D) incomparable.

4. How does Lindiel feel about approaching the Chieftain?

   A) She is confident her announcement of her discovery will be greeted with enthusiasm.
   B) She is afraid of how the Chieftain may react to her presence and her ideas.
   C) She is excited to meet one of her heroes face to face.
   D) She is worried that the Chieftain will be inconvenienced because it is late.

5. All of the following provide evidence for the answer to the previous question (question #4) EXCEPT:

   A) Lines 8-10 ("Certain … presence.")
   B) Lines 13-14 ("The chieftain's … imagination.")
   C) Lines 18-22 ("Just … door.")
   D) Lines 32-33 ("She … misunderstood.")

6. Throughout the passage, Lindiel speaks to Arandala in a manner that is

   A) aggressive but not threatening.
   B) irreverent but not offensive.
   C) dominant but not abusive.
   D) courteous but not completely submissive.

7. Which choice best describes the purpose of the first paragraph?

   A) It shows how far Lindiel has traveled.
   B) It criticizes the customs of the village.
   C) It shows the danger in which Lindiel has placed herself.
   D) It explains the origins of traditional beliefs.

8. As used in line 28, the phrase "had already done violence to protocol" most nearly means

   A) had physically harmed others in the village by being careless.
   B) had blatantly violated the accepted rules of behavior.
   C) had a history of committing brutal acts, although she was only following orders from her superiors.
   D) had shown great passion for tradition, causing her to sometimes celebrate too aggressively.

9. Why does Lindiel say that, "The knowledge I wish to share demanded to reach your ears without delay" (lines 43-44)?

   A) She believes the opportunity to relocate the village safely to a northern valley will be short-lived.
   B) She was afraid someone else might discover that the river was dry and tell the Chieftain first.
   C) She fears her parents will be upset that she traveled so far north without an elder to guide her.
   D) She knows that the Chieftain is not aware of the hardships the villagers are enduring.

10. Which choice provides the strongest evidence in support of the answer to the previous question?

    A) Lines 57-59 ("Thank you .... grounds.")
    B) Lines 75-76 ("Of course … greatly,")
    C) Lines 88-89 ('But chieftain … routes.")
    D) Lines 92-95 ("We could … enemies.")

11. What is the significance of Arandala's discovery that her family is preparing for a journey (line 112)?

    A) It indicates that her family will go against her wishes and act on Lindiel's suggestion.
    B) Arandala has already expressed her desire to rest (lines 61-62, "And you … bed?"), so we know she is too tired to travel.
    C) Arandala loves the enthusiasm of children and thus will be excited to travel with her own children.
    D) Because this land has cold nights (line 17), travel will be extremely difficult for her family.

SAMPLE TEST 1
Section 1: Reading Test

Questions 12-21 are based on the following passage and accompanying graphical information.

    The long-term success of any company depends heavily on recruiting and keeping a highly skilled, dedicated workforce. An editorial article in Chasing Down the Money magazine recently proposed that a
5 high rate of employee turnover is a major red flag for Wall Street investors. Companies that retained their employees for an average of more than six years were consistently rated as more worthy of investor support than those that didn't. Not surprisingly, then, many
10 company executives are eager to learn more about how to keep employees happy and foster in them a sense of loyalty to the organization.
    It would seem obvious that paying workers well should form the centerpiece of any long-term employee
15 retention plan. As it turns out however, the question of how compensation influences employee contentment and loyalty is more complex than it would initially appear. Sociologists Ahlik Russell and Carrie Kensington studied the salary structures and worker
20 turnover rates of two companies in depth throughout 2004 and 2005, focusing on employees who had been hired in 2001.
    Company A's employees were earning a slightly lower average hourly wage than those of Company B at
25 the outset of the study, but received frequent, significant raises throughout the study period. From mid-2004 onward, employees of Company A earned significantly more than their Company B counterparts. And yet, during the two-year span of the study,
30 Company B retained over 90% of its employees who had been hired in 2001. Meanwhile, Company A lost over 35% of its 2001 hires to voluntary resignation. Why would the company that pays it employees more generously have such a difficult time keeping those
35 employees?
    Russell and Kensington believe they have the answer. The central issue, they contend, is that executives attach a different meaning to employee compensation than the employees themselves do. To
40 those writing the checks, salaries are an incentive to inspire future effort, like a carrot held out before a horse. Executives therefore tend to think that the most effective strategy is to keep wages low for newer employees, while offering promises of significant raises
45 for those who are "team players" and commit to serving the organization for many years.
    Those receiving the checks, however, see salaries differently. They focus on a paycheck's literal meaning: it is payment for work already done. Therefore, if
50 workers are paid less than they believe their work was truly worth, they develop feelings of resentment that cannot easily be smoothed over, even by significant boosts in their salaries later. By the time managers believe workers have proven their loyalty and
55 deserve to be rewarded for it, many of those workers are already sending out job applications.
    Psychologists have long understood that differing value systems can lead to conflict between groups of people. "The strange thing is," says Dr.
60 Madison Lopez of the Hosenfeld Institute, "human beings are naturally social and keenly interested in the thoughts and feelings of their fellow humans. Yet most people are actually inept at discerning what those thoughts and feelings might be." If
65 indeed the executives of organizations like Company A are failing to understand their employees' point of view, their efforts to persuade workers to commit to the company for the long term might actually be having the opposite effect. New
70 employees are often the workers most focused on their careers as a cornerstone of their overall happiness. If they believe that company executives are undervaluing their hard work, they may find it hard to ever trust management, even if they are
75 treated very well in later years. By contrast, those who have already made a long-term commitment to the company tend to look beyond the workplace (for example, to relationships with family and friends) to find their deeper happiness, and are therefore less
80 inclined to take a company's compensation practices personally.
    Those who work in management may protest that employees have an equal obligation to learn to understand the point of view of executives making
85 salary decisions. Russell and Kensington disagree. "Executives need to remember," Kensington has stated, "that although the company is the center of their world, the same will not be true for most employees, nor should it be." Employees cannot
90 protect their assets in the ways that partners in the corporation can. They know that if the company should fail, they will have little protection from lasting financial hardship. The central message conveyed by Russell and Kensington's work is
95 clear: If a company wishes to keep its employees for the long term, the best policy is to show appreciation for them early, rather than trying to coerce them into staying by delaying any reward for their efforts.

Figure 1: Comparison of average wages of workers hired in 2001 at Factories A and B.

12. The authors discuss the editorial article from Chasing the Money magazine (lines 3-9) in order to

    A) establish the importance of a stable workforce for a company's success.
    B) show that Wall Street is a center of business activity.
    C) show that many companies have a high rate of employee turnover.
    D) criticize dishonest practices among Wall Street investors.

13. The word "foster" in line 11 most nearly means

    A) discourage.
    B) cultivate.
    C) exaggerate.
    D) alienate.

14. The authors indicate that executives value employee salaries as

    A) a way to reward employees for a job well done.
    B) a way to demonstrate their generosity and popularity.
    C) a deduction that reduces the company's overall tax liability.
    D) a way to motivate employees to work harder in the future.

15. Which choice offers the clearest evidence to support the answer to the previous question?

    A) Lines 13-15 ("It would … plan.")
    B) Lines 39-42 ("To … horse.")
    C) Lines 49-53 ("Therefore, … later.")
    D) Lines 69-72 ("New … happiness.")

16. The passage indicates that employees

    A) share their bosses' views on the meaning of salaries.
    B) appreciate raises more if they have to wait a long time to receive them.
    C) attach a different meaning and value to their salaries than their bosses do.
    D) do not consider their salaries to be an important consideration when deciding whether to stay at a company.

17. Which choice provides the clearest evidence to support the answer to the previous question?

    A) Lines 29-31 ("And yet … 2001.")
    B) Lines 33-35 ("Why … them?")
    C) Lines 48-49 ("They … done.")
    D) Lines 53-56 ("By … applications.")

18. As used in line 63, "discerning" most nearly means

    A) ignoring.
    B) accepting.
    C) altering.
    D) perceiving.

19. The authors quote Dr. Madison Lopez (lines 59-64) primarily in order to

    A) respond to a likely objection to their conclusion.
    B) show how their study relates to a broader issue.
    C) question a commonly held belief.
    D) make a transition to a new, unrelated topic.

20. The results of the study (lines 29-32), together with the graph shown in Figure 1, suggest

   A) that employees are more likely to be loyal to a company if they are rewarded with raises early in their tenure with the company.

   B) that worker happiness has increased more overall at Company A than at Company B.

   C) that receiving raises only after several years working at a company inspires deeper loyalty in employees.

   D) that increasing employee wages raises a company's perceived value among Wall Street investors.

21. The authors would most likely recommend to executives at Company A to

   A) change the company's salary structure so that employees receive raises sooner after joining the organization.

   B) hire more employees who list loyalty as one of their strengths on their job application forms.

   C) reduce employee salaries until they are equal to the salaries of employees at Company B, thus reducing expenses and increasing profits.

   D) continue offering raises primarily to employees with many years of service to the company, to encourage all workers to commit to Company A for the long term.

Questions 22-32 are based on the following passage and additional information provided.

The province of Western Idleston depends on angling—recreational fishing, for those unfamiliar with the jargon—as a driving force in its economy. Government officials and conservation biologists face
[5] the daunting challenge of balancing the wishes of anglers with the health of aquatic ecosystems. One of the most important steps taken toward achieving that balance was the introduction in 1962 of the "closed seasons," periods each spring during which fishing
[10] for certain species is prohibited. Closed seasons are intended to prevent the harvesting of mature fish that are guarding nests during the spawning season. Although fish do not care for their offspring, they do aggressively protect the eggs they have buried in the
[15] riverbed or lake bottom. That protection is essential if the next generation of fish is to survive. What follows is an excerpt from a report published by biologist Dr. Julia Ahmed about the efficacy of closed seasons in maintaining healthy fish populations.

[20] In the province of West Idleston, we have four major species of game fish. Two of these species—welkfish and boskit—belong to the dark-spined family, while the other two—snupper and longfin blue—are of the family known as double-finned.
[25] Dark-spined fish spawn from approximately March 25 through May 4, whereas double-finned fish spawn later, from about April 10 through May 15. Accordingly, the closed seasons for dark-spined and double-finned fish are March 20 – May 10 and
[30] April 5 – May 21, respectively. Of great concern to both anglers and conservation experts should be the question of whether the periods from March 20 through April 4 and from May 11 through May 21, when fishing for one family of fish is open while
[35] fishing for the other is closed, pose a threat to the survival of treasured fish species.

During the period of March 20 – April 4, for example, an angler can legally fish for double-finned fish even though it is the closed season for
[40] dark-spined fish. For many years, it was assumed that as long as dark-spined fish caught unintentionally during this time period were immediately released, no harm would be done. A recent study by my colleague, Fei Huong, however, casts doubt upon this belief.
[45] Dr. Huong discovered that fish injured due to angling, whether through angler negligence or simply due to deep ingestion of a hook or lure, will abandon their nest-guarding responsibilities as they heal. Therefore, it is critically important to determine whether current
[50] closed seasons adequately protect each species from accidental catching by anglers pursuing another type of fish.

My research indicates that the probability of such accidental catching is in fact quite high. Unfortunately,
[55] fish do not sort themselves in aquatic ecosystems according to their families. I have shown in my study that boskit and snuppers prefer the same habitats, for example. Almost anywhere boskit are found, snuppers exist there in great numbers as well. Furthermore, the
[60] two species attack similar prey, and so will often be drawn to the same lures or bait. Similarly, where there are welkfish, there are often also longfin blues.

Further research is needed to determine whether species that favor the same habitat actually benefit
[65] from each other's presence, or whether they choose the habitat independently. Large-scale capture and relocation plans could be considered in the case of independence. For the immediate future, however, I recommend extending the closed season to
[70] March 20 – May 21 for all four fish species.

The table shows the presence of each species of game fish (columns) in various habitats (rows), represented as a percent of the total game fish population in that habitat.

Fish species

	Welkfish	Snupper	Boskit	Longfin blue
Still, weedy, shallow	2.3%	49.2%	42.1%	6.4%
Still, muddy, deep	5.7%	39.8%	43.3%	11.2%
Flowing, weedy, shallow	14.9%	35.1%	31.2%	18.8%
Flowing, sandy, shallow	45.9%	1.6%	2.3%	50.2%
Flowing, rocky, deep	87.4%	3.8%	3.8%	5.0%

SAMPLE TEST 1
Section 1: Reading Test

22. The primary purpose of the introduction (lines 1-18) is

    A) To provide background information to help the reader understand the significance of Dr. Ahmed's work.
    B) To describe a mistaken belief that Dr. Ahmed refutes in her article.
    C) To explain the differences between angling and fishing.
    D) To question the validity of Dr. Ahmed's article by examining the methods used in the study.

23. The words "spawning" and "spawn" in lines 12, 24, and 26 refer to

    A) fish battles over territory.
    B) fish feeding frenzies.
    C) fish reproduction.
    D) fish hibernation.

24. A fishing guide claims that fish sharing the same habitat are usually of the same family. Which of the following statements from the passage contradicts the guide's claim?

    A) Lines 24-25 ("Dark-spined … May 4,")
    B) Lines 25-26 ("whereas … May 15.")
    C) Lines 56-58 ("I … example.")
    D) Lines 69-70 ("Large-scale … independence.")

25. In the second paragraph of the passage (lines 19-35), which issue does Dr. Ahmed claim should be important to all those with an interest in angling?

    A) Whether certain types of lures are more likely to attract particular fish species
    B) Whether fish can be more easily caught in certain types of habitats
    C) Whether anglers obey laws concerning closed seasons for fishing
    D) Whether the timing of closed seasons is detrimental to fish populations

26. Dr. Ahmed's main purpose for referring to the work of Dr. Huong is to

    A) explain the techniques used to determine the health of fish populations.
    B) establish a reason for concern about accidental catching of fish during the closed season.
    C) present a differing few about the distribution of fish species in Western Idleston waters.
    D) present a hypothesis about the reasons a fish may deeply ingest a lure.

27. What point is Dr. Ahmed making in lines 61-63 ("Furthermore … bait.")?

    A) That it is not realistic for anglers fishing in an area containing both boskit and snuppers to expect to catch only one of the two species.
    B) That using a lure is a more effective way to fish for boskit and snuppers than using live bait.
    C) That because boskit and snuppers are predators, greater attention should be paid to the survival of the prey animals on which these species depend.
    D) That boskit and snuppers work together to hunt for food.

28. Based on the table, which choice gives the correct percentages of double-finned fish in flowing, weedy, shallow habitats?

    A) 14.9% and 35.1%
    B) 35.1% and 31.2%
    C) 18.8% and 35.1%
    D) 31.2% and 14.9%

29. Does the data in the table support Dr. Ahmed's primary claim about the likelihood of accidental fish catching during closed seasons?

   A) No, because for every habitat, there is only one prevalent species of fish.

   B) No, because for all but one habitat, the percentage of welkfish is closest to the percentage of boskit and the percentage of snupper is closest to the percentage of longfin blue.

   C) Yes, because for all but one habitat, the percentage of welkfish is closest to the percentage of snupper and the percentage of boskit is closest to the percentage of longfin blue.

   D) Yes, because for all but one habitat, the percentage of welkfish is closest to the percentage of longfin blue and the percentage of snupper is closest to the percentage of boskit.

30. According to the table, which of the following pairs of percentages for flowing, sandy, shallow habitats provides evidence in support of the answer to the previous question?

   A) 45.9% and 1.6%

   B) 50.2% and 45.9%

   C) 1.6% and 45.9%

   D) 2.3% and 50.2%

31. Why does Dr. Ahmed call for further research regarding whether different species of fish benefit from each other's presence (lines 65-68)?

   A) Because such information is needed in order to determine whether fish of one particular species can be relocated without harming another species

   B) Because such information could be used to help anglers have more success catching fish

   C) Because her primary claim cannot be verified without such additional information

   D) Because providing anglers with such information would reduce the likelihood of accidental catching of species during the closed season

32. Based on the table, is there any habitat for which it might be safe to have a different closed season for dark-spined fish than for double-finned fish?

   A) Yes—still, weedy, shallow habitat

   B) Yes—flowing, weedy, shallow habitat

   C) Yes—flowing, rocky, deep habitat

   D) No

SAMPLE TEST 1
Section 1: Reading Test

Questions 33-42 are based on the following passage.

This passage is adapted from a letter written by Abigail Adams to John Adams on March 31 and April 5, 1776, several months before the signing of the Declaration of Independence.

I wish you would ever write me a letter half as long as I write you. What sort of defense can Virginia make against our common enemy? Is it so situated as to make an able defense? Are not the gentry lords and the common
[5] people all vassals, are they not like the uncivilized natives Britain represents us to be? I hope their riflemen, who have shown themselves very savage and bloodthirsty, are not a specimen of the generality of the people. I am willing to allow the colony of Virginia great merit for
[10] having produced a General Washington, but they have been shamefully duped by a Governor Dunmore.

I have sometimes been ready to think that the passion for liberty cannot be equally strong in the breasts of those who have been accustomed to depriving their fellow
[15] creatures of freedom. Of this I am certain, that such passion is not necessarily founded upon that generous and Christian principle of doing to others as we would have others do unto us.

The town in general is left in a better state than we
[20] expected, more owing to a precipitous flight of the inhabitants than to any regard for its survival. Some individuals at least discovered a sense of honor and justice and have left behind the rent they owed to the owners of the houses in which they had resided, and
[25] either left the furniture unharmed or included sufficient funds to make it good.

Others have committed abominable ravages. The mansion house of your president is safe and the furniture unhurt, while the house and furniture of the Solicitor
[30] General have fallen prey to his own merciless allies Surely even such fiends feel a reverential awe for virtue and patriotism, while detesting patricide and treachery.

I feel very differently at the approach of spring than I did a month ago. We knew not then whether we could
[35] plant or sow with safety, whether after our toil we would be able to reap the fruits or our own industry, whether we could rest in our own cottages, or whether we would be driven from the sea coast to seek shelter in the wilderness. Now we feel as if we might sit under our own vines and
[40] eat the good of the land.

I feel a gaiety of heart to which I was previously a stranger. I think the sun looks brighter, the birds sing more melodiously, and nature puts on a more cheerful countenance. We feel a temporary peace, and the poor
[45] fugitives are returning to their deserted habitations.

Though we feel joy, we sympathize with those who are trembling, lest the lot of Boston should be theirs. Yet they cannot be in similar circumstances unless cowardice should take possession of them. They have time and have
[50] received warning, that they may see the evil and shun it.

I long to hear that you have declared independence. And by the way, in the new Code of Laws which I suppose it will be necessary for you to
[55] make, I desire you would remember the ladies, and be more generous and favorable to them than your ancestors. Do not put such unlimited power in the hands of the husbands. Remember all men would be tyrants if they could. If particular care and attention is
[60] not paid to the ladies, we are determined to foment our own rebellion, and will not hold ourselves bound by any laws written in a manner such that we had neither voice nor representation.

That those of your sex are naturally tyrannical
[65] is a truth so thoroughly established as to admit of no dispute, but such of you as wish to be happy willingly give up the harsh title of master for the more tender and endearing one of friend. Why then, not put it beyond the power of the vicious and the
[70] lawless to act toward us with cruelty and indignity with impunity. Men of sense in all ages abhor those customs which treat women as the vassals of your sex. Regard us then as beings placed by providence under your protection, and in imitation of the
[75] Supreme Being, make use of that power only for our happiness.

I want to hear much more often from you than I do. March 8 was the last date of any that I have yet received. You inquire as to whether I am making
[80] saltpeter*. I have not yet attempted it, but after soap making believe I shall make the experiment. I know of but one person in this part of the town who has made any, that is Mr. Tertias Bass, who has got very near a hundred weight which has been found to be
[85] very good. I have lately seen a small manuscript describing the proportions for the various sorts of powder for cannon, small arms, and pistols. If it would be of any service to you, I will get it transcribed and send it to you.
[90] I need not say how much I am ever your faithful friend.

*Saltpeter: a chemical compound, potassium nitrate, used as a fertilizer, food preservative, and primary component of gunpowder.

33. Ms. Adams's reason for presenting the examples of Washington and Dunmore (lines 10 and 11) was

A) to acknowledge that Virginia has contributed to the independence effort, while explaining her reasons for distrusting the colony.

B) to criticize Virginia's admiration of military generals and disrespect toward civilian leaders such as governors.

C) to analyze the differences between General Washington and Governor Dunmore.

D) to suggest that General Washington's success would not have been possible without Governor Dunmore, and that the people of Virginia are unaware of that fact.

34. Which of the following choices best describes Ms. Adams's two main purposes in writing this letter?

A) to describe various styles of furniture and houses found in the town and their current state of repair.

B) to describe conditions in the town and to stress the importance of an issue to be considered in drafting new laws.

C) to discuss prospects for a successful farming season with a fruitful harvest and describe the projects she and others in the town have undertaken.

D) to explain her reasons for writing long letters and express her wish to reduce their length by half.

35. The main point made in lines 33-45 ("I feel … habitations.") is that

A) after a period of boredom, life in the town has become joyful and exciting again.

B) after a period of hard work, the people of the town are now relaxing and resting.

C) after a period of uncertainty and fear, the town feels safe again, so that normal activities may resume.

D) after a period of quiet reflection, she has finally decided which course of action to take.

36. Ms. Adams's main purpose in listing the examples in lines 42-44 ("I think … countenance.") is

A) to illustrate the recent improvement in her mood.

B) to provide a detailed description of natural phenomena in the region.

C) to urge Mr. Adams to take more time to appreciate nature's beauty.

D) to persuade Mr. Adams to visit more often.

37. Ms. Adams feels that the people of towns gripped by fear have no reason to believe they will suffer the same fate as the people of Boston because

A) they are aware of the looming danger and have time to prepare for it.

B) they are too far from the sea coast to be in any real danger.

C) they are fugitives with no permanent homes.

D) they have different enemies than the people of Boston had.

38. The passage shows that Ms. Adams saw American independence as an opportunity to

A) end all tyranny, since there would be no monarchy in the United States.

B) prove to the British that American colonists were not savages.

C) promote generosity among people.

D) improve conditions for women.

39. Which of the following best describes Ms. Adams's tone when writing about the opportunity mentioned in the previous question?

A) Gentle and supportive

B) Objective and scientific

C) Assertive and confrontational

D) Sarcastic and humorous

40. As used in line 60, "foment" most nearly means

A) torment.

B) forgo.

C) incite.

D) suppress.

41. The main point Ms. Adams is making in lines 52-76 is

A) that women need the protection of men and laws should reflect that need.

B) that men cannot be trusted not to abuse any power the law gives them over women.

C) that it is kinder to refer to a person as one's friend than as one's master.

D) that all people should obey the law, regardless of whether they had a say in how those laws were written.

42. The paragraph consisting of lines 77 through 89 suggests that Mr. Adams inquired about the making of saltpeter primarily because

A) he is curious about the activities of Ms. Adams and other people of the town.

B) he anticipates it being very useful during the busy farming season soon to begin.

C) of its value in the event of war.

D) of the need to preserve food since supplies run low at the end of winter.

Questions 43-52 are based on the following passages.

Passage 1

In the modern era, the thought of exploring the unknown generally sets people looking to the heavens. However, a vast treasure of undiscovered wonders lies hidden from us right here on Earth, literally beneath our
5   feet. Giant caves are known to extend for 40, 50, or even hundreds of miles beneath innocent-seeming hills. Venturing into their depths has always been the impossible dream of adventuring, as the risks to human explorers and the possibility of destroying unique
10 ecosystems together acted as a giant, metaphorical 'DO NOT ENTER" sign.

All of that may change thanks to the development of new, submersible drones that can function in total darkness and can easily withstand the massive pressures
15 that may be encountered in underground waterways. As cave expert Addison McNeil explains, "The greatest obstacle to deep cave expeditions has always been the impossibility of extended, safe dives in waterways that include treacherous cascades in utter blackness, still
20 pools that become disorienting swirls of silt the moment a diver enters, and streams that seem to stop dead at cave walls, sneaking onward to the other side through half-inch crevices up to 30 feet below the surface." The new drones can be
25 of even a half dozen of them would not bankrupt an exploration project. If a drone encounters a dead end, it can simply deactivate itself and sink harmlessly to the bottom of the pool or stream, where it will resist corrosion and decay for millions of years.
30 Since 2012, over a dozen companies have devoted substantial resources to developing cave-probing drones, including DiveScore Corporation, which claims to have created a drone that can function under extreme water pressure for up to 4 years. Underwater, Inc. plans to
35 soon unveil an advanced drone that can dispatch nanoprobes (microscopic data collecting devices) to delve into the tiniest crevices or carry data back to researchers if the drone is unable to return from the dive.

The use of these deep diving robots offers the
40 promise of extraordinary advancements in scientific knowledge. Biologists estimate that we have only identified 25% of the plant and animal species on Earth, and believe that the majority of unknown species live in high pressure, deep water environments like open ocean
45 and massive caves. "Every time we encounter new species in an environment we consider exotic," says ecologist Kayla Washington, "we are forced to reconsider everything we thought we knew about how life as we know it came into being." Many scientists thus
50 believe that deep cave exploration will greatly advance our understanding of the conditions under which life can exist. Ironically, that is one of the central questions of interest as we ponder launching human beings toward the stars.

Passage 2

55 Tremendous excitement is radiating throughout the scientific community these days, sparked by promising developments in the design and manufacturing of specialized drones that could be used in deep cave exploration. Proponents of the use
60 of these drones argue that at long last, scientists have a way to learn the secrets of the underground deep without the loss of life or potentially devastating environmental impacts associated with human cave-diving missions.
65 The logic behind the optimism is seductive. Drones are expendable in a way human lives are not. Because they do not need to eat, drink, or eliminate waste, they will not despoil fragile habitats the way human explorers inevitably would, even if human
70 divers exercised the greatest of care. "The scarcity of resources in under-Earth environments is incomprehensible to those of us who live on the surface," explains geologist Mayong Shin of the Carlinong Institute. "A single diver dropping a single
75 apple seed would have an impact comparable to campers leaving 200,000 gallons of ice cream in a forest. The behavior of species could be changed forever." The use of drones utterly eliminates this concern, seemingly affording scientists the
80 opportunity to study the farthest reaches of any cave without harming a single organism.

Such an optimistic view, however, is based on the erroneous assumption that just because drones wouldn't have the same impacts as human divers,
85 they would have no impact at all. Even if scientists are convinced that submersible drones will not damage deep cave ecosystems in the ways humans would, the possibility remains that they will cause harm in other, unforeseen ways. Almost all deep
90 cave-dwelling creatures are sightless (for eyesight is of no value in total darkness), and therefore depend on sound, smell, and vibrations of air and water to find their way around or hunt for food. Even the quietest drones are not silent, and even the smallest
95 nanoprobe still causes a microscopic ripple in the water. In the fragile depths of the Earth, a seemingly

insignificant intrusion might trigger a tragedy of astonishing proportions.

    We must also ask what will happen after drones bring images of the unimaginable beauty of the underground world up to the surface for all to see. Can humankind be trusted to exercise restraint, or will a mad rush into the deep ensue, with horrific consequences? Human history is woefully lacking in proof that our species is capable of knowing of the existence of a wondrous place, yet choosing to leave it alone.

43.

The author of Passage 1 indicates that the use of submersible drones could have which positive result?

A) It could lead to new opportunities for human exploration of deep caves.

B) It could lead to the discovery of new materials of great economic value in caves.

C) It could advance the scientific understanding of the nature and development of life.

D) It could lead to the development of new technologies that will be useful for space travel.

44.

Which choice provides the clearest evidence for the answer to the previous question?

A) Lines 16-23 ("The greatest … surface.")
B) Lines 26-29 ("If … years.")
C) Lines 34-38 ("Underwatter … dive.")
D) Lines 45-49 ("Every … being.")

45.

As used in lines 23 and 37, "crevices" most nearly means

A) cracks.
B) rivers.
C) surface depressions.
D) muddy deposits.

46.

The author's primary purpose in mentioning two companies in lines 30-38 is to

A) emphasize the potential economic benefits of deep cave exploration.
B) show the widespread interest in developing drone technology for cave exploration.
C) highlight the controversy over who stands to profit from deep cave exploration.
D) promote investment in companies working on cave exploration technology.

47.

What is the main parallel the author of Passage 1 draws between deep cave exploration and space exploration?

A) Both endeavors use technology that is rapidly growing more sophisticated.
B) Both endeavors involve great risk of loss of life and damage to fragile environments.
C) Both endeavors seek to answer the question of when, where, and how life comes into existence.
D) Both endeavors involve great expense and therefore can only succeed with the involvement of major compaies.

48.

The central claim of Passage 2 is that although the use of drones eliminates many of the risks traditionally associated with deep cave exploration,

A) it is too expensive to be practical.
B) it will require use of massive amounts of energy and therefore poses and environmental threat.
C) it will not allow for gathering the quantities of data that are needed to truly understand deep cave environments.
D) it may involve other risks that have not yet been fully considered.

49.

As used in line 65, "seductive" most nearly means

A) deceptively attractive.
B) completely irrefutable.
C) complex.
D) elusive.

50.

Which statement best describes how Passages 1 and 2 are related to each other?

A) Passage 2 offers specific illustrations of general ideas presented in Passage 1.
B) Passage 2 expresses concerns about the possibilities discussed in Passage 1.
C) Passage 2 offers general conclusions based on specific examples presented in Passage 1.
D) Passage 2 questions the accuracy of the descriptions of new technologies provided in Passage 1.

51.
The author of Passage 2 would most likely respond to the claim made about drones deactivating themselves in lines 26-29 of Passage 1 by claiming that

A) technology is not reliable and the drone's deactivation mechanism might fail.

B) it cannot be known for certain that a drone sinking in an underground waterway would be harmless.

C) a drone deactivating itself would result in the loss of massive amounts of data, rendering the exploration attempt worthless.

D) retrieval of deactivated drones would be extremely expensive, a cost that advocates for deep cave exploration have not considered.

52.
Which choice provides the clearest evidence in support of the answer to the previous question?

A) Lines 59-64 ("Proponents … missions.")

B) Line 66 ("Drones … not.")

C) Lines 93-98 ("Even … proportions.")

D) Lines 104-107 ("Human … alone.")

STOP

If you have finished this section before time expires, you may check your work. You cannot return to this section once you move on to the next section.

STOP!

If you have finished this section before time expires, you may check your work. You cannot return to this section once you move on to the next section.

www.eggheadprep.com

ANSWERS, SECTION 1
SAMPLE TEST 1 — READING

1. D
2. A
3. C
4. B
5. C
6. D
7. C
8. B
9. A
10. D
11. A
12. A
13. B
14. D
15. B
16. C
17. C
18. D
19. B
20. A
21. A
22. A
23. C
24. C
25. D
26. B
27. A
28. C
29. D
30. B
31. A
32. C
33. A
34. B
35. C
36. A
37. A
38. D
39. C
40. C
41. B
42. C
43. C
44. D
45. A
46. B
47. C
48. D
49. A
50. B
51. B
52. C

eggheadprep.com

SECTION 2: WRITING & LANGUAGE TEST

35 MINUTES, 44 QUESTIONS

DIRECTIONS

Below you will find a number of reading passages. Each one is accompanied by a series of questions. A note before each passage will tell you which questions are related to that passage. Some questions will require you to consider possible revisions to the passage to help the writer express the ideas more clearly or effectively. Other questions will ask you to consider ways to edit the passage to correct errors in punctuation, word usage, or sentence structure. Some questions and passages include graphics, such as tables and graphs. As you make your decisions about possible changes, you should take the graphics into consideration along with the text.

Some questions will refer to a specific, underlined portion of the passage. Others will ask you to focus on a particular location within the passage. There will also be questions that ask you to think about the passage as a whole. Numbers enclosed in parentheses and written with a Q, such as (Q14) indicate the number of the question associated with that portion of the passage. Numbers bracketed in plain text, like [2], are used to identifying sentences within the passage.

Read each passage and then choose the answer to each question that best improves the writing of the passage or brings the particular phrase or sentence into agreement with the conventions of standard written English. If you believe the best choice is to leave the indicated portion of the passage as it is, choose the option, "NO CHANGE."

Questions 1 – 11 are based on the following passage.

Beavers Know Best:
The Importance of Natural Dams

River canoeing is a very popular leisure activity throughout the United States. To facilitate river recreation, managers of parks and natural areas often remove beaver dams from waterways. In recent years, **(Q1)** for example, many people have started to wonder if that practice is more harmful to the environment than was previously believed.

1.
A) NO CHANGE
B) also,
C) however,
D) thus,

SAMPLE TEST 1
Section 2: Writing & Language Test

The primary reason for beaver dam removal is easy to understand. Portaging—the process of carrying a canoe over land around an obstruction in the river—is very difficult for novice paddlers. Those who manage natural areas want to make outdoor recreation accessible for everyone. Problems occur, however, when efforts to open up the wilderness to human visitors put at risk **(Q2)** the very plant and animal life those visitors came to see.

[1] Only recently have scientists begun to understand the extraordinary array of benefits that beaver dams provide for aquatic ecosystems. [2] Fish, amphibians, and waterfowl all benefit from the deep, calm pools that beaver dams create. [3] Rivers and streams with beaver dams at regular intervals have steadier, more sustained water flows **(Q4)** like those without dams. [4] Water flow is especially important in an era when severe droughts and floods are becoming more common **(Q5)** and people are becoming lazy and don't want to paddle a canoe. [5] In areas of the US where cities and counties have historically spent millions of dollars building levees to mitigate flooding, officials are now discovering that beavers will happily do the necessary work for free if given the chance. [6] **(Q6)** In spite of all these discoveries, officials have begun to investigate how humans and beavers might work together to protect rivers for everyone.

2.
- A) NO CHANGE
- B) the safety of those visitors.
- C) the revenue those visitors bring to a town.
- D) the reputation of the park and its staff.

3.

The author is considering adding this sentence:

Animals that feed on fish and amphibians, such as otters, eagles, osprey, and bears, have greater reproductive success because prey species are more abundant.

What would be the most appropriate place to add this sentence?

- A) Before sentence 1
- B) After sentence 2
- C) After sentence 4
- D) After sentence 5

4.
- A) NO CHANGE
- B) than those without dams.
- C) then those without dams.
- D) instead of those without dams.

5.

The author is considering deleting the underlined phrase. Should the writer make this change?

- A) No, because the phrase provides a transition to the next idea.
- B) No, because it provides key information that supports the author's main point.
- C) Yes, because it starts with the word, "and."
- D) Yes, because the phrase is not relevant to the paragraph.

6.
- A) NO CHANGE
- B) Ignoring
- C) In protest to
- D) In light of

[1] The primary challenge officials face is balancing the needs of human outdoor enthusiasts with the needs of the organisms that call wild areas home. [2] Some wildlife advocates have proposed leaving all beaver dams alone and simply telling paddlers to make the best of it. [3] However, that approach would be shortsighted: canoeists would inevitably attempt to push their way through dams, **(Q7)** destroyed the dams and sending a cascade of debris downriver. [4] More creative-thinking scientists have put forth a novel idea: creating portable "drag-around portages" that enable canoeists to paddle onto a small ramp along the shore and then easily drag their canoe around the dam to resume their journey.

Before **(Q9)** inciting such a plan, experts will need to analyze all the costs involved. Nevertheless, the very fact such a plan has been proposed represents a step in the right direction. Wilderness enthusiasts, conservation **(Q10)** experts; and local and national governments officials must work together to find ways to change our relationship with beavers into one of cooperation rather than **(Q11)** friendship.

7.
- A) NO CHANGE
- B) destroying
- C) having destroyed
- D) will destroy

8. The author is considering adding this sentence after sentence [4].

When beavers relocate their dams, the portage ramp could simply be moved to the new dam site, while the old dam is carefully dismantled.

Should the author make this change?
- A) Yes, because it highlights another advantage of the portage system being discussed.
- B) Yes, because it explains why environmental protection is important.
- C) No, because it is not relevant to the passage.
- D) No, because it should be inserted after sentence [3] instead.

9.
- A) NO CHANGE
- B) inclining
- C) infiltrating
- D) implementing

10.
- A) NO CHANGE
- B) experts: and
- C) experts, and
- D) experts: and,

11.
- A) NO CHANGE
- B) working together
- C) collaboration
- D) conflict

SAMPLE TEST 1
Section 2: Writing & Language Test

Questions 12-22 are based on the following passage and the graphics below.

Holiday Cheer or December Drear?

Consumers in the country of Northern Landia often find themselves struggling to pay off debts in February and March. Economists have long assumed that the cause of those debts was obvious: extravagant spending in November and December on winter holiday gifts. For the week of December 7-13, 2015, an average Northern Landia consumer spent **(Q12)** about $170 on food and $340 on other expenditures. Those amounts were **(Q13)** significantly higher for the week of February 22-28, 2016.

12. Which option most accurately represents the information provided by the graph?
    A) NO CHANGE
    B) about $130 on food
    C) over $180 on food
    D) about $150 on food

13.
    A) NO CHANGE
    B) significantly lower
    C) about the same
    D) not known

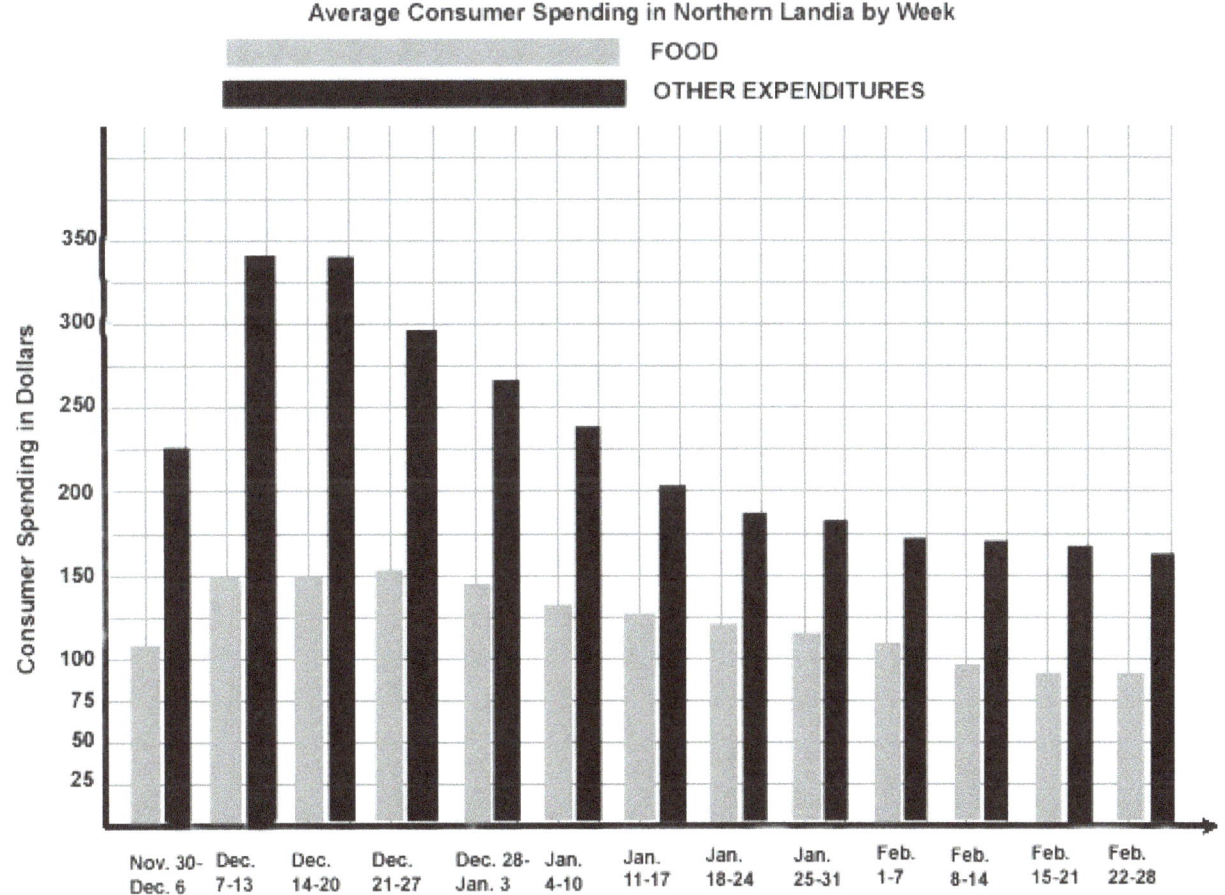

Northern Landians celebrate a variety of holidays throughout December, most of which involve some form of gift giving. **(Q14)** Therefore, many holiday celebrations center on the preparation of a traditional feast requiring the purchase of specialty grocery items. Experts have generally seen the increase in consumer spending in early winter as **(Q15)** exclusively being caused by this. However, as the graph shows, consumer spending **(Q16)** drops off immediately after the last of the holidays, on December 29th. **(Q17)** Diane Kowalska an economist at the Davidson Institute; has suggested there may be another cause for increased consumer spending that has been overlooked: seasonal depression.

14.
- A) NO CHANGE
- B) However,
- C) Nevertheless,
- D) In addition,

15.
- A) NO CHANGE
- B) exclusively caused by holiday-related expenses.
- C) exclusively caused by this increase.
- D) not really due to this.

16.
- A) NO CHANGE
- B) rises throughout December.
- C) remains well above late winter levels through early January, long after the last holiday on December 29th.
- D) drops off sharply before December 14th, even though the last holiday does not occur until December 29th.

17.
- A) NO CHANGE
- B) Diane Kowalska, an economist at the Davidson Institute,
- C) Diane Kowalska, an economist, at the Davidson Institute,
- D) Diane Kowalska: an economist at the Davidson Institute,

SAMPLE TEST 1
Section 2: Writing & Language Test

Kowalska, who has studied consumer behavior in Northern Landia for over 25 years, points out that November and December are the cloudiest months of the year in the country. Icy rains fall **(Q18)** incandescently, driven by relentless winds. On the rare days when the sun does shine, the brightening of the skies is short-lived, as daylight lasts a mere six hours. These constant environmental stresses take **(Q19)** it's toll on both the mind and the body. By early December, Kowalska observes, many Northern Landians feel downhearted and exhausted.

Psychologists have understood for many years that depression can alter a person's appetite. Kowalska has proposed that increased food expenditures in December may actually be a reflection of consumers' need to find comfort as their moods sag, **(Q20)** as similar to an indication of widespread holiday cheer. Likewise, increased spending on non-food items may stem from a need to fight the feeling of monotony that arises during seemingly endless strings of could-darkened days.

18. Which choice most likely expresses the author's intended meaning?
    A) NO CHANGE
    B) incessantly,
    C) incrementally,
    D) incidentally

19.
    A) NO CHANGE
    B) its
    C) they're
    D) their

20.
    A) NO CHANGE
    B) with regard to
    C) as opposed to
    D) in accordance with

[1] Kowalska acknowledges that more data is needed in order to determine the extent to which dreary weather, not holiday cheer, drives consumer spending in December in Northern Landia. [2] She has proposed a five-year study of consumers from every region of the country. [3] The results of such a study could fundamentally change the way Northern Landians think about the winter holiday season. [4] According to psychologists, a connection between seasonal depression and increased consumer spending could fuel an escalating cycle. [5] Old beliefs about holiday spending as an indicator of the health of the economy may be replaced by new concerns over the health of the populace. [6] Consumers might spend more money because they are feeling low and then feel guilty about their financial recklessness, **(Q22)** which is caused by deeper depression and even more irresponsible spending.

21. To make this paragraph as logical as possibly, sentence 4 should be placed

    A) in its current location.
    B) before sentence 3.
    C) after sentence 5.
    D) after sentence 6.

22. Which of these choices best expresses the idea of an escalating cycle?

    A) NO CHANGE
    B) causing deeper depression and even more irresponsible spending.
    C) which prevents deeper depression and even more irresponsible spending.
    D) which is how the economy can grow stronger.

SAMPLE TEST 1
Section 2: Writing & Language Test

Questions 23-33 are based on the following passage.

Can Powering Down Help the Mind Power Up?

It is virtually impossible to make it through a day in 2016 without being bombarded by advertisements for the latest gadgets. Laptops, tablets, and smartphones keep many people connected to the worldwide web every waking moment. As a freelancer, I have welcomed the "work from anywhere" possibilities of the present age with enthusiasm. Yet as I **(Q23)** increase to find myself interrupting conversations and dinner dates to connect with a screen, I have started to wonder what other connections I am losing. I struggle more often with memory and **(Q24)** concentration, friends have not asked me for help remembering things. It is as if I have lost the ability to solve problems in my own mental space, without interacting with a device. In the midst of pondering what to do about this situation, I came upon an interesting article **(Q25)** over the benefits of a daily "unplugging" routine.

23.
A) NO CHANGE
B) increase in
C) increasingly
D) more frequent

24.
A) NO CHANGE
B) concentration, and friends because of this had not asked me for help remembering things.
C) concentration: friends cannot remember things, and I have trouble asking them.
D) concentration; friends do not ask me for help remembering things anymore.

25.
A) NO CHANGE
B) about
C) into
D) upon

The article was published in 2014 by *The Dauntless Mind* magazine. The authors, Doctors Emma Nguyen and Jacob Mustafi, explain that there is a limit to how much information the human mind can process in a day. For almost all of human history, an average person spent several hours a day interacting with his or her surroundings in a very limited way, processing only basic sensory input. **(Q26)** On the other hand, the person's mind was free to wander, spinning daydreams in a state of relaxation. It turns out that those daydreams were **(Q27)** also just diversions, however. They allowed the brain to perform daily maintenance on its systems, keeping the mind sharp.

26.
- A) NO CHANGE
- B) As a result,
- C) Unfortunately,
- D) Coincidentally,

27.
- A) NO CHANGE
- B) altogether
- C) entirely
- D) not

28. The author is considering adding the following sentence at the end of the paragraph:

Modern imaging technology can be used to scan the brain and study its health, but the procedure is expensive.

Should this sentence be added?

- A) Yes, because it provides information that supports the main idea of the paragraph.
- B) Yes, because it provides a transition to the paragraph that comes next.
- C) No, because such technology does not exist.
- D) No, because it presents information that is only vaguely related to the rest of the paragraph and does not support the paragraph's main idea.

The authors conducted a study in **(Q29)** the year, 2013, asking participants to spend a minimum of 1 hour each day completely separated from any devices with screens. The participants could, for example, listen to music on a vinyl record, read a book, or simply gaze out a window and let their minds wander. The researchers found that **(Q30)** 56 percent of participants experienced greater difficulty remembering things as a result of spending time "unplugged." The results of the study strongly suggest that powering down devices for a short time each day can greatly improve a person's mental performance.

29.
A) NO CHANGE
B) 2013,
C) 2013;
D) throughout the year, 2013,

30.
At the end of this paragraph, the author will include the following graphic:

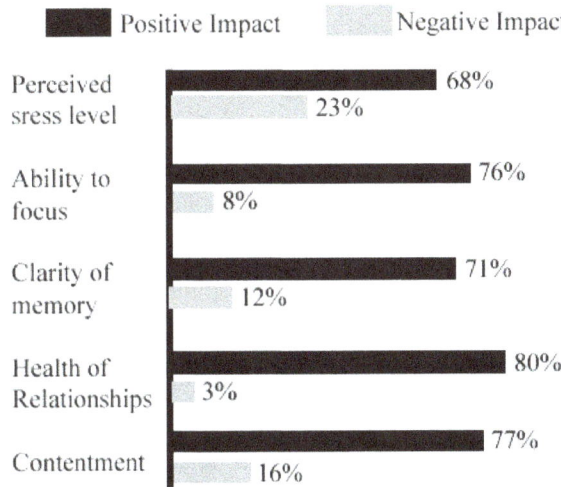

Which of the following choices would most appropriately complete the sentence with accurate information that supports the main idea of the paragraph?

A) NO CHANGE
B) participants believed that 80 percent of their relationship problems were caused by "unplugged time."
C) 71 percent of participants believed their clarity of of memory improved as a result of spending time "unplugged."
D) participants believed that their overall contentment increased by 16 percent as a result of spending time "unplugged."

[1] The first day, I barely made it 20 minutes before intense anxiety drove me to turn on my phone and check for messages and social media updates. [2] Over the course of the next several weeks, however, I became more comfortable with "unplugged" time, and even started looking forward to it eagerly each day. **(Q32)** [3] Sitting quietly and reading a Sherlock Holmes novel one evening, my phone was so far from my mind that I was astonished to see it within arm's reach when I finally looked up from my book. [4] I realized at that moment that a fundamental change had occurred in the way I spend my days. [5] Soon after, I began to recognize a variety of positive effects of that change.

First and foremost, my ability to focus mentally had improved dramatically. I no longer struggled to remember names, places, or details. I could maintain my concentration on a single task for hours at a time, and thus delve deeper into problems and generate more creative solutions. I have been amazed by all the other benefits of my "unplugged" time **(Q33)** regimen: better sleep, improved relationships, fewer health problems, and a more optimistic outlook on my life. I can't recommend daily "unplugged" time highly enough!

31.

The author wishes to add the following sentence to the first paragraph shown on this page:

After reading the article, I decided to try incorporating "unplugged" time into my daily routine.

The most logical placement of this sentence would be:

A) before sentence 1
B) after sentence 1
C) after sentence 3
D) after sentence 4

32.

A) NO CHANGE
B) Sitting quietly and reading a Sherlock Holmes novel one evening my
C) As I sat quietly reading a Sherlock Holmes novel one evening, my
D) I sat quietly and read and Sherlock Holmes novel one evening, my

33.

A) NO CHANGE
B) regimen
C) regimen;
D) regimen,

SAMPLE TEST 1
Section 2: Writing & Language Test

Questions 34-44 are based on the following passage.

In Defense of Hands-On Education

Throughout most of the twentieth century, almost all American high schools offered courses in manual arts, such as sewing, woodworking, cooking, and auto repair. The manual arts were generally divided into two broad groups: home economics, **(Q34)** which included skills seen as "domestic," such as sewing and cooking; and industrial arts (also called "shop"), which encompassed a broad range of disciplines associated with professional trades. For decades, most schools segregated students by gender, allowing girls to enroll only in home economics courses, while boys had access only to industrial arts classes. Fortunately, this shameful, discriminatory practice has come to an end, but in many schools, the entire manual arts curriculum has been eliminated in the process. Many experts are wondering if, **(Q35)** admittedly with the best of intentions, school systems are now depriving students of an essential component of a complete education.

Human infants gain much of their early understanding of the world by clasping objects in **(Q36)** one's hands. Skillful manipulation of small tools has long been recognized by biologists as one of the driving forces in the development of modern human intelligence. **(Q37)** Nevertheless, many public schools have chosen to disregard the central role manual skills play in training the mind to handle complex tasks. **(Q38)** Appropriately, now that their species has achieved intellectual greatness primarily by mastering manual tasks, human beings seem to view dedication to such tasks as a sign of low intelligence.

34.
A) NO CHANGE
B) that also included
C) that talks about
D) which should be including

35.
A) NO CHANGE
B) adversely with the best of intentions,
C) with the best of intentions, accordingly
D) admittedly since having intentions of the best,

36.
A) NO CHANGE
B) his or her
C) their
D) they're

37. Which option is most effective in setting up the information that follows?
A) A lot of people think that manual arts don't belong in a school setting.
B) It is therefore not surprising that a 2003 study showed that students who train in the manual arts exhibit greater patience in analyzing complicated problems than students without such training.
C) Small tools are used less in the present century than in previous eras, due to the prevalence of automated systems that can perform a variety of tasks that used to require many workers.
D) Also, a lot of simple tasks can now be done without even using one's hands, by using sophisticated digital technology.

38.
A) NO CHANGE
B) Ironically,
C) Apologetically,
D) Consequently,

Many experts believe the root of the problem is a widely held, but mistaken, belief that an individual may be talented with his or her hands, or with his or her mind, but not both. Many parents actually fear that allowing their child to study the manual arts will hinder the child's intellectual growth. Sadly, the majority of public high schools **(Q39)** reconstruct this misconception by scheduling classes in such a way that taking both manual arts and academic courses is a practical impossibility. The inevitable result is that all students, whether they choose to explore the manual arts or to focus on academic courses, receive an incomplete education.

The first step toward addressing this problem is to demonstrate the connection between manual arts training and the development of problem-solving abilities. Cognitive scientist Cassandra Yang has made an important contribution to that effort. In 2006, she showed that on average, expert auto mechanics exhibit greater skill at pure problem-solving tasks than high school **(Q40)** teachers do. This was because of the use of college entrance exams. Many **(Q41)** carpenter's also completed the exams, earning an average score higher than first-year college students. To date, not a single study has produced significantly different results.

39.
   A) NO CHANGE
   B) reconsider
   C) resolve
   D) reinforce

40.
   A) NO CHANGE
   B) teachers do, as measured by performance on college entrance exams.
   C) teachers do, and this can also be seen because of college entrance exams being used.
   D) teachers, based on when the results are taken from scores related to taking college entrance exams.

41.
   A) NO CHANGE
   B) carpenters also completed
   C) carpenter's completion of
   D) carpenters as well completed

42.
The author is considering adding the following sentence to the second paragraph on this page:

The tools required to teach manual arts are affordable to purchase and last for many years.

Should the writer make this addition to the paragraph?

   A) Yes, because it supports the main idea of the paragraph.
   B) Yes, because it is answers a question raised earlier in the passage and therefore strengthens the main argument being presented here.
   C) No, because it undermines the main idea that schools should offer courses in manual arts.
   D) No, because it blurs the focus of the paragraph by presenting an idea that is not relevant to the main argument being made.

Perhaps the strongest argument in favor of including manual arts training in the American high school curriculum, however, comes from the students themselves. Students constantly clamor for more high school courses focusing on skills that are "useful in real life." The obvious future usefulness of manual arts expertise **(Q43)** which offers powerful motivation for young people to throw themselves into a sewing or woodworking class with gusto. Of course, those same students will also be subtly gaining the intellectual agility to handle complex problems **(Q44)** he or she will encounter in the sciences and humanities later. But that can be our little secret.

43.
A) NO CHANGE
B) that
C) therefore
D) DELETE the underline portion.

44.
A) NO CHANGE
B) one
C) they
D) we

STOP!

If you have finished this section before time expires, you may check your work. You cannot return to this section once you move on to the next section.

www.eggheadprep.com

ANSWERS, SECTION 2
SAMPLE TEST 1 — WRITING & LANGUAGE

1. C
2. A
3. B
4. B
5. D
6. D
7. B
8. A
9. D
10. C
11. D
12. D
13. B
14. D
15. B
16. C
17. B
18. B
19. D
20. C
21. C
22. B
23. C
24. D
25. B
26. B
27. D
28. D
29. B
30. C
31. A
32. C
33. A
34. A
35. A
36. C
37. B
38. B
39. D
40. B
41. B
42. D
43. D
44. C

SECTION 3: MATH TEST
NO CALCULATOR, 25 MINUTES, 20 QUESTIONS

DIRECTIONS

For questions 1–15, solve the problem and choose the best answer from the options provided. For questions 16–20, solve the problem and type in your answer. Further instructions for typing in your answer are provided before question 16.

NOTES

1. Calculator use is not permitted for this section. You will distort your score if you use one.
2. All variables and expressions represent real numbers unless stated otherwise.
3. Unless otherwise indicated, figures shown have been drawn to scale.
4. All figures lie in a plane unless stated otherwise.
5. The domain of a function f is the set of real numbers for which f(x) is a real number, unless stated otherwise.

REFERENCE

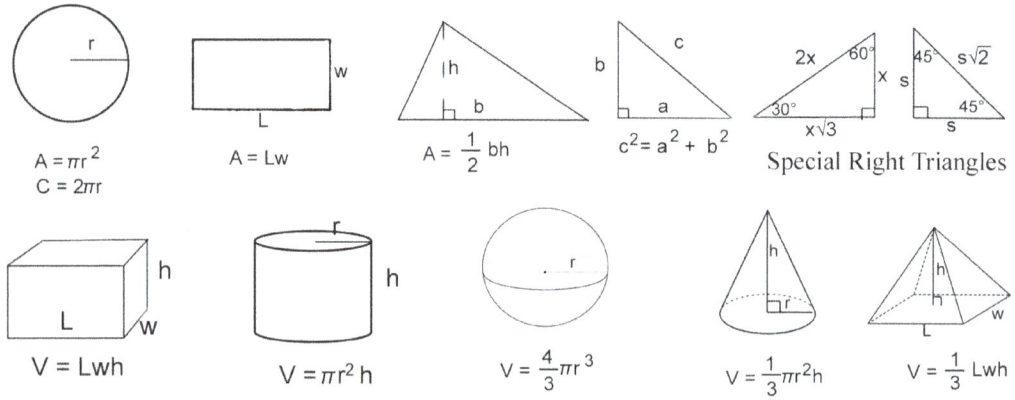

A full circle has 360 degrees of arc.

A full circle has 2π radians of arc.

The sum of the measures of the angles in a triangle is 180°.

EGGHEAD PREP

SAMPLE TEST 1
Section 3: Math, No Calculator

1. Tisha and her mother spent a week fishing. Tisha caught T fish per day for 7 days. Her mother caught M fish per day for 6 days and did not fish on the last day. Which expression represents the total number of fish Tisha and her mother caught that week?

   A) $42TM$
   B) $7M + 6T$
   C) $13TM$
   D) $7T + 6M$

2. If $r = \dfrac{t+5}{4}$ and $r = 4$, what is the value of t?

   A) 11
   B) 9/4
   C) 21
   D) 3

3. What is the value of $(7 - 2i) - (4 + 5i)$ if $i = \sqrt{-1}$?

   A) $3 + 3i$
   B) $11 - 7i$
   C) $3 - 7i$
   D) $11 + 3i$

4. An economist predicts that the price p of one gallon of gas, in U.S. dollars, in terms of the number of months m since January 1, 2016 will be:
   $$p = 1.68 + .07m$$
   Based on the economist's model, what will be the increase in the price of a gallon of gas each month?

   A) $1.75
   B) $0.07
   C) $1.68
   D) $0.14

5. Which of the following is equivalent to the expression,
   $$(-4mn^2 + 3m^2n + 4mn) + (-4n^2 - mn^2 - 8m^2n)?$$

   A) $-8mn4 + 2m3n3 - 4m3n2$
   B) $-5mn2 - 5m2n + 4mn - 4n2$
   C) $-8m + 2mn - 4m$
   D) $-10m2n2$

6. Jenna opens a savings account by depositing some money into it. Starting the next day, she withdraws the same amount of money from the account each day. She does not make any additional deposits. The amount of money in the account at the end of each day is given by the equation, $M = 800 - 20d$, where M is the amount of money in U.S. dollars, and d is the number of days after that date she opened the account. What does the number 800 mean in this equation?

   A) Jenna withdraws $800 each day from the account.
   B) Jenna will run out of money in 800 days.
   C) Jenna starts each day with $800 in the account.
   D) Jenna initially deposited $800 into the account.

7. If $\dfrac{m}{2r} = 3$, what is the value of $\dfrac{18r}{m}$?

   A) 2
   B) 9
   C) 3
   D) 6

8. A scientist discovers a lake that initially has Z zooplankton (tiny, floating organisms) in it. She believes that q percent of the zooplankton population is dying off each year due to pollution. She uses the formula,
   $$D = \dfrac{\dfrac{q}{7300}\left(1 + \dfrac{q}{7300}\right)^n}{\left(1 + \dfrac{q}{7300}\right)^n - 1} Z$$
   to predict D, the number of zooplankton that die every 5 days. Z is the original zooplankton population and n is the number of 5-day periods until the populations has completely died away.

Which of the following gives Z in terms of D, n, and q?

A) $Z = \dfrac{\dfrac{q}{7300}\left(1+\dfrac{q}{7300}\right)^n}{\left(1+\dfrac{q}{7300}\right)^n - 1} D$

B) $Z = \left(\dfrac{7300}{q} - 1\right) D$

C) $Z = \left(\dfrac{q}{7300} - 1\right) D$

D) $D = \dfrac{\left(1+\dfrac{q}{7300}\right)^n - 1}{\dfrac{q}{7300}\left(1+\dfrac{q}{7300}\right)^n} Z$

9.

Let $h(x) = 17 - bx2$.

For the function h defined by the above equation, $h(4) = 12$. What does $h(-4)$ equal?

A) 12
B) 1
C) −12
D) −1

10.
$$5x - 2y = 12$$
$$-6y - 2x = 2$$

If the solution to the above system of equations is (x,y), then $(x,y) = ?$

A) (2,1)
B) (−2,5)
C) (2,−1)
D) (−3,2)

11.

A line in the xy-plane has a slope of $-\dfrac{3}{5}$ and passes through the origin. Which of the following points must be on the line?

A) (−3,5)
B) (0,5)
C) (10,−6)
D) (0,−5)

12.
$$p = 0.78 + 0.11w$$
$$a = 0.62 + 0.15w$$

These equations represent the price per pound of pears (p) and apples (a), in dollars, w weeks after January 1, 2016. What was the price per pound of pears when it was equal to the price per pound of apples?

A) $4.00
B) $1.22
C) $3.50
D) $2.17

13.

What is the value of $\dfrac{3^y}{27^x}$ if $-y + 3x = -15$?

A) 315

B) $\left(\dfrac{1}{3}\right)^{-5}$

C) $\left(\dfrac{1}{9}\right)^{2}$

D) The value cannot be determined from the given information.

14.

If $m + n = 10$ and $(mx + 1)(nx - 5) = 21x2 + cx - 5$ for all x values, what are two possible values of c?

A) −35 and 3
B) −32 and −8
C) 7 and 3
D) −15 and 7

SAMPLE TEST 1
Section 3: Math, No Calculator

15. Which of the following expressions is equivalent to
$$\frac{1}{\frac{1}{x-1}+\frac{1}{x+4}} \text{ if } x > 0?$$

A) $x2 + 3x - 4$

B) $\dfrac{x^2 + 3x - 4}{2x + 3}$

C) $\dfrac{2x + 3}{x^2 + 3x - 4}$

D) $2x + 3$

DIRECTIONS

For questions 16 – 20, solve the problem and type in your answer. Please follow these guidelines:

1. No questions have negative answers.

2. If a problem has more than one correct answer, any of those answers will be accepted as correct. Please enter only one answer.

3. Do not type in mixed numbers. A number such as 2 ¼ should be entered as 2.25 or 9/4. Mixed numbers will be misinterpreted by the computer.

4. If a decimal answer does not terminate after 3 decimal places, enter three decimal places only. You may either round or truncate the decimal. For example, 3/8 may be entered as 3/8 or .375, because the decimal ends there; 7/9 may be entered as 7/9, .777, or .778. Fractions should be reduced to simplest terms. For example, you should enter 1/2 instead of 2/4.

16.
$$2x - y = 4$$
$$x + 3y = 9$$

Based on the system of equations above, what is the value of y?

17. A team of researches wishes to set up a floating net across a river to capture platypuses for a scientific study. The net must stretch from the Canoe Landing (point C) to the Fishing Pier (point D). The lengths DF, FN, NY, and FY measure 1000 feet, 400 feet, 320 feet, and 360 feet, respectively. Find the value of x, the length of the net.

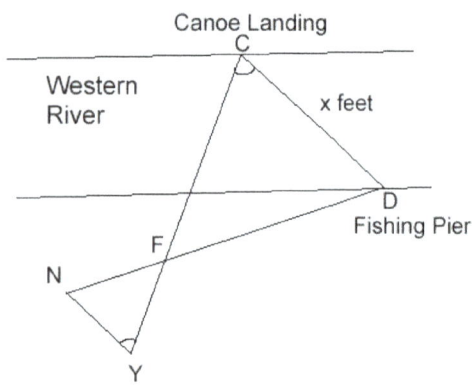

18. If $w > 0$ and $w^2 - 25 = 0$, then $w = ?$

19. If $3y = \sqrt{5x}$ and $y = 2\sqrt{5}$, then what is the value of x?

20. One angle in a right triangle measure $t°$. If $\cos t° = \frac{5}{13}$, what is $\sin(90° - t°)$?

STOP

If you have finished this section before time expires, you may check your work. You cannot return to this section once you move on to the next section.

STOP!

If you have finished this section before time expires, you may check your work. You cannot return to this section once you move on to the next section.

www.eggheadprep.com

ANSWERS, SECTION 3
SAMPLE TEST 1 — MATH, NO CALCULATOR

1. D
2. A
3. C
4. B
5. B
6. D
7. C
8. D
9. A
10. C
11. C
12. B
13. A
14. B
15. B

───────

16. 2
17. 800
18. 5
19. 36
20. 5/13 or .384 or .385

EGGHEAD PREP

SECTION 4: MATH TEST
CALCULATOR, 55 MINUTES, 38 QUESTIONS

DIRECTIONS

For questions 1–30, solve the problem and choose the best answer from the options provided. For questions 31–38, solve the problem and type in your answer. Further instructions for typing in your answer are provided before question 31.

NOTES

1. Calculator use is permitted for this section.
2. All variables and expressions represent real numbers unless stated otherwise.
3. Unless otherwise indicated, figures shown have been drawn to scale.
4. All figures lie in a plane unless stated otherwise.
5. The domain of a function f is the set of real numbers for which f(x) is a real number, unless stated otherwise.

REFERENCE

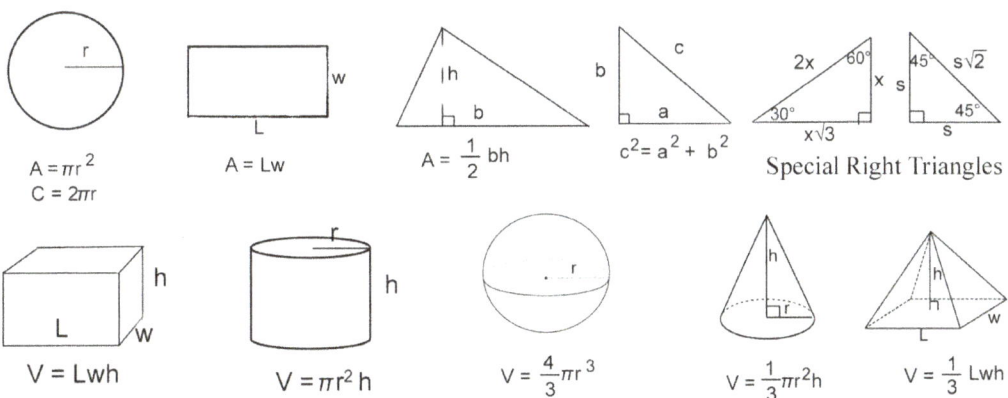

A full circle has 360 degrees of arc.
A full circle has 2π radians of arc.
The sum of the measures of the angles in a triangle is 180°.

eggheadprep.com

1.

In order to run tests on a racecar's engine, a mechanic runs the engine at various speeds, measured in revolutions per minute (rpms), over the course of roughly one and a half hours. On which interval is the engine speed strictly decreasing then strictly increasing?

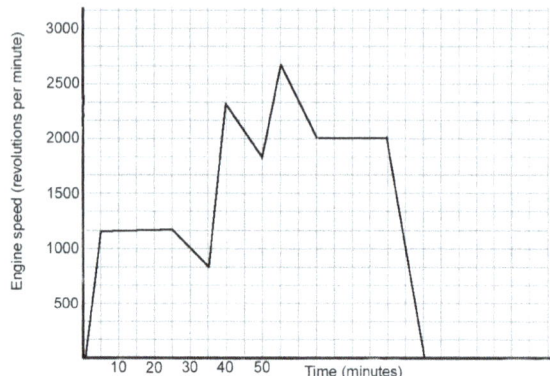

A) Between 20 and 35 minutes
B) Between 35 and 50 minutes
C) Between 25 and 40 minutes
D) Between 50 and 80 minutes

2.

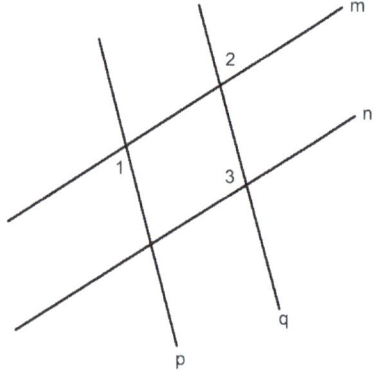

In the figure shown, lines m and n are parallel, and lines p and q are parallel. If the measure of angle *1* is 78°, what is the measure of angle 3?

A) 102°
B) 78°
C) 90°
D) 120°

3.

If $32 - 3x$ is 8 more than 6, what is the value of $6x$?

A) 6
B) 11.33
C) 68
D) 36

4. If $W = kL$, where k is a constant, and $W = 21$ when $L = 3$, what is the value of W when $L = 7$?

A) 21
B) 25
C) 35
D) 49

5.
$$1 \text{ kiloliter} = 1{,}000 \text{ liters}$$
$$10 \text{ deciliters} = 1 \text{ liter}$$

To perform a certain experiment, a chemistry lab needs 1 deciliter of a special liquid. The lab currently has one 4-kiloliter container of the liquid. How many times will the chemists be able to run the experiment using their current supply of the liquid?

A) 40,000
B) 4,000
C) 40
D) 0.0004

6. Which of the following graphs displays a strong positive relationship between X (horizontal axis) and Y (vertical axis)?

A)
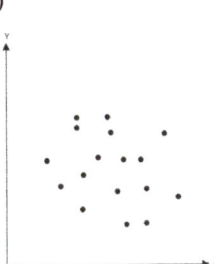

B)
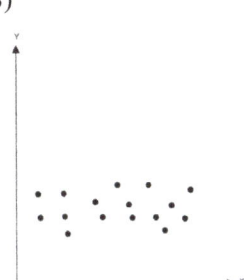

C)
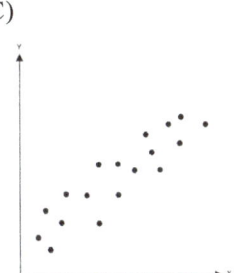

D)
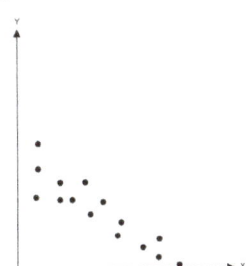

7. Which of the following numbers is NOT a solution to the inequality, $5x - 3 < 6x + 2$?

   A) -3
   B) -7
   C) -1
   D) 0

8. **Attendance at five basketball games on Jan. 2, 2016**

   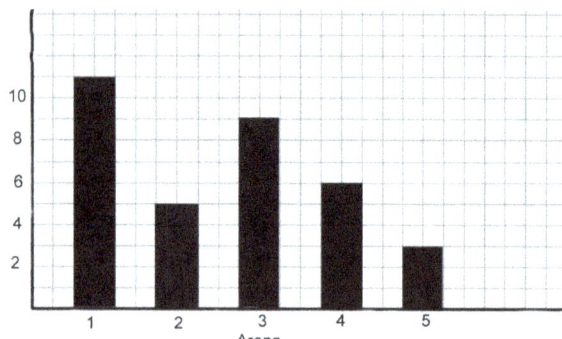

   The attendance at basketball games held at 5 different arenas on January 2, 2016 is shown in the graph above. If the total attendance at all 5 games was 34,000, how should the vertical axis be labeled?

   A) Number of people in attendance
   B) Number of people in attendance (in hundreds)
   C) Number of people in attendance (in thousands)
   D) Number of people in attendance (in hundred thousands)

9. For which of the following values of x is the expression $|x - 5| + 4$ equal to 1?

   A) 0
   B) 1
   C) 2
   D) No such value of x exists.

Questions 10 and 11 refer to the following information:

The speed of a sound wave traveling through water depends on the temperature of the water. If v represents the speed of the sound wave, in miles per hour, then v is given approximately by,

$$v = 3{,}121.5 + 2.37T,$$

where T is the temperature of the water in degrees Fahrenheit (°F).

10. Which of these equations expresses the water temperature T in terms of the speed v of the sound wave?

    A) $T = \dfrac{2.37}{v - 3{,}121.5}$
    B) $T = \dfrac{v - 3{,}121.5}{2.37}$
    C) $T = \dfrac{3{,}121.5 - v}{2.37}$
    D) $T = \dfrac{v + 3{,}121.5}{2.37}$

11. If a sound wave travels through water at 3,350 miles per hour, which of the following is the best estimate of the temperature of the water?

    A) 95°F
    B) 96°F
    C) 97°F
    D) 98°F

12.

Dance Style

	Ballroom	Swing	Aerial	Total
Female	27	42	74	143
Male	12	71	17	100
Total	39	113	91	243

A group of high school students were required to study a dance style for their physical education class. The above table shows the styles of dance that male and female students selected. Which of these groups represented approximately 17% of the students?

A) Female students selecting swing dance

B) Male students selecting aerial dance

C) Male students selecting ballroom dance

D) Female students selecting aerial dance

13.

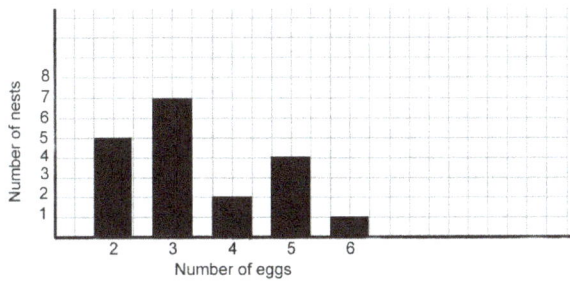

The histogram shown displays the number of eggs found in various sparrow nests. Which of the following numbers is closest to the average (arithmetic mean) number of eggs per nest?

A) 2

B) 3

C) 4

D) 5

14.

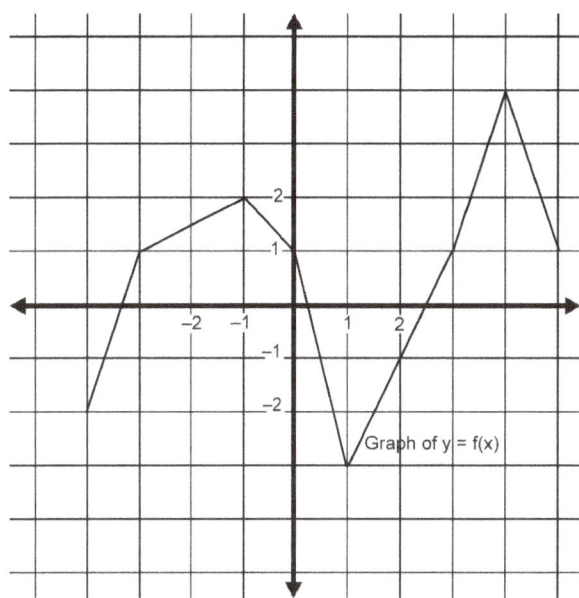

Shown is the complete graph of a function f on the xy-plane. For what value of x is the value of $f(x)$ at its maximum?

A) –4

B) –1

C) 1

D) 4

15.

Shown are the diameters of 24 elm trees, in inches. All of the trees are 50 years old.

Diameter of tree (inches)

27	27	28	28	28	29
30	31	31	31	31	34
34	34	34	35	35	35
35	35	36	36	36	37
37	38	38	38	38	39
39	40	40	40	41	67

The measurement 67 inches has been classified as an outlier. Which of the follow will change the most if the outlier is removed?

A) Median

B) Range

C) Mean

D) They will change by the same amount.

Use the following graph for questions 16 and 17.

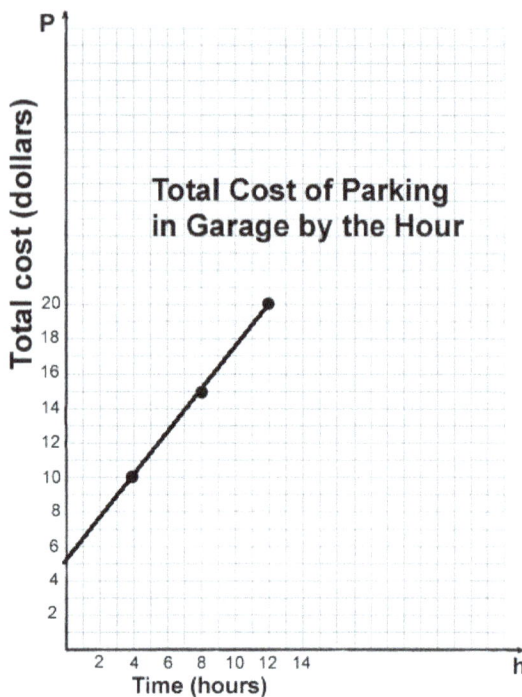

The graph displays the total cost P, in U.S. dollars, to park in a garage for h hours.

16. What is the meaning of the P-intercept in this situation?

    A) The average time a vehicle stays in the garage is 5 hours.
    B) It costs $5.00 per hour to park in the garage.
    C) There is an initial cost of $5.00 to park in the garage.
    D) There are currently 500 cars in the garage.

17. Which of the following equations expresses P in terms of h?

    A) $P = \frac{5}{4}h + 5$
    B) $P = 4h + 5$
    C) $P = 5 + \frac{4}{5}$
    D) $P = 5h$

18. A hardware store sells hammers for $8.75 each and screwdrivers for $5.50 each. Tamara runs a carpentry school and purchased a large order of hammers and screwdrivers from the store. If Tamara paid $990.50 for a total of 134 tools, how many screwdrivers did she purchase?

    A) 78
    B) 71
    C) 65
    D) 56

19. Given that

$$W > -3M + Q$$
$$\text{and} \quad W < 2M + P$$

If $(M, W) = (0,0)$, what must be true of the numbers P and Q?

    A) $Q > P$
    B) $|Q| < P$
    C) $Q < P$
    D) No conclusion can be made from the given information.

SAMPLE TEST 1
Section 4: Math, Calculator

20.

Incidents of Fighting with Other Males in One Month

	None	1 – 8	9 – 16	17 – 24	Total
Prairie	8	27	14	3	52
Forest	13	31	3	1	48
Total	21	58	17	4	100

The table shows data collected in a study of male deer in a region that has both prairie and forest habitats. The researchers attached tracking devices to 100 male deer and recorded the number of times each deer fought with another male over territory or mates during a single month. The male deer were divided into two groups, based on whether each deer lived primarily in a prairie or a forest habitat.

If a single male deer is chosen at random from among all the male deer that engaged in at least 9 fights, what is the probability that deer belonged to the Forest group?

A) $\frac{3}{48}$

B) $\frac{4}{100}$

C) $\frac{4}{48}$

D) $\frac{4}{21}$

21.

Which of the following equations describes a circle in the xy-plane with its center at $(5,0)$ and containing the point $(4, \frac{12}{5})$?

A) $(x + 5)^2 + y^2 = \frac{13}{5}$

B) $(x - 5)^2 + y^2 = \frac{169}{25}$

C) $(x + 5)^2 + y^2 = \frac{169}{25}$

D) $(x - 5)^2 + (y - \frac{144}{25})^2 = 25$

22.

Angelo bought a new snowboard on sale for 30% off the original price. He paid a total of D dollars, which included sales tax of 7%. Let X equal the original price of the snowboard. Which equation represents X in terms of D?

A) $X = (1.07)(0.70)D$

B) $X = \frac{D}{(1.07)(0.70)}$

C) $X = (0.77)D$

D) $X = \frac{D}{1.77}$

For questions 23 and 24, use the information provided in the table below.

Total Sales in Various Store Departments at Quincy's

Date in June 2015

	10	11	12	13
Women's	24,975	21,301	20,213	19,875
Men's	18,196	14,250	19,118	20,328
Infants'	9,320	11,990	10,317	10,622
Appliances	32,570	37,413	35,719	34,892
Furniture	12,764	9,327	11,495	14,213

The table displays the daily sales, in U.S. dollars, for various departments of a large store called Quincy's during a 4-day period in June 2015.

23. Which of the following departments had a ratio of June 13 sales to June 11 sales that was closest to the Women's department's ratio of June 13 sales to June 11 sales?

   A) Men's
   B) Infants'
   C) Appliances
   D) Furniture

24. Which of the following is the best estimate of the average rate of change of daily sales in the Furniture department from June 10 to June 13?

   A) $480 per day
   B) $1,450 per day
   C) $360 per day
   D) $2,440 per day

25. The play area in an elementary school is square in shape, with sides of length 10 yards. The children become fascinated with the speckled design of the large tiles making up the floor. Their teacher challenges them to figure out how many dots there are on the entire floor of the play area. Ten students volunteer to help. Each student picks a different tile and counts the dots. Each tile is a square with side length 1 yard. The table below shows the results.

Student	Number of dots counted on tile
Ahmed	87
Aisha	73
Bethany	51
Cassidy	92
Jacob	86
Madison	77
Pablo	68
Rochelle	97
Steven	82
Tristan	70

What is a reasonable estimate of the total number of dots on the play area floor?

   A) 80
   B) 800
   C) 8,000
   D) 80,000

26. The manufacturer of cereal brand X claims that its boxes contain 40% more cereal than boxes of cereal brand Y. Assuming the manufacturer's claim is true, if boxes of brand X contain 917 grams of cereal, how many grams of cereal are in a box of brand Y?

   A) 526
   B) 550
   C) 613
   D) 655

27.

A rock is launched upward from the ground with initial speed 56 feet per second. Its height above the ground after t seconds is given by the equation the equation below:

$$h = -16t^2 + 56t$$

How long will it take the rock to fall to the ground?

A) 3.5 seconds
B) 4.5 seconds
C) 16.0 seconds
D) 56.0 seconds

28.

$$y \leq \tfrac{3}{4}x - 2$$
$$y > 2x - 8$$

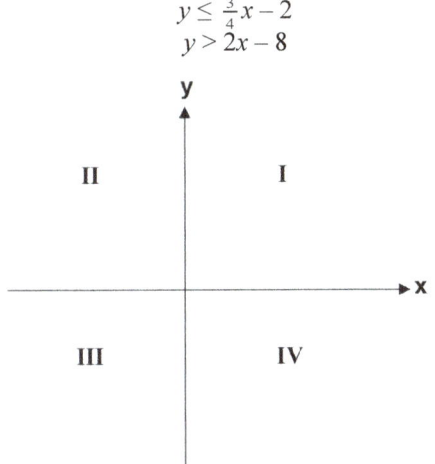

If a student graphed the system of inequalities shown above on the xy-plane shown, which quadrant would not contain any solutions of the system?

A) I
B) II
C) III
D) IV

29.

Consider the graph of $y = -2x^2 + 8x + 10$

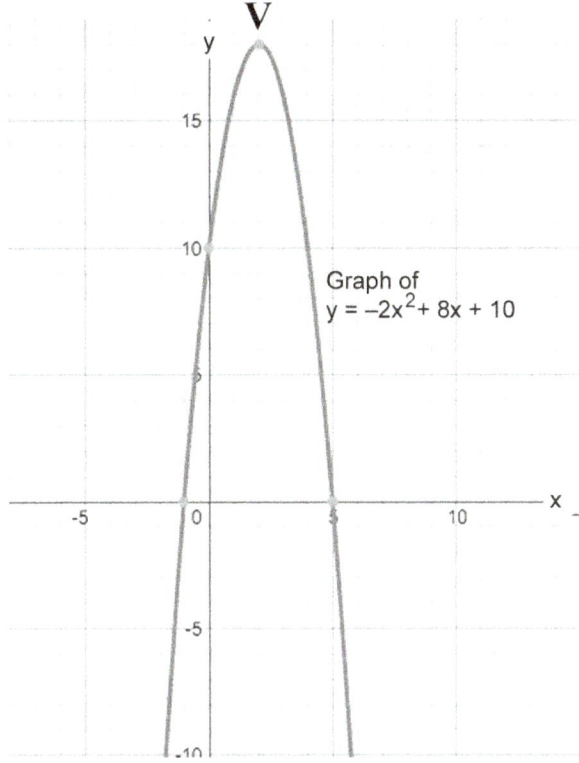

Which of the following equations is equivalent to the equation graphed above, and contains the coordinates of the vertex V as constants in the equation?

A) $y = -2(x - 2)^2 + 18$
B) $y = -2(x - 5)(x + 1)$
C) $y = -2(x - 2)(x + 18)$
D) $y = -2x(x - 4) + 10$

30.

For a certain polynomial p(x), the value of p(–4) is 5. Which of the following statements about p(x) must be true?

A) $x + 4$ is a factor of p(x).
B) $x - 5$ is a factor of p(x).
C) The remainder when p(x) is divided by $x + 4$ is 1.
D) The remainder when p(x) is divided by $x + 4$ is 5.

DIRECTIONS

For questions 31–38, solve the problem and type in your answer. Please follow these guidelines:

1. No questions have negative answers.

2. If a problem has more than one correct answer, any of those answers will be accepted as correct. Please enter only one answer.

3. Do not type in mixed numbers. A number such as 2 ¼ should be entered as 2.25 or 9/4. Mixed numbers will be misinterpreted by the computer.

4. If a decimal answer does not terminate after 3 decimal places, enter three decimal places only. You may either round or truncate the decimal. For example, 3/8 may be entered as 3/8 or .375, because the decimal ends there; 7/9 may be entered as 7/9, .777, or .778. Fractions should be reduced to simplest terms. In other words, you should enter 1/2 instead of 2/4.

31.

Number of Visitors to Website A Worldwide Each Year from 1999 to 2005

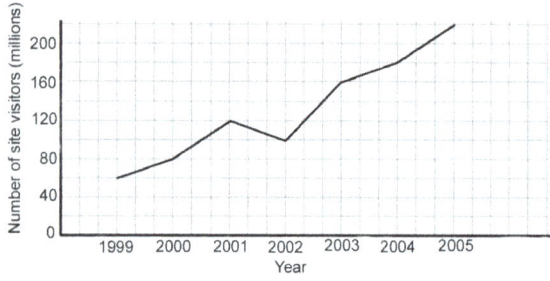

Based on the graph above, the number of visitors to Website A in 2000 was what fraction of the number of visitors in 2004?

32.

Rebecca has attempted at least 7 shots but at most 15 shots in every basketball game her team has played this season. If she has taken a total of 90 shots this season, what is a possible number of games she has played?

33.

A massage therapist offers 20-minute treatments. If she is available for appointments 8 hours each day, what is the maximum total number of treatments she can give on the days Wednesday, Thursday, and Friday?

34.

A rock band has rented a 1300 cubic foot storage space for gear. The keyboard, amplifiers, and drums take up 800 cubic feet of space. The band also wishes to store boxes of CDs in the space. Each box has a volume 2.5 cubic feet. Assuming the boxes can be arranged so that all available space is used, what is the highest number of CD boxes the band can store in the space?

35.

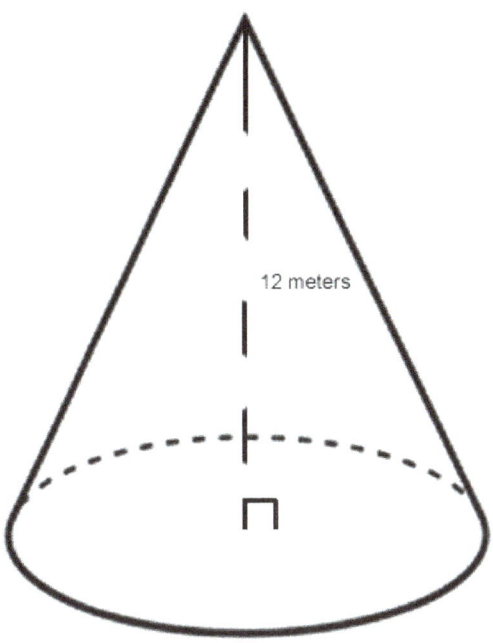

The cone shown above represents a pile of sand at a construction site. If the volume of the pile is 100π cubic meters, what is the <u>diameter</u> of the cone, in meters?

For questions 36 and 37, use the following information:

Danesha deposits $500 into a savings account that pays 3% annual interest, compounded annually. She makes no additional deposits or withdrawals. She uses the equation,

$$D = 500(b)^x$$

to calculate the number of dollars D in the account after x years.

36. What must be the value of b in this equation?

37. Danesha's cousin, Jackie, made a deposit the same day Danesha did. Jacques deposited $450 into an account that pays 3.8% annual interest, compounded annually. Let J represent the number of dollars in Jackie's account after x years. Find the value of $|J - D|$ after 20 years to the nearest whole dollar.

38.
$$g(x) = \frac{3x}{(x+1)^2 - 6(x+1) + 9}$$

For what value of x is the function g defined by the equation above not defined?

STOP

If you have finished this section before time expires, you may check your work. You cannot return to this section once you move on to the next section.

EGGHEAD PREP™
Get cracking.

STOP!

If you have finished this section before time expires, you may check your work. You cannot return to this section once you move on to the next section.

www.eggheadprep.com

ANSWERS, SECTION 4
SAMPLE TEST 1 — MATH, CALCULATOR

1. C
2. A
3. D
4. D
5. A
6. C
7. B
8. C
9. D
10. B
11. B
12. A
13. B
14. D
15. B
16. C
17. A
18. D
19. C
20. D
21. B
22. B
23. C
24. A
25. C
26. D
27. A
28. B
29. A
30. D

---

31. 8/18 or 4/9 or .444
32. 6, 7, 8, 9, 10, 11 or 12
33. 72
34. 200
35. 10
36. 103/100 or 1.03
37. 45, 46, or 47
38. 2

eggheadprep.com

ANSWER EXPLANATIONS
SAMPLE TEST 1 — SECTION 1, 2, 3, 4

NOTE: The SAT Reading Test emphasizes <u>evidence-based</u> analysis of the passages. While reading the passages, you will no doubt form opinions regarding whether the results of an experiment described should be trusted, or whether there are reasons beyond those presented in the passage for characters to act as they do. Those opinions may be perfectly valid, but when answering the questions, it is important to remember to draw conclusions based <u>solely</u> on evidence that is explicitly presented in the passage, not on your own personal feelings.

TEST SECTION 1: READING

1. Throughout the passage, we learn that the village is suffering many hardships caused at least in part by conflicts with other villages ("our enemies," line 88). In lines 80-96, we learn that Lindiel is trying to persuade the Chieftain to relocate the village, even though the Chieftain advocates keeping the village where it is. Thus, Lindiel is challenging the Chieftain's decision and suggesting a change of strategy. Note also that Lindiel is concerned about committing an "act of rebellion" (line 8), so she is clearly aware that she is not showing the expected obedience to the will of the Chieftain. **The correct answer is (D).**

2. Although answers (B), (C), and (D) all describe commonly used devices to develop a story, this passage centers on the conversation between Lindiel and the Chieftain, Arandala. **The correct answer is (A).**

3. The word "intolerable" always suggests a circumstance or situation that is beyond what people can reasonably be asked to endure (*tolerate*). Of the choices, the only one that implies a similar meaning is (C), unacceptable. Answer (D), incomparable, would imply that no similar situation has ever existed. That may be true of some intolerable situations, but the passage does not provide evidence for such a conclusion about the situation in which Lindiel and Arandala find themselves. **The correct answer is (C).**

4. Although the passage suggests that Lindiel respects and admires Arandala and hopes she will be open to the suggestion of relocating the village, a number of clues (see question #5) show us that she is very nervous about visiting the Chieftain's home. **The correct answer is (B).**

5. Answers (A), (B), and (D) all refer to sentences that describe Lindiel's fear of negative consequences resulting from her visit to the Chieftain. They all support the conclusion that Lindiel is afraid of the Chieftain's reaction, corresponding to the correct answer, (B), to question #4. Answer (C), however, refers to a sentence that describes an occurrence (the appearance of evening stars) that brings Lindiel comfort. Therefore, it does NOT provide relevant support for the answer to question #4. **The correct answer is (C).**

SAMPLE TEST 1
Answer Explanations

6. Lindiel is very polite and respectful in speaking with the Chieftain. See, for example, lines 36-38 ("Great Chieftain … time.") and lines 41-44 ("Begging … delay.") She is not aggressive or dominant. Although the word "irreverence" generally implies a lack of respect for tradition—of which Lindiel could fairly be accused—it most often describes disrespectfulness expressed in a humorous or offensive way. Lindiel's statements in the passage are neither humorous nor offensive. The word "courteous" refers to politeness, and so is very appropriate as a description of Lindiel's tone. Yet because Lindiel holds her ground after being challenged by the Chieftain (lines 88-95, "But Chieftain, … enemies."), her attitude could not be described as submissive. **The correct answer is (D).**

7. Although the first paragraph introduces the reader to some of the customs and traditions of the village, it neither criticizes those customs nor explains their origins. The paragraph makes no mention of the distance Lindiel has traveled. It does make clear, however, that Lindiel is taking a great risk (see, for example, lines 6-7, "Few who … about it."). **The correct answer is (C).**

8. Nowhere in the passage is there any indication that Lindiel has ever committed acts of violence or brutality, or that she has any tendency to celebrate in an inappropriate manner. The passage does make clear, however (see, for example, the first paragraph), that Lindiel has acted in a way that is not consistent with village customs. **The correct answer is (B).**

9. Answer (D) may be ruled out immediately, because the passage makes clear (lines 72-74) that the Chieftain knows of the suffering of the villagers. The passage gives no indication that Lindiel fears competition from other villagers, or that her parents would object to her travels. There is, however (see the explanation for question #10, below), strong evidence in the passage supporting the conclusion that Lindiel believes the opportunity to travel will soon be gone. **The correct answer is (A).**

10. In lines 92-95, Lindiel explains that relocating the village would require two weeks' time. She also points out that the dry riverbed that they would use to travel northward will no longer be dry after the mountain snows melt, also in about two weeks. Therefore, the trip must be undertaken very soon if it is to be successful. These lines therefore support answer (A) to question #9, which is the correct answer for that question. **The correct answer is (D).**

11. Answer (B), (C), and (D) all make accurate references to details provided in the passage: Arandala was ready to retire to bed when Lindiel arrived (line 62); Arandala does have a love of childish enthusiasm (lines 63-66); and the night would be cold (line 17). However, the wording of line 112 ("Instead, she found them readying for a journey") shows that Arandala is surprised that her family is preparing to travel. In other words, the family had no prior plans for a trip, which makes answers (B), (C), and (D) all unreasonable. Because the travel preparations have apparently just begun, the evidence suggests that they are connected to the conversation between Lindiel and Arandala, which in turn implies that the family wishes to journey northward as Lindiel has suggested. **The correct answer is (A).**

12. A "red flag" is an indication of danger or a cause for concern. Therefore, lines 3-9 state that investors view a high rate of employee turnover as a sign that a company is struggling or will have problems in the future. Low turnover—that is, a stable workforce—would thus be viewed favorably. **The correct answer is (A).**

13. To foster means to encourage or promote the development of something. Development may be thought of as growth. To cultivate something means to support its growth. Therefore, in the context of line 11, "foster" and "cultivate" would be very similar in meaning. **The correct answer is (B).**

14. In lines 39-42, the authors state that executives view salaries like a carrot dangled in front of a horse—a possible future reward (incentive) that will spur workers to put forth greater effort. Although the passage does discuss salaries as a reward for work already completed, the authors make clear that it is *employees*, not executives, who view salaries in that way. The passage makes no mention of the ideas presented in answers (B) and (C). **The correct answer is (D).**

15. As noted in the explanation for question #14, lines 39-42 explain executives' view of salaries as an incentive system. **The correct answer is (B).**

16. Lines 47-48 provide a clear answer for this question: "Those receiving the checks, however, see salaries differently." In other words, employees do not attach the same meaning to their salaries as executives do. **The correct answer is (C).**

17. As noted in the explanation for question #16, lines 47-48 clearly support answer (C) for that question. Those lines, however, are not represented in the answer choices for question #17. It is therefore necessary to find other lines in the passage that support the conclusion that employees do not share the view of employers that salaries should serve as incentives to motivate future effort. In lines 48-49, the authors state that employees view their paychecks as compensation for work already completed, *not* as an incentive. Therefore, these lines strongly support the conclusion that employees and employers attach different meanings to salaries, corresponding to correct answer to question #16. **The correct answer is (C).**

18. To "discern" means to recognize, identify, or perceive something. "Perceiving" is therefore a synonym for "discerning" in the context of line 63. **The correct answer is (D).**

19. Up until line 56, the authors of the passage have focused on providing evidence for their claim that a common cause of employee unhappiness is a difference of opinion between employees and employers about the meaning of worker salaries. In lines 57-59, the authors point out that many other types of conflicts arise from disagreements between groups of people about how an action or object should be interpreted or valued. Dr. Lopez's comments expand on that observation. Therefore, the authors are quoting her to support the proposition that the employer-employee misunderstanding stems from a widespread problem in human communication. **The correct answer is (B).**

SAMPLE TEST 1
Answer Explanations

20. The third paragraph of the passage (lines 23-35) explains that employees of Company B have been far more loyal to their employer (that is, have stayed at their jobs longer) than those of Company A. The graph shows that Company B workers received significant salary increases during their first two years of working for the company (2001-2003). Therefore, the study and the graph together suggest that employees who receive wage increases soon after becoming employed at a company are more likely to stay with that company than employees who have to wait a long time for raises. **The correct answer is (A).**

21. Since the conclusion suggested by the passage and the graph is that early raises promote employee loyalty more effectively than delayed raises (see the above explanation for question #20), **the correct answer is (A).**

---

22. The very first sentence of the passage makes clear that angling is a type of fishing, so answer (C) can be ruled out immediately. The paragraph as a whole presents general background information, but does not mention any specific beliefs people hold, ruling out answer (B). Furthermore, the paragraph does not in any way describe Dr. Ahmed's methods or question their validity, ruling out answer (D). **The correct answer is (A).**

23. There is a key contextual clue in line 13: immediately after the word "spawning" is first used in the passage, both offspring and eggs are mentioned. Based on these clues, it should be clear that spawning refers to reproduction. **The correct answer is (C).**

24. In lines 56-58, Dr. Ahmed states that boskit and snuppers, fish of different families, prefer the same habitats. She uses the example specifically to support her point in the previous sentence that "fish do not sort themselves in aquatic ecosystems according to their families." Both that statement and the specific example given in lines 56-58 directly contradict the guide's claim. **The correct answer is (C).**

25. In lines 29-35, Dr. Ahmed makes clear that the purpose of her study was to determine whether the specific timing of the closed seasons is detrimental to fish survival. She further states that both those who fish (anglers) and those who work to protect ecosystems (conservation experts) should be very interested in the results of her work. **The correct answer is (D).**

26. The introduction to the passage (first paragraph) makes clear that the purpose of closed seasons is to protect fish while they are spawning and guarding egg nests. In lines 44-48, Dr. Ahmed states that Dr. Huong's work shows that fish injured by anglers, even if they are returned to the water, often abandon their nests, greatly reducing their offspring's likelihood of survival. Dr. Ahmed concludes that accidental catching of fish during the closed season for that particular species is potentially an issue of great concern. **The correct answer is (B).**

eggheadprep.com

27. The fact that boskit and snuppers are both drawn to the same lures or bait in no way implies that they work together to hunt. Such cooperation is never mentioned in the passage, so answer (D) must be ruled out. Dr. Ahmed actually does not even mention what the prey species are that these fish hunt, so answer (C) is also clearly inappropriate. Finally, although Dr. Ahmed mentions the use of both lures and bait (that is, live bait), she suggests no conclusion about which fishing technique is more effective for catching the fish species she studied. Therefore, answer (B) must be ruled out as well. **The correct answer is (A).**

28. Lines 22-23 of the passage explain that the double-finned fish species are snupper and longfin blue. These species are represented in the second and fourth columns of the table. Flowing, weedy, shallow habitats are represented in row 3 of the table. Therefore, the correct values are the second and fourth entries in row 3, which are 35.1% and 18.8%. **The correct answer is (C).**

29. In the third and fourth rows of the table, the entries in the first and fourth columns (welkfish and longfin blue) are very close to each other in value. In the first and second rows, the entries in the second and third columns (snupper and boskit) are very close to each other in value. In all four of these rows (that is, all but the fifth row of the table), the percentage of welkfish is much closer to that of longfin blue than it is to those of snupper and boskit. Similarly, the percentage of snupper is much closer to that of boskit than it is to those of welkfish and longfin blue. **The correct answer is (D).**

30. To support the answer to question #29, and Dr. Ahmed's claims as well, we need to find two percentages in the appropriate row of the table that fit the pattern Dr. Ahmed identifies in the passage. Flowing, sandy, shallow habitats are represented in the table's fourth row. The percentages of welkfish (45.9%) and longfin blue (50.2%) are very similar, supporting both answer (D) from question #29 and Dr. Ahmed's claim that "where there are welkfish, there are often also longfin blues" (lines 63-64). **The correct answer is (B).**

31. None of Dr. Ahmed's observations, and none of her conclusions, pertain in any way to helping anglers catch more fish. Therefore, answer (B) cannot be correct. It has been established in questions #29 and #30 that Dr. Ahmed's primary claims are well supported by existing data, so answer (C) can be ruled out as well. Finally, Dr. Ahmed specifically recommends (lines 70-73) that the closed seasons be extended because there is no known way to reduce accidental catching of species during a closed season, ruling out answer (D). Dr. Ahmed's brief mention of the possibility of relocation shows that **the correct answer is (A).**

32. The fifth row of the table shows that in flowing, rocky, deep habitat, welkfish, of the dark-spined family, is the only prevalent species. Therefore, many of the concerns Dr. Ahmed expresses about periods when the season is closed for one family of fish but open for the other family would not apply in that habitat. **The correct answer is (C).**

SAMPLE TEST 1
Answer Explanations

33. In lines 4-8 ("Are not … people."), Ms. Adams makes clear that she has reservations about Virginia's participation in the Revolutionary War. The fact that she praises Virginia as the birthplace of Washington, however, shows that she recognizes the colony's importance to the broader war effort. Her statement that Virginians were "shamefully duped" (line 11) by Governor Dunmore is an additional indication of distrust toward the colony. Ms. Adams is clearly making a distinction between Washington (whom she clearly admires) and Dunmore (whom she holds in low regard), which might suggest answer (C), but she does not *analyze* (that is, study or describe in detail) the differences between the two men. **The correct answer is (A).**

34. Throughout lines 12-51 and 79-89, Ms. Adams reports on recent developments in the town. In lines 52-76, she makes her case that if and when independence is won, any new code of laws should address a long history of discrimination against women. Therefore, she does indeed describe conditions in town and raise an issue to be considered when drafting new laws. **The correct answer is (B).**

35. In lines 34-38 ("We knew … wilderness."), Ms. Adams states that a month earlier, the people of the town were hesitant to plant crops or even stay in their homes, for fear that the region would be invaded. In lines 39-45 ("Now we … habitations."), she indicates that the sense of immediate danger has passed and that those who did leave are returning to their homes. **The correct answer is (C).**

36. There are two key pieces of evidence in determining the answer to this question. First, in the lines cited in the question (lines 42-44), Ms. Adams makes statements that could not be literally true. For example, she states that, "nature puts on a more cheerful countenance" (lines 43-44). "Countenance" means face or facial expression, which of course nature does not have in a literal sense. From this evidence we know that Ms. Adams is speaking of her *perceptions*, not of actual, natural phenomena. Secondly, in lines 41-42 ("I feel … stranger."), Ms. Adams speaks directly about her mood, an indication that the paragraph will focus on that topic. **The correct answer is (A).**

37. In lines 49-51, Ms. Adams indicates that residents of the towns in question have been warned of the possible dangers and given sufficient time to ready themselves to respond. **The correct answer is (A).**

38. In lines 55-57, Ms. Adams writes, "I desire you would remember the ladies, and be more generous and favorable to them than your ancestors." She is explicitly calling for better treatment of women. **The correct answer is (D).**

39. Ms. Adams threatens in lines 61-63 that if their demands are not met, she and other women will stage a rebellion and defy any laws created without consulting them. These are very strong and confrontational words. **The correct answer is (C).**

40. The meanings of "foment" include to cause, instigate, arouse, provoke, or incite. **The correct answer is (C).**

eggheadprep.com

41. In lines 57-59, Ms. Adams warns against giving too much power to men ("the husbands"), because "all men would be tyrants if they could." Later (lines 68-71), she urges lawmakers to "put it beyond the power of the vicious" (that is, make it illegal) to treat women cruelly. These statements make clear that Ms. Adams sees in men a tendency to abuse any power placed in their hands. **The correct answer is (B).**

42. Although saltpeter was used as both a fertilizer and a food preservative, the fact that Ms. Adams specifically mentions the use of the powder for "cannons, small arms, and pistols" (line 87) clearly indicates a focus on the military uses of saltpeter. **The correct answer is (C).**

---

43. The author of Passage 1 explicitly states in lines 49-52 that, "Many scientists ... believe that deep cave exploration will greatly advance our understanding of the conditions under which life can exist." Only answer (C) expresses a similar idea. **The correct answer is (C).**

44. As noted in the previous explanation, answer (C) for question #43 is very well supported by lines 49-52. However, none of the choices presented here mention those lines. We must therefore find additional support for the previous answer. The quote from Kayla Washington provides the needed evidence, because Ms. Washington specifically describes the influence of the discovery of a new species on our understanding of the history of life. **The correct answer is (D).**

45. The word "crevice" is most often used to describe a small crack or opening. Without even knowing that, however, it would be possible to discern the answer to this question by examining the contexts in which the word is used in the passage. In both instances, we have indications that a crevice can be very small (lines 22-23, "half-inch," and line 37, "tiniest") and can be passed through. Of the answer choices, only cracks could have those properties. **The correct answer is (A).**

46. The paragraph in question makes clear that the companies named are just two of many that are pursuing projects related to submersible drones. The fact that so many companies see value in such projects is certainly an indication of "widespread interest." **The correct answer is (B).**

47. In the last two sentences of Passage 1 (lines 49-54), the author notes the value of deep cave exploration in enhancing our understanding of the nature and origins or life, and observes that space exploration is, at least in part, motivated by similar interests. **The correct answer is (C).**

48. In lines 85-89, the author of Passage 2 claims that, "Even if scientists are convinced that submersible drones will not damage deep cave ecosystems in the ways humans would, the possibility remains that they will cause harm in other, unforeseen ways." Answer (D) summarizes this opinion. **The correct answer is (D).**

49. The word "seductive" generally implies attractive in some sense. Because this passage states that the use of submersible drones may have more negative consequences than many people believe, there is a clear suggestion that in this case, the attractiveness obscures hidden risks. In other words, it is "deceptive." **The correct answer is (A).**

SAMPLE TEST 1
Answer Explanations

50. As noted in the explanation for question #48, the author of Passage 2 is cautioning people against the sort of optimism expressed by the author of Passage 1 about the possibilities that submersible drones present. However, Passage 2 does not directly dispute any of the descriptions of the new technologies offered in Passage 1; it only questions whether all the possible implications of the use of those technologies have been considered. This important distinction rules out answer (D). **The correct answer is (B).**

51. Passage 2 does not discuss either the reliability of drone technology or the costs associated with the use of drones, so answers (A) and (D) may be eliminated immediately. Nor does Passage 2 raise the issue of lost data in the event of a drone deactivating itself. Therefore, answer (C) must also be ruled out. That leaves only answer (B), which reiterates the author's concern about unforeseen consequences. **The correct answer is (B).**

52. Only the lines cited in answer (C) address the possible impacts of a small disturbance of a deep cave environment. The sinking of a deactivated drone would constitute just such a small disturbance, making these lines relevant to the answer to question #51. **The correct answer is (C).**

TEST SECTION 2: WRITING AND LANGUAGE

NOTE: As the instructions for this test section clearly state, the goal when answering questions is to bring each passage into compliance with the conventions of standard written English. Standard written English is a form of the English language specifically developed to facilitate clear communication in writing, even between people who speak very different forms of English. Therefore, many of the correct answers may seem different from the choices you would make in your everyday speech. That does not mean there is anything wrong with the version of spoken English you have learned. To perform well on this test section, you must learn to make distinctions between the English you speak on a daily basis and the guidelines governing word choices, punctuation, and sentence structure in standard written English.

1. The phrase "for example" should only be used to introduce a specific instance illustrating a general point just made. The sentence referenced in question #1 does not mention any specific examples of river recreation or beaver dam removal, so the phrase cannot be correct as it is. The desired word should indicate contrast, since the sentence points out that previously held beliefs are now being called into question. The word "however" is the only one among the choices that conveys such a contrast. **The correct answer is (C).**

2. The sentence as written is both logical and compliant with standard written English conventions. There is no reason to alter it. **The correct answer is (A).**

3. Since sentence 2 mentions fish and amphibians, it is most logical to add a sentence about predators that feed on these animals immediately after it. **The correct answer is (B).**

4. Sentence 3 is setting up a comparison between streams with beaver dams and those without. The words "steadier" and "more sustained" indicate inequality: one type of stream has more desirable characteristics; the other type has less desirable characteristics. It is therefore important to use a word that indicates a comparison of unequal quantities or amounts. The best word for this purpose is **than** (not "then," which is an indicator of time or consequence). **The correct answer is (B).**

5. It is perfectly acceptable to begin a phrase with the word "and" as long as other conventions of standard written English are followed. The problem with the underlined phrase is that it falls between two closely related observations about the relationship between beaver dams and drought-flood cycles, but discusses a matter utterly unrelated to that relationship. In fact, the question of whether people are lazy is not connected to any of the issues discussed in the paragraph. **The correct answer is (D).**

6. This is a case where two similar sounding phrases convey very different meanings. "In spite of" is generally used to describe a situation in which a decision is made that seems contradictory to the course of action suggested by the evidence. For example, "In spite of the fact that it was raining fiercely, John chose to walk to the store without his umbrella." For sentence 6 of this paragraph, what is needed is a phrase to indicate the officials are taking the available evidence into consideration and acting upon it in a logical way. The phrase, "in light of" serves this purpose. **The correct answer is (D).**

SAMPLE TEST 1
Answer Explanations

7. The verb tense chosen should indicate that the canoeists would destroy the dams *while they are pushing their way through* and *as a consequence of trying to push through*. The present progressive ("ing") form of a verb best conveys these meanings. **The correct answer is (B).**

8. The proposed sentence definitely does highlight an advantage of the portage ramps that is not otherwise explicitly mentioned in the passage. Therefore, the sentence would be a useful addition to the passage, so a "Yes" answer is appropriate. The sentence does not, however, address the issue of why environmental protection is important. **The correct answer is (A).**

9. The sentence requires a word that indicates putting a plan into action. "Inciting" is related to that process, in that the word conveys the idea of rousing others to act, but generally, one can only "incite" beings that can deliberately respond to the call—that is, animals, usually humans. "Implementing" more directly express the idea of putting ideas into action, and is more appropriate to apply to something abstract or inanimate, like a plan. **The correct answer is (D).**

10. In most cases, the items (in this case, types of people) in a list should be separated by commas. There are instances when it is necessary to use semicolons (;) instead of commas, but the list "dividers" should *never* be a mixture of commas and semicolons. In addition, a comma should *not* follow the "and" introducing the last item in the list. **The correct answer is (C).**

11. The words "rather than" indicate that the final word in the sentence should be very different in meaning from "cooperation," perhaps even opposite in meaning. "Friendship" is therefore an unacceptable word choice, since friendship and cooperation are similar, not contrasting, in meaning. Answers choices (B) and (C) are even more similar in meaning to "cooperation," and therefore must be ruled out. **The correct answer is (D).**

---

12. The gray bar (food spending) above the label **Dec. 7-13** on the horizontal axis extends up only to the $150 mark on the vertical axis. Therefore, **the correct answer is (D).**

13. Both the gray bar (food spending) and the black bar (other expenditures) above the label **Feb. 22-28** on the horizontal axis are noticeably shorter than the corresponding bars above the label **Dec. 7-13**. Therefore, consumer spending in both categories was much lower during the indicated week in February than during the indicated week in December. **The correct answer is (B).**

14. The word "therefore" implies that the statement about to be made is a consequence of the ideas or information just presented. The act of gift giving does not automatically imply preparation of a traditional meal as a consequence, so "therefore" is not an appropriate word in this context. What is needed is a word or phrase suggesting that the holidays Northern Landians celebrate in December involve *both* gift giving *and* preparation of special meals. "In addition" is an appropriate phrase for this purpose. **The correct answer is (D).**

egghead prep.com

15. In standard written English, it is conventional to avoid using the word "this" to vaguely refer to ideas or phenomena described in the previous sentence or sentences. It is desirable to use a more specific description. The phrase "this increase" is preferable to the single word "this," but that choice would be illogical in the context of the sentence containing the underlined phrase, because it would imply that experts believe the cause of an increase is the increase itself. Rather, the passage makes clear that the experts have believed in the past that the only cause of the December increase in consumer spending in Northern Landia is expenditures related to the holidays. **The correct answer is (B).**

16. The graph actually shows that consumer spending (in both categories) is much higher from November 30 through January 10 than it is in February (late winter). Spending does not rise throughout December. In fact, it begins to decline after December 20 (*not* before December 14), though the decline is gradual, not sharp. **The correct answer is (B).**

17. The words, "an economist at the Davidson Institute," act as a supplemental phrase—a phrase that provides additional information about the person just introduced, Diane Kowalska. Supplemental phrases are always set off by commas at both ends, and not interrupted in the middle by a comma unless absolutely necessary for clarity. **The correct answer is (B).**

18. "Incandescently" means in a manner that involves heating, resulting in the emission of light. The word "incandescently" might therefore be used in a poetic description of rain. The tone of this passage, however, is journalistic, not poetic, so "incandescently" would be an inappropriate word choice. "Incessantly" means "endlessly" or "without interruption." Both meanings would be consistent with a description of cloudy, dark days that cause depression. **The correct answer is (B).**

19. The word "stresses" is plural in form. Therefore, the appropriate pronoun is "they" (not "it"). The sentence requires the possessive form of "they," which is "their." "They're" is incorrect, because it is a contraction of "they are." Any sentence in which "they're" is used must make sense if "they're" is replaced by the two words, "they are." Here, that substitution would result in an illogical sentence: *These constant environmental stresses take they are toll on both the mind and the boy.* **The correct answer is (D).**

20. The author is implying setting up a contrast between spending driven by holiday joy and spending as a compensation for seasonal depression. That is, the author wishes to place these two concepts in **opposition** to each other to emphasize the distinction between them. **The correct answer is (C).**

21. The "escalating cycle" described in sentence 4 is explained in sentence 6. Therefore, the paragraph would be most logical if sentence 4 immediately preceded sentence 6. In other words, sentence 4 should come *after* sentence 5, not before it. **The correct answer is (C).**

SAMPLE TEST 1
Answer Explanations

22. As noted in the explanation for question #21, sentence 6 is intended to describe the "escalating cycle" mentioned in sentence 4. A cycle occurs when a pattern feeds its own repetition. In this case, depression causes reckless spending, which in turn causes feelings of guilt, which fuel depression, which triggers additional spending, starting the whole process over again. The answer choice that best describes such a cyclical pattern is answer (B). **The correct answer is (B).**

---

23. The phrase, "increase to find," would mean "increase for the purpose of finding," which does make sense in the context of the sentence. Therefore, a change is required. The underlined phrase is intended to modify the word "find." Since "find" is a verb, the most appropriate modifier is an adverb. Since "ly" is a common ending for adverbs, it makes sense to look for an answer choice with that ending. Answer (C) contains a word ending in "ly," and "increasingly find" would mean "find more and more often," which expresses the author's intended meaning. **The correct answer is (C).**

24. The phrases, "I struggle more often with memory and concentration," and "friends have not asked me for help remembering things," are both complete sentences. Therefore, in order to include them both in the same sentence, a semicolon (;) must be employed. The other problem with the sentence as originally written is that it implies friends have *never* asked the author for help remembering things, suggesting that his or her memory was never very good in the first place. Both of these issues are corrected in answer choice (D). **The correct answer is (D).**

25. The word most commonly used in a description of an article's topic is *about*. For example, "I read a newspaper story about the kidnapping in Platterston." The word "on" can also be used: "A saw an interesting on the upcoming election." Words like "around" and "over" are used in place of "about" or "on" in some versions of spoken English, but not in standard written English. **The correct answer is (B).**

26. The author is suggesting that the freedom to daydream arose from the limited interactions described in the previous sentence. Therefore, the underlined phrase should be replaced with a phrase indicating that the fact a person's mind was free to wander was a consequence of the circumstances just described. The phrase "as a result" serves this purpose. **The correct answer is (B).**

27. The underlined word and answer choices (B) and (C) all suggest that the daydreams were only diversions, nothing more. But the next sentence of the passage clearly indicates that daydreams played an important role in maintaining the health of the brain. Therefore, the daydreams were *more* than diversions. Only answer choice (D), "not," conveys an idea consistent with this conclusion. **The correct answer is (D).**

eggheadprep.com

28. The paragraph as a whole is devoted to a discussion of the relationship between mental "down time," during which aimless daydreaming can occur, and the health of the brain. It does not focus on clinical assessment of brain health. Therefore, in order for the proposed sentence to be an appropriate addition to the paragraph, it would need to offer a connection between the use of brain scanning techniques and the author's assertion of the value of daydreaming activity. Because no such connection is made, **the correct answer is (D).**

29. It is inappropriate to place a comma between the phrase, "the year," and the numerical representation of the year. The underlined phrase therefore needs to be replaced. A comma after the year number is appropriate, however, because it separates the description of when the study occurred from the description of how it was conducted. Notice that answers (B) and (C) do not include the phrase "the year" at all. That phrase is actually unnecessary, since the number 2013 will immediately be recognized by the reader as a year number in this context. However, the semicolon (;) in answer (C) is inappropriate. **The correct answer is (B).**

30. Careful study of the graphic reveals that each black bar represents the percent of respondents who believed that the particular variable represented by that row was affected positively by spending time "unplugged," while each gray bar represents the percent who believed the variable was negatively affected. For example, 76% of respondents believed "unplugged time" had a positive effect on their ability to focus, whereas only 8% believed ability to focus was negatively affected by "unplugged time." (The fact that the percentages do not add up to 100% simply indicates that some respondents believed there was no effect at all, either positive or negative.) "Positively affected" and "improved" are very similar in meaning. Answer (C) thus best expresses information shown in the graph. **The correct answer is (C).**

31. In its current form, the paragraph begins in a disorienting way. (The first day of what?) The proposed additional sentence explains that reading the article described in the previous two paragraphs motivated the author to make a lifestyle change. With this introduction, the phrase "the first day" would make sense. Therefore, the new sentence should come at the very beginning of the paragraph. **The correct answer is (A).**

32. In the current construction of sentence 3, the verb "sitting" would be attached to the first noun to appear after the completion of the phrase about sitting and reading. In other words, the sentence in its current form implies that the author's phone was reading the novel. Option (C) eliminates this silly implication by rewording the sentence in a way that shows clearly that the author was the one sitting and reading, while still showing how the author's activities, state of mind, and phone were all related. Although option (D) also provides the correct subject (the author) for the verb "sat," it does not show how the elements of the sentence are connected. **The correct answer is (C).**

33. The punctuation following the word "regimen" should clearly indicate that a list is being introduced. A colon (:) is ideal for that purpose. Therefore, no change is required. **The correct answer is (A).**

SAMPLE TEST 1
Answer Explanations

34. A descriptive phrase introduced by a comma calls for the word, "which," not "that." For example, "The picture of my grandfather, which hung in the living room above the sofa, reminded me daily of what my family had endured over the years." Therefore, answers (B) and (C) should be eliminated. Choice (D) is unnecessarily wordy and does not match the verb tense (past) of the sentence as a whole. **The correct answer is (A).**

35. Neither "adversely" nor "accordingly" is an appropriate adverb in this context. The first would imply that the good intentions themselves (rather than the poor choices made based on those intentions) cause negative consequences. The second would imply that the good intentions were appropriate for, perhaps even consequences of, the negative impacts next described. Replacing "best of intentions" with "intentions of the best" complicates the language for no particular purpose. Therefore, it is best to leave the underlined portion as it is. **The correct answer is (A).**

36. The subject of the sentence is "infants," which is plural. Therefore, any pronoun used in reference to that subject should also be plural, which rules out options (A) and (B). Remember that "they're" is only appropriate when it can be logically be replaced by "they are," for which it is a contraction. Here, the resulting sentence would be illogical: "Human infants gain much of their early understanding of the world by clasping objects in they are hands." What is needed instead is a possessive form of "they," which is "their." **The correct answer is (C).**

37. The added sentence should connect to the previous statement that tool manipulation played an important role in the growth of human intelligence. It should also set up the sentence to come by providing evidence that discontinuing manual arts education is detrimental to students' development. Only option (B) accomplishes both of these purposes. **The correct answer is (B).**

38. It certainly would not be "appropriate" for human beings to view engagement in the activities that may have contributed the most to the rise of human intellect as a sign of inferior intelligence. It definitely would be ironic (that is, essentially the opposite of what would actually make sense), however. **The correct answer is (B).**

39. The evidence presented earlier in the passage shows that the fear described in the previous sentenced is actually unfounded (that is, it has no basis in fact). The sentence in which the underlined word appears is intended to point out that in spite of the evidence, schools engage in practices, such as restrictive scheduling procedures, that seem to suggest the fear is justified. That is, the actions of the schools make the fear stronger, or *reinforce* it. **The correct answer is (D).**

40. In standard written English, the use of "this" to vaguely refer to an idea, fact, or opinion expressed in a previous sentence is discouraged. Sometimes, a more specific phrase can be substituted for "this." In other cases, sentences can be combined, eliminating the need for the word altogether. Option (C) represents an attempt to combine the sentences, but still uses the word "this" inappropriately. Option (D) is awkwardly worded and unnecessarily long. Option (B) expresses the same ideas as sentence (D) in a far "cleaner" manner. **The correct answer is (B).**

41. "Also" would be a simpler choice here than "as well," so option (D) should be eliminated. The "s" at the end of "carpenter" is intended to indicate a plural (more than one carpenter), NOT a possessive form (that which belongs to a carpenter), so an apostrophe should not be used. **The correct answer is (B).**

42. School officials would definitely be interested in the information presented in the proposed sentence. But the fact that a sentence contains useful information does not necessarily mean it would make a good addition to a paragraph. Each sentence in a paragraph should support the paragraph's main idea. The main idea of the second paragraph on this page is that it is possible, through experiments and observations, to establish a connection between training in the manual arts and development of the mind. Therefore, the proposed sentence is off topic. **The correct answer is (D).**

43. The sentence can be brought into compliance with the conventions of standard written English simply by taking out the word "which." The sentence also remains completely logical if that change is made. Therefore, deletion of the underlined word is the simplest, most effective rewrite. **The correct answer is (D).**

44. The subject of the sentence is the plural, "students." Therefore, the pronoun to be used here should also be plural, so answers (A) and (B) should be eliminated. Since it is unreasonable to assume that either the author or the reader is included among the students described, answer (D), "we" is an inappropriate choice. **The correct answer is (C).**

SAMPLE TEST 1
Answer Explanations

TEST SECTION 3: MATH—NO CALCULATOR

NOTE: Most problems in math can be solved using multiple different methods. In these explanations, the most standard methods taught in US middle school and high school mathematics are shown. You may have employed a different method that is equally valid.

1. Since Tisha fished 7 days fishing and caught T fish per day, she caught a total of $7T$ fish. Her mother caught M fish per day but only fished on 6 days, so the total number of fish caught by Tisha's mother is $6M$. These results should be added to calculate the total number of fish caught by Tisha and her mother: $7T + 6M$, or $6M + 7T$. **The correct answer is (D).**

2. Substitute the value 4 for r and then perform standard steps from algebra:

   $4 = \dfrac{t+5}{4}$ multiply both sides by 4 to get

   $16 = t + 5$ subract 5 from both sides

   $11 = t$

   The correct answer is (A).

3. First we distribute the (−) sign across the second set of parentheses to get,

   $7 - 2i - 4 - 5i.$

   Next, combine like terms, yielding $3 - 7i$. **The correct answer is (C).** (Note that it is not necessary to use the information that $i = \sqrt{-1}$.)

4. The quantity "increase in price each month," which could also be worded, "increase in price per month," is a rate of change. In an equation of the form, $y = a + bx$, the coefficient of x, which is the number b, is the rate of change, also called the slope. The equation given in the problem, $p = 1.68 + .07m$, matches the form, $y = a + bx$, with p in place of y and m in place of x. Therefore, the desired rate of change is the number in the b position for this equation form, which is 0.07. **The correct answer is (B).**

5. Because the quantities are to be added, the parentheses may be dropped. It is then necessary to combine like terms, which are those terms that have the same variables and same exponents on those variables. The steps are:

   $-4mn^2 + 3m^2n + 4mn + -4n^2 - mn^2 - 8m^2n$
   $= -4mn^2 - mn^2 + 3m^2n - 8m^2n + 4mn + -4n^2$
   $= -5mn^2 - 5m^2n + 4mn - 4n^2$

   The correct answer is (B).

6. As in problem #4, the equation given in the problem, $M = 800 - 20d$, is in the form, $y = a + bx$. The number b, as explained above (problem #4), represents the rate of change, which would be the amount by which number of dollars in the account decreases (since b is negative) per day. In such equations, the number a represents the **initial value**, that is, the amount in the account when $d = 0$. In other words, the number a stands for how much money Jenna deposited when she created the account. The number 800 is in the a position in the equation. **The correct answer is (D).**

7. Multiply both sides of the first equation by $2r$ to get, $m = 6r$. Next, substitute $6r$ for m in the second equation:

$$\frac{18r}{6r} = \frac{18}{6} = 3$$

The correct answer is (C).

8. The equation looks extremely complicated. In part, a problem like this one is testing whether you are intimidated by complex-looking math problems. The important thing to realize is that everything except the Z on the right side of the "=" sign takes the form of a fraction. Therefore, the equation can be thought of as, more simply:

$$D = \frac{a}{b} Z$$

To solve, multiply both side by the reciprocal of $\frac{a}{b}$, which is $\frac{b}{a}$

$$\frac{b}{a} D = Z, \text{ or } Z = \frac{b}{a} D$$

The correct answer should therefore take the form,

Z = (reciprocal of original fraction) * D

The answer that takes this form is (D). **The correct answer is (D).**

9. Note that $h(4) = 17 - b(4)^2 = 17 - 16b$, and we are told this result equals 12. Now plug in -4 for x: $h(-4) = 17 - b(-4)^2$, but since $(-4)^2 = 16$, the result is once again $17 - 16b$. We know this expression is equal to 12 based on our previous work. **The correct answer is (A).**

SAMPLE TEST 1
Answer Explanations

10. First rearrange the second equation so that the order of variables is the same as in the first. Then use standard algebra techniques:

    $5x - 2y = 12$

    $-2x - 6y = 2$ Multiply the first equation by -3 to get

    $-15x + 6y = -36$

    $-2x - 6y = 2$ Add the two equations to get

    $-17x = -34$ Divide both sides by -17 to get $x = 2$.

    Now plug 2 in for x in the first of the original equations:
    $5(2) - 2y = 12$
    $10 - 2y = 12$ Subtract 10 from both sides and divide both sides by -2:
    $-2y = 2$
    $y = -1$

    Since $x = 2$ and $y = -1$, **the correct answer is (C).**

11. Using the equation $y = mx + b$, in which m is the slope of the line and b is the line's y-intercept, we can represent the line described in the problem by the equation, $y = -\frac{3}{5}x + 0$, or more simply, $y = -\frac{3}{5}x$. Since the line crosses the y-axis at (0, 0), it cannot cross the y-axis at any other point, so answers (B) and (D) can be ruled out. It remains to determine which of the points given in answers (A) and (C) satisfy our equation. Testing the point given in answer (A) yields

    $5 = -\frac{3}{5}(-3)$, but

    $5 \neq \frac{9}{5}$

    Since the point given in answer (A) does not satisfy the equation, (A) must be eliminated. The point (10, –6), however, does satisfy the equation. **The correct answer is (C).**

12. Since we want the price per pound of pears (p) and apples (a) to be equal, we set the expressions for the two prices equal to each other and solve using standard algebra methods:

    $0.78 + 0.11w = 0.62 + 0.15w$ Subtract 0.11w from both sides:
    $0.78 = 0.62 + 0.04w$ Subtract 0.62 from both sides, then divide by 0.04:
    $0.16 = 0.04w$
    $4 = w$

egghead prep.com

Note that we have found the value of w, the number of weeks after January 1, 2016. The problem asks for the price per pound of pears, p. So we must plug in the value 4 for w in the formula for p:

$p = 0.78 + 0.11(4) = 0.78 + 0.44 = 1.22$. **The correct answer is (B).**

13. Begin by rearranging the equation, $-y + 3x = -15$, to get y by itself:

$$-y + 3x = -15 \quad \text{Add y to both sides}$$
$$3x = -15 + y \quad \text{Add 15 to both sides}$$
$$3x + 15 = y$$

Now, replace y by $3x + 15$ in the given fraction. Also rewrite 27 as 3^3, so that the numerator and denominator of the fraction have the same base, 3:

$$\frac{3^{3x+15}}{(3^3)^x} = \frac{3^{3x+15}}{3^{3x}} \quad \text{(Denominator simplified using the exponent property,} \quad (a^b)^c = a^{bc})$$

$$= 3^{3x+15-3x} \quad \text{(Simplified using the property,} \quad \frac{a^b}{a^c} = a^{b-c})$$

$$= 3^{15}$$

The correct answer is (A).

14. The expression, $(mx + 1)(nx - 5)$ can be expanded (an operation many students learn by the acronym, FOIL). The result is, $mnx^2 - 5mx + 1nx - 5$. Since we know from the information given in the problem that $(mx + 1)(nx - 5) = 21x^2 + cx - 5$, it must be true that

$$mnx^2 - 5mx + 1nx - 5 = 21x^2 + cx - 5 \quad (1)$$

By comparing the x^2 terms on the left and right sides of equation (1) above, we see that $mn = 21$. We also know from the given information for the problem that $m + n = 10$. Therefore, m and n add up to 10 but have a product of 21. Two such numbers are 7 and 3. We conclude that $m = 3$ and $n = 7$, or $m = 7$ and $n = 3$. Plugging the first pair of values in for m and n in equation (1) above gives us

$$3(7)x^2 - 5(3)x + 1(7)x - 5, \text{ which equals}$$
$$21x^2 - 8x - 5.$$

Comparing this expression with the right side of equation (1) above, we see that $-8 = c$. Note that answer (B) is the only answer to include -8 as a value of c. (Using $m = 7$ and $n = 3$ in equation (1) above yields the other value of c, -32, though this work is not necessary.) **The correct answer is (B).**

SAMPLE TEST 1
Answer Explanations

15. We will simplify the denominator of the large fraction first:

$$\frac{1}{\frac{1}{x-1} + \frac{1}{x+4}} = \frac{1}{\frac{x+4}{(x-1)(x+4)} + \frac{x-1}{(x-1)(x+4)}} \quad \text{(Creating common denominator)}$$

$$= \frac{1}{\frac{x+4+x-1}{(x-1)(x+4)}} = \frac{1}{\frac{2x+3}{(x-1)(x+4)}} \quad \text{Now use the fact that } \frac{1}{\frac{a}{b}} = \frac{b}{a} \text{ to get}$$

$$= \frac{(x-1)(x+4)}{2x+3}$$

To completely match one of the answer choices, we would need to expand (FOIL) the numerator, but that is not actually necessary. Note that of the choices, only (B) has the correct denominator. **The correct answer is (B).**

---

16. Solve the system using standard methods of algebra:

$$2x - y = 4$$
$$x + 3y = 9 \quad \text{Multiply the second equation by } -2 \text{ to get}$$

$$2x - y = 4$$
$$-2x - 6y = -18 \quad \text{Add the two equations to get}$$

$$-7y = -14 \quad \text{Divide both sides by } -7$$
$$y = 2$$

The correct answer is 2.

17. Here is the diagram from the problem with the specified lengths included:

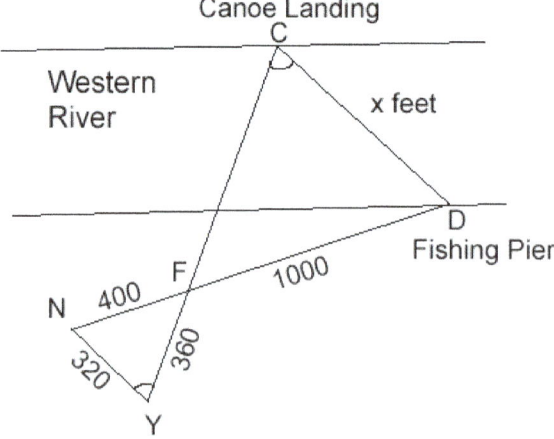

According to the principle of similar triangles from geometry,

$$\frac{NF}{DF} = \frac{NY}{DC}$$ Plugging in the numbers from above yields,

$$\frac{400}{1000} = \frac{320}{x}$$ which simplifies to, $\frac{2}{5} = \frac{320}{x}$. Cross multiply to get

$2x = 1600$ Divide both sides by 2 to get

$x = 800$

The correct answer is 800.

18. Adding 25 to both sides of the given equation yields $w^2 = 25$. Since we know $w > 0$, we can simplify take the positive square root of 25 to solve for w. **The correct answer is 5.**

19. First, multiply the second equation by 3 on both sides, so that the two equations are now

$$3y = \sqrt{5x} \quad \text{and} \quad 3y = 6\sqrt{5}$$

Since the expressions on the right sides of the two equations both equal $3y$, they are equal to each other. Set them equal and use standard algebra methods:

$\sqrt{5x} = 6\sqrt{5}$ Square both sides, making sure to square the 6 :
$5x = 36 * 5$ Dividing both sides by 5 eliminates both 5's, leaving
$x = 36$

The correct answer is 36.

20. A basic property of trigonometry states that $\cos t° = \sin(90° - t°)$ and $\sin t° = \cos(90° - t°)$, for **any** angle of $t°$. Therefore, **the correct answer is 5/13, or 0.385, or 0.384.**

SAMPLE TEST 1
Answer Explanations

TEST SECTION 4: MATH—CALCULATOR

NOTE: Most problems in math can be solved using multiple different methods. In these explanations, the most standard methods taught in US middle school and high school mathematics are shown. You may have employed a different method that is equally valid.

1. Strictly decreasing means the graph should display a purely downward trend when read from left to right; strictly increasing means the graph should display a purely upward trend when read from left to right. Therefore, we are looking for an interval over which, when read from left to right, the graph first goes downward, then upward. Answer (A) can be ruled out because during the interval from 20 to 25 minutes, there is neither an upward nor a downward trend. Answer (B) describes an interval over which the trend of the graph is upward then downward, the opposite of what we are seeking. Answer (D) describes an interval that, like the interval in answer (A), contains a section of the graph that neither increases nor decreases. Only the interval described in answer (C) corresponds to a segment of the graph that, when read from left to right, goes downward first then upward, as required. **The correct answer is (C).**

2. Angle 1 and angle 2 have equal measures, since they are alternate exterior angles on the lines p and q, with transversal m. Therefore, angle 2 measures 78°. Angle 2 and angle 3, however, are not equal in measure. Angle 3 has the same measure as the angle immediately to the left of angle 2 (those two angles form a pair of corresponding angles on parallel lines *m* and *n*, with transversal *q*). Therefore, the sum of the measures of angle 2 and angle 3 is 180°. The measure of angle 3 is then 180° − 78° = 102°. **The correct answer is (A).**

3. The given information corresponds to the equation, $32 - 3x = 6 + 8$, which equals 14. Rearramge the equation to get the term "$3x$" by itself:

    $32 - 3x = 14$ Add 3x to both sides to get
    $32 = 14 + 3x$ Subtract 14 from both sides to get
    $18 = 3x$

    Now multiply both sides of the final equation by 2 to get $36 = 6x$. **The correct answer is (D).**

4. Begin by plugging 21 in for W and 3 in for L in the given equation to get, $21 = k(3)$. Dividing both sides of this equation by 3 yields, $7 = k$. Since k is a *constant*, we may continue to use the value 7 for k even if the values of L and W change. To solve the problem, plug in 7 for k and 7 for L in the given equation: $W = 7(7) = 49$. **The correct answer is (D).**

5. It is necessary to either convert 4 kiloliters into deciliters, or 1 deciliter into kiloliters. Either option will work. The following method converts 4 kiloliters to deciliters:

$$4 \text{ kiloliters} \times \frac{1000 \text{ liters}}{1 \text{ kiloliter}} \times \frac{10 \text{ deciliters}}{1 \text{ liter}} \quad \text{All units except kiloliters cancel out,} \quad \text{leaving}$$

$$\frac{4(1000)(10)}{1} \text{ deciliters, or } 40,000 \text{ deciliters}$$

Since only 1 deciliter is needed to run the experiment, the chemists can run the experiment 40,000 times. **The correct answer is (A).**

6. A strong positive relationship is displayed in a graph that clearly shows Y increasing as X increases. That is, the trend should be clearly upward if the scatterplot is read from left to right. Only answer choice (C) shows such a graph. **The correct answer is (C).**

7. Here are the steps to solve the inequality for x:

   $5x - 3 < 6x + 2$ Subtract 6x from both sides to get
   $-1x - 3 < 2$ Add 3 to both sides to get
   $-1x < 5$ Multiply or divide both sides by -1; the inequality reverses
   $x > -5$

   Therefore, any number greater than –5 is a solution. The only choice that does NOT show an answer greater than –5 is (B). **The correct answer is (B).**

8. By reading the vertical axis, we can determine that the heights of the five bars of the graph are (from left to right): 11, 5, 9, 6, and 3. The sum of these numbers is $11 + 5 + 9 + 6 + 3 = 34$. Since we are told the total attendance was 34 *thousand* (34,000), the numbers on the vertical axis must be in thousands. **The correct answer is (C).**

9. By definition, the absolute value of any expression is at least zero. We therefore know that $|x - 5| \geq 0$. Therefore (adding 4 to both sides of this inequality), we know that $|x + 5| + 4 \geq 4$. A value of 1 for the expression, $|x + 5| + 4$, therefore, is impossible. **The correct answer is (D).**

10. Here are the steps to rearramge the equation to get the variable T by itself:

    $v = 3,121.5 + 2.37T$ Subtract 3,121.5 from both sides to get
    $v - 3,121.5 = 2.37T$ Divide both sides by 2.37 to get
    $\frac{v - 3,121.5}{2.37} = T$, or $T = \frac{v - 3,121.5}{2.37}$

The correct answer is (B).

SAMPLE TEST 1
Answer Explanations

11. One way to solve this problem would be to plug in 3,350 for v in the equation we just found for problem #10, and thus calculate T. That method, however, is dependent on solving problem #10 correctly. The safe approach is to return to the original equation, $v = 3{,}121.5 + 2.37T$, plug in 3,350 for v, and solve for T:

    $3{,}350 = 3{,}121.5 + 2.37T$ Subtract 3,121.5 from both sides to get

    $228.5 = 2.37T$ Divide both sides by 2.37 to get

    $96.41 = T$

    This result is closest to answer (B), 96°. **The correct answer is (B).**

12. For each answer choice, divide the number of students in that group by the total number of students, 243. For answer (A), the number of female students who selected swing dance was 42, and $42/243 \approx 0.1728$, or 17.28%. For answer (B), the number of male students who selected aerial dance is 17, and $17/243 \approx 0.06996$, or 6.996%. For answer (C), the number of male students who selected ballroom dance was 12, and $12/243 \approx 0.04938$, or 4.938%. For answer (D), the number of female students who selected aerial dance is 74, and $74/243 \approx 0.3045$, or 30.45%. The only choice that yields a result close to 17% is answer (A). **The correct answer is (A).**

13. Correctly reading the graph is very important. The leftmost bar tells us that there were 5 nests with 2 eggs. The second bar in from the left tells us there were 7 nests with 3 eggs. Continuing to read the bars left to right, there were 2 nests with 4 eggs, 4 nests with 5 eggs, and 1 nest with 6 eggs. The total number of nests was therefore $5 + 7 + 2 + 4 + 1 = 19$. To calculate the average number of eggs per nest, we must add up all the eggs (accounting for every single nest) and then divide by the total number of nests:

    $$\frac{2+2+2+2+2+3+3+3+3+3+3+3+4+4+5+5+5+5+6}{19}$$

    which equals 3.421. This number is closest to answer (B), 3. **The correct answer is (B).**

14. The maximum of f occurs at the highest point on the graph, which is the point (4, 4). Therefore, the *x*-value is 4. **The correct answer is (D).**

15. Removing an outlier has little, if any, effect on the median of a data set, so answer (A) can be eliminated. The mean (average) of a data is always more affected by the removal of an outlier than the median is. Therefore, these values do not change by the same amount, which means that answer (D) can be eliminated. All that remains is to determine which changes more if the outlier is removed, the mean or the range. The range is defined as the maximum minus the minimum. With the value 67 included in the set, the range is $67 - 27 = 40$. With the value 67 removed, the range is $41 - 27 = 14$. Therefore, removing the outlier changes the range by $40 - 14 = 26$, a very large change. Since the calculation of the mean uses *all* the values in the data set, not just the highest and lowest values, it will not change as dramatically as the range if a single value at either the high or low end is removed from the set. **The correct answer is (B).**

16. The P-intercept is the point (0, 5) on the vertical axis. Its coordinates indicate that when h = 0, P = $5.00, or, in words, that it costs $5.00 to park in the garage for 0 hours. We interpret this result to mean that the cost of parking in the garage starts at $5.00, even before the car has been parked for any duration of time. This cost is known as a "startup" or "initial" cost. **The correct answer is (C).**

17. In an equation of the form, y = mx + b, b is the y-intercept and m is the slope. Therefore, for an equation in the form, P = mh + b, b is the P-intercept, which we know from problem #16 is 5, and m is the slope. To determine the correct answer, we must calculate the slope of the line. Notice that the points (0, 5) and (4, 10) are both on the line. We calculate the slope using the standard formula from algebra:

$$\frac{y_2 - y_1}{x_2 - x_1} = \frac{10 - 5}{4 - 0} = \frac{5}{4} = m$$

Only answer (A) displays the correct values for both m and b. **The correct answer is (A).**

18. Using the total number of tools Tamara purchased, the total cost, and the cost of each type of tool, the given information can be translated into the system of equations,

$$H + S = 134$$
$$8.75H + 5.50S = 990.50$$

Subtracting S from both sides of the first equation yields, H = 134 − S. We then substitute this expression for H in the second equation to get, 8.75(134 − S) + 5.50S = 990.50. We now solve using standard algebra methods:

$8.75(134 - S) + 5.50S = 990.50$ Using the distributive property, we get
$1,172.5 - 8.75S + 5.50S = 990.50$ Combine like terms and subtract 1,172.5 from both sides :
$-3.25S = -182$ Divide both sides by − 3.25 to get
$S = 56$

The correct answer is (D).

19. Begin by plugging in the given values, 0 for M and 0 for W. The result is the new pair of inequalities,

$$0 > -3(0) + Q, \text{ or } 0 > Q, \text{ or } Q < 0$$

and $$0 < 2(0) + P, \text{ or } 0 < P, \text{ or } P > 0$$

In other words, Q is negative and P is positive. Q must therefore be less than P. **The correct answer is (C).**

20. The columns with headings 9 – 16 and 17 – 24 represent male deer that engaged in at least 9 fights. Therefore, the total number of male deer that engaged in at least 9 fights was 14 + 3 + 3 + 1 = 21. The number of male deer that engaged in at least 9 fights AND belonged to the forest group was 3 + 1 = 4. Therefore, the probability is 4 / 21. **The correct answer is (D).**

SAMPLE TEST 1
Answer Explanations

21. The equation, $(x - h)^2 + (y - k)^2 = r^2$ represents a circle with center (h, k) and radius r. For a circle with center $(5, 0)$, the left side of this equation should take the form, $(x - 5)^2 + (y - 0)^2$, which can be more simply written as, $(x - 5)^2 + y^2$. The only answer choice that displays a correct left side of the equation is (B). We therefore do not have to do any further work. **The correct answer is (B).**

22. If the sale price was 30% off the original price, then Angelo paid 100% – 30% = 70% of the original price. If X is the original price, then $(0.70)X$ represents 70% of the original price. If 7% sales tax was added to the cost, then the total cost was 100% + 7% = 107% of the previous expression, that is, $(1.07)(0.70)X$. Therefore, $D = (1.07)(0.70)X$. The answer choices, however, require an equation in which X is by itself. Divide both side by $(1.07)(0.70)$ to get

$$\frac{D}{(1.07)(0.70)} = X ,$$

which is equivalent to answer (B). **The correct answer is (B).**

23. Using the first row of the table, calculate the ratio of June 13 sales to June 11 sales in the Women's department: $19{,}875 / 21{,}301 \approx 0.933$. We are looking for another department with a ratio of June 13 sales to June 11 sales that is close to 0.933. Note that in Women's, June 13 sales were *lower* than June 11 sales, so we must find another department for which June 13 sales were *lower* than June 11 sales. Therefore, we can rule out Men's and Furniture. We calculate the ratio for Infants as $10{,}622 / 11{,}990 \approx 0.886$, and the ratio for Appliances as $34{,}892 / 37{,}413 \approx .9326$. The value 0.9326 is very close to 0.933, so Appliances is the correct department. **The correct answer is (C).**

24. The average rate of change is defined as the change in sales divided by the number of days that have gone by:

$$\frac{\text{June 13 sales } - \text{ June 10 sales}}{3 \text{ days}} = \frac{14{,}213 - 12{,}764}{3}$$

which equals $483 per day. Answer (A) is closest to this value. **The correct answer is (A).**

25. The average number of dots counted by the a single student is,

$$\frac{87 + 73 + 51 + 92 + 86 + 77 + 68 + 97 + 82 + 70}{10} = 78.3 ,$$

which suggests that each tile has approximately 80 dots on it. Since each tile is a square with sides of length 1 yard, the area of a single tile is 1 square yard. However, the total area of the floor of the play space, which measures 10 yards on each side, is
10 yd × 10 yd = 100 square yards. Therefore, the floor of the play area is made up of 100 tiles, so the best estimate of the total number of dots is 80 × 100 = 8,000. **The correct answer is (C).**

26. If boxes of cereal brand X contain 40% more cereal than boxes of cereal brand Y, then the amount of cereal in a box of brand X is 100% + 40% = 140% of the amount of cereal in a box of brand Y. That is, $X = (1.00 + 0.40)Y$, or $X = 1.40Y$. We plug in the given value for X and solve for Y:

$$917 = 1.40Y \quad \text{Divide both sides by 1.40 to get}$$
$$655 = Y$$

The correct answer is (D).

NOTE: Many students will mistakenly assume that since boxes of brand X have 40% more cereal than boxes of brand Y, it must be true that boxes of brand Y have 40% less cereal than boxes of brand X. That is incorrect. We can see from the answer that boxes of brand Y have 655 / 917 ≈ 0.71 = 71% of the amount of cereal that boxes of brand X have. That means that boxes of brand Y have 100% – 71% = 29% less cereal than boxes of brand X. This discrepancy shows that percent problems are asymmetrical: you cannot replace a percent increase in one direction with the same percentage as a decrease in the opposite direction. It is therefore very important to set up percent problems very carefully.

27. The rock will hit the ground when the value of h is zero, so we plug in 0 for h to get, $0 = -16t^2 + 56t$. This equation can be factored as $0 = t(-16t + 56)$. Each factor may then be set equal to zero. The equation, $t = 0$, would just give 0 seconds as a solution, which is not a reasonable answer. Therefore, we solve the equation given by the other factor:

$$-16t + 56 = 0 \quad \text{Subtract 56 from both sides to get}$$
$$-16t = -56 \quad \text{Divide both sides by } -16 \text{ to get}$$
$$t = 3.5 \text{ seconds}$$

The correct answer is (A).

SAMPLE TEST 1
Answer Explanations

28. The graph below shows the solution set to the system of inequalities (indicated by the "diamonds" pattern of crossing thin lines).

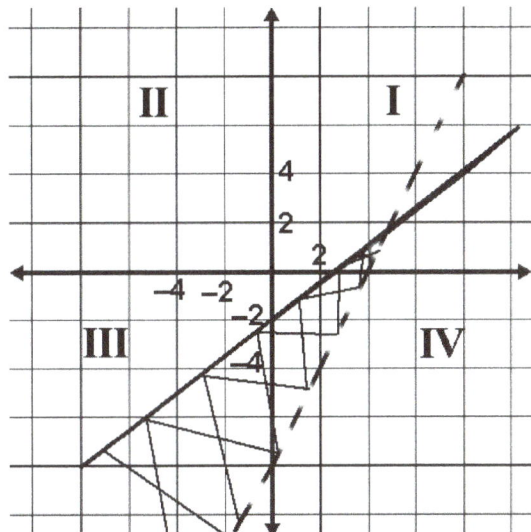

The solution set contains points in quadrants I, III, and IV, but not in quadrant II.
The correct answer is (B).

29. Because the problem refers to the equations as equivalent, we know they are all correct equations for the parabola. We need the one in vertex form, which is the form, $y = a(x - h)^2 + k$, where the coordinates of the vertex are (h, k). The graph shows that the vertex has coordinates (2, 18), so the correct equation is, $y = -2(x - 2)^2 + 18$. **The correct answer is (A).**

30. This problem refers to a very specific theorem from algebra, called the Remainder Theorem, typically studied in Advanced Algebra (Algebra II). The theorem states that if $p(x)$ is divide by $x - r$, then the remainder from the division will equal $p(r)$. In problem #30, r would be the value –4. The expression $x - r$ must then equal $x - (-4)$, or $x + 4$. Therefore, the Remainder Theorem, as applied to this problem, states that if $p(x)$ is divided by $x + 4$, the remainder will be $p(-4)$, which is 5. This statement matches answer choice (D). **The correct answer is (D).**

---

31. Based on the graph, the number of visitors to Website A in 2000 was 80 and the number of visitors in 2004 was 180. Therefore, the fraction requested in the problem is

$$\frac{80}{180} = \frac{8}{18} = \frac{4}{9} = 0.444$$

The correct answer is 4/9, or 0.444.

egghead prep.com

32. According to the information in the problem, Rebecca may have attempted exactly 7 shots in each game. In that case, she has played 90 ÷ 7 = 12.857 games, but the number of games must be a whole number. The answer should be rounded **down** to 12 games, because 7 shots × 13 games would equal 91 shots, more than Rebecca took. It is also possible that Rebecca took exactly 15 shots in each game. In that case, the number of games would be 90 ÷ 15 = 6. Because the number of shots in any game could be anywhere from 7 to 15, inclusive, the number of games could be anywhere from 6 to 12, inclusive. **Any of the following numbers is a correct answer: 6, 7, 8, 9, 10, 11, 12.**

33. Since 60 minutes divided by 20 minutes is 3, we know that the therapist can complete three 20-minute treatments each hour. Therefore, during an 8-hour day, she can complete 8(3) = 24 treatments. For three days, the maximum number of treatments would be 24(3) = 72. **The correct answer is 72.**

34. Since the keyboard, amplifiers, and drums take up 800 cubic feet of space, the band has 1300 – 800 = 500 cubic feet of space remaining for CD boxes. Therefore, the maximum number of boxes that the band can store in the space is 500 cubic feet divided by 2.5 cubic feet per box. 500 ÷ 2.5 = 200. **The correct answer is 200.**

35. Use the formula for volume of a cone shown on the instructions page. Plug in 100π for the volume and 12 for the height, and solve for r :

    $100\pi = \frac{1}{3}\pi r^2 (12)$ Multiply 1/3 by 12 to get

    $100\pi = 4\pi r^2$ Divide both sides by 4 π to get

    $\frac{100\pi}{4\pi} = \frac{100}{4} = 25 = r^2$ Take the positive square root of both sides

    $5 = r$

    Therefore, the radius of the cone is 5 meters. However, the problem asks for the *diameter* of the cone, which is 2(5 meters) = 10 meters. **The correct answer is 10.**

36. Since the balance in the account is **growing** by 3% per year, the growth factor in the exponential formula must be 100% + 3% = 103% = 1.03. **The correct answer is 1.03.**

    NOTE: *Many students learn the compound interest formula, $A = P(1 + r)^x$ for annually compounded interest. Substituting $500 for P (the initial investment, or principle) and 0.03 (that is, 3%) for r gives us, $A = 500(1 + 0.03)^x$, or $A = 500(1.03)^x$. This is another way to see that b = 1.03.*

SAMPLE TEST 1
Answer Explanations

37. Since Jackie's principle (initial) amount is $450 and her account pays 3.8% annually compounded interest, the amount of money in her account is given by $J = 450 (1.038)^x$. (See the explanation for problem #36 above.) Now we calculate the amount of money in each account after 20 years.

    The amount in Danesha's account is, $D = 500(1.03)^{20} \approx 903.06$

    The amount in Jackie's account is, $J = 450(1.038)^{20} \approx 948.77$

    Therefore, $|J - D| \approx |948.77 - 903.06| = |45.71| = \$45.71$. To the nearest whole dollar, this amount is $46. **The correct answer is 46.**

38. The function will not be defined if the denominator of the fraction equals zero. Therefore, we set the denominator equal to zero and solve the equation using standard algebra methods:

$(x+1)^2 - 6(x+1) + 9 = 0$	Rewrite the first expression in order to expand (FOIL)
$(x+1)(x+1) - 6(x+1) + 9 = 0$	Expand (FOIL) first expression, use distributive property on second
$x^2 + x + x + 1 - 6x - 6 + 9 = 0$	Combine like terms to get
$x^2 - 4x + 4 = 0$	Now factor (or use quadratic formula)
$(x-2)(x-2) = 0$	Set individual factors equal to zero and solve
$x - 2 = 0$	
$x = 2$	

    The correct answer is 2.

SCORING CONVERSION
RAW TO SCALED SCORE CONVERSION CHARTS

Sample Test 1:

A. SECTION 1: Conversion Chart for Reading Test:

RAW SCORE (# of correct answers)	READING TEST SCORE		RAW SCORE (# of correct answers)	READING TEST SCORE
0	10		27	26
1	10		28	26
2	10		29	27
3	11		30	28
4	12		31	28
5	13		32	29
6	14		33	29
7	15		34	30
8	15		35	30
9	16		36	31
10	17		37	31
11	17		38	32
12	18		39	32
13	19		40	33
14	19		41	33
15	20		42	34
16	20		43	35
17	21		44	35
18	21		45	36
19	22		46	37
20	22		47	37
21	23		48	38
22	23		49	38
23	24		50	39
24	24		51	40
25	25		52	40
26	25			

EGGHEAD PREP

SAMPLE TEST 1
Scoring Conversion

B. SECTION 2: Conversion Chart for Writing and Language Test

RAW SCORE (# of correct answers)	WRITING AND LANGUAGE TEST SCORE		RAW SCORE (# of correct answers)	WRITING AND LANGUAGE TEST SCORE
0	10		23	25
1	10		24	25
2	10		25	26
3	10		26	26
4	11		27	27
5	12		28	28
6	13		29	28
7	13		30	29
8	14		31	30
9	15		32	30
10	16		33	31
11	16		34	32
12	17		35	32
13	18		36	33
14	19		37	34
15	19		38	34
16	20		39	35
17	21		40	36
18	21		41	37
19	22		42	38
20	23		43	39
21	23		44	40
22	24			

C. Evidence-Based Reading and Writing Section Score

To calculate the Evidence-Based Reading and Writing Section Score, add the Reading Test Score (10 – 40) to the Writing and Language Test Score (10 – 40), and then multiply that total by 10.

For example, if the Reading Test Score is 27 and the Writing and Language Test Score is 34, then the Evidence-Based Reading and Writing Section Score is,

$$27 + 34 = 61 \times 10 = 610.$$

eggheadprep.com

D. Sections 3 and 4: Math Test Score

The raw scores from Section 3 (Math—No Calculator) and Section 4 (Math—Calculator) should be added together to create the Math Raw Score. For example, if there were 18 correct answers in Section 3 (Math—No Calculator) and 24 in Section 4 (Math—Calculator), the Math Raw Score would be 18 + 24 = 42.

MATH RAW SCORE (Total # of correct answers, Sections 3 and 4 combined)	MATH SECTION SCORE		MATH RAW SCORE (Total # of correct answers, Sections 3 and 4 combined)	MATH SECTION SCORE
0	200		30	530
1	200		31	540
2	210		32	550
3	230		33	560
4	240		34	560
5	260		35	570
6	280		36	580
7	290		37	590
8	310		38	600
9	320		39	600
10	330		40	610
11	340		41	620
12	360		42	630
13	370		43	640
14	380		44	650
15	390		45	660
16	410		46	670
17	420		47	670
18	430		48	680
19	440		49	690
20	450		50	700
21	460		51	710
22	470		52	730
23	480		53	740
24	480		54	750
25	490		55	760
26	500		56	780
27	510		57	790
28	520		58	800
29	520			

SAMPLE TEST 2

Including...

▶ SECTION 1: READING TEST   138

▶ ANSWERS, SECTION 1   154

▶ SECTION 2: WRITING & LANGUAGE TEST   155

▶ ANSWERS, SECTION 2   171

▶ SECTION 3: MATH TEST   172

▶ ANSWERS, SECTION 3   178

▶ SECTION 4: MATH TEST   179

▶ ANSWERS, SECTION 4   191

▶ ANSWER EXPLANATIONS   192

▶ SCORING CONVERSION   223

SECTION 1: READING TEST

65 MINUTES, 52 QUESTIONS

DIRECTIONS

Each group of questions below is based on a passage or pair of passages. Read each passage carefully, then choose the best answer to each question based on what is stated in or suggested by the passage(s). The questions may also refer to any graphical displays that accompany the passage(s), such as tables or graphs.

Questions 1-11 are based on the following passage.

This passage is adapted from Federalist Paper Number 85, written by Alexander Hamilton in anticipation of the upcoming vote on adopting the document that would become the U.S. Constitution.

To the People of the State of New York:

    It is remarkable, the resemblance that the plan of the convention holds to the act which organizes the government of this state, not less with regard to many of the supposed defects than to the real excellences of
5 the former. Among the pretended defects are the re-eligibility of the Executive, the want of a council, the omission of a formal bill of rights, the omission of a provision respecting the liberty of the press. These and several others which have been noted in the
10 course of our inquiries are as much chargeable on the existing constitution of this state as on the one proposed for the Union; and a man must have slender pretensions to consistency who can rail at the latter for imperfections which he finds no difficulty in
15 excusing in the former.
    The additional securities to republican government, to liberty and to property, to be derived from the adoption of the plan under consideration, consist chiefly in the restraints which the preservation
20 of the Union under its rule will impose on local factions and insurrections, and on the ambition of powerful individuals in single states, who may become despots of the people; in the diminution of the opportunities for foreign intrigue, which the
25 dissolution of the Confederacy* would invite and facilitate; in the prevention of extensive military establishments, which could not fail to grow out of wars between the states in a disunited situation; in the express guarantee of a republican form of government
30 to each; in the absolute and universal exclusion of titles of nobility; and in the precautions against the repetition of those practices on the part of the state governments which have undermined the foundations of property and credit, have planted mutual distrust in
35 the breasts of all classes of citizens, and have occasioned an almost universal weakening of morals.
    Concessions on the part of the friends of the plan that it has not a claim to absolute perfection,
40 have afforded matter of no small triumph to its enemies. "Why," say they, "should we adopt an imperfect thing? Why not amend it and make it perfect before it is irrevocably established?" This may be plausible enough, but plausible only. In
45 the first place I remark that the extent of these concessions of imperfection has been greatly exaggerated. They have been stated as amounting to an admission that the plan is radically defective, and that without material alterations the rights and
50 the interests of the community cannot be safely confided to it. This, as far as I have understood the meaning of those who have made the concessions, is an entire perversion of their sense. No advocate of the measure can be found who will not declare
55 as his sentiment that the system, though it may not be perfect in every part, is, upon the whole, a good one; is the best that the present views and circumstances of the country will permit; and is such a one as promises every type of security which a
60 reasonable people can desire.
    I answer in the next place that I should esteem it the extreme of imprudence to prolong the precarious state

of our national affairs, and to expose the Union to the jeopardy of successive
65 experiments, in the chimerical pursuit of a perfect plan. I never expect to see a perfect work from imperfect humanity. The result of the deliberations of all collective bodies must necessarily be a compound, as well of the errors and prejudices, as
70 of the good sense and wisdom, of the individuals of whom they are composed. The compacts which are to embrace thirteen distinct states in a common bond of amity and union must as necessarily be a compromise of as many
75 dissimilar interests and inclinations. How can perfection spring from such materials?

  The reasons assigned in an excellent little pamphlet lately published in this city** are unanswerable in the thoroughness with which they
80 show the utter improbability of assembling a new convention, under circumstances in any degree so favorable to happy issue, as those under which the recent convention met, deliberated, and concluded. It may be in me a defect of political
85 fortitude, but I acknowledge that I cannot entertain an equal tranquility with those who would treat the dangers of a longer continuance in our present situation as imaginary. A nation, without a national government, is, in my view, an awful
90 spectacle.

* *Hamilton refers here to the Articles of Confederation, the document that had bound the states together after the Revolutionary War, which was to be either supplanted by the U.S. Constitution or discarded if no new agreement could be reached.*

** *The pamphlet was titled, "An Address to the people of the state of New York."*

1. What was Hamilton's primary objective in writing this article?
   A) To present a general summary of varying opinions about a specific topic
   B) To persuade people to pursue one specific course of action
   C) To reflect on the question of humanity's drive to achieve perfection
   D) To examine in detail one specific benefit offered by the document being discussed

2. All of these passages provide evidence for the answer to the previous question EXCEPT:
   A) Lines 47-51 ("They have … to it.")
   B) Lines 55-60 ("though … desire.")
   C) Lines 61-63 ("I answer ... affairs,")
   D) Lines 84-90 ("It may … spectacle.")

3. As used in lines 12-13, the phrase "slender pretensions to consistency" most nearly means
   A) aspirations of being thin on a consistent basis.
   B) strong tendencies toward consistency.
   C) unexplainable aversions to consistency.
   D) little hope of convincing others of one's consistency.

4. The main purpose of the second paragraph (lines 16-37) is to
   A) lament the moral decline of America.
   B) explain that despots cannot exist in America since there is no noble class.
   C) advocate for a strong U.S. military.
   D) list some of the benefits of adopting the Constitution.

5. Which of the following is NOT a reason that Hamilton cites as having been offered for opposing the adoption of the Constitution?
   A) It lacks a Bill of Rights.
   B) The Executive (President) would be eligible to serve multiple terms.
   C) Its adoption would result in higher taxes.
   D) It lacks explicit protections for a free press.

6. As used in lines 38, 46, and 52, "concessions" most nearly means

   A) diversions.
   B) permissions.
   C) acknowledgements.
   D) successions.

7. What is the primary point Hamilton makes about his and others' statements that the proposed Constitution is imperfect in lines 38-76?

   A) The Constitution should not be adopted until all imperfections are fully addressed and corrected.
   B) A perfect document cannot be created, and waiting for one will make the country vulnerable.
   C) Any imperfections in the Constitution can be fixed through the amendment process later.
   D) No one has actually pointed out a specific flaw in the proposed Constitution.

8. As used in line 65, "chimerical" most nearly means

   A) unrealistic.
   B) inconsequential.
   C) amusing.
   D) hostile.

9. What does Hamilton believe to be the inevitable outcome of successful negotiations between parties with different interests and desires?

   A) One group having its wishes fulfilled while the other is left empty-handed
   B) An agreement that embodies both the good and the bad qualities of those who participated in the negotiations
   C) A solution that represents only the very best ideas brought to the negotiations by the participants
   D) Unresolved tensions that lead to war

10. Which choice provides the strongest evidence in support of the answer to the previous question?

    A) Lines 1-5 ("It is .... former.")
    B) Lines 44-47 ("In the ... exaggerated.")
    C) Lines 51-53 ('This, ... sense.")
    D) Lines 67-71 ("The result ... composed.")

11. What opinion is Hamilton expressing in referring to the recent pamphlet (lines 77-84, "The reasons ... concluded.")

    A) The drafting of the Constitution has raised many questions that simply cannot be answered, and all citizens must accept that fact.
    B) Finding a suitable location for such a large convention as is required to draft a Constitution is extremely difficult, making it impractical to hold a second convention.
    C) Current circumstances are particularly favorable to the drafting and adoption of a Constitution; such conditions may not arise again.
    D) Although many people see the drafting of a Constitution as cause for happiness, there are others who view the event negatively.

Questions 12-21 are based on the following passage.

This passage is adapted from "In Stasis," by Karin E. Dahlin. ©2010 K. E. Dahlin and Coeval *literary journal. Reprinted by permission of the author.*

Joan Didion keeps a notebook stuffed to the covers with pocket-sized images, spilling out the silliest of details—a woman in a hotel bar wearing a dirty *crepe-de-Chine* wrapper, a sauerkraut recipe she prepared on
[5] Fire Island. What's important is that she remembers how it felt to be herself in that moment: how she wanted to befriend the woman in the bar, how safe she felt the night she ate that sauerkraut. *"Remember what it was to be me*: that is always the point," she wrote.

[10] At twenty years old, I am doing my best to begin assembling my own collections of memory, my own jumble of half-accurate recollections. I take on this project in a small, stove-heated cabin in the mountains of Oregon. Here in Lincoln City, a few students and
[15] professors have gathered for four months of study. Just before I came here, my older brother, Joel, moved to Maryland: we are a continent's width apart. Months have passed since we last had a chance to speak. I am acutely aware of the ease with which the days slip past.

[20] As I sit down to write, though, I feel as if time has stopped. No, that's not quite it. Maybe it's more accurate to say that time, all of it, has come spinning onto my desk like, say, this morning's snow might if I propped open my bedroom window.

[25] Memory is a time-shifter; it is a mode of return. Not a return to names and dates and places, mind you. No, it's a return to that pliable, round feeling—the one that lives just below your ribs, ignorant of the rolling forward of time that you feel just behind the bridge of
[30] your nose. You realize: I'm everywhere, and I am peering past these lashes at all of it. I'm watching time spin.

1. Nectar

My family was just beginning a new term in
[35] Venezuela. I was in third grade, Joel in fifth. During our apartment hunt, we stayed in a weary, mission-owned building we called "the dorm." In past years, it had housed boarding students for the international elementary school; now it served as missionary housing
[40] and as long-term storage.

A giant garage sprawled near the end of the driveway. Its doors and windows gaped to reveal an assortment of stacks and heaps, homes to who-knows-what odd treasures, relics of past years, waiting
[45] patiently to never be recovered. They choked under decades of darkness and dust.

A peevish old playground dozed just across the driveway from the garage, nothing but a swingset, a netless basketball hoop, and a tangle of metal bars that
[50] had made up a jungle gym in its youth. The playground felt magnificent and stately, with mango trees stretching upward to form a ceiling as high as a ballroom's.

Joel, scholarly in this thick-rimmed glasses,
[55] scrambled quickly up the snarl of bars. In time, I learned to follow. The peak of the jungle gym was the highest point within our reach. Still, perched atop it, I felt miles beneath the mango canopy. A glance upward sent me swimming, as if I were
[60] swinging by my toes on the highest branch, whispering secrets to the giggling baby fruit.

Eventually, the mangoes grew dark on their thinning stems, weary of clinging to swaying limbs. With a shrug, they loosened their hold and fell,
[65] eager to nest into the earth and age black and pungent. What a sight it was, every crack of the playground oozing with sweet, thick juice. With every breath, I drank heavily of black and red and orange.

[70] Once, while gingerly poking through the undergrowth to reach the swings, I stumbled upon one bright mango that had freed itself just before its time. I reached down, pulling it carefully from the company of its older companions. Its lively peel was
[75] smooth and unbruised, though I imagined the weight of the smallest fly could deflate it, buckling its smooth curves and leaving the body formless, dripping through my fingers.

I broke its skin with my baby teeth. The juice
[80] ran warm and sharp on my tongue.

Memory is a plump fruit whose skin can be opened with a touch. At the slightest puncture, it spills free.

12. Which of the following best describes the nature of the passage?

    A) A warning about the inaccuracy of childhood memories and a guide to developing a sharper, more reliable memory as an adult
    B) A description of a specific relationship between childhood experiences and adult life
    C) An examination of cultural differences between the US and Venezuela.
    D) A meditation on the nature of memory and the creative retelling of a specific memory

13. Which of the following is the most likely reason the writer chose to mention her brother in line 16?

    A) To emphasize her loneliness in the remote Oregon cabin
    B) To set up a contrast between the passage of present day time and the timelessness of memories
    C) To describe a conflict within her family that is affecting her feelings toward her memories
    D) To introduce a method of measuring distance that will be used throughout the passage

14. Which choice provides the best evidence in support of the answer to the previous question?

    A) Lines 18-23 ("I am ... desk")
    B) Lines 35-37 ("I was ... dorm.")
    C) Lines 54-55 ("Joel ... bars.")
    D) Lines 58-61 ("A glance ... fruit.")

15. Which choice offers the most logical reason the writer may have chosen to include the description of the garage in lines 41-46?

    A) To draw a parallel with the cabin in Oregon
    B) To portray the hazards to children that existed at "the dorm"
    C) To suggest symbolically the how much is lost when memories fade away
    D) To draw a contrast between Venezuelan and North American architecture

16. Which choice offers the clearest evidence to support the answer to the previous question?

    A) Lines 39-40 ("now ... storage.")
    B) Lines 42-43 ("Its doors ... heaps")
    C) Lines 44-46 ("relics ... dust.")
    D) Lines 47-48 ("A peevish ... swingset")

17. As used in line 58, the word "canopy" most nearly means

    A) sunset.
    B) panoply.
    C) skyline.
    D) treetops.

18. As used in line 66, the word "pungent" most nearly means

    A) strongly fragrant.
    B) deeply wrinkled.
    C) surprisingly resilient.
    D) eerily silent.

19. Which of the following represents a plausible symbolic interpretation of the mango that "freed itself just before its time" (lines 72-73)?

    A) It represents the writer's childhood yearning to climb to the top of the tallest trees.
    B) It mirrors the writer's youth and her future separation from her brother.
    C) It represents the yearning of oppressed people to "taste" freedom.
    D) It represents humanity's destructive impulses toward nature.

20. Which choice provides the best evidence in support of the answer to the previous question?

    A) Lines 66-67 ("What ... juice.")
    B) Lines 73-74 ("I reached ... companions.")
    C) Lines 76-78 ("buckling ... fingers.")
    D) Lines 79-80 ("I broke ... tongue.")

21. What point is the writer making in the final paragraph (lines 80-83, "Memory … free.")?

   A) Memories are too often consumed by our "appetite" for wealth and we should be more careful to protect them.

   B) The triggering of a memory is always a deeply painful experience.

   C) A small event can set in motion a rich cascade of memories that lie just below the surface of our consciousness.

   D) Many of a person's strongest memories are associated with the food the person ate during childhood.

Questions 22-32 are based on the following passage and additional information provided.

The Rise of the Broad Bay Musicians' Collective

The image most Americans carry in their minds of the music business is one of a vast wasteland of exploitation in which a privileged few live like royalty while millions of sincere artists struggle on the brink of
5   starvation. Furthermore, most people believe they know the reason behind the reality: only music that appeals to the most generic popular tastes generates substantial revenues, so that even an acknowledged virtuoso must expect to live as a pauper if his or her music lies outside
10 those narrow boundaries. So pervasive is this conception of the industry that even savvy insiders have never bothered to question it. Suddenly, a small group of little-known musicians from the little-known city of Broad Bay, Connecticut is threatening to turn decades of
15 thinking on its head.

Violinist and bandleader Cassie Jackson, whose music blends bluegrass, classical, and East Asian operatic styles, knows what it means to eke out a living at the distant fringes of public awareness. She didn't set out to
20 change the realties of the industry. She didn't believe such a change was even possible. All she set out to do was answer a friend's unexpected and confounding question. "It was after a really beautiful show with a great crowd," Jackson explains. "My friend saw me leaving the club
25 with just a few crumpled ten-dollar bills as my meager reward for all the effort. I expected a lecture about how I needed a real job, or perhaps a lament that no one was appreciating my art. Instead, she asked me, 'How can you be so selfish?'"

30 In the wake of the lengthy argument that followed, Jackson stumbled her way to a flash of insight. In many occupations, the driving force behind campaigns for higher wages—and behind workers' willingness to endure massive hardship as part of those campaigns—is the hope
35 workers hold that their children might be treated better than they have been. Underneath that seemingly self-sacrificing vision lurks a complex tangle of motives, including both the genuinely loving desire to provide a better life for one's descendants and the somewhat
40 egocentric notion that one's children should follow in one's footsteps. To be sure, other factors are at play, including a sense of loyalty to coworkers and, in some cases, a sincere willingness to fight for the abstract cause of justice for all. But Jackson was certain that questions of
45 personal legacy stood at the center of it all. That realization brought another along on its coattails: due to their deeply ingrained acceptance of the music business status quo, every musician she had ever known felt that the best way to ensure a better life for his or her children
50 was to discourage those children from ever becoming involved with music. In fact, many performers openly expressed a hope that their careers would never bring financial success, just so that their heirs would feel no temptation to follow the same poverty-inducing
55 path in life.

None of that, however, offered an explanation for her friend's seemingly preposterous accusation. Fitting that puzzle piece into place required a second, much calmer conversation with the friend in
60 question. "You see," the friend offered, "there's someone whom you can't talk out of a life in music, and who depends on you as utterly as your son for financial support. That person is you, ten years from now."

65 The revelation hit Jackson's ears like a thunderclap. Within a few weeks, she had launched the Respect Your (Future) Self Broad Bay Musicians' Collective. The loosely organized union swiftly drew attention for its boisterous street demonstrations and
70 very vocal sit-ins at cafés and other music venues. The immediate results of their efforts were jail time and blacklisting by every music venue within 30 miles. In time, however, venue managers began to feel the sting of decreased patronage caused by their
75 inability to provide quality entertainment. Even when they presented bands that played cover versions of all the latest pop hits, their clubs wallowed as dusty rooms full of forlorn, empty seats if the musicians lacked the skill of pros like Jackson. All the old
80 assumptions began to fall by the wayside. Perhaps the public, at least at a local level, actually did care about something other than the latest trend, after all.

It is too early too know how lasting or how widespread the impact of Jackson's efforts will be.
85 But for the moment, and for the first time ever, the violin prodigy, like many of her colleagues, is being treated like a professional and earning an income commensurate with that status. "The person I've done it all for is just a gleam in my eye right now,"
90 she quips. "But I think when I finally meet her, I might just like her."

SAMPLE TEST 2
Section 1: Reading Test

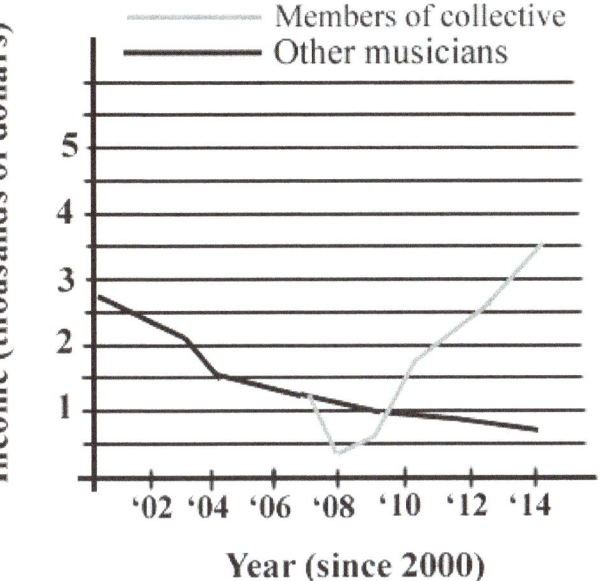

Average Monthly Income of Musicians in the Broad Bay Area Since 2002

22. As used in line 11, the word "savvy" most nearly means

    A) cynical.
    B) critical.
    C) popular.
    D) knowledgeable.

23. The primary purpose of the first paragraph (lines 1-15) is

    A) to explain long-held beliefs about the nature of the economics of the music business.
    B) to demonstrate the pervasiveness of popular music in American daily life.
    C) to criticize the American public's tastes in music.
    D) to emphasize the fact that only famous musicians can influence the future of the industry.

24. Which choice offers the most likely explanation for why Ms. Jackson found her friend's question (lines 28-29) "confounding?" (Line 22)?

    A) She had taken the time to talk with her friend during a busy night, which was not a selfish act.
    B) She did not expect to see her friend that night, and so was not prepared to answer her questions.
    C) She had just completed an evening of working very hard for very little pay, an act not normally considered selfish.
    D) She, like most people, did not understand the complicated economics of the music business and so was not qualified to explain them.

25. Which choice provides the best evidence for the answer to the previous question?

    A) Lines 19-21 ("She didn't … possible.")
    B) Lines 24-26 ("My friend … effort.")
    C) Lines 26-28 ("I expected … art.")
    D) Lines 30-31 ("In the … insight.")

26. What does Ms. Jackson believe is the most important reason that workers in many occupations have been willing to take great risks to fight for higher wages?

    A) They want to be able to move to better neighborhoods so their children can attend better schools.
    B) They are tired of seeing less qualified workers succeed by riding on the coattails of those who are very skilled.
    C) They are afraid they will lose the respect of their communities if they don't stand up for themselves.
    D) They have dreams of their children choosing the same career they've chosen, and want their children to be well paid if they do so.

27. Which choice provides the best evidence for the answer to the previous question?

    A) Lines 36-41 ("Underneath … footsteps.")
    B) Lines 41-44 ("To be … all.")
    C) Lines 45-46 ("That … coattails:")
    D) Lines 56-57 ("None … accusation.")

28. Which choice correctly identifies the "old assumptions" referred to in line 79?

A) Lines 1-5 ("The image … starvation.")
B) Lines 5-10 ("Furthermore … boundaries.")
C) Lines 16-19 ("Violinist … awareness.")
D) Lines 31-36 ("In many … been.")

29. As used in line 88, "commensurate with" most nearly means

A) at odds with.
B) posing a threat to.
C) corresponding to.
D) generated by.

30. Based on the graph, during what year did Ms. Jackson start the Respect Your (Future) Self Broad Bay Musicians' Collective?

A) 2003
B) 2005
C) 2007
D) 2009

31. Which feature of the graph corresponds to the events described in lines 71-73 ("The immediate … miles.")

A) The steady decline of the black line
B) The sharp ascent of the gray line after 2008
C) The crossing of the two lines in approximately 2009
D) The sharp decline of the gray line from 2007 to 2008

32. Does the graph suggest that Ms. Jackson's mission has been successful overall?

A) Yes, because from 2008 onward, the incomes of members of the collective have risen dramatically.
B) Yes, because musicians who are not members of the collective have seen a gradual increase in their incomes.
C) No, because the average monthly incomes of musicians who are not members of the collective were higher in 2012 than those of members of the collective.
D) No, because the incomes of members of the collective have both fallen and risen, so there is no clear trend.

SAMPLE TEST 2
Section 1: Reading Test

Questions 33-42 are based on the following passage.

This passage is adapted from "What Is Man?" by Mark Twain.

Old Man: What are the materials of which a steam engine is made?
Young Man: Iron, steel, brass, white-metal, and so on.
O.M.: Where are these found?
Y.M.: In the rocks.
O.M.: In a pure state?
Y.M.: No—in ores.
O.M.: Are the metals suddenly deposited in the ores?
Y.M.: No—it is the patient work of countless ages.
O.M.: You could make the engine out of the rocks themselves?
Y.M.: Yes, a brittle one and not valuable.
O.M.: To make a fine and capable engine, how would you proceed?
Y.M.: Drive tunnels and shafts into the hills; blast out the iron ore; crush it, smelt it, reduce it to pig-iron; put some of it through the Bessemer process and make steel of it. Mine and treat and combine several metals of which brass is made.
O.M.: Then?
Y.M.: Out of the perfected result, build the fine engine.
O.M.: You would require much of this engine?
Y.M.: Oh, indeed yes.
O.M.: It could drive lathes, drills, planers, punches, polishers—in a word, all the cunning machines of a great factory?
Y.M.: It could.
O.M.: What could the stone machine do?
Y.M.: Drive a sewing machine, possibly—nothing more.
O.M.: People would admire the metal engine and rapturously praise it?
Y.M.: Yes.
O.M.: The merits of the metal machine would be far above those of the stone one?
Y.M.: Of course.
O.M.: Personal merits?
Y.M.: *Personal* merits? How do you mean?
O.M.: It would be personally entitled to the credit of its own performance?
Y.M.: The engine? Certainly not.
O.M.: Why not?
Y.M.: Because its performance is not personal. It is the result of the law of its construction. It is not a *merit* that it does the things which it is set to do—it can't *help* doing them.
O.M.: And it is not a personal demerit in the stone machine that it does so little?
Y.M.: Certainly not. It does no more and no less than the law of its make permits and compels it to do. There is nothing *personal* about it; it cannot choose. In this process of "working up to the matter," is it your idea to work up to the proposition that a human and a machine are about the same thing, and that there is no personal merit in the performance of either?
O.M.: Yes—but do not be offended. What makes the grand difference between the stone engine and the steel one? Shall we call in training, education? Shall we call the stone engine a savage and the steel one civilized? The original rock contained the stuff of which the steel one was built—but along with a lot of sulphur and stone and other obstructing inborn heredities, brought down from the old geologic ages—prejudices, let us call them. Prejudices which nothing in the rock itself had either *power* to remove or *desire* to remove. Prejudices must be removed by *outside influences* or not at all.
Y.M.: Very well. Go on.
O.M.: The iron's prejudice against ridding itself of the cumbering rock. To make it more exact, the iron's absolute *indifference* as to whether the rock be removed or not. Then comes the outside influence and grinds the rock to powder and sets the ore free. The *iron* in the ore is still captive. An outside influence smelts it free of the clogging ore. The iron is emancipated iron, but indifferent still to further progress. An outside influence beguiles it into the Bessemer furnace and refines it into steel of the first quality. It is educated now—its training is complete.
Y.M.: And you have thus arrived at your proposition about a human?
O.M.: Yes—human, the machine, the impersonal engine. Whatsoever a man is, is due to his *make*, and to the *influences* brought to bear upon it by his heredities, his habitat, his associations. He is moved, directed, commanded, by *exterior* influences, solely. He *originates* nothing, not even a thought.
Y.M.: Oh, come! Where, then, did I get my opinion that this which you are talking is all foolishness?
O.M.: It is a quite natural opinion—indeed, an inevitable opinion—but you did not create the materials out of which it was formed. They are odds and ends of thoughts, impressions, feelings, gathered unconsciously from a thousand books, a thousand conversations, and from streams of thought and feeling which have flowed down into your brain out of the brains of centuries of ancestors. *Personally* you did not create even the smallest microscopic fragment of the materials out of which your opinion is made; and personally you cannot claim even the slender credit of putting the borrowed materials

together. That was done automatically by your mental machinery, in strict accordance with the law of that
100 machinery's construction.

Y.M.: That position is untenable—I may say ludicrously untenable.

O.M.: What makes you think so?

Y.M.: I don't merely think it, I know it. Suppose I resolve
105 upon a course of thought, and study, and reading, with deliberate purpose of changing my opinion on this matter; and suppose I succeed. That is not the work of an exterior impulse, the whole of it is mine and personal; for I originated the project.

110 **O.M.:** Not a shred of it. It grew out of this talk with me. But for that, the idea would not have occurred to you. No human ever originates anything.

Y.M.: But Shakespeare's creations—

O.M.: Shakespeare created nothing. He was a machine,
115 and machines do not create.

Y.M.: Where was his excellence, then?

O.M.: In this: He was not a sewing machine, like you and me: He was a Gobelin loom*. The threads and the colors came into him *from the outside*; outside influences framed
120 the patterns in his mind and started up his complex and admirable machinery, and it *automatically* turned out that pictured and gorgeous fabric which still compels the astonishment of the world. If Shakespeare had been born and bred on a barren and unvisited rock in the ocean, his
120 mighty intellect would have had no outside material to work with, and so Shakespeare would have produced nothing.

* A style of loom manufactured in France, known for its use in creating elaborate tapestries

33.
Which of the following best describes the structure and content of the passage as a whole?

A) A heated, emotional argument between two characters over the merits and demerits of various people and their inventions

B) A discussion of technological developments in which one character answers technical questions about the process of manufacturing various types of machines

C) A logical debate in which one character presents a view on the nature of humanity while another states objections that the author believes readers will raise

D) A friendly conversation between two characters about changing times and how best to adapt to them through industrial progress

34.
As used in line 25, "cunning" most nearly means

A) devious.
B) sophisticated.
C) massive.
D) dangerous.

35.
As used in line 31, "rapturously" most nearly means

A) religiously.
B) reluctantly.
C) moderately.
D) lavishly.

36.
The phrase "personal merits" in line 36 refers to

A) desirable qualities that arise from conscious choices.
B) the morally virtuous traits of a person.
C) awards received for exemplary ethical conduct.
D) exceptional qualities of all kinds.

37.
Which choice provides the strongest evidence in support of the answer to the previous question?

A) Lines 33-34 ("**O.M.:** The merits … one?")
B) Lines 42-45 ("**Y.M.:** Because … them.")
C) Lines 55-58 ("**O.M.:** Yes— … education?")
D) Lines 58-60 ("The original … built—")

38. What is the Old Man's purpose in presenting the example of the two machines?

   A) To criticize humanity's obsession with technology
   B) To examine the environmental impacts of mining and large-scale manufacturing
   C) To demonstrate the importance of external influences in the development of a person
   D) To show that people who have access to more advanced technology accomplish greater things than those with access to less advanced technology

39. Based on the discussion of the two machines and subsequent debate about humans, does the Old Man believe there is a connection between education and the ongoing presence of prejudices in human society?

   A) No, because a certain amount of prejudice is inevitable in society, no matter what efforts are made to combat it.
   B) No, because most people already have the ability to overcome their prejudices even without education; they just choose not to use that ability.
   C) Yes, because without training, people demonstrate neither the willingness nor the ability to overcome prejudices.
   D) Yes, because education often reinforces prejudices so that they are passed on to future generations.

40. As used in line 87, "inevitable" most nearly means

   A) undesirable.
   B) indefensible.
   C) impressive.
   D) expected.

41. What is implied by the description of Shakespeare as a "Gobelin loom" in line 118?

   A) That Shakespeare's works include particularly vivid descriptions of texture and color
   B) That Shakespeare's mind was, by its nature, more sophisticated than the minds of most people
   C) That Shakespeare's works showed many French influences, just as British and American weaving styles had been influenced by the invention of the Gobelin loom.
   D) That Shakespeare wove together the themes and stories in his works like the threads of an intricate tapestry

42. Which of the following possible reasons for the author's choice to introduce the topic of Shakespeare into the passage is supported by lines 117-127 ("O.M.: In this … nothing.") of the passage?

   A) The author wished to present a clear contradiction to the Old Man's unreasonable claims.
   B) The author wished to show that his characters should not be believed because they are inferior to Shakespeare as "machines."
   C) The author wished to show that Shakespeare's writings are not worthy of the admiration they receive.
   D) The author wished to emphasize what can be lost if people do not have access to the outside influence of education.

Questions 43-52 are based on the following passage and additional information.

This passage describes a fictitious experiment and scientific hypothesis about the causes of earthquakes.

The Ocean Beneath Us: A New Conception of Earthquakes.

For decades, geologists have understood that earthquakes are caused by the movements of tectonic plates—the massive slabs of earthen crust that have defined the past and present shapes and positions of the
5 continents. As the plates drift ever so lazily about on the planet's surface, they collide and rub against each other, creating seismically unstable regions where earthquakes occur frequently. Yet for all the sophistication of the theories accounting for the movements of the great
10 plates, the dream of predicting earthquakes in a reliable way that saves lives remains as elusive as that of discovering living dragons.

The problem is that although it is well known that the grinding of tectonic plates as they fight for the same
15 stretch of real estate leads to the unleashing of seismic waves that we experience as earthquakes, there is no apparent rhyme or reason to when those unleashing events occur. One daring scientist, Dr. Liesl Castonelli, has proposed a way to search for order amidst the chaos:
20 Go deeper.

Tectonic plates float atop Earth's upper mantle, a roiling, ultra hot, gooey stew of ultra-pressurized water and molten metallic elements. Dr. Castonelli has proposed that the mantle actually moves like a viscous
25 ocean, oozing around in waves of varying sizes. She points out that all manner of oceanic surface phenomena seemed random and unexplainable until very recently, when great progress was made in detecting, measuring, and tracking the movements of deep ocean waves that
30 are invisible to us surface dwellers. We now know that most of the action on the surface of the sea is actually a *reaction* to the movement of these mighty waves of the deep. Castonelli speculated that a similar phenomenon may occur in the realm of the mantle.

35 In Castonelli's model, earthquakes would be triggered by what amount to surface disturbances of the mantle's molten ocean. That such disturbances originate from deep "sea" waves is plausible: the primary cause of such waves in water oceans is temperature variation
40 within the liquid, and there is plenty of that in the turbulent realm of the mantle. Since plates float on the surface, they respond to the "ripples" by vibrating; and since we live on top of the plates, we vibrate with them.

Testing Castonelli's hypothesis proved to be no
45 simple matter. For starters, replicating the temperatures in the upper mantle is beyond challenging: every material available for human use would melt at such temperatures, so containment of the fluid would be an impossibility. Secondly, no one knows for sure the
50 exact composition of the mantle. Finally, the fault lines that form where plates rub elbows are deep, long, and incredibly complex in shape. To build an accurate scale model of a single fault could take several years.

55 Nevertheless, Castonelli and her team believe they have created a usable surrogate for a true replica of the mantle; they call it the "pudding pond." Within the giant tank, a foul-smelling brown sludge ("Don't ask what's in it," Castonelli warns) plays the role of
60 the upper mantle, while plates constructed with the help of Hollywood set designers creep along the surface at imperceptible speeds. Randomly placed heating elements throughout the tank supply the temperature variations needed to stimulate the
65 formation of subsurface waves. Of course, due to the extreme thickness of the liquid, nothing happens quickly.

After several months of running the painfully slow simulations, Castonelli's team seems to have
70 found the results they sought: evidence that deep waves can form even in an ultra-heavy, gunky fluid; that there is a predictability to the formation of deep waves based on temperature patterns; and that deep waves ultimately have an impact at the surface.

75 Scientists are now pondering the question of how to further explore Castonelli's ideas. To a layperson, it might seem natural as a next step to drill down to the upper mantle itself. The dangers involved in such an operation go far beyond what
80 most would imagine, however. "The first rule of studying earthquakes," says Castonelli, "is don't cause them."

SAMPLE TEST 2
Section 1: Reading Test

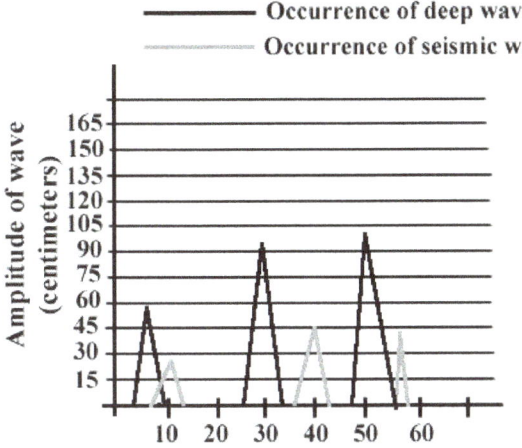

Observation of Deep Waves and Seismic Surface Disturbances in "Pudding Tank" Simulation, April 1 – May 31, 2015

43. The main purpose of the first paragraph (lines 1-12) is to

A) present a common misconception about a the nature of a well-known phenomenon so that the writer can later correct the misconception.

B) summarize the results of a specific research study about the movements of tectonic plates and the effects of those movements.

C) provide a summary of current knowledge about a phenomenon and point out the limitations of that knowledge.

D) highlight a scientific controversy surrounding multiple, conflicting theories that have been offered as explanations for a phenomenon.

44. As used in line 5, "lazily" most nearly means

A) slowly.
B) without motivation.
C) apathetically.
D) inattentively.

45. What is the main argument Dr. Castonelli is making in the third paragraph (lines 21-34)?

A) Water in the upper mantle is highly pressurized, which is why it does not boil.

B) Molten metals make up a large part of the upper magma, making it very heavy.

C) Many ocean phenomena have never been explained, so it is reasonable to believe that the same will be true for seismic activity.

D) Events observed on the surface of water oceans were not well understood until detailed information about subsurface activity was gathered.

46. Why does Dr. Castonelli believe that the upper mantle may experience deep waves similar to those in water oceans?

A) Extreme temperature variations within a fluid, a common cause of water waves, are prevalent in the mantle.

B) The deepest points in the oceans are very close to the mantle, and therefore the two realms should behave in about the same way.

C) Large waves within the mantle have been directly observed by scientists.

D) The rotation of Earth on its axis would naturally disturb the mantle, likely creating waves.

47. The article cites many reasons that it was not possible for Dr. Castonelli's team to build a tank that duplicated conditions in the mantle. Which of the following was NOT a reason?

A) The extreme heat would destroy the tank.

B) There is no way to generate deep waves within a tank.

C) The exact composition of the mantle cannot be replicated because it isn't known.

D) It is impractical to build true reproductions of the shapes of fault lines.

48. As used in line 56, "surrogate" most nearly means

A) complement.
B) building material.
C) surrounding building.
D) substitute.

49. Does the passage present specific evidence that the experiment may lead to better earthquake forecasting in the future?

    A) Yes, in lines 70-71 ("evidence … fluid;")
    B) Yes, in lines 72-73 ("that … patterns;")
    C) Yes, in lines 75-76 ("Scientists … ideas.")
    D) No.

50. The last paragraph (lines 75-82) explains that trying to directly study the upper mantle would be extremely dangerous because

    A) No human could survive the intense pressure and heat.
    B) Drilled passages could collapse, trapping researchers and valuable equipment.
    C) The powerful drill required could cause severe injury or death if it malfunctions.
    D) The drilling process might trigger seismic activity.

51. According to the graph, how many deep waves occurred during the course of the experiment?

    A) 3
    B) 4
    C) 5
    D) 6

52. How does the graph support Dr. Castonelli's hypothesis?

    A) Deep waves are always larger than seismic waves.
    B) The amplitude (size) of deep waves increased through the course of the experiment.
    C) Surface seismic activity always followed the development of deep waves.
    D) The amplitude (size) of seismic waves appears unrelated to the amplitude of deep waves.

STOP

If you have finished this section before time expires, you may check your work. You cannot return to this section once you move on to the next section.

EGGHEAD PREP™
Get cracking.

STOP!

If you have finished this section before time expires, you may check your work. You cannot return to this section once you move on to the next section.

www.eggheadprep.com

ANSWERS, SECTION 1
SAMPLE TEST 2 — READING

1. B
2. A
3. D
4. D
5. C
6. C
7. B
8. A
9. B
10. D
11. C
12. D
13. B
14. A
15. C
16. C
17. D
18. A
19. B
20. B
21. C
22. D
23. A
24. C
25. B
26. D
27. A
28. B
29. C
30. C
31. D
32. A
33. C
34. B
35. D
36. A
37. B
38. C
39. C
40. D
41. B
42. D
43. C
44. A
45. D
46. A
47. B
48. D
49. B
50. D
51. A
52. C

EGGHEAD PREP

SECTION 2: WRITING & LANGUAGE TEST

35 MINUTES, 44 QUESTIONS

DIRECTIONS

Below you will find a number of reading passages. Each one is accompanied by a series of questions. A note before each passage will tell you which questions are related to that passage. Some questions will require you to consider possible revisions to the passage to help the writer express the ideas more clearly or effectively. Other questions will ask you to consider ways to edit the passage to correct errors in punctuation, word usage, or sentence structure. Some questions and passages include graphics, such as tables and graphs. As you make your decisions about possible changes, you should take the graphics into consideration along with the text.

Some questions will refer to a specific, underlined portion of the passage. Others will ask you to focus on a particular location within the passage. There will also be questions that ask you to think about the passage as a whole. Numbers enclosed in parentheses and written with a Q, such as (Q14) indicate the number of the question associated with that portion of the passage. Numbers bracketed in plain text, like [2], are used to identifying sentences within the passage, whereas a number surrounded by dashes, like –2– identifies a paragraph.

Read each passage and then choose the answer to each question that best improves the writing of the passage or brings the particular phrase or sentence into agreement with the conventions of standard written English. If you believe the best choice is to leave the indicated portion of the passage as it is, choose the option, "NO CHANGE."

eggheadprep.com

Questions 1 – 11 are based on the following passage.

Specializing in Everything: The Modern School's Dilemma

The present era has often been referred to as "the age of specialization," a time during which people are **(Q1)** increased in how much they are expected to develop one specific skill around which to build a career. **(Q2)** For example, many professionals actually find themselves needing to master a far more diverse set of tasks than their predecessors in their fields. Musicians spend more time on marketing and social media-related tasks than they do on writing songs. A single staff member at a pre-K education facility might manage student enrollment, staff hiring, and public relations matters. **(Q3)** A sanitation worker has better equipment than was available in the past to help reduce injuries on the job. In light of these trends, recent fears that an overly specialized workforce wouldn't have the flexibility to respond to changing circumstances have begun to give way to worries that highly skilled specialists will be impossible to find when needed in the future.

1.
   A) NO CHANGE
   B) increasingly expected
   C) being increased in what is expected
   D) expected to be increasing

2.
   A) NO CHANGE
   B) Therefore,
   C) One of the reasons for this change is that
   D) In reality, however,

3. Which of the following would best serve as another illustrative example of the point the writer wishes to make?

   A) NO CHANGE
   B) A sanitation worker is no longer on the bottom of the salary scale, and is in fact paid quite well by today's standards.
   C) A sanitation worker needs a lot more than a strong back, as the job now requires operation of sophisticated machinery and in-cab computers.
   D) A sanitation worker still struggles to receive the respect he or she deserves for doing a difficult and important job.

Art schools find themselves at the epicenter of the debate over the proper balance between training students to master a specific craft and preparing them for a world that will ask far more of them than the creation of artwork. Tasks historically associated with business school courses **(Q4)** take up an ever-growing portion of an artist's work time. A typical day requires **(Q5)** so many non-artistic tasks for them to complete that one artist jokingly remarked, "I will consider my career as a full-time artist to be a smashing success if it allows me to be a part-time artist." As a consequence of these changing realities, art schools feel pressure to provide courses on persuasive writing, analytical data processing, and **(Q6)** social networks. Unfortunately, as long-time sculpture and ceramics instructor Dr. Macy Thornburton observes, "We can't just add years to college. The only way to teach a greater diversity of skills is to reduce the time we devote to teaching the core skills needed to make art."

4. The author is considering adding the following information at this point:

   —maintaining a website, researching markets, and preparing and distributing promotional email messages, for example—

   Would this addition be appropriate here?

   A) Yes, because it provides specific examples of the types of tasks mentioned in the sentence.
   B) Yes, because it illustrates the specific amount of time these tasks require of an artist.
   C) No, because it interrupts the flow of the sentence to provide irrelevant details.
   D) No, because it blurs the focus of the paragraph by discussing a subject different from types of schools.

5.
   A) NO CHANGE
   B) the completion of so many non-artistic tasks
   C) so many non-artistic tasks for their completing
   D) them to complete so many tasks non-artistically

6.
   A) NO CHANGE
   B) artists using social networks.
   C) to develop social networks.
   D) social networking.

The question of how best to serve tomorrow's artists has thus brought art schools face to face with the most fundamental questions of what it means to be an artist. **(Q7)** A few decades ago, the idea of an art school student minoring in data management systems would have seemed absurd. Additionally, after graduating, many of them now pursue exhibit curation careers requiring extensive computer expertise, so that the choice seems perfectly natural. The entire nature of an artist's relationship with the public has changed as well. Gone are the days when an artist worked in isolation, unconcerned with the hustle and bustle of mainstream life. Although art school courses in effective social networking most obviously benefit students wishing to work in the commercial realm, **(Q8)** yet even artists on the far fringes of public awareness must skillfully navigate such networks if they are to survive. **(Q9)** Uniquely equipped with excellent studio facilities for artistic work, it is imperative that art schools provide the non-artistic training aspiring artists need today. Otherwise, art students would be forced to simultaneously attend multiple colleges, since no business school could match the outstanding studio facilities an art school provides for aspiring artists in all media.

7. Which choice offers the best option for combining the two underlined sentences?

   A) A few decades ago, the idea of an art school student minoring in data management systems would have seemed absurd, but with many graduates now pursuing exhibit curation careers requiring extensive computer expertise, the choice seems perfectly natural.

   B) As it happens, many art school graduates now pursue exhibit curation careers requiring extensive computer expertise, which means that it's absurd for a student to minor in data management systems.

   C) A few decades ago, the idea of an art school student minoring in data management systems would have seemed absurd, many graduates, actually, are now pursuing exhibit curation careers requiring extensive computer expertise.

   D) A few decades ago, the idea of an art school student minoring in data management systems would have seemed absurd, which is why it seems perfectly natural that many graduates are now pursuing exhibit curation careers requiring extensive computer expertise.

8.
   A) NO CHANGE
   B) because
   C) and
   D) DELETE the underlined portion.

9. Which choice best sets up both the rest of this sentence and the sentence that follows?

   A) NO CHANGE
   B) Although a lot of great artists dropped out of art school before graduating,
   C) However reluctant they may be to do so,
   D) When it comes to providing studio facilities for artistic work,

None of these observations are intended to suggest, however, that art school administrators' concerns about the long-term effects of curriculum changes are not valid. If tomorrow's artists spend too much time learning skills related to brand promotion, **(10)** numbers problems, and search engine optimization, they will have no time left for matters like concept and content. Their artwork will suffer as a result. Art schools, and all of us, must commit to finding a way forward **(11)** that supports the success of artists without costing too much money.

10.
- A) NO CHANGE
- B) problems related to the use of numbers
- C) issues concerning math
- D) data analysis

11. Which choice most clearly reflects the point the author is making in this paragraph?
- A) NO CHANGE
- B) that supports the success of artists without contributing to the failure of art itself.
- C) that supports the success of artists by encouraging them to use their diverse skills to work multiple jobs to support themselves.
- D) that insures a successful career for any student who enrolls at an art school.

Questions 12-22 are based on the following passage.

One Quilt, A Thousand Intricacies

–1–

Archaeologists enthusiastically celebrated the 2014 discovery of a fully intact, sealed stone vault amidst the ruins of Pahuatanaca, a town buried by the eruption of the Mt. Rona volcano in the 15th century. **(Q12)** Their reaction, however, paled in comparison to the unbridled elation of arts and crafts experts when the vault was opened last month to reveal **(Q13)** it's contents; 47 breathtaking, perfectly preserved wool quilts. The quilts of Pahuatanaca have been described in legends for centuries, but no one knew if the items themselves had ever actually existed. As one art historian who witnessed the opening of the vault observed, the discovery is akin to a person stumbling upon **(Q14)** architect, Maya Lin's, 2-acre Vietnam Veterans Memorial after years of being told the monument was fictitious.

12.
A) NO CHANGE
B) They're
C) There
D) Theirs

13.
A) NO CHANGE
B) its contents;
C) it's contents,
D) its contents:

14.
A) NO CHANGE
B) architect Maya Lin's
C) architect, Maya Lin's
D) architect Maya Lin's,

–2–

Animals played central roles in Pahuatanacan religious life, so their prevalence among the images presented on the quilts comes as no surprise. No one could have imagined, however, the level of realism of the images. A single lizard's eye appears to have been fashioned from over 300 individual threads. For clarity, the image rivals any captured by the best high-definition camera on the market today. **(Q15)** Similarly, the human figures that appear on the quilts are rather **(Q16)** crude, they seem to have been created with a specific intention of avoiding accurate representation. Such a choice on the part of the weavers would be consistent with the beliefs held in many cultures about the dangers of faithfully representing the human form in artwork.

–3–

The comparison to Lin's masterpiece is appropriate, for the quilts of Pahuatanaca, true to the legends, are massive. The 47 quilts contained in the vault would together cover 1.5 acres, an area nearly the size of a World Cup soccer field. The coyote portrayed on one of the quilts would dwarf a semi truck. Impressive though the epic dimensions of the quilts are, however, it was the level of detail anthropologists discovered when they studied a quilt under a microscope that has most amazed scientists. The illustration of a parrot, for example, includes a single feather woven from threads of 14 different colors, **(Q17)** and this is because parrots are very colorful in the tropics. Over 35 different animals species appear in the artwork of the quilts, all presented in dazzling colors.

15.
A) NO CHANGE
B) For instance,
C) By contrast,
D) Alternatively,

16.
A) NO CHANGE
B) crude, the figures
C) crude,
D) crude and

17. Which choice gives a second supporting example that is most like the example already presented in this sentence?

A) NO CHANGE
B) and it also looks like it is ready to take flight.
C) and a lizard has such perfectly rendered stripes that biologists have identified its exact species.
D) other images also employ many colors.

—4—

The human figures are far less colorful than their animal (Q18) counterparts. The activities in which they are engaged reveal much about everyday life in Pahuatanaca. Not surprisingly, images of hunting, farming, and food preparation predominate. The images also make clear, though, that Pahuatanacan interest in art was not limited to quilt making. One very striking panel shows a gathering in what appears to be a room in an adobe house. The people are being entertained by a dancer twirling ribbons, a musician playing a wooden flute, and (Q19) a singer or storyteller sitting on a high stool in a corner.

18. Which choice most logically combines the first two sentences of the paragraph?

A) counterparts, but the
B) counterparts—the
C) counterparts, so the
D) counterparts; similarly, the

19. Which choice best matches the phrasing pattern established previously in the sentence?

A) NO CHANGE
B) a singer or storyteller is in a corner sitting on a high stool.
C) in a corner there is a high stool on which a singer or storyteller is sitting.
D) there is also a singer or storyteller sitting on a high stool in a corner.

—5—

For the present, the vault has been resealed to protect the quilts from harm while their fate is determined. There is good reason to be mindful of a **(Q20)** conservators' observation at a recent press conference that "a single day of exposure to modern urban pollution might inflict two decades' worth of wear" on the quilts. **(Q21)** Representing one of the very rare instances when reality surpasses legend, everyone with access to the vault must show great care toward these incomparable works of traditional art. In time, suitable display cases will be created, so that the lost quilts of Pahuatanaca may be enjoyed by all.

Question 22 asks about the passage as a whole.

20.
A) NO CHANGE
B) conservator's observation
C) conservators observing
D) conservator observed

21.
A) NO CHANGE
B) Representing one of the very rare instances when reality surpasses legend, these incomparable works of traditional art must be treated with great care by everyone with access to the vault.
C) Everyone with access to the vault, representing one of the very rare instances when reality surpasses legend, must show great care toward these incomparable works of traditional art.
D) Everyone representing one of the very rare instances when reality surpasses legend must show great care, with access to the vault, toward these incomparable works of traditional art.

22.
To make the passage as a whole most logical, paragraph 2 should be placed
A) after paragraph 5.
B) after paragraph 4.
C) after paragraph 3.
D) in its current location.

Questions 23-33 are based on the following passage.

This passage describes an environmental crisis on a fictional planet similar to Earth.

Fargonites, the human-like inhabitants of planet Fargon, have long understood that forests **(Q23)** growing along the shores of rivers and streams (known as riparian forests here on Earth) help to prevent erosion that can fill waterways with silt, decimating fish populations. Such erosion is a major concern on Fargon, where the average depth of rivers and streams planet-wide has decreased by 65 percent **(Q24)**.

What Fargonites did not realize for a long time, however, is that there is a fundamental connection between the health of riparian forests and the size of wild populations of large, land-dwelling predators. A 20-year study **(Q25)** has revealed, that in areas where the planet's two largest land-dwelling predators, the lupinine and the ursalot, are abundant, waterways are cleaner, deeper, and support significantly greater numbers of fish than waterways surrounded by land where the two predator species are

23.
A) NO CHANGE
B) growing along the shores of rivers and streams (known as riparian forests here on Earth), they also help
C) that grow along the shores of rivers and streams (known as riparian forests here on Earth) and help
D) growing along the shores of rivers and streams (known as riparian forests here on Earth), where they help

24. At this point, the writer wishes to add this information:

> since huge areas of forest were cleared to make room for large-scale agriculture 350 years ago

Should the writer add this information here?

A) Yes, because it explains the connection between between loss of forests and erosion that fills in waterways.
B) Yes, because it explains how forests, stream depths, and fish populations contribute to a healthy environment.
C) No, because it contradicts the previous statement that forests help to protect rivers and streams from erosion.
D) No, because it blurs the focus of the article by mentioning agriculture, which is not the main topic being investigated.

25.
A) NO CHANGE
B) has revealed: that
C) has revealed; that
D) has revealed that

scarce. In fact, **(Q26)** greater than 25 predators in an area surrounding a waterway can restore fish populations to historically normal levels.

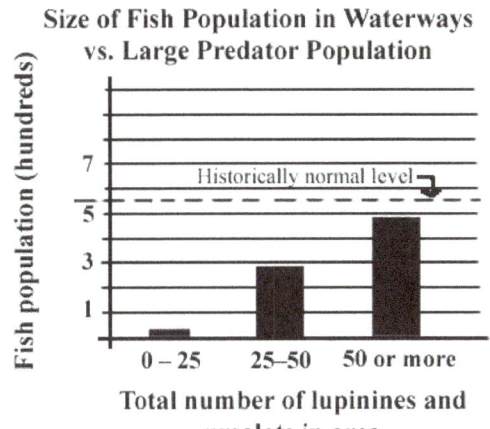

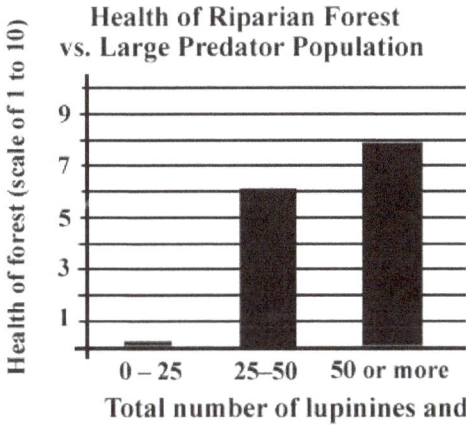

Two Fargonite scientists, Kwazmak and Jurgstor, believe they have discovered the explanation for this phenomenon. When large predators are scarce, animals that feed on leaves and twigs will stay in the same section of riparian forest for several weeks, until the trees and shrubs there are so compromised that the entire stretch of forest will die off within a few years. Without a strong presence of large predators, riparian areas **(Q27)** are, thus, eventually reduced to wastelands of rotting tree trunks by the **(Q28)** voracious feeding of stationary herbivores. Without living tree roots to hold it in place, the soil in such regions disintegrates into fine silt that washes away with every rainfall. As a result, the cool, deep pools in nearby streams become stagnant mud puddles.

26.
A) NO CHANGE
B) the presence of only 25 or more predators in an area surrounding a waterway can help restore fish populations to about half of historically normal levels.
C) Forest die off increases as the number of predators increases.
D) even with only 25 or more predators in an area surrounding a waterway, the health of the riparian forest is inversely proportional to the size of the large predator population.

27.
A) NO CHANGE
B) are, nonetheless,
C) are, conversely,
D) are

28.
A) NO CHANGE
B) capacious
C) sporadic
D) murderous

On the other hand, when riparian areas play host to a healthy population of large predators, plant-eating animals must stay constantly on the move. This "migratory grazing" actually **(Q29)** disintegrates the health of riparian forests, since only the weakest trees and shrubs die from the limited damage that the grazers inflict.

[1] Although many Fargonite scientists had speculated that the presence of large predators influenced forest hardiness, few had supposed that **(Q30)** there was such a strong connection between them and the health of fish populations. [2] And yet Kwazmak and Jurgstor believe that, if anything, their initial findings underestimated the positive impacts of the presence of land-dwelling predators. [3] Further analysis, they assert, suggests that waterways in regions with significant populations of lupinines and ursalots can support well over 15 times more fish than waterways surrounded by areas in which plant-eating animals live unmolested by predators. **(Q31)**

Kwazmak and Jurgstor point out, however, that **(Q32)** the increasing of numbers of lupinines and ursalots may cause problems in some areas. There may, for example, be tragic consequences if these predators exist in great numbers in an area where the Fargonite population is dense. Their findings do show, however, how dramatically the management of one wildlife population affects other species. "Our main contention," they explain, "is that you can't maintain a healthy population of any one animal or plant unless you understand the big picture." Evidently, near-river, **(Q33)** or riparian—ecosystems have a lot to teach everyone, on any planet.

29.
A) NO CHANGE
B) accentuates
C) improves
D) exacerbates

30.
A) NO CHANGE
B) there was such a strong connection between those and
C) they had such a strong connection with
D) there was such a strong connection between that presence and

31. The writer is considering adding the following sentence to the previous paragraph.

> The recent study results have therefore created quite a stir.

Where is the most logical place to add this sentence?
A) Before sentence 1
B) After sentence 1
C) After sentence 2
D) After sentence 3

32.
A) NO CHANGE
B) an increase in the population
C) rising the number
D) this increasing amount

33.
A) NO CHANGE
B) or, riparian; ecosystems
C) or riparian, ecoystems
D) or riparian ecosystems,

SAMPLE TEST 2
Section 2: Writing & Language Test

Questions 34-44 are based on the following passage.

A Rhodes By Any Other Name

    A sudden job transfer in 2015 necessitated my purchasing a new home in western Kansas, a vast region **(Q34)** <u>by which</u> I had never laid eyes on a single **(Q35)** <u>square foot,</u> without even seeing a video of the house or property. Making such an important decision based on a leap of faith represented a major **(Q36)** <u>accession</u> from my usual approach to living, which is measured and cautious. However, rental units are few and far between on the western plains, and landlords are suspicious of outsiders who seem a little too eager to move to a town that would be easy to miss even if you walked toward it in a straight line from a mile away. Those who come suddenly tend to leave just as swiftly, and quite often, **(Q37)** <u>they do so after helping a lot of the people of the town with their problems.</u>

34.
- A) NO CHANGE
- B) of which
- C) whereupon
- D) thereof

35.
- A) NO CHANGE
- B) square foot;
- C) square foot
- D) square foot:

36.
- A) NO CHANGE
- B) concession
- C) violation
- D) departure

37. Which option would best account for the attitude toward outsiders described in the previous sentence?
- A) NO CHANGE
- B) they do so before anyone in the town has the opportunity to really know them.
- C) they do so filled with regret because they can't stay longer.
- D) they do so with a lot of the townspeople's hard-earned money stuffed in their pockets.

[1] Upon arriving at my new residence, I began to wonder if there was a bit of truth in all the old **(Q38)** tales about everything being bigger in the West then in the East. [2] It was a full week before I had explored every room and closet of the enormous house, and another before I ventured up into the attic. [3] What I found there topped anything I might have **(Q39)** expected, besides: a vintage Rhodes electric piano, caked in a half inch of dust and grime. [4] As I've said, my approach to life is measured and cautious, so I made the common sense decision to sell the Rhodes and later purchase a digital instrument. [5] I had grown up playing piano and had long intended to acquire a keyboard and rekindle my old passion for music. [6] But a Rhodes is a really, weird, fickle version of a piano. [7] A little online research brought me to the blog of Stephan Yorgerson, **(Q40)** believing that within a few years, digital pianos will be able to perfectly replicate the sound of a vintage Rhodes, in addition to the sounds of thousands of other instruments. [8] Furthermore, a new digital piano would cost less than the estimate Yorgerson's website provided for the cost of restoring the neglected instrument I had inadvertently acquired. **(Q41)**

38.
- A) NO CHANGE
- B) tales about everything being bigger in the West, then
- C) tales about everything being bigger in the West than
- D) tails about everything being bigger in the West than

39.
- A) NO CHANGE
- B) expected:
- C) expected, nevertheless:
- D) expected, hence:

40.
- A) NO CHANGE
- B) whom believes
- C) he believes
- D) who believes

41.
To make this paragraph most logical, sentence 4 should be placed
- A) where it is now
- B) after sentence 5
- C) after sentence 7
- D) after sentence 8

The responses I received to my online classified ad soon had me doubting whether Yorgerson's **(Q42)** acclaims were as valid as they seemed. Offers poured in from a dozen countries, including Brazil, Finland, Thailand, **(Q43)** and New Zealand also. Many of the bids came from veteran keyboard players who acknowledged that they already owned multiple acoustic and digital pianos. They seemed willing to all but climb over each other's backs to get their hands on a dust-encrusted relic that was a half dozen repairs away from sounding a single note.

I do not know whether I was moved more by those surprising developments or by my strange new surroundings. Something about the endless procession of rolling Kansas hills made me appreciate, indeed yearn for, uniqueness in a way I never had before. **(Q44)** Has digitalization sent us racing toward a future where we are all as indistinguishable as blades of grass? I doubted that, but I didn't doubt the rightness of the idea slowly taking shape in my mind in spite of all the logic that told me to reject it. Two days after placing the online ad, I deleted it and began placing orders for replacement parts for a vintage Rhodes.

42.
 A) NO CHANGE
 B) claims
 C) accusations
 D) admissions

43.
 A) NO CHANGE
 B) and New Zealand.
 C) and New Zealand additionally.
 D) as well as also New Zealand.

44. At this point, the author is considering whether to add the following sentence.

> I was tired of all the pressure to conform that I always felt from television and online commercials.

Should the writer add this sentence in this location?

 A) No, because it contradicts the previous sentence.
 B) No, because it blurs the article's focus by introducing an entirely new motivation for the author's actions that is not further explained.
 C) Yes, because it provides examples of specific trends towards the loss of uniqueness that the author fears.
 D) Yes, because it elaborates on the reasons for the author's sudden move to Kansas, which precipitated all the other events described.

STOP

If you have finished this section before time expires, you may check your work. You cannot return to this section once you move on to the next section.

STOP!

If you have finished this section before time expires, you may check your work. You cannot return to this section once you move on to the next section.

www.eggheadprep.com

ANSWERS, SECTION 2
SAMPLE TEST 2 — WRITING & LANGUAGE

1. B
2. D
3. C
4. A
5. B
6. D
7. A
8. D
9. C
10. D
11. B
12. A
13. D
14. B
15. C
16. D
17. C
18. A
19. A
20. B
21. B
22. C
23. A
24. A
25. D
26. B
27. D
28. A
29. C
30. D
31. B
32. B
33. C
34. B
35. A
36. D
37. D
38. C
39. B
40. D
41. D
42. B
43. B
44. B

eggheadprep.com

SECTION 3: MATH TEST

NO CALCULATOR, 25 MINUTES, 20 QUESTIONS

DIRECTIONS

For questions 1–15, solve the problem and choose the best answer from the options provided. For questions 16–20, solve the problem and type in your answer. Further instructions for typing in your answer are provided before question

NOTES

1. Calculator use is not permitted for this section. You will distort your score if you use one.
2. All variables and expressions represent real numbers unless stated otherwise.
3. Unless otherwise indicated, figures shown have been drawn to scale.
4. All figures lie in a plane unless stated otherwise.
5. The domain of a function f is the set of real numbers for which f(x) is a real number, unless stated otherwise.

REFERENCE

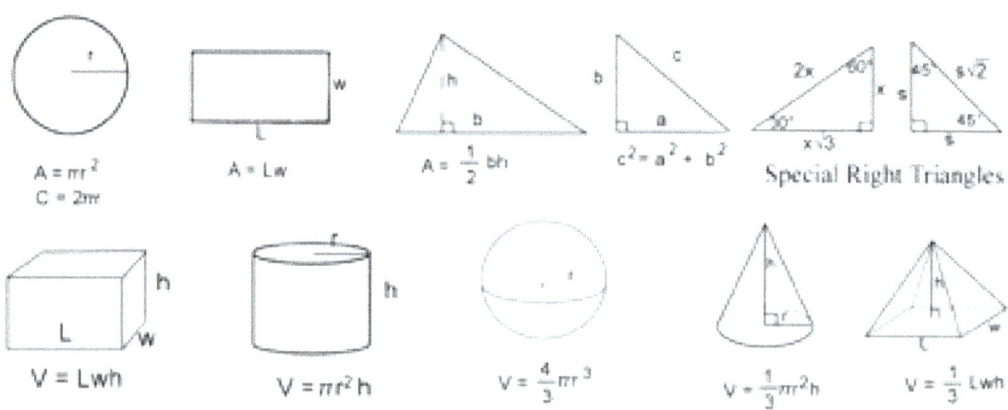

A full circle has 360 degrees of arc.
A full circle has 2π radians of arc.
The sum of the measures of the angles in a triangle is 180°.

EGGHEAD PREP

SAMPLE TEST 2
Section 3: Math, No Calculator

1. If 7x + 4 = 13, then 14x + 2 = ?
   A) 13
   B) 15
   C) 18
   D) 20

2. $$x + y = 5$$
   $$2x - 3y = 5$$
   Which of the following ordered pairs (x, y) is a solution to the system of equations shown above?
   A) (–4, 1)
   B) (4, 1)
   C) (2, 3)
   D) (3, 2)

3. A rental service provides laptop computers for professionals attending a conference. The cost, in dollars, for a company to rent laptops during the conference is given by the expression 200 + 18ad, where a is the number of laptops the company rents and d is the number of days for which the laptops are rented. Which of the following choices best describes the meaning of the number 18 in this expression?
   A) The company requires at least 18 laptops for the conference.
   B) After the initial fees are paid, the cost of any rental increases by $18 for each added day.
   C) In addition to any other fees, the rental service charges $18 per day for each laptop.
   D) The rental price includes the use of each laptop for up to 18 days.

4. $$\sqrt{3m^2 - 2} - w = 0$$
   If the value of w in the above equation is 5 and m > 0, what is the value of m?
   A) 1
   B) 2
   C) 3
   D) 4

5. $$16a^4 + 8a^2b^2 + b^4$$
   Which of the following choices is equivalent to the above expression?
   A) $(16a^2 + b^2)^2$
   B) $(4a^2 + b^2)^2$
   C) $(2a + b)^4$
   D) $(16a + b)^4$

6. If $\dfrac{y^{r^2}}{y^{q^2}} = y^{36}$, $y \geq 2$, and $r - q = 9$, what must be the value of $r + q$?
   A) 4
   B) 12
   C) 27
   D) 36

7.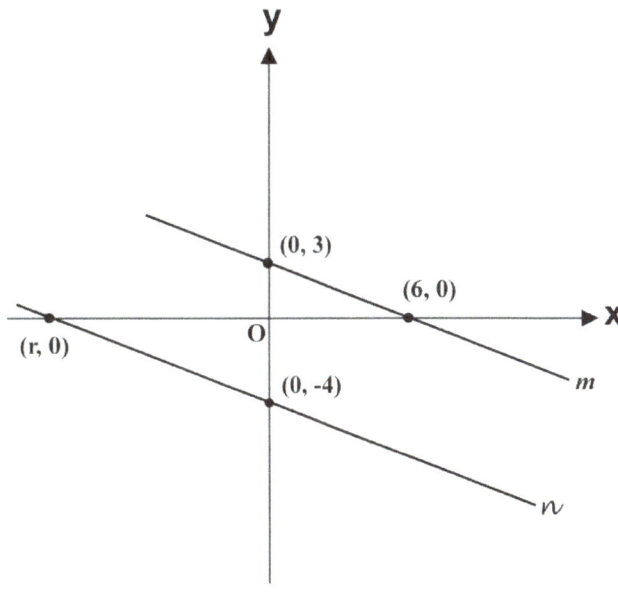

In the xy-plane shown, lines m and n are parallel. Which of the following is the value of r?
   A) –10
   B) –8
   C) –6
   D) –4

8. Line *l* has slope –3 and passes through the point (–1, 8). Line *t* contains the two points (2, –1) and (–1, 2). Let the ordered pair (*b*, *c*) represent the point where lines *l* and *t* intersect. What is the value of $c - b$?

A) –3
B) –2
C) –1
D) 2

9. $$pQ = 450$$
The formula above shows the relationship between the between the number of prairie dogs, *p*, and the number of quail, *Q*, on a wildlife preserve in North Dakota at any given time. If the number of quail is less than 80, what is the minimum number of prairie dogs that could be present?

A) 4
B) 5
C) 6
D) 7

10. Which of the following equations represents a graph in the *xy*-plane for which *y* is always greater than or equal to –2?

A) $y = x^3 - 3$
B) $y = x^2 - 3$
C) $y = |x| - 3$
D) $y = |x - 3|$

11. $$L = \frac{M}{P - M}$$
A head mechanic uses the formula above to determine the number of lug nuts needed to service *M* vehicles based on a tire performance rating *P* reported to her by her crew. Which of the following correctly expresses the number of vehicles in terms of the other two variables?

A) $M = \dfrac{LP}{L+1}$
B) $M = LP - LM$
C) $M = \dfrac{L}{1+L}$
D) $M = \dfrac{P}{L+1}$

12. Given that $i = \sqrt{-1}$, which of the following expressions is equivalent to,
$$\frac{2-7i}{6+2i}?$$

A) $\dfrac{1}{20} - \dfrac{23}{20}i$
B) $\dfrac{-1}{20} - \dfrac{23}{20}i$
C) $\dfrac{2}{6} + \dfrac{7}{2}i$
D) $\dfrac{1}{3} - \dfrac{7}{2}i$

13. What is the sum of all solutions *x* of the equation,
$$3x^2 + 15x - 24 = 0?$$

A) –5
B) $3\sqrt{5}$
C) $3\sqrt{5}$
D) 5

SAMPLE TEST 2
Section 3: Math, No Calculator

14. For all real values of x except -2, the expression $\dfrac{3x+7}{x-2}$ is equal to which of the following?

    A) $3 - \dfrac{7}{2}$

    B) $\dfrac{3+7}{-2}$

    C) $3 + \dfrac{1}{x-2}$

    D) $3 + \dfrac{13}{x-2}$

15. A car is purchased for $16,500. Each year, it loses 14.5% of its value. Which of the following functions g models the value of the car t years after it is purchased?

    A) $g(t) = 16500\,(0.145)^t$

    B) $g(t) = 16500\,(0.855)^t$

    C) $g(t) = 0.145\,(16500)^t$

    D) $g(t) = 0.855\,(16500)^t$

DIRECTIONS

For questions 16 – 20, solve the problem and type in your answer. Please follow these guidelines:

1. No questions have negative answers.
2. If a problem has more than one correct answer, any of those answers will be accepted as correct. Please enter only one answer.
3. Do not type in mixed numbers. A number such as 2 ¼ should be entered as 2.25 or 9/4. Mixed numbers will be misinterpreted by the computer.
4. If a decimal answer does not terminate after 3 decimal places, enter three decimal places only. You may either round or truncate the decimal. For example, 3/8 may be entered as 3/8 or .375, because the decimal ends there; 7/9 may be entered as 7/9, .777, or .778. Fractions should be reduced to simplest terms. For example, you should enter 1/2 instead of 2/4.

16. $$3(2x^2 - 1) + 4x(2 + 3x) = ax^2 + bx + c$$

    In the above equation, a, b, and c are constants. If the equation is true for all real values of x, what is the value of the constant a?

17.

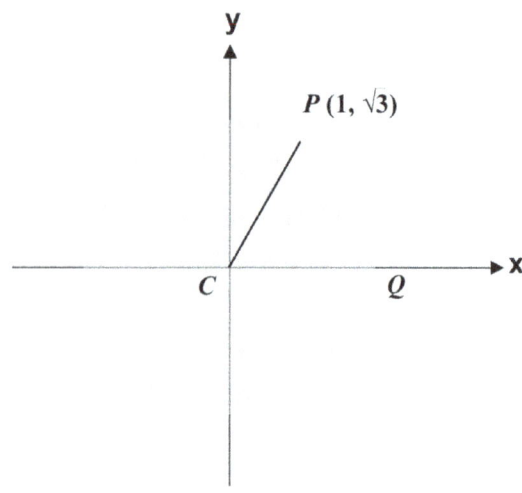

In the figure above, C is the center of the circle on the xy-plane. If the measure of ∠QCP is $\dfrac{\pi}{n}$ radians, what is the value of n?

18.

A female wozzula bear weighs about 150 pounds, whereas a male weighs about 450 pounds. If the total weight of wozzula bears at Honeyland National Park is 1800 pounds, and the park has at least one female wozzula bear and at least one male wozzula bear, what is one possible number of female wozzula bears in the park?

19.

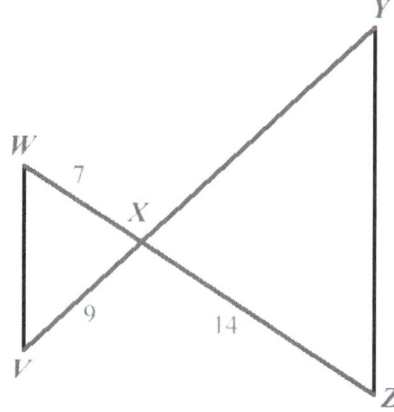

In the figure above, $\overline{WV}$ is parallel to $\overline{YZ}$. X is the intersection point of $\overline{WZ}$ and $\overline{VY}$. What is the length of segment $\overline{VY}$?

20.

$$3x + 5y = 45$$
$$cx + dy = 15$$

In the above equations, c and d are constants. If the system has infinitely many solutions, what is the value of $\dfrac{c}{d}$?

STOP

If you have finished this section before time expires, you may check your work. You cannot return to this section once you move on to the next section.

STOP!

If you have finished this section before time expires, you may check your work. You cannot return to this section once you move on to the next section.

www.eggheadprep.com

ANSWERS, SECTION 3

SAMPLE TEST 2 — MATH, NO CALCULATOR

1. D
2. B
3. C
4. C
5. B
6. A
7. B
8. A
9. C
10. D
11. A
12. B
13. A
14. D
15. B

---

16. 18
17. 3
18. 3 or 6 or 9
19. 27
20. 3/5 or .6

SECTION 4: MATH TEST
CALCULATOR, 55 MINUTES, 38 QUESTIONS

DIRECTIONS

For questions 1–30, solve the problem and choose the best answer from the options provided. For questions 31–38, solve the problem and type in your answer. Further instructions for typing in your answer are provided before question 31.

NOTES

1. Calculator use is permitted for this section.
2. All variables and expressions represent real numbers unless stated otherwise.
3. Unless otherwise indicated, figures shown have been drawn to scale.
4. All figures lie in a plane unless stated otherwise.
5. The domain of a function f is the set of real numbers for which f(x) is a real number, unless stated otherwise.

REFERENCE

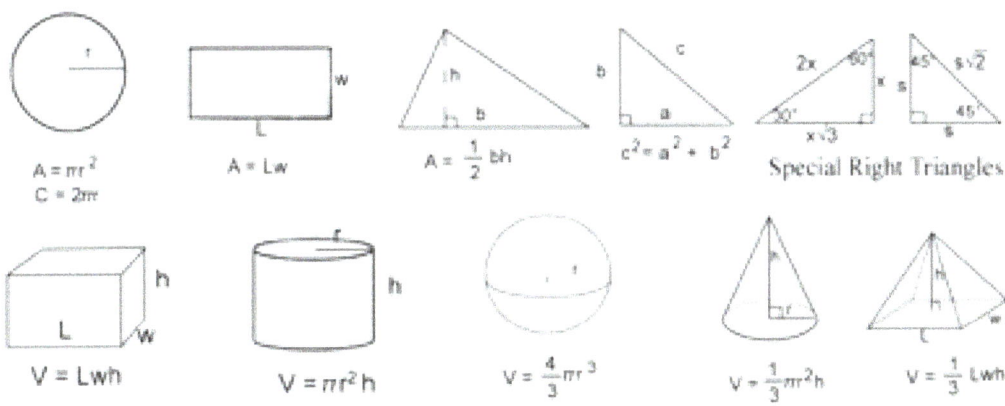

A full circle has 360 degrees of arc.
A full circle has 2π radians of arc.
The sum of the measures of the angles in a triangle is 180°.

eggheadprep.com

1. A researcher presents a survey question to 9 randomly selected people out of every 300 people who enter an arena to watch a basketball game. At this rate, how many people will be asked the survey question if 18,000 people attend the game?

   A) 460
   B) 500
   C) 540
   D) 580

2. $$m = 16 + 4.5q$$
   When a chemist adds 10 grams of a certain solid to a mixture of 5 deciliters of water and q deciliters of liquid quantonium, the solid takes m minutes to dissolve, as given by the above equation. What is the value of q when m is 79?

   A) 1.56
   B) 10
   C) 14
   D) 283.5

3. A grocery store has a nutritional information kiosk where customers can look up articles on various food-related topics. The customer can then either read the article on the kiosk screen or print it out to read at home. The kiosk charges $0.07 to read the article on screen and $0.33 to print it. Which of the following represents the amount of money, M (in dollars) that the store collects through the kiosk if R articles are read by customers on screen and P articles are printed?

   A) $M = 0.07R + 0.33P$
   B) $M = 0.07R - 0.33P$
   C) $M = 0.07P + 0.33R$
   D) $M = 0.07P - 0.33R$

4. If 3 times the number n is subtracted from 7, the result is 19. What is the result when 2 times n is added to 10?

   A) −4
   B) 0
   C) 2
   D) 19

5. Consider the equation,
   $$y = x^2 - 10x + 16,$$
   which represents a parabola in the xy-plane. All of the following equations are equivalent to the given equation. Which one displays the x-intercepts of the parabola as coefficients or constants?

   A) $y - 16 = x^2 - 10x$
   B) $y = (x - 8)(x - 2)$
   C) $y = x(x - 10) + 16$
   D) $y + 9 = (x - 5)^2$

Questions 6 and 7 refer to the following information.

The decibel level of the noise in a children's play area is directly proportional to the number of children present. The decibel level is 84 when 7 children are present.

6. What would be the decibel level of the noise in the playroom if 10 children were present?

   A) 87
   B) 120
   C) 168
   D) 240

7. Of the noise in the play area, 73% is caused by talking, laughing, and yelling; the rest of the noise is caused by foot-stomping and the sounds made by toys. If there are 7 children present, how many decibels of noise are caused by foot-stomping and toy sounds?

   A) 66.00
   B) 61.32
   C) 34.00
   D) 22.68

8. The Northwest Angle in northern Minnesota is a small area of land on the shore of Lake of the Woods that, due to an irregularity of the US-Canadian border, the US Postal Service can only reach by boat. Each bag of letters the boat carries weighs 45 pounds. Each bag of packages weighs 70 pounds. Let L be the number of letter bags the boat carries and P be the number of package bags. If the boat can carry up to either 25 bags or a total weight of 1,400 pounds, which system of inequalities represents this situation?

   A) $\begin{cases} 45L + 70P \leq 1{,}400 \\ L + P \leq 25 \end{cases}$

   B) $\begin{cases} \dfrac{L}{45} + \dfrac{P}{70} \leq 1{,}400 \\ L + P \leq 25 \end{cases}$

   C) $\begin{cases} 45L + 70P \leq 25 \\ L + P \leq 1{,}400 \end{cases}$

   D) $\begin{cases} L + P \leq 1{,}400 \\ \dfrac{L}{45} + \dfrac{P}{70} \leq 25 \end{cases}$

9. At the start of a board game, each player has N "power points." A player gains 4 additional power points each time he or she completes a journey. If a player who has completed 40 journeys has 760 points, what is the value of N?

   A) 720
   B) 600
   C) 480
   D) 160

10.

Number of 8-hour days Jenai works each week	3
Number of machines she uses to process orders	4
Number of tasks that must be completed to process each order	13
Number of orders Jenai can process per hour	37
Number of orders that make up a batch	10
Number of orders Jenai must process	9,582

Jenai processes orders at a factory. The table above shows information about the number of orders she has to process, how the processing is done, her pace of work, and her work schedule. Based on the information in the table, which of these choices is closest to the number of weeks it will take Jenai to processes all of the orders?

A) 11
B) 9
C) 7
D) 6

11. For a function f, $f(-3) = 7$ and $f(4) = 5$. For a function g, $g(4) = -3$ and $g(5) = -1$. What is the value of $g(f(4))$?

A) 7
B) 5
C) −1
D) −3

12. A city official wanted to study whether the people of the small town of Coos Bay, Oregon supported or opposed the building of a new high-rise resort hotel that would increase tourism but would also partially block many residents' view of the bay. On a Saturday afternoon, she asked the opinions of 83 local residents who were hiking on the Bay View Trail. Of the residents she surveyed, 4 refused to answer the question. Which of the following reasons would an expert most likely give for saying that the survey would not yield a reliable conclusion about the opinions of all the people of Coos Bay?

A) Population size
B) Non-participation bias (the number of people who refused to respond)
C) Sample size
D) The location at which the official conducted the survey

13.

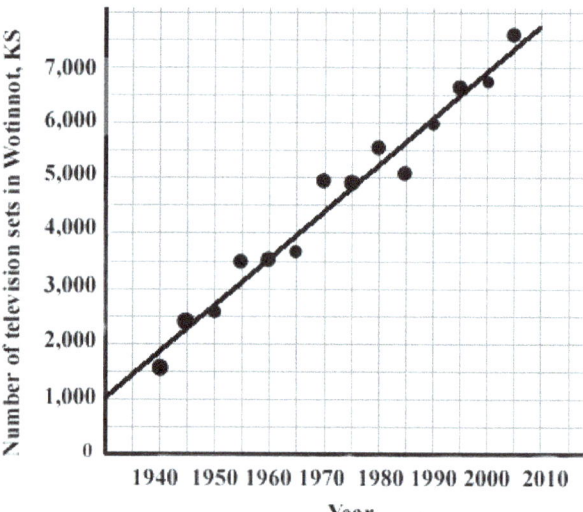

Television Ownership in the Town of Wotinott, Kansas

According to the line of best fit shown in the scatterplot above, which of the following is the best estimate of the year in which television set ownership in Wottinott reached 5,500 sets?

A) 1968
B) 1978
C) 1983
D) 1988

SAMPLE TEST 2
Section 4: Math, Calculator

14. On July 1, 2006, wildlife experts determined that 43 blue herons live along the Roon River. They believe that the population ceiling (the largest population possible before the herons are at risk due to disease or an insufficient food supply) for blue herons along the river is 70. Each year, the population increases by 8 herons. If Y represents the number of years since July 1, 2006, which inequality could be solved to determine the set of years for which the population of herons was at or below the ceiling?

    A) $43Y + 8 \leq 70$
    B) $8Y + 43 \leq 70$
    C) $70 - 8Y \leq 43$
    D) $8 - 70 \leq 43Y$

15. The moon travels roughly 1,500,000 miles while making one orbit of Earth. If the time required for one orbit is roughly 27 days, which of the following is closest to the orbital speed of the moon?

    A) 230,000 miles per hour
    B) 56,000 miles per hour
    C) 15,000 miles per hour
    D) 2,300 miles per hour

16. The length of a Davidson cruising boat, in meters, is approximately 30% less than the length of a Wattleford cruising boat. If the length of a Wattleford cruising boat is 50 meters, what is the length, in meters, of a Davidson cruising boat?

    A) 15
    B) 20
    C) 35
    D) 65

17. **Results on the Playbook Quiz for the Stony Falls High School Girls' Basketball Teams**

	Passed quiz	Did not pass quiz
Brought playbook home	12	5
Did not bring playbook home	9	16

The 42 girls who play on the three basketball teams (varsity, junior varsity, and 9th grade) at Stony Falls High School were given a playbook to study. Some of the players were allowed to bring the playbook home, while others were not. The table above summarizes the results when the players took a quiz on the playbook. If a player is chosen at random from among those who did not pass the quiz, what is the probability she brought the playbook home?

A) $\dfrac{5}{16}$

B) $\dfrac{5}{21}$

C) $\dfrac{5}{17}$

D) $\dfrac{5}{12}$

18. The 45 towns in the small nation of Spoonland have a mean population of 23,000 people and a median population 39,000 people. Which of the following scenarios could account for the difference between the mean and the median?

    A) There are some towns that have very small populations.
    B) There are a few towns that have very large populations.
    C) A significant number of the towns have populations between 23,000 and 39,000.
    D) Most of the towns have populations that are not very different from each other.

Questions 19 and 20 refer to the following information.

A child psychologist chose 200 children randomly from each of two large summer camps and asked them how many pets their families have. The results are shown in the table below.

Pet Ownership

Number of Pets	Camp Happy	Camp Joyous
0	30	40
1	80	90
2	50	50
3	30	20
4	10	0

There are a total of 1,800 children at Camp Happy and 1,400 at Camp Joyous.

19. Which of the following is the median number of pets for all of the children who were surveyed?

A) 4
B) 3
C) 2
D) 1

20. Based on the survey results, which of these choices most accurately expresses the relationship between the expected number of children with 2 pets at Camp Happy and the expected number of children with two pets at Camp Joyous?

A) The total number of children with 2 pets is expected to be the same at both camps.
B) The total number of children with 2 pets is expected to be 400 more at Camp Happy.
C) The total number of children with 2 pets is expected to be 100 more at Camp Joyous.
D) The total number of children with 2 pets is expected to be 100 more at Camp Happy.

21. Consider the circle in the xy–plane represented by the equation,

$$x^2 + y^2 - 6x + 4y = 12.$$

What is the radius of the circle?

A) 3
B) 5
C) 12
D) 25

Questions 22 and 23 refer to the following information.

$$E = \frac{N}{3q^2}$$

A scientist has developed a new energy source called a Quasmatron. She explains that the energy, E, that a Quasmatron installation can generate is given by the formula above, where N is the number of Quasmatrons and q is the quasmatic resistance of each Quasmatron.

22. Which of the following correctly expresses the square of the quasmatic resistance in terms of the energy generated and the number of Quasmatrons?

A) $q^2 = \dfrac{E}{3N}$

B) $q^2 = \dfrac{N}{3E}$

C) $q^2 = \dfrac{EN}{3}$

D) $q^2 = \dfrac{3N}{E}$

23. Quasmatron installation I has 9 times the energy output of Quasmatron installation II. Assuming the two installations have the same number of Quasmatrons, the quasmatic resistance of each Quasmatron at installation I must be what fraction of the Quasmatic resistance of each Quasmatron at installation II?

A) $\dfrac{1}{81}$

B) $\dfrac{1}{9}$

C) $\dfrac{1}{3}$

D) $\dfrac{1}{2}$

24. A store manager is required to provide an estimate each month of the number of hours h of work that members of the staff missed during that month due to illness, where $h > 60$ for any given month. For two randomly chosen months each year, the regional managers conduct an in-depth audit to determine the exact number of work hours w that the store staff missed that month due to illness. The store manager receives a bonus if the estimate was within 8 hours of the exact number. If the store manager receives the bonus, which of the following relationships must be true?

A) $-8 < w + h < 8$

B) $-8 < w - h < 8$

C) $w + h > 60$

D) $w < h - 8$

25.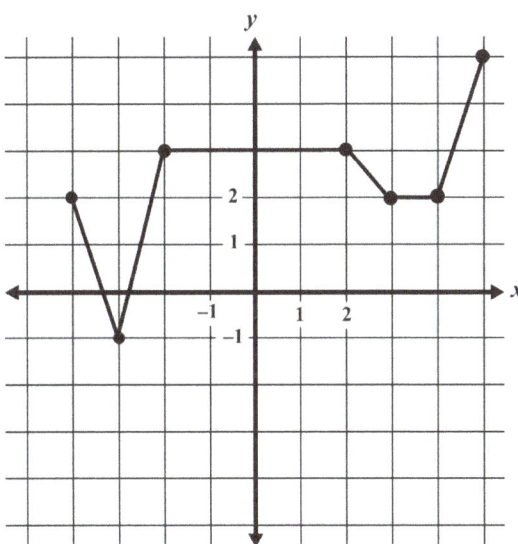

The complete graph of a function f on the xy–plane is shown above. Which of the following is/are equal to 3?

I. $f(3)$
II. $f(0.5)$
III. $f(-1)$

A) I only

B) I and II only

C) II and III only

D) I, II, and III

26.

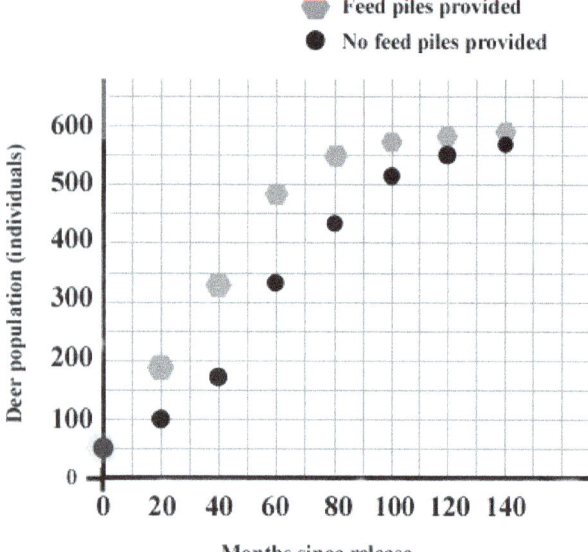

One hundred deer were captured from an overpopulated area and relocated to two new habitats. Fifty deer were released in a habitat where feed piles were provided for a number of years after the release; the other 50 deer were released into a Wildlife Refuge where no feed piles were provided. The graph shows the deer populations in the two habitats at 20-month intervals after the initial release. Which statement accurately describes the relationship between the average rates at which the deer populations in the two habitats changed?

A) In every 20-month interval, the rate of change of the deer population for which feed piles were provided was greater than that of the deer population that did not receive feed piles.

B) In every 20-month interval, the rate of change of the deer population for which no feed piles were provided was greater than that of the deer population that received feed piles.

C) In the intervals from 0 to 20 months and 20 to 40 months, the rate of change of the deer population that did not receive feed piles was greater than that for the deer population that received feed piles, whereas from 80 to 100 months and 100 to 120 months, the rate of change of the deer population that received feed piles was greater.

D) In the intervals from 0 to 20 months and 20 to 40 months, the rate of change of the deer population that received feed piles was greater than that for the deer population that did not receive feed piles, whereas from 80 to 100 months and 100 to 120 months, the rate of change of the deer population that did not receive feed piles was greater.

27. The graph of a linear function g in the xy-plane has intercepts at the points $(r, 0)$ and $(0, w)$. If $r - w = 0$ and $r \neq 0$, which statement must be true about the slope of the graph of g?

A) It is negative.
B) It is positive.
C) It is zero.
D) It could be either positive or negative, but is not zero.

28.
$$x = 5$$
$$x + cy^2 = d$$

For which values of the constants c and d will the system of equations shown above have exactly two real solutions?

A) $c = 4, d = 3$
B) $c = -3, d = 6$
C) $c = -6, d = 6$
D) $c = -6, d = 3$

29.

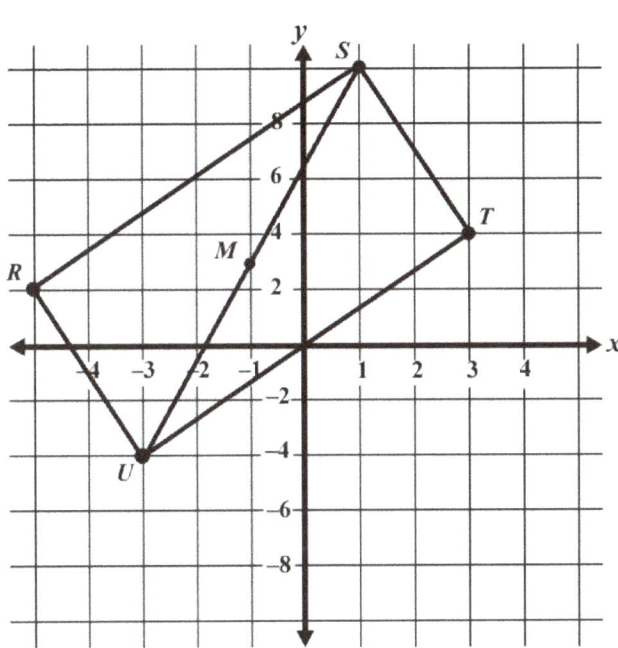

In the figure above, RSTU is a rectangle. M is the midpoint of the diagonal US. The coordinates of S are (1, 10) and those of M are (−1, 3). What is an equation for the line containing the points R and T?

A) $y = \dfrac{1}{4}x + 4$

B) $y = \dfrac{1}{4}x + \dfrac{13}{4}$

C) $y = 4(x − 3)$

D) $y = 4x − 8$

30.

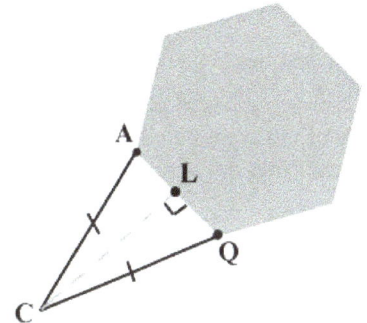

The figure above shows a regular hexagon with sides of length s and an isosceles triangle, AQC. The segment $\overline{AC}$ has length 12 cm. If the area of the hexagon is $54\sqrt{3}$ square cm, what is the area, in square cm, of triangle AQC?

A) $10\sqrt{3}$

B) $12\sqrt{3}$

C) $9\sqrt{15}$

D) $12\sqrt{15}$

DIRECTIONS

For questions 31–38, solve the problem and type in your answer. Please follow these guidelines:

1. No questions have negative answers.
2. If a problem has more than one correct answer, any of those answers will be accepted as correct. Please enter only one answer.
3. Do not type in mixed numbers. A number such as 2 ¼ should be entered as 2.25 or 9/4. Mixed numbers will be misinterpreted by the computer.
4. If a decimal answer does not terminate after 3 decimal places, enter three decimal places unless otherwise instructed. You may either round or truncate the decimal. For example, 3/8 may be entered as 3/8 or .375, because the decimal ends there; 7/9 may be entered as 7/9, .777, or .778. Fractions should be reduced to simplest terms. In other words, you should enter 1/2 instead of 2/4.
5. Do not include a comma within any number. For example, for the number 3,750, simply enter 3750.

31.

If m minutes and 40 seconds is equal to 520 seconds, what is the value of m?

32.

A forest ranger reports that an ancient redwood tree grows in height at a rate of 0.25 feet per year. Based on the forest ranger's report, how many years will it take for the tree to grow 11 feet?

33.

Terrence and Felicia worked at a car wash for a total of 400 hours one summer. If Felicia worked for 60 more hours than Terrence did, how many hours did Terrence work at the car wash that summer?

34.

The graph of the function $f(x) = -2x^2 + bx + 27$ in the xy–plane contains the point $(-3, 3)$. What is the value of b?

35.

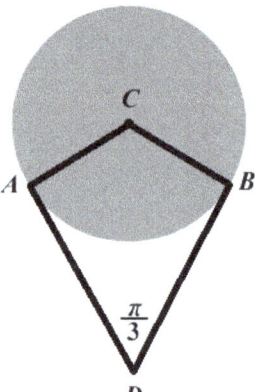

In the figure above, C is the center of the circle. Line segment DB is tangent to the circle at B; line segment DA is tangent to the circle at A. The measure of angle D is shown in radians. Given that circle C has circumference 84 meters, what is the length, in meters, of minor arc AB?

36.

Delfayo was given some old seashells by his grandfather to start a collection. From that date forward, Delfayo added the same number of seashells to his collection every year. The total number of seashells, S, in Delfayo's collection after Y years is given by the equation,

$$S = 25Y + 43.$$

Based on the equation, how many seashells did Delfayo add to his collection each year?

Questions 37 and 38 refer to the following information.

An inventor has created the first robots that "reproduce"—that is, that can build robots similar to themselves without human assistance. Currently, the inventor has 200 of these robots. The number of robots that will exist a month from now, $N_{\text{next month}}$, is related to the current number, $N_{\text{this month}}$, by the equation shown below.

$$N_{\text{next month}} = N_{\text{this month}} + 0.15\left(N_{\text{this month}}\right)\left(\frac{M - N_{\text{this month}}}{M}\right)$$

The constant M in the formula represents the maximum number of robots that the factory's power supply can support.

37.

According to the formula, if $M = 700$, what will be the number of robots two months from now? (Round your answer to the nearest whole number.)

38.

The inventor would like to increase the rate at which new robots are produced by increasing the power supply for the factory. If the inventor's goal is to increase from the current 200 robots to 225 robots next month, how many robots must the factory be equipped to support? (Round your answer to the nearest whole number.)

STOP

If you have finished this section before time expires, you may check your work. You cannot return to this section once you move on to the next section.

STOP!

If you have finished this section before time expires, you may check your work. You cannot return to this section once you move on to the next section.

www.eggheadprep.com

ANSWERS, SECTION 4
SAMPLE TEST 2 — MATH, CALCULATOR

1. C
2. C
3. A
4. C
5. B
6. B
7. D
8. A
9. B
10. A
11. C
12. D
13. C
14. B
15. D
16. C
17. B
18. A
19. D
20. D
21. B
22. B
23. C
24. B
25. C
26. D
27. A
28. D
29. B
30. C

---

31. 8
32. 44
33. 170
34. 2
35. 28
36. 25
37. 221
38. 1200

eggheadprep.com

ANSWER EXPLANATIONS

SAMPLE TEST 5 — SECTION 1, 2, 3, 4

NOTE: The SAT Reading Test emphasizes <u>evidence-based</u> analysis of the passages. While reading the passages, you will no doubt form opinions regarding whether the results of an experiment described should be trusted, or whether there are reasons beyond those presented in the passage for characters to act as they do. Those opinions may be perfectly valid, but when answering the questions, it is important to remember to draw conclusions based <u>solely</u> on evidence that is explicitly presented in the passage, not on your own personal feelings.

TEST SECTION 1: READING

1. Hamilton states (lines 55-58) that "the system [that is, the proposed Constitution], though it may not be perfect in every part, is, upon the whole a good one; is the best that the present views and circumstances of the country will permit; and is such a one as promises every type of security which a reasonable people can desire." He later (lines 85-88) forcefully warns against the dangers of any further delay ("continuance") in adopting the Constitution. Therefore, it is clear that he has written the paper for the specific purpose of persuading readers to advocate for adoption of the Constitution. **The correct answer is (B)**.

2. Answers (B) and (D) both include passages already mentioned in the explanation of the answer to question #1 (above), and therefore certainly provide evidence in support of that answer. The use of words such as "imprudence" and "precarious" in lines 61-63 further demonstrate Hamilton's belief that is imperative that the Constitution be swiftly adopted, so answer (C) supports the correct answer to question #1 as well. The only remaining choice is answer (A). In lines 47-51, Hamilton acknowledges the arguments presented by those opposing adoption of the Constitution. Although Hamilton goes on to present reasons why readers should disregard those arguments, *his objectives cannot be clearly determined simply by reading lines 47-51*, and so those lines do not provide evidence in support of the correct answer to question #1. **The correct answer is (A).**

3. A "pretension" is essentially a claim that one possesses a certain trait or status. Therefore, to say people have "pretensions to consistency" implies that they are asserting that they are consistent. "Slender" does mean thin or slim, but its meaning can be either literal or figurative. As a modifier of "pretensions," its meaning is similar to "slim" in the context of a statement like, "they have a slim chance of getting out of this mess," which means that there is little hope. In other words, Hamilton is asserting that there is not much of a chance that any claim of consistency put forth by the men he is describing will be believed. **The correct answer is (D).**

4. At the beginning of the second paragraph (lines 16-19), Hamilton declares, "The additional securities to republican government, to liberty and to property, to be derived from the adoption of the plan under consideration [that is, the Constitution], consist chiefly…" This introduction shows that

SAMPLE TEST 2
Answer Explanations

he intends to describe some of the reasons why he advocates adoption of the Constitution. The only answer that correctly describes this intention is answer (D). **The correct answer is (D).**

5. The term "re-eligibility" used in lines 5-6 implies that the Executive (i.e., President) could campaign for multiple terms in office. As long as this meaning is understood, it is clear that Hamilton refers to all of the reasons described in answer choices (A), (B), and (D) in lines 5-8. He does not, however, mention any possible impact of the Constitution on tax rates. **The correct answer is (C).**

6. In the lines mentioned, Hamilton is observing that even advocates for the Constitution have willingly admitted that the document is not perfect. That is, they have *acknowledged* the imperfections of the document. The words proposed in answer choices (A), (B), and (D) are not logical in the context of the third paragraph (lines 38-60). **The correct answer is (C).**

7. Hamilton's description of the country's "precarious state of affairs" and warning against "[exposing] the Union to the jeopardy of successive experiments" certainly imply that he believes the country will be in a vulnerable state if the Constitution is not adopted. By asking the rhetorical question, "How can perfection spring from such materials?" in lines 75-76, he clearly implies that perfection is impossible, and that delaying action in the hope of attaining perfection would be an ill-advised course of action. Both of these observations point to answer (B), while simultaneously ruling out answer (A). Although at other points in the Federalist Papers, Hamilton and his allies did point out that the Constitution could later be improved through the addition of amendments (as it has been), he does not make that case in this article. And since he has already acknowledged the flaws others claimed existed in the Constitution (lines 5-8, for example), answer (D) can be ruled out as well. **The correct answer is (B).**

8. In its most common use, "chimerical" refers to a thing or outcome that, although many may hope for it, is actually nonexistent or impossible to achieve. (The root word, "Chimera," was the name of a mythological monster.) **The correct answer is (A).**

9. In lines 67-71, Hamilton asserts, "The result of the deliberations of all collective bodies must necessarily be a compound, as well of the errors and prejudices, as of the good sense and wisdom, of the individuals of whom they are composed." "Errors and prejudices" are obviously undesirable qualities, while "good sense and wisdom" are desirable. Hamilton implies some mixture of both is to be expected when an agreement between parties is forged. **The correct answer is (B).**

10. As noted in the explanation for question #9 above, lines 67-71 very clearly express Hamilton's view that negotiations between groups with differing objectives will result in an agreement that embodies both the good and the bad qualities of the participating groups. These lines, therefore, clearly support answer (B) to question #9. Lines 1-5 describe the similarities between the proposed Constitution and the existing Constitution of New York state, which is irrelevant to question #9. Lines 44-47 and lines 51-53 both express Hamilton's belief that the concessions made by advocates for adoption of the Constitution have been exaggerated, but do not address Hamilton's views on the expected results of negotiations. **The correct answer is (D).**

eggheadprep.com

11. Answer (A) is a bit of a trap answer, in that the lines referred to in the question do contain the word, "unanswerable." However, when one considers the entire phrase, "unanswerable in the thoroughness with which they show the utter improbability…," it becomes clear that Hamilton intends "unanswerable" to mean something along the lines of "irrefutable." Continuing, Hamilton speaks of the utter improbability "of assembling a new convention, under circumstances to any degree so favorable to happy issue…" "Happy issue" is a fanciful way of saying, "a desirable outcome." He is thus implying that the pamphleteer has claimed that present conditions are the best one could realistically hope to have for the drafting of a Constitution that serves the best interests of the nation. **The correct answer is (C).**

---

12. Although the author acknowledges that memories are an imperfect record of past events (see line 12 and lines 25-26, for example), she definitely does not offer any suggestions for improving the sharpness of one's memory. Therefore, answer (A) can be immediately eliminated. The author does draw parallels between her past experiences and present circumstances (for example, by mentioning her brother multiple times throughout the passage), but she does not at any point investigate a *specific relationship* between her childhood experiences and her life as an adult. Therefore, though not outlandish, answer (B) is incorrect. Differences between Venezuela and the US are apparent from the passage, but they are clearly not the author's primary topic, which rules out answer (C).

One excellent way to discern the main purpose of an essay is to focus on the first part of the passage and the last. In the first paragraph (lines 1-9), the author emphasizes Joan Didion's desire to remember events as she experienced them. The author then begins the second paragraph (lines 10-19) by discussing her desire to preserve and make sense of her own memories. She finishes the passage (lines 81-83) by drawing a comparison between memory and the mangoes she recalls from her childhood. Therefore, **the correct answer is (D).**

13. After mentioning her brother, the author, in line 19, states that she is "acutely aware of the ease with which the days slip past," implying that she has been perceiving time as moving by swiftly. Yet as she transitions to writing about her memories, she observes (lines 20-21) that she feels "as if time has stopped," then expands on this idea, ultimately referring to memory as a "time-shifter" (line 25). She is therefore drawing a clear contrast between the persistent ticking of present-moment time and the ambiguous time of memory. **The correct answer is (B).**

14. Lines 18-23 of the passage contain most of the statements mentioned above in the explanation of the answer to question #13. Those lines therefore provide strong support for that answer. Answers (B) and (C) both reference lines in which the author's brother is mentioned, but in both cases, the lines in question simply narrate specific events and do not provide any insight into the author's intention in line 16. Therefore, those lines are irrelevant to question #13. Lines 58-61, while beautifully poetic, once again focus on one specific moment and provide no insight that would be relevant to question #13. **The correct answer is (A).**

15. In the lines referred to in the question, the author describes the contents of the garage as "relics of past years," then later suggests that those relics would "never be recovered" and states that they are "choked under decades of darkness and dust." There is a strong implication that the neglect has in some way damaged the relics or resulted in their loss, and that either outcome is tragic. Only answer (C) expresses these ideas. **The correct answer is (C).**

16. As noted in the explanation to the answer for question #15, the author's description of "relics of past years" that will "never be recovered" reveals her reason for including the description of the garage in the

SAMPLE TEST 2
Answer Explanations

passage. These phrases are found within lines 44-46, corresponding to answer (C). In lines 39-40 and 42-43, corresponding to answer choices (A) and (B), the author describes the garage vividly, but she does not yet reveal her reasons for doing so, which means that those answer choices do not *specifically* support the correct answer to question #15. The lines mentioned in choice (D) merely mention the garage in passing as a transition to the description of the playground, and therefore are not relevant to question #15. **The correct answer is (C).**

17. If you are familiar with the word "canopy," then you will immediately recognize answer (D) as correct. If not, there are many contextual clues that make the meaning of the word clear. In the previous paragraph (lines 51-53), the author describes "mango trees stretching upward to form a ceiling…" Naturally, that ceiling would be the object of the author's upward gaze from the top of the jungle gym. It is therefore clear that "canopy" must refer to the treetops. **The correct answer is (D).**

18. Once again, this question is most easily answered if you already know the meaning of "pungent," which usually describes a strong smell or taste. But as with question #17, the meaning of the word can also be grasped from the context in which it is used. In lines 66-68, the author describes "sweet, thick juice" that she "drinks" with every breath. This implies that she is describing a quality of the mangoes that one can experience by inhaling, which could only be true of their smell, or fragrance. **The correct answer is (A).**

19. This is the subtlest type of question that appears on the SAT Reading Test, in that it asks you to speculate about a meaning that is NOT explicitly presented in the passage. The fact that the author refers to the mango as falling from the tree "before its time" (line 72), suggests that it is "younger" than the other mangoes. This conclusion is confirmed in the next sentence (lines 73-74), which reads, "I reached down, pulling it carefully from the company of its older companions." We know from line 16 that the author's brother, Joel, is older than she is. We also know that in early adulthood, when she wrote the passage, she found herself separated from her brother, just as the immature mango becomes separated from its "older companions." Therefore, it is reasonable to conclude that the author is drawing a parallel between the mango's life cycle and her own history with her brother. **The correct answer is (B).**

20. As noted above in the explanation for question #19, it is in lines 73-74 that the author most clearly makes a connection between the mango and her relationship with her brother. None of the other answer choices offered here suggest that connection. **The correct answer is (B).**

21. Although the word "puncture" can certainly imply pain, which would suggest answer (B), the fact that the author describes memory as a "plump fruit" (line 80) shows that she is describing a phenomenon that, in her view, is defined more by beauty than by anguish. The key ideas in lines 80-83 are that a memory's "skin" can be opened "with a touch," and that it "spills free" at the "slightest puncture." These images strongly suggest that something very small can trigger a large flow of memories. Answer (C) best expresses these ideas. **The correct answer is (C).**

---

22. The word "savvy" generally implies that a person is shrewd or knowledgeable. The context is also helpful here. It is clear from the sentence as a whole (lines 10-12) that the author believes that "savvy insiders" are less likely to believe a widely held misconception than most people would be. This clue narrows the answer choices to answer (A), "cynical," (which implies a general distrust of mainstream ideas, but not necessarily superior knowledge), and answer (D), "knowledgeable." The word that better matches the positive tone of the paragraph is "knowledgeable." **The correct answer is (D).**

eggheadprep.com

23. There are clues throughout the first paragraph that point to the answer to this question. Phrases like "image most Americans carry in their minds," "most people believe they know," and "so pervasive is this conception" all indicate that the author is describing widely held beliefs. The phrase "decades of thinking" in the final sentence (lines 12-15) makes clear that the beliefs in question have been held for a long time. All of these clues make clear that **the correct answer is (A).**

24. Lines 24-26 fall between the lines referenced in the question, and point the way to the correct answer. Ms. Jackson says, "My friend saw me leaving the club with just a few crumpled ten-dollar bills as my meager reward for all the effort." In other words, she had worked very hard but was paid very little, just as described in answer choice (C). **The correct answer is (C).**

25. As indicated in the explanation for question #24 above, lines 24-26 of the passage clearly support the correct answer for that question. Therefore, **the correct answer for question #25 is (B).**

26. In lines 39-41, the author mentions "the somewhat egocentric notion that one's children should follow in one's footsteps." The implication is that many people hope their children will pursue the same career that they have pursued. This evidence alone is sufficient to conclude that **the correct answer is (D).**

27. In the explanation for question #26 above, the importance of lines 39-41 is stressed. These lines are included among the lines referenced in answer (A). Lines 41-44, referenced in answer choice (B), do suggest additional reasons why people might fight for better wages, but none of those reasons are mentioned in the answer choices for question #26. Therefore, those lines cannot support the correct answer to the previous question and answer (B) must be eliminated. Answer choices (C) and (D) reference lines that have only words, not ideas, in common with the answer choices for question #26, and so are incorrect. **The correct answer is (A).**

28. It is the sentence that immediately follows the mention of "old assumptions" that provides us with the answer to this question: "Perhaps the public … actually did care about something other than the latest trend, after all." This sentence clearly reference the sentence in lines 5-10 ("Furthermore … boundaries.") **The correct answer is (B).**

29. Lines 86-88 describe Ms. Jackson "being treated like a professional and earning an income commensurate with that status." The upbeat tone of the sentence clearly implies that the income is appropriate for (that is, corresponding to status as) a professional, a conclusion supported by the upward trend of the gray line on the graph. Answers (A) and (B) can thus both be eliminated, since both imply conflict, rather than agreement, between Ms. Jackson's professional status and her income. Answer (D) is nonsensical, in that it suggests that status creates income. **The correct answer is (C).**

30. The key above the graph indicates that the gray line represents members of the musicians' collective. Since that line doesn't appear until about '07 (year 2007), it is reasonable to conclude that 2007 was the year the collective was founded. **The correct answer is (C).**

31. The musicians who joined the collective were "blacklisted" (line 72), meaning that they were denied opportunities to perform. The lines referenced in the question further state that some of those

SAMPLE TEST 2
Answer Explanations

musicians even went to jail. These circumstances would obviously result in a significant decrease in income for musicians in the collective (gray line of graph), represented by the downward trend from about 2007 to 2008. **The correct answer is (D).**

32. As identified in the answer to question #31 (see above), the brief downward trend exhibited by the gray line of the graph corresponded to the immediate backlash musicians experienced upon forming the collective. Notice that from that point ('08 on the horizontal axis) onward, the trend of the gray line is strongly upward, indicating a dramatic rise in income for members of the collective, even as income for other musicians continued to decline. Note that the latter eliminates answer choice (B). **The correct answer is (A).**

---

33. Emotionally charged language is not present in the passage, even when the two characters are directly contradicting each other's views. Therefore, answer (A) must be eliminated. Although the passage does contain some discussion of technical matters related to machine-making, both the Old Man and the Young Man acknowledge that they are discussing machines for the purpose of analyzing human nature (lines 51-53 and line 79, for example), and not in relation to technological advances, which rules out both answer (B) and answer (D). **The correct answer is (C).**

34. Both "sophisticated" and "devious" are meanings of the word "cunning," whereas "massive" and "dangerous" are not. Therefore, the correct answer must be either choice (A) or choice (B). In context, the word cunning is used to describe *machines*, which cannot be devious. (Perhaps machines that mislead and lie will exist some day, but they certainly didn't exist in the early 1900s!) A machine can, however, be quite sophisticated. **The correct answer is (B).**

35. The words "rapture" and "praise" both do have religious connotations, particularly for Christians. However, it would make no sense to speak of "religiously praising" a machine. Both answers (B) and (C) suggest limited or qualified praise, whereas it is clear from lines 30-35 that both the Old Man and the Young Man believe the metal machine would be praised heavily. The word "lavish" can be used to imply a very great amount, of praise especially. Therefore, **the correct answer is (D).**

36. In lines 42-45, the Young Man says of the metal machine, "its performance is not personal. It is the result of the law of its construction. It is not a *merit* that it does the things which it is set to do—it can't *help* doing them." He is clearly indicating that a *personal merit* would arise from the person or object in question making a choice to do a better thing as opposed to a worse thing. He believes that a machine has no such power of choice, and therefore cannot have *personal* merits. **The correct answer is (A).**

37. As noted in the explanation for question #36 above, it is in lines 42-45 that the Young Man explains the view of "personal merits" that he and the Old Man apparently share, represented in answer (A) for question #36. Answer choice (B) refers to these specific lines. Therefore, **the correct answer is (B).**

38. In lines 58-60, the Old Man explicitly states that the "original rock contained the stuff of which the steel [machine] was built." He then goes on (lines 60-84) to explain that the stone machine and the metal machine differ only in the outside influences exerted upon them, asserting that a similar

phenomenon occurs with people. Note that the Old Man focuses on how external influences shape a person, not on what people can accomplish using machines. **The correct answer is (C).**

39. The Old Man (lines 62-64) describes the elements present in the rock that prevent it from functioning as a sophisticated engine as "prejudices," drawing a clear parallel with the prejudices human beings carry in their minds. He states that the rock had neither the power nor the desire to rid itself of those prejudices, and would do so only in the presence of outside influences—which he also refers to as "education" and "training" (line 57). All of this evidence shows clearly that **the correct answer is (C).**

40. The standard meaning of "inevitable" is "unavoidable." But in the context of line 87, "inevitable" describes an opinion. It would be strange to call an opinion "unavoidable." Therefore, we search for a word that is near to "unavoidable" in meaning, but could also modify the word, "opinion." "Expected" is such a word. **The correct answer is (D).**

41. In lines 117-118, the Old Man describes the Young Man and himself as "sewing machines," but Shakespeare as a "Gobelin loom," a far more sophisticated machine. He is therefore suggesting that Shakespeare's mind was, in its very makeup, a superior "machine" to most human brains. **The correct answer is (B).**

42. Because the Old Man refers to Shakespeare's writings as a "pictured and gorgeous fabric which still compels the astonishment of the world" (lines 122-123), answer (C) can be eliminated immediately. In lines 123-127, the author's purpose becomes clear, as the Old Man asserts that without outside influences (which he has previously termed, "education"), Shakespeare, in spite of his natural brilliance, would have "produced nothing." The clear implication is that if people do not have access to education, many possible great achievements will never occur. **The correct answer is (D).**

---

43. In lines 1-8, the author describes scientists' current, and impressive, understanding of the motion of tectonic plates. Lines 8-12 ("Yet for … dragons."), however, make clear that however impressive that knowledge may be, it lacks a crucial element: a methodology for predicting earthquakes. Therefore, the author uses the paragraph both to summarize current knowledge and point out limitations of that knowledge. **The correct answer is (C).**

44. In everyday speech, the word "lazily" could have any of the four meanings proposed in the answer choices. However, answers (B), (C), and (D) all describes states of mind, and therefore could not apply to inanimate objects like tectonic plates. **The correct answer is (A).**

45. In lines 25-30, the author states that Dr. Castonelli "points out that all manner of oceanic surface phenomena seemed random and unexplainable until very recently, when great progress was made in detecting, measuring, and tracking the movements of deep ocean waves that are invisible to us surface dwellers." Answer choice (D) paraphrases this statement. The other answer choices do not accurately summarize the ideas of the third paragraph. **The correct answer is (D).**

SAMPLE TEST 2
Answer Explanations

46. The key to this question may be found in lines 38-41: "the primary cause of such waves in water oceans is temperature variation within the liquid, and there is plenty of that in the turbulent realm of the mantle." This statement is paraphrased in answer (A). No other answer choice accurately reflects Dr. Castonelli's views, as described in the third and fourth paragraphs (lines 21-43). **The correct answer is (A).**

47. The reasons given in answers (A), (C), and (D) are all explicitly mentioned in the fifth paragraph (lines 44-54) of the passage. The reason given in answer (B) is never mentioned in the passage. **The correct answer is (B).**

48. "Substitute" is the most common meaning of "surrogate," indicating that answer (D) is correct. Answers (A), (B), and (C) all imply that "a true replica of the mantle" (lines 56-57) exists, which, as has been established in lines 44-54, is not true. **The correct answer is (D).**

49. A big clue for this question is the fact that to forecast means to predict. Thus, the fact that the author states in lines 72-73 that "there is a predictability to the formation of deep waves based on temperature patterns…" indicates that Dr. Castonelli's research may lead to better forecasting techniques. **The correct answer is (B).**

50. Dr. Castonelli is quoted as saying (lines 80-82), "The first rule of studying earthquakes is don't cause them." She is therefore implying that drilling down to the upper mantle could actually cause earthquakes, that is, seismic activity. **The correct answer is (D).**

51. As indicated in the key above the graph, the black lines indicate deep wave activity. Those black lines shown three clear peaks, and therefore, three deep waves. **The correct answer is (A).**

52. The gray lines (representing seismic waves, as indicated by the key above the graph) also show three clear peaks, each coming soon after one of the peaks shown in black. Therefore, seismic activity always *follows* the formation of a deep wave. **The correct answer is (C)..**

TEST SECTION 2: WRITING AND LANGUAGE

NOTE: As the instructions for this test section clearly state, the goal when answering questions is to bring each passage into compliance with the conventions of standard written English. Standard written English is a form of the English language specifically developed to facilitate clear communication in writing, even between people who speak very different forms of English. Therefore, many of the correct answers may seem different from the choices you would make in your everyday speech. That does not mean there is anything wrong with the version of spoken English you have learned. To perform well on this test section, you must learn to make distinctions between the English you speak on a daily basis and the guidelines governing word choices, punctuation, and sentence structure in standard written English.

1. What is needed is a way to clearly and simply convey the idea that there is an increasing amount of pressure on people to specialize in their learning. The underlined phrase and answer choice (C) are both intended to make this point, but are unnecessarily wordy and break from the conventions of standard written English in multiple ways. Answer choice (D) incorrectly alters the meaning of the sentence by implying that it is skill development that is increasing, rather than the level of expectation regarding such development. Answer choice (B) conveys the correct meaning without wasted words. **The correct answer is (B).**

2. The phrase "for example" should only be used to introduce a specific instance illustrating a general point just made. The sentence referenced in question #2 does not mention any specific examples of people under pressure to specialize. In fact, it asserts that many professionals need a variety of skills, not just one particular skill. Therefore, the sentence is intended to show a *contrast* between the phenomenon described in the previous sentence and actual circumstances in the workplace. "However" is commonly used to indicate a contrast. **The correct answer is (D).**

3. The previous two sentences present examples of people whose career responsibilities include many tasks not traditionally associated with a their occupations. Therefore, if what is desired is another example to illustrate the idea being discussed, we should search for the answer choice that describes sanitation workers performing a variety of tasks. Answer (C) is the only answer choice that fits this description. **The correct answer is (C).**

4. Since the proposed addition does not in any way discuss specific amounts of time associated with the various tasks, answer (B) may be ruled out immediately. The key issue to consider is whether the added text would enhance or diminish the clarity of the sentence in question, "Tasks historically … time." The proposed addition specifically addresses the question, "What sorts of tasks might those be?" Therefore, it *improves* the clarity of the sentence, as suggested by answer (A). **The correct answer is (A).**

5. The underlined phrase has a couple of problems. First, the word "them" would have to refer to the "one artist" described, since that artist is the only person mentioned in the sentence. While it is increasingly common to use "they/them" as a singular pronoun in standard written English, it is still helpful to readers to find a different way to construct the sentence to avoid such use if possible. The larger problem is that as constructed, the underlined phrase suggests that the day requires *tasks*, when in fact the intended meaning is that the day requires the tasks *to be completed*. Answer choice

SAMPLE TEST 2
Answer Explanations

(B) offers a construction that does not require a pronoun such as "them" AND emphasizes that is the *completion* of the tasks that is necessary. **The correct answer is (B).**

6. The issue behind this question is *parallel structure*. To help the reader process a list, all items in the list should be presented in the same style and grammatical format to the greatest extent possible. Each of the other courses is described using an adjective, such as "persuasive," and a gerund—that is, an "-ing" verb form—such as "writing." We should find an answer choice that uses a similar construction to describe the third course. Therefore, the best choice is "social networking." **The correct answer is (D).**

7. The intended meaning of the pair of sentences is that the idea of an art student minoring in data management systems no longer seems absurd in light of present-day realities. Neither answer (B) nor answer (D) suggests this meaning, so those answers must be eliminated. Answers (A) and (C) both correctly express the idea of changing times, but answer choice (C) fails to clearly delineate the contrast between past and present perceptions of students' course selections. By setting up the combined sentence in two halves, the first ending with, "seemed absurd," the second ending with, "seems perfectly natural," answer choice (A) most clearly describes the change that has occurred. **The correct answer is (A).**

8. The word "even," which appears immediately after the underline "yet," effectively communicates the idea of contrast that the author wishes to convey. Therefore, the word "yet" is not needed. **The correct answer is (D).**

9. Art schools are indeed very well equipped with studio facilities, but that has nothing to do with providing non-artistic training for students. Hence, the underlined portion fails to set up the rest of the sentence, and answer (A) can be eliminated. Answer (D) is even worse, in that it implies that the goal of providing non-artistic training can somehow be achieved simply by offering studio facilities. Since the entire passage focuses on ways that schools can better prepare students who *stay in school* for the life that awaits them after graduation, the information presented in answer (B) is irrelevant to both the sentence in question and the passage as a whole. **The correct answer is (C).**

10. Like question #6, this question deals with *parallel structure*. To help the reader process a list, all items in the list should be presented in the same style and grammatical format to the greatest extent possible. "Brand promotion" and "search engine optimization" are both technical terms for specific types of work, whereas "numbers problems" is a very vague, informal term that could refer to many different things. "Data analysis" better matches the formality and precision of the other terms used in the list. **The correct answer is (D).**

11. One should never conclude an essay with a statement unrelated to any of the topics discussed in the essay. Since no previous sentence in the passage has made any reference to costs, answer (A) may be ruled out. The previous sentence, "Their artwork will suffer as a result," raises a concern about the future of art if schools focus too much on non-artistic skill training. The conclusion should blend this idea with the essay's general theme of reinventing art schools to improve students' chances of career success. **The correct answer is (B).**

12. The reaction being described is the reaction of (that is, "belonging to") the archaeologists described in the previous sentence. Therefore, a pronoun implying possession is required. Both "their" and "theirs" are possessive forms of they/them. However, "theirs" is generally used to *end* a phrase indicating possession (for example, "the reaction was *theirs*"), not to introduce one. Therefore, the word "their" is the proper choice. **The correct answer is (A).**

13. The contents being described are the contents of (that is, "belonging to") the vault. So once again, a possessive pronoun is required. The possessive form of "it" is "its" (*no* apostrophe). Therefore, the correct answer choice must be (B) or (D). The phrase, "47 breathtaking, perfectly preserved wool quilts," effectively answers the question raised by the previous part of the sentence: *What is in the vault?* The required punctuation mark in such a case is a colon (:). **The correct answer is (D).**

14. In the underlined portion, "Maya Lin's" is set off by commas. Commas are used to set off *supplemental* phrases, that is, phrases that could be deleted without altering the meaning of the sentence. For example, in the sentence, "I went to play with my brother, Jonathan Wilkes, last night," the name Jonathan Wilkes is a supplemental phrase, since it is not essential to the meaning of the sentence. But for the sentence in question here, the phrase, "Maya Lin's" is *essential* to the meaning of the sentence. Without it, the sentence would read, "…stumbling upon architect 2-acre Vietnam…," which is nonsensical. Since the phrase is essential, it should NOT be set off by commas. **The correct answer is (B).**

15. The previous two sentences describe the sophistication and exacting attention to detail that the quilt makers exhibited in their portrayal of animals. The sentence in question here describes human figures seen on the quilts as *crude*, the opposite of sophisticated. Therefore, the sentence should begin with a word or phrase that conveys contrast. Clearly, answer choice (C) accomplishes this purpose. **The correct answer is (C).**

16. Notice that the following could both stand as complete sentences:

"By contrast, the human figures that appear on the quilts are rather crude."

and

"They seem to have been created with a specific intention of avoiding accurate representation."

Because each phrase is in fact a complete sentence, combining them as a single sentence would require the use of a semicolon. Since no answer choice offers this option, it is necessary to select an option that alters the second phrase so it is no longer a complete sentence on its own. Option (B) simply replaces "they" with the specific noun to which it already refers, which is not a significant change. Answer choice (C) would confuse the reader by implying the beginning of a list of qualities: "…are rather crude, seem to have been created with a specific intention of avoiding accurate representation" (*and??*). **The correct answer is (D).**

SAMPLE TEST 2
Answer Explanations

17. A "second supporting example" should be a description of another animal and the level of detail with which it is portrayed in the quilts. Only answer choice (C) fits this description. **The correct answer is (C).**

18. There is a clear contrast suggested by the first two sentences of paragraph #4. The first sentence suggests that the human figures shown in the quilts are less impressive to look at than the animal figures. The second sentence emphasize that, in spite of their lack of visual appeal, the human figures have much to teach us. Therefore, the two sentences should be joined in a manner that provides a cue that the second half of the compound sentence will to some degree stand in contrast to the first half. The word "but" nicely conveys contrast. **The correct answer is (A).**

19. Here is another question dealing with *parallel structure*. To help the reader process a list, all items in the list should be presented in the same style and grammatical format to the greatest extent possible. The previous phrases in the list—"dancer twirling ribbons" and "musician playing a wooden flute"—name a type of performer and then describe what he or she is doing. The phrase, "singer or storyteller sitting…" nicely follows this pattern. The best choice, therefore, is to leave the sentence as it is. **The correct answer is (A).**

20. The observation "belongs to" the conservator, so it is correct to use an apostrophe and an "s" to convey possession. However, placing the apostrophe after the "s" implies that the opinion belongs to *multiple* conservators, since the word "conservators" is plural in form. Because the word prior to the underlined phrase is "a," we know only *one* conservator is being described. Therefore, the apostrophe should come before the "s." **The correct answer is (B).**

21. According to the conventions of standard written English, the introductory phrase, "Representing one of the very rare instances when reality surpasses legend," will be assumed to apply to the first noun or noun phrase that appears after the introductory phrase. As written, therefore, the sentence would imply that *everyone with access to the vault* represents one of the very rare instances when reality surpasses legend. That is nonsensical and clearly does not convey the author's intended meaning. Rather, it is the *quilts* that represent one of the very rare instances when reality surpasses legend. Therefore, we need an answer in which the first noun phrase after the introductory phrase clearly refers to the quilts. Since "these incomparable works of traditional art" is a noun phrase describing the quilts, **the correct answer is (B).**

22. Paragraph 3 begins by referring back to Maya Lin's Vietnam Veterans Memorial, mentioned at the end of paragraph 1. Therefore, paragraph 3 should be placed immediately after paragraph 1. Paragraph 2 continues the discussion of portrayals of animals in the quilts that began in the latter part of paragraph 3. Therefore, paragraph 2 should be placed immediately after paragraph 3. Notice also that paragraph 2 transitions from discussing portrayals of animals to describing portrayals of humans, the primary topic of paragraph 4. The most logical paragraph order for the passage is thus 1-3-2-4-5. **The correct answer is (C).**

---

23. The underlined phrase accurately conveys the author's intended meaning without violating any conventions of standard written English, strongly suggesting that answer (A) is correct. Answer choice (C) is a pretty effective decoy, however. The phrase "that grow" is a perfectly acceptable

eggheadprep.com

replacement for "growing" (in fact, many writers would prefer it), but the addition of "and" creates a problem. The problem arises because the entire phrase, "that grow along the shores of rivers and streams (known as riparian forests here on Earth) and help to prevent erosion that can fill waterways with silt, decimating fish populations," reads as one long very introduction to an additional part of the sentence that does not exist. Because answer (C) is not a viable option, **the correct answer is (A).**

24. The simplest reason why the correct answer must be one of the two "Yes" options is that the phrase, "has decreased by 65 percent" does not convey any useful information unless the writer explains the timeline over which the decrease has occurred. There is thus a clear need for a phrase that states when the decrease began, as the proposed addition does. The proposed addition does not, however, offer the explanations described in answer choice (B). **The correct answer is (A).**

25. The word "that" is introducing the answer to the question, *What has the study revealed?* When used in this way, the word "that" should never be preceded by a comma or any other punctuation mark. **The correct answer is (D).**

26. The second graph clearly shows that a larger number of predators results in *healthier* riparian forests, so answers (C) and (D) may be ruled out immediately. Answers (A) and (B) convey very similar interpretations of the graph, so this question must center on subtle details of the two choices. The phrase "greater than" implies *more than* 25, but the middle bar of the second graph corresponds to a number of predators from 25 to 50—that is, 25 *or more*. Therefore, answer (B) more accurately describes the information in the graph than the underlined passage, in addition to complying more fully with conventions of standard written English. **The correct answer is (B).**

27. The sentence does not in any way require the word "thus," since the first part of the sentence has already cued the reader that a conclusion will be drawn in the second part. A word implying contrast would be completely inappropriate, which rules out answer choices (B) and (C). **The correct answer is (D).**

28. The word "voracious" means either desiring or consuming large quantities of food, so the word clearly fits with the meaning of the sentence. "Murderous" might be used poetically for the same purpose, but such usage would be inappropriate for a scientific article. **The correct answer is (A).**

29. The graphs have already made clear that the presence of large predators results in healthier forests, so it would be illogical to state that the "migratory grazing" behavior that herbivores develop when such predators are present damages the forests. The word "improves" simply and clearly conveys the author's intended meaning. **The correct answer is (C).**

30. The problem with the use of a general or demonstrative pronoun such as "them," "they," or "those" in this context is that the reader cannot be sure whom or what the pronoun represents. The predators? The forests? The scientists? A more specific phrase is needed, such as "that presence," which very clearly refers back to "the presence of large predators." **The correct answer is (D).**

31. The presence of the word "therefore" in the proposed addition is a cue that the new sentence should come immediately after a sentence that explains *why* the study results created a stir. Sentence

SAMPLE TEST 2
Answer Explanations

1 answers that question by explaining that scientists had previously underestimated the importance of large predator presence for forest health. **The correct answer is (B)**.

32. Answers choices (C) and (D) both fail to comply with the conventions of standard written English. The word "rising" is used incorrectly in answer (C) (the appropriate word would be *raising*), while the word "amount" is inappropriate in answer (D) (the appropriate word would be *number*). The phase "the increasing of numbers" has a reasonably clear meaning, but is an awkward construction for the reader to untangle. We simply need an answer choice that expresses the same idea in clearer language, without violating standard written English conventions. Therefore, **the correct answer is (B).**

33. The phrase "or riparian" has been included by the author to remind the reader that "near-river" and "riparian" are synonymous. Such a phrase may be set off either by commas or by dashes, but the *same* punctuation mark should be used at both ends of the phrase. This rule eliminates answers (A) and (B). In answer (D), the second comma comes to late. "Ecosystems" correctly completes both the phrase "near-river ecosystems" and the phrase "riparian ecosystems," and therefore should come *after* the commas or dashes that set off "or riparian." **The correct answer is (C).**

---

34. The phrase, "by which" would either be used indicate something in near proximity to the place just mentioned (western Kansas, in this case) or to signal a clarification or consequence of the previous statement. Since none of those situations applies here, the underlined phrase must be replaced. Both "whereupon" and "thereof" are decoys. The words "where" and there" can refer to location, which seems appropriate for the context. But the full words have meanings that wouldn't make sense in the sentence. For example, "whereupon" actually means "very soon after," a reference to time, not place. Thus, answers (A), (C), and (D) must all be eliminated. **The correct answer is (B).**

35. The entire phrase, "a vast region of which I had never laid eyes on a single square foot" serves as a supplemental phrase within the sentence. Therefore, it should be set off by commas at both ends. Since the phrase is already punctuated as required, no change is necessary. **The correct answer is (A).**

36. The context of the sentence makes clear that the needed word should emphasize that buying a home without even seeing it is not consistent with the author's usual, measured approach to life. Both "violation" and "departure" would emphasize the contrast between the author's normal habits and this specific decision. However, "violation *from*" is not a construction that complies with the conventions of standard written English ("violation *of*" would be the standard construction). Therefore, answer (C) must be eliminated, and **the correct answer is (D).**

37. The previous sentence states that landlords on the western plains are *suspicious* of outsiders, meaning that they do not view outsiders as trustworthy. The most logical answer choice, therefore, would be one that implies that the basis for this distrust is past experience with outsiders who did the landlords or townspeople harm. Answer (D) is the only choice fitting that description. **The correct answer is (D).**

38. This question deals with the distinction between "then," an adverb that can mean, among other things, "at that particular time," "after (X) occurred," or "for the reasons stated." The word "than" is most commonly used to introduce the second item in a comparison: "Everyone on the basketball team is taller than Joe." Since sentence 1 presents a comparison between life in the West and life in the East, "than" is the appropriate word to use before "in the East." There is no need for a comma before the word "than." **The correct answer is (C).**

39. The description of the Rhodes piano answers the question posed in the first half of the sentence, namely, *What did the author find in the attic?* So it is correct to use a colon. However, the word "besides" is unnecessary and distracting. The sentence would be improved by deleting that word. Therefore, **the correct answer is (B).**

40. The phrase "believing that" requires a subject (a person or other entity that holds the belief in question), which, based on the previous phrase, could either be "me" (the author) or the blog. We know that the author does not have the expertise to make the judgment described after the phrase "believing that," and obviously, a piano cannot "believe" anything. Rather, the author intends to associate the belief with Stephan Yorgerson. In order to make that connection, the author must add a pronoun to refer to Yorgerson. "He" is a pronoun, but using "he" would create two phrases that could stand as complete sentences:

"A little online research brought me to the blog of Stephan Yorgerson."

and

"He believes that within a few years, digital pianos will be able to perfectly replicate the sound of a vintage Rhodes, in addition to the sounds of thousands of other instruments."

To be combined as one sentence, these phrases would need to be separated by a semicolon rather than a comma. Therefore, answer (C) must be eliminated, leaving the options "who" and "whom" for the needed pronoun representing Yorgerson. Since the pronoun will function as the subject for the verb "believes," "who" is the proper choice. **The correct answer is (D).**

41. The reader cannot be expected to understand why selling the Rhodes and subsequently purchasing a digital instrument would be the "common sense decision" until he or she becomes aware of the information provided in sentences 7 and 8. Therefore, sentence 4 should come after both of those sentences. **The correct answer is (D).**

42. Context suggests that the underlined word is supposed to convey a meaning along the lines of "beliefs" or "assertions." Accusations and even, in certain contexts, admissions could be seen as types of assertions. However, the opinions attributed to Yorgerson in the previous paragraph are not well described by either of these words. The word "acclaims" is clearly inappropriate, since it implies enthusiastic praise, which definitely does not describe Yorgerson's statements. We have therefore ruled out answers (A), (C), and (D). **The correct answer is (B).**

43. There is no need for the word "also," since it would only serve the purpose already served by the word "and." The only non-redundant choice is answer (B). **The correct answer is (B).**

44. In effective writing, authors never introduce information "out of left field" in a concluding paragraph. Nowhere in the passage has the author given any indication that commercials had any influence on his feelings or actions. To suddenly introduce that topic while bringing the essay to a conclusion would only serve

to confuse the reader. Therefore, the author should NOT add the proposed sentence. However, the proposed sentence does not in any way contradict the previous sentence. Therefore, **the correct answer is (B).**

TEST SECTION 3: MATH—NO CALCULATOR

NOTE: Most problems in math can be solved using multiple different methods. In these explanations, the most standard methods taught in US middle school and high school mathematics are shown. You may have employed a different method that is equally valid.

1. Solving the given equation.

$$7x + 4 = 13 \quad \text{subtract 4 from both sides to get}$$
$$7x = 9 \quad \text{divide both sides by 9}$$
$$x = \frac{9}{7}$$

Therefore, $14x + 2 = 14(\frac{9}{7}) + 2 = 18 + 2 = 20$. **The correct answer is (D).**

2. Multiplying the top equation by 3 throughout yields the new system,

$$3x + 3y = 15$$
$$2x - 3y = 5$$

Adding the two equations yields $5x = 20$, or $x = 4$. This value may be substituted into either of the given equations to determine the value of y, but note that it is already clear that **the correct answer is (B).**

3. Imagine that the company rents just one laptop for one day. The cost would be $200 + 18(1)(1) = \$218$. If the company rents two laptops for one day, the cost would be $200 + 18(2)(1) = \$236$. On the other hand, if the company rents one laptop for two days, the cost would be $200 + 18(1)(2) = \$236$. Note that increasing either the number of laptops *or* the number of days by 1 increases the total cost by $18 (that is, $236 - 218$). Therefore, $18 must be the cost of one laptop for a single day. **The correct answer is (C).**

4. We substitute the value 5 in for w in the equation and solve for m:

$$\sqrt{3m^2 - 2} - 5 = 0 \quad \text{add 5 to both sides to get}$$
$$\sqrt{3m^2 - 2} = 5 \quad \text{square both sides to get}$$
$$3m^2 - 2 = 25 \quad \text{add 2 to both sides and divide both sides by 3 to get}$$
$$m^2 = 9 \quad \text{take the positive square root of both side (since m} > 0\text{) to get}$$
$$m = 3$$

The correct answer is (C).

5. Standard factoring techniques may be employed to determine the answer. Note, however, that answers (A) and (D) may be ruled out immediately, because $(16a^2)^2 = 256a^4$ and $(16a)^4 = 65{,}536\,a^4$, both of which fail to

SAMPLE TEST 2
Answer Explanations

match any term in the given expression. Therefore, this problem can also be solved by expanding answers (B) and (C) to determine which choice yields an expression matching the given one. Expanding answer (B) yields,

$$16a^4 + 4a^2b^2 + 4a^2b^2 + b^4 = 16a^4 + 8a^2b^2 + b^4,$$

so **the correct answer is (B).**

6. Applying exponent laws, we subtract the exponents that appear in the fraction. We then factor the resulting exponent:

$$y^{r^2 - q^2} = y^{(r+q)(r-q)}$$

Since this expression must equal y^{36}, we know that $(r + q)(r - q) = 36$. Since $r - q = 9$, we have $(r + q)(9) = 36$. Dividing both sides by 9 yields $r + q = 4$. **The correct answer is (A).**

7. Nonvertical lines that are parallel have equal slopes. We therefore apply the slope formula to each line, setting the results equal to each other:

$$\frac{y_2 - y_1}{x_2 - x_1} = \frac{-4 - 0}{0 - r} = \frac{0 - 3}{6 - 0} \quad \text{simplify to get}$$

$$\frac{4}{r} = \frac{-1}{2} \quad \text{now cross multiply to get}$$

$$8 = -1r, \text{ or, multiplying both sides by } -1, -8 = r.$$

The correct answer is (B).

8. First find the slope of the line through (2, –1) and (–1, 2):

$$\frac{y_2 - y_1}{x_2 - x_1} = \frac{2 - (-1)}{-1 - 2} = \frac{3}{-3} = -1$$

Next find an equation for each line. The first line has slope –3, so its equation is $y = -3x + b$. Substituting the coordinates of the point (–1, 8) into this equation yields, $8 = -3(-1) + b$, or $8 = 3 + b$, or $b = 5$. Therefore, the first line has equation, $y = -3x + 5$. The second line has slope –1 (see above), so its equation is $y = -x + b$. Substituting the coordinates of the point (2, –1) into this equation yields, $-1 = -2 + b$, or $b = 1$. Therefore, the second line has equation, $y = -x + 1$. To find the coordinates of the point of intersection, set the expressions for y from these two equations equal to each other:

$$-3x + 5 = -x + 1 \quad \text{add x to both sides to get}$$
$$-2x + 5 = 1 \quad \text{subtract 5 from both sides to get}$$
$$-2x = -4 \quad \text{divide both sides by } -2 \text{ to get}$$
$$x = 2$$

egghead prep.com

Therefore, the x-coordinate of the point of intersection is 2, and the y-coordinate (using the equation of the second line) is, –(2) + 1 = –1. Hence, the intersection point is (2, –1), and this is the point described as (b, c) in the problem. Finally, then, c – b = –1 – 2 = –3. **The correct answer is (A).**

9. If the number of prairie dogs, p, were exactly 80, then the number of quail, Q, would be simply 450 ÷ 80, or 5.625. (Clearly, that exact number of quail is impossible.) Since the number of prairie dogs is *less than* 80, the number of quail must be *greater than* the number we just found in order to keep the product, pQ, equal to 450. Therefore, the minimum number of quail is the smallest whole number *greater than* 5.625, which is 6. **The correct answer is (C).**

10. Note that if one plugs the value 0 in for y in any of the equations proposed in answers (A), (B), or (C), the resulting value is –3, which is *less than* –2. So those answers can be eliminated, leaving only answer (D). To confirm that answer (D) is correct, note that for any real number r, $|r| > 0$. Therefore, y will always be greater than zero in the equation proposed in answer (D), and hence certainly greater than or equal to –2. **The correct answer is (D).**

11. Since the problem states that M represents the number of vehicles, we must rearrange the equation to get M by itself:

$$L = \frac{M}{P - M}$$ multiply both sides by (P – M) to get

$$L(P - M) = M$$ use the distributive property to get

$$LP - LM = M$$ add LM to both sides so that M appears on only one side:

$$LP = LM + M$$ factor out an M on the right side to get

$$LP = M(L + 1)$$ divide both sides by L + 1 to get

$$\frac{LP}{L + 1} = M.$$

The correct answer is (A).

12. Multiply the numerator and denominator of the fraction by 6 – 2i, the complex conjugate of 6 + 2i, and simplify:

$$\frac{2 - 7i}{6 + 2i} \cdot \frac{6 - 2i}{6 - 2i} = \frac{12 - 4i - 42i + 14i^2}{36 - 12i + 12i - 4i^2}$$ use the fact that $i^2 = -1$:

$$= \frac{12 - 46i + 14(-1)}{36 - 4(-1)} = \frac{12 - 46i - 14}{36 + 4} = \frac{-2 - 46i}{40}$$

$$= \frac{-2}{40} - \frac{46}{40}i = \frac{-1}{20} - \frac{23}{20}i$$

The correct answer is (B).

SAMPLE TEST 2
Answer Explanations

13. Begin by factoring out a 3 to get, $3(x^2 + 5x - 8) = 0$, then divide both sides by 3 to get, $x^2 + 5x - 8 = 0$. Now use the quadratic formula:

$$x = \frac{-5 \pm \sqrt{5^2 - 4(1)(-8)}}{2(1)} = \frac{-5 \pm \sqrt{57}}{2}$$

The sum of the solutions is therefore,

$$\frac{-5 + \sqrt{57}}{2} + \frac{-5 - \sqrt{57}}{2} = \frac{-10}{2} = -5.$$

The correct answer is (A).

14. Perform the division:

$$\require{enclose}\begin{array}{r} 3 \\ x-2 \enclose{longdiv}{3x+7} \\ \underline{3x-6} \\ 13 \end{array}$$

Since the quotient is 3 and the remainder is 13, the expression may be written as in answer choice (D). **The correct answer is (D).**

15. Since the car loses 14.5% of its value each year, it *retains* 100% − 14.5% = 85.5% of its value each year. Therefore, in the exponential function equation, $g(t) = ab^t$, $b = 0.855$, while a has the initial value, 16,500. The resulting equation is, $g(t) = 16500(0.855)^t$. **The correct answer is (B).**

---

16. Simplify the left side of the equation by applying the distributive property and combining like terms:

$$3(2x^2 - 1) + 4x(2 + 3x) = ax^2 + bx + c$$
$$6x^2 - 3 + 8x + 12x^2 = ax^2 + bx + c$$
$$18x^2 + 8x - 3 = ax^2 + bx + c$$

In order for the equation to be true for all real values of x, the x^2-term on the left side must equal the x^2-term on the right side. In other words, $18 = a$. **The correct answer is 18.**

17. Draw a vertical segment from the point P down to the x-axis:

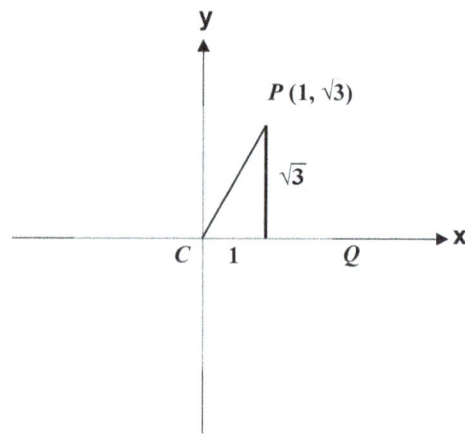

The resulting right triangle shows us that $\tan(\angle QCP) = \frac{\sqrt{3}}{1} = \sqrt{3}$. This value for the tangent function occurs for an angle of 60°, or $\pi/3$ radians. Therefore, n must equal 3. **The correct answer is 3.**

18. Let F equal the number of female wozzula bears and M the number of male wozzula bears in the park. The given information may be expressed as, $150F + 450M = 1800$. Rearrange the equation to get F by itself (because the problem asks for a possible number of *female* bears):

$150F + 450M = 1800$ divide all terms by 10 to simplify the equation   :

$15F + 45M = 180$ subtract $45M$ from both sides to get

$15F = 180 - 45M$ divide all terms by 15 to get F by itself   :

$F = 12 - 3M$

The following table shows the values of F corresponding to various values of M, according to the formula just derived.

M	F
1	9
2	6
3	3
4	0

Note that we start with the value $M = 1$ because we know there is at least one male bear in the park. And because we know there is also at least one female bear, the last row of the table may be disregarded. Therefore, the number of female bears, F, must be 3, 6, or 9. **Any of the numbers 3, 6, or 9 is a correct answer.**

SAMPLE TEST 2
Answer Explanations

19. The parallel segments ensure that alternate interior angle pairs ($\angle W$ and $\angle Z$, $\angle V$ and $\angle Y$) have equal measures. Therefore, the triangles are similar, with vertices corresponding according to the statement, D$WXV \sim$ DZXY. According to geometry principles for similar triangles, then,

$$\frac{WX}{ZX} = \frac{VX}{YX} \quad \text{plug in the known measurements to get}$$

$$\frac{7}{14} = \frac{9}{x} \quad \Rightarrow \quad \frac{1}{2} = \frac{9}{x}$$

Cross multiplication yields $x = 18$ for the length YX, or XY. Note that for our final answer, we want the length VY, and that $VY = VX + XY$. Therefore, $VY = 9 + 18 = 27$. **The correct answer is 27.**

20. For the system of equations to have infinitely many solutions, the two equations must be equivalent. Note that $45 \div 3 = 15$. Therefore, if the equations are equivalent, then dividing the entire first equation by 3 must yield the second equation. We therefore have,

$$\frac{3x}{3} + \frac{5y}{3} = \frac{45}{3} = 15, \quad \text{and this equation must be the same as,}$$

$cx + dy = 15$. In order for the equations to be the same, we must have

$\frac{3}{3} = c$ and $\frac{5}{3} = d$. That is, $c = 1$ and $d = \frac{5}{3}$. Therefore,

$$\frac{c}{d} = \frac{1}{\frac{5}{3}} = \frac{1}{1} \cdot \frac{3}{5} = \frac{3}{5}.$$

Therefore, $c / d = 3 / 5$. **The correct answer is 3/5 or 0.6.**

TEST SECTION 4: MATH—CALCULATOR

NOTE: Most problems in math can be solved using multiple different methods. In these explanations, the most standard methods taught in US middle school and high school mathematics are shown. You may have employed a different method that is equally valid.

1. The given information may be expressed as a proportion:

$$\frac{9}{300} = \frac{x}{18000}$$ Cross multiply to get

$$162,000 = 300x$$ Divide both sides by 300 to get

$$540 = x$$

The correct answer is (C).

2. The contextual information about the chemist and the dissolving solid is actually irrelevant to the mathematical issue of solving the problem. We simply plug 79 in for m in the equation and solve:

$$79 = 16 + 4.5q$$ subtract 16 from both sides to get

$$63 = 4.5q$$ divide both sides by 4.5 to get

$$14 = q$$

The correct answer is (C).

3. Since reading costs a customer $0.07, the amount of money collected if R articles are read is $0.07R$. Likewise, since printing costs a customer $0.33, the amount of money collected if P articles are printed is $0.33P$. Therefore, the total amount of money collected is $0.07R + 0.33P$. **The correct answer is (A).**

4. The given information may be expressed as the equation, $7 - 3n = 19$. Subtracting 7 from both sides yields $-3n = 12$. Dividing both sides by -3 gives the result, $n = -4$. This, however, is NOT the final answer! The second sentence of the problem states that we now must calculate the value of $10 + 2n$, which is $10 + 2(-4) = 10 - 8 = 2$. **The correct answer is (C).**

5. The *factored* form of the equation of a parabola, $y = a(x - r)(x - s)$, displays the two x-intercepts, namely, r and s. Only answer (B) is in this form. **The correct answer is (B).**

6. The given information may be expressed as the equation, $D = kC$, where D is the decibel level, C is the number of children present, and k is a constant. Since the decibel level is 84 when 7 children are present, we have, $84 = k(7)$. Dividing both sides by 7 yields $12 = k$. Our equation is now, $D = 12C$. (Since k is a constant, its value cannot change once that value has been determined.) Therefore, if 10 children are present, $D = 12(10) = 120$. **The correct answer is (B).**

7. Since 73% of the noise is caused by talking, laughing, and yelling, 100% − 73% = 27% must be caused by foot-stomping and toy sounds. We already know that with 7 children present, the decibel

SAMPLE TEST 2
Answer Explanations

level of the noise is 84. Therefore, the number of decibels attributable to foot-stomping and toy noises is 27% of 84, which is 0.27(84) = 22.68. **The correct answer is (D).**

8. Since L and P represent the numbers of the two types of bags, and the total number of bags must be less than or equal to 25, we have the inequality, $L + P \leq 25$. This fact alone eliminates answers (C) and (D). To get the total weight of the letters and packages, we should *multiply* the number of bags of each type by the weight of such bags. This multiplication creates the expression, $45L + 70P$. This total weight must be less than or equal to 1,400 pounds, hence the inequality, $45L + 70P \leq 1,400$. **The correct answer is (A).**

9. Since a player starts a game with N power points and gains 4 more power points for each completed journey, the player's total number of points after J journeys would be $N + 4J$. We are told that with 40 journeys completed, this total is 760. This information gives us the equation, $N + 4(40) = 760$, which simplifies to $N + 160 = 760$. Subtracting 160 from both sides yields the answer, $N = 600$. **The correct answer is (B).**

10. The tricky part about this problem is that the table includes a large amount of information that is not needed to solve the problem. The relevant information is that Jenai works three 8-hour days each week and can process 37 orders per hour. Three 8-hour days equals 24 total hours, so in one week, Jenai processes 37(24) = 888 orders. The total number of orders she must process is 9,582, so it will take Jenai 9,582 ÷ 888 = 10.79 weeks to process all the orders. This number is much closer to 11 than to any other answer choice. **The correct answer is (A).**

11. To evaluate $g(f(4))$, we start with the *inside* expression. We therefore begin by evaluating $f(4)$, which we have been told equals 5. The problem now reduces to evaluating $g(5)$, which we have been told equals –1. **The correct answer is (C).**

12. The number of people who refused to respond (4) is quite small in comparison to the number of people who were asked to participate in the survey (83). Therefore, non-participation bias is not an issue, and answer (B) can be eliminated. The size of a population is not a reasonable basis for an objection to the results of a survey, since that element is beyond the researcher's control. And given that Coos Bay is described as a small town, it is reasonable to assume that 83 is a sample size that is neither too small nor too large. We have thus ruled out answers (A) and (C), leaving only answer (D). The reason answer (D) makes sense is that the researcher asked her question only of people who were hiking on a trail called the Bay View Trail. It is reasonable to suspect that people who make frequent use of that trail would be more likely to object to anything that obstructs residents' view of the bay than people who do not hike the trail. Therefore, due to the location at which the survey was conducted, the sample may not accurately represent the town as a whole. **The correct answer is (D).**

13. First notice that the graph contains a point very close to (5500, 1985). Therefore, the answer is either (C) or (D). Now notice that the line of best fit actually intersects the horizontal gridline corresponding to 5,500 television sets owned slight *before* crossing the vertical gridline corresponding to the year 1985. Therefore, the answer should be a year slightly *before* 1985. **The correct answer is (C).**

14. The number 43 is the *initial value* for the number of herons. In a model of the form, $mx + b$, the initial value is the number b. The population increase of 8 herons per year is a *rate*, represented by the number m in the above expression. Therefore, a correct model for the heron population is, $8Y + 43$. We want this number to be "at or below," in other words, *less than or equal to* the ceiling, which is 70. From all of this information, we generate the inequality, $8Y + 43 \leq 70$. **The correct answer is (B).**

15. This problem can be readily solved using the unit conversion methods taught in chemistry and physics classes. The given information tells us that the moon travels at a rate of 1,500,000 miles per 27 days. The conversion proceeds as follows.

$$\frac{1,500,000 \text{ miles}}{27 \text{ days}} \cdot \frac{1 \text{ day}}{24 \text{ hours}} = \frac{1,500,000(1) \text{ miles}}{27(24) \text{ hours}} = \frac{1,500,000 \text{ miles}}{648 \text{ hours}}$$

$$\approx \frac{2,314.8 \text{ miles}}{1 \text{ hour}}$$

This result is very close to answer choice (D). **The correct answer is (D).**

16. Since the length of a Davidson boat is 30% *less than* that of a Wattleford boat, the length of the Davidson boat is 100% − 30% = 70% of the length of a Wattleford boat. Therefore, the length of a Davidson boat is 70% of 50, which is 0.70(50) = 35 meters. **The correct answer is (C).**

17. The last column of the table represents players who did not pass the quiz, so the total number of such players is 5 + 16 = 21. Of those, only 5 brought the playbook home. Therefore, the desired probability is 5 / 21. **The correct answer is (B).**

18. It is always important to remember that the mean of a data set is much more affected by outliers than is the median. Since the mean is far below the median for the data set described, it is reasonable to conclude that there must be outliers at the *low* end of the data set. This logic suggests the existence of towns with very small populations. Therefore, **the correct answer is (A).**

19. The median is the *middle number* (or average of the pair of middle numbers) in a data set. We know that the total number of children surveyed was 400 (200 from each camp). Therefore, if we start from the top of the table, we will reach the median as soon as the totals of the numbers in the columns for Camp Happy and Camp Joyous exceeds 200 (half of 400). The first row gives us 30 + 40 = 70 children. Adding the second row to this total, we get 70 + 80 + 90 = 240 children, a number greater than 200. Therefore, we have already reached the median in the second row of data, which corresponds to 1 pet owned. **The correct answer is (D).**

SAMPLE TEST 2
Answer Explanations

20. For Camp Happy, 50 of the 200 *surveyed* children owned 2 pets. There were 1,800 children at the camp. This information can be expressed as a proportion that can be solved to find the expected number of children at the camp with two pets.

$$\frac{50}{200} = \frac{H}{1,800} \quad \text{cross multiply to get}$$

$90,000 = 200H$ divide both sides by 200 to get

$450 = H$,   which is the expected number of children with 2 pets at Camp Happy.

Similarly, 50 out of the 200 *surveyed* children at Camp Joyous owned 2 pets, and there were 1,400 children at the camp:

$$\frac{50}{200} = \frac{J}{1,400}$$

$70,000 = 50J$

$350 = J$,   which is the expected number of children with 2 pets at Camp Joyous.

Therefore, the expected number is higher by 100 (450 – 350) at Camp Happy. **The correct answer is (D).**

21. The equation, $(x – h)^2 + (y – k)^2 = r^2$ represents a circle with center (h, k) and radius r. We must transform the given equation into this form through the process called *completing the square*.

$$x^2 + y^2 - 6x + 4y = 12$$
$$x^2 - 6x + y^2 + 4y = 12$$
$$(x^2 - 6x + 9) + (y^2 + 4y + 4) = 12 + 9 + 4$$
$$(x - 3)^2 + (y + 2)^2 = 25$$

Comparing the final line to the general equation given above, we see that $r^2 = 25$, so $r = 5$. **The correct answer is (B).**

22. We must rearrange the equation to isolate the expression q^2.

$$E = \frac{N}{3q^2} \quad \text{multiply both sides by} \quad 3q^2 \text{ to get} \quad 3q^2 E = N.$$

Dividing both sides by 3 and by E yields, $q^2 = \frac{N}{3E}$.

The correct answer is (B).

23. Because we are assuming the two installations have the same number N of Quasmatrons, we can choose the simplest possible number for N, namely, 1. Since installation I has 9 times the energy output of installation II, let's say for simplicity that the energy output of installation II is 1 unit, so that the output from installation I is 9 units. We therefore have, for installation I, $E = 9$ and $N = 1$. Use the equation found in problem #22 to find the value of q for this installation:

$$q^2 = \frac{1}{3(9)} = \frac{1}{27} \quad \Rightarrow \quad q = \sqrt{\frac{1}{27}} \approx 0.19245.$$

For installation II, $E = 1$ and $N = 1$, so

$$q^2 = \frac{1}{3(1)} = \frac{1}{3} \quad \Rightarrow \quad q = \sqrt{\frac{1}{3}} = 0.57735.$$

Therefore, the fraction in question is $\frac{0.19245}{0.57735} \approx .33333\ldots = 1/3$. **The correct answer is (C).**

24. In order for the manager to receive the bonus, the quantities h and w must <u>differ</u> by no more than 8. We find the difference by subtracting the two quantities and taking the absolute value of the result. Therefore, one way to express this relationship is the absolute value inequality, $|w - h| < 8$. Algebra rules dictate that this inequality may be rewritten as $-8 < |w - h| < 8$. **The correct answer is (B).**

25. The graph shows that $f(x) = 3$ (that is, the y-coordinate equals 3) for any x value from -2 to 2, as well as for one x value slightly greater than 4. The x values -1 and 0.5 are within the interval, $-2 \geq x \leq 2$, but the x value 3 is not. Therefore, choices II and III are correct, but choice I is incorrect. **The correct answer is (C).**

26. Careful study of the graph reveals that the curve suggested by the gray hexagons (representing the population of deer that received feed piles) climbs more steeply than the curve suggested by the black circles (representing the population that did not receive feed piles) for about the first 40 months. Therefore, the rate of change of population was greater for the deer that received feed piles than for those that didn't over the time interval from 0 to 40 months. Between 80 and 120 months, however, the curve suggested by the black circles climbs more steeply than the one suggested by the gray hexagons. Hence, for the interval from 80 to 120 months, the rate of change of population was greater for the deer that did *not* receive feed piles than for the deer that received feed piles. Only answer (D) accurately summarizes these conclusions. **The correct answer is (D).**

27. Notice first that the statement, $r - w = 0$, can be rewritten (by adding w to both sides) as, $r = w$. Therefore, we may replace w with r throughout the problem. We now find the slope between the two points, $(r, 0)$ and $(0, r)$.

$$\frac{y_2 - y_1}{x_2 - x_1} = \frac{r - 0}{0 - r} = \frac{r}{-r} = -1$$

Therefore, the slope is negative. **The correct answer is (A).**

SAMPLE TEST 2
Answer Explanations

P. 219

28. First, rewrite the second equation with x by itself (subtract cy^2 from both sides): $x = -cy^2 + d$. This equation represents a parabola with a horizontal axis of symmetry and its vertex at $(d, 0)$. The parabola will open to the right if $-c > 0$, that is, if $c < 0$. It will open to the left if $-c < 0$, that is, $c > 0$. Meanwhile, the equation $x = 5$ represents a vertical line crossing the x-axis at $(5, 0)$. In order for the parabola to cross this vertical line twice, we need one of the following two statements to be true:

I. The vertex of the parabola, $(d, 0)$, is to the *left* of $(5, 0)$ and the parabola opens to the *right*. In other words, $d < 5$ and $c < 0$.

–OR–

II. The vertex of the parabola, $(d, 0)$, is to the *right* of $(5, 0)$ and the parabola opens to the *left*. In other words, $d > 5$ and $c > 0$.

Answer choice (D) satisfies the conditions of statement II. No other answer choice satisfies the condition of either statement I or statement II. **The correct answer is (D).**

29. This problem contains a great deal of unneeded information. In order to write the equation of the line through R and T, we simply need the coordinates of those two points. From the graph, we can tell that the coordinates of R are $(-5, 2)$ and those of T are $(3, 4)$. Now find the slope between these two points:

$$\frac{y_2 - y_1}{x_2 - x_1} = \frac{4 - 2}{3 - (-5)} = \frac{2}{8} = \frac{1}{4}$$

We now know that the equation of the line takes the form, $y = \frac{1}{4}x + b$. Plug in the coordinates of either point R or point T for x and y to solve for b. Let's use the coordinates of T, $(3, 4)$.

$$4 = \frac{1}{4}(3) + b \quad \Rightarrow \quad 4 = \frac{3}{4} + b \quad \text{now get a common denominator}$$

$$\frac{16}{4} = \frac{3}{4} + b \quad \text{subtract } \frac{3}{4} \text{ from both sides to get}$$

$$\frac{13}{4} = b$$

The correct answer is (B).

eggheadprep.com

30. Here is the figure with the given length marked and auxiliary segments added.

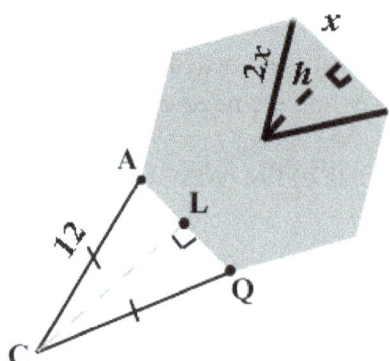

Notice that the added triangle is equilateral with sides of length $2x$. The interior of the hexagon is composed of six such triangles. Use the Pythagorean Theorem to express h in terms of x.

$$x^2 + h^2 = (2x)^2 \implies x^2 + h^2 = 4x^2 \quad \text{subtract } x^2 \text{ from both sides}$$
$$h^2 = 3x^2 \quad \text{take positive square roots on both sides to get}$$
$$h = \sqrt{3}x$$

Therefore, the area of the equilateral triangle is $\frac{1}{2}(base)(height) = \frac{1}{2}(2x)(\sqrt{3}x) = \sqrt{3}x^2$.

Since we know that six such triangles make up the interior of the hexagon, and that the interior has an area of $54\sqrt{3}$, we can solve for x.

$$6(\sqrt{3}x^2) = 54\sqrt{3} \quad \text{divide both sides by } \sqrt{3} \text{ to get}$$
$$6x^2 = 54 \quad \text{divide both sides by 6 to get}$$
$$x^2 = 9 \implies x = 3.$$

Using the symmetry of the hexagon, we now know that the length AL is also 3 and the length AQ, the base of triangle AQC, is 6. Use the Pythagorean Theorem again to solve for the length LC.

$$3^2 + LC^2 = 12^2 \implies 9 + LC^2 = 144 \implies LC^2 = 135$$
$$LC = \sqrt{135} = \sqrt{9} \cdot \sqrt{15} = 3\sqrt{15}$$

Finally, the area of triangle AQC is found by using the length AQ as the base and the length LC as the height in the calculation,

$$\frac{1}{2}(base)(height) = \frac{1}{2}(6)(3\sqrt{15}) = 9\sqrt{15} \text{ square cm.}$$

The correct answer is (C).

SAMPLE TEST 2
Answer Explanations

31. Since a minute is equal to 60 seconds, m minutes is $60m$ seconds. Therefore, the given information may be expressed as the equation, $60m + 40 = 520$. Subtracting 40 from both sides yields, $60m = 480$. Dividing both sides by 60 gives us $m = 8$. **The correct answer is 8.**

32. If the tree grows 0.25 feet per year, that means it will grow $0.25y$ feet in y years. The problem can therefore be expressed as the equation, $0.25y = 11$. Dividing both sides by 0.25 gives us $y = 44$. **The correct answer is 44.**

33. Let T be the number of hours Terrence worked at the car wash and F the number of hours Felicia worked. The given information may be translated into the equations, $F = T + 60$ and $F + T = 400$. We use the first equation to substitute for F in the second equation, giving us, $(T + 60) + T = 400$. Combining like terms yields, $2T + 60 = 400$. Subtracting 60 from both sides, we get $2T = 340$. Dividing both sides by 2, we find that $T = 170$, so Terrence worked for 170 hours. **The correct answer is 170.**

34. Since the graph of any function is based on the relationship, $y = f(x)$, we may replace $f(x)$ in the given equation with y, giving us $y = 2x^2 + bx + 27$. Now plug in the given coordinates (–3, 3) for x and y and solve for b.

$$3 = -2(-3)^2 + b(-3) + 27 \implies 3 = -2(9) - 3b + 27$$
$$3 = -18 - 3b + 27 \implies 3 = 9 - 3b$$
$$-6 = -3b \implies 2 = b$$

The correct answer is 2.

35. It is necessary to find the measure of angle C. The measure of angle D, $\pi/3$ radians, equates to 60°. We know angles A and B are right angles, because a tangent to a circle is always perpendicular to the radius with which it intersects. The angles of quadrilateral $ACBD$ must add up to 360° because any quadrilateral can be divided into two triangles, each of which has an angle sum of 180°. We therefore have, $90 + 60 + 90 + m\angle C = 360$, or $240 + m\angle C = 360$, or $m\angle C = 120°$. We now use the geometry formula for arc length.

$$\text{Length} = \frac{\text{measure of central angle}}{360}(\text{circumference})$$
$$\text{Length} = \frac{120}{360}(84) = 28 \text{ meters}$$

The correct answer is 28.

36. We are looking for the *rate of change* of the number of shells (in shells per year), which should be found in the "m" position of an equation in the form, $y = mx + b$. The number in that position in the equation, $S = 25Y + 43$, is 25. **The correct answer is 25.**

eggheadprep.com

37. Since we know there are currently 200 robots, the value of $N_{\text{this month}}$ is 200. We plug this value, along with the specified value for M, 700, into the given formula:

$$N_{\text{next month}} = 200 + (0.15)(200)\left(\frac{700 - 200}{700}\right)$$

$$= 200 + 30\left(\frac{5}{7}\right) = 221.428\ldots$$

The correct answer is 221.

38. This problem asks us to solve for M, given that $N_{\text{this month}} = 200$ and $N_{\text{next month}}$ is to be 225. Plug these values into the given formula and solve for M.

$$225 = 200 + 0.15(200)\left(\frac{M - 200}{M}\right)$$

$$225 = 200 + 30\left(\frac{M - 200}{M}\right) \quad \text{subtract 200 from both sides to get}$$

$$25 = 30\left(\frac{M - 200}{M}\right) \quad \text{divide both sides by 30,} \quad \text{then multiply both sides by M}$$

$$0.8333\ldots = \frac{M - 200}{M}$$

$$0.8\overline{3}M = M - 200 \quad \text{subtract M from both sides,} \quad \text{then divide by} \quad -1.\overline{6}$$

$$-0.1\overline{6}M = -200$$

$$M = 1200$$

The correct answer is 1200.

SCORING CONVERSION
RAW TO SCALED SCORE CONVERSION CHARTS

Sample Test 2:

A. SECTION 1: Conversion Chart for Reading Test:

RAW SCORE (# of correct answers)	READING TEST SCORE		RAW SCORE (# of correct answers)	READING TEST SCORE
0	10		27	25
1	10		28	26
2	10		29	27
3	11		30	27
4	12		31	28
5	13		32	28
6	14		33	29
7	15		34	29
8	15		35	30
9	16		36	30
10	17		37	31
11	18		38	31
12	18		39	32
13	19		40	32
14	19		41	33
15	20		42	33
16	20		43	34
17	21		44	34
18	21		45	35
19	22		46	35
20	22		47	36
21	23		48	37
22	23		49	37
23	24		50	38
24	24		51	39
25	24		52	40
26	25			

eggheadprep.com

B. SECTION 2: Conversion Chart for Writing and Language Test

RAW SCORE (# of correct answers)	WRITING AND LANGUAGE TEST SCORE		RAW SCORE (# of correct answers)	WRITING AND LANGUAGE TEST SCORE
0	10		23	25
1	10		24	25
2	10		25	26
3	11		26	26
4	12		27	27
5	13		28	27
6	14		29	28
7	14		30	29
8	15		31	29
9	16		32	30
10	17		33	31
11	17		34	31
12	18		35	32
13	18		36	33
14	19		37	33
15	20		38	34
16	20		39	35
17	21		40	36
18	22		41	37
19	22		42	38
20	23		43	39
21	23		44	40
22	24			

C. Evidence-Based Reading and Writing Section Score

To calculate the Evidence-Based Reading and Writing Section Score, add the Reading Test Score (10 – 40) to the Writing and Language Test Score (10 – 40), and then multiply that total by 10.

For example, if the Reading Test Score is 27 and the Writing and Language Test Score is 34, then the Evidence-Based Reading and Writing Section Score is,

$$27 + 34 = 61 \times 10 = 610.$$

SAMPLE TEST 2
Scoring Conversion

D. Sections 3 and 4: Math Test Score

The raw scores from Section 3 (Math—No Calculator) and Section 4 (Math—Calculator) should be added together to create the Math Raw Score. For example, if there were 18 correct answers in Section 3 (Math—No Calculator) and 24 in Section 4 (Math—Calculator), the Math Raw Score would be 18 + 24 = 42.

MATH RAW SCORE (Total # of correct answers, Sections 3 and 4 combined)	MATH SECTION SCORE		MATH RAW SCORE (Total # of correct answers, Sections 3 and 4 combined)	MATH SECTION SCORE
0	200		30	550
1	200		31	560
2	210		32	570
3	230		33	570
4	250		34	580
5	270		35	590
6	290		36	600
7	300		37	610
8	320		38	620
9	330		39	630
10	340		40	640
11	360		41	650
12	370		42	650
13	380		43	660
14	390		44	670
15	400		45	680
16	420		46	690
17	430		47	690
18	440		48	700
19	450		49	710
20	460		50	720
21	470		51	730
22	480		52	740
23	490		53	750
24	500		54	760
25	510		55	770
26	510		56	780
27	520		57	790
28	530		58	800
29	540			

eggheadprep.com

SAMPLE TEST 3

Including...

- ▶ SECTION 1: READING TEST — 228
- ▶ ANSWERS, SECTION 1 — 245
- ▶ SECTION 2: WRITING & LANGUAGE TEST — 246
- ▶ ANSWERS, SECTION 2 — 263
- ▶ SECTION 3: MATH TEST — 264
- ▶ ANSWERS, SECTION 3 — 270
- ▶ SECTION 4: MATH TEST — 271
- ▶ ANSWERS, SECTION 4 — 283
- ▶ ANSWER EXPLANATIONS — 284
- ▶ SCORING CONVERSION — 318

eggheadprep.com

SECTION 1: READING TEST

65 MINUTES, 52 QUESTIONS

DIRECTIONS

Each group of questions below is based on a passage or pair of passages. Read each passage carefully, then choose the best answer to each question based on what is stated in or suggested by the passage(s). The questions may also refer to any graphical displays that accompany the passage(s), such as tables or graphs.

Questions 1-11 are based on the following passage.

This passage is adapted from Emma, *by Jane Austen.*

Emma Woodhouse, handsome, clever, and rich, with a comfortable home and happy disposition, seemed to unite some of the best blessings of existence, and had lived nearly twenty-one years in
5   the world with very little to vex her.
   She was the younger of two daughters of a most affectionate, indulgent father, and had, in consequence of her sister's marriage, been mistress of his house from a very early period. Her mother had
10 died too long ago for her to have more than an indistinct remembrance of her caresses; her presence had been supplied by an excellent woman as governess, who had fallen little short of a mother in affection.
15 Sixteen years had Miss Taylor been in Mr. Woodhouse's family, less as a governess than a friend, very fond of both daughters, but particularly of Emma. Even before Miss Taylor had ceased to hold the nominal office of governess, the mildness of her
20 temper had hardly allowed her to impose any restraint. And the shadow of authority now long passed away, they had been living together as friend and friend very mutually attached, with Emma doing just what she liked—highly esteeming Miss Taylor's
25 judgment, but directed by her own.
   The real evils, indeed, of Emma's situation were the power of having rather too much her own way, and a disposition to think a little too well of herself; these were the disadvantages which threatened to
30 alloy her many enjoyments. The danger, however, was at present so unperceived, that it did not by any means rank as misfortune with her.
   Sorrow came, a gentle sorrow, but not at all in the shape of any disagreeable consciousness. Miss Taylor
35 married. It was on the wedding day of this beloved friend that Emma first sat in mournful thought of any continuance. The wedding over, her father and her were left to dine together, with no prospect of a third to cheer the long evening. Her father composed
40 himself to sleep after dinner, and she had then only to sit and think of what she had lost.
   The event had every promise of happiness for her friend. Mr. Weston was a man of exceptional character, easy fortune, suitable age, and pleasant
45 manners. And there was some satisfaction in considering with what self-denying, generous friendship she had always wished and promoted the match, but it was a black morning's work for her. The want of Miss Taylor would be felt every hour of
50 every day. She recalled her past kindness, how she had taught and how she had played with her from five years old, how she had devoted all her powers to amuse her in health, and to nurse her through the illnesses of childhood. A large debt of gratitude was
55 owed here; but the intercourse of the last seven years, the equal footing and perfect unreserve which had soon followed Isabella's marriage, upon their being left to each other, was yet a dearer, tenderer recollection. She had been a friend and companion
60 such as few possessed: intelligent, well-informed, useful, and peculiarly interested in Emma herself, in every pleasure, every scheme of hers.
   How was she to bear the change? It was true that her friend was going only half a mile from them, but
65 Emma was aware that great must be the difference between a Mrs. Weston, a half mile away, and a

Miss Taylor in the house. With all her advantages, natural and domestic, she was now in great danger of suffering from intellectual solitude. She dearly loved
70 her father, but he was no companion for her. He could not meet her in conversation, rational or playful.
   The evil of the actual disparity in their ages (and Mr. Woodhouse had not married early) was much increased by his constitution and habits—for, having
75 been a valetudinarian all his life, refraining from any strenuous activity of mind or body, he was a much older man in ways than in years. And though everywhere beloved for the friendliness of his heart and his amiable temper, his talents could not have
80 recommended him at any time.
   Highbury, the large and populous village, almost amounting to a town, to which Hartfield did really belong, afforded her no equals. She had many acquaintances in the place, for her father was
85 universally civil, but not one among them who could be accepted in lieu of Miss Taylor for even half a day. It was a melancholy change, one Emma could not but sigh over, and wish for impossible things till her father awoke and made it necessary to be cheerful. He
90 was a nervous man, easily depressed; fond of everybody that he was used to, and hating to part with them—hating, in fact, change of any kind.

1. Which of the following is the best description of the passage?
   A) A young woman offers a critique of the institution of marriage.
   B) A young woman ponders her prospects after a major change in her circumstances.
   C) A young woman grieves as she remembers her deceased mother.
   D) The narrator describes a small town and the way distance affects the relationships between the townspeople.

2. As used in line 12, "supplied" most nearly means
   A) equipped.
   B) provided.
   C) replaced.
   D) recalled.

3. The passage most clearly implies that Emma was
   A) willful.
   B) naive.
   C) pessimistic.
   D) unreliable.

4. Which option provides the strongest evidence in support of the answer to the previous question?
   A) Lines 1-5 ("Emma … her.")
   B) Lines 23-27 ("with Emma … way.")
   C) Lines 36-37 ("Emma … continuance.")
   D) Lines 67-69 ("With all … solitude.")

5. As used in line 30, "alloy" most nearly means
   A) blend.
   B) exaggerate.
   C) accompany.
   D) impair.

6. The main purpose of the third paragraph (lines 15-25) is
   A) to show that "governess" is an empty title that doesn't give a person any real authority.
   B) to discuss the importance of restraining one's temper.
   C) to show that a governess often has a closer relationship with a young girl than her parents do.
   D) to establish the depth and duration of the friendship between two of the main characters.

7. What does the passage show about Emma's attitude toward Miss Taylor's wedding?
   A) She believes her friend has made a grave mistake that will cause her great suffering.
   B) She believes her friend will be happy, but is uncomfortable with the custom that requires her to change her name.
   C) She advocated for the marriage and believes it will work out well, but fears a life without having her best friend readily available to her.
   D) She is unhappy about the wedding because she will now have to bear all the burden of caring for her father and buoying his spirits.

8. What primary meaning is conveyed by lines 72-77 ("The evil ... years.")?
   A) Emma's father's cautiousness had resulted in him living in a manner befitting of someone much older than he actually was.
   B) Emma's father had a sinister side that caused him to look more advanced in years than his way of life would have suggested.
   C) Emma's father had developed a number of bad habits that would likely shorten his life by many years.
   D) Emma's father was often viewed in a negative light because he waited so many years to get married.

9. As presented in the passage, Emma's father is best described as
   A) Stern and unyielding, with little interest in conversation.
   B) Kind-hearted and gentle, but lacking any truly impressive qualities.
   C) Cold and distant, but deeply passionate about his beliefs.
   D) Calm and composed, even under very trying circumstances.

10. Which choice provides the strongest evidence in support of the answer to the previous question?
    A) Lines 37-41 ("The wedding ... lost.")
    B) Lines 72-74 ("The evil ... habits—")
    C) Lines 77-80 ('And though ... time.")
    D) Lines 83-85 ("She had ... civil,")

11. What possible connection exists between the fourth paragraph (lines 26-32) and the last paragraph (lines 81- 92)?
    A) The "unperceived" dangers threatening Emma that are mentioned in the fourth paragraph may be a result of the growing size of the town in which she lives.
    B) The fact that Emma perceived no misfortune in her situation, as described in the fourth paragraph, will make it easier for her to be cheerful for her father's sake.
    C) Since Emma has many acquaintances because of her father, she will not have to face the dangers hinted at in the fourth paragraph alone.
    D) Together, the two paragraphs suggests that Emma's arrogance may hinder her ability to make new friends after Miss Taylor's departure.

Questions 12-21 are based on the following passage about a fictional business venture.

If You Didn't Watch It, You Missed It!

A great many people today would be hard pressed to remember the last time they went even two full days without accessing the internet. Yet although those living in such a privileged state would struggle to
[5] believe it, well over half of people living today do not have access to the worldwide web. Television ownership continues to rise around the globe, however, meaning that in many places, watching TV programs live as they are broadcast remains the norm. How
[10] strange that thought must seem to North American Millennials, who consume almost all of their favorite shows solely through online streaming services.

In the eyes of many who live in wealthy nations, planning one's viewing around a preset broadcast
[15] schedule is an amusingly antiquated notion. Their feelings are not unfounded: traditional TV network schedules were based on the assumption of a 40-hour work week, an almost laughable proposition in an era when many Americans work multiple jobs totaling 55
[20] or more hours per week just to make ends meet. Streaming allows people to create their own "broadcast" schedules built around their scant leisure time. Watching television in the traditional way also requires planting oneself in a single room for an hour or
[25] more, an utterly foreign concept to many people today. And if that block of time should be interrupted by an important phone call right at the moment of the show's big reveal, the entire experience can be ruined. Given the choice, surely almost all people would opt to stream
[30] their entertainment. Watching on a tablet or smartphone frees the viewer up to tackle chores all over the house without missing a moment. Furthermore, the mere presence of that precious pause button, with its power to eliminate any worry of an unwelcome intrusion
[35] drowning out the best part of the show, would appear to be enough to tip the scales in favor of streaming once and for all.

Entrepreneur Andrew Bennett of Philadelphia isn't so sure about that, however. Bennett spent much of
[40] 2013 and 2014 traveling abroad, and returned home convinced that traditional television viewing offers rewards that on-demand streaming simply cannot match. "All over the world," he observes, "I saw people gathered around TV sets, watching with a shared
[45] excitement, an electricity in the air, that I haven't experienced in my own country since I was a young child in the 1970s." That realization got him thinking about the inherent intensity of now-or-never experiences. The thrill of riding a roller coaster lies in
[50] the finality of that moment when the safety bars lock down and the cars lurch into motion. Imagine the adrenaline loss if riders had a pause button at their disposal. And what magic would there be in watching an eagle suddenly dive out of the sky to catch a fish if
[55] one could simply turn away with a shrug, secure in the knowledge that the experience could be repeated any time?

Early in 2015, Bennett put ideas into action by
[60] founding the Now or Never (NoN) television network. The network offers just seven hours of programming per day, all of it on a strict schedule, and all of it centered on live events occurring at the very moment they are aired. None of the programs are made available
[65] to online streaming services, and every broadcast is transmitted with an encoded signal that thwarts any effort to capture the show on a DVR for later viewing. Programs include rare music and dance events, such as a remarkable, one-night-only joint performance by
[70] operatic tenor David Connelly and former Alvin Ailey Company lead dancer Cheryl Bates Monroe; compelling conversations with scientists, authors, and visual artists; and lively debates about important issues like global climate change.

[75] A year of abysmal ratings and little or no advertiser support brought Bennett a seemingly endless stream of messages from friends and family inquiring as to whether he had lost his grip on reality. The tide appears to have turned with the dawn of 2016, however, with
[80] viewership of NoN climbing by over two million per month. Ironically, the growing success of the network has been bolstered greatly by the internet itself. Suddenly, gathering up one's social network buddies for a "virtual viewing party," during which everyone
[85] watches a NoN broadcast and shares the excitement of every moment by participating in a chat or video call, is all the rage. Not surprisingly, older viewers, who have not embraced the streaming lifestyle in significant numbers, love the new network as well. Bennett's own
[90] generation, Generation X, is the demographic most resistant to the concept thus far. But with all signs indicating that the hunger for one-time-only entertainment is alive and well, Bennett believes that winning over his peers is, appropriately enough, just a
[95] matter of time.

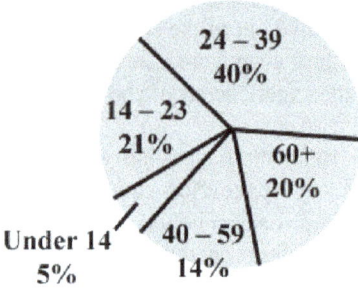

Figure 1: Ages of NoN Viewers in the U.S.

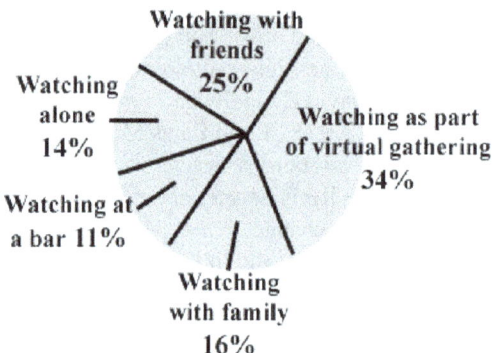

Figure 2: Viewer's Social Environment While Watching NoN

12. What is the primary purpose of the second paragraph (lines 13-37)?
   A) It identifies the questions that the experts mentioned in the article refused to address.
   B) It points out the reasons why people might not embrace the concept behind the venture described in the article.
   C) It provides specific illustrations related to data presented in the previous paragraph.
   D) It analyzes the worldwide wealth gap and its effect on the global economy.

13. Which of the following is NOT a reason that the author explicitly presents to explain why people prefer streaming shows over watching live TV broadcasts?
   A) the incompatibility of broadcast schedules with the work schedules of many North Americans
   B) the ability to pause a show and resume watching after an interruption
   C) the option of skipping over commercials if one pays a subscription fee
   D) the inconvenience of remaining in one place throughout a live broadcast

14. As used in line 22, "scant" most nearly means
   A) limited
   B) hectic
   C) excessive
   D) relaxing

15. The main idea of the third paragraph (lines 38-57) is that
   A) world travel can help a person understand other cultures.
   B) Americans have more of a thrill-seeking nature than people of many other cultures.
   C) in some respects, traditional television viewing is better than streaming shows online.
   D) the amount of time North Americans spend online has resulted in a loss of contact with nature.

SAMPLE TEST 3
Section 1: Reading Test

16. Which choice provides the clearest evidence in support of the answer to the previous question?

    A) Lines 38-40 ("Entrepreneur … abroad.")
    B) Lines 43-47 ("All over … 1970s.")
    C) Lines 49-51 ("The thrill … motion.")
    D) Lines 53-57 ("And what … time?")

17. How do the examples of the roller coaster (lines 49-53) and the eagle (lines 53-57) support the introduction of the concept behind NoN in the next paragraph?

    A) They provide examples of the type of programming the new network offers.
    B) They illustrate the excitement generated by experiences that cannot be repeated, or stopped once they have begun.
    C) They remind the reader of the types of experiences Americans miss out on as a result of spending so much time online.
    D) They provide evidence for claims made about the NoN broadcast schedule and the unique aspects of the broadcast signal.

18. As used in line 74, "abysmal" most nearly means

    A) offensive.
    B) abstract.
    C) impressive.
    D) poor.

19. Which of the following options provides the strongest evidence in support of the conclusion that there was a great deal of doubt about whether NoN would succeed?

    A) Lines 63-66 ("None … viewing.")
    B) Lines 67-73 ("Programs … change.")
    C) Lines 74-77 ("A year … reality.")
    D) Lines 80-81 ("Ironically … itself.")

20. Which option is supported by the data in the first figure?

    A) People age 60 or over watch NoN less frequently than people age 23 or under.
    B) The number of people ages 14-23 who watch NoN and the number of people ages 40-59 who watch NoN are about equal.
    C) People of ages 24-39 are less likely to watch NoN than people age 60 or over.
    D) The number of people under age 14 who watch NoN is less than the number of people ages 40-59 who watch NoN.

21. Taken together, the two figures suggest which conclusion about the majority of people who watch NoN?

    A) They are younger than age 40 and prefer to watch NoN in the company of others.
    B) They are younger than age 40 and prefer to watch NoN without the distraction of having friends or family members present.
    C) They are 23 years of age or younger and watch NoN only as part of virtual gatherings.
    D) They are 60 years of age or older and prefer not to watch NoN in bars.

eggheadprep.com

Questions 22-32 are based on the following passage.

This passage is adapted from "Reconstruction," by Frederick Douglass, published in the Atlantic Monthly in 1866, one year after the end of the U.S. Civil War.

Whether the tremendous war so heroically fought and so victoriously ended shall pass into history a miserable failure, barren of permanent results—a scandalous and shocking waste of blood and treasure; an attempt to re-
5 establish a Union by force, which must be the merest mockery of a Union; an effort to bring under Federal authority states into which no loyal man from the North may safely enter, and to bring men into the national councils who deliberate with daggers and vote with
10 revolvers, and who do not even conceal their deadly hate of the country that conquered them—or whether, on the other hand, we shall, as the rightful reward of victory over treason, have a solid nation, entirely delivered from all contradictions and social antagonisms, a nation based
15 upon loyalty, liberty, and equality, must be determined one way or the other by the present session of Congress. The last session really did nothing which can be considered final as to these questions. The Civil Rights Bill, the Freedmen's Bureau Bill, and the proposed
20 constitutional amendments, with the amendment already adopted and recognized as the law of the land, do not reach the difficulty, and cannot, unless the whole structure of the government is changed from a government by states to something like a despotic central government,
25 with power to control even the municipal regulations of states. As long as there remains such an idea as the right of each state to control its own local affairs—an idea, by the way, more deeply rooted in the minds of men of all sections of the country than perhaps any one other
30 political idea—no general assertion of human rights can be of any practical value. To change the character of the government at this point is neither possible nor desirable. All that is necessary to be done is to make the government consistent with itself, and thus render the rights of the
35 states compatible with the sacred rights of human nature.

Slavery, like all other great systems of wrong, founded in the depths of human selfishness, and existing for ages, has not neglected its own conservation. It has steadily exerted an influence upon all around it favorable
40 to its own continuance. And today it is so strong that it could exist, not only without law, but even against law. Custom, manners, morals, religion, are all on its side everywhere in the South; and when you add the ignorance and habit of servility of the ex-slave to the intelligence
45 and accustomed authority of the master, you have the conditions, not out of which slavery will again grow, but under which it is impossible for the Federal government to wholly destroy it, unless the Federal government be armed with despotic power, to blot out State authority,
50 and to station a Federal officer at every crossroad. This, of course, cannot be done, and ought not even if it could. The true way and the easiest way is to make our government entirely consistent with itself, and give to every loyal citizen the elective franchise—a right
55 and power which will be ever-present, and will form a wall of fire for the citizen's protection.

There is cause to be thankful even for rebellion. It is an impressive teacher, though a stern and terrible one. One of the invaluable
60 compensations of the late Rebellion is the highly instructive disclosure it made of the true source of danger to republican government. Whatever may be tolerated in monarchical and despotic governments, no republic is safe that tolerates a privileged class,
65 or denies to any of its citizens equal rights and equal means to maintain them. What was theory before the war has been made fact by the war.

It is no disparagement to truth that it can only prevail where reason prevails. War begins where
70 reason ends. The thing worse than rebellion is the thing that causes rebellion. What that thing is, we have been taught to our cost. It remains now to be seen whether we have the needed courage to have that cause entirely removed from the Republic. At
75 any rate, to this grand work of national regeneration and entire purification Congress must now address itself, with full purpose that the work shall this time be thoroughly done. The deadly upas*, root and branch, leaf and fiber, body and sap, must be utterly
80 destroyed. Authority and power are here commensurate with the duty imposed. There are no cloud-flung shadows to obscure the way. Truth shines with brighter light and more intense heat at every moment, and a country torn and rent and
85 bleeding implores relief from its distress and agony.

*A tropical Asian tree of the mulberry family that produces a toxic latex historically used for poison arrow tips.

SAMPLE TEST 3
Section 1: Reading Test

22. As used in line 3, the word "barren" most nearly means

    A) infertile.
    B) devoid.
    C) restrictive.
    D) uninhabited.

23. Which of the following is a fear about the fate of the United States after the Civil War that the author explicitly expresses?

    A) The tremendous loss of life that occurred during the war will result in a long-lasting labor shortage, impoverishing both the North and the South.
    B) Eventually, the practice of slavery will become legal again in a number of states.
    C) The work of Congress may be hindered by the destructive intentions of representatives from states that have been forced to rejoin the Union.
    D) Pressing concerns about rebuilding the country will result in a neglect of other important matters such as environmental conservation.

24. Which choice provides the strongest evidence in support of the answer to the previous question?

    A) Lines 3-6 ("A scandalous … Union;")
    B) Lines 6-11 ("an effort … them—")
    C) Lines 36-38 ("Slavery … conservation.")
    D) Lines 40-41 ("And today … law.")

25. What does the author see as a problem with legislation currently under consideration, such as the Civil Rights Bill?

    A) The bills will be weakened by too many amendments.
    B) The President has the power to veto the bills, so it is a waste of time to consider them.
    C) The laws would likely be overturned in the next election cycle, before there were ever enforced.
    D) The laws would not produce the desired effects without massive Federal intervention in many states.

26. Which option offers the strongest evidence in support of the answer to the previous question?

    A) Lines 14-16 ("A nation … Congress.")
    B) Lines 18-21 ("The Civil … adopted")
    C) Lines 21-25 ("do not … states.")
    D) Lines 32-35 ("All that … nature.")

27. Which two ideas does the author identify as being currently at odds with each other?

    A) Sovereignty of states and equal rights for all citizens
    B) Destructive intentions and the continuation of a "system of wrong"
    C) Rebellion and education
    D) Truth and reason

28. What does the author recommend as the single action Congress can take that would be most likely to guarantee equal rights for all?

    A) Deploying Federal law enforcement agencies to every region of the country
    B) Granting the right to vote to all citizens
    C) Providing better teachers for the school system
    D) Ensuring that the huge cost of the Civil War is not passed on to future generations

29. Which option offers the strongest evidence in support of the answer to the previous question?

    A) Lines 31-32 ("To change … desirable.")
    B) Lines 48-50 ("Federal … crossroad.")
    C) Lines 53-56 ("and give … protection.")
    D) Lines 58-59 ("It is … one.")

30.

In the third paragraph (lines 57-67), the author identifies "the true source of danger to republican government." Which of the following best characterizes that danger?

- A) Compensation of those who are in rebellion, whichencourages them to continue engaging in violentactivities
- B) The acceptance of a system under which differentgroups of people receive different treatment fromthe government
- C) The establishment of a monarchy, which wouldlead to despotism
- D) Lack of disclosure about the inner workings ofgovernment

31.

Which option provides the strongest evidence in support of the answer to the previous question?

- A) Lines 59-60 ("One of … Rebellion")
- B) Lines 61-62 ("instructive … government.")
- C) Lines 62-63 ("Whatever … governments,")
- D) Lines 64-66 ("no republic … them.")

32.

As used in line 85, "implores" most nearly means

- A) pleads for
- B) resists
- C) curtails
- D) receives

SAMPLE TEST 3
Section 1: Reading Test

Questions 33-42 are based on the following pair of passages.

Passage 1, by Leroy Biltonase, January 2016

As a forty-year resident of Oak Springs City, I know the roads here as well as anyone. I have also worked as a civil engineer for almost two decades, helping to design the East Side and West Side bridges in 1997. Like most
5   Oak Springs City residents, I am deeply concerned about the ever-worsening traffic that is turning our roads and highways into parking lots.

Elected officials triumphantly brandish dazzling images of what our city will look like if we devote
10 massive amounts of taxpayers' hard-earned money to building light rail and trolley systems. The personal automobile is one of the most enduring symbols of American freedom, and now politicians are trying to maneuver us into paying for a plan that will wrest that
15 symbol from our hands and homes, as they force us all into plastic chairs on mass transit. We are told that we must renounce the obvious solution to our current woes—widening the highways—and think about the long term instead. But a little research reveals that short-term and
20 long-term goals are not in conflict, after all.

Let's examine the situations in two cities, both a few hundred miles from here: Calinoma City and Oreton Valley. Calimona City leaders authorized an ambitious highway expansion project in 1995. Since that same date,
25 efforts to improve transportation in Oreton Valley have focused entirely on mass transit development, with highway widening abandoned completely. Based on the ominous predictions of our own current leaders, one would figure Calinoma City to be commuter's worst
30 nightmare, while the good citizens of Oreton Valley zip around with carefree ease in high-tech trains and buses. But the numbers tell a very different story: the average commuting time per mile in Calinoma City is 43% *less* than the average commuting time per mile in Oreton
35 Valley, which in turn is roughly equal to the average commuting time here in Oak Springs City. The implications could not be any clearer. Widening highways works, while building transit systems doesn't.

But of course, we will be told that for the benefit of
40 future generations, we must also consider the environmental impacts of any transit decisions made. Proponents of mass transit will speak of reducing harmful emissions by encouraging commuters to trade their car keys for train tickets. Their intention, however, is not
45 "encouragement," but rather, the deliberate dismantling of our individual rights by so neglecting the state of our roads that we have no choice but to accept the means of getting around town that they wish to foist upon us.

Consider this question, however: Wouldn't a 43%
50 reduction in commuting time guarantee a 43% reduction in emissions *right now?*

Passage 2, response from statistical analyst Dr. Rosemary Wilson of Oak Springs University

As a resident of Oak Springs City and a daily commuter, I sympathize fully with Mr. Biltonase's frustration with the current state of traffic in this region.
55 All of us would live more calmly and happily if it were a little less stressful to get to and from work each day. However, Mr. Biltonase errs in concluding based on the very limited data he studied that our best solution would be to invest in widening highways rather than in a viable
60 mass transit system. Having analyzed traffic data from over 400 cities worldwide, I know that the broad trends are discordant with the unusual cases upon which Mr. Biltonase chooses to focus. I need not elaborate on those general trends, however, for simply digging a little deeper
65 into the numbers Mr. Biltonase himself trumpeted reveals that he has overlooked some important facts.

First of all, as can readily be verified by a review of state records, Oreton Valley embarked on a three-year highway widening program, every bit as impressive as
70 Calinoma City's 1995 plan, in 1988. It is thus misleading to claim that Oreton Valley has "abandoned completely" the widening of roadways. More importantly, both cities based their road expansion plans on 40-year population growth projections. The explosion of the high-tech
75 industry has fueled an unprecedented population boom in Oreton Valley since 2001; the current population is nearly twice what was projected for the year 2028. Meanwhile, Calinoma City has stagnated, with no significant growth in population since 2005, and a total population far below
80 what was projected 20 years ago. The anemic growth of Calinoma City has left the city utterly unable to pay for all that 1995 work, which was authorized based on tax revenue projections, which in turn were based on the population projections. Everything but the roads, from
85 schools to sewer systems, is in a woeful state of disrepair as the city buckles under the weight of debts incurred building highway lanes for which there still is no need.

As for the matter of emissions reductions, here it is necessary to call upon the broader data. Studies have
90 shown repeatedly that when highways are widened, people move farther from their workplaces, taking advantage of the increased speed of the drive. That means that although their commute time *per mile* decreases, their total time commuting remains about the same, at least for
95 the short term. Over the years, as people flock to more

distant suburbs, widened highways receive a dramatic increase in vehicle volume, and the entire metro area ends up with greater traffic woes than ever.

    Finally, consider the fact that in cities like New York
100 and Paris, many people choose not to own an automobile because they feel no need for one, thanks to excellent transit systems. Can something really be called a symbol of freedom if a person is forced to own it by the lack of other options? Isn't choice synonymous with freedom?

33. For Passage 1, which choice offers the most logical explanation of the author's intention in the first paragraph (lines 1-7)?

A) He wishes to point out the importance of two specific bridges to transportation within the city.

B) He wishes to reveal his age and awaken memories of a simpler time in the past.

C) He wishes to establish his credentials to comment on the plans proposed by elected leaders.

D) He wishes to give background information about the geography of the city.

34. Which specific objection to the transportation plans presented by elected officials does the author of Passage 1 put forth in the second paragraph (lines 8-20)?

A) The plans will force residents to give up driving, and thus surrender their liberty.

B) The plans will cost more than the plan he favors.

C) The plans represent an apparently obvious solution, and therefore probably won't work out.

D) The plans put short-term gains ahead of long-term goals.

35. Which choice provides the clearest evidence for the answer to the previous question?

A) Lines 8-11 ("Elected … systems.")

B) Lines 11-16 ("The personal … transit.")

C) Lines 16-18 ("We are … highways—")

D) Lines 19-20 ("But … all.")

36. As used in line 29, "figure" most nearly means

A) expect.

B) represent.

C) compute.

D) drawing.

37.

Which of the following best describes the purpose of the third paragraph (lines 21-38) of Passage 1?

A) To give context to the transportation problem in Oak Springs City by describing the surrounding geography and how it affects commuting times.

B) To show that results of transportation improvement plans in two cities are consistent with those predicted for Oak Springs City

C) To show that two cities with very different transportation improvement plans have roughly equal commuting times

D) To show that in two cities, the results of transportation improvement efforts were the opposite of what the leaders of Oak Springs City would predict

38.

Which option best describes the relationship between the two passages?

A) Passage 2 expands on the claims made in Passage 1 and presents more detailed evidence to support them.

B) Passage 2 offers an emotional response to the factual report presented in Passage 1.

C) Passage 2 provides a detailed description of the plan opposed by the author of Passage 1.

D) Passage 2 directly refutes the arguments presented in Passage 1 by citing specific evidence.

39.

Which of the following is the best summary of the opinion expressed in Passage 2 regarding the conclusion drawn in Passage 1 about the effectiveness highway widening (lines 37-38, "Widening … doesn't.")?

A) The conclusion presented in Passage 1 is essentially correct, but additional factors such as population must be considered in order to fully understand the implications of that conclusion.

B) The conclusion presented in Passage 1 is essentially correct, and further analysis reveals that an even stronger conclusion about the value of the highway expansion is justified.

C) The conclusion presented in Passage 1 is not valid because current traffic situations in both Calinoma City and Oreton Valley are more attributable to population trends than to highway planning.

D) The conclusion presented in Passage 1 is not valid because it is based on inaccurate data that was falsified by a pro-highway political lobby.

40.

As used in line 62, "discordant" most nearly means

A) unpleasant.

B) in agreement.

C) in conflict.

D) complementary.

41.

How, specifically, does the author of Passage 2 respond to the claim made by the author of Passage 1 that commuting times in Calinoma City are significantly shorter than in Oreton Valley and Oak Springs City, resulting in lower emissions?

A) She asserts that the measurement, commuting time per mile, is not a reliable predictor of emissions.

B) She claims that a 43 percent difference in commuting time per mile is not significant, since the distance involved is so short.

C) She disputes the claim that the average commuting time per minute is about the same in Oreton Valley and Oak Springs City.

D) She states that commuting time is irrelevant when a city is facing a major budget crisis due to unpaid debts.

42. Which option provides the strongest evidence in support of the answer to the previous question?

   A) Lines 77-80 ("Meanwhile … ago.")
   B) Lines 84-87 ("Everything … need.")
   C) Lines 92-95 ("That … term.")
   D) Lines 102-104 ("Can … freedom?")

SAMPLE TEST 3
Section 1: Reading Test

Questions 43-52 are based on the following passage and additional information.

In the following passage, a fictional scientist describes fictional events in a fictional location. (The reference to events in the U.S. is factually accurate, however.) The phrase "colony failure" refers to a situation in which the population of a bat colony falls so low that the colony will eventually die out completely.

    Many people are aware of the high mortality rate occurring within bat colonies in the northeast US due to the fungal infection known as "white nose syndrome." Here in the small nation of Two Islands, we face a bat
5 crisis of our own. The bat species that lives here, *leptonycteris islandius* (commonly known as the striped-wing bat), is the primary pollinator of our crops, serving much the same function as bees in many countries. Over the last twenty years, an alarming increase in colony
10 failures threatens the survival of the entire species, and hence, of our agricultural industry.
    Striped-wing bats are the favored hosts for a tiny parasitic worm, *pirofilaria dysfunctor* (Piro worm). Although the presence of these worms in a bat's system
15 does not directly cause serious illness or death, it may have indirect effects. For example, it is suspected that the parasites deplete a bat's immune system, leading to increased vulnerability to secondary viral, fungal, or bacterial infections that often prove fatal.
20 Our islands also play host to a unique genus of flowering plants, the *triberitum* genus, consisting of species *triberitum eastior*, *triberitum westernia*, and several others. These plants produce an enzyme, beritase, which is poisonous to Piro worms but harmless
25 to bats. Once plentiful, triberitum plants are now found only in remote areas of the islands because of large-scale harvesting during the 1990s, driven by a global craze in which *triberitum* extracts were touted as an herbal miracle drug.
30 I propose that bats that feed on plants rich in beritase excrete the enzyme in the guano (excrement) that lines their caves, protecting them from an excessive presence of Piro worms. Without feeding at least occasionally on plants that provide the enzyme, bats
35 might become defenseless against Piro worms, and could thus be at higher risk of fatal secondary infections. Furthermore, efforts to directly eradicate Piro worms from caves may be counterproductive. Synthetic pesticides could be as damaging to bats' immune
40 systems as they are to the worms themselves. Trying to employ natural methods to alleviate the problem would pose its own challenges, as determining the proper quantity of natural beritase to apply would be pure guesswork. On the other hand, if bats have access to
45 triberitum plants, they might instinctively know how much beritase enzyme to consume and excrete. Experimental testing of these hypotheses is therefore recommended. In the feeding territories of several currently healthy bat colonies, a number of
50 *triberitum* plants could be introduced amidst the wildleaf, bucknettle, and ferndaisy flowers on which striped-wing bats principally feed at present. Because bat colonies are highly territorial about their feeding grounds, healthy colonies that feed in regions where
55 *triberitum* plants are not introduced will serve as control groups. Researchers could then introduce Piro worms into the caves of the control and experimental colonies, carefully making note of any changes in the bats' feeding habits in response to the infestation, as well as of
60 any impact the presence of Piro worms has on the health of the colonies.
    It would be important to conduct this experiment on both East Island and West Island, since the populations of bats on our two main islands have
65 been separated for several thousand years and may be significantly genetically different from each other.

FIGURE:

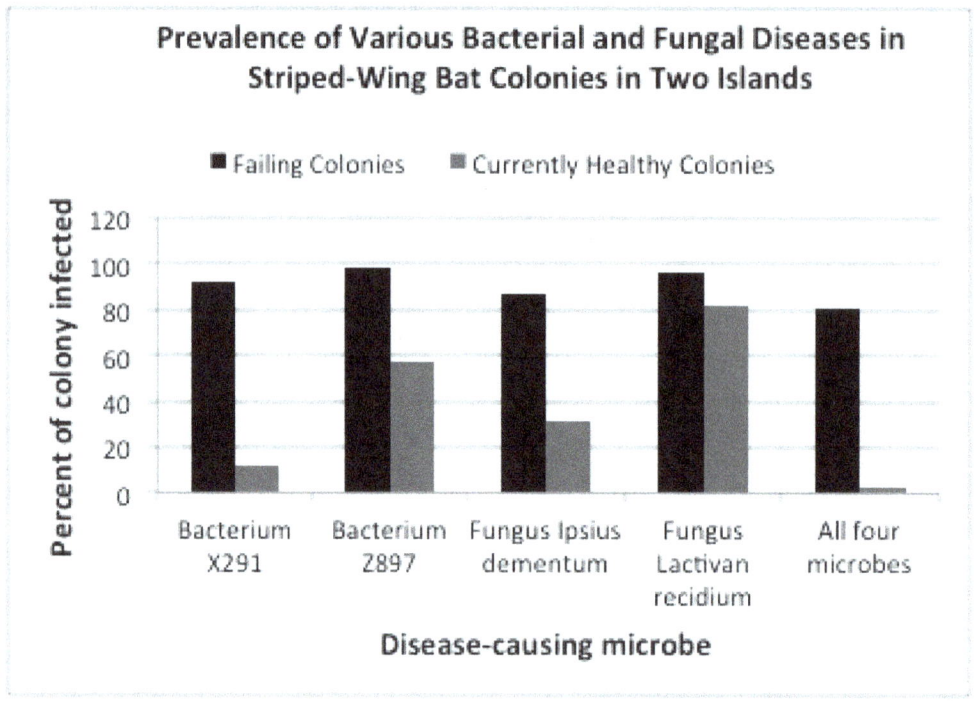

43. As used in line 29, "touted" most nearly means

   A) recommended.
   B) evaluated.
   C) mocked.
   D) discredited.

44. In what way do the words "propose," "might," "could," and "may" help to indicate the scientist's intention in the fourth paragraph (lines 30-46)?

   A) They show the scientist's uncertainty, suggesting that the experiment described may not be worth pursuing because there is a good chance it will produce no useful results.
   B) They allow the scientist to convey the belief that global trade is the primary cause of bat colony failures without having to express that belief in a confrontational way.
   C) They contribute to the overall critical tone of the article, making clear the scientist's skepticism about previous research on bat colony failures.
   D) They remind the reader that, regardless of the scientist's level of confidence regarding the stated hypotheses, they have not yet been tested.

45. In lines 47-48, the scientist states that, "Experimental testing of these hypotheses is therefore recommended." Which of the following is a hypothesis that would be tested in the proposed research study?

   A) Striped-wing bats that feed on *triberitum* plant nectar and are exposed to Piro worms are likely to develop fungal, bacterial, or viral infections.
   B) Striped-wing bat colonies that feed on *triberitum* plant nectar will likely show greater resistance to Piro worm infestations than those that do not.
   C) Striped-wing bats in failing colonies are likely to spread secondary infections to human populations in nearby towns.
   D) Direct application of the beritase enzyme to the walls of striped-wing bat caves can effectively reduce bats' vulnerability to Piro worm infestations.

46. Which option offers the strongest evidence in support of the answer to the previous question?

   A) Lines 14-17 ("Although … system")
   B) Lines 25-29 ("Once … drug")
   C) Lines 30-33 ("I … worms.")
   D) Lines 37-40 ("Furthermore, … themselves")

SAMPLE TEST 3
Section 1: Reading Test

47. Which of the following best expresses the scientist's view on the use of synthetic pesticides to prevent Piro worm infestations in bat caves?

   A) It may have some negative side effects, but protecting bat colonies is worth the risk.
   B) It is not advisable due to the risk of harm to the bats.
   C) It is definitely preferable to treating bat caves with natural beritase.
   D) It should not be undertaken until the risks to human visitors to the caves are assessed.

48. The main purpose of the fifth paragraph (lines 47-61) is to

   A) describe a possible experiment that would test whether dietary changes affect the vulnerability of bat colonies to Piro worms.
   B) analyze the differences in nutrient content among several plant species on which striped-wing bats typically feed.
   C) predict how a previously abandoned experiment described in the third paragraph (lines 20-29) would most likely have ended.
   D) summarize the results of an experiment that contradicted the scientist's hypothesis about the role of bucknettle in the diet of striped- wing bats.

49. An unstated assumption made by the scientist about wildleaf, bucknettle, and ferndaisy is

   A) that these plants are members of the genus triberitum.
   B) that these plants provide all the nutrition striped-wing bats need to remain healthy.
   C) that these plants usually grow only where *triberitum* plants are plentiful.
   D) that these plants do not produce beritase.

50. Based on the Figure, in what percent of healthy striped-wing bat colonies were bats affected by all four microbes?

   A) Less than 5 percent
   B) Just over 10 percent
   C) Just under 60 percent
   D) Approximately 80 percent

51. Based on the data in the table, which of the four microbes affects the lowest percentage of failing striped-wing bat colonies?

   A) X291
   B) Z897
   C) ipsius dementum
   D) lactivan recidium

52. Does the Figure provide evidence in support of the belief that Piro worm infestation makes bats more vulnerable to secondary infections, and thus colonies more prone to failure?

   A) Yes, because every pathogen listed occurs
   B) with greater frequency in failing colonies than in healthy colonies.
   C) Yes, because the percentages in the table clearly indicate that infection with microbes contributes significantly to colony failure.
   D) No, because the Figure does not provide direct evidence that bacteria and fungi cause colony failure.
   E) No, because the Figure does not provide information on whether the colonies were infested with Piro worms.

STOP

If you have finished this section before time expires, you may check your work. You cannot return to this section once you move on to the next section.

EGGHEAD PREP™
Get cracking.

STOP!

If you have finished this section before time expires, you may check your work. You cannot return to this section once you move on to the next section.

www.eggheadprep.com

ANSWERS, SECTION 1
SAMPLE TEST 3 — READING

1. B
2. C
3. A
4. B
5. D
6. D
7. C
8. A
9. B
10. C
11. D
12. B
13. C
14. A
15. C
16. B
17. B
18. D
19. C
20. D
21. A
22. B
23. C
24. B
25. D
26. C
27. A
28. B
29. C
30. B
31. D
32. A
33. C
34. A
35. B
36. A
37. D
38. D
39. C
40. C
41. A
42. C
43. A
44. D
45. B
46. C
47. B
48. A
49. D
50. A
51. C
52. D

eggheadprep.com

SECTION 2: WRITING & LANGUAGE TEST
35 MINUTES, 44 QUESTIONS

DIRECTIONS

Below you will find a number of reading passages. Each one is accompanied by a series of questions. A note before each passage will tell you which questions are related to that passage. Some questions will require you to consider possible revisions to the passage to help the writer express the ideas more clearly or effectively. Other questions will ask you to consider ways to edit the passage to correct errors in punctuation, word usage, or sentence structure. Some questions and passages include graphics, such as tables and graphs. As you make your decisions about possible changes, you should take the graphics into consideration along with the text.

Some questions will refer to a specific, underlined portion of the passage. Others will ask you to focus on a particular location within the passage. There will also be questions that ask you to think about the passage as a whole. Numbers enclosed in parentheses and written with a Q, such as (Q14) indicate the number of the question associated with that portion of the passage. Numbers bracketed in plain text, like [2], are used to identifying sentences within the passage, whereas a number surrounded by dashes, like –2– identifies a paragraph.

Read each passage and then choose the answer to each question that best improves the writing of the passage or brings the particular phrase or sentence into agreement with the conventions of standard written English. If you believe the best choice is to leave the indicated portion of the passage as it is, choose the option, "NO CHANGE."

Questions 1 – 11 are based on the following passage.

An Elevator Ride to the Roses: The Rooftop Garden Movement

A variety of recent research papers have demonstrated that workers exhibit greater **(Q1)** productivity, loyalty, and contentment when their workplace **(Q2)** is located close to modern transit facilities. Many companies now search for new office and factory locations with those benefits in mind, but firms with existing facilities surrounded only by asphalt and concrete find themselves unable to satisfy their staff's need for fresh air and sunshine. The rooftop garden movement offers new hope to employers without the resources to relocate. "At first, it feels pretty strange taking an elevator to go outdoors," as one employee in a building with a newly-installed rooftop garden observes, "but now, I eat lunch surrounded by the flowers every day the weather allows it." Although the initial costs of creating such a garden are substantial, the long-term payoffs for employees and employers **(Q3)** likewise more than outweigh the short-term expense.

1.
   A) NO CHANGE
   B) productiveness, loyalness, and contentedness
   C) productivity, loyalty, and also are more content
   D) productivity, loyalty, being more likely to show contentment

2. Which of the following provides the most appropriate introduction to the passage?
   A) NO CHANGE
   B) provides them with healthy food choices in the cafeteria.
   C) offers them convenient access to parks and other "green" spaces.
   D) holds regular events to celebrate employees' birthdays and important achievements.

3.
   A) NO CHANGE
   B) similarly
   C) analogously
   D) alike

The health benefits of regular exposure to outdoor air, especially outdoor air purified and oxygen-enriched by the photosynthesis processes of plants, are well documented, and include better respiratory function, decreased frequency of headaches, improved emotional health, and higher energy levels throughout the day. (Q4) Consistently high daytime energy levels and robust respiratory health contribute significantly to a person's ability to sleep deeply at night, which (Q5) is essential for good health. This combination of factors may explain why employees at locations with either nearby parks or accessible rooftop gardens miss significantly fewer workdays due to illness than those at facilities without such features. The central library in one major U.S. city (Q6) enjoyed a major increase in employees posting positive reviews of their workplace on social media after installing a roof garden. As one physician who reviewed the case observed, although the (Q7) libraries indoor air filtration systems are state of the art, they cannot compete with living plants when it comes to providing health- supporting air.

4. At this point, the author is considering adding the following sentence:

> One study found that employees who regularly spend time outdoors are 33 percent more likely to report for work on time that those who rarely spend time outdoors.

Should the author make this change?

A) Yes, because it presents statistical data that supports the main theme of the paragraph and will be examined further in the next several sentences.

B) Yes, because it explains the scientific basis for the health effects of exposure to outdoor air.

C) No, because the study may be flawed since it doesn't take into account other factors like traffic and weather conditions.

D) No, because it interrupts the discussion of specific health benefits of exposure to outdoor air.

5.
A) NO CHANGE
B) is being
C) have been seen as
D) are

6. Which option best supports the statement made in the preceding sentence?

A) NO CHANGE
B) saw a 28 percent decrease in employee sick days after
C) experienced a 30 percent increase in positive publicity after
D) is still recovering from the exorbitant cost of

7.
A) NO CHANGE
B) library's indoor air filtration systems'
C) library's indoor air filtrations systems
D) libraries' indoor air filtration system's

(Q8) Rooftop gardens also offer substantial long-term financial benefits besides improving employee health. They often lower heating and cooling costs by 15 percent or more. The soil and mulch provide extra insulation, while the plants absorb much of the sun's heat before it can seep into the building. After creating a roof garden for its national headquarters building in Madison, Wisconsin, one company experienced quarterly energy savings of over $85,000 **(Q9)** per three months.

8. In context, which option offers the best way to combine the two underlined sentences?

   A) Often lowering heating and cooling costs by 15 percent or more, rooftop gardens improve
   B) employee health and offer substantial long-term financial benefits.
   C) In addition to improving employee health, rooftop gardens offer substantial long-term financial benefits, often lowering heating and cooling costs by 15 percent or more.
   D) The long-term financial benefits of rooftop gardens, besides improving employee health, often include lowering heating and cooling costs by 15 percent or more.
   E) Rooftop gardens, which improve employee health and offer substantial long-term financial benefits, often lower heating and cooling costs by 15 percent or more.

9.
   A) NO CHANGE
   B) every three months.
   C) each three-month time period.
   D) DELETE the underlined portion and end the sentence with a period.

The most daunting and costly challenges companies face when launching a rooftop garden project are acquiring the massive amount of soil required and transporting it all up to the roof. **(Q10)** Consequently, companies can begin sending food and paper waste from cafeterias up to the roof for composting a year or two in advance of building the garden, greatly reducing the amount of soil that must be delivered to the facility. Particularly efficient companies have also installed new pipes to reclaim gray **(Q11)** water, this being water from sinks used for hand- and dishwashing, for irrigation use. Through careful planning, employers can minimize the startup costs associated with a roof garden, and then "harvest" cost savings for decades, all while providing a healthy and happy environment for employees.

10.
- A) NO CHANGE
- B) As an alternative,
- C) Nonetheless,
- D) Ultimately,

11.
- A) NO CHANGE
- B) water, this is water from sinks used for hand- and dishwashing, for
- C) water—that is, water from sinks used for hand- and dishwashing—for
- D) water: which could also be water from sinks used for hand- and dishwashing,

SAMPLE TEST 3
Section 2: Writing & Language Test

Questions 12-22 are based on the following passage, which describes fictitious events in a fictitious country.

The Crisis That Gave Rise to Lasting Cultural Change

The world-famous Pony Express of the American West may well have been only the second most impressive human-animal partnership in the history of letter delivery. In the early twentieth century, the people of the vast desert nation of Sandimar prided **(Q12)** themselves on their simple, village-centered lifestyle, taking no interest in the "communication age" dawning in other parts of the world. Everything changed when a mysterious disease began spreading rapidly across the land, sending thousands of men to their beds for months at a time. **(Q13)** In spite of having survived childhood diseases, Emsun Putainy and Inpon Siotaex, two respected leaders from a **(Q14)** western village. They began recruiting expert camel riders from far and wide to carry messages between the many suffering towns. Within a few years, a vast network of camel trails zigzagged across the country, serving as communication lifelines. The Riders of Sandimar, who together represented the first countrywide mail delivery service in a land with no national government, **(Q15)** was extraordinary, maintaining an unblemished record of breathtakingly fast delivery in spite of all the hazards of desert travel. Suddenly, a nation in which long-distance communication had previously been all but nonexistent had vaulted to the forefront of a new global era.

12.
- A) NO CHANGE
- B) their selves on their
- C) oneself on one's
- D) himself or herself on his or her

13. Which option introduces the sentence in the most logical way?
- A) NO CHANGE
- B) They had played together for many years as children, and as a result,
- C) In response to the growing crisis,
- D) DELETE the underlined portion.

14.
- A) NO CHANGE
- B) western village,
- C) western village;
- D) western village—they

15.
- A) NO CHANGE
- B) was extraordinary because it maintained
- C) were extraordinary by having maintained
- D) were extraordinary, maintaining

(Q16) That success, however, seemed doomed to be short-lived, as rider after rider succumbed to the debilitating ailment ravaging the nation. Thanks to all the inter-village communication that had occurred, however, Putainy and Siotaex realized that the disease only affected men. (Modern biologists have discovered that the illness was caused by a parasite found in camel fur that bonds with a protein unique to the human Y chromosome, which women do not have.) Women did not customarily travel in the Sandimar of that era, **(Q17)** so the leaders' idea to turn the delivery service over to female camel riders was initially greeted with hostility, even resistance. In time, however, Sandimarians recognized that without the message delivery service, there was no hope of saving any village, and so began to welcome the brave women riders of the desert to their towns with open arms. As the number of men incapacitated by the disease continued to grow, the riders expanded their role in Sandimarian life. By the 1930s, not only were they the carriers of all the news of the land, **(Q18)** but also served as master carpenters and food gatherers for the towns they visited.

When Putainy and Siotaex themselves took to their beds after contracting the nameless disease, even the management and leadership of the delivery service fell upon the shoulders of women. They answered the call in heroic fashion, continually improving upon the already dazzling delivery speeds for which the camel riders were becoming known around the world. It was clear that no matter what might lie ahead for the ailing men of the land, the gender dynamics of Sandimar had changed forever. **(Q19)**

16. The author is considering deleting the first sentence of this paragraph. Would that change be appropriate?
    A) Yes, because the sentence does not connect logically with the previous paragraph.
    B) Yes, because the health of the camel riders is not relevant at this point in the passage.
    C) No, because it provides further justification for the claims made in the previous paragraph.
    D) No, because it provides a logical transition from the previous paragraph.

17.
    A) NO CHANGE
    B) so it was hostility, even resistance, that initially greeted the leaders' idea to turn the delivery service over to female camel riders.
    C) so the leaders' idea to turn the delivery service over to female camel riders was initially greeted with hostility.
    D) so there was an initial greeting of hostility, even resistance, to the leaders' idea to turn the delivery service over to female camel riders.

18.
    A) NO CHANGE
    B) but they also served
    C) also having served
    D) but also serving

19. Which choice follows the previous sentence most logically?
    A) It simply didn't make sense anymore to see women merely as assistants to men.
    B) Camels were the perfect animals for the grueling work, due to their exceptional speed, endurance, and tolerance of brutal desert conditions.
    C) Many countries later developed message delivery services that were inspired by the amazing camel riders of Sandimar.
    D) Often, letters made the journey from one end of Sandimar to the other in only four days, which may not seem all that fast by today's standards, but was an incredible achievement at that time.

SAMPLE TEST 3
Section 2: Writing & Language Test

Flourishing in their new roles as independent leaders and exhibiting unrivaled **(Q20)** bravery: the riders extended their range to reach the remotest villages of the most desolate expanses of the great desert. Eventually, one of them came upon a tiny, uncharted town where not one of the twelve men who lived there showed any sign of the **(Q21)** spiteful disease. A medicine woman there had created a blend of herbs that cured the ailment in hours. Thanks to the camel riders, the cure soon reached every sick man in the country. Sadly, much of the world has utterly forgotten the brief era when a bizarre infection sidelined half of a nation's population and transformed the people's belief system. But the women letter carriers of Sandimar will forever be remembered in **(Q22)** their homeland.

20.
- A) NO CHANGE
- B) bravery, and so
- C) bravery,
- D) bravery;

21. Which word choice both logically completes the sentence and maintains the tone established in the passage?
- A) NO CHANGE
- B) crummy
- C) unpropitious
- D) horrific

22. The author is considering expanding the underlined portion of the final sentence to read:

> their homeland, where they are celebrated in songs, stories, and even a newly passed national law declaring that "camel rider" shall be classified as a feminine word form in the Sandimarian language for as long as the language is spoken.

Should this information be added to the passage in this place?

- A) Yes, because it answers a question raised earlier in the passage.
- B) Yes, because it provides examples demonstrating how revered the female camel riders are in Sandimar.
- C) No, it should appear earlier in the passage, since it would serve as a logical transition between the next-to-last and final paragraphs.
- D) No, because it contradicts the main points presented in the passage.

Questions 23-33 are based on the following passage describing a fictional product.

Life in the Forest Fast Lane

Although it is officially classified as a fertilizer, the new product RocketGrow, developed by a New Jersey chemist, is unlike any plant growth supplement ever previously created. The chemical compound is intended to reduce the high mortality rate of young trees by accelerating their growth to mature size. **(Q23)** Many tree species have been shown to grow up to 12 times faster during their first 10 years of life when they are treated with RocketGrow. This rapid growth enables park managers and homeowners to replace majestic trees lost to storms or disease in mere years, instead of decades. Impressively, a sapling requires only two applications of the compound during the first year after it is planted, at a cost of a few dollars each time. Nevertheless, RocketGrow is not the cure-all for reforestation that it may at first appear to be; those considering using it would do well to learn about the both the advantages and disadvantages of its use.

23. Which option represents the most effective way to combine the underlined sentences?

   A) When treated with RocketGrow, many tree sprecies have been shown to grow up to 12 times faster during their first 10 years of life, enabling park managers and homeowners to replace majestic trees lost to storms or disease in mere years, instead of decades.

   B) Park managers and homeowners are allowed to replace majestic trees lost to storms or disease in mere years—instead of decades—because RocketGrow, when used as a treatment for many tree species, causes them to grow up to 12 times faster.

   C) Many tree species have been shown to grow, when they are treated with RocketGrow, up to 12 times faster during their first 10 years of life, enabling majestic trees lost to storms or disease to be replaced in mere years by park managers or homeowners, instead of decades.

   D) In mere years, instead of decades, park managers and homeowners are able to replace majestic trees, lost to storms or disease, because RocketGrow results in many tree species growing up to 12 times faster when it is used to treat the trees during their first 10 years of life.

SAMPLE TEST 3
Section 2: Writing & Language Test

[1] RocketGrow works by stimulating ultra-rapid water circulation within the tree's tissues, **(Q24)** by which resulting in dramatically accelerated photosynthesis. [2] Although a RocketGrow-treated ash or oak will **(Q25)** chute upward as spectacularly as the product name promises, the development of **(Q26)** its innate immune system will be suppressed, making it more vulnerable to disease later in life. [3] This side effect of the compound's use is of particular concern to homeowners **(Q27)** that hope to one day see grandchildren enjoying their yard's stately shade trees. [4] Some tree species do not benefit from treatment with RocketGrow as much as others **(Q28)** had done, however, and some suffer significant negative effects. [5] In addition, some tree varieties, especially those that traditionally produce softer wood, tend to sprout weak limbs due to the poor formation of internal connective tissues during the period of accelerated growth.

[6] Consider Colorado spruce trees, both green and blue **(Q29)** varieties, for example—when treated with RocketGrow, they developed limbs so brittle that even 15 pounds of force snapped the branches off instantly. [7] To treat such species with the compound in any area where playful children are likely to be present would be an invitation for lawsuits. **(Q30)**

24.
A) NO CHANGE
B) which is
C) and thus
D) DELETE the underlined portion.

25.
A) NO CHANGE
B) root
C) shoot
D) scoot

26.
A) NO CHANGE
B) their
C) it's
D) they're

27.
A) NO CHANGE
B) which
C) whom
D) who

28.
A) NO CHANGE
B) do,
C) have done,
D) would do,

29.
A) NO CHANGE
B) varieties. For example,
C) varieties, for example:
D) varieties for example—

30.
To make this paragraph most logical, sentence 4 should be placed
A) where it is now.
B) after sentence 1.
C) after sentence 2.
D) after sentence 5.

Lastly, entomologists have discovered that treatment of a tree with RocketGrow may hinder the tree's ability to support other organisms within its ecosystem. Although it is rarely given much thought by humans, one of the most important roles that trees play is serving as host and home for a huge diversity of insect life. Those insects in turn serve as food for woodpeckers and numerous other bird species, and also fortify twigs and leaves with additional proteins that benefit browsers like moose and deer. Scientists have known for centuries that trees growing in isolation support fewer insect species than those growing in thickly vegetated or wooded areas. In fact, among untreated trees, as can be seen from the graph, those in wooded areas play host to **(Q31)** about ten percent more insect species than those that are isolated. As the data shows, however, treated trees **(Q32)** in wooded areas support only a small number of insect species, though they do support more species if they are isolated.

31. Which of the following is an accurate description of the data conveyed by the graph?

    A) NO CHANGE
    B) slightly fewer insect species than
    C) about one third as many insect species as
    D) nearly twice as many insect species as

32. Which of the following represents an accurate interpretation of the graph?

    A) NO CHANGE
    B) show a reduced ability to support diverse insect species when they are isolated, but not when they are in wooded areas.
    C) support significantly fewer insect species than untreated trees in both isolated and wooded environments.
    D) support fewer insect species when they are located in wooded areas, though isolation has less of an effect than is the case with untreated trees.

Therefore, treating saplings with RocketGrow is best seen as a short-term solution in areas with a desperate need for shade trees, as well as a potentially effective way to rapidly sequester large amounts of carbon and slow the progression of global climate change. But when it comes to nurturing and protecting healthy, vibrant forest ecosystems, **(Q33)** <u>it is necessary to realize that some scientists pay too much attention to things like wood strength and insect species, which most people don't really care about.</u>

33. The author wishes for the final paragraph to convey both the most promising uses of RocketGrow and the influence RocketGrow's shortcomings should have on decision-making. Which option best accomplishes the author's goal?

A) NO CHANGE

B) it must be recognized that using RocketGrow will produce far more rapid growth than leaving trees untreated.

C) it appears that for the foreseeable future, nature's way will remain the best approach the benefits of using RocketGrow still outweigh

D) any negative impacts, and this should be considered by both forest rangers and homeowners.

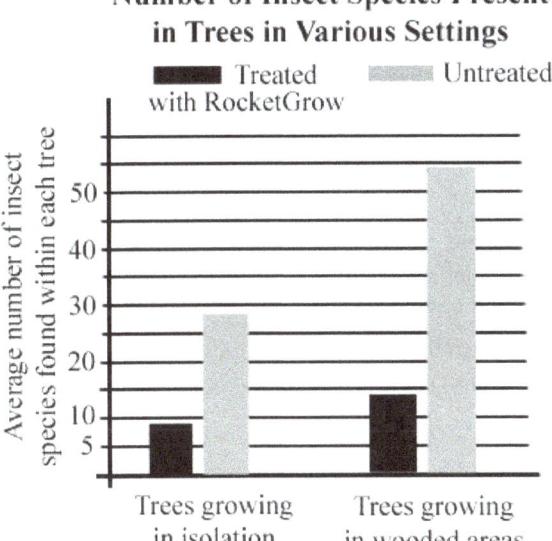

Number of Insect Species Present in Trees in Various Settings

Questions 34-44 are based on the following passage about a fictional coastal town.

Whale of an Officer

From the towering figure of Admiral Nelson in London's Trafalgar Square to broad-shouldered likenesses of Commodore Barry in the U.S. and Ireland to the battle-ready representation of Yi Sun-Sin in **(Q34)** Seoul. These statues and sculptures all over the world show humanity's enduring fascination with great heroes of the sea. Calling to mind an iconic maritime sculpture of a non-human figure is a decidedly more difficult task, however. Many people might name Copenhagen's *The Little Mermaid*—Edvard Eriksen's creation, based on the famous Hans Christian Andersen **(Q35)** tale; as one example, but the sculpture actually represents Princess Ariel after her transformation into a human woman. Interestingly, some of humanity's oldest ocean-themed artistic creations, including carvings on sea cliffs found on several continents, **(Q36)** depicts ocean creatures as protectors of human settlements. It now appears that this ancient tradition has not utterly disappeared from human culture, **(Q37)** even though the modern scientific understanding of marine animals has resulted in people no longer seeing them as mythical creatures.

34.
- A) NO CHANGE
- B) Seoul; these statues and sculptures
- C) Seoul. Statues and sculptures
- D) Seoul, statues and sculptures

35.
- A) NO CHANGE
- B) tale, as
- C) tale—as
- D) tale as

36.
- A) NO CHANGE
- B) depict
- C) depicting
- D) was depicting

37. If the author wishes to link the first paragraph to the ideas that follow in the next two paragraphs, which option will best accomplish that objective?
- A) NO CHANGE
- B) at least if one is to judge by one thriving seaside town.
- C) even though most people still think of human beings when they are asked to picture maritime heroes.
- D) even though many centuries have passed since those ancient carvings were produced.

[1] The small city of Port Humberstrand, an unassuming town with a fishing-based economy, plays home to a unique group of defenders of the coast. [2] For decades, the people of Port Humberstrand lived in fear of occasional incursions into their quiet bay by pods of marauding orcas, giant predators that slaughtered seals and dolphins by the dozens and weren't above seeking human prey as well. [3] **(Q38) Then, in 1947, Olten Parletine, a solitary fisherman saw** the bay's two pods of resident orcas—which are smaller and far less aggressive than their nomadic, deep sea cousins—array themselves in a defensive formation and turn back just such invading force. [4] So grateful was he that he dumped his entire catch of salmon overboard as a thank you gift to the local pods. [5] Within a few years, the resident orca pods were proudly serving as the guardians of Humberstrand Bay, fending off nomadic pods and arbitrating sea lion territorial disputes, not to mention **(Q39)** intimidating foreign fishing vessels. [6] In the wake of the incident Parletine witnessed, many other fishermen and fisherwomen began rewarding the resident orcas for any protective services they provided. [7] Since 1974, a two-week festival has been held every summer to honor Port Humberstrand's "Orca Coast Guard." **(Q40)**

38.
   A) NO CHANGE
   B) Then, in 1947, Olten Parletine a solitary fisherman, saw
   C) Then, in 1947, Olten Parletine; a solitary fisherman saw
   D) Then, in 1947, Olten Parletine, a solitary fisherman, saw

39.
   A) NO CHANGE
   B) intimidated
   C) have intimidated
   D) would intimidate

40. Within this paragraph, the most logical place for sentence 6 is
   A) where it is now
   B) after sentence 3
   C) after sentence 4
   D) after sentence 7

So beloved are the resident orcas that in 1994, the city's mayor **(Q41)** unfurled an ambitious plan to raise money for the production of a dozen statues portraying the then-living members of the pods. An internet campaign brought in money from around the world, allowing construction of the statues to begin in 1997. Now complete, the statues depict the whales in sailors' uniforms, including stripes on their fins denoting military ranks **(Q42)** as an indication of the high regard in which each individual guardian of the bay is held. The largest, oldest orca, given the name Deep Lightning by fishing crews, sports the uniform of an admiral and leaps above an invading deep sea orca in full retreat. A powerful

41.
- A) NO CHANGE
- B) unveiled
- C) abandoned
- D) enforced

42. Which option most effectively introduces the examples that follow this sentence?
- A) NO CHANGE
- B) to the delight of tourists, who come to the summer festival primarily for entertainment.
- C) as a satirical commentary on humans' fascination with dressing up animals like dogs and cats.
- D) to show that orcas are capable of exhibiting remarkable teamwork in hunting and other activities.

female bears a captains's stripes as she aggressively turns back a boatful of fish poachers from the West. **(Q43)** People unfamiliar with the story of the orcas of Port Humberstrand may find the statues puzzling at first, but the message behind the artwork is, in the end, as clear as the waters of the bay: through their **(Q44)** remarkable demonstrations of speed and power, the members of the Orca Coast Guard have proven that these magnificent creatures, though admittedly frightening, are often misunderstood.

43.

At this point, the author is considering adding this sentence:

Humberstrand Bay covers approximately 130 square miles and experiences dramatic tidal variations, with extreme tidal events raising or lowering the water level by over 25 feet.

Should the author add this sentence?

A) Yes because it shows the connection between the geography of the bay and the need for an "Orca Coast Guard."

B) Yes, because it helps to show how isolated Port Humberstrand is from other fishing towns.

C) No, because it fails to explain the cause of the dramatic tidal variations it describes.

D) No, because it provides supplemental information that is not relevant to this paragraph.

44.

A) NO CHANGE

B) longevity, intelligence, and consistent behavioral patterns, the members of the Orca Coast Guard have given scientists an extraordinary opportunity to learn the secrets of one of the sea's most charismatic species.

C) tireless efforts to protect the city of Port Humberstrand, the members of the Orca Coast Guard have proven themselves as worthy of admiration as any human naval hero in history.

D) presence as top predators in a bay that would otherwise be overrun by herbivorous species, permanently damaging the marine ecosystem, the members of the Orca Coast Guard have shown the value of biodiversity in habitats all over the world.

STOP

If you have finished this section before time expires, you may check your work. You cannot return to this section once you move on to the next section.

STOP!

If you have finished this section before time expires, you may check your work. You cannot return to this section once you move on to the next section.

www.eggheadprep.com

ANSWERS, SECTION 2
SAMPLE TEST 3 — WRITING & LANGUAGE

1. A
2. C
3. D
4. D
5. A
6. B
7. C
8. B
9. D
10. B
11. C
12. A
13. C
14. B
15. D
16. D
17. C
18. B
19. A
20. C
21. D
22. B
23. A
24. D
25. C
26. A
27. D
28. B
29. C
30. B
31. D
32. C
33. C
34. D
35. C
36. B
37. B
38. D
39. A
40. C
41. B
42. A
43. D
44. C

SECTION 3: MATH TEST
NO CALCULATOR, 25 MINUTES, 20 QUESTIONS

DIRECTIONS

For questions 1–15, solve the problem and choose the best answer from the options provided. For questions 16–20, solve the problem and type in your answer. Further instructions for typing in your answer are provided before question 16.

NOTES

1. Calculator use is not permitted for this section. You will distort your score if you use one.
2. All variables and expressions represent real numbers unless stated otherwise.
3. Unless otherwise indicated, figures shown have been drawn to scale.
4. All figures lie in a plane unless stated otherwise.
5. The domain of a function f is the set of real numbers for which f(x) is a real number, unless stated otherwise.

REFERENCE

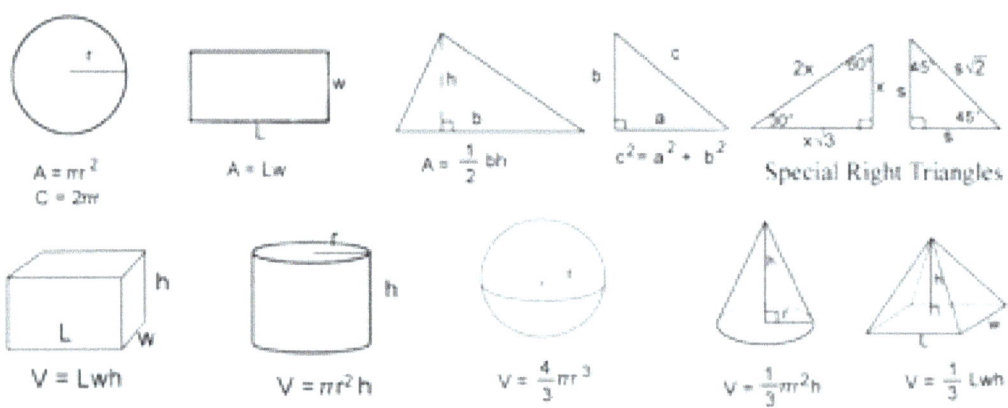

A full circle has 360 degrees of arc.
A full circle has 2π radians of arc.
The sum of the measures of the angles in a triangle is 180°.

SAMPLE TEST 3
Section 3: Math, No Calculator

1. If $5m = 35$, what is the value of $2m + 6$?
   A) 7
   B) 14
   C) 20
   D) 35

2. A farmer will be spraying several growing fields of identical size with an organic fertilizer. The cost of applying the spray is $nCAT$, where n is the number of fields and C is a constant with units of dollars per square yard. A is the area of each field in square yards. T is calculated by dividing the temperature in degrees Fahrenheit by 75° Fahrenheit. (Higher temperatures increase evaporation and thus affect the amount of fertilizer required.) If the farmer decides to switch to a less expensive organic fertilizer, which of the numbers in the equation would change?
   A) n
   B) C
   C) A
   D) T

3. The number of people who attended Jessica's birthday party was three times the number of people who attended her summer solstice game night. If 45 people attended her birthday party and s people attended her summer solstice game night, which equation accurately represents this information?
   A) $3s = 45$
   B) $45s = 3$
   C) $\dfrac{s}{3} = 45$
   D) $s + 3 = 45$

4. For all positive values of x, which of the following is equal to $x^{\frac{3}{4}}$?
   A) $\sqrt[3]{x^4}$
   B) $\sqrt[3]{x^{\frac{1}{4}}}$
   C) $\sqrt[4]{x^3}$
   D) $\sqrt[4]{x^{\frac{1}{3}}}$

5.
$$3x + 6y = -3$$
$$5x - 2y = -17$$
If the ordered pair (x, y) is a solution to the above system of equations, what is the value of $2x + y$?
   A) -20
   B) -5
   C) -3
   D) 1

6. If $\dfrac{4}{x} = \dfrac{6}{x+6}$, what is the value of $\dfrac{1}{3}$?
   A) 12
   B) 6
   C) 3
   D) $\dfrac{1}{3}$

7. A line in the xy-plane is represented by the equation, $y = ax - 7$, where a is a constant. If the point (u, v) is on the line, and neither u nor v equals zero, what is the slope of the line in terms of u and v?
   A) $\dfrac{u+7}{v}$
   B) $\dfrac{u+7}{v}$
   C) $\dfrac{v-7}{u}$
   D) $\dfrac{v+7}{u}$

8. The function g is represented by a polynomial expression. If the graph of g contains the points $(-3, 0)$, $(-1, -2)$, $(0, 1)$, and $(2, 0)$, which of the following must be a factor of g?
   A) $x + 3$
   B) $x + 1$
   C) $x + 2$
   D) $x - 1$

egghead prep.com

9.

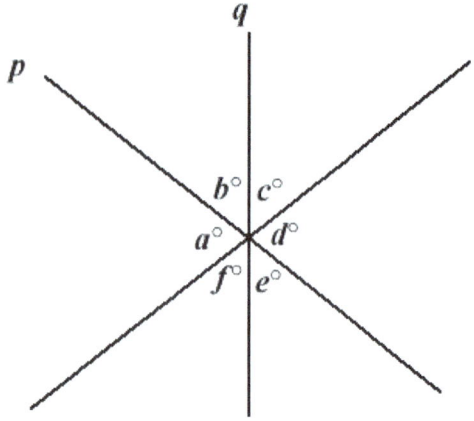

NOTE: This figure is not drawn to scale.

If $a + b = c + d$ in the figure above, which of these statements must be true?

I. $b = f$
II. $c = e$
III. $a = c$

A) I and II only
B) II and III only
C) I and III only
D) I, II, and III

10.
$$2x + ky = -6$$
$$-5x + 4y = 8$$
If the system of equations above has no solutions, what is the value of the constant k?

A) 3
B) −3
C) $\dfrac{8}{5}$
D) $-\dfrac{8}{5}$

11.
$$y = (x + 6)^2$$
The equation above represents a parabola in the xy-plane. The parabola intersects the line $y = 16$ in two points, P and Q. What is the distance from P to Q?

A) $\sqrt{6}$
B) 8
C) $2\sqrt{3}$
D) 12

12.
$$\dfrac{16x^2 - 20x + 17}{kx + 5} = -8x - 10 + \dfrac{67}{kx + 5}$$

The equation above is true for all values of x, $x \neq \dfrac{-5}{k}$. What is the value of the constant k?

A) −20
B) −2
C) 2
D) 20

13.
$$y = a(x + 3)(x - 5)$$
The graph of the equation shown above, where a is a constant, is a parabola in the xy-plane. If the vertex of the parabola is (h, k), what is the value of k in terms of a?

A) −16a
B) −15a
C) −2a
D) 3a

SAMPLE TEST 3
Section 3: Math, No Calculator

14.

$$P = \frac{4}{7}(L + 20)$$

The equation shows how the weight P, in pounds, of a package is related to the length L of the package, measured in inches. Based on the equation, which of the following statements must be true?

I. If the length of the package increases by $\frac{4}{7}$ of an inch, the weight will increase by 1 pound.

II. If the length of the package increases by 1 inch, the weight will increase by $\frac{4}{7}$ of a pound.

III. An increase of 1 pound in the weight of the package corresponds to an increase of 1.75 inches in length.

A) I only
B) II only
C) I and II only
D) II and III only

15.

What are the solutions of the equation,
$4x^2 - 24x + 12 = 0$?

A) $\dfrac{-3 \pm \sqrt{63}}{2}$
B) $6 \pm \sqrt{6}$
C) $3 \pm \sqrt{6}$
D) $6 \pm 2\sqrt{6}$

DIRECTIONS

For questions 16 – 20, solve the problem and type in your answer. Please follow these guidelines:

1. No questions have negative answers.
2. If a problem has more than one correct answer, any of those answers will be accepted as correct. Please enter only one answer.
3. Do not type in mixed numbers. A number such as 2 ¼ should be entered as 2.25 or 9/4. Mixed numbers will be misinterpreted by the computer.
4. If a decimal answer does not terminate after 3 decimal places, enter three decimal places only. You may either round or truncate the decimal. For example, 3/8 may be entered as 3/8 or .375, because the decimal ends there; 7/9 may be entered as 7/9, .777, or .778. Fractions should be reduced to simplest terms. For example, you should enter 1/2 instead of 2/4.

16.

If
$$\frac{9}{8}x - \frac{3}{8}x = \frac{2}{5} + \frac{11}{10},$$
what is the value of x ?

17.

$$x^4(x^2 - 13) = -36x^2$$

Given that $x > 0$, give one possible solution of the equation shown above.

18. In the sport of Gonk Honk, there are two ways to score: a *gonk* and a *honk*. A *honk* is worth 9 more points than a *gonk*. If a team that scored 4 *gonks* and 2 *honks* has a total of 120 points, how many points is a *gonk* worth?

20. In triangle *EFG*, the measure of ∠E is 90°. *EG* = 9 and *FG* = 15. Triangle *JIH* is similar to triangle *EFG*. The vertices *J*, *I*, and *H* correspond to the vertices *E*, *F*, and *G*, respectively, of the original triangle *EFG*. Each side of triangle *JIH* is twice the length of the corresponding side of triangle *EFG*. What is the value of cos *I* ?

19.

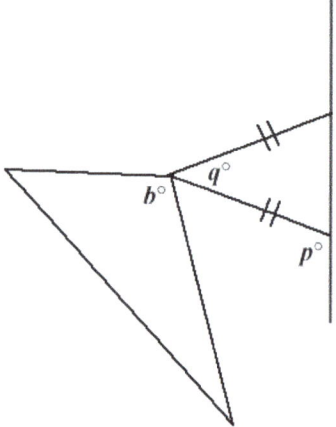

NOTE: This figure is not drawn to scale.

In the figure above, the triangle on the right is isosceles, as shown. If $q + 2b = 180$ and $b = 40$, what is the value of $2b + p$?

STOP

If you have finished this section before time expires, you may check your work. You cannot return to this section once you move on to the next section.

EGGHEAD PREP™
Get cracking.

STOP!

If you have finished this section before time expires, you may check your work. You cannot return to this section once you move on to the next section.

www.eggheadprep.com

ANSWERS, SECTION 3
SAMPLE TEST 3 — MATH, NO CALCULATOR

1. C
2. B
3. A
4. C
5. B
6. C
7. D
8. A
9. A
10. D
11. B
12. B
13. A
14. D
15. C

---

16. 2
17. 2 OR 3
18. 17
19. 220
20. 24/30 OR 12/15 OR 4/5 OR .8

EGGHEAD PREP

SECTION 4: MATH TEST
CALCULATOR, 55 MINUTES, 38 QUESTIONS

DIRECTIONS

For questions 1–30, solve the problem and choose the best answer from the options provided. For questions 31–38, solve the problem and type in your answer. Further instructions for typing in your answer are provided before question 31.

NOTES

1. Calculator use is permitted for this section.
2. All variables and expressions represent real numbers unless stated otherwise.
3. Unless otherwise indicated, figures shown have been drawn to scale.
4. All figures lie in a plane unless stated otherwise.
5. The domain of a function f is the set of real numbers for which f(x) is a real number, unless stated otherwise.

REFERENCE

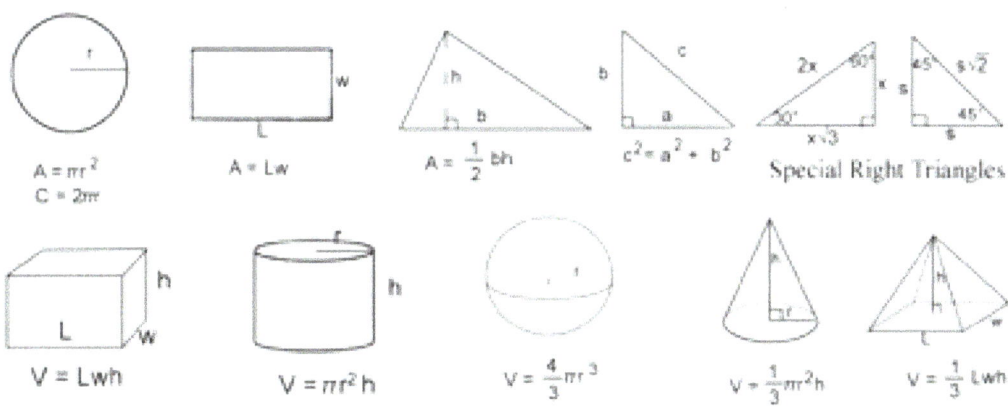

A full circle has 360 degrees of arc.
A full circle has 2π radians of arc.
The sum of the measures of the angles in a triangle is 180°.

eggheadprep.com

1.

Boat Cruise

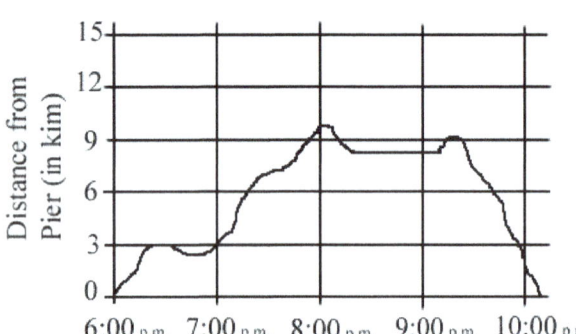

A group of people went on a boat cruise on a Saturday evening. The graph above shows the boat's distance from the pier through the course of the evening. For nearly an hour, the boat stayed anchored in place so the passengers could go for a moonlight swim. Based on the graph, which of the following times is closest to the time when the moonlight swim began?

A) 7:30 p.m.
B) 8:20 p.m.
C) 9:10 p.m.
D) 10:10 p.m.

2.

Coyotes Living in U.S. Urban Areas

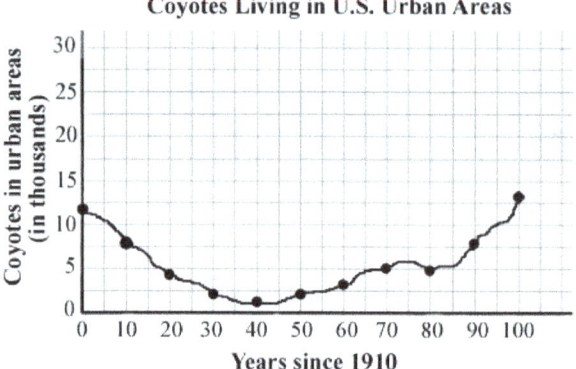

The graph above shows the total number of coyotes living in US urban areas, in thousands, from 1910 through 2010. Based on the graph, which of the following is an accurate description of the data?

A) The number of coyotes living in US urban areas generally decreased each decade from 1910 through 2010.

B) The number of coyotes living in US urban areas generally increased each decade from 1910 through 2010.

C) The number of coyotes living in US urban areas remained about the same throughout the period from 1910 through 2010.

D) The number of coyotes living in US urban areas decreased from 1910 through 1950, then generally increased after that.

SAMPLE TEST 3
Section 4: Math, Calculator

3.

Year in School

School	Junior	Senior	Total
Western H.S.	27	18	45
Eastern H.S.	15	31	46
Total	42	49	91

Juniors and seniors from two different high schools, Western H.S. and Eastern H.S., were selected to have their artwork exhibited at the city museum for a month. Each student was allowed to submit one piece of artwork. The table above shows the number of juniors and seniors selected from each school. If a piece of artwork from the exhibit is selected at random, what is the probability that the artist was a junior at Western H.S. or a senior at Eastern H.S.?

A) $\dfrac{1}{2}$

B) $\dfrac{42}{49}$

C) $\dfrac{45}{91}$

D) $\dfrac{45}{91}$

4.

$$7x^3 - 8x - 6$$
$$4x^3 + 5x - 3$$

Which of the following expressions represents the sum of the polynomials above?

A) $11x^3 - 3x - 9$
B) $11x^3 - 3x + 9$
C) $11x^6 - 3x^2 - 9$
D) $11x^6 - 3x^2 + 9$

5. A local clothing manufacturer makes sweatshirts and skirts. Approximately 3% of the sweatshirts and 12% of the skirts that the manufacturer made in 2012 had a special logo on them commemorating the 150th anniversary of the founding of the town. If the manufacturer made 985 sweatshirts and 780 skirts in 2012, which number is closest to the total number of items of clothing the manufacturer made with the special logo?

A) 30
B) 94
C) 123
D) 142

6.

x	2	3	4	5
$g(x)$	4	1	−2	−5

The table above shows some of the values of a function g. If g is a linear function, which of these rules defines g?

A) $g(x) = -x + 6$
B) $g(x) = -2x + 8$
C) $g(x) = -3x + 10$
D) $g(x) = -4x + 12$

7. A bicyclist travels 6 km in 18.3 minutes. If she maintains the same pace, which of the following is closest to the distance she will travel in 3 hours?

A) 1 km
B) 60 km
C) 330 km
D) 1,060 km

8. The average number of housecats per square mile in the town of Omerville from 2002 to 2014 is modeled by the line of best fit with equation $C = 93.4 - 8.29x$, where C is the average number of cats per square mile and x is the number of years since 2002. Which of these statements best describes the meaning of the number −8.29 in this equation?

A) In 2014, on average, there were 8.29 fewer cats per square mile in Omerville than in 2002.

B) In 2002, there were, on average, 8.29 cats per square mile in Omerville.

C) The number 8.29×12 represents the total number of cats in Omerville in 2014.

D) From 2002 to 2014, it is estimated that the average number of cats per square mile in Omerville decreased by 8.29 per year.

9. If $\frac{5}{8}p = \frac{3}{5}$, what is the value of p?

A) $\frac{24}{25}$

B) $\frac{25}{24}$

C) $\frac{8}{3}$

D) $\frac{8}{3}$

10. If the function g has exactly four distinct zeros, which of these choices could represent a complete graph of g on the xy-plane?

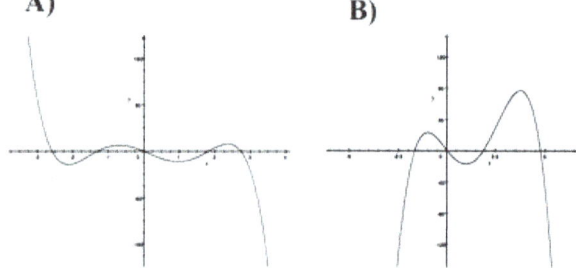

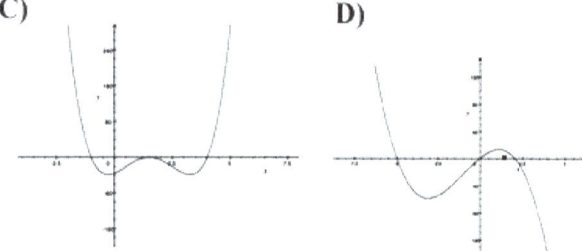

Questions 11 and 12 refer to the following information.

Liquid	Buoyancy constant (N / m³)
Water	9,810
Seawater	10,100
Cooking oil	8,980
Isopropyl alcohol	7,710
Liquid nitrogen	7,940
Cane molasses	13,830
Gasoline	7,060

The table above shows the buoyancy constants for various liquids. The buoyant force on an object submerged in a liquid can be calculated using the formula F = BV, where F is the buoyant force in Newtons, B is the liquid's buoyancy constant measured in Newtons per cubic meter, and V is the volume of the object in cubic meters.

11. Which value best approximates the buoyant force, in Newtons, on an object of volume 1.4 m3 that is submerged in liquid nitrogen?

A) 5,670

B) 9,880

C) 11,120

D) 13,730

12. When submerged in cooking oil, a certain object is acted on by a buoyant force of 25,500 Newtons. In which liquid would the same object be acted on by a buoyant force of approximately 28,700 Newtons?

A) water

B) seawater

C) isopropyl alcohol

D) cane molasses

13.

The heart of a very small animal beats an average of 11.3 times per second. Which of the following equations represents the number of heartbeats h that the animal has in m **minutes**?

A) $h = \dfrac{11.3m}{60}$

B) $h = 11.3m$

C) $h = 11.3m + 60$

D) $h = 11.3(60m)$

14.
$$d = 9p^2 + cp + z$$
The equation above gives the number of days it takes for a biologist to be able to individually identify p penguins, where c and z are constants that depend on weather conditions and the time of year. Which of the following correctly expresses c in terms of d, p, and z?

A) $c = d - z - 9p$

B) $c = \dfrac{d - z - 9}{p}$

C) $c = \dfrac{d + z + 9}{p}$

D) $c = \dfrac{d + z + 9}{p}$

15.

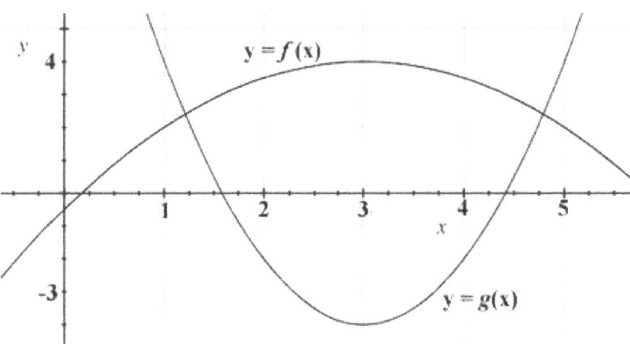

The image above shows the graphs of two functions f and g. For what value of x does it appear that $f(x) + g(x) = 0$?

A) 1.25

B) 1.6

C) 3

D) 4.75

16.

The headmaster at the School for Magical Arts and Sciences wished to determine if a new type of wand would help students cast spells more effectively. From the 4,500 students at the school, the headmaster randomly selected a sample of 180 students. Half of the selected students received the new type of wand. The other half received wands that looked like the new type of wand, but were actually the same as the wands they were already using. The data gathered in the study showed that overall, students who received the new type of wand had significantly more success casting spells than those who received wands that were the same as their existing wands. Based on the design of the study and the results obtained, which of the following conclusions would be appropriate?

A) The new type of wand is likely to help students achieve greater success in casting spells.

B) Using the new type of wand results in a dramatic increase in a student's ability to cast spells.

C) The new type of wand is more powerful than any other type of wand for casting spells.

D) Every student who uses the new type of wand will experience an improved ability to cast spells.

17.
Collapsed stars such as white dwarfs contain some of the densest matter in the universe. Suppose that at one stage of a star's collapse, a teaspoon of material from the star, if brought to Earth, would weigh as much as 11 average-sized cars. If an average-sized car weighs $1\frac{3}{4}$ tons, which choice would be closest to the weight on Earth, in tons, of 36 teaspoons of material from the collapsing star?

A) 225

B) 395

C) 695

D) 2,770

Questions 18 and 19 refer to the following information.

In economics, the supply S of a product is the number of units of that product that manufacturers are willing and able to produce. The demand D for the product is the number of units of that product that consumers are willing and able to purchase. Both supply and demand depend on the price P of the product, in dollars. For a new product called the Norbinator, the demand function $D(P)$ and supply function $S(P)$ are described by the following equations:

$$S(P) = 0.75P + 120$$
$$D(P) = 235 - 2.5P$$

18. How will the number of Norbinators supplied by manufacturers change if the price increases by $12?

A) The supply will increase by 12 units.

B) The supply will decrease by 12 units.

C) The supply will increase by 129 units.

D) The supply will increase by 9 units.

19. *Market balance* occurs when supply and demand are equal. Which of the following is closest to the price at which market balance will occur for Norbinators?

A) $35

B) $94

C) $103

D) $160

20. Of the four situations described below for the declining value of an automobile, which option would yield an exponential decrease of the value?

A) Each successive year, the value of the automobile decreases by 4.7% of the original price of the automobile.

B) Each successive year, the value of the automobile decreases by 5.8% of the current value of the automobile.

C) Each successive year, the value of the automobile decreases by $750.

D) Each successive year, the value of the automobile decreases by $300 plus 4.7% of the original price of the automobile.

21.

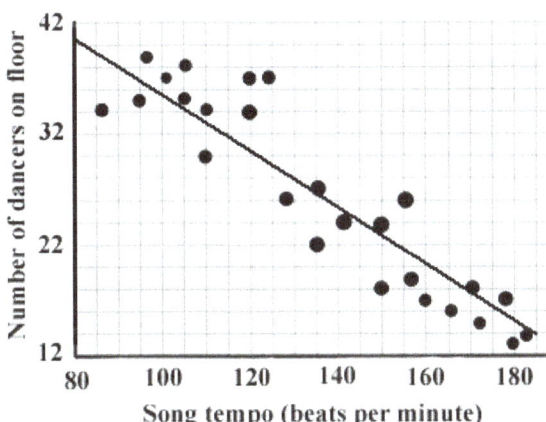

Number of People Dancing vs. Song Tempo

Tasha works as a DJ for blues-swing dance events. On a certain night, she played 26 songs, making note of the tempo of each song and the number of people who danced to it. Her data is displayed in the scatterplot above, along with the line of best fit. For the song with tempo 165 beats per minute, the actual number of people who danced was about how many less than the number predicted by the line of best fit?

A) 2
B) 3
C) 4
D) 5

22.

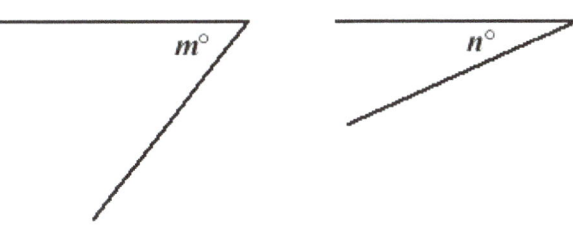

NOTE: These figures are not drawn to scale.

The figures above represent two acute angles. It is known that $\cos(m°) = \sin(n°)$. If $m = 4x - 14$ and $n = 2x + 2$, what is the value of x?

A) 9.5
B) 13
C) 17
D) 26

23. The director of a choir is paid a certain amount of money for the choir's performance at a cathedral. After paying expenses and his own salary, the director has d dollars to distribute to the members of the choir. If he pays each member $104, there will be $12 remaining. In order to pay each member $107, he would need $204 more than the d dollars he has. How many members does the choir have?

A) 17
B) 64
C) 72
D) 204

24.

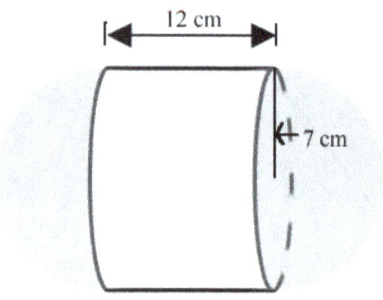

A balloon is shaped like a right circular cylinder with hemispheres built upon both of its bases, with measurements as shown above. Which number is closest to the volume of the balloon, in cubic centimeters?

A) 1,436.8
B) 1,847.3
C) 2,656.6
D) 3,284.0

25. Three numbers, x, y, and w satisfy the equation:

$$x + y + w = 1,560$$

If w is 40% more than $x + y$, what must be the value of w?

A) 1,114.3
B) 910
C) 650
D) 445.7

26. A landscape architect altered the design of a rectangular garden, decreasing the length of the garden by 25% while increasing the width by r percent. If these changes decreased the area of the garden by 4%, what is the value of r?

A) 4
B) 21
C) 28
D) 29

27. A line in the xy–plane goes through the points $(n, 27)$ and $(3, n)$. If the line also contains the origin, which of the following is a possible value of n?

A) 9
B) 6
C) 3
D) 0

28.

Preferred Mascot for Xenon Middle School

Grade of Student	Honey badger	Fishing cat
7th		
8th		
Total	136	25

Xenon Middle School will have a new mascot in 2017. School administrators have narrowed the choices to a honey badger and a fishing cat. Every 7th and 8th grade student at Xenon was asked to declare his or her preference between the two choices. The incomplete table above summarized the results of the survey. There were four times as many 7th graders who preferred the honey badger as there were 7th graders who preferred the fishing cat. There were seven times as many 8th graders who preferred the honey badger as 8th graders who preferred the fishing cat. A total of 25 students preferred the fishing cat. Which of the following choices is closest to the probability that a student selected at random from among those who preferred the honey badger is a 7th grader?

A) 0.38
B) 0.52
C) 0.62
D) 0.80

SAMPLE TEST 3
Section 4: Math, Calculator

29. The number of baseball teams competing in the qualifying tournaments for the Little League World Series that have at least one female player is expected to increase by 18 percent every 5 years. If there are currently 25 teams with at least one female player, which expression could be used to estimate the number of such teams N years from now?

A) $25(.18)^{5N}$

B) $25(1.18)^{5N}$

C) $25(.18)^{\frac{N}{5}}$

D) $25(1.18)^{\frac{N}{5}}$

30.
$$4x - n = 9x + 3$$
$$4y - m = 9y + 3$$

In the system of equations shown above, n is equal to $m + \frac{1}{3}$. Which of the following must be true?

A) x minus y is -1

B) x plus y is $\frac{1}{3}$

C) x minus y is $\frac{1}{3}$

D) y minus x is $\frac{1}{15}$

DIRECTIONS

For questions 31–38, solve the problem and type in your answer. Please follow these guidelines:

1. No questions have negative answers.
2. If a problem has more than one correct answer, any of those answers will be accepted as correct. Please enter only one answer.
3. Do not type in mixed numbers. A number such as 2 ¼ should be entered as 2.25 or 9/4. Mixed numbers will be misinterpreted by the computer.
4. If a decimal answer does not terminate after 3 decimal places, enter three decimal places unless otherwise instructed. You may either round or truncate the decimal. For example, 3/8 may be entered as 3/8 or .375, because the decimal ends there; 7/9 may be entered as 7/9, .777, or .778. Fractions should be reduced to simplest terms. In other words, you should enter 1/2 instead of 2/4.
5. Do not include a comma within any number. For example, for the number 3,750, simply enter 3750.

31.
Times of Various Competitors for 400-meter Obstacle Course

Name	Time (sec.)	Name	Time (sec.)
Chandra	87	Naomi	81
Philip	84	Toby	71
Daneesha	73	Jacob	98
Madison	96	Brenda	70
Benjamin	91	Daniel	88
Addison	93	Riley	86

The table above shows the times, in seconds, of 12 competitors in a 400-meter obstacle course race. What was the mean time, in seconds, of these 12 competitors? (Round your answer to the nearest tenth.)

32.
Tickets to a recent performance by the band SHARP at Weston Middle School cost $5 for students and $7 for parents. If Ms. Davis spent at least $22 but no more than $36 on s student tickets and 1 parent ticket, what is one possible value of s?

33.
Points M and N are on a circle with center C. The measure of angle MCN is $\dfrac{4\pi}{3}$ radians. The area of the sector formed by angle MCN represents what fraction of the area of circle C?

34.
$$(-4x^2 + 7x - 5) - 3(2x^2 - 4x - 3)$$
If the expression shown above is rewritten in the form $ax^2 + bx + c$, where a, b, and c are constants, what is the value of b?

35.
$$y \geq 20x$$
$$y \geq -10x + 6000$$
The point (u, v) in the xy-plane lies in the solution set of the above system of inequalities. What is the minimum possible value of v?

36.
Sheila needs to play 15 rounds of golf and have an average score of 74 or below to qualify for a national tournament. She believes that the lowest score she can possibly achieve for any round is 64. Assuming her belief is correct, if Sheila's average score for her first 9 rounds is 78, what is the highest possible score she can have for her 10th round and still have a chance to qualify for the tournament?

SAMPLE TEST 3
Section 4: Math, Calculator

Questions 37 and 38 refer to the following information.

When web designers create a website for a business, it is important for them to consider how many visitors the site will typically need to accommodate at a time. One statistician has proposed that a good formula to estimate the number of visitors V to a site at any given time is, $V = 0.8LT$, where L is the average number of new visitors to the site per second, and T is the average number of seconds each visitor stays on the site. (This formula is a variation of Little's Law for physical stores.)

For example, the owner of Finagling, Inc., estimates that an average of 7 new visitors come to the company's website every second and each visitor stays on the site for an average of 45 seconds, so that the number of visitors at any given time is approximately $V = 252$.

37. The same formula can be applied to any specific page or section of the website. Suppose a particularly popular page of the Finagling, Inc. website draws 2 new visitors per second, and each visitors stays on the page for an average of 1 minute, 40 seconds. About what number of visitors does that page have at any given time?

38. Finagling, Inc.'s main competitor is Wangling, LLC. Suppose the Wangling, LLC website has an average of 600 new visitors every **minute** and the visitors stay on the site for an average of 22 seconds. The average number of visitors to the Wangling, LLC website at any time is what percent less than the average number of visitors to the Finagling, Inc. website at any time? (NOTE: Round your answer to the nearest whole percent and ignore the percent symbol for your answer. For example, if the answer is 53.957%, round to 54% and simply enter 54 as your answer.)

STOP

If you have finished this section before time expires, you may check your work. You cannot return to this section once you move on to the next section.

STOP!

If you have finished this section before time expires, you may check your work. You cannot return to this section once you move on to the next section.

www.eggheadprep.com

ANSWERS, SECTION 4
SAMPLE TEST 3 — MATH, CALCULATOR

1. B
2. D
3. C
4. A
5. C
6. C
7. B
8. D
9. A
10. B
11. C
12. B
13. D
14. C
15. C
16. A
17. C
18. D
19. A
20. B
21. B
22. C
23. C
24. D
25. B
26. C
27. A
28. A
29. D

30. D

31. 84.8
32. 3 OR 4 OR 5
33. 4/6 OR 2/3 OR 0.667 OR 0.666
34. 19
35. 4000
36. 88
37. 160
38. 30

eggheadprep.com

ANSWER EXPLANATIONS

SAMPLE TEST 3 — SECTION 1, 2, 3, 4

NOTE: The SAT Reading Test emphasizes <u>evidence-based</u> analysis of the passages. While reading the passages, you will no doubt form opinions regarding whether the results of an experiment described should be trusted, or whether there are reasons beyond those presented in the passage for characters to act as they do. Those opinions may be perfectly valid, but when answering the questions, it is important to remember to draw conclusions based <u>solely</u> on evidence that is explicitly presented in the passage, not on your own personal feelings.

TEST SECTION 1: READING

1. Note that the first three paragraphs (lines 1-32) provide a general overview of Emma Woodhouse's background. The fourth paragraph (lines 33-41) begins, "Sorrow came, a gentle sorrow, but not at all in the shape of any disagreeable consciousness." The next two sentences explain that as a result of Miss Taylor's marriage, Emma felt persistent sadness (a "mournful thought of any continuance") for the very first time. We therefore conclude that the marriage of Miss Taylor was a pivotal moment in Emma's life. Most of the rest of the passage is devoted to Emma's concerns about how she will find happiness in Miss Taylor's absence. Because the exploration of those concerns could reasonably be described as Emma "ponder[ing] her prospects," and because the passage makes clear that Miss Taylor's marriage affected Emma's life greatly, **the correct answer is (B)**.

2. The words presented in answer choices (A), (B), and (C) are all accepted meanings of the word "supplied." Only answer (D) can be immediately eliminated, since "recalled" has no meaning in common with the word "supplied." In present-day usage, choices (A) and (B) are the meanings most commonly associated with the word "supplied." However, the context of the sentence in which the word "supplied" is used in the passage (lines 9-14) makes clear that the governess served, in effect, as a *substitute* for a mother in Emma's life. That is, Miss Taylor in some sense *replaced* Emma's mother. **The correct answer is (C).**

3. Notice, first of all, that we are instructed to identify what the passage *most clearly* implies about Emma's personality. We therefore look for direct statements about Emma's temperament, not subtle implications. In any case, absolutely nothing said in the passage calls Emma's reliability into question, so answer (D) may be ruled out immediately. Although Emma is certainly pessimistic about her possibilities for finding happiness in the wake of Miss Taylor's departure, it is stated quite clearly in the passage (lines 1-2) that she has, by nature, a "happy disposition." We therefore rule out answer (C). Growing up in isolation is often associated with naiveté, but we find no clear evidence of naiveté on Emma's part in the passage. Though plausible, then, answer (B) is incorrect. Notice, however, that lines 23-27 refer to Emma "doing just what she liked" and "having rather too much her own way." The word "willful" describes a stubborn insistence on doing what one wants to do. **The correct answer is (A).**

EGGHEAD PREP

SAMPLE TEST 3
Answer Explanations

4. As noted in the explanation for the answer to question #3 above, the strongest evidence for that answer is to be found in lines 23-27. **The correct answer is (B).**

5. You may be aware that to "alloy" metals is to blend or mix them. That meaning, however, would not make sense within the context of the statement (lines 29-30) in which the word "alloy" is used in the passage. The words "disadvantages" and "threatened" make clear that Emma's traits described in lines 26-28 could *harm* her prospects for happiness. Because impair means hinder or harm, **the correct answer is (D).**

6. In lines 16-18, we learn that Emma saw Miss Taylor less as a governess than as a friend, and that Miss Taylor was "particularly" fond of Emma. Lines 22-23 state that Miss Taylor and Emma lived as "friend and friend very mutually attached." Therefore, the depth of the friendship between these two characters is clearly a central theme of the paragraph, as indicated in answer choice (D). Choice (A) is alluring, however. It is certainly true that the paragraph implies that possessing the title of governess did not mean that Miss Taylor was an authority figure in Emma's life. However, the observation that "the mildness of [Miss Taylor's] temper had hardly allowed her to impose any restraint" (lines 19-21) shows that the reason for Miss Taylor's lack of authoritative power was her own personality, not an inherent lack of value in the title, "governess." **The correct answer is (D).**

7. Lines 45-50 hold the key to answering this question correctly. In those lines, we learn that Emma had always "wished and promoted the match," that is, advocated for the marriage to occur. But she had also considered doing so to be "a black morning's work for her," implying that she believed she would suffer as a result of the marriage actually occurring. She believed, in fact, that "The want [that is, absence] of Miss Taylor would be felt every hour of every day." We must therefore identify the answer choice that describes both Emma's support of the marriage and her worry about the life that would await her after the marriage occurred. Only answer choice (C) clearly expresses both ideas. **The correct answer is (C).**

8. The phrase, "[t]he evil of the actual disparity in their ages," implies that the mere fact that a large difference in age existed between Emma and her father would have been hard on Emma under any circumstances. But the phrase, "was much increased by his constitution and habits," indicates that the most important issue is not Mr. Woodhouse's biological age, but rather his manner of living. The next several lines then explain that Mr. Woodhouse's lifestyle, particularly his avoidance of strenuous activity, has made him, as we would say today, old before his time ("a much older man in ways than in years"). The answer choice that best expresses these ideas is (A). **The correct answer is (A).**

9. Lines 77-80 state with regard to Emma's father, "And though everywhere beloved for the friendliness of his heart and his amiable temper, his talents could not have recommended him at any time." Here, "recommended" is used to mean something like "distinguished," or "set apart from the crowd." In other words, Mr. Woodhouse is universally viewed as kind and likable, but lacking any abilities that would truly impress people. These observations are well summarized in answer choice (B). **The correct answer is (B).**

eggheadprep.com

10. As noted in the explanation for question #9 above, it is in lines 77-80 that Mr. Woodhouse's nature is summarized most clearly. Therefore, those lines provide the clearest evidence in support of the correct answer for question #9. **The correct answer is (C).**

11. In the fourth paragraph (lines 26-32), the reader is warned that Emma is disposed to "think a little too well of herself," which is essentially the definition of arrogance. In the final paragraph (lines 81-92), the reader learns that Emma does not view anyone in all of Highbury as her equal. She therefore believes that no one can take Miss Taylor's place in her life, a belief that lies at the root of her melancholy mood. In short, Emma's excessively high opinion of herself seems destined to result in her isolation. Answer (D) summarizes these thoughts. **The correct answer is (D).**

---

12. In the paragraph, the author describes the incompatibility of traditional TV broadcast schedules with present-day work schedules (lines 16-20), the unease most people today would feel at the thought of committing an uninterrupted hour to watching a television broadcast (lines 23-25), and the possibility that a traditional TV viewing experience could be ruined by a single interruption (lines 26-28). All of these considerations would generally deter people from getting excited about a concept like the NoN television network. Therefore, **the correct answer is (B).**

13. All of the answer choices offer legitimate reasons why a person might prefer watching streaming content to viewing live TV broadcasts. We must determine which of the reasons are explicitly put forth by the author of the passage, however. As noted above in the explanation for question #12, the reason described in answer choice (A) is discussed in lines 16-20 of the passage. The reason proposed in choice (B) is discussed in lines 26-28 and lines 32-35. The reason described in choice (D), again as noted above in the explanation for question #12, is discussed in lines 23-25. The remaining answer choice, (C), presents a reason that is not mentioned in the passage. **The correct answer is (C).**

14. The word "scant" generally implies barely adequate or in very short supply. Further evidence for the answer to this question can be found in lines 19-20. Given that "many Americans work multiple jobs totaling 55 or more hours per week just to make ends meet," they certainly cannot have much free time. All of these clues point us toward answer (A), "limited." **The correct answer is (A).**

15. Quite often, the main idea of a paragraph is set forth in the paragraph's first sentence or two. In the first sentence of the third paragraph (lines 38-39), the reader is told that Andrew Bennett has doubts about the conclusion suggested at the end of the second paragraph. In the second sentence (lines 39-43), the author notes that Bennett returned home from his travels "convinced that traditional television viewing offers rewards that on-demand streaming simply cannot match." Answer choice (C) paraphrases this statement. **The correct answer is (C).**

16. As noted in the explanation for question #15 above, lines 39-43 provide strong support for the correct answer to that question. However, those lines are not referenced in any of the answer choices offered for question #16. Note, however, that in lines 43-47, Bennett himself is quoted, elaborating on the experiences that led him to believe that traditional TV viewing is in some ways superior to on-demand streaming. Bennett speaks specifically of a unique form of excitement that does not exist when programs are available at any time. Therefore, since lines 43-47 expand on the idea presented

SAMPLE TEST 3
Answer Explanations

in lines 39-43, the best answer choice is the one that references lines 43-47. **The correct answer is (B).**

17. Answer (D) may be ruled out immediately, because nothing in the descriptions of the roller coaster and the eagle connects in any way to aspects of the NoN broadcast signal. And while it may be true that NoN programming includes shows about roller coasters and eagles, no such programs are mentioned in the passage, so answer (A) must be eliminated as well. Answer choice (C) offers a very plausible reason why the descriptions may be included in the passage, but an objective reading of the passage as a whole reveals that neither the author nor Bennett at any time criticizes Americans for spending time online. Therefore, though not outlandish, answer (C) is incorrect. **The correct answer is (B).**

18. The word "abysmal" usually describes something that is very bad or appalling. Therefore, answers (A) and (D) are both reasonable choices. Answers (B) and (C) can be ruled out, since those words do not have meanings in common with the word "abysmal." To choose between answers (A) and (D), consider the context in which the word is used. It would be quite normal to refer to a TV network's ratings as "poor" (that is, very bad) but strange to call them "offensive" (that is, causing deep hurt for many people). **The correct answer is (D).**

19. As has been noted in the explanation for question #18 above, the NoN network had very bad ratings during its first year (line 74), which would certainly be a good reason to doubt its viability as an enterprise. The observation (lines 75-77) that Bennett received a "seemingly endless stream of messages from friends and family inquiring as to whether he had lost his grip on reality," implies that even those closest to Bennett believed his network was destined to fail. Therefore, lines 74-77 provide strong evidence for the conclusion proposed in the question, that there was a great deal of doubt about whether NoN would succeed. **The correct answer is (C).**

20. Note, first of all, that Figure 1 solely presents data about the ages of viewers of the NoN network. For example, the figure tells us that 20% of the network's viewers are 60 years of age or older. The chart does *not* provide any information about how frequently viewers of various ages watch the network. Therefore, answer (A) can be eliminated immediately. We now look for the statement that is most clearly true based on the figure. Note that according to the chart, only 5% of NoN viewers are under 14, while 14% fall in the 40-59 age range. Therefore, the statement made in answer choice (D) is clearly correct. **The correct answer is (D).**

21. From the first figure, combining the percentages for age groups Under 14, 14-23, and 24-39, we conclude that 40% + 21% + 5% = 66% of NoN viewers are under age 40, which is a clear majority. From the second figure, we see that only 14% of NoN viewers prefer to watch the network alone, so that 100% – 14% = 86% of viewers prefer to watch in the company of others. Answer choice (A) summarizes both of these conclusions. **The correct answer is (A).**

---

22. "Restrictive" is neither a logical word choice within the context of the sentence nor an accepted meaning of the word "barren," so answer (C) can be eliminated. The words presented in answers (A), (B), and (D) all share at least one meaning in common with "barren," however. The phrase "uninhabited of permanent results" is clearly nonsensical, so answer (D) is incorrect. In a poetic

setting, it would not be unthinkable to write, "infertile of permanent results," which would suggest that the effort in question cannot "give birth" to permanent results. However, it is clear from the passage as a whole that Mr. Douglass believes that the Civil War *could* yield permanent results if the right actions are taken in its wake. Therefore, the word "infertile" would not be consistent with Douglass's message. **The correct answer is (B).**

23. Any one of the concerns proposed in the four answer choices might have been put forth by a politician or activist after the Civil War. From lines 36-41 of the passage, we know that Douglass feared that forms of slavery would continue to exist even after slavery was outlawed. However, he does not at any point suggest that slavery may become legal again. Nor does he mention the possibility of a labor shortage. And although he uses the word "conservation" (line 38), he is clearly referring to the continuation of slavery, not environmental issues. We are thus left with answer (C) as the only viable possibility. Note that in lines 8-11, Douglass warns that men are being brought into the "national councils" (that is, Congress) who represent states that have been forced to rejoin the Union, and that these men have no intention of contributing constructively to the work of Congress. Answer choice (C) expresses these concerns. **The correct answer is (C).**

24. As noted above in the explanation for question #23, lines 8-11 provide clear support for the answer to that question. Since those lines are among the lines referenced in answer choice (B), **the correct answer is (B).**

25. In lines 21-25, Douglass states that the bills in question "do not reach the difficulty," meaning that they do not address fundamental issues in a manner that would be likely to create lasting change. He further asserts that they cannot have the desired impact "unless the whole structure of the government is changed from a government by states to something like a despotic central government, with power to control even the municipal regulations of states." In other words, he believes that the proposed laws could only have their intended effects if the federal government forcefully imposed its will upon state and local governments. This opinion is summarized in answer choice (D). **The correct answer is (D).**

26. As noted above in the explanation for question #25 above, lines 21-25 provide clear and strong evidence in support of the answer to that question. Therefore, **the correct answer is (C).**

27. In lines 26-31, Douglass asserts that, "As long as there remains such an idea as the right of each state to control its own local affairs [that is, state sovereignty] … no general assertion of human rights can be of any practical value." The statement offers a clear indication that Douglass believed that, under the conditions of his time, state sovereignty and equal rights for all were incompatible goals. **The correct answer is (A).**

28. Douglass does mention (line 50) the possibility of deploying federal officers throughout the land, but he also states that it should not be done (line 51), so answer choice (A) must be eliminated. He also metaphorically describes rebellion (that is, the Civil War) as a "teacher" (line 58) but he does not comment on the American school system, which rules out answer (C). He does not at any point mention the cost of the Civil War, so answer (D) is clearly incorrect. In lines 52-54, however, he asserts that "[t]he true way and the easiest way is to make our government entirely consistent with

SAMPLE TEST 3
Answer Explanations

itself, and give to every loyal citizen the elective franchise [right to vote]." Therefore, **the correct answer is (B).**

29. As noted in the explanation for question #28 above, lines 52-54 of the passage clearly support the correct answer to that question. Those lines overlap with lines 53-56, referenced in answer choice (C), and quite importantly, the statement about the "elective franchise" is included within lines 53-56. **The correct answer is (C).**

30. Within the paragraph (lines 64-66), Douglass states that, "no republic is safe that tolerates a privileged class, or denies to any of its citizens equal rights and equal means to maintain them." He is denouncing unequal treatment under the law. Answer (B) identifies such unequal treatment as the "true source of danger" of which Douglass writes. **The correct answer is (B).**

31. As noted in the explanation for question #30 above, lines 64-66 provide the evidence needed to answer that question correctly. T**he correct answer is (D).**

32. The word "implore" generally implies begging or urging. Only answer choice (A) offers a word or phrase with a similar meaning. **The correct answer is (A).**

---

33. There is no consequential geographic information about the city included in the first paragraph (numerous cities have an East Side and a West Side), so answer (D) must be ruled out immediately. Although the author's mention of the East Side and West Side bridges suggests that they are significant structures, he does not discuss their importance to transportation in any meaningful way, which eliminates answer choice (A). Since the author does not, in fact, reveal his age (we only know that he is *at least* forty; he could be far older), answer (B) cannot be correct. Therefore, **the correct answer is (C).**

34. In line 12, the author describes the personal automobile as "one of the most enduring symbols of American freedom." Then, in lines 14-15, he warns that the transportation plan under consideration will "wrest [take by force] that symbol from our hands and homes." Answer choice (A) paraphrases this argument. **The correct answer is (A).**

35. As noted in the explanation for question #34 above, lines 12, 14, and 15 provide the clearest evidence in support of the answer to that question. All of these lines are included among the lines referenced in answer choice (B). Therefore, **the correct answer is (B).**

36. "Represent" does not have meanings in common with "figure" (although *representation* does), so answer (B) is incorrect. Answer choices (A), (C), and (D) are all accepted meanings of the word "figure." However, it is clear from the context of the sentence (lines 27-31), that the author's intended meaning for "figure" is along the lines of, "suppose," "imagine," or "predict." In other words, he is describing what he believes most people would *expect* to be true. **The correct answer is (A).**

37. As noted in the explanation for question #36 above, in lines 27-31, the author lays out his understanding of what Oak Springs City leaders would expect to occur in Calinoma City and Oreton

Valley based on the transportation plans of the two cities. In line 32, he asserts that "the numbers tell a very different story," implying that what has actually occurred is very different from what Oak Springs City leaders would have predicted. Therefore, answer (D) accurately describes the author's purpose. **The correct answer is (D).**

38. The author of Passage 2 directly address the points made in Passage 1, without resorting to emotionally charged language. Passage 2 does not provide a detailed description of Oak Springs City's transportation plan, and it certainly does not provide evidence in support of the arguments presented in Passage 1. We have thus ruled out answer choices (A), (B), and (C). The author of Passage 2 signals early in the passage that she intends to refute the arguments present in Passage 1 by stating (line 7) that "Mr. Biltonase errs in" his conclusions. In the second paragraph (lines 67-87) she presents a great deal of specific evidence pertaining to the situations in Calinoma City and Oreton Valley. Therefore, answer choice (D) describes the relationship between the passages well. **The correct answer is (D).**

39. As noted in the explanation for question #38 above, the author of Passage 2 states that the author of Passage 1 errs in his conclusions, so it is highly unlikely that she would view the conclusion discussed in this question as "essentially correct." For this reason, answers (A) and (B) must be eliminated. At no point, however, does the author of Passage 2 accuse the author of Passage 1 of using data that was falsified in any way by anyone. Answer (D) is therefore incorrect. We are left with answer choice (C), which accurately summarizes the arguments presented in the second paragraph of Passage 2 (lines 67-87). **The correct answer is (C).**

40. The root word of "discordant" is *discord*, which refers to conflict or disharmony. Therefore, "in agreement" and "complementary" are clearly unreasonable answers. When applied to music or to sound generally, "discordant" often means "unpleasant," but that word choice would be inappropriate in this case: a statement that "the broad trends are unpleasant with the unusual cases upon which Mr. Biltonase chooses to focus" would be strange and very difficult for the reader to comprehend. However, the meaning of the statement, "the broad trends are *in conflict* with the unusual cases upon which Mr. Biltonase chooses to focus" (emphasis added) is crystal clear in meaning. **The correct answer is (C).**

41. In lines 92-95, the author of Passage 2 points out that a reduction in commuting time *per mile* does not result in a reduction in emissions if *total* commuting time remains the same. She is suggesting, then, that data on commuting time per mile does not give an accurate indication of emissions levels. This view is summarized in answer choice (A). **The correct answer is (A).**

42. As noted in the explanation for question #41 above, lines 92-95 provide the basis for answering that question correctly. Therefore, **the correct answer is (C).**

---

43. The word "tout" most often connotes a very aggressive attempt to sell a product or promote an idea. The context in which the word "touted" is used in the passage (lines 27-29, especially the word "craze") suggests just such a meaning. Answer choices (C) and (D) must therefore be eliminated. The tricky issue is that the words proposed in answer choices (A) and (B) are both rather mild in comparison to the likely meaning of "touted" in the passage. However, the word proposed in

answer choice (A), "recommended," is similar in meaning to "promoted," and therefore has at least some overlap in meaning with "touted," which cannot be said of answer choice (B). Answer (A) is therefore the only reasonable answer. **The correct answer is (A).**

44. The scientist begins the fourth paragraph with the words "I propose," indicating that he or she is at least fairly confident about the hypotheses he or she is about to put forward. The reader learns from the fifth paragraph (lines 47-61), however, that although these hypotheses *could* be tested, experimentally, the experiments have not yet been attempted. It would therefore be unreasonable for the scientist to claim that the hypotheses are definitely true, even if he or she feels deeply that they are. The indefinite language of the fourth paragraph thus allows the scientist to present the hypotheses without making unsupported claims about their accuracy. Answer choice (D) makes this point clearly. The other answer choices propose explanations that are not supported by evidence in the passage. **The correct answer is (D).**

45. In lines 30-33, the scientist proposes "that bats that feed on plants rich in beritase excrete the enzyme in the guano (excrement) that lines their caves, protecting them from an excessive presence of Piro worms." Because the experiment suggested by the scientist would involve studying bat colonies with and without access to plants rich in beritase, and studying the effects of an introduction of Piro worms into the colonies, it would test the specific hypothesis described in lines 30-33. This hypothesis is summarized in answer choice (B). **The correct answer is (B).**

46. As noted in the explanation for question #45 above, it is in lines 30-33 that the scientist presents the hypothesis to which that question refers. Therefore, **the correct answer is (C).**

47. In lines 38-40, the scientist warns that "[s]ynthetic pesticides could be as damaging to bats' immune systems as they are to the worms themselves." His or her primary concern about the use of such pesticides, therefore, is the risk of doing harm to bats. **The correct answer is (B).**

48. The third paragraph (lines 20-29) does not even describe an experiment, abandoned or otherwise, so answer (C) is clearly incorrect. As mentioned above in the explanation for question #44, the experiment described in the fifth paragraph has not yet been attempted, and so nothing about the results of the experiment could be known. Answer (D) is therefore incorrect. Although the passage does discuss differences in nutrient content among various plant species, that discussion occurs primarily in the *third* paragraph (lines 20-29), not the fifth paragraph, which rules out answer (B). The remaining option is answer (A), which correctly states that the fifth paragraph describes a *possible* experiment—that is, an experiment that could be performed, but has not yet been performed. **The correct answer is (A).**

49. In describing the possible experiment (fifth paragraph, lines 47-61), the scientist specifically proposes introducing *triberitum* plants, which are known to produce beritase (lines 23-25) amidst wildleaf, bucknettle, and ferndaisy flowers. Such an introduction would be of no experimental value if wildleaf, bucknettle, or ferndaisy also produced beritase. The scientist must therefore believe that these flowers do *not* produce beritase. **The correct answer is (D).**

50. The required information may be found in the fifth pair of vertical bars shown in the Figure, on the far right. The gray vertical bar, representing healthy colonies, is barely visible, and therefore represents an infection rate under 5%. **The correct answer is (A).**

51. The key for the Figure indicates that black vertical bars represent infection rates among failing colonies. The black bars show that of the four microbes represented in the Figure and the answer choices, the fungus *ipsius dementum* is the least prevalent in failing colonies, with an infection rate just over 80%. Therefore, **the correct answer is (C).**

52. The data displayed in the Figure strongly suggests that certain microbes contribute greatly to striped-wing bat colony failure, since for all microbes except *lactivan recidium*, the percentage of bats affected by the microbe is far higher in failing colonies than in healthy colonies. However, the scientist's primary hypothesis (lines 30-33) deals with the relationship between colony health and Piro worm infestation. Since the Figure provides the reader with no information about the presence or absence of Piro worm infestations in the colonies studied, it does not provide any support for the scientist's assertion that Piro worm infestation makes bats more likely to contract other infections, and colonies more likely to fail. **The correct answer is (D).**

SAMPLE TEST 3
Answer Explanations

TEST SECTION 2: WRITING AND LANGUAGE

NOTE: As the instructions for this test section clearly state, the goal when answering questions is to bring each passage into compliance with the conventions of standard written English. Standard written English is a form of the English language specifically developed to facilitate clear communication in writing, even between people who speak very different forms of English. Therefore, many of the correct answers may seem different from the choices you would make in your everyday speech. That does not mean there is anything wrong with the version of spoken English you have learned. To perform well on this test section, you must learn to make distinctions between the English you speak on a daily basis and the guidelines governing word choices, punctuation, and sentence structure in standard written English.

1. This question tests your understanding of *parallel structure*. To help the reader process a list, all items in the list should be presented in the same style and grammatical format to the greatest extent possible. Notice that the underlined portion already exhibits this structure: "productivity," "loyalty," and "contentment" are all nouns describing characteristics an employee might have. Answers choices (C) and (D) do not exhibit parallel structure. Answer (B) may seem appealing because all three words end in "-ness," but "productiveness" is a far more awkward word than "productivity," and "loyalness" is not a word at all. Therefore, **the correct answer is (A).**

2. The primary topic of the passage as a whole is rooftop gardens. Therefore, it would be most natural for the introductory sentence to mention outdoor spaces in some fashion. Notice also that the second sentence of the passage mentions a workplace staff's "need for fresh air and sunshine," providing additional evidence that the correct answer choice for this question is one that emphasizes access to the outdoors. Only answer choice (C) has such an emphasis. **The correct answer is (C).**

3. The needed word should communicate as simply as possible that there are long-term payoffs for *both* employees and employers. The word that accomplishes this goal while complying with the conventions of standard written English is "alike," choice (D). The words "likewise" and "similarly" get the idea across, but these words are conventionally used when the two entities being compared are mentioned in separate sentences. For example, "Wolves learn obedience to the alpha male-female pair at an early age. Similarly (or likewise), domestic dogs are more likely to live happily if they receive obedience training within the first year of their lives." Therefore, though not outlandish, choices (A) and (B) are incorrect. **The correct answer is (D).**

4. The proposed addition is certainly relevant to the passage as a whole, in that it describes a positive outcome that arises when employees spend time outdoors. Notice, however, that both the first sentence ("The health … day.") and the second sentence ("Consistently … health.") of the paragraph discuss particular *health* benefits of time spent outdoors. Since the proposed addition discusses a benefit not related to health, it should be *not* be added at the indicated point in the passage. Answer (D) best summarizes this reasoning. **The correct answer is (D).**

5. The word "which" preceding the question number marker in the passage refers to the ability just mentioned (a person's ability to sleep). Since "ability" is singular, a singular verb is required, which rules out choices (C) and (D). The two-word phrase, "is being," conveys the same information as

the single word "is," so for the sake of simplicity, the one-word option is preferable. **The correct answer is (A).**

6. The previous sentence ("This combination … features.") raises the issue of missed workdays due to illness. It would be most logical for the sentence about the central library to address the same issue. Of the answer choices, only option (B) discusses the matter of sick days, so **the correct answer is (B).**

7. The indoor air filtration systems are part of ("belong to") the (one) central library. Therefore, the underlined portion should begin with the possessive form of the singular noun, *library*, which is *library's*. No other change is required. **The correct answer is (C).**

8. The previous paragraph (previous page of test) focused on the health benefits of rooftop gardens. This paragraph focuses on financial benefits. It would therefore be best to combine the paragraph's first two sentences in such a way that the first part of the sentence creates a link to the previous paragraph, while the second part shifts the focus to the new topic. Option (A) presents the ideas in a jumbled order that would disorient a reader. Option (C) has a similarly distracting order of ideas, since the link back to the previous paragraph is sandwiched between two phrases outlining the new topic of financial benefits. Option (D) would be a well-constructed sentence for certain contexts, but it reads more like a conclusion than a transitional sentence. Notice how the sentence in option (B) follows the most logical order of ideas, first referencing the topic just discussed in the previous paragraph, then introducing the new idea of financial benefits, and then elaborating on that new idea. Among the options put forth in the answer choices, this presentation is most helpful to the reader. **The correct answer is (B).**

9. The word "quarterly" means four times per year. Since a year consists of 12 months, and $12 \div 4 = 3$, quarterly implies once every three months. Therefore, the phrase "per three months" is redundant and should be deleted. **The correct answer is (D).**

10. "Consequently" implies that the phenomenon to be described next occurs *as a result* (consequence) of the circumstances just described. In this case, the implication would be that sending food and paper waste from cafeterias up to the roof is somehow made possible by acquiring and transporting soil. That does not make sense. What the author seems to be suggesting is that sending food and paper waste up to the roof is a different way to begin creating a rooftop garden than purchasing and hauling huge quantities of soil. Therefore, the author is proposing an *alternative* to soil acquisition. **The correct answer is (B).**

11. In the underlined portion, the author is offering a mid-sentence explanation of the term, "gray water." The most common and most widely understood way to set off such an explanation from the rest of the sentence is with a dash (—) at each end of the explanation. This construction is shown in answer choice (C). Notice that if you deleted the explanation marked off by the dashes in option (C), the result would still be a perfectly logical sentence: "Particularly efficient companies have also installed new pipes to reclaim gray water for irrigation use." The fact that the deletion does not alter the meaning of the sentence shows that answer choice (C) is properly constructed. **The correct answer is (C).**

SAMPLE TEST 3
Answer Explanations

12. The noun phrase replaced by the pronoun "themselves" in the underlined portion is "the people of … Sandimar. "People" is a plural noun, so a plural pronoun is required. We therefore rule out answer choices (C) and (D). The pronoun construction "their selves" does not comply with the conventions of standard written English, whereas the option "themselves" does. **The correct answer is (A).**

13. The phrase "in spite of" suggests that the circumstance about to be described would tend to reduce the likelihood of the outcome that occurred (in this case, that outcome is the founding of the delivery service by the two men). If anything, a background surviving childhood diseases would make the men *more* likely to respond effectively to the threat posed by an epidemic. Therefore, "In spite of" is an illogical beginning for the sentence and a change is necessary. Whether the leaders played together as children is irrelevant to the passage, so answer (B) is incorrect. Option (C) nicely links the sentence in question to the preceding sentence by indicating that the course of action undertaken by the two men was a response to the epidemic just described. This option improves the logic of the paragraph. **The correct answer is (C).**

14. Even with the improvement that results from making the change suggested in the correct answer to question #13, there is still a large problem with the portion of the passage to which this question refers. The construction, "In response to the growing crisis, Emsun Putainy and Inpon Siotaex, two respected leaders from a western village," is not a complete sentence. (It never answers the question, *What did the leaders do in response to the crisis?*) Therefore, neither a period nor a semicolon is a correct punctuation mark at the end of the construction. Hence, answers (A) and (C) are incorrect. Consider the result of making the change proposed in choice (B): "In response to the growing crisis, Emsun Putainy and Inpon Siotaex, two respected leaders from a western village, began recruiting expert camel riders from far and wide to carry messages between the many suffering towns." This sentence is clear in meaning and complies with all conventions of standard written English. Meanwhile, answer choice (D) would complicate the sentence by adding an unneeded word ("they"). Even if choice (D) complied with standard written English conventions (which it does not), it would be an inferior choice to answer (B). **The correct answer is (B).**

15. The phrase, "who together … government," is a supplemental phrase (note that it is set off by commas at both ends). The subject of the sentence is actually the "Riders of Sandimar," which is plural in form. Therefore, a plural verb form is required, that is, "were" instead of "was." No other change is required. **The correct answer is (D).**

16. Whenever possible, an interior paragraph (a paragraph that is neither the first nor the last) of an essay or article should begin with a *transitional sentence*. A transitional sentence makes reference to the paragraph just concluded before introducing the new topic to be discussed. The sentence the author is considering deleting here is a very effective transitional sentence, and so should be kept. **The correct answer is (D).**

17. The underlined portion complies with the conventions of standard written English, but it is redundant and clumsy. Hostility *is* resistance; in fact, it is one of the strongest forms of resistance. The word "even" that follows the comma after "hostility" suggests that the next word or phrase will be more forceful than the word "hostility," which "resistance" is not. Reversing the order of appearance of the two words "hostility" and "resistance" would be acceptable, as it would at least

eggheadprep.com

create a logical progression from the weaker word to the stronger word. However, the construction would still be redundant, and that change is not included among the available options, anyway. The best way to improve the sentence is to simply delete the comma and the words "even resistance." Answer (C) presents this option. **The correct answer is (C).**

18. For this question, it is likely that neither the underlined portion nor any of the answer choices will sound right to you. The reason is that the question deals specifically with the "not only … but also" construction, which is often employed in written English but rarely used in speech. The conventional rule for the construction is that one must be able to delete all the words from "not only" through "but" (OR all the way through "also"—the "also" may be either deleted or kept) and still have a coherent, logical sentence. Let's attempt this deletion with all four options, beginning with the underlined portion:

(A – NO CHANGE) "By the 1930s, served as master carpenters and food gatherers for the towns they visited." OR "By the 1930s, also served as master carpenters and food gatherers for the towns they visited." This construction is an incomplete sentence, for it has no subject. (*Who* also served in those capacities?)

(B) "By the 1930s, served as master carpenters and food gatherers for the towns they visited." OR "By the 1930s, they also served as master carpenters and food gatherers for the towns they visited." The second construction is a complete sentence, and its subject, "they," clearly refers back to the women riders discussed in the previous sentence.

(C) "By the 1930s, having served as master carpenters and food gatherers for the towns they visited." OR "By the 1930s, also having served as master carpenters and food gatherers for the towns they visited." Neither of these constructions is a complete sentence.

(D) "By the 1930s, serving as master carpenters and food gatherers for the towns they visited." OR "By the 1930s, also serving as master carpenters and food gatherers for the towns they visited." Once again, neither construction is a complete sentence.

With the deletion, then, only option (B) can yield a complete sentence that is clear in meaning and compliant with the conventions of standard written English. **The correct answer is (B).**

19. The previous sentence ends with the statement that "the gender dynamics of Sandimar had changed forever." The term "gender dynamics" refers to relationships between men and women in a society. Therefore, in order to follow the previous sentence logically, the answer choice should discuss such relationships. Only answer (A) does so. **The correct answer is (A).**

20. The standard punctuation of the sentence would be to use a comma, not a semicolon (;) or colon (:), after the word "bravery." No other change is required. **The correct answer is (C).**

21. The word "spiteful" implies malicious intent. Since a disease has no consciousness, it cannot have intent. "Unpropitious" refers to circumstances that make a favorable outcome unlikely. The presence of the disease in the country, therefore, was certainly unpropitious, but it would be strange to apply that adjective to the disease itself. Without doubt, the disease was crummy, but that word

SAMPLE TEST 3
Answer Explanations

would not fit well with the generally formal tone of the passage. "Horrific" means, "causing horror," which the epidemic surely did. Use of the word "horrific" would be consistent with the author's tone throughout the passage. **The correct answer is (D).**

22. The author is ending the passage with the assertion that the women riders "will forever be remembered in their homeland." Without specific examples of how the riders are remembered, that statement could sound hollow. Readers might interpret it as wishful thinking, rather than as honest reporting of the facts. Therefore, providing examples of the ways in which the people of Sandimar honor the women riders would bolster the author's conclusion significantly. In short, it would improve the passage to make the proposed addition, for the reason stated in answer choice (B). **The correct answer is (B).**

---

23. A strong case could be made that the author would be better served by *not* combining the two sentences, due to the length and complexity of the resulting construction. However, that option is not presented among the answer choices. We must therefore find the answer choice that conveys the large amount of information contained in the two sentences most simply. One approach to this problem is to examine the underlying logical connections between the ideas. Those connections could be summarized as,

Trees are treated with RocketGrow ⇒ Growth is accelerated ⇒ Lost trees replaced more quickly.

The best answer choice is the one that presents the ideas in this order, which is option (A). **The correct answer is (A).**

24. Deleting the two underlined words leaves a perfectly logical sentence that conveys the author's intended meaning: "RocketGrow works by stimulating ultra-rapid water circulation within the tree's tissues, resulting in dramatically accelerated photosynthesis." Any other option, including leaving the underlined text in place, would complicate the sentence without adding meaning. **The correct answer is (D).**

25. The phrase "as the product name promises" indicates that the author wishes for the underlined word to be a verb with a meaning similar to "rocket" or "grow." The word "chute" is a noun, describing a vertical or sloping channel, slide, or narrow passage (such as a laundry chute, through which dirty laundry travels downward to a laundry room). Because it is a noun, not a verb, and because items travel *downward*, not upward, through a chute, the word "chute" must be replaced. The word "shoot" is a verb that can mean to "move suddenly or with great speed." Thus, the phrase "shoot upward" would very much mimic the product name, RocketGrow. **The correct answer is (C).**

26. The pronoun refers back to the ash or oak, and therefore should be singular. (Note that ash *and* oak would be a plural subject.) Since the innate immune system is part of ("belongs to") the tree, the pronoun should be possessive. The possessive form of the singular pronoun "it" is "its" (no apostrophe). Therefore, the underlined word is correct. **The correct answer is (A).**

27. The pronoun in the underlined position will refer back to the homeowners. Standard written English conventions specify that when referring to people, the word "who" should be used, rather than "that" or "which." **The correct answer is (D).**

28. It is worth noting that simply deleting the underlined words, while keeping the comma, would be an excellent rewrite of the sentence. That option is not offered among the answer choices, however. The next best option is to make sure that the verb tense at the indicated point matches the verb tense used earlier in the sentence within the phrase, "do not benefit." That tense is simple present tense. Among the answer choices, only choice (B), "do," is in simple present tense. **The correct answer is (B).**

29. The phrase "both green and blue varieties" is a supplemental phrase (note that it is set off by commas at both ends), and so could be deleted without altering the sentence's meaning. Mentally making this deletion, we are left with, "Consider Colorado spruce trees, for example…" We can now see clearly that "for example" completes the thought begun with the phrase, "Consider Colorado spruce trees." Therefore, "for example" cannot be moved to the next sentence, and answer choice (B) is incorrect. Now notice that the statement, "when treated with RocketGrow…," effectively answers a question raised by the first part of the sentence. (*What happens to Colorado spruce trees?*) Therefore, the standard punctuation mark is a colon. **The correct answer is (C).**

30. Sentences 2, 3, 5, 6, and 7 all describe either negative side effects that might result from the use of RocketGrow or the dangers posed by such side effects. Sentence 4 (as corrected—see the explanation for #28 above) states, "Some tree species do not benefit from treatment with RocketGrow as much as others do, however, and some suffer significant negative effects." This statement would serve as an excellent introduction to the examples presented in sentences 2, 3, 5, 6, and 7. Therefore, sentence 4 should be placed immediately before those sentences, right after sentence 1. **The correct answer is (B).**

31. The graph shows that untreated trees growing in isolation support an average of about 28 or 29 insect species, whereas untreated trees growing in wooded areas support almost 55 insect species. Since $28 \times 2 = 56$ and $29 \times 2 = 58$, it is quite accurate to say that untreated trees in wooded areas support "nearly twice as many" insect species as those growing in isolation. **The correct answer is (D).**

32. The graph shows that treated trees growing in wooded areas do indeed support only a small number of insect species—an average of only about 14. However, treated trees growing in isolation support even *fewer* insect species, an average of about nine. Therefore, both the underlined text and answer choice (B) fail to accurately convey the information displayed in the graph. Because both of the black bars on the graph are significantly shorter than the corresponding gray bars, the difference between the heights of the black bars might not seem consequential to you at first. However, an increase from 9 to 14 supported insect species, which is a 56% increase, is actually quite significant. Therefore, the claim made in answer choice (D) that "isolation has less of an effect" on treated trees is not strongly supported by the data. What is crystal clear from the graph is that in both isolated and wooded areas, treated trees support far fewer insect species than their untreated counterparts. This conclusion is plainly stated in answer choice (C). **The correct answer is (C).**

SAMPLE TEST 3
Answer Explanations

33. The concluding sentence of an essay should in some way summarize the points made in the essay. Because the sentence referred to in this question began, "But when it comes to nurturing and protecting healthy, vibrant forest ecosystems," it should end with a statement that encapsulates the author's beliefs about the effects of treatment with RocketGrow on tree health. The author has made a strong case in the preceding paragraphs that trees not treated with RocketGrow (that is, grown "nature's way") are overall much healthier than trees treated with the product. Hence, **the correct answer is (C).**

---

34. In spite of its length, the phrase, "From the towering … of Yi Sun-Sin in Seoul," is not a complete sentence; it has no verb. The statement, "These statues and sculptures…," is a continuation of the thought begun in that opening phrase. Therefore, it makes sense to join the introductory phrase and the statement about "statues and sculptures all over the world" as a single sentence, which can be accomplished by replacing the period with a comma. (It would not be appropriate to use a semicolon, since we have already determined that the phrase preceding the proposed comma could not stand as a complete sentence.) The construction of the resulting (rather long) sentence renders the word "these" unnecessary. Answer choice (D) shows the needed changes. **The correct answer is (D).**

35. The author has chosen to mark the beginning of the phrase that provides historical information about the *Little Mermaid* with a dash, a perfectly acceptable choice. Having made that choice, however, the author must mark the end of the phrase with a dash as well. (NOTE: The phrase providing historical information could be seen as a supplemental phrase, which would normally be set off by commas. However, dashes are often used to prevent confusion when a supplemental phrase has a comma within it.) **The correct answer is (C).**

36. Since "depicting" cannot stand on its own as a verb (it needs a "helping verb"), answer choice (C) must be eliminated. The subject of the sentence is "artistic creations," which is plural. Therefore, a plural form of the verb "depict" is required. "Depicts" is singular and incorrect; "depict" is plural. **The correct answer is (B).**

37. The key aspect of this question is that we are asked to choose an option that links the first paragraph to the next two paragraphs. The next two paragraphs focus entirely on past and present events in Port Humberstrand, which is a seaside town. Answer choice (B) would therefore serve as a transitional sentence by linking the statements in the first paragraph to the information that follows. **The correct answer is (B).**

38. It would be appealing to reduce the number of commas in the underlined portion, but that cannot be done without failing to comply with the conventions of standard written English. The phrase, "a solitary fisherman," is a supplemental phrase; deleting it would not affect the meaning of the sentence. A supplemental phrase must always be set off from the rest of the sentence *at both ends*, usually with commas. Therefore, commas must precede the name "Parletine" *and* the word "saw." Only answer choice (D) has all the necessary commas in their proper places. **The correct answer is (D).**

eggheadprep.com

39. This question tests your understanding of *parallel structure*. To help the reader process a list, all items in the list should be presented in the same style and grammatical format to the greatest extent possible. Notice the sequence of words describing actions in the sentence: *serving*, *fending*, *arbitrating*. To create parallel structure, the next "action word" should also have an "-ing" ending if possible. Therefore, the underlined word is completely appropriate. **The correct answer is (A).**

40. The phrase "in the wake of…" generally suggests the immediate aftermath of an occurrence. The wording of the passage thus implies that the events described in sentence 6 occurred *before* those described in sentence 5. It would therefore be most logical to place sentence 6 before sentence 5—that is, immediately after sentence 4. **The correct answer is (C).**

41. The word "unfurled" very specifically refers to the billowing motion that occurs when something made of fabric is freed from restraints. For example, it is common to speak of a flag or sail being unfurled. Therefore, "unfurled" is an inappropriate word choice in this context. It is clear that the intended meaning of the underlined word is essentially, "revealed." The answer choice closest to "revealed" in meaning is choice (B), "unveiled" (which literally means to pull back a veil, bringing an object or person into view). **The correct answer is (B).**

42. Previous statements in the passage have certainly made clear that all of the whales in the "Orca Coast Guard" are held in very high regard by the people of Port Humberstrand. Stripes and other ornamentations denoting military rank have long been associated with showing proper respect toward those who have distinguished themselves through dedicated service. It is therefore reasonable to conclude that the purpose of the stripes is indeed to show how highly regarded the whales are. No change is necessary. **The correct answer is (A).**

43. The paragraph up until the indicated point has recounted the story of how the statues came into existence and described the statues themselves. The next sentence after the indicated position describes possible reactions to the statues. Since the proposed addition does not even mention the orca statues, it is clearly not relevant to the paragraph. **The correct answer is (D).**

44. The concluding sentence of an essay or article should in some way summarize and tie together the main points the author has presented. The focus of this passage has been on the remarkable relationship between the people of Port Humberstrand and their beloved "Orca Coast Guard." In particular, the author has emphasized the bravery of the whales and their dedication to keeping the bay safe. Answer (C) summarizes these points in persuasive language, and very nicely links the conclusion back to the introductory remarks about statues of human military heroes. **The correct answer is (C).**

SAMPLE TEST 3
Answer Explanations

TEST SECTION 3: MATH—NO CALCULATOR

NOTE: Most problems in math can be solved using multiple different methods. In these explanations, the most standard methods taught in US middle school and high school mathematics are shown. You may have employed a different method that is equally valid.

1. Starting with $5m = 35$, divide both sides by 5 to get $m = 7$. Now plug this value for m into the expression, $2m + 6$.

$$2(7) + 6 = 14 + 6 = 20.$$

The correct answer is (C).

2. We need to analyze the meaning of each symbol in the expression $nCAT$ to determine which of the quantities would change in value if the farmer switches to a less expensive fertilizer. We are told that n represents the number of growing fields, which is clearly unaffected by the cost of the fertilizer. Likewise, the cost of the fertilizer would not affect the size of the fields, so A, the area of each field, would not change if the cost of the fertilizer were reduced. Notice, finally, that although the description of its meaning is complicated, the value T can be calculated solely from the *temperature*, and so would not be affected by a change in the fertilizer cost. To be specific, the problem tells us that T = (Temperature in °F) ÷ (75° F). For example, if the temperature were 100° F, then T would equal 100° / 75° = 1.333…, and this value for T would be correct no matter what the cost of the fertilizer might be. We have now ruled out answer choices (A), (C), and (D). **The correct answer is (B).**

3. The first sentence of the problem may be represented as a "word equation" as follows.

(number of people at b-day party = 3 • (number of people at solstice game night)

We substitute 45 for the number of people at the birthday party and s for the number of people at the solstice game night to arrive at the equation,

$$45 = 3 \cdot s, \text{ or simply, } 45 - 3s, \text{ which is equivalent to } 3s = 45.$$

The correct answer is (A).

4. By definition,

$$x^{\frac{m}{n}} = \sqrt[n]{x^m}, \text{ where } n \neq 0.$$

Therefore, $x^{\frac{3}{4}} = \sqrt[4]{x^3}$.

The correct answer is (C).

eggheadprep.com

5. To solve the system, first multiply the lower equation by three to make the coefficients of y opposites, then add the two equations.

$$\begin{cases} 3x + 6y = -3 \\ 3(5x - 2y) = (-17)(3) \end{cases} \Rightarrow \begin{cases} 3x + 6y = -3 \\ 15x - 6y = -51 \end{cases} \text{ adding the equations yields}$$

$$18x = -54 \quad \text{dividing both sides by 18 yields}$$

$$x = -3$$

We must now plug this x-value into either of the two original equations to find the value of y. Using the first equation, $3(-3) + 6y = -3 \Rightarrow -9 + 6y = -3$. Adding 9 to both sides, we get $6y = 6$, so dividing both sides by 6 yields, $y = 1$. We have found that $x = -3$ and $y = 1$. Therefore, $2x + y = 2(-3) + 1 = -6 + 1 = -5$. **The correct answer is (B).**

6. Using the standard algebra method of cross multiplication to solve the proportion, we get the equation, $4(x + 6) = 6x$. Use the distributive property to simplify to, $4x + 24 = 6x$. Subtracting $4x$ from both sides yields, $24 = 2x$, and finally, dividing both sides by 2 yields, $12 = x$. Therefore,

$$\frac{x}{4} = \frac{12}{4} = 3$$

The correct answer is (C).

7. The equation takes the form, $y = mx + b$, with a in the "m" position. Therefore, a is the slope of the line. We plug in the coordinates u and v for x and y in the equation $y = ax - 7$ and solve for a.

$$y = ax - 7 \Rightarrow v = a(u) - 7$$
$$v = au - 7 \quad \text{add 7 to both sides to get}$$
$$v + 7 = au \quad \text{divide both sides by } u \text{ to get}$$
$$\frac{v + 7}{u} = a$$

The correct answer is (D).

8. The given points $(-1, -2)$ and $(0, 1)$ are actually irrelevant to the problem. What is important is that the points $(-3, 0)$ and $(2, 0)$ tell us that $g(-3) = 0$ and $g(2) = 0$. In other words, -3 and 2 are both zeros of the function g. The Factor Theorem for polynomials states that if k is a zero of a polynomial function g, then $(x - k)$ is a factor of $g(x)$. Therefore, g has factors $(x - (-3))$ and $(x - 2)$, or more simply, $(x + 3)$ and $(x - 2)$. Only the first of these appears as an answer choice, choice (A). **The correct answer is (A).**

9. Using the vertical angle pairs, we know that $a = d$, $b = e$, and $c = f$. This means, for example, that we can substitute a for d in the equation, $a + b = c + d$, yielding, $a + b = c + a$. Subtracting a from both sides gives us $b = c$. Notice that we now know that $b = c$ and $c = f$, so by the Transitive Property, $b = f$. Statement I is therefore true. We also have $b = c$ and $b = e$, so, also by the Transitive Property, $c = e$, and statement II is true as well. Notice, however, that we only know of

SAMPLE TEST 3
Answer Explanations

a that $a = d$, and there is no other quantity known to be equal to *d*. Therefore, there is no way to create a link between the value of *a* and the value of *c*. We must conclude that statement III may NOT be true. **The correct answer is (A).**

10. One option to solve this problem is to use standard algebra methods to attempt to solve the system. For example, we could multiply the first equation by 5 and the second equation by 2 and then add the equations.

$$\begin{cases} 5(2x + ky) = (-6)5 \\ 2(-5x + 4y) = 8(2) \end{cases} \Rightarrow \begin{cases} 10x + 5ky = -30 \\ -10x + 8y = 16 \end{cases}$$ add the two equations to get

$5ky + 8y = -14$ factor out a *y* on the left side to arrive at

$y(5k + 8) = -14$ divide both sides by $(5k + 8)$, which yields

$$y = \frac{-14}{5k + 8}$$

The system will have no solutions if the expression for *y* is undefined, which in turn will occur if the denominator of the fraction is zero. We therefore solve the equation, $5k + 8 = 0$. Subtracting 8 from both sides yields, $5k = -8$, and dividing both sides by 5 gives us, $k = -8/5$. **The correct answer is (D).**

11. We are looking for the intersection points of the two graphs, $y = (x + 6)^2$ and $y = 16$. If we employ the standard algebra method of setting the two expressions for *y* equal to each other, we have the equation, $(x + 6)^2 = 16$. Taking both the positive and the negative square roots of both sides yields two possibilities, $x + 6 = 4$ or $x + 6 = -4$. In both equations, subtract 6 from both sides to get, $x = -2$ or $x = -10$. Therefore, the points *P* and *Q* have coordinates $(-2, 16)$ and $(-10, 16)$, respectively. (Note that because one of the intersecting graphs is the line, $y = 16$, it was already known that both *P* and *Q* would have *y*-coordinate 16.) The distance between these two points may be calculated using the Distance Formula. More simply, since the segment connecting them is horizontal (they have the same *y*-coordinate), the distance is $|-10 - (-2)| = |-10 + 2| = |-8| = 8$. **The correct answer is (B).**

12. Here is one of many methods to solve this problem.

$$\frac{16x^2 - 20x + 17}{kx + 5} = -8x - 10 + \frac{67}{kx + 5}$$ subtract $\frac{67}{kx + 5}$ from both sides to get

$$\frac{16x^2 - 20x + 17}{kx + 5} - \frac{67}{kx + 5} = -8x - 10$$

Use the fact that the two fractions have the same denominator to combine them:

$$\frac{16x^2 - 20x + 17 - 67}{kx + 5} = \frac{16x^2 - 20x - 50}{kx + 5} = \frac{-8x - 10}{1}$$ now cross multiply to get

$16x^2 - 20x - 50 = (kx + 5)(-8x - 10)$ expand (FOIL) the right side to get

$16x^2 - 20x - 50 = -8kx^2 - 10kx - 40x - 50$

eggheadprep.com

For these two expressions to be equal for all values of x, the coefficient of x^2 on the left side must equal the coefficient of x^2 on the right side. That is, $16 = -8k$. Dividing both sides by -8 yields, $-2 = k$. **The correct answer is (B).**

13. We expand (FOIL) the expression on the right side and then distribute a over the result.

$$y = a(x+3)(x-5) = a(x^2 - 5x + 3x - 15)$$
$$= a(x^2 - 2x - 15) = ax^2 - 2ax - 15a$$

An algebra theorem specifies that the vertex of a parabola with an equation written in the form, $y = ax^2 + bx + c$, occurs at the x-value, $x = -\frac{b}{2a}$. Applying that formula here yields the result, $x = -\frac{(-2a)}{2(a)} = \frac{2a}{2a} = 1$. We can use the original (given) equation to find the y-coordinate corresponding to $x = 1$: $y = a(1+3)(1-5) = a(4)(-4) = -16a$. **The correct answer is (A).**

14. Apply the distributive property to rewrite the given equation:

$$P = \frac{4}{7}(L + 20) \Rightarrow P = \frac{4}{7}L + \left(\frac{4}{7}\right)20 \Rightarrow P = \frac{4}{7}L + \frac{80}{7}$$

The resulting equation is in the form, $y = mx + b$, so $4/7$ is the slope of the line, or *rate of change* of the value of P. One standard interpretation of this rate of change is that for every 1-unit increase in the value of L, there will be an increase of $4/7$ of a unit in the value of P. This interpretation is expressed in statement II, so that statement is true. A reciprocal relationship must exist if we reverse the order of the variables in the interpretation of the rate of change. In other words, for every 1-unit increase in the value of P, there must be an increase of $7/4$ of a unit in the value of L. Since $7/4 = 1.75$, statement III is also true. Without further analysis, we can now conclude that **the correct answer is (D).**

15. First divide both sides of the equation (and thus, all terms) by 4 to get the simpler equation, $x^2 - 6x + 3 = 0$. Now solve by using the quadratic formula.

$$x = \frac{-(-6) \pm \sqrt{(-6)^2 - 4(1)(3)}}{2(1)} = \frac{6 \pm \sqrt{36-12}}{2} = \frac{6 \pm \sqrt{24}}{2}$$
$$= \frac{6 \pm \sqrt{4} \cdot \sqrt{6}}{2} = \frac{6 \pm 2 \cdot \sqrt{6}}{2} = \frac{6}{2} \pm \frac{2\sqrt{6}}{2} = 3 \pm \sqrt{6}$$

The correct answer is (C).

---

16. There are many ways to solve this problem, including multiplying both sides of the equation by a common denominator for all the fractions. The least common denominator would be 40. However,

SAMPLE TEST 3
Answer Explanations

since the two terms on the left side already have the same denominator, and finding a common denominator for the two fractions on the right side is a simple matter, we will proceed by combining the fractions on each side of the equals sign.

$$\frac{9}{8}x - \frac{3}{8}x = \frac{2}{5} \cdot \frac{2}{2} + \frac{11}{10} \quad \Rightarrow \quad \frac{6}{8}x = \frac{4}{10} + \frac{11}{10} \quad \text{which simplifies to}$$

$$\frac{3}{4}x = \frac{15}{10} \quad \Rightarrow \quad \frac{3}{4}x = \frac{3}{2}, \text{ or } \frac{3x}{4} = \frac{3}{2}$$

Cross multiplication of the last equation yields, $6x = 12$. Dividing both sides by 6 gives us the answer, $x = 2$. **The correct answer is 2.**

17. Because it is stated that $x > 0$, we know that $x \neq 0$. Therefore, we can safely divide both sides of the equation by x^2 to get, $x^2(x^2 - 13) = -36$. Using the distributive property on the left side yields, $x^4 - 13x^2 = -36$. Now add 36 to both sides to get, $x^4 - 13x^2 + 36 = 0$. This equation can be factored as, $(x^2 - 9)(x^2 - 4) = 0$, and factored further to yield the equation, $(x + 3)(x - 3)(x + 2)(x - 2) = 0$. Setting each individual factor equal to zero gives us the answers, $x = -3, 3, -2, 2$. However, -3 and -2 must be eliminated since it was given that $x > 0$. **The correct answer is either 2 or 3.**

18. The statement, "A *honk* is worth 9 more points than a *gonk*," may be expressed as the equation, $h = g + 9$, where h represents the point value of a *honk* and g represents the point value of a *gonk*. The statement that "a team that scored 4 *gonks* and 2 *honks* has a total of 120 points" may be expressed as, $4g + 2h = 120$. The first equation tells us that we may substitute the expression $g + 9$ in for h in the second equation: $4g + 2(g + 9) = 120$. Now solve this equation.

$$4g + 2(g+9) = 120 \quad \text{use the distributive property to simplify:}$$
$$4g + 2g + 18 = 120 \quad \text{combine like terms to get}$$
$$6g + 18 = 120 \quad \text{subtract 18 from both sides, then divide both sides by 6:}$$
$$6g = 102 \quad \Rightarrow \quad g = 17$$

The correct answer is 17.

eggheadprep.com

19. Since $b = 40$, the first equation may be rewritten as, $q + 2(40) = 180$, or $q + 80 = 180$. Subtracting 80 from both sides yields, $q = 100$. Here is the drawing with the values of b and q in place, and two additional angles marked.

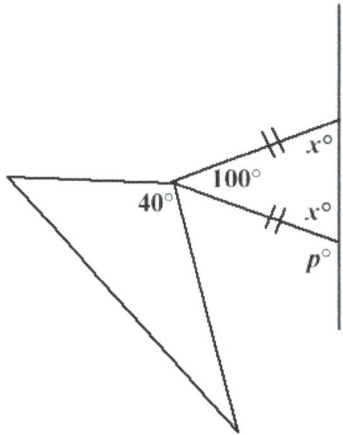

Note that two different angles are marked as measuring x degrees. It is valid to mark the figure in this way because the markings on the original figure showed that those two angles are the base angles of an isosceles triangle, and therefore must have equal measures. Using the fact that the interior angles of a triangle have a sum of $180°$, we have the equation, $100 + x + x = 180$. Subtracting 100 from both sides and combining like terms yields, $2x = 80$. Dividing both sides by 2, we get $x = 40$. The value of x is not the final answer, however. Now notice that the lower of the two angles marked as x degrees forms a straight line with the angle marked p degrees. Therefore, $x + p = 180$, or $40 + p = 180$. Subtracting 40 from both sides, we get $p = 140$. Therefore, the value of $2b + p$ is $2(40) + 140$, or $80 + 140$, which is 220. **The correct answer is 220.**

20. Notice that the given information tells us that $\angle I$ of triangle JIH corresponds to angle F of triangle EFG. Since corresponding angles of similar triangles have equal measures, we know that $m\angle I = m\angle F$. Below is a drawing of triangle EFG, as described in the problem. As you will see, there is no need to draw the second triangle, JIH.

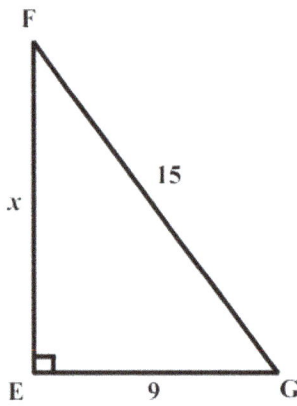

SAMPLE TEST 3
Answer Explanations

Use the Pythagorean Theorem to solve for the missing side length: $x^2 + 9^2 = 15^2$, which simplifies to, $x^2 + 81 = 225$. Subtract 81 from both sides to get, $x^2 = 144$. Taking the positive square root of both sides yields, $x = 12$. Now, in a right triangle,

$$\text{cosine of an angle} = \frac{\text{length of leg adjacent to that angle}}{\text{length of hypotenuse}}$$

Therefore, $\cos(\angle F) = \frac{12}{15} = \frac{4}{5}$. Because we have already determined that $m\angle I = m\angle F$, $\cos(\angle I)$ must have the same value as $\cos(\angle F)$. **The correct answer is 4 / 5 or 0.8.**

TEST SECTION 4: MATH—CALCULATOR

NOTE: Most problems in math can be solved using multiple different methods. In these explanations, the most standard methods taught in US middle school and high school mathematics are shown. You may have employed a different method that is equally valid.

1. While the boat is anchored, its distance from the pier remains constant. Therefore, we should look for a segment of the graph that is horizontal (no increase or decrease in distance from the pier). The horizontal segment of the graph begins shortly after 8:00 p.m. and ends just after 9:00 p.m. Therefore, the moonlight swim must have *begun* shortly after 8:00 p.m. Choice (B) is the only reasonable answer. **The correct answer is (B).**

2. It may be tempting to choose answer (C), because the graph shows that the number of coyotes living in US urban areas in 2010 (year 100 on the horizontal axis) was approximately 13,000, which is not much different from the number in 1910 (year zero on the horizontal axis). However, to say that the number of coyotes living in US urban areas "remained about the same *throughout* the period" (emphasis added) would imply that the population graph is nearly a horizontal line, which is clearly not the case. Therefore, answer (C) is incorrect. Rather, we should choose an answer that describes a downward trend followed by an upward trend. Only choice (D) fits this description. **The correct answer is (D).**

3. Because the piece of artwork is to be chosen randomly, the number of possible creators of the selected piece is simply the total number of students whose work was chosen for the exhibit, 91. The number of juniors from Western H.S. whose artwork was selected for the exhibit was 27, while the number of seniors from Eastern H.S. whose work was selected was 31. Therefore, the probability is calculated as,

$$\frac{27 + 31}{91} = \frac{58}{91}$$

The correct answer is (C).

4. We add the polynomials by adding like terms:

$$7x^2 + 4x^2 = 11x^2$$

$$-8x + 5x = -3x$$

$$-6 + (-3) = -9$$

Therefore, the sum is $11x^2 - 3x - 9$. **The correct answer is (A).**

5. The number of sweatshirts with the logo is 3% of 985, or 0.03(985), which equals 29.55. (Obviously, the number of sweatshirts should be a whole number, but we will deal with that issue at the end of the problem.) The number of skirts with the logo is 12% of 780, or 0.12(780), which is 93.6. Therefore, the total number of items of clothing with the logo is about 29.55 + 93.6, or 123.15. Again, all of these numbers should be rounded to whole numbers, but since it is now clear

SAMPLE TEST 3
Answer Explanations

that answer choice (C) is the option closest to the actual total by far, there is no need to analyze the situation any further. **The correct answer is (C).**

6. There are many ways to solve this problem, but all of them revolve around the fact that because g is a linear function, we know it can be represented by an equation of the form, $g(x) = mx + b$. One way to find the value of m, the slope of the line, is to represent two columns of the table as ordered pairs. For example, we could use the points (2, 4) and (3, 1). Using the slope formula,

$$m = \frac{y_2 - y_1}{x_2 - x_1} = \frac{1 - 4}{3 - 2} = \frac{-3}{1} = -3$$

We now know that $g(x) = -3x + b$. Notice that at this point, we already know that choice (C) is the only one that could possibly be correct. To verify the answer, however, you might wish to determine the value of b. To do so, substitute the values from any column of the table for x and $g(x)$ in the equation just found and solve for b. Let's use the point (2, 4) again, which gives us, $4 = -3(2) + b$. Simplification yields, $4 = -6 + b$. Adding 6 to both sides yields, $10 = b$. Therefore, the equation for the function is, $g(x) = -3x + 10$. **The correct answer is (C).**

7. We can solve this problem by using the unit conversion technique most commonly taught in chemistry and physics classes.

$$\frac{6 \text{ km}}{18.3 \text{ minutes}} \times \frac{60 \text{ minutes}}{1 \text{ hour}} \times (3 \text{ hours})$$
$$= \frac{6 \times 60 \times 3}{18.3 \times 1 \times 1} \text{ km} = \frac{1,080}{18.3} \text{ km} = 59.016 \text{ km}$$

Among the answer choices, only choice (B) is close to 59.016. **The correct answer is (B).**

8. The given equation, $C = 93.4 - 8.29x$, takes the form, $y = a + bx$. In such an equation, the coefficient of x, which is the number b, is the slope. Therefore, -8.29 is the slope of the line, or *rate of change* of the function. The standard interpretation of this rate of change is that for each 1-unit increase in the value of x (years since 2002), there has been a decrease of 8.29 units (that is, 8.29 cats per square mile) in the value of C. Therefore, the average number of cats has *decreased* at an average rate of 8.29 cats per year. Choice (D) correctly states this conclusion. **The correct answer is (D).**

9. We can solve this equation for p by multiplying both sides of the equation by the reciprocal of the fraction, 5 / 8.

$$\frac{5}{8}p = \frac{3}{5} \quad \text{multiply both sides by the reciprocal of } \frac{5}{8}, \text{ which is } \frac{8}{5}, \text{ then simplify:}$$

$$\left(\frac{8}{5}\right)\left(\frac{5}{8}p\right) = \left(\frac{3}{5}\right)\left(\frac{8}{5}\right) \quad \Rightarrow \quad p = \frac{24}{25}$$

The correct answer is (A).

eggheadprep.com

10. A graph with four distinct zeros must cross or touch the *x*-axis exactly four times. Only the graph shown in choice (B) fits this description. **The correct answer is (B).**

11. We are given that the volume is 1.4 m³, which is the value of *V* in the formula $F = BV$. From the table, we know that the buoyancy constant for liquid nitrogen is $B = 7,940$ N / m³. Therefore, the value of *F* (the buoyant force), in Newtons, is $7,940(1.4) \approx 11,116$. Only answer choice (C) is close to the value 11,116. **The correct answer is (C).**

12. We are given that the buoyant force *F* is 25,500 Newtons. From the table, for cooking oil, $B = 8,980$ N / m³. Plugging these values into the formula $F = BV$ gives us the equation, $25500 = 8980(V)$, where *V* is the volume of the object in m³. Dividing both sides of the equation by 8,980 yields, $2.84 \approx V$ (in units of m³). Now use this value for *V*, along with the new value 28,700 Newtons for *F*, to generate the equation, $28700 = B(2.84)$, where B is the buoyancy constant in N / m³. Dividing both sides of the equation by 2.84 yields, $10,105.6 \approx B$ (in units of N / m³). The only liquid shown in the table for which *B* is close to the value 10,105.6 N / m³ is seawater, for which $B = 10,100$ N / m³. **The correct answer is (B).**

13. We can solve this problem by using the unit conversion technique most commonly taught in chemistry and physics classes.

$$h = \frac{11.3 \text{ heartbeats}}{1 \text{ second}} \cdot \frac{60 \text{ seconds}}{1 \text{ minute}} \cdot m \text{ minutes} = \frac{11.3(60)(m) \text{ heartbeats}}{1},$$

which is equal to $11.3(60m)$. **The correct answer is (D).**

14. Here are the steps to rearrange the equation to get *c* by itself.

$d = 9p^2 + cp + z$ subtract *z* from both sides to get

$d - z = 9p^2 + cp$ subtract $9p^2$ from both sides to get

$d - z - 9p^2 = cp$ separately divide each term by *p*, which yields

$\dfrac{d}{p} - \dfrac{z}{p} - 9p = c$ combine the first two fractions, which have the same denominator

$\dfrac{d-z}{p} - 9p = c$

NOTE: The fact that that an answer choice has the term, $-9p$, separated from the fraction is a cue to perform the division term-by-term when dividing by *p*. As it happens, that answer is correct. **The correct answer is (C).**

15. It might be tempting for this problem to choose one of the *x*-values at which the two curves intersect, or an *x*-value where one of the curves crosses the *x*-axis. Such points are very often important in algebra, but they are not relevant to this problem. To see why, start with the given equation, $f(x) + g(x) = 0$, and subtract $f(x)$ from both sides to get, $g(x) = -f(x)$. We are thus looking for an *x*-value for which the *y*-coordinate on the graph of *g* is the *opposite* of the *y*-coordinate on the graph of *f*. Notice that at $x = 3$, the *y*-coordinate on the graph of *f* appears to 4, while the

SAMPLE TEST 3
Answer Explanations

y-coordinate on the graph of *g* appears to be –4. These coordinates satisfy the condition, $g(x) = -f(x)$. Therefore, 3 is the desired *x*-value. **The correct answer is (C).**

16. We should rule out choice (C) immediately. We have no idea if every possible type of wand was tested in the study, so the conclusion presented in answer (C) is unfounded. We should also rule out choice (B). We know only that students who used the new type of wand "had significantly more success." "Significantly more success" indicates a level of increase in spell-casting success that is not likely to occur randomly, but it definitely does *not* mean the increase is "dramatic." Finally, answer choice (D) is also significantly flawed. We know only that *overall*, students experienced more success with the new type of wand, which does not mean that *every* student who used the new type of wand was more successful than students who did not use the new type. The remaining option, answer (A), summarizes the most reasonable conclusion that can be drawn from the available information about the study. **The correct answer is (A).**

17. If each average-sized car weights $1\frac{3}{4}$ tons = 1.75 tons, then the weight of 11 average-sized cars is (1.75 tons)(11) = 19.25 tons. Therefore, if brought to Earth, a single teaspoon of material from the collapsing star would weigh 19.25 tons. The weight of 36 teaspoons of the material, in tons, would then be 36(19.25) = 693. Answer (C) is the only choice close to 693. **The correct answer is (C).**

18. There are many ways to solve this problem. One method would be to calculate $S(P)$ for some value of *P* of your choice, then increase your value of *P* by 12 and recalculate $S(P)$, and then, finally, compare your two values for $S(P)$. The most direct approach, however, is to recognize that both the expression for $S(P)$ and the expression for $D(P)$ take the form, $mx + b$. For $S(P)$, the number in the "*m*" position is 0.75, so 0.75 is the slope of the graph of $S(P)$, or the *rate of change* of *S*. The standard interpretation of this rate of change is that for each 1-unit increase in the value of *P*, there will be an increase of 0.75 units in the value of *S*. In other words, if the price increased by $1.00, the supply would increase by 0.75 units. Therefore, if the price increases by $12, the supply will increase by 0.75(12) = 9 units. **The correct answer is (D).**

19. Since we are looking for the price at which supply and demand will be equal, we set the expressions for $S(P)$ and $D(P)$ equal to each other: $0.75P + 120 = 235 - 2.5P$. Subtracting 120 from both sides gives us, $0.75P = 115 - 2.5P$. We next add $2.5P$ to both sides to arrive at, $3.25P = 115$. Dividing both sides by 3.25 yields the answer, $P = \$35.3846...$ Rounding this price to the nearest whole dollar, we get $35, which matches choice (A). **The correct answer is (A).**

20. Let *P* be the original price of the automobile, let *Y* be the number of years since the automobile was purchased, and let *V* be the automobile's value after *Y* years.

(A) 4.7% of the original price would be $0.047P$. Since the automobile loses this much of its value every year, after *Y* years, it will have lost $(0.047P)Y = 0.047PY$ dollars in value. Therefore, the value after *Y* years would be, $V = P - 0.047PY$, which is not an exponential function.

(B) Because the automobile *loses* 5.8% of its current value each year, it must *retain* 100% – 5.8% = 94.2% of its current value every year. Because the amount of value retained depends on the *current value*, not the original value, we must apply the percentage repeatedly to obtain the value after each successive year. After one year, the value would be $0.942P$. After two years, it would be $0.942(0.942)P = (0.942)^2 P$. After three years, the value would be $0.942(0.942)(0.942)P = (0.942)^3 P$. Hence, after Y years, the value would be given by the formula, $V = (0.942)^Y P$, or $V = P(0.942)^Y$. This equation matches the standard form, $y = ab^x$, of an exponential function.

(C) The answer choice describes a constant decrease. The rate of change is -750. Hence, the equation would take the form, $y = mx + b$. Specifically, the formula would be, $V = -750Y + P$, which is not an exponential equation.

(D) By basing our work on the analysis completed above for option (A) above, we produce the formula, $V = P - (300 + 0.047PY)$. This is not an exponential equation.

The correct answer is (B).

21. Scanning upward from the number 165 on the horizontal axis to the dot immediately above it, we see that 16 people danced to the song with a tempo of 165 beats per minute. Continuing to read upward, we see that the line of best fit passes through the point (165, 19). In other words, the line of best fit predicts that 19 people will dance to a song with a tempo of 165 beats per minute. Since $19 - 16 = 3$, the actual number of people who danced to the song is 3 less than the line of best fit would predict. **The correct answer is (B).**

22. A major theorem from trigonometry states that for any angle $x°$, $\cos(90 - x°) = \sin(x°)$. Since $\cos(m°) = \sin(n°)$, we conclude that $m = 90 - n$. Now substitute the expressions given for m and n into this equation: $4x - 14 = 90 - (2x + 2)$. Distributing the subtraction over the parentheses yields, $4x - 14 = 90 - 2x - 2$. Combining like terms on the right side, we get, $4x - 14 = 88 - 2x$. Now add 14 to both sides to get, $4x = 102 - 2x$. Adding $2x$ to both sides yields, $6x = 102$. Finally, divide both sides by 6 to get $x = 17$. **The correct answer is (C).**

23. Translating the given information into equations is challenging. The first important observation we need to make is that since the director will need to pay expenses and his own salary no matter how many members the choir has or how much each member gets paid, we do not need to include those amounts in our equations. Let m stand for the number of members in the choir. If the director pays each member $104, then the total amount he pays to members, in dollars, will be $104m$. We are told that if he starts with d dollars and pays out the amount just expressed to the members, there will be $12 remaining. We can express this information as, $d - 104m = 12$. Now, if he pays each member $107, he will pay out a total of $107m$. We are told that he could do this if he received $204 more than d dollars. We are to assume that in the scenario just described, there would be no money leftover. The equation is therefore, $d + 204 - 107m = 0$. Subtracting 204 from both sides of this equation gives us, $d - 107m = -204$. We now solve the system of two equations that we have generated.

$$\begin{cases} d - 104m = 12 \\ d - 107m = -204 \end{cases}$$ multiply both sides of the second equation by -1 to get

$$\begin{cases} d - 104m = 12 \\ -d + 107m = 204 \end{cases}$$ adding the two equations gives us,

$$3m = 216$$

SAMPLE TEST 3
Answer Explanations

Dividing both sides of the last equation by 3, we get $m = 72$. **The correct answer is (C).**

24. Using the formula for volume of a cylinder, being careful to remember that the "height" of a cylinder is the distance between its circular bases (which is measured horizontally for this figure), we calculate the volume of the cylinder as $V = \pi r^2 h$, that is, $V = \pi (7)^2 (12) \approx 1{,}847.26$ cubic centimeters. Remember that this is only the volume of the cylindrical center section, *not* the entire balloon. Notice next that the two hemispheres could be combined to make a complete sphere. We calculate the volume of that sphere as,

$$V = \frac{4}{3}\pi r^3 = \frac{4}{3}\pi(7)^3 \approx 1{,}436.76 \text{ cubic centimeters.}$$

Therefore, the total volume of the balloon is about $1{,}847.26 + 1{,}436.76 = 3{,}284.02$ cubic centimeters. This result matches choice (D) very closely. **The correct answer is (D).**

25. If w is 40% *more* than the quantity $x + y$, then w is 100% + 40% = 140% of the quantity $x + y$. In symbols, $w = 1.40(x + y)$. Dividing both sides by 1.40, we get,

$$\frac{w}{1.40} = x + y.$$

We now substitute this expression in for $x + y$ in the given equation, $x + y + w = 1{,}560$.

$\frac{w}{1.40} + w = 1{,}560$ subtract w from both sides and place the right side over 1

$\frac{w}{1.40} = \frac{1560 - w}{1}$ cross multiply and use the distributive property:

$w(1) = 1.40(1560 - w) \Rightarrow w = 2184 - 1.40w$ add $1.40w$ to both sides

$2.40w = 2184$ divide both sides by 2.40 to arrive at the answer

$w = 910$

The correct answer is (B).

26. Because we are given neither the length nor the width of the original rectangular design, and are not asked to determine those measurements, we may safely assume that they do not affect the answer. To minimize the number of variables we need to use, then, we will arbitrarily pick values for the length and width. When working with percents, the number 100 is particularly easy to work with, so we'll set the length at 100 and make the width, say, 50. (Making the width 100 also would make the original design square, a very special case, which could yield misleading results.) The area of the original garden would then be $100(50) = 5{,}000$ square units. Decreasing the length by 25% means we *retain* 100% − 25% = 75% of the original length. The length of the redesigned garden is therefore $0.75(100) = 75$. Now, we need to increase the width by an unknown percentage, r. Assuming that r is the decimal form of the percent, the new width would be $(1 + r)(50)$, which equals $50 + 50r$. The area of the new garden would be $75(50 + 50r)$, or $3{,}750 + 3{,}750r$ square units. We are told that this area represents a 4% *decrease* from the original area of 5,000 square units, which means we *retain*

100% − 4% = 96% of the original area. Therefore, the new area is 0.96(5000) = 4,800 square units. Setting the two expressions for the area of the new rectangle equal to each other, we have 3750 + 3750r = 4800. Subtracting 3750 from both sides gives us, 3750r = 1050. Dividing both sides by 3750 yields the answer, r = 0.28. Since we used r to represent the *decimal* form of the percent, the true value of r is 28%. **The correct answer is (C).**

27. We are told, in effect, that the three points, (n, 27), (3, n), and (0, 0) all lie on the same line. Therefore, if we calculate the slope between any two of these points, we will always get the same value. We will use the slope formula to compute the slope between (n, 27) and (0, 0), and between (3, n) and (0, 0). We will then set the results equal to each other.

$$\text{slope between } (n, 27) \text{ and } (0, 0) = \frac{-27}{0-n} = \frac{-27}{-n} = \frac{27}{n}$$

$$\text{slope between } (3, n) \text{ and } (0, 0) = \frac{0-n}{0-3} = \frac{-n}{-3} = \frac{n}{3}$$

$$\text{Hence, } \frac{27}{n} = \frac{n}{3} \Rightarrow 27(3) = n(n) \Rightarrow 81 = n^2$$

The two solutions of this equation are n = 9 and n = −9. The first value appears as answer choice (A); the second does not appear in the answer choices. **The correct answer is (A).**

28. Note first that if h 7th graders preferred the honey badger, then 136 − h 8th graders preferred the honey badger. Similarly, if f 7th graders preferred the fishing cat, then 25 − f 8th graders preferred the fishing cat. Here is the table with this information added.

Grade of Student	Honey badger	Fishing cat
7th	h	f
8th	136 − h	25 − f
Total	136	25

The information given in the problem may now be expressed as the equations, $h = 4f$ and 136 − h = 7(25 − f). Substituting the expression for h from the first equation into the second equation gives us, 136 − 4f = 7(25 − f). Apply the distributive property on the right side to get, 136 − 4f = 175 − 7f. Subtracting 136 from both sides and adding 7f to both sides yields, 3f = 39. Now divide both sides by 3 to get, f = 13. We now know that 13 7th graders preferred the fishing cat, and therefore that h = 4(13) = 52 seventh graders preferred the honey badger. The probability that a student chosen randomly from among those who preferred the honey badger is a 7th grader is thus 52 / 136 ≈ 0.38. **The correct answer is (A).**

29. Repeated increase or decrease by a specific percentage gives rise to an exponential function with an equation of the form, $y = ab^x$, where a is the initial (beginning) quantity and b is the growth factor *per single time period*, x. Note that in this problem, the specified time period is 5 years. Therefore, after 5 years, the value of x will be 1. After 10 years, the value of x will be 2, and so on. Following this pattern, we see that after N years, the value of x will be $N / 5$. Since the number of teams with at least one female player is expected to *increase* by 18 percent per 5-year time period, the growth

SAMPLE TEST 3
Answer Explanations

factor b is 100% + 18% = 118% = 1.18. Therefore, the correct expression for the number of teams with at least one female player N years from now is, $25(1.18)^{\frac{N}{5}}$. **The correct answer is (D).**

30. One of many valid approaches to solving this problem is to rearrange the two equations to get n and m by themselves. For the first equation, $4x - n = 9x + 3$, begin by subtracting $4x$ from both sides, which yields, $-n = 5x + 3$. Multiply both sides by -1 to get, $n = -5x - 3$. For the second equation, $4y - m = 9y + 3$, begin by subtracting $4y$ from both sides to get, $-m = 5y + 3$. Multiplying both sides by -1 yields, $m = -5y - 3$. Since $n = m + \frac{1}{3}$, we now have the equation, $-5x - 3 = -5y - 3 + \frac{1}{3}$. We now rearrange this equation to get x and y on the same side of the equals sign.

$$-5x - 3 = -5y - 3 + \frac{1}{3} \quad \text{add 3 to both sides to get}$$

$$-5x = -5y + \frac{1}{3} \quad \text{add } 5y \text{ to both sides to get}$$

$$-5x + 5y = \frac{1}{3} \quad \text{multiply each term by } \frac{1}{5} \text{ to get}$$

$$-x + y = \frac{1}{15}, \quad \text{or} \quad y - x = \frac{1}{15}$$

The correct answer is (D).

---

31. The mean is the *average* of the times, so it is found by adding all of the times and then dividing the sum by the number of times, which is 12. Therefore,

$$\text{mean} = \frac{87 + 84 + 73 + 96 + 91 + 93 + 81 + 71 + 98 + 70 + 88 + 86}{12}$$

$$= \frac{1,018}{12} = 84.8\overline{3}$$

We are instructed to round the answer to the nearest tenth, so **the correct answer is 84.8 .**

32. Because student tickets cost $5 and adult tickets cost $7, the information about Ms. Davis's ticket purchases may be expressed as, $22 \leq 5s + 7(1) \leq 36$, or more simply, $22 \leq 5s + 7 \leq 36$. Subtracting 7 from all three parts of the inequality yields, $15 \leq 5s \leq 29$. Dividing all three parts by 5 gives us, $3 \leq s \leq 5.8$. Therefore, s could be any whole number (since one cannot purchase part of a ticket) that is greater than or equal to 3 and less than or equal to 5.8. Only the numbers 3, 4, and 5 satisfy these conditions. **The correct answer is 3 or 4 or 5.**

33. We know that a complete revolution around a circle equates to 2π radians. Therefore, the angle MCN represents

$$\frac{\frac{4\pi}{3}}{2\pi} = \frac{\frac{4\pi}{3}}{\frac{2\pi}{1}} = \frac{4\pi}{3} \cdot \frac{1}{2\pi}$$

$$= \frac{4\pi}{6\pi} = \frac{4}{6} = \frac{2}{3} \text{ of the circle.}$$

Consequently, the area of the sector formed by angle MCN represents 2 / 3 of the area of the circle. **The correct answer is 2 / 3 or 0.667 or 0.666.**

34. We distribute the –3 over the second set of parentheses and then combine like terms:

$$(-4x^2 + 7x - 5) - 3(2x^2 - 4x - 3) = -4x^2 + 7x - 5 - 6x^2 + 12x + 9$$
$$= -10x^2 + 19x + 4$$

Since b is the coefficient of x in the expression, $ax^2 + bx + c$, we have, $b = 19$. **The correct answer is 19.**

35. Notice that v is the y-coordinate of a point in the solution set of the system. We set the two $mx + b$ expressions for y equal to each other to find the intersection point of the lines that bound the solution set: $20x = -10x + 6000$. Adding $10x$ to both sides yields, $30x = 6000$. Dividing both sides by 30 gives us, $x = 200$. The y-coordinate of the intersection point is therefore $y = 20(200) = 4000$. Since both inequalities take the form, "y is *greater than* or equal to ($mx + b$ expression)," we know that the solution set lies *above* the point of intersection. Hence, y must be greater than or equal to 4000 for all points in the solution set. The value 4000 is thus the minimum possible value a y-coordinate in the solution set can have. **The correct answer is 4000.**

36. Because we are interested only in Sheila's average score, we may assume that she had a score of 78 for each of her first 9 rounds. Let x equal Sheila's score for her 10th round. In the best case scenario, Sheila would have a score of 64, her lowest possible score, for her 11th, 12th, 13th, 14th, and 15th rounds. In order for Sheila to have a chance to qualify for the national tournament, it must be true that the average of her first 9 rounds with a score of 78 for each round, her tenth round with a score of x, and her (hypothetical) 11th through 15th rounds with a score of 64 for each round is less than or equal to 74. We can express this information as an inequality and solve for x.

$$\frac{78 + 78 + 78 + 78 + 78 + 78 + 78 + 78 + 78 + x + 64 + 64 + 64 + 64 + 64}{15} \leq 74$$

$\frac{702 + x + 320}{15} \leq 74 \Rightarrow \frac{1022 + x}{15} \leq 74$ multiply both sides by 15 to get

$1022 + x \leq 1110$ subtracting 1022 from both sides yields,

$x \leq 88$

SAMPLE TEST 3
Answer Explanations

Therefore, Sheila must have a score of 88 or lower for her 10th round to still have any chance of qualifying for the tournament. In other words, the highest possible score she can have for her 10th round is 88. **The correct answer is 88.**

37. We are given that the page draws 2 new visitors per second, so the value of L for the page is 2. A time of 1 minute, 40 seconds equates to 60 seconds + 40 seconds = 100 seconds, so the value of T for this page is 100. Using the formula, $V = 0.8LT$, we calculate that for this page, $V = 0.8(2)(100) = 160$. **The correct answer is 160.**

38. Note that we know from the information provided that the number of visitors at any given time to Finagling, Inc.'s website is 252. Now, we are told that the Wangling, Inc. website attracts 600 new visitors per **minute**, which we need to convert to visitors per **second**.

$$\frac{600 \text{ visitors}}{1 \text{ minute}} \times \frac{1 \text{ minute}}{60 \text{ seconds}} = \frac{600}{60} \text{ visitors per second,}$$

which simplifies to 10 visitors per second. Since each visitor stays for an average of 22 seconds, we have, $V = 0.8(10)(22) = 176$ visitors to the Wangling, Inc. website at any time. The difference between the number of visitors to the Finagling, Inc. website at any time and the number of visitors to the Wangling, Inc. website at any time is therefore, $252 - 176 = 76$. We now calculate what percent of 252 the number 76 is, in order to express the number of visitors to Wangling, Inc.'s website as a *percent less than* the number of visitors to Finagling, Inc.'s website.

$$\frac{76}{252} \approx 0.30158 \approx 30.158\%$$

Per the instructions provided in the problem, we should type in this answer as 30. **The correct answer is 30.**

SCORING CONVERSION
RAW TO SCALED SCORE CONVERSION CHARTS

Sample Test 3:

A. SECTION 1: Conversion Chart for Reading Test:

RAW SCORE (# of correct answers)	READING TEST SCORE		RAW SCORE (# of correct answers)	READING TEST SCORE
0	10		27	27
1	10		28	27
2	10		29	28
3	11		30	28
4	12		31	29
5	13		32	29
6	14		33	29
7	14		34	30
8	15		35	30
9	16		36	31
10	17		37	31
11	17		38	32
12	18		39	32
13	19		40	33
14	19		41	33
15	20		42	34
16	21		43	34
17	21		44	35
18	22		45	36
19	22		46	36
20	23		47	37
21	24		48	38
22	24		49	38
23	25		50	39
24	25		51	40
25	26		52	40
26	26			

EGGHEAD PREP

SAMPLE TEST 3
Scoring Conversion

B. SECTION 2: Conversion Chart for Writing and Language Test

RAW SCORE (# of correct answers)	WRITING AND LANGUAGE TEST SCORE		RAW SCORE (# of correct answers)	WRITING AND LANGUAGE TEST SCORE
0	10		23	26
1	10		24	26
2	10		25	27
3	11		26	27
4	12		27	28
5	13		28	29
6	14		29	29
7	15		30	30
8	15		31	30
9	16		32	31
10	17		33	32
11	18		34	33
12	19		35	33
13	19		36	34
14	20		37	34
15	21		38	35
16	22		39	35
17	22		40	36
18	23		41	37
19	24		42	38
20	24		43	39
21	25		44	40
22	25			

C. Evidence-Based Reading and Writing Section Score

To calculate the Evidence-Based Reading and Writing Section Score, add the Reading Test Score (10 – 40) to the Writing and Language Test Score (10 – 40), and then multiply that total by 10.

For example, if the Reading Test Score is 27 and the Writing and Language Test Score is 34, then the Evidence-Based Reading and Writing Section Score is,

$$27 + 34 = 61 \times 10 = 610.$$

D. Sections 3 and 4: Math Test Score

The raw scores from Section 3 (Math—No Calculator) and Section 4 (Math—Calculator) should be added together to create the Math Raw Score. For example, if there were 18 correct answers in Section 3 (Math—No Calculator) and 24 in Section 4 (Math—Calculator), the Math Raw Score would be 18 + 24 = 42.

MATH RAW SCORE (Total # of correct answers, Sections 3 and 4 combined)	MATH SECTION SCORE		MATH RAW SCORE (Total # of correct answers, Sections 3 and 4 combined)	MATH SECTION SCORE
0	200		30	570
1	200		31	580
2	210		32	580
3	230		33	590
4	250		34	600
5	270		35	610
6	290		36	620
7	300		37	630
8	320		38	630
9	330		39	640
10	340		40	650
11	360		41	660
12	370		42	660
13	380		43	670
14	390		44	680
15	410		45	680
16	420		46	690
17	430		47	690
18	440		48	700
19	450		49	710
20	460		50	710
21	470		51	720
22	480		52	730
23	490		53	740
24	500		54	750
25	510		55	770
26	530		56	780
27	540		57	790
28	550		58	800
29	560			

SAMPLE TEST 4

Including...

▶ SECTION 1: READING TEST   322

▶ ANSWERS, SECTION 1   340

▶ SECTION 2: WRITING & LANGUAGE TEST   341

▶ ANSWERS, SECTION 2   357

▶ SECTION 3: MATH TEST   358

▶ ANSWERS, SECTION 3   364

▶ SECTION 4: MATH TEST   365

▶ ANSWERS, SECTION 4   377

▶ ANSWER EXPLANATIONS   378

▶ SCORING CONVERSION   409

eggheadprep.com

SECTION 1: READING TEST
65 MINUTES, 52 QUESTIONS

DIRECTIONS
Each group of questions below is based on a passage or pair of passages. Read each passage carefully, then choose the best answer to each question based on what is stated in or suggested by the passage(s). The questions may also refer to any graphical displays that accompany the passage(s), such as tables or graphs.

Questions 1-11 are based on the following passage.

The narrator of this passage is a fictional explorer seeking to reach the summit of the highest mountain in her country.

As quickly as we lay them down, blowing snow erases any trace of our footprints, the mountain as impervious to our progress as the memories of the world's men and women will be to our
5   achievements—if there should even be any of the latter. Promises of medals of gold still echo in our ears from the day of our departure on this excursion of folly, but we know well that the reward reaped by those whose footprints lie buried beneath us was not a
10 gold medal but an icy coffin. It seems to me that some time in the past, I know not whether it was weeks or decades ago, all the forces imposing themselves on my life seemed perfectly aligned and this endeavor, the right and inevitable outcome of all events that
15 preceded it. Now, whatever purpose may drive this progression of trudging souls no art or science I know can divine.
   Surely, those who assert that we are advancing the cause of knowledge have but the most fragile grasp
20 on sanity. What truths can a person aspire to read upon an endless page of featureless white? What use serves the summit? What malady will it cure? What advantage of sight has it to offer that the more accessible peaks of the South, humbler only by a
25 matter of a few dozen meters, do not? No, the relentless winds of ice that dull our senses rather remind us by the moment that this lofty wasteland does not provide knowledge; it destroys it. As much as I am any longer certain of anything, I know that we
30 few who have embarked on this path shall reach the height of it with minds as empty as the sky for which we reach. We will be capable of knowing as much as we will find—nothing.
   And yet, it is that very thought, however mightily
35 I have struggled to arrive at it, that now gives me pause. For is not my ability to ponder the nothingness that awaits us itself a measure of the progress of our understanding? To our ancestors, the forbidding peak that looks down mockingly on our halting advance
40 was a place of gods and menacing beasts. The very notion that the secrets the clouds obscure are no secrets at all began to dawn upon my people precisely and only because previous attempts to surmount this boundary of our land, however futile they may have
45 been, evoked no response from above and changed not one of our circumstances. We who shiver on this unyielding path feel no fear to match those of our forbearers who never aspired to travel it. No horror we may find at the apex, no torment of wind or snow
50 or cold beyond measure, could ever so control us as the demons and monsters with which our fancy populates places our eyes have not beheld.
   Boldly onward, then, we trudge, even as dullness increasingly overwhelms our consciousness. We
55 climb not to discover, but to fail to discover. It was not myths that advanced humankind, but the destruction of myths. If we should conquer, we will in the conquering prove there was no foe. If we should return alive, then by that fact alone we will free all
60 who shall call us "ancestor" from the shackles of superstition.

This passage was adapted from B. Siems, "The Height of Tomorrow," ©2016.

SAMPLE TEST 4
Section 1: Reading Test

1. What is the narrator implying in lines 1-5 ("As quickly … achievements")?
   A) The snow has made the mountain trail utterly impassable, so she and her party will need to turn back.
   B) She does not expect her endeavor to be remembered, even if it is successful.
   C) She is worried that she and her companions will get lost because they can neither remember the route they've taken nor see their own footprints.
   D) She views the act of reaching the mountain peak as a great achievement.

2. The narrator suggests that those who previously attempted to climb the mountain
   A) discovered important medicines.
   B) succeeded but did not receive the medals they had been promised.
   C) did not survive the journey.
   D) encountered terrifying animals.

3. Which option provides the strongest evidence in support of the answer to the previous question?
   A) Lines 6-10 ("Promises … coffin.")
   B) Line 22 ("What … cure?")
   C) Lines 38-40 ("To our … beasts.")
   D) Lines 43-46 ("previous … circumstances.")

4. Over the course of the narrative, there is a shift in the narrator's attitude. Which choice best describes that shift?
   A) From fear of failure to certainty of success
   B) From distrust of human progress to celebration of it
   C) From disrespect for her ancestors to veneration of them
   D) From doubt about the value of the expedition to a strong belief in its importance

5. Which option provides the strongest evidence in support of the answer to the previous question?
   A) Lines 18-20 ("Surely … sanity.") and lines 53-54 ("boldly … consciousness.")
   B) Lines 15-18 ("Now, … divine.") and lines 57-61 ("If we … susperstition.")
   C) Lines 38-40 ("To our … beasts.") and lines 46-48 ("We who … travel it.")
   D) Lines 1-6 ("As quickly … latter.") and lines 54-55 ("We climb … discover.")

6. As used in line 16, "divine" most nearly means
   A) holy.
   B) discover.
   C) disprove.
   D) deny.

7. The narrator's purpose in asking the questions in lines 20-25 ("What truths … do not?") is
   A) to explain her people's belief that reaching a mountain summit can cure the malady of poor eyesight.
   B) to share her belief that the attempt to reach the summit is an act of arrogance, and suggest that her people should be more humble.
   C) to explain that her people have limited knowledge of the world because they have not learned to read.
   D) to convey her feeling that reaching the mountain peak will serve no useful purpose.

8. What specific negative effect of the altitude, cold, and snow does the narrator mention?
   A) Loss of appetite
   B) Difficulty breathing due to low oxygen levels
   C) Difficulty in maintaining clarity of thought
   D) Severe headaches

9. As used in line 51, "fancy" most nearly means
   A) imagination
   B) liking
   C) elaborate
   D) delicate

10. Why does the narrator come to believe it will be significant for her and her companions to find nothing of interest at the summit?

   A) It will convince others not to risk their lives to make the climb.
   B) Their minds will be too weak to process anything they might discover, anyway.
   C) Proof that nothing exists there will dispel fears of the unknown that hinder human progress.
   D) Encountering wildlife there would be extremely dangerous, especially because they are weak from the climb.

11. Which option provides the strongest evidence in support of the answer to the previous question?

   A) Lines 6-8 ("Promises … folly")
   B) Lines 32-33 ("We will … nothing.")
   C) Lines 38-40 ("To our … beasts.")
   D) Lines 48-52 ("No horror … beheld.")

Questions 12-22 are based on the following passage and supplemental information describing fictional scenarios and data.

The ease with which the young manipulate technology, and the parallel floundering of older generations in the presence of button-laden gadgets, has become such a universally accepted notion that few
[5] would think to question its validity. New parents consider their future humiliation in the face of their children's adept handling of all things technological to be as inevitable as teenage rebellion. The correlation between age and technological proficiency is not nearly
[10] as clear-cut as popular culture would have us believe, however. Some have even suggested that in the near future, there will be "generational inversion"—a phenomenon in which an older generation possesses demonstrably superior command of new technology
[15] than a younger one.

General statistics on the amount of time people spend interacting with technology continue to suggest that the realm of cutting-edge gadgets yet belongs to the young. For the purpose of measuring personal
[20] comfort and skill with various devices, however, such data offer a dull edge where razor-keen parsing of the numbers is needed. We know, for example, that 15 years ago, the majority of American teens did not carry cell phones, though most adults had adopted the
[25] technology. Today, cell phone ownership among teens virtually equals that among adults, and with regard to time spent on the device on a daily basis, the youth prevail by a good margin. But it is also true that whereas the adults of the early 2000s found their handheld
[30] phones baffling, many today employ them for far more sophisticated purposes than do their children. Similarly, studies indicate that the average American adult of age 25 to 45 runs over 12 computer (desktop or laptop) applications per day, nearly twice the number run by
[35] children ages 10 to 16. On the other hand, adults above age 35 remain far more likely than younger people to describe technology as "confusing" or "intimidating." Those results alone caution us to temper any assertion that a generational inversion is under way.

[40] Only at the older end of the generational spectrum are there clear patterns that align with popular belief. Adults over the age of 55 lag far behind all younger groups in their use of, openness to, and facility with technological devices. Indeed, it was precisely those
[45] generations that gave rise to the comedic cliché of an eleven-year-old ably programming the family's TV recording device while his or her parents gawked in amazement. Many people between the ages of 40 and 55 were those child tech wizards, but fully expected to
[50] one day watch their own children with equal awe. Whether or not a full-scale inversion is upon us, there can be little doubt that those expectations have not been fully borne out. The question is, why not?

No one would suggest that the reason the old mode
[55] of generational change with respect to technology is no longer valid is that the pace of change in technology has slowed. Any such assertion is manifestly false. Indeed, several experts believe the exact opposite, that any inversion now occurring is a direct consequence of
[60] the dizzying acceleration of technological change that began in the early 1990s. Those who were children or young adults at any time between 1990 and 2004, these analysts suggest, made a cognitive leap that no previous generation had made. As Dr. Carissa Gelpin of the
[65] Reiswig Center for Technical Research observes, "These are people who, from a very young age, had to face the reality that any gadget they employed and any skill they acquired might be obsolete within a few years. In response to this initially terrifying revelation,
[70] they focused not so much on developing expertise with any particular device as on adaptability as a primary life skill." As a result, they are remarkably deft at transferring yesterday's know-how to an entirely different context, be it the latest app or even an entirely
[75] new operating system.

Of course, those who have come of age since 2010 have experienced equally rapid change in the world around them, but there is a key difference. Much of the focus in the tech world in recent years has been on
[80] improving the user's experience. Ever-improving voice recognition software, for example, is on the verge of eliminating any need for a youngster to even ponder the intricacies of a device's operating system. To oversimplify the situation somewhat, many of today's
[85] adults developed their thinking skills in response to their perception that if they did not adapt to technology, they could not survive. To an extent, the youth of today believe that if they wait a while, technology will adapt to them. In that regard at least, a very profound
[90] inversion has occurred, after all.

Chart 1

Age Distribution of US Citizens owning three or more software-running* devices

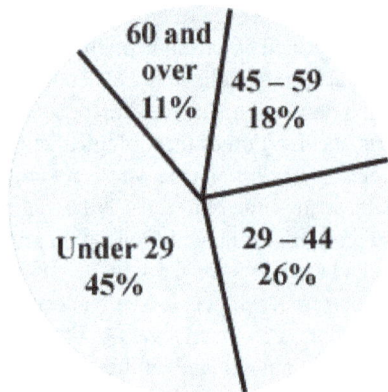

*Software-running devices include desktop and laptop computers, smartphones, and tablets.

Chart 2

Average Annual Growth Rates in Software-Running Device Ownership

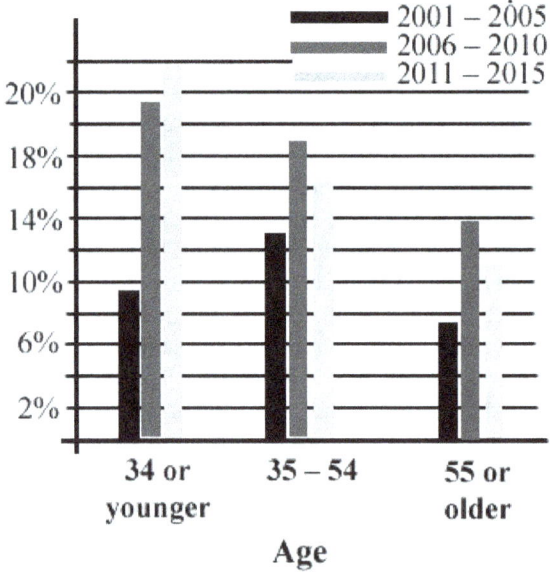

12. Which is the best description of the author's purpose in the first paragraph (lines 1-15)?

A) To present a commonly held belief about technology and then call it into question

B) To discuss feelings of humiliation experienced by children and their parents

C) To examine trends in technology, especially the need to simplify devices with too many buttons

D) To explore the relationship between popular culture and the rebelliousness of teenagers

13. Which of these conclusions is implied by the second paragraph (lines 16-39)?

A) Data on use of technological devices is often too broad in nature to reveal significant generational trends; closer examination reveals numerous apparent contradictions.

B) The rise of cell phone use is strongly associated with dangerous driving habits among teenagers, because teens spend significantly more time on their phones than adults.

C) Young people own fewer technological devices than those over the age of 35, but they use their devices for a greater variety of sophisticated purposes.

D) As people grow older, they are less likely to find complex technology confusing or difficult to use.

14. As used in line 38, "temper" most nearly means

A) strengthen.

B) moderate.

C) exaggerate.

D) protest.

15. What is meant by the first sentence of the third paragraph (lines 40-41, "Only ... belief.")?

    A) Like the color spectrum, popular beliefs about technology form patterns that are familiar but also display great variety.
    B) Older generations of Americans frequently align themselves against popular trends.
    C) The widely held belief that technological savvy decreases with age is consistent with the evidence only among older age groups.
    D) As people grow older, their behavior falls into more predictable patterns, often based on adherence to popular beliefs.

16. Which option provides the best supporting evidence for the answer to the previous question?

    A) Lines 42-44 ("Adults ... devices.")
    B) Lines 48-50 ("Many ... awe.")
    C) Lines 51-53 ("Whether ... borne out.")
    D) Lines 54-57 ("No one ... slowed.")

17. As used in line 72, "deft" most nearly means

    A) silly.
    B) clumsy.
    C) outspoken.
    D) proficient.

18. Based on the arguments presented in the final two paragraphs (lines 54-90), the author believes the primary cause of any generational inversion occurring with regard to technology is

    A) The pace of change in technology has slowed, making it easier for older Americans to stay up to date.
    B) Today's youth have access to more technology than any generation in history.
    C) Improving user interfaces are making it simpler for people of all ages to interact with their devices.
    D) An era of rapid change stimulated unique growth in one generation's ability to adapt.

19. Which option provides the best supporting evidence for the answer to the previous question?

    A) Lines 54-57 ("the reason ... slowed.")
    B) Lines 69-72 ("In response ... skill.")
    C) Lines 76-78 ("Of course ... them")
    D) Lines 80-83 ("Ever-improving ... system.")

20. The author of the passage would probably describe Chart 1 as

    A) strongly supportive of the arguments put forth in the passage because ownership of devices is broken down by age group.
    B) an attempt to defend an opinion with which the author does not agree by using data that is probably not accurate.
    C) likely accurate, but of limited relevance to the passage because a person's level of technological mastery and the manner in which devices are used are not described in the data.
    D) interesting but extremely difficult to interpret because there is no accompanying historical information to put the data in context.

21. According to Chart 2, which choice characterizes the years 2006 – 2010?

    A) The highest rate of growth in device ownership during the period 2001 – 2015 for two of the three age groups
    B) Gradual decline in device ownership across all age groups
    C) The lowest rate of growth in device ownership during the period 2001 – 2015 across all age groups
    D) A decline in device ownership to below 2001 – 2006 levels, in some cases by more than half, depending on the age group

22. What general conclusion can be drawn about device ownership and age group based solely on Chart 2?

   A) Throughout the period 2001 – 2015, Americans of age 55 or over owned fewer devices than their younger counterparts.

   B) Americans age 34 and younger will continue to have the highest growth rate in the number of devices they own.

   C) Throughout the period 2001 – 2015, the rate at which device ownership increased was lowest among Americans age 55 or over.

   D) With the exception of Americans age 35 – 54, the data show a consistent pattern of the growth rate in device ownership rising and then falling again during the period 2001 – 2015.

SAMPLE TEST 4
Section 1: Reading Test

Questions 23-32 are based on the following passage.

This passage is adapted from "What Is a University?" by John Henry Newman, written around the year 1835.

If I were asked to describe as briefly and popularly as I could what a University was, I should draw my answer from its ancient designation as a *Studium Generale*, or "School of Universal Learning." This
[5] description implies the assemblage of strangers from all parts in one spot: *From all parts*, else, how will you find professors and students for every department of knowledge? and *In one spot*, else, how can there be any school at all? Accordingly, in its simple and rudimental
[10] form, it is a school of knowledge of every kind, consisting of teachers and learners from every quarter. Many things are requisite to complete and satisfy the idea embodied in this description; but such as this a University seems to be in its essence, a place for the
[15] communication and circulation of thought, by means of personal intercourse.

If this be a University, then a University does but answer a necessity of our nature, and is but one specimen that does so in one particular medium, out of
[20] many that might be cited in others. Mutual education, in a large sense of the word, is one of the great and incessant occupations of human society, carried on partly with set purpose, and partly not. Now, in this process, books, I need scarcely say, are one special
[25] instrument, emphatically so in this age. Considering the prodigious powers of the press, and how they are developed at this time in the never-intermitting issue of periodicals, tracts, pamphlets, works in series, and light literature, we must allow there never was a time fairer
[30] for dispensing with every other means of disseminating information and instruction. What can we want more, you will say, for the intellectual education of the whole person, and for every person, than so exuberant, diversified, and persistent a promulgation of all kinds
[35] of knowledge? Why, you will ask, need we go up to knowledge, when knowledge comes down to us? Works larger and more comprehensive than those which have gained for ancients an immortality issue forth every morning, and are projected onwards to the
[40] ends of the earth at the rate of hundreds of miles a day. Our seats are strewn, our pavements are powdered, with swarms of little tracts.

I allow all this, and much more; such certainly is our popular education, and its effects are remarkable.
[45] Nevertheless, after all, even in this age, whenever people are really serious about getting what, in the language of trade, is called "a good article," when they aim at something precise, something refined, something really luminous, they go to another market;
[50] they avail themselves, in some shape or other, of the rival method, the ancient method, of oral instruction, of present communication between one person and another, of teachers instead of solitary learning, of the personal influence of a master and
[55] the humble initiation of a disciple, and, in consequence, of great centers of pilgrimage and throng, which such a method of education necessarily involves. This, I think, will be found to hold good in all those departments or aspects of
[60] society that possess an interest sufficient to bind us together. It holds in the political world, and in the high world, and in the religious world. And it holds also in the literary and scientific worlds.

If the actions of people may be taken as any
[65] test of their convictions, then we have reason for saying this: that the province and the inestimable benefit of books is that of being a record of truth and an authority of appeal, an instrument of teaching when in the hands of a teacher; but also
[70] that, if we wish to become exact and fully furnished in any branch of knowledge which is diversified and complicated, we must consult the living and listen to their living voices. I am not bound to investigate the cause of this, and anything I may say will, I am
[75] conscious, be short of its full analysis. Perhaps we may suggest simply that no books can get through the number of minute questions which it is possible to ask on any extended subject, or can hit upon the varied difficulties which are severally felt by each
[80] reader in succession. Or again, that no book can convey the special spirit and delicate peculiarities of its subject with that rapidity and certainty which attend on the sympathy of mind with mind, through the eyes, the look, the accent, and the manner, in
[85] casual expressions thrown off at the moment, and the unstudied turns of familiar conversation. Whatever be the cause, the fact is undeniable. The general principles of any study you may learn by books at home; but the detail, the color, the tone, the air,
[90] the life that makes it live in us: you must catch all these from those in whom it lives already.

23. As used in line 1, the word "popularly" is most similar in meaning to
   A) famously.
   B) in keeping with current trends.
   C) accessibly.
   D) crowd-pleasingly

24. Which of the following is NOT a characteristic that the author explicitly identifies with a university in the first paragraph (lines 1-16)?
   A) Face-to-face interaction between students and teachers
   B) Extracurricular activities to promote community leadership
   C) The presence of people from a wide variety of back- grounds
   D) Centralization of activities in a single location

25. As used in line 12, the word "requisite" is most similar in meaning to
   A) excluded.
   B) requited.
   C) acquired.
   D) required.

26. In the second paragraph (lines 17-42), what observation does the author make about the age in which he lives?
   A) Newspapers are gaining excessive power, an issue that must be addressed without delay.
   B) A university is the only place where significant learning occurs because in all other settings, people are concerned only with their occupations.
   C) As a result of the accelerating pace of life, cities are suffering from major problems with litter, compromising the beauty of streets and sidewalks.
   D) The dawn of mass-scale printing has made information available to the general public as never before, leading some to wonder if other methods of education are obsolete.

27. Which option offers the strongest evidence in support of the answer to the previous question?
   A) Lines 20-23 ("Mutual … partly not.")
   B) Lines 25-27 ("Considering … issue")
   C) Lines 28-31 ("periodicals … instruction.")
   D) Lines 40-42 ("Our seats … tracts.")

28. As used in lines 29 and 43, "allow" essentially means
   A) authorize.
   B) acknowledge.
   C) permit.
   D) disagree.

29. Which of the following points does the author present in the final paragraph as an advantage of education at a university?
   A) Face-to-face communication is enhanced by the use of nonverbal cues.
   B) Regular exams motivate students to keep reviewing material on a daily basis.
   C) Universities offer the best opportunity to learn the general principles of a subject, without getting bogged down in details.
   D) At a university, students have the opportunity, with a teachers' help, to investigate whether people's actions are aligned with their beliefs.

30. Which option offers the strongest evidence in support of the answer to the previous question?
   A) Lines 64-69 ("If the … teacher")
   B) Lines 73-75 ("I am … analysis.")
   C) Lines 80-86 ("Or again … conversation.")
   D) Lines 87-89 ("Whatever … home;")

31.

Which of the following best expresses the author's beliefs about schools, learning, and education?

A) In-person instruction from a qualified teacher is an irreplaceable component of a complete education.

B) Because attending a university often requires traveling a great distance at considerable expense, it is wise to consider studying a trade instead.

C) In ancient times, universities were important centers of learning, but they are no longer needed due to the wide variety of other forms of education now available.

D) Education should be specialized rather than general to ensure that those who attend a university will graduate with skills directly applicable to a career.

32.

Which option provides the strongest evidence in support of the answer to the previous question?

A) Lines 2-4 ("I should ... Learning") and lines 18-20 ("and is ... others.")

B) Lines 4-6 ("This description ... spot") and lines 45-47 ("Nevertheless, ... article,")

C) Lines 58-63 ("This, I ... worlds.")

D) Lines 87-91 ("The general ... already.")

Questions 33-42 are based on the following pair of passages, adapted from an 1887 US Senate debate over a women's suffrage Constitutional amendment.

Passage 1: Testimony by Senator Brown of Georgia

    Mr. President, the resolution proposing an amendment to the Constitution of the United States, conferring the right to vote upon women, is one of paramount importance, as it involves great questions far
5 reaching in their tendency, which seriously affect the very pillars of our social fabric, which involve the peace and harmony of society, the unity of the family, and much of the future success of our Government.
    I believe that the Creator intended that the sphere of
10 the males and females of our species should be different, and that their duties and obligations, while they differ materially, are equally important and honorable, and that each sex is well qualified by natural endowments for the discharge of the important duties which pertain to each.
15 We find an abundance of evidence, both in the works of nature and in the Divine revelation, that the family properly regulated is the foundation of society, and that it is provided that the man shall be the head of the family.
    Man, by reason of his physical strength, is qualified
20 for the discharge of those duties that require strength and ability to combat the sterner realities and difficulties in life. He discharges such labors as require greater physical strength and endurance than the female sex are usually found to possess. It is not only his duty to provide for and
25 protect the family, but also to represent the family in discharging the laborious obligations which the family owes to the state, and which obligations must be discharged by the head of the family. Among other duties which the head of the family owes the state is military
30 duty, which he is able to discharge, and which the female members of the family are unable to discharge.
    As it is the duty of the male sex to perform obligations to the state, to society, and to the family, it is also their duty to aid in the government of the state, which
35 is simply a great aggregation of families.
    On the other hand, the Creator has assigned to woman very laborious and responsible duties, by no means less important than those imposed upon the male sex, though entirely different in their character. She alone
40 is fitted for the discharge of the sacred trust of wife and the endearing relation of mother. If the wife and the mother is required to leave the sacred precincts of home and attempt to do military duty when the state is in peril, if she is to take part in all the unsavory work that may be
45 deemed necessary for the triumph of her party, and if on election day she is to leave her home and press her way through the crowds to the precinct to deposit her ballot, how is she to attend to her more sacred, delicate, and refining trust, to which we have already referred, and for
50 which she is peculiarly fitted by nature?

Passage 2: Testimony by Senator Blair of New Hampshire

    If there be any principle upon which our form of government is founded, and wherein it is different from aristocracies, monarchies, and despotisms, it is this: Every human being of mature powers, not disqualified by
55 ignorance, vice, or crime, is the equal of, and is entitled to all the rights and privileges which belong to any other such human being under the law. The exclusion of women from the suffrage can be justified upon proof, and only upon proof, that by reason of her sex she is
60 incompetent to exercise that power. No such proof exists.
    There is no legal or natural connection between the right or liability to fight and the right to vote. Society has well established the distinction, fixing forty-five years as the age at which obligation for military duty terminates,
65 while the right of suffrage continues as long as the mind lasts. There are at least three million more male voters in our country than the population liable by law to perform military duty. Further, the right to fight may be exercised voluntarily, and the liability to fight may be enforced by
70 the community. The extent to which the physical forces of society may be called upon in self-defense is measured not by age or sex, but by necessity. It cannot be claimed that woman has no right to vote because she is not liable to fight, for she is so liable, and the freest government on
75 the face of the earth has reserved the right to place her on the forefront of battle. More than this, woman has the right, and often has exercised it, to go there.
    The claim that woman is represented in government by the other sex is not well founded. It cannot be claimed
80 that she is a free being already represented, for she can only be represented according to her will, by the exercise of her will through the suffrage itself. I quote briefly from the report of the committee*:
    The rights for the maintenance of which human
85 *governments are constituted are life, liberty, and property. These rights are common to men and women alike, and every citizen is entitled to demand from the sovereign power the full protection of those rights.*
    This right to the protection of all other rights
90 *appertains to the individual, not to the family alone, or to any form of association. Probably not more than five-eighths of the men of legal age, qualified to vote, are heads of families, and not more than that proportion of adult women are united with men in the legal merger of*
95 *married life. It is, therefore, quite incorrect to speak of the state as an aggregate of families duly represented at the ballot box by their male head. The relation between*

the government and the individual is direct; all rights are individual rights.

100   *The distinction between human beings by reason of sex is a physical distinction. The soul is of no sex.*

**The Senate committee that drafted the amendment*

33. As used in line 5, "tendency" is closest in meaning to

   A) inclination
   B) impact
   C) tenability
   D) habit

34. Which option is NOT one of the possible negative outcomes suggested by Senator Brown in Passage 1 as a result of adoption of the amendment?

   A) Impaired functioning of the US government
   B) Strife and discord in domestic politics
   C) The weakening of the US military
   D) Harmful effects on families

35. Which of the following best summarizes Senator Brown's primary argument against the amendment, as presented in Passage 1?

   A) Men and women perform different roles in society; asking women to take up duties currently assigned to men would impair their ability to fulfill those duties that are uniquely theirs.
   B) Because men are generally physically stronger than women, it is reasonable to conclude that men are also better equipped mentally to handle the responsibilities of voting.
   C) Female voters would advance an agenda that excessively regulates the lives of families and impedes the economic growth of the nation.
   D) If empowered to vote, women would place a greater number of more intense, demanding obligations upon men, rather than attempt to take on such challenges as military duty themselves.

36. Which option offers the strongest evidence in support of the answer to the previous question?

   A) Lines 15-17 ('We find … society,")
   B) Lines 24-28 ("It is … family.")
   C) Lines 28-31 ("Among … discharge.")
   D) Lines 45-50 ("if on … nature?")

37. Which statement best summarizes the nature of the two passages and their relationship to each other?

   A) Passage 1 provides a general summary of issues surrounding the adoption of the amendment; Passage 2 explores those issues in greater detail.

   B) Passage 1 cites specific evidence supporting the claim that the amendment is flawed and potentially harmful; Passage 2 acknowledges the validity of that evidence but points out its limitations.

   C) Passage 1 presents a logical progression of arguments against adoption of the amend- ment; Passage 2 attempts to discredit those arguments primarily through an appeal to the emotions.

   D) Passage 1 puts forth arguments based on traditional beliefs, abstract ideas, and generalizations; Passage 2 refutes those arguments by calling upon specific evidence.

38. Which option best summarizes Senator Blair's main purpose(s) in the first paragraph (lines 1-10 of Passage 2?

   A) To enumerate the differences between the founding principles of the US system of government and those of other systems of government

   B) To assert that because women are inherently entitled entitled to the same rights as men, they can only be excluded from voting if it becomes established that they are unfit to vote

   C) To lament rising levels of ignorance, vice, and crime in America, and to link those issues to a lack of maturity among American citizens

   D) To discuss the power that voting represents, and to speculate on the various negative impacts that may arise from abuse of that power by those not competent enough to use it wisely.

39. As used in lines 62 and 69, "liability" is closest in meaning to

   A) weakness.
   B) proneness.
   C) dishonesty.
   D) compulsion.

40. All of the following are specific claims Senator Blair makes in response to Senator Brown's assertion of a link between voting rights and the obligation of military duty EXCEPT

   A) The law states that no one shall be required to serve in the military who has not yet had the opportunity to vote in elections.

   B) Voting rights and military service are governed by different rules with regard to age.

   C) Many women have voluntarily demonstrated their fitness for service in battle.

   D) A large number of men are exempted from military duty but still maintain their voting rights.

41. Which of the following statements summarizes specific evidence offered by the Senate committee (as quoted by Senator Blair in Passage 2) in response to Senator Brown's claim in Passage 1 that men, in their role as heads of families, represent women when voting?

   A) Men are more concerned than women with physical characteristics, and therefore cannot understand the wishes of women's souls.

   B) A significant number of men do not represent families, and a significant number of women are not part of households with a male head of family.

   C) Although it is reasonable to characterize the state as an aggregation of families, many families do not own property, and therefore are not guaranteed protection of their rights.

   D) In instances when every citizen was given the authority to interact with a government directly, the result was excessive demands, showing that the power of male voters should be limited.

42. Which option most directly supports the correct answer to the previous question?

   A) Lines 84-88 ("The rights ... rights.")
   B) Lines 91-95 ("Probably ... life.")
   C) Lines 97-99 ("The relation ... rights.")
   D) Lines 100-101 ("The distinction ... sex.")

Questions 43-52 are based on the following passage and additional information.

The following passage describes fictional events in a fictional location on Earth.

For centuries, travelers have reported that the continent of Hyberntam, at least in certain regions, offers something unforgettable: the most flavorful water on Earth. In the early twentieth century, scientists
[5] discovered the surprising truth behind the tales: In several areas of the continent, natural water supplies from lakes and rivers have extraordinarily high levels of the rare element methenium. The element is inert and entirely harmless, but its presence in drinking water fuels
[10] an almost miraculous explosion of taste.

Although many celebrated the methenium discovery as a shining example of science decoding an ancient mystery, those in the scientific community knew they had only answered one question with a still more
[15] baffling one. Given the relative scarcity of the element near Earth's surface, geologists asked, where did all that methenium come from? Because many of the lakes of Hyberntam are deep and fed by underground springs, it seemed natural to suppose that the methenium source
[20] must itself lie deep underground. The high level of earthquake, volcano, and geyser activity across much of Hyberntam would seem to support a belief that the molten stew at the heart of the world regularly spews its contents upward in the area occupied by the continent.
[25] Since the chemical composition of the core has not been completely catalogued, there may well be rich reserves of methenium lurking there. For these reasons, the Core Source Hypothesis was widely accepted for decades as the best explanation for Hyberntam's unique waters.

[30] It was, of all people, a travel agent who muddied the scientific waters, so to speak. Paodif Jansingisk spent much of the 1990s meticulously gathering anecdotal information from his clients about where the best of the best Hyberntamian water was to be found, hoping to
[35] assemble an exclusive, "insider's guide" for tourists that would give him an edge over his competitors. Each time he received a report of a town with exceptionally memorable water, he marked that town with a pin on a map he kept carefully hidden. To his astonishment, over
[40] the course of two years, the pins formed into a nearly perfect circle. Fortunately for us all, Jansingisk then put personal gain aside and informed the scientific community of his research.

After several years of collecting and analyzing
[45] water samples from all over Hyberntam and meticulously recording every result on the most detailed maps available, scientists confirmed that the lakes and rivers richest in methenium form a ring with a radius of approximately 80 kilometers, with the city of Gandocrast
[50] at its center. In fact, if one were to march directly toward Gandocrast starting from a distance of 500 or more kilometers away, one would discover a generally steady increase in the concentration of methenium in the waters along the way, reaching a peak at
[55] "Jansingisk's Ring," as the circle of waters is now known. Then, against all expectation, methenium levels would suddenly decline as one continued the march to Gandocrast. In the end, one would find oneself in a rather ill-fated city, home of the most
[60] ordinary drinking water in all of Hyberntam.

Recognizing that such a pattern is completely inconsistent with the Core Source Hypothesis—which would predict essentially random distribution of methenium across the continent—scientists looked for
[65] a new source of the flavor enhancer. Once again, the extraordinary stories of travelers had spurred an advance in scientific knowledge. The most radical hypothesis put forth, nicknamed the Deep Asteroid Explanation (DAE), proposed that millions of years
[70] ago, a large, methenium-rich asteroid collided with Earth's surface in the area of modern-day Hyberntam, subsequently becoming buried under hundreds of meters of ash and pyroclastic rock from volcanic eruptions triggered by the ensuing earthquakes all over
[75] the world. Confirmation for DAE came in 2012, when exploratory drilling and sample analysis confirmed the existence of a buried crater heavily sprinkled with fragments of methenium-laden ores that, based on their atomic signatures, did not originate on Earth. The
[80] asteroid remnants lie at the junction of several large underground waterways, located, in a bit of cruel irony, directly beneath Gandocrast itself.

Hydrologists know why it is that the city closest to this water-sweetening treasure trove finds itself
[85] envying its neighbors' water supplies. Underground waters, they explain, wend their way toward the surface slowly, over the course of many kilometers, before finally reaching a lake or river. Jansingisk's Ring lies at a sweet spot in terms of distance from the
[90] asteroid impact site, the region where the majority of those hidden streams share their bounty with freshwater bodies within our reach. As the blended waters head toward the sea, they become diluted by rainwater and glacial melt, lowering methenium
[95] levels.

Scientists acknowledge that even with all the evidence supporting it, DAE does not put to rest every question about the legendary waters of Hyberntam. As they continue the search for answers, city leaders in
[100] Gandocrast have a more practical matter on their minds: the digging of some very, very deep wells.

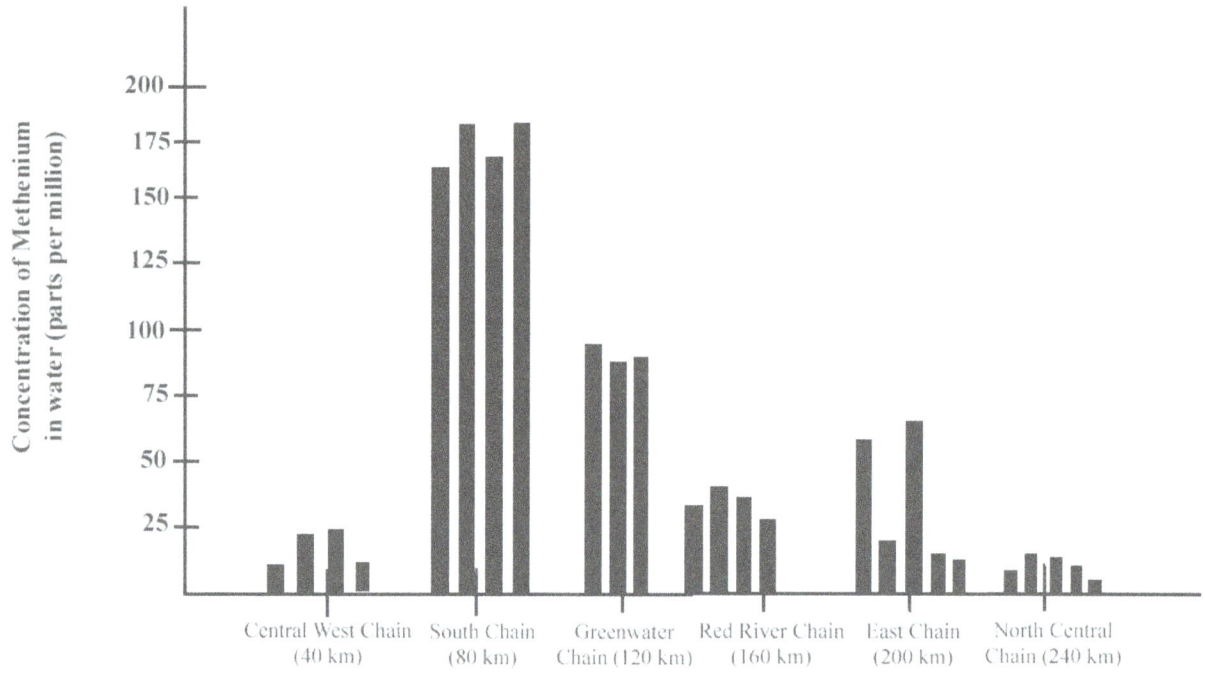

Levels of Methenium in Various Chains of Lakes on the Continent of Hyberntam

43. The main purpose of the passage is to

A) describe discoveries about the potentially harmful effects of exposure to the element methenium and examine how those discoveries might affect tourism in Hyberntam.

B) give a detailed explanation of the physical properties of underground waterways.

C) describe a strange phenomenon and explore how possible explanations for it have been tested against evidence.

D) examine the mechanisms by which material from Earth's core reaches the planet's surface.

44. What does the author suggest about the relationship between reports from non-scientists like travelers and the conduct of scientific research?

A) The author indicates that since non-scientists are not trained in the gathering and analysis of data, their stories should be disregarded by scientists.

B) The author indicates that scientists are often wrong in their hypotheses, so it is better to trust one's own experience and "everyday" people like travelers than to pay attention to scientific theories.

C) The author believes a primary responsibility of scientists is to prove that widely told stories are fabricated and exaggerated, so that such stories can be replaced by scientific truth.

D) The author conveys the idea that non-scientists can sometimes be a source of information about fascinating matters that can be further studied scientifically.

SAMPLE TEST 4
Section 1: Reading Test

45.
Which option offers the strongest evidence in support of the answer to the previous question?

A) Lines 11-15 ("Although … one.")
B) Lines 30-36 ("It was … competitors.")
C) Lines 65-67 ("Once … knowledge.")
D) Lines 96-98 ("Scientists … Hyberntam.")

46.
What was one outcome of the discovery of Jansingisk's Ring?

A) The existence of the ring largely disproved the previously widely accepted Core Source Hypothesis.
B) Discovering the ring gave Jansingisk a major competitive advantage in the travel and tourism business.
C) The discovery of the ring confirmed the Core Source Hypothesis by disproving the Deep Asteroid Explanation (DAE).
D) As a result of discovering the ring, scientists were able to identify methenium as the cause of the unique flavor of Hyberntamian water.

47.
Which option offers the strongest evidence in support of the answer to the previous question?

A) Lines 4-8 ("In the … methenium.")
B) Lines 31-36 ("Paodif … competitors.")
C) Lines 50-56 ("In fact … known.")
D) Lines 61-65 ("Recognizing … enhancer.")

48.
What important discovery made during drilling operations in 2012 gave positive confirmation of the Deep Asteroid Explanation (DAE)?

A) The city of Gandocrast lies directly above a major junction of underground waterways.
B) Underground waterways feed many of the deep lakes in Hyberntam.
C) The methenium found in ore samples came from a source in space.
D) Water from underground sources often blends with rainwater and glacial melt.

49.
Which option offers the strongest evidence in support of the answer to the previous question?

A) Lines 17-20 ("Because … underground.")
B) Lines 76-79 ("exploratory … Earth.")
C) Lines 79-82 ("The asteroid … itself.")
D) Lines 92-95 ("As the … levels.")

50.
What reason does the author imply for the digging of new, deep wells in Gandocrast (lines 100-101)?

A) The city wishes to have methenium-rich drinking water, like other regions in Hyberntam.
B) City officials in Gandocrast wish to conduct further research to verify the Deep Asteroid Explanation.
C) Previous drilling has destabilized the layers of volcanic buildup beneath Gandocrast; corrective measures are needed to ensure the safety of the city.
D) Fragments of the asteroid contain high levels of Uranium and other energy sources.

51.
Which conclusion is most strongly supported by the data shown in the figure?

A) The concentration of methenium in bodies of fresh-water in Hyberntam is highest approximately 80 kilometers from Gandocrast.
B) The presence of unusually high levels of methenium in freshwater in Hyberntam is the direct result of an asteroid-Earth collision millions of years ago (DAE).
C) The exceptional taste of drinking water in Hyberntam is caused by high levels of methenium.
D) methenium is an inert element that is perfectly safe for human consumption.

52. In the final paragraph (lines 96-101), the author states that "DAE does not put to rest every question about the legendary waters of Hyberntam." What specific issue represented by the data in the figure supports the idea that further research is still necessary?

A) The figure does not display any data about lakes in Gandocrast, so it does not confirm that that drinking water in Gandocrast is "ordinary."

B) Methenium levels in the Central West Chain of Lakes are significantly lower than those in the South Chain, even though the Central West Chain is closer to Gandocrast.

C) It cannot be determined from the data presented in the figure which, if any, of the chains of lakes lie on Jansingisk's Ring.

D) Two of the lakes in the East Chain have much higher levels of methenium than would be predicted by DAE based on their distance from Gandocrast.

STOP

If you have finished this section before time expires, you may check your work. You cannot return to this section once you move on to the next section.

EGGHEAD PREP™
Get cracking.

STOP!

If you have finished this section before time expires, you may check your work. You cannot return to this section once you move on to the next section.

www.eggheadprep.com

ANSWERS, SECTION 1
SAMPLE TEST 4 — READING

1. B
2. C
3. A
4. D
5. B
6. B
7. D
8. C
9. A
10. C
11. D
12. A
13. A
14. B
15. C
16. A
17. D
18. D
19. B
20. C
21. A
22. C
23. C
24. B
25. D
26. D
27. C
28. B
29. A
30. C
31. A
32. D
33. B
34. C
35. A
36. D
37. D
38. B
39. D
40. A
41. B
42. B
43. C
44. D
45. C
46. A
47. D
48. C
49. B
50. A
51. A
52. D

EGGHEAD PREP

SECTION 2: WRITING & LANGUAGE TEST

35 MINUTES, 44 QUESTIONS

DIRECTIONS

Below you will find a number of reading passages. Each one is accompanied by a series of questions. A note before each passage will tell you which questions are related to that passage. Some questions will require you to consider possible revisions to the passage to help the writer express the ideas more clearly or effectively. Other questions will ask you to consider ways to edit the passage to correct errors in punctuation, word usage, or sentence structure. Some questions and passages include graphics, such as tables and graphs. As you make your decisions about possible changes, you should take the graphics into consideration along with the text.

Some questions will refer to a specific, underlined portion of the passage. Others will ask you to focus on a particular location within the passage. There will also be questions that ask you to think about the passage as a whole. Numbers enclosed in parentheses and written with a Q, such as (Q14) indicate the number of the question associated with that portion of the passage. Numbers bracketed in plain text, like [2], are used to identifying sentences within the passage, whereas a number surrounded by dashes, like –2– identifies a paragraph.

Read each passage and then choose the answer to each question that best improves the writing of the passage or brings the particular phrase or sentence into agreement with the conventions of standard written English. If you believe the best choice is to leave the indicated portion of the passage as it is, choose the option, "NO CHANGE."

eggheadprep.com

Questions 1 – 11 are based on the following passage.

The book, author, and researchers described in this passage are fictitious.

In the late 1950s, Japanese American chemist Philip Katayama was asked to write a book about his life as the successful son of immigrant parents. To all appearances, Katayama gave the editors and publishers exactly what they wanted: a story that, **(Q1)** though it included occasional episodes of racism and discrimination predominantly sounded an optimistic note in celebration of the American Dream. Schools and politicians embraced the book instantly as proof positive that the US truly is a land of limitless opportunity for all, **(Q2)** it bore the cryptic title, *First Words, Second Thoughts, and Three Strands of Barbed Wire*. **(Q3)** Similarly, many years passed before anyone gave the title any serious thought.

1.
- A) NO CHANGE
- B) though it included occasional episodes of racism and discrimination;
- C) though it included occasional episodes of racism and discrimination—
- D) though it included occasional episodes of racism and discrimination,

2.
- A) NO CHANGE
- B) even though it bore
- C) it also bore
- D) because it bore

3.
- A) NO CHANGE
- B) Nevertheless,
- C) By contrast,
- D) In fact,

When the mystery of the strange title's true meaning was finally **(Q4)** unsettled by statistician Deborah Huntinger in 1975, **(Q5)** those who had previously lauded the book suddenly changed their tune. Huntinger had suspected that the words, "First Words, Second Thoughts" actually provided the key to a code. She carefully went through the book and circled the first word of every second sentence, then had a typist prepare a manuscript consisting of just those words. Upon adding appropriate punctuation, Huntinger discovered that Katayama had secretly embedded in his seemingly patriotic memoir a stinging condemnation of the US Government for the interment of his family and other Japanese Americans during World War II. The hidden narrative vividly described the rough treatment of Katayama's parents by National Guard soldiers and **(Q6)** recounting the flurries of racial insults young Philip heard as the family was stripped of their belongings and herded onto trains with little more than the clothes on their backs.

4. Although many political leaders and schoolteachers attacked Katayama for his deception, others celebrated him as a hero for telling a story that no US publisher in the 1950s would have knowingly put into print. Journalists of all backgrounds rushed to gather more stories of the forced relocation of Japanese Americans during the war. The reporters who participated in (Q7) this helped to prevent the loss of an important, if shameful, chapter in American history.

5.
   A) NO CHANGE
   B) unchallenged
   C) unraveled
   D) untrammeled

6. Which option best connects the sentence with the previous paragraph?
   A) NO CHANGE
   B) many people were amazed at how clever Katayama had been in disguising his thoughts.
   C) a lot of other people acknowledged that they had solved the mystery as well.
   D) it became trendy to give books unusual titles as a way to generate interest and boost sales.

7.
   A) NO CHANGE
   B) recounts
   C) recounted
   D) had recounted

8.
   A) NO CHANGE
   B) this effort
   C) it
   D) these

(Q8) As a result of all that research, a barrage of books began to appear in the early 1980s, finally granting the American public access to the horrible truth about life in the internment camps. They are known collectively as the Barbed Wire Bibliography. Many of the books reveal realities that Katayama was only able to hint at in his secret code. There are numerous accounts describing malnutrition and dangerously poor sanitation in the camps, abuse by camp guards, and **(Q9)** telling about years of postwar financial hardship caused by the government's refusal to return seized property to the victims of forced relocation.

9. Which option offers the best way to combine the two underlined sentences?
   A) A barrage of books, collectively known as the Barbed Wire Bibliography, that finally granted the American public access to the horrible truth about life in the internment camps as a result of all that research, began to appear in the early 1980s.
   B) As a result of all that research, a barrage of books began to appear in the early 1980s, collectively known as the Barbed Wire Bibliography, which were finally granting the American public access to the horrible truth about life in the internment camps.
   C) A barrage of books, finally granting the American public access to the horrible truth about life in the internment camps, began to appear as a result of all that research in the early 1980s, which came to be known as the Barbed Wire Bibliography.
   D) As a result of all that research, a barrage of books, collectively known as the Barbed Wire Bibliography, began to appear in the early 1980s, finally granting the American public access to the horrible truth about life in the internment camps.

10.
   A) NO CHANGE
   B) they are telling about
   C) about
   D) DELETE the underlined portion.

Fittingly, Katayama himself made one of the most significant contributions to the Barbed Wire Bibliography. **(Q10)** Freed from the constraints placed upon him by publishers in the past, he expanded the skeletal narrative he had hidden in that first, controversial book into a three-volume series that is viewed to this day as the definitive account of the horrors of forced relocation. Upon its publication in 1987, the book, cheekily titled *Last Words from the Barbed Wire Code Writer*, spent over five months on the national bestseller list, cementing Katayama's position as one of the great political activists of the American twentieth century. **(Q11)** His courage in devising an ingenious way to tell a truth no one wanted to hear continues to inspire oppressed people all over the world.

11.
Which option best connects the sentence with previous information in the passage and sets up the rest of the sentence?

A) NO CHANGE
B) Enticed by the prospect of selling more books,
C) Using the same code he had previously employed,
D) Although he is no longer working as a chemist,

12.
At this point, the author is considering adding the following sentence.

> Even though many people were angry with Katayama in the past because of his use of a secret code to hide his meaning, he is viewed in a positive light today.

Should the author make this addition in this place?

A) Yes, because it provides historical context for recent developments described in the paragraph.
B) Yes, because it reminds the reader that Katayama's earlier work drew a negative reaction.
C) No, because it unnecessarily repeats information from earlier in the paragraph and earlier in the passage.
D) No, because it makes a claim that contradicts the evidence presented in the passage.

Questions 12-22 are based on the following passage.

NOTE: The claims made in this passage have not been substantiated; the research cited is fictitious.

Change Your Shirt? Not So Fast

A variety of high-tech synthetic fibers may revolutionize the clothing industry over the next decade. Be that as it may, many consumers still strongly prefer their clothes to be made of natural fibers because they believe fabrics made from such fibers are better for the environment and their own skin than **(Q12)** when stores sell fabrics fashioned from synthetics. As part of the latest "all natural" craze, **(Q13)** even seeking out clothes made exclusively from natural fibers that have not been treated with any of the chemical dyes or protectants **(Q14)** that are employed in manufacturing clothes according to methods viewed as traditional. The results of several recent studies, **(Q15)** consequently, suggest that purchasing natural fibers may not have the desired positive effects on either the health of one's skin or the health of the environment.

13.
- A) NO CHANGE
- B) those
- C) the selling of
- D) DELETE the underlined portion.

14.
- A) NO CHANGE
- B) even having sought out
- C) to seek out even
- D) some people even seek out

15.
- A) NO CHANGE
- B) that are employed in the traditional manufacturing of clothing, which is therefore less natural.
- C) that are not employed in manufacturing clothes in a natural way, but only in using traditional methods.
- D) traditionally employed in manufacturing clothes.

16.
- A) NO CHANGE
- B) in addition
- C) on the other hand
- D) incidentally

Although adherents to the principle that natural is always better **(Q16)** pretend that wearing only clothes made from tried-and-true fibers like cotton and hemp reduces a person's risk of developing skin sensitivities and allergies, there is not a shred of scientific evidence in support of that belief. **(Q17)** On the contrary, multiple studies have indicated that skin allergies are far more often triggered by natural fibers than by synthetics. As Dr. Jackson Westberg of the Northern Plains Dermatology Institute observes, "Whether it is due to the material itself or to the way natural fibers tend to trap irritants like detergent residue or pet dander we cannot say, but there is no doubt that a person is far more likely to develop a rash from wearing wool than from wearing rayon." **(Q18)** Now, it may well be that the lack of allergies to synthetic fibers among the human population is simply due to the fact that the fibers have not been around for long. Nevertheless, a belief that wearing natural fiber-based clothing protects a child's skin cannot be defended based on the available evidence.

17.
- A) NO CHANGE
- B) portend
- C) contend
- D) preserve

18.
- A) NO CHANGE
- B) Likewise,
- C) As a consequence,
- D) As one would expect,

19. At this point, the author wishes to insert the following sentence.

> According to the US Department of Commerce, the manufacture of synthetic fibers contributes $547 billion to the US economy every year.

Should the author add the sentence in this place?

- A) Yes, because it adds information gathered from a highly respected government agency.
- B) Yes, because it provides additional scientific evidence that natural fibers are better for a person's skin.
- C) No, because the information it provides is not related to the scientific evidence being discussed in the paragraph.
- D) No, because the figure cited does not take into account the amount of money lost to taxes, license fees, insurance, and other costs.

Nor does the evidence lend much support to the notion that buying clothes made only of untreated natural fibers **(Q19)** help the environment. Certainly, it is true that untreated natural fibers will break down in a landfill long before synthetic fabrics. The problem is that "all natural" clothing also tends to break down rapidly long before it even goes to the landfill: the material, frays, tears, and disintegrates quickly, forcing the consumer to replace clothing frequently. One study, in fact, found that those who buy only natural fiber-based clothing must replace their clothes four times more frequently than consumers who buy primarily synthetics. That's an enormous amount of waste, no matter how fast it may decompose. **(Q20)**

20.
   A) NO CHANGE
   B) helps
   C) have helped
   D) are helping

21. At this point, the author wants to strengthen the paragraph's claim that clothing made from synthetic fibers is not necessarily harmful to the environment. Which option represents the best way to accomplish this goal?

   A) Furthermore, a growing number of companies offer recycling of synthetic fabrics, so that synthetic fiber-based clothing need not go into landfills at all.
   B) In order to claim that their clothing is made from natural fibers, however, manufacturers must submit fabric samples to independent agencies for rigorous testing to verify that no synthetic fibers have been used.
   C) The reality is that many US states are running out of landfill space due to the extremely long time it takes many disposable items to decompose.
   D) Workers at factories where synthetics-based clothing is manufactured wear masks and gloves to protect themselves from harmful dust, just like their counterparts at factories manufacturing clothing from natural fibers.

In short, based on the best evidence available, there is no reason to believe that consumers dedicated to purchasing natural fabrics are helping either themselves or the environment. Nevertheless, that doesn't mean **(Q21)** their not accomplishing anything positive at all. There is some evidence, for example, suggesting that the cause of economic justice can be served by consumers buying natural fiber-based clothing, provided that such clothing is also certified as Fair Trade. A great many people have a hand in the making of a traditional wool **(Q22)** sweater, including, farmers, herders, shearers, skirters, yarn spinners, and many more. If all of them are paid fairly for their work, then natural fiber wearers have something to be proud of, after all.

22.
A) NO CHANGE
B) they're not
C) there are not
D) they're are not

23.
A) NO CHANGE
B) sweater, including
C) sweater including:
D) sweater including,

Questions 23-33 are based on the following passage.

True Colors: It Is All About the Trim

A person's color preferences not only supply fodder for **(Q23)** combative first date conversations **(Q24)** they also provide genuine insight into the ways people are affected by their environment, at least if several psychology researchers are to be believed. Gathering information about individuals' attitudes toward various colors has always been an arduous, labor-intensive process, so much so that large-scale research on the matter was a practical impossibility. Although the traditional, time-consuming methods of collecting such data **(Q25)** do not yield results that would be meaningful to modern researchers, modern satellite imaging software has opened up new possibilities for investigation.

[1] In Landistrania, a vast country with multiple distinct biomes (regions characterized by their geography and plant and animal life), researcher Pved Nbokatun launched an ambitious study in 1971. [2] Nbokatun believed that the environment in which an individual grows up influences his or her color choices. [3] Researchers were dispatched across the nation to record the most common colors people chose when painting their homes. [4] They hoped to determine whether any discernible patterns existed that would suggest a connection between home color and the surrounding landscape. [5] Simply gathering the data took over a

24. 2
The author wants to have a gently mocking, somewhat sarcastic tone, without any suggestion of bitterness. Which word choice would be best for this purpose?

A) NO CHANGE
B) idiotic
C) bizarre
D) scintillating

25. 24.
A) NO CHANGE
B) but also provide
C) also these provide
D) also providing

26. Which option effectively sets up the contrast the author intends to draw within the sentence while remaining consistent with the rest of the passage?

A) NO CHANGE
B) no longer serve any useful purpose
C) can still be of great value in research studies
D) remain the only reliable way to collect data that yields meaningful results

decade; compiling and analyzing it all required more time still. [6] As a result, the value of the work was widely questioned by **(Q26)** <u>experts. Experts</u> dismissed the study as an exercise in futility. **(Q27)**

Four decades after Nbokutan's ill-fated venture began, psychologist Phora Mrunamo decided to revisit the matter of color preference and environmental influences by employing an ultra-modern tool: the satellite images internet users peruse on a daily basis when trying to find their way across town. Not all features of a house **(Q28)** <u>are visible</u> in such images, but colors can be seen clearly. Mrunamo's second innovation was a **(Q29)** <u>shift of focus instead</u> of looking at the principle color used in painting the house, she focused on the color of the trim. It turns out that, according to a number of studies Mrunamo **(Q30)** <u>cites in her report</u>, homeowners remain very consistent in their choices of trim colors through the years, even if they radically change the overall color of their houses.

27.
- A) NO CHANGE
- B) experts, so these experts
- C) experts, who
- D) experts, but they

28.

To improve the overall flow and logical development of this paragraph, the author wants to add this sentence:

> To make matters worse, many of the first houses studied had already been repainted in new colors by the time the data collection concluded.

The most logical place for this sentence would be after

- A) sentence 2
- B) sentence 3
- C) sentence 4
- D) sentence 5

29.
- A) NO CHANGE
- B) is visible
- C) have been visible
- D) are being visible

30.
- A) NO CHANGE
- B) shift of focus, instead
- C) shift of focus—instead,
- D) shift of focus: instead

31.
- A) NO CHANGE
- B) sites in her report
- C) sites from her report
- D) sights in her report

Mrunamo's findings strongly suggest that Nbokutan may have been right, after all. She found a significant correlation between trim color choices and the nature of the surrounding landscape. As the figure shows, green trim predominates in towns surrounded by deciduous forests; red trim is most common where coniferous forests prevail; white trim is seen most frequently on the prairies; and dark trim (brown or black) is a popular choice in the deserts. **(Q31)** As fascinating as these discoveries may be, however, **(Q32)** <u>there remains much to be learned about they're</u> true meaning. As Mrunamo herself points out, her investigation has not answered the question of whether the decisive influence on a homeowner's color choice is the natural landscape or simply a desire to fit in with his or her neighbors. Only old-fashioned methods can answer that question—human researchers must ask homeowners how they came to choose their house trim colors. It may well turn out that homeowners' responses to such questions are not merely a source of confirmation of Nbokutan's original hypothesis but **(Q33)** <u>are also a source of significant insights into the many factors that influence a person's tastes.</u>

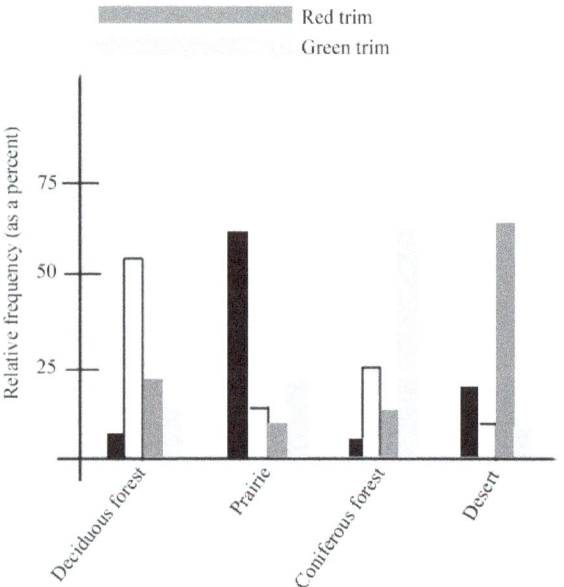

32.

The author wants the information in this paragraph to reflect the information displayed in the graph as accurately as possible. Assuming that all other aspects of the previous sentence would remain unchanged, in which order should the four trim color choices appear in order to accomplish the author's goal?

A) NO CHANGE
B) "white," "green," "dark," "red"
C) "red," "green," "dark," "white"
D) "dark," "green," "white," "red"

33.

A) NO CHANGE
B) there remains much to be learned about their
C) their remains much to be learned about their
D) they're remains much to be learned about there

34.

Which option represents the most effective conclusion for the sentence and paragraph?

A) NO CHANGE
B) also show how satellite images of a house fail to represent the house's features in detail.
C) also explain why people change the main color of their houses less often than the trim color.
D) are also unreliable as a basis for conclusions, since many people will answer dishonestly to protect their privacy.

SAMPLE TEST 4
Section 2: Writing & Language Test

Questions 34-44 are based on the following passage

Paying It By Ear: A Career in Recording

If you have a great ear for music and a love of sophisticated gadgets, or if you have ever wondered why your favorite CD or album sounds better than all the rest, a career in the music recording industry may be right for you. If you wish to determine whether you would like to pursue such a career and, if so, learn how best to prepare yourself for the challenge, there **(Q34)** would have been a variety of specific things you can do to find the answers you need.

First of all, you need to learn a little about what recording engineers actually do. Movie and television portrayals of the recording process tend to depict engineers merely as glorified button-pushers, relaxing in comfortable chairs while musicians do all the work. In reality, an audio engineer's work begins hours before the "record" button is lit. The engineer makes all the decisions about the setup to be used for the **(Q35)** session the microphones to be used, the placement of those microphones, the arrangement of the instruments within the space, and the locations of any sound-muffling dividers, and therefore plays a vital role in sculpting the sound of the recording.

Getting the right gear into the right places represents only the first step in turning a song into a great **(Q36)** recording, though. Because even the world's finest microphones in the most perfect positions cannot yield a good recording if the musicians don't feel comfortable. **(Q37)** Engineers must remember that musicians often

35.
- A) NO CHANGE
- B) has been
- C) are
- D) is

36.
- A) NO CHANGE
- B) session—the microphones to be used, the placement of those microphones, the arrangement of the instruments within the space, and the locations of any sound-muffling dividers—
- C) session: the microphones to be used, the placement of those microphones, the arrangement of the instruments within the space, and the locations of any sound-muffling dividers;
- D) session; the microphones to be used, the placement of those microphones, the arrangement of the instruments within the space, and the locations of any sound-muffling dividers—

37.
- A) NO CHANGE
- B) recording—though, because
- C) recording, though, because
- D) recording though; because

38.
At this point, the author wishes to add the following sentence.

> Musicians who are uneasy can't record good music, no matter how ideal the setup of the studio may be.

Should the author add this sentence in this place?

- A) Yes, because it provides a specific example to support the claim made in the previous sentence.
- B) Yes, because it adds important information that provides context for the rest of the paragraph.
- C) No, because it blurs the focus of the paragraph by introducing material that is not relevant.
- D) No, because it only restates the ideas already expressed in the previous sentence.

come into a studio feeling very nervous and can therefore rapidly become frustrated with themselves, each other, or the recording process as a whole. The best engineers **(Q38)** project a calm, confident demeanor that musicians find very reassuring as they struggle to find their groove. **(Q39)** Nevertheless, anyone considering a career as a recording engineer should consider studying group dynamics and stress reduction techniques to become **(Q40)** effective negotiators and resourceful managers of high-pressure situations. In addition, because recording sessions often stretch late into the night, recording professionals should learn about proper nutrition and sleep hygiene to maintain good health even when working unusual hours.

[1] It is essential to take a diverse array of courses providing technical education, both in the use of physical components (microphones, cables, mixing boards, etc.) and in the use of complex computer software. [2] Many recording engineers actually **(Q41)** begin their college experiences at the outset by studying materials science, which is a great way to become familiar with the acoustic properties of the many physical objects present in a studio. [3] Courses in electrical engineering are tremendously valuable, since electrical issues are the most common cause of ruined recording sessions. [4] A recording engineer also needs a great deal of specialized training. [5] And do

39.
- A) NO CHANGE
- B) have a tremendous amount of technical know-how
- C) have a volatile temper
- D) offer complicated instructions

40.
- A) NO CHANGE
- B) However,
- C) Likewise,
- D) Therefore,

41.
- A) NO CHANGE
- B) both effective negotiators and resourceful managers
- C) an effective negotiator and a resourceful manager
- D) effective and resourceful both as negotiators and as managers

42.
- A) NO CHANGE
- B) start the onset of their college work
- C) instigate their college experiences
- D) begin their college careers

not forget that at the center of any career in recording is the music itself. [6] Studying music theory will help you to understand the language musicians speak, enabling you to acquire a **(Q42)** vague awareness of the critical moments that make or break the recording of a song. [7] Finally, because a recording engineer must keep track of a huge amount of information during every session, it is important to take courses in data organization and management. [8] While it is certainly not for everyone, **(Q43)** audio engineering can be an exciting and fulfilling professional pursuit for those with the right temperament and preparation. **(Q44)**

43.
A) NO CHANGE
B) keen
C) minimal
D) cute

44.
A) NO CHANGE
B) it is a good idea to select audio engineering because it
C) the choice of a career in audio engineering
D) choosing to work at audio engineering

45. The most logical placement of sentence 4 within this paragraph would be
A) before sentence 1
B) after sentence 2
C) where it is now
D) after sentence 5

STOP

If you have finished this section before time expires, you may check your work. You cannot return to this section once you move on to the next section.

EGGHEAD PREP™
Get cracking.

STOP!

If you have finished this section before time expires, you may check your work. You cannot return to this section once you move on to the next section.

www.eggheadprep.com

ANSWERS, SECTION 2
SAMPLE TEST 4 — WRITING & LANGUAGE

1. D
2. B
3. D
4. C
5. A
6. C
7. B
8. D
9. D
10. A
11. C
12. B
13. D
14. D
15. C
16. C
17. A
18. C
19. B
20. A
21. B
22. B
23. D
24. B
25. C
26. C
27. D
28. A
29. D
30. A
31. B
32. B
33. A
34. C
35. B
36. C
37. D
38. A
39. D
40. C
41. D
42. B
43. A
44. A

SECTION 3: MATH TEST

NO CALCULATOR, 25 MINUTES, 20 QUESTIONS

DIRECTIONS

For questions 1–15, solve the problem and choose the best answer from the options provided. For questions 16–20, solve the problem and type in your answer. Further instructions for typing in your answer are provided before question

NOTES

1. Calculator use is not permitted for this section. You will distort your score if you use one.
2. All variables and expressions represent real numbers unless stated otherwise.
3. Unless otherwise indicated, figures shown have been drawn to scale.
4. All figures lie in a plane unless stated otherwise.
5. The domain of a function f is the set of real numbers for which f(x) is a real number, unless stated otherwise.

REFERENCE

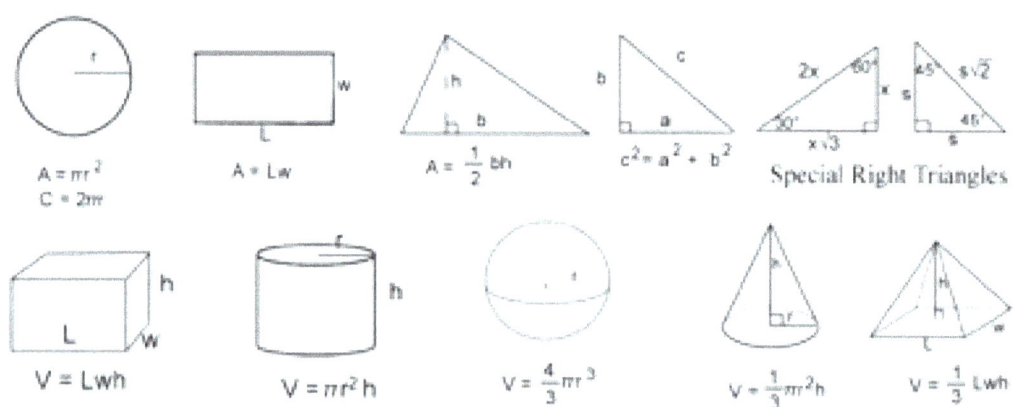

A full circle has 360 degrees of arc.
A full circle has 2π radians of arc.
The sum of the measures of the angles in a triangle is 180°.

EGGHEAD PREP

SAMPLE TEST 4
Section 3: Math, No Calculator

1.
$$f(x) = k - \frac{4}{3}x$$
In the function shown above, k is a constant. If $f(9) = -15$, what is the value of $f(-3)$?
   A) -27
   B) -15
   C) -3
   D) 1

2. Which of the following expressions can have the value 0 for one or more values of x?
   A) $|x - 3| + 2$
   B) $|x + 3| + 2$
   C) $|x - 3| - 2$
   D) $|3 - x| + 2$

3. If $f(x) = -3x + 4$, what is the value of $f(-4x)$?
   A) $12x^2 - 16x$
   B) $12x + 4$
   C) $-12x + 4$
   D) $12x - 4$

4.
$$\frac{y}{x} = 5$$
$$4(x + 1) = y$$
If (x, y), where $x \neq 0$, is the solution to the above system of two equations, then $x = $?
   A) 4
   B) 8
   C) 20
   D) 32

5. If $\frac{a + 2b}{b} = \frac{3}{5}$, which choice must also be true?
   A) $\frac{a + b}{b} = \frac{2}{5}$
   B) $\frac{a - 2b}{b} = -\frac{17}{5}$
   C) $\frac{a}{b} = \frac{13}{5}$
   D) $\frac{a}{b} = -\frac{7}{5}$

6. Which expression below is equivalent to, $2(3x + 2)(5x + 1)$?
   A) $30x^2 + 4$
   B) $30x^2 + 26x + 4$
   C) $16x^2 + 6$
   D) $60x$

7. Which equation describes a line parallel to the line, $y = -4x + 7$?
   A) $12x + 3y = -9$
   B) $x + 4y = 8$
   C) $4x - y = 6$
   D) $5x - 2y = 7$

8.
$$\sqrt{x + r} = x - 5$$
In the equation shown above, $r = 1$. What is the solution set of the equation?
   A) $\{3\}$
   B) $\{1\}$
   C) $\{8\}$
   D) $\{3, 8\}$

9. To improve its public image, a company with a record of environmentally harmful activities joins a website called HighFiveForNature.com. The website allows consumers to give a "high five" to any company that does something positive for the environment. During week 8 of the company's membership on the site, it receives 17 high fives. If the company's goal for week 20 is to receive 32 high fives, what must be true about how the number of high fives it receives changes between week 8 and week 20?

A) The number of high fives must increase by an average of 4 high fives every 5 weeks.

B) The number of high fives must increase by an average of 1.25 high fives each week.

C) The number of high fives must increase by an average of $\frac{5}{8}$ high fives per week.

D) The number of high fives must increase by an average of 2.5 high fives per week.

10.
$$x = -3y + 6$$
$$y = (4x + 6)(x - 8)$$

The system of equations shown above has how many solutions (x, y)?

A) Infinitely many

B) 2

C) 1

D) none

11. If $\frac{z+7}{z-3} = 12$, what must be the value of z?

A) $\frac{43}{11}$

B) $-\frac{29}{13}$

C) $\frac{13}{4}$

D) -4

12.

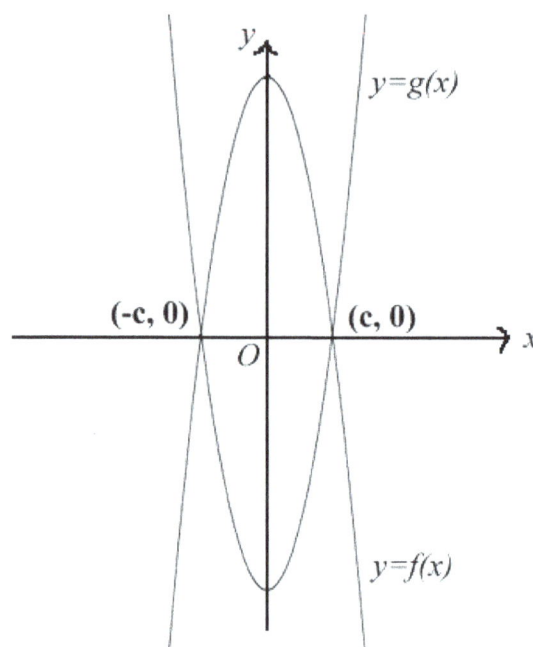

The figure above shows the graphs of two functions f and g, where $f(x) = -18x^2 + 8$ and $g(x) = 18x^2 - 8$. As shown, the two graphs intersect at the points $(-c, 0)$ and $(c, 0)$. What is the value of c?

A) 8

B) 2

C) $\frac{2}{3}$

D) $\frac{1}{2}$

13. Geena and Kelly played a trivia quiz and decided to cooperate rather than compete with each other. Geena earned x points, while Kelly earned 1 point less than Geena earned. At the end of the game, they were awarded a 40% bonus for working together, and then the total number of points was divided evenly between them. Which expression represents the number of points each of them had in the end?

A) $0.4x - 0.4$

B) $0.4x + 1.0$

C) $1.4x - 1.4$

D) $1.4x - 0.7$

SAMPLE TEST 4
Section 3: Math, No Calculator

14.
$$x^2 - 4m = \frac{n}{3}x$$

The letters m and n in the above quadratic equation represent constants. What are the possible values of x?

A) $x = \dfrac{n}{2} \pm \dfrac{\sqrt{n^2 + 4}}{2}$

B) $x = \dfrac{n}{6} \pm \dfrac{\sqrt{n^2 + 4}}{6}$

C) $x = \dfrac{n}{2} \pm \dfrac{\sqrt{n^2 + 144m}}{6}$

D) $x = \dfrac{n}{6} \pm \dfrac{\sqrt{n^2 + 144m}}{6}$

15. Suppose the expression,
$$\frac{2 + 4i}{4 + 3i}$$
is rewritten in the form, $a + bi$, where $i = \sqrt{-1}$. What would be the value of b?

A) $\dfrac{2}{5}$

B) $\dfrac{4}{3}$

C) 10

D) 16

DIRECTIONS

For questions 16 – 20, solve the problem and type in your answer. Please follow these guidelines:

1. No questions have negative answers.
2. If a problem has more than one correct answer, any of those answers will be accepted as correct. Please enter only one answer.
3. Do not type in mixed numbers. A number such as 2 ¼ should be entered as 2.25 or 9/4. Mixed numbers will be misinterpreted by the computer.
4. If a decimal answer does not terminate after 3 decimal places, enter three decimal places only. You may either round or truncate the decimal. For example, 3/8 may be entered as 3/8 or .375, because the decimal ends there; 7/9 may be entered as 7/9, .777, or .778. Fractions should be reduced to simplest terms. For example, you should enter 1/2 instead of 2/4.

16.
$$-x^3 + 7x^2 - 3x + 21 = 0$$
What real value of x is a solution to the above equation?

17.

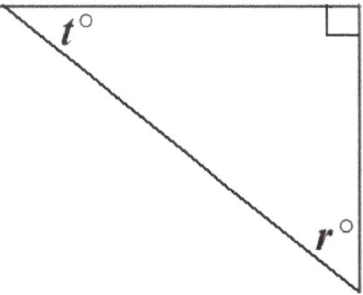

In the triangle shown, the cosine of $r°$ is 0.47. What is the sine of $t°$?

18.

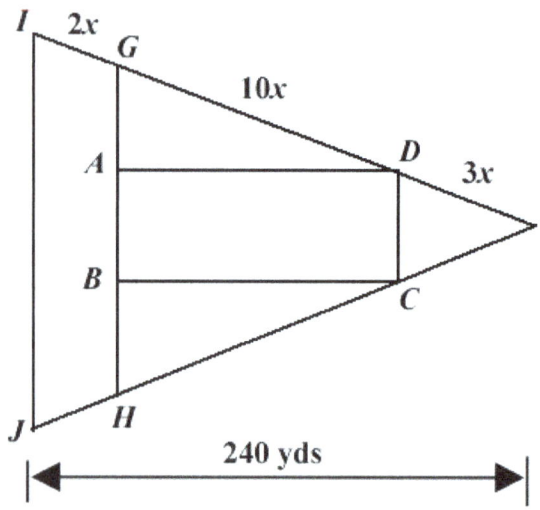

As shown in the figure above, a sports playing field, represented by rectangle ABCD, must fit within a triangular plot of land. Segments $\overline{IJ}$, $\overline{GH}$, and $\overline{DC}$ are parallel. (The trapezoidal area, IGHJ, cannot be used for the playing field due to flooding issues.) What is the maximum possible length (measured as the length BC or AD) that the field can have?

19. The number of bonobos a primate researcher encounters during the course of a day is related to the researcher's distance from the center of the bonobos' territory. At a distance of 90 meters from the center of the territory, the researcher encounters 31 bonobos throughout the day. At a distance of 130 meters from the center of the territory, the researcher encounters only 3 bonobos that day. If the number of bonobos encountered during a day decreases by a constant number b for each additional 10 meters from the center of the territory, what is the value of b?

20.
$$-9x - 5y = -2$$
$$6x + 10y = 28$$

If the solution to the above system of equations is (x, y), what is the value of y?

STOP

If you have finished this section before time expires, you may check your work. You cannot return to this section once you move on to the next section.

STOP!

If you have finished this section before time expires, you may check your work. You cannot return to this section once you move on to the next section.

www.eggheadprep.com

ANSWERS, SECTION 3
SAMPLE TEST 4 — MATH, NO CALCULATOR

1. D
2. C
3. B
4. A
5. D
6. B
7. A
8. C
9. B
10. B
11. A
12. C
13. D
14. D
15. A

---

16. 7
17. 0.47 OR .47
18. 160
19. 28/4 OR 14/2 OR 7
20. 4

EGGHEAD PREP

SECTION 4: MATH TEST
CALCULATOR, 55 MINUTES, 38 QUESTIONS

DIRECTIONS

For questions 1–30, solve the problem and choose the best answer from the options provided. For questions 31–38, solve the problem and type in your answer. Further instructions for typing in your answer are provided before question 31.

NOTES

1. Calculator use is permitted for this section.
2. All variables and expressions represent real numbers unless stated otherwise.
3. Unless otherwise indicated, figures shown have been drawn to scale.
4. All figures lie in a plane unless stated otherwise.
5. The domain of a function f is the set of real numbers for which f(x) is a real number, unless stated otherwise.

REFERENCE

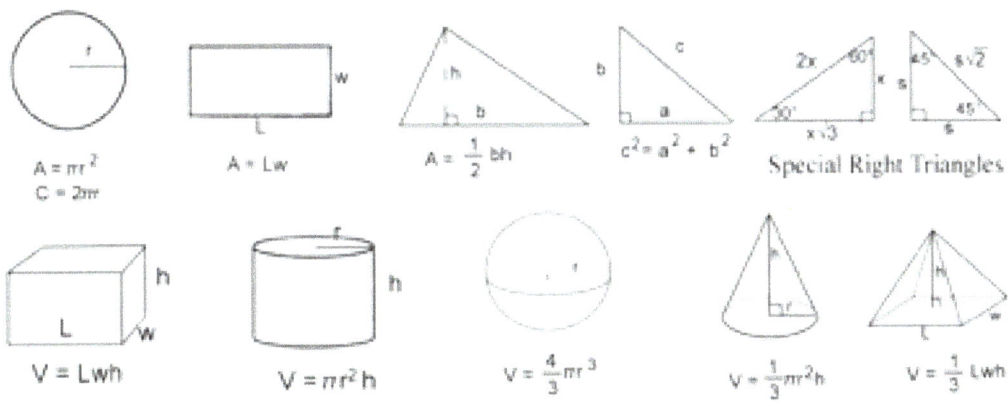

A full circle has 360 degrees of arc.
A full circle has 2π radians of arc.
The sum of the measures of the angles in a triangle is 180°.

eggheadprep.com

1. A 2-by-4 board is 6 feet long. It is cut in half and then each section is cut into fourths. What is the length, in inches, of each of the resulting sections of board? (1 foot = 12 inches)

   A) 3
   B) 6
   C) 9
   D) 12

2. Jaclyn is a sheet metal worker at a factory. At present, she can process 85 units of sheet metal per hour. In order to qualify for a 20% raise, she needs to be able to process 120 units per hour. She believes that she will be able to increase her work rate by 7 units per hour every week. Let w be the number of weeks from today. Which of the following inequalities could be solved to determine how long it will take Jaclyn to qualify for the raise?

   A) $85 + 7w \geq 120$
   B) $85w + 7 \geq 120$
   C) $85 - 7w \leq 120$
   D) $7w + 20 \geq 85$

3. The annual membership fee to join a certain health club is $840. The membership fee covers unlimited visits to the club, but there is an additional charge of $25 for each personal training session. If Marcel's total cost for membership and personal training sessions for 2015 was $990, how many personal training sessions did Marcel have in 2015?

   A) 4
   B) 6
   C) 8
   D) 25

4. At any point along a river, the speed v of the current is equal to the flow rate, F, divided by the cross-sectional area of the river, A. What is the cross-sectional area of the river, in square meters, at a point where the speed of the current is 2 meters per second and the flow rate is 800 cubic meters per second?

   A) 1600
   B) 800
   C) 400
   D) .0025

5. Wildlife experts captured a random sample of 40 deer in a national forest in Wisconsin, taking a blood sample from each deer before releasing it back into the wild. They discovered that 42.5% of the deer were infected with the parasite, gumilitius ungulatum. If there are 350 deer in the national forest, about how many of them would be expected to be infected with the parasite?

   A) 17
   B) 40
   C) 140
   D) 150

6. In a basketball game, Madison scored 13 more points than Kaitlyn. If the two players scored a total of 49 points, how many points did Kaitlyn score?

   A) 13
   B) 18
   C) 31
   D) 36

7. A line m in the xy-plane passes through Quadrants I, III, and IV, but does not contain any points in Quadrant II. Which statement must be true?

   A) Line m has a positive slope.
   B) Line m has a negative slope.
   C) The slope of line m is zero.
   D) The slope of line m is undefined.

8.

Chimpanzee Preference in Button Pushing

	Red	Blue	White	Green	Total
Circle	13	8	6	4	31
Square	15	10	13	16	54
Oval	8	0	2	5	15
Total	36	18	21	25	100

During a recent research study, a chimpanzee entered a room where there was a console with a variety of buttons of different shapes and colors. Initially, all the buttons were lighted. When a button was pressed, it went dark until the chimpanzee pressed a different button; then it lit up again. The chimpanzee was prompted by a trainer to continue pressing buttons. When the chimpanzee had pressed 100 lighted buttons, a window opened, granting the chimpanzee access to food. The above table shows the lighted buttons the chimpanzee chose to press, by shape and color. What proportion of the lighted buttons the chimpanzee pressed consisted of buttons that were square and green?

A) $\dfrac{8}{27}$

B) $\dfrac{16}{25}$

C) $\dfrac{1}{4}$

D) $\dfrac{4}{25}$

Questions 9 and 10 refer to the following information.

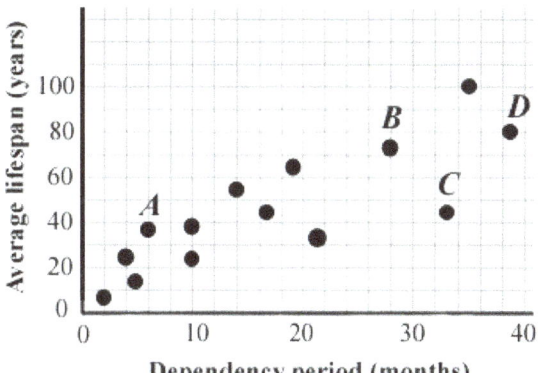

The above scatterplot was created to examine a possible relationship between the dependency period (that is, how long offspring remain wholly dependent on one or both parent and the average lifespan of 14 animal species.

9. Which choice is closest to the dependency period, in months, of the animal with the longest average lifespan?

A) 35
B) 38
C) 80
D) 100

10. Of the points labeled with letters, which represents the animal with the highest ratio of average lifespan (in year to dependency period (in months)?

A) A
B) B
C) C
D) D

11.

Number of Ants of Various Species in Various Environments, in hundreds

Species (common name)

Habitat	Red wood-land	Red grass-land	Black - hairy	Black - biting	Total
A	357	123	67	420	967
B	217	168	112	301	798
C	48	97	199	106	450
D	79	276	312	129	796
Total	701	664	690	956	3,011

A researcher wants to determine if different species of ants will work together cooperatively to obtain food if their environment requires such cooperation. She creates four habitats, each requiring different levels of large-scale cooperation to secure resources, and puts ants of four different species into each habitat. Based on the table, if a single black ant is selected at random, which answer is closest to the probability that the black ant was from Habitat C?

A) 0.10
B) 0.20
C) 0.30
D) 0.70

12. In the xy-plane, the graph of the equation, $y = f(x)$ has x-intercepts at –5, 2, and 5. Which of the following equations could define the function f ?

A) $f(x) = (x - 5)(x + 2)(x + 5)$
B) $f(x) = (x - 5)^2(x + 2)$
C) $f(x) = (x + 5)(x - 2)(x - 5)$
D) $f(x) = (x + 2)(x + 5)^2$

13. Amal deposits $700 into a savings account that pays r % interest, compounded quarterly. The balance in the account, in dollars, after one year will be given by the expression below.

$$750\left(1 + \frac{r}{400}\right)^4$$

Which of the expressions shown below accurately represents how much less money will be in the account after one year if the interest rate is 2% than if the rate is 6% ?

A) $750\left(1 + \frac{6-2}{400}\right)^4$

B) $\dfrac{750\left(1 + \frac{2}{400}\right)^4}{750\left(1 + \frac{6}{400}\right)^4}$

C) $750\left(1 + \frac{\frac{2}{6}}{400}\right)^4$

D) $750\left(1 + \frac{6}{400}\right)^4 - 750\left(1 + \frac{2}{400}\right)^4$

14. Daniel applies a plant-based, organic antifungal compound to his shower to eliminate mildew. The amount of mildew remaining at various times is displayed in the table below.

Time since application, in minutes	Amount of mildew (grams)
0	400
15	200
30	100
45	50
60	25

Which type of function would provide the best model for the relationship between time since application and number of grams of mildew?

A) Exponential growth
B) Exponential decay
C) Increasing linear
D) Decreasing linear

SAMPLE TEST 4
Section 4: Math, Calculator

Questions 15 and 16 refer to the following information.

A rock band needs to hire a sound engineer and rent audio gear for an outdoor concert. The table below shows the cost to hire an engineer and the hourly rental costs for audio gear for three different audio services stores.

Store	Cost of engineer, E	Rental cost of PA system, P (dollars per hour)	Rental Cost of microphones & cables, M (dollars per hour)
Slammin' Sound	220	20	15
Awesome Audio	175	30	20
Music Mania	190	25	15

The total cost in dollars, y, of hiring the engineer and renting the audio gear from any given store for x hours is given by the equation,
$$y = E + (P + M)x$$

15. For what number of hours, x, will the total cost of hiring the engineer and renting the audio gear be lower at Slammin' Sound than at Awesome Audio?

    A) $x < 4.5$
    B) $x > 4.5$
    C) $x < 3$
    D) $x > 3$

16. The relationship between the total cost, y, of hiring the engineer and renting the audio gear at Music Mania and the number of hours of the rental, x, is graphed in the xy-plane. What does the slope of the line represent?

    A) The total cost of hiring the engineer and renting the audio gear at Music Mania
    B) The total cost of renting the audio gear at Music Mania
    C) The total hourly cost of renting the audio gear at Music Mania
    D) The total hourly cost of hiring the engineer and and renting the audio gear at Music Mania

17. Which of the following scatterplots exhibits a relationship that would be most reasonably modeled by an equation of the form,
$$y = ab^x,$$
where a and b are constants, $a > 0$ and $b > 1$?

A)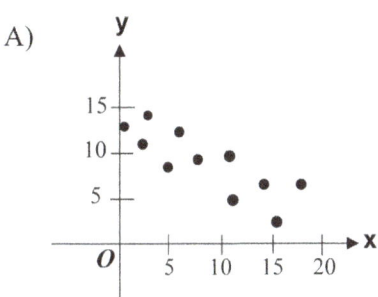

B)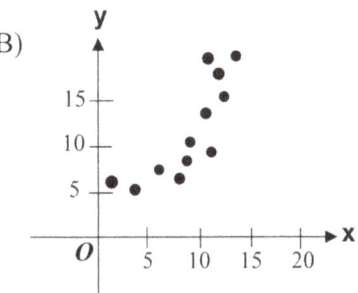

C)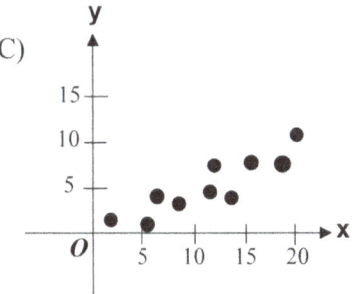

D)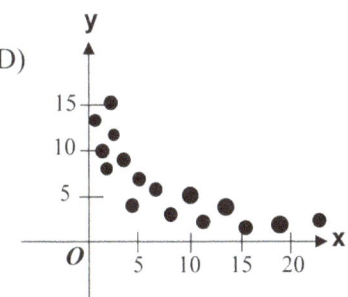

18. If $4r + 3 \leq 8$, what is the greatest possible value of $4r - 3$?

    A) 2
    B) 3
    C) 5
    D) 8

19. Kerry has a number of drinking cups lined up in a rack that holds them in place. Each cup is in the shape of a right circular cone with a diameter of 10 centimeters. She pours orange juice from a two-quart carton into the first cup, filling it completely. If the height of the orange juice in the cup is 7 centimeters, what is the largest number of cups Kerry can fill completely using the two-quart carton of orange juice? (NOTE: There are about 946 cubic centimeters in a quart.)

    A) 3
    B) 5
    C) 10
    D) 11

Questions 20 and 21 refer to the following information.

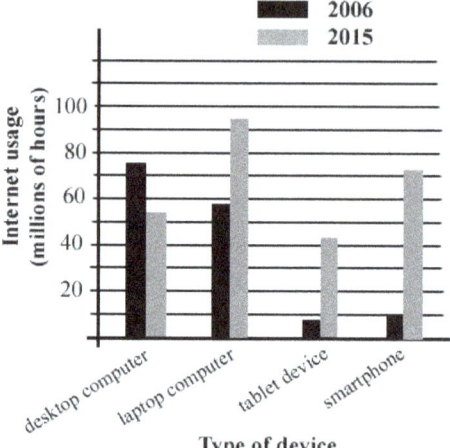

The above graph shows how much time residents of the city of West Mortland spent accessing the internet using various types of devices during the years 2006 and 2015.

20. Suppose a different graph displayed the same data in a scatterplot, with internet usage in 2006 on the x-axis and internet usage in 2015 on the y-axis for each type of device. How many points of the scatterplot would be below the line $y = x$?

    A) 4
    B) 3
    C) 2
    D) 1

21. Which of the following is the best estimate of the percent increase in the number of hours residents of West Mortland spent accessing the internet using laptop computers from 2006 to 2015?

    A) 28%
    B) 35%
    C) 58%
    D) 158%

22. If the weight of a shipping container is directly proportional to the square of its diagonal measurement, which of the functions graphed below could model the relationship between weight and diagonal measurement?

A)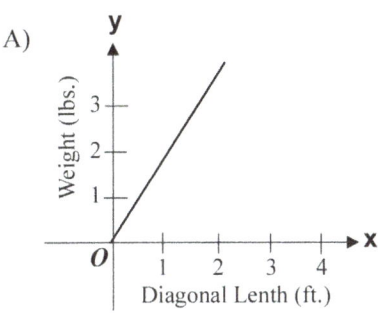

B)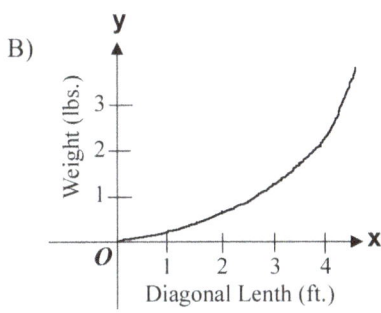

C)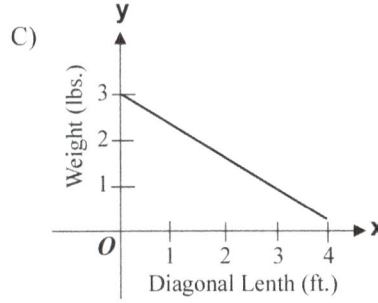

D)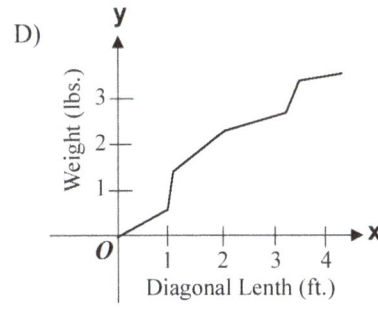

23.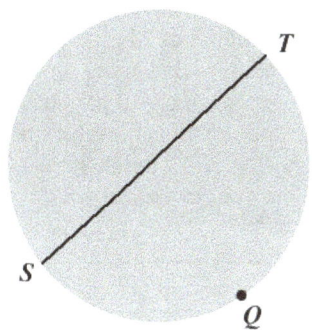

NOTE: This figure is NOT drawn to scale.

$\overline{ST}$ is a diameter of the circle shown above. If the arc SQT has length 15π meters, what is the radius of the circle, in meters?

A) 5
B) $\sqrt{30}$
C) 7.5
D) 15

24.
$$g(x) = 3x^3 - 12x^2 + 6x$$
$$h(x) = x^2 - 4x + 2$$

Given the polynomials g and h defined above, which function must be divisible by $3x + 4$?

A) $r(x) = g(x) + h(x)$
B) $s(x) = g(x) - h(x)$
C) $u(x) = g(x) + 4h(x)$
D) $v(x) = 3g(x) + 4h(x)$

25. The quality control manager of a cereal manufacturer inspects two batches of 30 cereal boxes to see how well the company is delivering on its promise to provide 23 ounces of cereal per box. The results of her inspections are shown in the tables below.

Batch 1

Weight of cereal in box (in ounces)	Frequency
25	1
24	5
23	19
22	4
21	1

Batch 2

Weight of cereal in box (in ounces)	Frequency
25	6
24	3
23	10
22	4
21	7

Which statement about the data displayed in the tables must be true?

A) The standard deviation of the data from Batch 1 is less than the standard deviation of the data from Batch 2.

B) The standard deviation of the data from Batch 1 is greater than the standard deviation of the data from Batch 2.

C) The standard deviation of the data from Batch 1 is equal to the standard deviation of the data from Batch 2.

D) The information provided is insufficient to determine how the standard deviations of the two data sets are related

26. Let u and v be two real numbers such that $-v > u > v$. Which of these statements must be true?
I. $u > 0$
II. $-v > |u|$
III. $v < 0$

A) I only
B) II only
C) I and II only
D) II and III only

27. The relative sanitation collection cost for a city in the US is defined as the ratio,

$$\frac{\text{average cost of sanitation collection in the city}}{\text{national average sanitation collection cost}},$$

which is expressed as a percent.

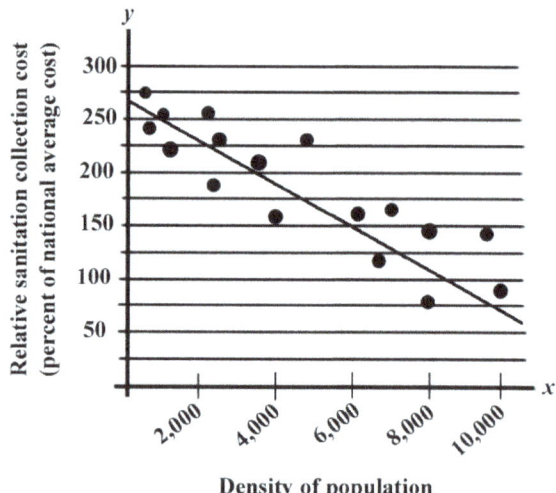

Density of population
(people per square mile)

The scatterplot shows the relative sanitation collection cost in 17 US cities, graphed in relation to the population density of each city. The line shown is the line of best fit, with equation $y = -0.016x + 258.43$. Which of the following is a reasonable interpretation of the number 258.43 in the equation?

A) The highest relative sanitation collection cost in a US city is about $258.43 per month

B) The highest relative sanitation collection cost in a US city is about 258.43% more than the lowest relative sanitation collection cost.

C) Even in US cities with very low population densities, the relative sanitation cost is usually not more than 258.43% of the national average.

D) Even in US cities with low population densities, the relative sanitation collection cost is never more than 258.43% of the national average.

SAMPLE TEST 4
Section 4: Math, Calculator

28. Let p equal the average (arithmetic mean) of $2x$ and -1. Let q equal the average of $4x$ and 6. Let r equal the average of $6x$ and 13. What is the average of p, q, and r in terms of x?

    A) $4x + 6$
    B) $2x + 3$
    C) $6x + 9$
    D) $4x + 9$

29.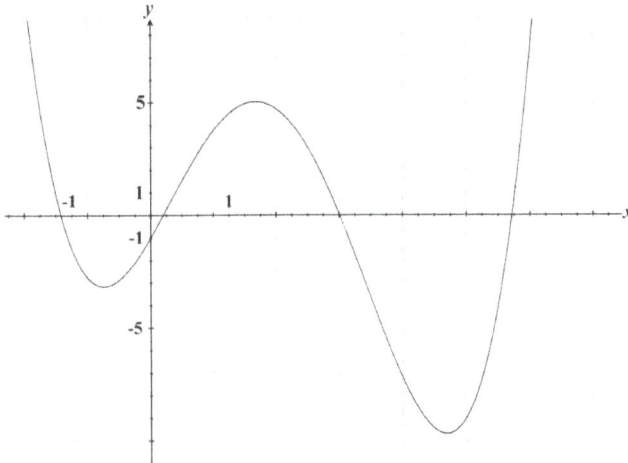

    Shown is the graph of
    $$f(x) = 0.5x^4 + bx^3 + cx^2 - 1$$
    in the xy-plane, where b and c are constants. If j is a constant and the equation $f(x) = j$ has four real solutions, which of the following is a possible value of j?

    A) 7
    B) 2
    C) -5
    D) -9.5

30. $$f(x) = (x - 10)(x + 4)$$
    Which choice is an equivalent form of the above function f in which the minimum value of f appears as a coefficient or constant?

    A) $f(x) = (x - 3)^2 - 49$
    B) $f(x) = x^2 - 40$
    C) $f(x) = x^2 - 6x - 40$
    D) $f(x) = (x + 3)^2 - 45$

DIRECTIONS

For questions 31–38, solve the problem and type in your answer. Please follow these guidelines:

1. No questions have negative answers.
2. If a problem has more than one correct answer, any of those answers will be accepted as correct. Please enter only one answer.
3. Do not type in mixed numbers. A number such as 2 ¼ should be entered as 2.25 or 9/4. Mixed numbers will be misinterpreted by the computer.
4. If a decimal answer does not terminate after 3 decimal places, enter three decimal places unless otherwise instructed. You may either round or truncate the decimal. For example, 3/8 may be entered as 3/8 or .375, because the decimal ends there; 7/9 may be entered as 7/9, .777, or .778. Fractions should be reduced to simplest terms. In other words, you should enter 1/2 instead of 2/4.
5. Do not include a comma within any number. For example, for the number 3,750, simply enter 3750.

31. A track and field athlete believes that her time for an 800-meter race is affected by the temperature. Let x represent the number of degrees Fahrenheit that the race day temperature is above or below 80° F. (The variable x is assigned a positive value if the temperature is above 80° F, a negative value if the temperature is below 80° F.) After analyzing her race times, the athlete proposes the formula,

    $$T = \frac{3x + 944}{8}$$

    as a model for the relationship between her race time T (in seconds) and the variable x as described above. According to the model, by how many seconds will the athlete's race time increase for each 1° F increase in temperature?

32. At a certain moment, there are 1400 visitors in a museum in New York. Visitors then begin leaving the museum at the rate of 9 visitors per minute. If no new visitors enter the museum, how many visitors will be in the museum after 80 minutes?

33. A florist currently has 140 red roses and 75 white roses in stock. If a new shipment of 30 white roses arrives, how many red roses should the florist order if he wants $\frac{5}{8}$ of his roses to be red?

34. In the country of North Uxiki, weight is measured in a unit called the *stum*, where 1 *stum* equals approximately 8.43 ounces. A *stum* is also equal to 11 smaller units of weight called *pebbs*. Based on these relationships, a weight of 105 *pebbs* is equivalent to how many **pounds**, to the nearest hundredth? (1 pound = 16 ounces)

35.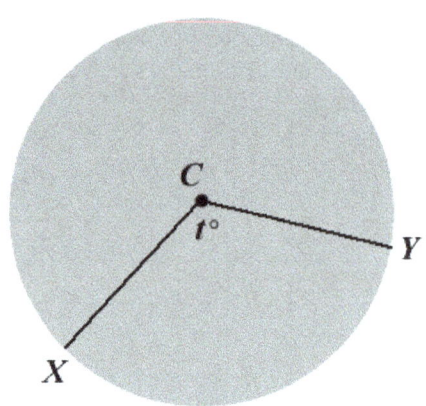

NOTE: This figure is not drawn to scale.

Point C is the center of the circle shown, which has a radius of 15 cm. If the length of minor arc XY (the arc intercepted by $\angle XCY$) is between 19 cm and 20 cm, what is one possible **integer** value of t?

36. $$N = \frac{1}{3}kP^2$$

Felipe is highly sensitive to the smell of pepper. If he is in a room where pepper is present, Felipe will sneeze N times per hour. The number N can be calculated by using the formula above, where P is the number of grams of pepper present and k is a constant that depends on the size of the room. Felipe's doctor uses the formula to calculate how many times Felipe will sneeze per hour in a certain room if P grams of pepper are present, and how many times Felipe will sneeze per hour in the same room when $2.5P$ grams of pepper are present. What is the ratio of the number of sneezes per hour Felipe will have with the higher amount of pepper present to the number of sneezes he will have with the lower amount of pepper present? (Express your answer as a fraction or decimal.)

SAMPLE TEST 4
Section 4: Math, Calculator

Questions 37 and 38 refer to the following information.

The current value of a vintage guitar is $3700. A collector believes that the value of the guitar will increase by 13% each year for the next 5 years. The collector uses the formula

$$D = 3700(r)^t$$

to calculate the dollar value D of the guitar after t years.

37. What value should the collector use for r?

38. To the nearest dollar, what does the collector believe the value of the guitar will be after five years? (Do not type in the $ sign with your answer.)

STOP

If you have finished this section before time expires, you may check your work. You cannot return to this section once you move on to the next section.

EGGHEAD PREP™
Get cracking.

STOP!

If you have finished this section before time expires, you may check your work. You cannot return to this section once you move on to the next section.

www.eggheadprep.com

ANSWERS, SECTION 4
SAMPLE TEST 4 — MATH, CALCULATOR

1. C
2. A
3. B
4. C
5. D
6. B
7. A
8. D
9. A
10. A
11. B
12. C
13. D
14. B
15. D
16. C
17. B
18. A
19. C
20. D
21. C
22. B
23. D
24. C
25. A
26. D
27. C
28. B
29. B
30. A

---

31. 3/8 or .375 or 0.375
32. 680
33. 35
34. 5.03
35. 73 or 74 or 75 or 76
36. 25/4 or 6.25
37. 1.13
38. 6817

ANSWER EXPLANATIONS

SAMPLE TEST 5 — SECTION 1, 2, 3, 4

NOTE: The SAT Reading Test emphasizes <u>evidence-based</u> analysis of the passages. While reading the passages, you will no doubt form opinions regarding whether the results of an experiment described should be trusted, or whether there are reasons beyond those presented in the passage for characters to act as they do. Those opinions may be perfectly valid, but when answering the questions, it is important to remember to draw conclusions based <u>solely</u> on evidence that is explicitly presented in the passage, not on your own personal feelings.

TEST SECTION 1: READING

1. It is very helpful to know that as used in line 3, "impervious" essentially means, "utterly unaffected by." Within the sentence in question, the word suggests that the quick disappearance of the explorers' footprints is ensuring that the mountain will be completely unchanged by the mission. Applied to the latter part of the sentence, the word "impervious" suggests that the memories of the people of the world will also be unchanged by the mission—that is, that the expedition will be quickly forgotten. **The correct answer is (B)**.

2. The author states in lines 9-10 that, "the reward reaped by those whose footprints lie buried beneath us was not a gold medal but an icy coffin." The very clear implication is that previous explorers were never able to collect any rewards for their efforts because they died on the mountain. **The correct answer is (C).**

3. As noted in the explanation for question #2 above, lines 9-10 of the passage very clearly support the correct answer for that question. Because those lines are included among the lines referenced in answer choice (A), **the correct answer is (A).**

4. Examine lines 15-18, keeping in mind that the word "divine" in such a context means to discover, often by way of intuition or an educated guess: "Now, whatever purpose may drive this progression of trudging souls no art or science I know can divine." The author is stating here that she cannot even imagine a purpose for the expedition. Now consider the ending of the passage (lines 58-61): "If we should return alive, then by that fact alone we will free all who shall call us 'ancestor' from the shackles of superstition." This claim is a definitive statement of belief in the expedition's value. From these two excerpts alone, it is clear that the author has experienced a shift in her thinking, from believing that the mission has no purpose, to embracing its potential value. **The correct answer is (D).**

5. As noted in the explanation for question #4 above, lines 15-18 and 58-61 provide very strong evidence in support of the correct answer to that question. Because these lines are included among the lines referenced in answer choice (B), **the correct answer is (B).**

6. The word "holy" is an accepted meaning of the word "divine," indeed the most common meaning in modern usage. Consider how the sentence in question would read with the word "holy" inserted in place of "divine," however: "Now, whatever purpose may drive this progression of trudging souls no art or science I know can holy." The result is nonsense, since "holy" is an adjective, and the word following "can" needs to

EGGHEAD PREP

SAMPLE TEST 4
Answer Explanations

be a verb. The remaining three answer choices are all verbs, but as noted in the explanation for question #4 above, only "discover" is an accepted meaning of the word "divine." **The correct answer is (B).**

7. In lines 20-25, the author is posing rhetorical questions—questions intended to lead the reader to one specific conclusion. Use of rhetorical questions is very common in persuasive writing, since if the questions are cleverly posed, readers will feel like they reached the same conclusion as the author on their own. For example, in asking what malady the summit will cure, the author is clearly implying that the summit will cure no maladies. Further evidence of the author's intent can be found in lines 27-28 ("this lofty wasteland does not provide knowledge; it destroys it.") and lines 32-33 ("We will be capable of knowing as much as we will find—nothing.") It is clear, then, that the author wishes to use this paragraph to support her claim, made in lines 15-18, that the expedition is without purpose. **The correct answer is (D).**

8. In line 26, the author speaks of "relentless winds of ice that dull our senses." In lines 30-31, she adds that, "we few who have embarked on this path shall reach the height of it with minds as empty as the sky…" Both of these statements point very clearly toward answer (C). **The correct answer is (C).**

9. Depending on context, any one of the answer choices might be an appropriate meaning to associate with the word "fancy." Therefore, it is essential that we consider the context in which the word is used. Lines 51-52 refer to "the demons and monsters with which our fancy populates places our eyes have not beheld." The words "elaborate" and "delicate" would clearly be inappropriate replacements for "fancy" within this context, so answers (C) and (D) must be eliminated. The phrase, "our fancy populates places our eyes have not beheld," indicates *imagining* what one would find in a place where one has never been. Therefore, **the correct answer is (A).**

10. Consider lines 48-52: "No horror we may find at the apex, no torment of wind or snow or cold beyond measure, could ever so control us as the demons and monsters with which our fancy populates places our eyes have not beheld." The author is suggesting that even if something genuinely frightening were to exist at the summit, the fear of whatever that might be would not exert nearly as much power over people as their fear of the unknown. **The correct answer is (C).**

11. As noted in the explanation for question #10 above, lines 48-52 provide very clear evidence in support of the answer to that question. **The correct answer is (D).**

---

12. The phrase "universally accepted notion," which appears in line 4, gives a strong indication that the author is discussing a widely held belief. When the author later (lines 9-11) states that "[t]he correlation between age and technological proficiency is not nearly as clear-cut as popular culture would have us believe, however," it is a clear indication that he or she intends to call the widely accepted belief into question. Only answer choice (A) expresses these ideas. The other three answer choices all misrepresent the meanings of words used in the paragraph by taking them out of context. **The correct answer is (A).**

13. Answer choice (B) addresses a topic—the driving habits of teenagers—that is not even mentioned in the paragraph, and so is clearly incorrect. Answer choices (C) and (D) both directly contradict information presented in the paragraph. Answer (C) claims that young people use their phones for "a greater variety of sophisticated purposes" than those over age 35, but the paragraph itself notes (lines 30-31) that "whereas the adults of the early 2000s found their handheld phones baffling, many today employ them for far more sophisticated purposes than do their children." Choice (D) presents the assertion that "as people grow older, they are less likely to find complex technology confusing or difficult to use," which is essentially the opposite of the passage author's observation (lines 35-37) that, "On the other hand, adults above age 35 remain far

more likely than younger people to describe technology as 'confusing' or 'intimidating.'" Therefore, answers (B), (C), and (D) are clearly incorrect, and **the correct answer is (A).**

14. "Protest" is not an accepted meaning of the word "temper," so answer (D) must be eliminated. If you are familiar with tempered steel, then you know that the word "temper" can describe a process by which metals are made stronger. In certain contexts, therefore, "strengthen" would be very similar in meaning to "temper." However, note that lines 38-39 of the passage read, "Those results alone caution us to temper any assertion that a generational inversion is under way." It would be very strange to *caution* someone to *strengthen* his or her conclusion. Therefore, answer (A) is incorrect. Likewise, one definitely would not caution someone to exaggerate an assertion, so answer (C) may be eliminated. One very well might, however, caution someone to *moderate* an assertion, that is, to not overreach in drawing conclusions. **The correct answer is (B).**

15. As used in this context, "align with" is similar in meaning to "agree with" or "are consistent with." Therefore, the author is suggesting that popularly held beliefs about technology and age are essentially true for older age groups, even if they are often untrue for other age groups. **The correct answer is (C).**

16. Immediately after claiming that widely held beliefs about technology and age are largely accurate for older age groups, the author presents specific information (lines 42-44) about adults over 55—namely, that people in that age group are far less skillful with and accepting of new technology than people in all other age groups. This evidence is clearly consistent with the correct answer to question #15 (see above explanation). **The correct answer is (A).**

17. The most common meaning of the word "deft" is "skillful, adept, or proficient." That meaning is also consistent with the context in which the word is used in line 72. **The correct answer is (D).**

18. In lines 66-72, Dr. Carissa Gelpin observes that those who were children or young adults at any time between 1990 and 2004, "from a very young age, had to face the reality that any gadget they employed and any skill they acquired might be obsolete within a few years. In response to this initially terrifying revelation, they focused not so much on developing expertise with any particular device as on adaptability as a primary life skill." This statement is the basis of the paragraph's concluding sentence (lines 73-76), which asserts that a focus on adaptability gave one particular generation a unique advantage with regard to mastering new technological devices. **The correct answer is (D).**

19. The explanation for question #18 above shows clearly that the best support for the correct answer to that question is to be found in lines 66-76. Therefore, the best answer choice for question #19 is the one that references only lines within that range. The only choice that satisfies this criterion is answer (B). **The correct answer is (B).**

20. The focus of the passage as a whole is on *mastery* of technological devices, not simply ownership of the devices. Therefore, in the author's view, the information provided in Chart 1 would be only marginally relevant to the passage. Note also that at no point in the passage does the author suggest that available data on generational differences with respect to technology is either inaccurate or difficult to interpret without historical information, so we should rule out choices (B) and (D). **The correct answer is (C).**

21. Note that the graph key informs us that the middle bar in each group of three bars pertains to the years 2006 – 2010. The middle bar is the highest bar for age groups 35 – 54 and 55 or older, but not for the age group 34 or younger. Therefore, it is accurate to say that this time period saw the highest rate of growth in device ownership in two of the three age groups represented on the chart, as stated in answer choice (A). The other choices all make claims that are not consistent with the data displayed in Chart 2. **The correct answer is (A).**

SAMPLE TEST 4
Answer Explanations

22. For this question, it is critical to remember that, as explained at the top of Chart 2, the graph displays *annual growth rates* in device ownership, NOT the total number of devices owned. Therefore, answer (A) cannot be correct. Answer (B) presents a definitive conclusion about future developments; such conclusions can never be drawn based *solely* on data from a specific time period (in this case, 2001 – 2015). Therefore, answer (B) must be eliminated as well. Answer choice (D) misidentifies the age group in question: it is the age group 34 or younger that provides the exception to the "rising then falling" pattern described in the answer choice. (For the 34 or younger group, the growth rate in device ownership only rose and never fell within the time period covered by the graph.) As the only remaining choice, answer (C) must be correct. Note that this choice is consistent with the graph, since all three vertical bars for the 55 or older group are clearly shorter than the corresponding bars for the other two age groups. **The correct answer is (C).**

---

23. This is a vocabulary-related question for which we are entirely dependent on context, since all four answer choices are accepted meanings of the word "popularly." By examining the first sentence of the passage (lines 1-4), we can quickly begin eliminating choices. The phrase, "to describe as briefly and famously as I could what a University was," is not nonsensical, but it would convey an arrogance that is inconsistent with the author's overall tone. Specifically, he would be suggesting that his explanation will be exceptional and/or long remembered. We may therefore eliminate answer (A). Next notice that the fact the author is drawing his description from ancient sources makes it extremely unlikely that he would expect the description to be either crowd pleasing or in line with current trends. With choices (B) and (D) thus eliminated, we are left with choice (C); the word "accessibly" is a very logical replacement for "popularly" within the context of the sentence. **The correct answer is (C).**

24. Note the following phrases within the lines referenced in this question: "*In one spot*" (line 8), which clearly implies centralization in a single location; "teachers and learners from every quarter" (line 11), which implies that the institution will play host to people from many different backgrounds; and "by means of personal intercourse" (lines 15-16), which implies face-to-face conversation. Granted, personal intercourse needn't mean literal face-to-face contact today, thanks to cell phones, video conferencing, etc., but note that the passage was written before the telegraph was even in common use, let alone the telephone or internet. Therefore, answer choices (A), (C), and (D) all describe characteristics that the author explicitly mentions. **The correct answer is (B).**

25. The word "requisite" may be used as a noun meaning "requirement" or (as is the case in line 12 of this passage) as an adjective meaning "needed." If you are familiar with either of these meanings, you will be drawn immediately to answer choice (D), "required." The other answer choices would not make sense in the context of line 12 of the passage. **The correct answer is (D).**

26. Some of the older manuscripts used by SAT test writers have rather complex sentence constructions, as is the case with this tract. Be especially wary of questions about the main idea of a paragraph in such cases; the test writers often create decoy answers by taking a few key words from the paragraph completely out of context. Focus on the paragraph as a whole. The author is emphasizing that books and other written material are far more widely available than ever before. Notice, especially, lines 29-31, "[W]e must allow there never was a time fairer for dispensing with every other means of disseminating information and instruction." The author is acknowledging, in

other words, that a strong argument could be made that the dramatic increase in the availability of written material has rendered universities unnecessary. Answer choice (D) summarizes these ideas accurately. **The correct answer is (D).**

27. As noted in the explanation for question #26 above, lines 29-31 provide very strong evidence to support the correct answer for that question. These lines are among the lines referenced in answer choice (C). **The correct answer is (C).**

28. "Disagree" is not an accepted meaning of "allow" in any context, so choice (D) may be immediately eliminated. Although "authorize" definitely is an accepted meaning of "allow," it would be an inappropriate meaning in this context, because the sentence in which "allow" appears is describing an opinion or speculative conclusion. One can only *authorize* an activity, not a thought. "Permit" is essentially a less formal synonym for "authorize," so answer (C) should be eliminated along with answer (A). Note, finally, that the statement, "[W]e must *acknowledge* there never was a time fairer for dispensing with every other means of disseminating information and instruction," is very logical and clear in meaning. **The correct answer is (B).**

29. As noted in the explanation for question #26 above, it is important to focus on the *ideas* the author is presenting and not get bogged down by his complex sentence constructions. Consider lines 80-86: "Or again, that no book can convey the special spirit and delicate peculiarities of its subject with that rapidity and certainty which attend on the sympathy of mind with mind, through the eyes, the look, the accent, and the manner, in casual expressions thrown off at the moment, and the unstudied turns of familiar conversation." The phrase "sympathy of mind with mind" suggests closeness and intimacy. The references to a speaker's eyes, speech patterns, and mannerisms all identify nonverbal aspects of communication present only in face-to-face conversation, certainly not in books. **The correct answer is (A).**

30. As noted in the explanation for question #29 above, lines 80-86 clearly demonstrate the author's belief in the importance of nonverbal communication to teaching and learning, and so strongly support the correct answer for that question. **The correct answer is (C).**

31. An excellent place to look in an essay for a summary of the author's main points is the concluding sentence, found in lines 87-91 of this passage. The author writes, "The general principles of any study you may learn by books at home; but the detail, the color, the tone, the air, the life that makes it live in us: you must catch all these from those in whom it lives already." He is asserting here that to become truly knowledgeable about any subject, one must study under the tutelage of one who already possesses the required knowledge. In other words,, in spite of all the other means of acquiring knowledge available, face-to-face instruction from an expert remains essential to true learning. This conclusion is well summarized in answer choice (A). **The correct answer is (A).**

32. As noted in the explanation for question #31 above, lines 87-91 directly support the correct answer for that question. **The correct answer is (D).**

---

33. It is important to remember when working with older passages that the most common meanings assigned to words can change over time. Answer choice (A), "inclination," and (D), "habit"

represent the most common meanings of the word "tendency" as used today. However, inclinations and habits are, by their very nature, not "far-reaching," which is the adjective Senator Brown uses to describe the "tendency" of the questions raised by the resolution (lines 4-5). Notice the phrase right after the word "tendency" in the passage: "… which seriously affect the very pillars of our social fabric …" It is clear from this phrase that Senator Brown is speaking not of the inclination or habit of the resolution, but rather, its potential impact. **The correct answer is (B).**

34. In lines 5-8, Senator Brown warns that the resolution will "seriously affect the very pillars of our social fabric," including damage to "the peace and harmony of society," which implies that domestic discord would result if the resolution were to be passed; "the unity of the family," which implies that families would suffer negative consequences if the resolution were to be passed; and "much of the future success of our Government," which clearly implies that the functioning of the US government would be impaired if the resolution were to be passed. Therefore, the possibilities mentioned in answer choices (A), (B), and (D) are all explicitly mentioned by Senator Brown. **The correct answer is (C).**

35. Throughout the passage, Senator Brown attempts to make the case that his opposition to women's suffrage stems from the fact that "the Creator has assigned" different roles to men and women in society. As one hypothetical example, Senator Brown asks (lines 45-50), "if on election day [a woman] is to leave her home and press her way through the crowds to the precinct to deposit her ballot, how is she to attend to her more sacred, delicate and refining trust … for which she is peculiarly fitted by nature?" Only answer choice (A) specifically identifies the idea of different roles for men and women in society as the basis of Senator Brown's argument. **The correct answer is (A).**

NOTE REGARDING QUESTION #35: By no means are you expected to accept Senator Brown's argument. In fact, you very likely find it highly offensive, and would be well justified in feeling that way. Remember that for this test, you are analyzing the passage based on clear, explicit evidence. You are NOT expressing your agreement or disagreement with the author's arguments.

36. As noted in the explanation for question #35 above, lines 45-50 summarize the heart of Senator Brown's argument, and thus provide clear evidence in support of the answer to that question. **The correct answer is (D).**

37. Notice that throughout Passage 1, Senator Brown appeals to religious beliefs about the creation of men and women. In fact, he specifically names "Divine revelation" as a primary basis for his argument (line 16). His statements are all general, and many are hypothetical. Therefore, it is reasonable to say that, "Passage 1 puts forth arguments based on traditional beliefs, abstract ideas, and generalizations." Notice that, by contrast, Senator Blair presents very specific evidence, including the different age restrictions associated with voting and military service (lines 62-66), the difference between the number of men eligible to vote and the number subject to military service obligations (lines 66-68), and the fact that women have served in battle (lines 76-77). It is therefore quite correct to say that Passage 2 refutes the claims made in Passage 1 by presenting specific evidence. **The correct answer is (D).**

38. Lines 57-60 point very clearly to the correct answer to this question. Senator Blair asserts that "[t]he exclusion of women from the suffrage can be justified upon proof, and only upon proof, that by reason of her sex she is incompetent to exercise that power." Answer choice (B) accurately summarizes this statement. **The correct answer is (B).**

39. In many contexts, the word "liability" means "weakness." However, it would not make sense to say (lines 69-70) that, "the weakness to fight may be enforced by the community." One cannot enforce a weakness, so answer (A) is incorrect. The word "compulsion," however, can mean "legal obligation," and of course legal obligations absolutely can be enforced. Furthermore, this meaning of the word "compulsion" is also an accepted meaning of the word "liability." **The correct answer is (D).**

40. As noted in the explanation for question #37 above, Senator Blair specifically mentions the differing age restrictions for voting and for military service, the fact that many men are eligible to vote who are not subject to military service obligations, and the fact that women have ably served in battle. Therefore, answer choices (B), (C), and (D) all describe claims that Senator Blair puts forth in the passage. **The correct answer is (A).**

41. In lines 91-95, in which Senator Blair is quoting from the committee, the statement is made that, "Probably not more than five-eighths of the men of legal age, qualified to vote, are heads of families, and not more than that proportion of adult women are united with men in the legal merger of married life." These statistical estimations are summarized in answer choice (B). **The correct answer is (B).**

42. As noted in the explanation for question #41 above, lines 91-95 provided the statistical information upon which the answer to that question is based. **The correct answer is (B).**

---

43. The second paragraph (lines 11-29) describes the Core Source Hypothesis, a proposed scientific explanation for the high levels of methenium in the waters of Hyberntam. The next two paragraphs (lines 30-60) explain how that hypothesis proved to be inconsistent with the evidence. The fifth paragraph (lines 61-82) introduces the Deep Asteroid Explanation, and examines the evidence supporting that hypothesis. Therefore, answer choice (C) correctly summarizes the content and purpose of the passage. **The correct answer is (C).**

44. In the third paragraph (lines 30-43), the author describes the key role that travel agent Paodif Jansingisk played in solving the Hyberntam water mystery. The next three paragraphs (lines 44-95) detail the scientific research that transformed Jansingisk's strange observation into a breakthrough in the scientific fields of geology and hydrology. Therefore, the passage emphasizes how the work of non-scientists and the work of scientists complement each other in the pursuit of knowledge. Answer choice (D) is the only one that expresses this idea, since all of the others suggest an almost adversarial relationship between scientists and non-scientists. **The correct answer is (D).**

45. Because the correct answer to question #44 highlighted the complementary roles scientists and non-scientists play in the advancement of knowledge, we should look for lines that emphasize the connection between these two groups of people. Lines 65-67 satisfy this requirement, because they stress the important role that stories told by (presumably non-scientist) travelers played in the development of the Deep Asteroid Explanation. **The correct answer is (C).**

46. In lines 61-62, the author notes that the evidence gathered by researchers studying Jansingisk's Ring was "completely inconsistent with the Core Source Hypothesis." This essentially means that the new evidence disproved the hypothesis. **The correct answer is (A).**

SAMPLE TEST 4
Answer Explanations

47. As noted in the explanation for question #46 above, lines 61-62 provide critical evidence in support of the correct answer to that question. Since those lines are included among the lines referenced in answer choice (D), **the correct answer is (D).**

48. Lines 76-79 state that, "exploratory drilling and sample analysis confirmed the existence of a buried crater heavily sprinkled with fragments of methenium-laden ores that, based on their atomic signatures, did not originate on Earth." In other words, the ores came to Earth from somewhere in space. **The correct answer is (C).**

49. As noted in the explanation for question #48 above, the basis for the correct answer to that question may be found in lines 76-79. **The correct answer is (B).**

50. The author has explained that the reason water in Gandocrast lacks methenium is that the methenium-rich water below the city reaches Earth's surface many miles away. Since we know that residents of Gandocrast "envy" (line 85) the water elsewhere in Hyberntam, it stands to reason that, now that they know the primary methenium source lies directly beneath them, they would wish to access that source by drilling wells. **The correct answer is (A).**

51. Always be careful when drawing conclusions based on a graph to consider ONLY the data shown in the graph. As the title of the graph clearly states, the graph simply displays the level of methenium in various lakes in Hyberntam. The graph provides NO information about the source of the methenium or about the effects of methenium on either water flavor or human health. Therefore, **the correct answer is (A).**

52. The passage notes that Jansingisk's Ring, where the highest levels of methenium are found in lake water, is at a "sweet spot" (line 89) about 80 km from Gandocrast, "where the majority of those hidden streams share their bounty with freshwater bodies within our reach" (lines 90-92). It is next stated that as the water continues making its way to the sea, dilution by rainwater and glacial melt lowers methenium levels (lines 92-95). We would therefore expect methenium levels in lakes of the East Chain to be lower than methenium levels in the lakes of the Red River Chain, since the East Chain's greater distance from Jansingisk's Ring would imply more dilution. Because two lakes in the East Chain clearly violate this expected pattern, there is good reason to conduct further research. **The correct answer is (D).**

eggheadprep.com

TEST SECTION 2: WRITING AND LANGUAGE

NOTE: As the instructions for this test section clearly state, the goal when answering questions is to bring each passage into compliance with the conventions of standard written English. Standard written English is a form of the English language specifically developed to facilitate clear communication in writing, even between people who speak very different forms of English. Therefore, many of the correct answers may seem different from the choices you would make in your everyday speech. That does not mean there is anything wrong with the version of spoken English you have learned. To perform well on this test section, you must learn to make distinctions between the English you speak on a daily basis and the guidelines governing word choices, punctuation, and sentence structure in standard written English.

1. Because the phrase beginning with the word "though" is preceded by a comma, its ending must be marked with a comma as well. The addition of a comma after "discrimination" is the only needed change. **The correct answer is (D).**

2. The cryptic title of the book comes as a surprise, given the acclaim for the book described in the first half of the sentence. Presenting the surprise with no cue that it is coming disorients the reader. Therefore, the words "it bore" should be preceded by an indication that the information that follows is unexpected. The words "even though" serve well as such an indication. **The correct answer is (B).**

3. The word "Similarly" is inappropriate because the information presented in the final sentence of the paragraph is not similar to any other information mentioned earlier in the paragraph. Making the correct choice between answer options (B), (C), and (D) is a subtle matter, however. It is important to realize that both choice (B), "Nevertheless," and choice (C), "By contrast," suggest that a contrast or conflict exists between this sentence and the previous one. In reality, if either of these two choices were correct, they would likely both be correct. By that logic alone, both answer (B) and answer (C) can be eliminated. Careful reading shows that the final sentence of the paragraph actually expands on the information put forth in the previous sentence, rather than presenting a contrast to it. The phrase "In fact" nicely suggests this intention. **The correct answer is (D).**

4. The word "unsettled" would suggest that Huntinger's work triggered the re-evaluation of a mystery that was previously considered "settled" (that is, well understood). It would further imply that as a result of the re-evaluation, the mystery was subsequently viewed as confounding. Such a meaning is inconsistent with the information presented in the paragraph in which this sentence appears. Both answer choice (B), "unchallenged," and choice (D), "untrammeled, would suggest, either directly or poetically, that Huntinger's work left the mystery alone, which is certainly not the case. We have thus ruled out choices (A), (B), and (D). **The correct answer is (C).**

5. Answer choices (C) and (D) may be ruled out quickly, because the passage gives no indication whatsoever that the phenomena described in those two choices ever occurred. Answer choice (B) is a very tempting option, because the code Katayama employed, as described in the next several sentences of the paragraph, is indeed extraordinarily clever. It is critical to remember, however, that the first sentence of an interior paragraph (that is, any paragraph other than the first or last paragraph) of an essay should begin with a *transitional sentence*. A transitional sentence should connect the

SAMPLE TEST 4
Answer Explanations

new paragraph to the paragraph that preceded it. The sentence as constructed does exactly that, by mentioning the people who once touted Katayama's book as a shining example of the fulfillment of the American dream. No change is needed. **The correct answer is (A).**

6. Because the preceding verb in the sentence ("described") is in past tense, the underlined verb should also be in past tense. The past tense of "recount" is "recounted." Therefore, **the correct answer is (C).**

7. To avoid issues with lack of clarity, a writer should avoid using the word "this" in an essay to refer vaguely to information mentioned in the previous sentence(s). Whenever possible, the writer should explicitly provide the answer to the question, *"this what*?" Answer choice (B) is the only option that clarifies the meaning of the word "this." **The correct answer is (B).**

8. Note that the phrase, "As a result of all that research," refers to information presented in the previous paragraph, and thus serves as an excellent opening for a transitional sentence. That phrase, therefore, should be kept at the head of the sentence, which narrows the choices to answers (B) and (D). The two choices are very similar, but notice that choice (B) includes the phrase, "which were finally granting," whereas choice (D) has the much simpler construction, "finally granting." Since option (D) conveys the same information as option (B) in a simpler way, it is the more desirable construction. **The correct answer is (D).**

9. This question tests your understanding of *parallel structure*. To help the reader process a list, all items in the list should be presented in the same style and grammatical format to the greatest extent possible. Note that the gerund ("–ing" verb form) "describing" applies to all the occurrences mentioned in the sentences—poor sanitation, abuse, and financial hardship. Introducing the synonymous phrase "telling about" after the word "and" unnecessarily breaks the sentence's parallel structure. The phrase should be deleted. **The correct answer is (D).**

10. Answer choice (C) is clearly incorrect, since the paragraph makes very clear that Katayama did NOT employ a code when writing the book published in 1987. Answer choice (D) should be ruled out as well, because Katayama's current career is irrelevant to the paragraph and the entire passage. And while it may be true that Katayama found the prospect of selling more books enticing, we cannot know that with certainty based on the information presented in the passage. At a minimum, then, we must view choice (B) with suspicion. By contrast, we CAN know with certainty that Katayama no longer felt compelled to honor any publisher's directive to "write a book about his life as the successful son of immigrant parents." (The quotation is from the first paragraph of the passage.) Therefore, it is appropriate to say that he was freed from constraints. **The correct answer is (A).**

11. By this point in the passage, the author has very clearly described Katayama's journey from celebrated patriotic author to controversial figure to revered teller of uncomfortable truths. The proposed addition simply restates this information in a rather bland way that offers no new insights. Therefore, although the proposed sentence does not contradict the evidence presented earlier in the passage, adding it would serve no purpose. **The correct answer is (C).**

12. The intended comparison is between fabric types; the mention of stores is an irrelevant distraction. All that is needed is a simple word or phrase that either means "fabrics" or refers back to the earlier mention of fabrics within the sentence. Answer (C) is incorrect because it suggests that the *selling* of synthetic fabrics could harm people's skin, as opposed to the fabrics themselves. The demonstrative pronoun "those" is sufficient to refer back to the word "fabrics," creating a sentence that has a clear meaning and complies with all conventions of standard written English. (A demonstrative pronoun is a pronoun that has meaning only when clearly connected to a specific thing or concept, as when a child points and says, "I want those!"). **The correct answer is (B).**

13. As constructed, the sentence has a major structural problem: it has no subject. In other words, no answer to the question, "*Who* seeks out such clothes?" is provided. A noun, pronoun, noun phrase, or pronoun phrase is needed to answer that question and serve as the subject of the sentence. Only choice (D) has such a phrase, namely, "some people." Therefore, choice (D) is the only option that would bring the sentence into compliance with the conventions of standard written English. **The correct answer is (D).**

14. The last part of the sentence simply needs to explain that chemical dyes and protectants are customarily used in the manufacture of clothing. The underlined phrase, along with answer choices (B) and (C), employs an excess of words to attempt to explain this very simple idea. Choice (D), on the other hand, is concise and completely clear in meaning. Remember, part of good writing is keeping things simple whenever possible. **The correct answer is (D).**

15. The word "consequently" implies that a sentence describes a *consequence* of circumstances or information presented in the previous sentence(s). The last sentence of this paragraph, however, presents information that *contradicts* the ideas just discussed. Therefore, a word or phrase suggesting contrast or contradiction is required. Only choice (C), "on the other hand," satisfies this criterion. **The correct answer is (C).**

16. If a person *pretends* that wearing only clothes made from natural fibers is better for his or her skin than wearing clothes made from synthetic fibers, then that person doesn't really believe the claim is true, and so is definitely not "an adherent to the principle that natural is always better." Answer (A), therefore, cannot be correct. Context suggests that the correct word should have a meaning along the lines of either "believe" or "claim." "Contend" is a synonym for "claim." **The correct answer is (C).**

17. The information presented in the sentence—that skin allergies are more likely to be triggered by natural fiber-based fabrics than by fabrics made from synthetic fibers—directly contradicts the claim attributed to the "adherents" mentioned in the previous sentence. Therefore, the sentence should begin with a word or phrase alerting the reader to the contradiction. The phrase "On the contrary" serves this purpose very well, so no change is needed. **The correct answer is (A).**

18. The entire paragraph is devoted to testing the claim that wearing natural fibers protects a person from allergic reactions against the known scientific evidence. The proposed addition, which discusses an economic consideration, would therefore be completely off topic. **The correct answer is (C).**

SAMPLE TEST 4
Answer Explanations

19. We need to identify the subject to which the verb "help" relates. That subject is "buying clothes." Although "clothes" is a plural noun, as is "fibers" (which immediately precedes the word "help"), the phrase "buying clothes" refers to an action, and is thus considered singular. Therefore, the underlined verb should be the singular form "helps." **The correct answer is (B).**

20. Answer choice (D) points out a similarity between the manufacture of natural fiber-based clothing and the manufacture of clothing from synthetic fibers. Such a statement may be both informative and interesting, but it has no place in a paragraph devoted to highlighting a *difference* between the two types of clothing (specifically, the longer "lifespan" of synthetics-based clothes). Therefore, choice (D) is incorrect. Option (C) gives general information about waste disposal problems in the US, but does not link that information specifically to natural or synthetic fabrics, and therefore is not relevant to the paragraph. Choice (B) does not address waste disposal or any other environmental issue at all, and so is also irrelevant to the paragraph. Only option (A) remains, and that proposed addition would in fact strengthen the paragraph by highlighting a development that directly reduces the environmental impact of the manufacture and use of synthetic fiber-based clothing. **The correct answer is (A).**

21. In order for the sentence to be logical, the underlined portion should mean, "they are not." The word "their" is a possessive pronoun, referring to that which belongs to them, and therefore does not mean, "they are." The word "they're," however, is a contraction of the phrase "they are." Therefore, choice (B) conveys the desired meaning and is in compliance with the conventions of standard written English. Choice (C) is incorrect because "there" is not a pronoun, so the sentence would have no subject. Note, finally, that choice (D) has an incorrect repetition built into it. Since "they're" is a contraction of the two words "they are," choice (D) actually reads, "they are are not." **The correct answer is (B).**

22. According to the conventions of standard written English, when introducing a list by using the word "including," one should place a comma before "including" but NOT after it. For example, "There are many types of keyboard instruments, including pianos, synthesizers, and harpsichords." Choice (B) has the needed comma before "including" and no unnecessary comma after it. **The correct answer is (B).**

---

23. The underlined word, "combative," is neither mocking nor sarcastic, as it clearly and directly implies an argument. Therefore, a change is needed. The word "idiotic" could certainly be used in a mocking way, but it has a strong suggestion of bitterness, so answer choice (B) is inappropriate given the author's goals. A conversation about color preferences would hardly be bizarre, since such conversations are common, so the use of "bizarre" would simply be a poor word choice overall. We are therefore left with only choice (D), "scintillating," a word that generally has a meaning along the lines of fascinating or captivating. It is easy to see how such a word could be used to gently mock conversations that are typical of the awkward situation of a first date. **The correct answer is (D).**

24. There are not many situations in which the conventions of standard written English dictate only one specific word choice. One of those rare situations is the "Not only …" construction. By convention, if a sentence begins with "Not only," the second half of the sentence should begin with "but also." There is very little "wiggle room" with this construction. One should either use it in the

standard manner or avoid it altogether. Choice (B) is the only option that includes the needed phrase, "but also." **The correct answer is (B).**

25. Prior to the sentence in question, the author has in no way implied that traditional data collection methods are useless or fail to yield results of consequence. He or she has simply stated that they are extremely time-consuming. The implication is that such methods are, in fact, useful when it is feasible to employ them. The point the author wishes to make is that in situations where the logistical challenges posed by traditional data collection may have made a research study impossible to complete in the past, technological advancements can offer new hope for conducting the desired research. In short, the author does not wish to imply either that traditional methods are without value or that they are the only valuable methods. We therefore rule out choices (A), (B), and (D), and conclude that **the correct answer is (C).**

26. In most situations, writers try to avoid beginning a sentence with the same word that ended the previous sentence, as the repetition tends to throw the reader off balance. Therefore, a change is desirable here. Options (B), (C), and (D) all combine the last two sentences of the paragraph into a single sentence, but option (B) keeps the distracting repetition of the word "experts." Choice (D) is misleading, because the word "but" suggests a contrast is being set up, when in fact the second half of the sentence simply expands on the information presented in the first half. Therefore, choice (C) is the only one that eliminates the repetition and maintains the author's intended meaning, while complying with the conventions of standard written English. **The correct answer is (C).**

27. The proposed sentence describes a difficulty encountered when the original study was conducted. Because it begins with the phrase, "To make matters worse," it should appear *after* another sentence that describes one or more difficulties the researches struggled with while gathering data. Sentence 5 describes two such difficulties. Sentence 6 explains how such difficulties influenced the way experts viewed the study. Therefore, the proposed sentence should be inserted between sentence 5 and sentence 6. In other words, it should be placed after sentence 5. **The correct answer is (D).**

28. "Not all features" is a plural construction, so the plural form of the verb is required. Answer choice (B) is therefore incorrect. The underlined portion, "are visible," correctly employs a plural verb form and so complies with the conventions of standard written English. No change is needed. Answer choices (C) and (D) also include plural verb forms, but are clumsy and unnecessarily wordy. **The correct answer is (A).**

29. The phrase, "instead of looking at the principle color used in painting the house, she focused on the color of the trim," essentially answers a question raised in the first part of the sentence. (*What was the shift of focus that constituted Mrunamo's second innovation?*) In such a construction, the appropriate punctuation mark between the two parts of the sentence is a colon (:). **The correct answer is (D).**

30. This question is intended to test your ability to differentiate between soundalike words. The word "site" refers to a location. For example, "Shea Stadium was the site of an epic, 29-inning baseball game in 1983." The word "sight" refers to either the ability to see or something that one sees. For example, "That giant redwood tree is a memorable sight." The word "cite" means to quote or refer to

SAMPLE TEST 4
Answer Explanations

other writings, which is clearly the intended meaning of the underlined portion. Therefore, the choice of the word "cite" is entirely appropriate, and no change is needed. **The correct answer is (A).**

31. The graph shows that the most common trim color choice near deciduous forests is *white* (white graph bar). The most common trim color choice near coniferous forests is *green* (very light gray graph bar). The most common choice on the prairie is *dark trim* (black graph bar). Finally, the most common trim color choice in desert areas is *red* (darker gray bar). Therefore, the correct order is *white, green, dark, red*. **The correct answer is (B).**

32. The word "there" at the beginning of the underlined portion is correctly used. However, the word "they're" is incorrectly used at the end of the underlined portion. Remember that "they're" is a contraction of "they are," and so can only be used in a situation where the two-word phrase "they are" could reasonably be used instead. Consider the result of making this replacement in the underlined portion: "As fascinating as these discoveries may be, however, there remains much to be learned about they are true meaning." The sentence fails to comply with the conventions of standard written English and is very difficult to read. The meaning being discussed "belongs to" the discoveries Mrunamo made. What is needed, therefore, is the possessive form of the word "they," which is "their." Remember, however, that as noted at the beginning of this explanation, that change should only be made at the *end* of the underlined portion. **The correct answer is (B).**

33. Answer choice (C) includes inaccurate information (the passage states that homeowners change the main color of their houses *more* often than the trim color), and therefore must be eliminated. It is very hard to imagine how homeowners' responses to questions could demonstrate the limitations of satellite imaging, so choice (B) is far-fetched at best. While it may be true that some homeowners would respond dishonestly to questions about their color preferences, no mention of this possibility has been made in the passage, so choice (D) would be an inappropriate concluding sentence. The existing underlined passage is thus preferable to the other options. It would be best to leave it as it is. **The correct answer is (A).**

---

34. The phrase "a variety of specific things" is plural in form, so the verb in the underlined portion must be plural in form. Answers (B) and (D) are therefore incorrect. The construction "would have been" can be either singular or plural, and so complies with the conventions of standard written English. However, this construction implies that the "specific things" either only existed in the past or never existed at all, neither of which is true. Answer (A) is therefore incorrect as well. **The correct answer is (C).**

35. Notice first that everything between the word "session" and the comma that precedes, "and therefore" could be deleted without the sense of the sentence being lost: "The engineer makes all the decisions about the setup to be used for the session, and therefore plays a vital role in sculpting the sound of the recording." Therefore, the entire (long) phrase, "the microphones … dividers" is a *supplemental phrase*. Supplemental phrases are most often separated from the rest of the sentence with commas, but remember, a comma must appear at both the beginning and the end of the phrase. Neither the underlined portion as written nor any of the answer choices satisfies this requirement. However, it is also acceptable in some cases to separate a supplemental phrase through the use of a dash (—) at each end. In fact, dashes are the preferred choice when the supplemental phrase is

eggheadprep.com

very long and/or contains multiple commas of its own. Answer choice (B) correctly sets off the supplemental phrase with a dash at each end. **The correct answer is (B).**

36. It is not true that it is never acceptable in standard written English to begin a sentence with the word "Because." However, the conventions do place a clear restriction on when it can be done: the phrase that starts with "Because" must lead into another phrase that could stand on its own as a complete sentence. For example, *Because there is no late train out of the city on Fridays, Sheila has to make certain to leave the office by 5:30 p.m. sharp.* Notice that the phrase, "Sheila has to make certain to leave the office by 5:30 p.m. sharp," is a complete sentence. For question #36, then, we note that the phrase beginning with "Because" is not followed by a second, independent phrase (that is, a second phrase that could stand on its own as a sentence), so the sentence is incomplete. A change must be made. Remember that a semicolon is used to separate two phrases that could stand on their own as complete sentences. Since we have already determined that the phrase beginning with "Because" is NOT a complete sentence, choice (D) is incorrect. Although there could be a context in which the construction used in option (B) would be acceptable, there is no doubt that option (C) complies with the conventions of standard written English through its simple use of carefully placed commas. **The correct answer is (C).**

37. Note first that the previous sentence includes the phrase, "world's finest microphones in the most perfection positions," while the proposed addition includes the phrase, "no matter how ideal the setup of the studio may be." It should occur to you that these two phrases say essentially the same thing using different words. Now notice that the previous sentence ends with the phrase, "musicians don't feel comfortable," and the proposed new sentence begins with, "Musicians who are uneasy." Again, these two phrases are synonymous. Finally, observe that both sentences comment on the impact musicians' lack of comfort can have on a recording. It should now be very clear that the proposed sentence is merely a reformulation of the ideas in the previous sentence, and is therefore completely unnecessary. **The correct answer is (D).**

38. The previous sentence described musicians becoming frustrated with themselves and each other during recording sessions. It is highly unlikely that an engineer who offers complicated instructions or has a volatile temper would be helpful in such a situation. Answers (C) and (D) are thus illogical. It certainly is true that the best engineers have a tremendous amount of technical know-how, but it is difficult to see how such know-how would give reassurance to musicians in a moment of frustration. The underlined portion as written, however, is perfectly logical, in that it states that an engineer's calmness and confidence provide musicians with the reassurance they need. Therefore, the best choice by far is to leave the sentence as it is. The correct answer is (A).

39. The sentence is presenting a conclusion based on the observations made in the previous two sentences: *Because* musicians are often nervous and frustrated at a recording session, and *because* a calm, confident demeanor on the engineer's part can help diffuse tensions and put musicians at ease, those considering a career in recording engineering *should consider* studying group dynamics and stress reduction techniques. Words and phrases that cue the reader that a conclusion is about to be presented include "consequently," "hence," "therefore," and "as a result." Of these words and phrases, only "Therefore" appears among the answer choices, so that answer choice must be correct. The correct answer is (D).

SAMPLE TEST 4
Answer Explanations

40. The subject of the sentence, "anyone," is singular. People often find that fact surprising, but keep in mind that the word "anyone" is just the two-word phrase, "any one" written as a single word. It should certainly make sense to you that "one" is singular. The problem with the underlined portion, then, is that it is written in the plural ("negotiators" and "managers"). It simply needs to be rewritten in the singular ("negotiator" and "manager") in order to comply with the conventions of standard written English. The correct answer is (C).

41. Since "at the outset" means "from the beginning," to use both "begin" and "at the outset" in the same sentence is clumsy and redundant. The best answer choice is the one that eliminates the redundancy in the simplest possible way. Note also that it is more logical to speak of the way people "begin their careers" than the way they "begin their experiences." (A person can readily identify the moment when he or she begins a career, but in most cases, a person doesn't know that he or she is having "an experience" until the experience has already begun.) For these reasons, the correct answer is (D).

42. A "vague" awareness is not a particularly strong awareness, and so would be unlikely to be helpful to someone wishing to excel as a recording engineer. "Minimal" awareness would be even worse, in that in implies very little awareness at all. We have thus ruled out choices (A) and (C). Answer choice (D) is a decoy. You have probably heard of someone having *acute* hearing or eyesight, meaning very good ears or very sharp eyes, but "a cute" is not an acceptable substitute for the single word "acute." In the sentence in question, since we do not have the option of deleting, altering, or moving the word "a," we cannot create a construction using the word "acute" that complies with the conventions of standard written English. The phrase would have to be something like, "an acute awareness," which would require changing the word "a." The word "keen," however, is an excellent choice because it means "sharp" or "very well developed." Those meanings perfectly describe the kind of awareness an engineer should ideally have. The correct answer is (B).

43. For this question, it is simply necessary to recognize that options (B), (C), and (D) would all greatly lengthen the underlined portion, without altering or enhancing its meaning in any way. Such unnecessary wordiness is never considered good writing. The correct answer is (A).

44. It is necessary first to recognize why it is illogical for sentence 4 to be in its present location. Sentences 1, 2, and 3 have already described types of specialized training that a person needs in order to succeed as a recording engineer. To state that, "A recording engineer *also* needs a great deal of specialized training" (emphasis added), after presenting all of the information in those three sentences does not make sense. However, it would be perfectly logical to *introduce* the previous three sentences with sentence 4. If sentence 4 were placed at the head of the paragraph, then the word "also" would nicely serve as a transitional link connecting this paragraph to the previous one. (That single word would make clear that *in addition* to learning about group dynamics, stress reduction, proper nutrition, and sleep hygiene, a person who wishes to become a recording engineer should seek out specialized training as described in the new paragraph.) Therefore, sentence 4 should begin the paragraph. The correct answer is (A).

egghead prep.com

TEST SECTION 3: MATH—NO CALCULATOR

NOTE: Most problems in math can be solved using multiple different methods. In these explanations, the most standard methods taught in US middle school and high school mathematics are shown. You may have employed a different method that is equally valid.

1. Using the formula given for the function, we know that $f(9) = k - \frac{4}{3}(9) = k - 12$. Since we also know that $f(9) = -15$, we have the equation, $k - 12 = -15$. Adding 12 to both sides yields, $k = -3$. Hence, $f(x) = -3 - \frac{4}{3}x$, and so $f(-3) = -3 - \frac{4}{3}(-3) = -3 + 4 = 1$. **The correct answer is (D).**

2. Recall that $|y| \geq 0$ for any real number y. We therefore know that $|x - 3| \geq 0$ for any real number x. Adding 2 to both sides yields, $|x - 3| + 2 \geq 2$ for any real number x. Therefore, the expression shown in answer choice (A) cannot equal zero for any x value. The same analysis proves that answers (B) and (D) are incorrect as well. But the 2 is *subtracted* from the absolute value expression in option (C), creating a different situation. We still have, $|x - 3| \geq 0$ for any real number x. Subtracting 2 from both sides yields, $|x - 3| - 2 \geq -2$. Since $0 \geq -2$, the expression shown in answer choice (C) *could* equal zero. (In fact, it does equal zero if $x = 5$ or 1.) **The correct answer is (C).**

3. To evaluate $f(-4x)$, we plug in the expression $(-4x)$ for the x in the formula for the function f. $f(-4x) = -3(-4x) + 4 = 12x + 4$. **The correct answer is (B).**

4. Begin by multiplying both sides of the first equation by x (which is allowed because we know $x \neq 0$) to get, $y = 5x$. Substitute this expression for y in the second equation to get, $4(x + 1) = 5x$. Simplifying the left side using the distributive property yields, $4x + 4 = 5x$. Now simply subtract $4x$ from both sides to get, $4 = x$. **The correct answer is (A).**

5. Because two of the four answer choices involve the expression, a/b, it is likely that generating that expression will be very helpful. There is a sneaky way to accomplish this goal quite quickly, but we will demonstrate here the more standard method that most students would employ. Cross multiplication of the given equation gives us, $5(a + 2b) = 3b$. Now use the distributive property to simplify the left side, yielding, $5a + 10b = 3b$. Subtract $10b$ from both sides to get, $5a = -7b$. Now divide both sides by $5b$ to generate the expression, a/b:

$$5a = -7b \Rightarrow \frac{5a}{5b} = \frac{-7b}{5b} \Rightarrow \frac{a}{b} = -\frac{7}{5}$$

The correct answer is (D).

6. As a first step, expand (FOIL) the expression $(3x + 2)(5x + 1)$ to get, $15x^2 + 3x + 10x + 2$. Combining like terms yields the expression, $15x^2 + 13x + 2$. Now multiply by 2, using the distributive property: $2(15x^2 + 13x + 2) = 30x^2 + 26x + 4$. **The correct answer is (B).**

SAMPLE TEST 4
Answer Explanations

7. The given line is written in the form, $y = mx + b$, so we know that its slope, m, is –4. A line parallel to the given line will have the same slope, –4. You may be aware that the slope of a line written in the form, $Ax + By = C$, is equal to $-A/B$. If so, you can use that formula to calculate the slopes of the four lines given in the answer choices. If not, you will need to rewrite each line in $y = mx + b$ form, as follows.

$$\text{A)} \quad 12x + 3y = -9 \Rightarrow 3y = -12x - 9 \Rightarrow y = -4x - 3$$

$$\text{B)} \quad x + 4y = 8 \Rightarrow 4y = -x + 8 \Rightarrow y = -\frac{1}{4}x + 2$$

$$\text{C)} \quad 4x - y = 6 \Rightarrow -y = -4x + 6 \Rightarrow y = 4x - 6$$

$$\text{D)} \quad 5x - 2y = 7 \Rightarrow -2y = -5x + 7 \Rightarrow y = \frac{5}{2}x - \frac{7}{2}$$

Only answer choice (A) yields a value of –4 for m. **The correct answer is (A).**

8. Notice that both 3 and 8 appear twice among the answer choices. It is therefore efficient to test these values in the given equation. Here is the equation with $r = 1$ (its given value) and $x = 3$:

$$\sqrt{3+1} = 3 - 5 \Rightarrow \sqrt{4} = -2$$

This statement is *almost* true. The number –2 *is* a square root of 4. However, the symbol, $\sqrt{}$, specifically denotes the *nonnegative* square root of a number. Therefore, the above equation is false. The value of x cannot be 3, which means that answer choices (A) and (D) have been eliminated. Now here is the equation with $r = 1$ and $x = 8$:

$$\sqrt{8+1} = 8 - 5 \Rightarrow \sqrt{9} = 3$$

This statement is true, so 8 is a solution to the equation. **The correct answer is (C).**

9. Notice that each answer choice includes the unit, "high fives per week." The word *per* in the unit tells us that we are solving for a *rate of change*, that is, a slope. We may express the given information as ordered pairs of the form, (week number, number of high fives). The two ordered pairs are, (8, 17) and (20, 32). The rate of change (slope) between these two points is,

$$\frac{y_2 - y_1}{x_2 - x_1} = \frac{32 - 17}{20 - 8} = \frac{15}{12} = \frac{5}{4} = 1.25$$

Therefore, the number of high fives must increase at a rate of 1.25 high fives per week. **The correct answer is (B).**

10. We will actually demonstrate two methods to solve this equation, since they are both quite instructive, highlighting numerous concepts that are emphasized in the SAT Math Sections. For the first method, we use the information given in the first equation to substitute $-3y + 6$ in for x in the second equation. The result is, $y = (4(-3y + 6) + 6)(-3y + 6 - 8)$. Applying the distributive property yields, $y = (-12y + 24 + 6)(-3y + 6 - 8)$, which, upon combining like terms, becomes $y = (-12y + 30)(-3y - 2)$. We now expand (FOIL) the expression on the right side to get, $y = 36y^2 + 24y - 90y - 60$, or $y = 36y^2 - 66y - 60$. Subtracting y from both sides yields, $0 = 36y^2 - 67y - 60$. Now recall that for a quadratic equation, $ax^2 + bx + c = 0$, the *discriminant*,

which equals $b^2 - 4ac$, can be used to determine the number of real solutions the equation has. Here, $b^2 - 4ac = (-67)^2 - 4(36)(-60)$, which is very time-consuming to compute. Careful examination of signs, however, shows that the result will be positive. Hence, the equation has 2 real solutions. **The correct answer is (B).**

(Problem #10, continued—alternate solution)

The second method is to consider the graphs of the two equations. First, rewrite the first equation in the form, $y = mx + b$.

$$x = -3y + 6 \Rightarrow x - 6 = -3y \Rightarrow -\frac{1}{3}x + 2 = y, \text{ or, } y = -\frac{1}{3}x + 2$$

Hence, the line has slope $-\frac{1}{3}$ and y-intercept 2. This line is shown on the coordinate axes below. Now note that the second equation, if expanded, would take the form, $y = ax^2 + bx + c$, with $a > 0$ (specifically, $a = 4$), so the graph of the equation will be a parabola that opens upward. Set each of the factors on the right side of the given equation equal to zero to determine the zeros (x–intercepts) of the parabola. For the equation, $4x + 6 = 0$, subtract 6 from both sides to get $4x = -6$, then divide both sides by 4 to get $x = -6/4 = -1.5$. For the equation, $x - 8 = 0$, simply add 8 to both sides to get, $x = 8$. Therefore, the x–intercepts of the parabola are at $(-1.5, 0)$ and $(8, 0)$. Because you are working without a calculator for this test section, your graph will just be a rough sketch. We have therefore drawn the graph of the parabola very crudely below. You will see that even this "ugly" graph is more than adequate to solve the problem!

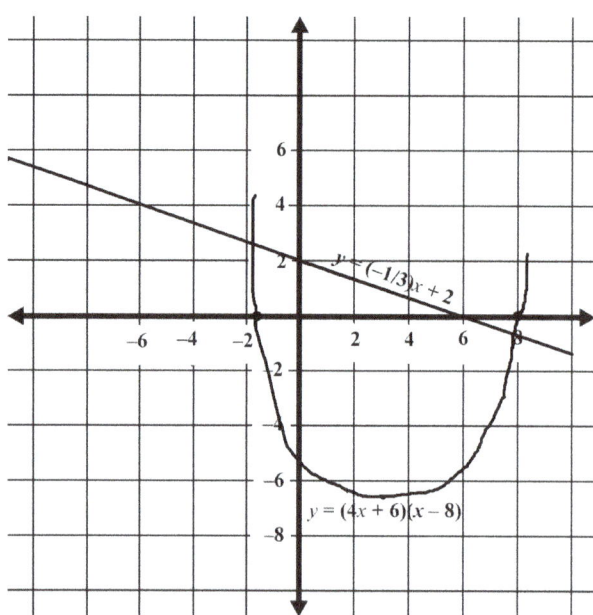

Notice that even with the parabola drawn so poorly, it is quite clear that the line intersects the parabola twice. Therefore, the system has two solutions. **The correct answer is (B).**

11. We will begin by multiplying both sides of the equation by $z - 3$, noting that if we arrive at the solution, $z = 3$, we will have a problem, because the fraction would have a denominator of zero. Let's just proceed with the algebra and hope for the best. The multiplication by $z - 3$ yields the equation, $z + 7 = 12(z - 3)$. Applying the distributive property to the right side gives us, $z + 7 = 12z - 36$. Adding 36 to both sides, we arrive at,

SAMPLE TEST 4
Answer Explanations

$z + 43 = 12z$. We next subtract z from both sides to get, $43 = 11z$, and finally divide both sides by 11 to obtain the result, $43/11 = z$. **The correct answer is (A).**

12. The standard method for finding the intersection point(s) of two function graphs is to set the expressions defining the two functions equal to each other. Here is the solution.

Set the expression for $f(x)$ equal to the expression for $g(x)$:

$-18x^2 + 8 = 18x^2 - 8$ add $18x^2$ to both sides to get

$8 = 36x^2 - 8$ add 8 to both sides to get

$16 = 36x^2$ divide both sides by 36 to get

$\dfrac{16}{36} = \dfrac{4}{9} = x^2$ and therefore,

$x = \pm\sqrt{\dfrac{4}{9}} = \pm\dfrac{2}{3}$, and these, then, are the possible values of c.

Since the graph clearly shows that $c > 0$, we choose the positive value. **The correct answer is (C).**

13. Since Geena earned x points and Kelly earned 1 point less than Geena, Kelly earned $x - 1$ points. Therefore, their initial point total was, $x + (x - 1) = 2x - 1$. The 40% bonus represents a 40% *increase* in their total score, so the total should be multiplied by 100% + 40% = 140%, or 1.40. Executing this multiplication and applying the distributive property, we arrive at a final point total of, $1.40(2x - 1) = 2.80x - 1.40$. If the total number of points was divided evenly between Geena and Kelly, then each player received half of this amount, or $1.40x - 0.70$. **The correct answer is (D).**

14. The equation is quadratic, and therefore must be solved either by the method of completing the square or by use of the quadratic formula. Either way, the algebra is intense. If you are not comfortable with extensive symbol manipulations, you may wish to simply skip a problem like this one. In any case, here are the steps to solve the equation using the quadratic formula.

$x^2 - 4m = \dfrac{n}{3}x \Rightarrow x^2 - \dfrac{n}{3}x - 4m = 0$ multiply both sides by 3 to get

$3x^2 - nx - 12m = 0$.   By the quadratic formula,

$x = \dfrac{-(-n) \pm \sqrt{(-n)^2 - 4(3)(-12m)}}{2(3)} = \dfrac{n \pm \sqrt{n^2 + 144m}}{6} = \dfrac{n}{6} \pm \dfrac{\sqrt{n^2 + 144m}}{6}$

The correct answer is (D).

15. To simplify the fraction, we multiply its numerator and denominator by the *complex conjugate* of the denominator. The complex conjugate of $4 + 3i$ is $4 - 3i$.

$$\frac{(2+4i)}{(4+3i)} \cdot \frac{(4-3i)}{(4-3i)} = \frac{8 - 6i + 16i - 12i^2}{16 - 12i + 12i - 9i^2}$$

$$= \frac{8 + 10i - 12(-1)}{16 - 9(-1)} = \frac{8 + 10i + 12}{16 + 9} = \frac{20 + 10i}{25}$$

$$= \frac{20}{25} + \frac{10}{25}i = \frac{4}{5} + \frac{2}{5}i$$

Comparing this result to the form, $a + bi$, we see that $b = 2/5$. **The correct answer is (A).**

---

16. Here is one method that can be used to solve the problem, the method of factoring by grouping.

$-x^3 + 7x^2 - 3x + 21 = 0$ Multiply both sides by -1 to get

$x^3 - 7x^2 + 3x - 21 = 0$

Now take out the common factor x^2 from the first two terms and the common factor 3 from the third and fourth terms:

$x^2(x - 7) + 3(x - 7) = 0 \Rightarrow (x - 7)(x^2 + 3) = 0$

Now set each factor equal to zero to find the solutions:

$x - 7 = 0 \Rightarrow x = 7$

$x^2 + 3 = 0 \Rightarrow x^2 = -3 \Rightarrow x = \pm\sqrt{-3} = \pm i\sqrt{3}$

Of the three solutions, only the value 7 is a real number. **The correct answer is 7.**

17. Notice that because the sum of the measures of the angles of a triangle is 180°, we have the equation, $t + r + 90 = 180$. Subtracting 90 from both sides yields, $t + r = 90$. Subtracting r from both sides then gives us, $t = 90 - r$. Therefore, $\sin(t°) = \sin(90° - r°)$. A basic theorem of trigonometry states that $\sin(90° - r°) = \cos(r°)$. Therefore, $\sin(90° - r°) = 0.47$. **The correct answer is 0.47.**

18. There is a very subtle principle of similar figures underlying this problem. Notice that the length BC (or AD) represents the same fraction of the total horizontal distance, 240 yards, as the length GD represents of the total diagonal distance, which is $2x + 10x + 3x$. Since $GD = 10x$, we have the proportion,

$$\frac{10x}{2x + 10x + 3x} = \frac{BC}{240}$$ which simplifies to,

$$\frac{10x}{15x} = \frac{BC}{240}, \text{ or } \frac{2}{3} = \frac{BC}{240}.$$

Cross multiplication yields, $2(240) = 3BC$, or $480 = 3BC$. Dividing both sides by 3 gives us, $160 = BC$. **The correct answer is 160.**

SAMPLE TEST 4
Answer Explanations

19. There are two key elements to this problem. First, we need to recognize the key words "for each," which identify the constant number b as a *rate of change*. Remember, rate of change is another term for slope, so this problem is actually asking us to calculate the slope of a linear function. Second, we must notice that the slope is defined in an unusual manner in this problem. The rate unit is not b bonobos per *meter*, but rather b bonobos per *ten meters*. Therefore, each distance measurement should be, in effect, counted in tens. In other words, 90 meters would be represented as the value 9, since it is made up of 9 sets of 10 meters. (That is, 90 ÷ 10 = 9.) Similarly, 130 meters should be represented as the value 13. We can therefore express the given information as the ordered pairs (9, 31) and (13, 3). To find the needed rate of change, use the slope formula:

$$\frac{y_2 - y_1}{x_2 - x_1} = \frac{3 - 31}{13 - 9} = \frac{-28}{4} = -7$$

Therefore, the number of bonobos encountered decreases by 7 for each additional 10 meters of distance from the center of the territory. **The correct answer is 7.**

20. Here is one of the many methods that can be used to solve the problem.

$$\begin{cases} -9x - 5y = -2 \\ 6x + 10y = 28 \end{cases}$$

Multiply the first equation by 2 and the second by 3 to get

$$\begin{cases} -18x - 10y = -4 \\ 18x + 30y = 84 \end{cases}$$ Add these two equations to get

$$20y = 80$$ Divide both sides by 20 to get

$$y = 4$$

The correct answer is 4.

TEST SECTION 4: MATH—CALCULATOR

NOTE: Most problems in math can be solved using multiple different methods. In these explanations, the most standard methods taught in US middle school and high school mathematics are shown. You may have employed a different method that is equally valid.

1. Because we are asked to calculate our final answer in inches, it is easiest to work in inches from the beginning. Since 1 foot = 12 inches, 6 feet = 6 × 12 = 72 inches. Cutting a board of length 72 inches in half yields two boards of length 72 ÷ 2 = 36 inches. If each of these boards is then cut into fourths, the resulting boards will have length 36 ÷ 4 = 9 inches. **The correct answer is (C).**

2. This situation is characterized by a constant rate of increase, and therefore can be modeled by an expression of the form $mx + b$, or rather, $mw + b$, where m is the rate of change, b is the initial value, and w is the number of weeks. Since Jaclyn can process 85 units per hour at present, the initial value, b, is 85. She expects the rate of increase of her output to be 7 units per hour each week, so the numerical value of the rate of change, m, is 7. Therefore, the expression, $7w + 85$, or $85 + 7w$, correctly models the situation. Notice that this expression only appears in answer choice (A). Furthermore, the inequality shown in choice (A) accurately expresses Jaclyn's wish to have an output of 120 *or more* units per hour. **The correct answer is (A).**

3. Notice the key words "for each" following the amount $25. The words and phrases "each," "for each," and "per" are always indicators of a *rate of change*. Therefore, the cost of membership in the club for a year has a rate of change of $25 per training session. Since this rate is constant, the situation can be modeled by an expression of the form, $mx + b$, and $m = 25$. The annual fee for membership in the club of $840 applies even with no training sessions, so 840 is the *initial value*—that is, the value of b. Therefore, the total cost of membership in the club for a year is $25x + 840$, where x equals the number of training sessions. Because Marcel's total cost for 2015 was $990, we have the equation, $25x + 840 = 990$. Subtracting 840 from both sides yields, $25x = 150$. Dividing both sides by 25 gives us the result, $x = 6$. **The correct answer is (B).**

4. The information provided in the first sentence may be expressed as the formula, $v = \frac{F}{A}$. We are given the value 2 meters per second for the speed, v, and 800 cubic meters per second for the flow rate, F. Plugging in these values gives us the equation, $2 = \frac{800}{A}$. Multiplying both sides by A (which cannot be zero since the river must have a positive cross sectional area), we get, $2A = 800$. Dividing both sides by 2 gives us, $A = 400$ square meters. **The correct answer is (C).**

5. Since the sample size is greater than 30 and the sample was randomly selected, the sample should be representative of the population as a whole. Therefore, the infection rate of 42.5% should apply to the population as well as to the sample. Hence, we would expect 42.5% of 350, or 0.425(350) ≈ 149 (the calculated value is exactly 148.75) deer in the forest to be infected with the parasite. Answer (D) is closest to this value. **The correct answer is (D)**

6. Let M equal the number of points Madison scored and K equal the number of points Kaitlyn scored. The given information may be translated into the two equations, $M = K + 13$ and $M + K = 49$. Substitute the expression $K + 13$ for M in the second equation to get, $(K + 13) + K = 49$, or $2K + 13 = 49$. Subtracting 13

SAMPLE TEST 4
Answer Explanations

from both sides yields, $2K = 36$. Divide both sides by 2 to get $K = 18$. Kaitlyn scored 18 points. **The correct answer is (B).**

7. Focus on the fact that the line contains points in quadrants I and III. All points in quadrant I have coordinates in the form (*positive*, *positive*). Points in quadrant III have coordinates in the form (*negative*, *negative*). Therefore, the slope of the line takes the form,

$$\frac{negative - positive}{negative - positive} = \frac{negative}{negative} = positive$$

Line *m* has a positive slope. **The correct answer is (A).**

8. We examine the row labeled "square" and the column labeled "green" and find that the box where they cross contains the value 16. Therefore, 16 of the pressed buttons were square and green. Since 100 buttons were pressed in all, the proportion of square green buttons is 16/100, or 4/25. **The correct answer is (D).**

9. The animal with the longest average lifespan is represented by the dot located at the highest position in the scatterplot. This point, which is not labeled, is to be found just above and to the left of point *D*. It aligns with 100 on the vertical axis, indicating an average lifespan of 100 years. It aligns with a number between 34 and 36 on the horizontal axis, indicating a dependency period of between 34 and 36 months. Answer choice (A), 35, is the only option between 34 and 36. **The correct answer is (A).**

10. The table below shows the calculation of the needed ratio for each of the four points. Values have been estimated where necessary; using slightly different estimates would not affect the result.

Point name	Dependency period (months)	Average lifespan (years)	Ratio of lifespan to dependency period
A	6	38	$38/6 \approx 6.3$
B	28	73	$73/28 \approx 2.6$
C	33	45	$45/33 \approx 1.4$
D	38.5	80	$80/38.5 \approx 2.1$

Point *A* yields the highest ratio by far. **The correct answer is (A).**

11. Note, first of all, that there are two types of black ants—black hairy and black biting. Both of those columns must be accounted for in our work. By definition, the needed probability is calculated as,

$$\frac{\text{Total number of black ants in habitat C}}{\text{Total number of black ants}} = \frac{199 + 106}{690 + 956} = \frac{305}{1{,}646} = 0.185\ldots \approx 0.19$$

Only answer choice (B), 0.20, is close to the value 0.19. **The correct answer is (B).**

12. We may assume that *f* is a polynomial function since all of the answer choices are polynomial functions. A major theorem of algebra states that if *r* is an *x*-intercept (also called a root or zero) of a polynomial function *f*, then $f(x)$ has a factor of the form, $(x - r)^n$, where *n* is a positive integer. Therefore, in this problem, $f(x)$ must have factors of the form, $(x - (-5))^n$, $(x - 2)^m$, and $(x - 5)^p$, or $(x + 5)^n$, $(x - 2)^m$, and $(x - 5)^p$, where *n*, *m*, and *p* are all positive integers. The only answer choice that takes this form (with the value 1 for *m*, *n*, and *p*) is (C) **The correct answer is (C).**

13. If the interest rate is 2%, then the value of r is 2. In this case, the amount of money in the account after one year will be,

$$750\left(1 + \frac{2}{400}\right)^4.$$

If the interest rate is 6%, then the value of r is 6. In this case, the amount of money in the account after one year will be,

$$750\left(1 + \frac{6}{400}\right)^4.$$

To find the difference between these two amounts of money, simply subtract the entire expressions:

$$\text{Difference between account balances} = 750\left(1 + \frac{6}{400}\right)^4 - 750\left(1 + \frac{2}{400}\right)^4$$

The correct answer is (D).

14. Notice that for each 15 minutes of time that elapses, the amount of mildew is cut in half. You may be aware that such a pattern is characteristic of an exponential function, in which case you can identify the correct answer immediately. If not, however, make a scatter plot of the data.

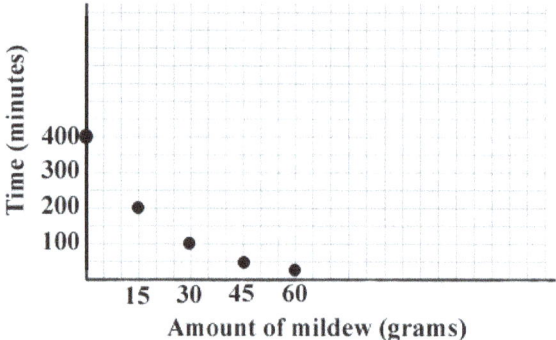

It should be clear that a straight line would not fit the data well, which eliminates answer choices (C) and (D). Since the graph shows a clear downward trend, it would not be reasonable to describe it using the word "growth," so answer (A) may be ruled out as well. **The correct answer is (B).**

15. At Slammin' Sound, the value of E is 220, the value of P is 20, and the value of M is 15. Therefore, for Slammin' Sound, the formula for total cost, y, in dollars, is

$$y = 220 + (20 + 15)x = 220 + 35x.$$

At Awesome Audio, the value of E is 175, the value of P is 30, and the value of M is 20. Therefore, for Awesome Audio, the formula for total cost, y, in dollars, is

SAMPLE TEST 4
Answer Explanations

$$y = 175 + (30 + 20)x = 175 + 50x.$$

The total cost will be lower at Slammin' Sound if $220 + 35x < 175 + 50x$. Subtracting 175 from both sides yields, $45 + 35x < 50x$. Next, subtract $35x$ from both sides to get, $45 < 15x$. Finally, divide both sides by 3 to obtain the solution set, $3 < x$. Remember now that if we reverse the order of the inequality statement, we must also reverse the inequality symbol. The proper form of the inequality with the variable x on the left, then, is $x > 3$. **The correct answer is (D).**

16. For Music Mania, $E = 190$, $P = 25$, and $M = 15$. Therefore, for Music Mania, the formula for total cost, y, in dollars, is $y = 190 + (25 + 15)x$, or $y = 190 + 40x$. By comparing this equation to the slope-intercept form of the equation of a line, $y = mx + b$, we can see that the slope, m, of the line is 40. The rate $40 per hour represents the total of the hourly rental costs for the PA system and the microphones and cables at Music Mania. Since the PA system and the microphones and cables are all audio gear, we could also say that $40 is the total hourly cost of renting audio gear at Music Mania. Be careful, however, to notice that this figure is the total *hourly* cost of renting the gear, not simply the total cost. **The correct answer is (C).**

17. In order to be modeled well by an equation of the form $y = ab^x$, where $a > 0$ and $b > 1$ (in other words, by an exponential growth function), the scatterplot should suggest a nonzero y-intercept and show a clear upward curve when read from left to right. Only answer choice (B) fits this description. **The correct answer is (B).**

18. Simply subtract 6 from both sides of the given inequality to get, $4r - 3 \leq 2$. Hence, the maximum possible value of $4r - 3$ is 2. **The correct answer is (A).**

19. The given information tells us that each cup is a right circular cone with a diameter of 10 centimeters and a height of 7 centimeters. Note that if the *diameter* is 10 centimeters, the *radius* is 5 centimeters. Using the formula for the volume of a cone, $V = \frac{1}{3}\pi r^2 h$, given in the test instructions, we compute the volume of a single cup as, $V = \frac{1}{3}\pi(5)^2(7) \approx 183.26$ cubic centimeters. Now, since there are 946 cubic centimeters in a quart, the two-quart pitcher contains $2(946) = 1,892$ cubic centimeters of orange juice. Therefore, the total number of cups Kerry can fill with orange juice is $1,892 \div 183.26 \approx 10.3$ cups. In other words, Kerry can fill 10 cups completely, but can only partially fill an 11th cup. The largest number of cups Kerry can fill *completely*, then, is 10. **The correct answer is (C).**

20. Since internet usage in 2006 is to be plotted on the horizontal axis for the scatterplot, it corresponds to the variable x. Since internet usage in 2015 is to be plotted on the vertical axis, it corresponds to the variable y. Now, in order for a point to be *below* the line $y = x$, the point must satisfy the condition, $y < x$. Combining all of this information, we see that we are determining the number of points in the scatterplot for which it would be true that

(internet usage in 2015) < (internet usage in 2006).

Referring to the original bar graph, then, we are looking for instances in which the gray bar is *shorter* than the black bar. This is only true in one case, desktop computers. Therefore, only one point of the scatterplot would be below the line $y = x$. **The correct answer is (D).**

21. The graph shows that internet usage in West Mortland on laptop computers was around 58 million or 59 million hours in 2006 (black bar above "laptop computer"). Internet usage in West Mortland on laptop computers was around 93 million or 94 million hours in 2015 (gray bar above "laptop computer"). Since 93

eggheadprep.com

$-58 = 94 - 59 = 35$, let's estimate that internet usage in West Mortland on laptop computers increased by 35 million hours from 2006 to 2015. To find the *percent* increase, we divide this amount by the original (that is, 2006) value, for which we will use the estimate of 58 million hours.

$$\frac{35 \text{ million hours}}{58 \text{ million hours}} \approx 0.603 \approx 60\%$$

Only answer choice (C), 58%, is close to 60%. **The correct answer is (C).**

22. Let W represent the weight of the container in pounds and D its diagonal measurement in feet. The given information may be expressed as, $W = kD^2$, where k is a constant. Because both weight and diagonal length are positive quantities, we may assume k is positive. Therefore, the graph of the relationship between weight and diagonal measurement should be a parabola that opens upward. Only option (B) fits this description. **The correct answer is (B).**

23. Because $\overline{ST}$ is a diameter of the circle, arc SQT represents half of the circle's circumference. That is, $15\pi = \frac{1}{2}C$, where C is the circumference. Multiplying both sides of this equation by 2 gives us, $30\pi = C$. According to the formula given in the test instructions, $C = 2\pi r$. We therefore know that $30\pi = 2\pi r$. Dividing both sides by 2π gives us, $15 = r$. The radius is 15 meters. **The correct answer is (D).**

24. The answer to this question is not immediately obvious. It is critically important to notice that in the expression for $g(x)$, there is a common factor of $3x$. Taking out this common factor, we can rewrite the formula for $g(x)$ as, $g(x) = 3x(x^2 - 4x + 2)$. Notice that the expression inside the parentheses is identical to the expression given for $h(x)$. Therefore, $g(x) = 3x \cdot h(x)$. We now use this fact to rewrite the expressions for $r(x)$, $s(x)$, $u(x)$, and $v(x)$.

$$r(x) = g(x) + h(x) = 3x \cdot h(x) + h(x) = h(x)(3x + 1)$$
$$s(x) = g(x) - h(x) = 3x \cdot h(x) - h(x) = h(x)(3x - 1)$$
$$u(x) = g(x) + 4h(x) = 3x \cdot h(x) + 4h(x) = h(x)(3x + 4)$$
$$v(x) = 3g(x) + 4h(x) = 3 \cdot 3x \cdot h(x) + 4h(x) = 9x \cdot h(x) + 4h(x) = h(x)(9x + 4)$$

In each case, we have taken out the common factor $h(x)$. Note that since $u(x) = h(x)(3x + 4)$, it is clearly divisible by $3x + 4$. **The correct answer is (C).**

25. Standard deviation is a measure of *spread*. Notice that in Batch 2, there were 13 cereal boxes with a weight of 25 or 21 ounces—that is, 13 boxes with a weight 2 ounces different from the central value of 23 ounces. In Batch 1, there were only 2 boxes with a weight 2 ounces different from the central value of 23 ounces. The weights in Batch 1 are more "clumped" near the center than those in Batch 2. In other words, Batch 2 has greater spread, and, therefore, a greater standard deviation. That is, (standard deviation of Batch 2) > (standard deviation of Batch 1), or (standard deviation of Batch 1) < (standard deviation of Batch 2). **The correct answer is (A).**

SAMPLE TEST 4
Answer Explanations

26. An algebra rule states that if a three-part inequality is true, then any inequality obtained by deleting one of the three elements of the inequality is also true, as long as the original left to right order is preserved. In other words, the statement, $-v > u > v$ implies that all of the following are true:

$$-v > u$$
$$u > v$$
$$-v > v$$

The third of these inequalities provides critical information. You may recognize immediately that $-v > v$ implies that v must be negative. But if not, simply add v to both sides to get, $0 > 2v$. Dividing both sides by 2 yields, $0 > v$, or $v < 0$. We therefore know that statement III must be true, which actually enables us to answer the question. Also note, however, that since u is between v and $-v$, a point with coordinate u would lie closer to zero on a number line than a point with coordinate v or $-v$. Therefore, u must have a smaller absolute value than v does, that is, $|v| > |u|$. By definition, since $v < 0$, $|v| = -v$. Combining the last two statements, we have, $-v > |u|$, and statement II is true as we require. **The correct answer is (D).**

27. Answer (A) may be ruled immediately, since it is based on interpreting 258.43 as a dollar amount. As the vertical axis label on the graph makes clear, 258.43 is a percentage. Answer (B) is also incorrect, since it has been explained in the problem that relative sanitation collection cost is based on comparison with the national average sanitation collection cost, NOT with the lowest relative sanitation collection cost. Now, the equation, $y = -0.016x + 258.43$ is in the form, $y = mx + b$. Therefore, 258.43 is the y-intercept of the line, or *initial value* of the linear function. The standard interpretation of the initial value of a linear model would suggest that according to the line of best fit, we should expect a city with a population density of 0 people per square mile to have a relative sanitation collection cost of 258.43. In other words, in such a city, the sanitation collection cost would be 258.43% of the national average sanitation collection cost. In reality, of course, there is no such thing as a city with 0 people per square mile. Noting that the line of best fit slopes downward from left to right, it would be more reasonable to conclude that the initial value implies that for a town with a very low population density (that is, getting close to 0 people per square mile), we would expect the sanitation collection cost to be a little below 258.43% of the national average cost. However, because the line of best fit only *approximately* matches the data, and actual data points lie both above and below the line of best fit, we cannot say that a town with very low population density *never* has a sanitation collection cost above 258.43% of the national average. Answer choice (D), therefore, presents a conclusion beyond what is reasonable. Answer choice (C) correctly summarizes the analysis just presented. **The correct answer is (C).**

28. Recall that the average of two values is found by adding the two values, then dividing the result by 2. By applying this principle, we can find expressions for the quantities p, q, and r.

$$p = \frac{2x + (-1)}{2} = \frac{2x - 1}{2} = \frac{2x}{2} - \frac{1}{2} = x - \frac{1}{2}$$

$$q = \frac{4x + 6}{2} = \frac{4x}{2} + \frac{6}{2} = 2x + 3$$

$$r = \frac{6x + 13}{2} = \frac{6x}{2} + \frac{13}{2} = 3x + \frac{13}{2}$$

We now find the average of p, q, and r by adding these expressions and dividing by 3.

$$\text{Avg.} = \frac{x - \frac{1}{2} + 2x + 3 + 3x + \frac{13}{2}}{3} = \frac{6x + \frac{12}{2} + 3}{3} = \frac{6x + 6 + 3}{3} = \frac{6x + 9}{3} = \frac{6x}{3} + \frac{9}{3},$$

which equals $2x + 3$. **The correct answer is (B).**

29. The graph of the function $y = j$ is a horizontal line with y-intercept j. In order for the equation, $f(x) = j$, to have four real solutions, the horizontal line $y = j$ must cross the graph of $y = f(x)$ exactly four times. Guided by the answer choices, we visualize horizontal lines with y-intercepts 7, 2, –5, and –9.5. Only the horizontal line with y-intercept 2 would cross the given graph four times. **The correct answer is (B).**

30. The minimum value of a function whose graph is a parabola that opens upward is the y-coordinate of the vertex. Recall that the coordinates of the vertex, (h, k), appear as constants in the vertex form of the equation of the parabola, $y = a(x - h)^2 + k$. Since only answer choices (A) and (D) are equations of parabolas in vertex form, one of those two choices must be correct. Based on the general vertex form given above, answer (A) indicates that the parabola's vertex is at the point $(3, -49)$. Answer (D) indicates a vertex at $(-3, -45)$. To see which one is correct, notice that the equation given in the problem is the *factored* form of the equation of the parabola, from which we can determine the x-intercepts. Specifically, the x-intercepts are found by solving the two equations, $x - 10 = 0$ and $x + 4 = 0$. Hence, the x-intercepts are 10 and –4. The x-coordinate of the vertex is the *average* of these two values, or $\frac{10 + (-4)}{2} = \frac{6}{2} = 3$. Since answer choice (A) is in vertex form, as required, and correctly indicates that 3 is the x-coordinate of the vertex, **the correct answer is (A).**

31. The problem is asking us to determine the *rate of change*, or slope, of the function T. In order to determine the slope, first rewrite the formula for T.

$$T = \frac{3x + 944}{8} = \frac{3x}{8} + \frac{944}{8} = \frac{3}{8}x + 118$$

The equation is now in the form, $y = mx + b$, so we can see immediately that the slope of the line is $\frac{3}{8}$. **The correct answer is 3/8 or 0.375.**

SAMPLE TEST 4
Answer Explanations

32. Because the visitors leave the museum at a constant rate, the situation may be modeled by an equation of the form $y = mx + b$, where y represents the number of visitors in the museum and x represents the number of minutes that have passed since visitors began leaving. Since there are 1400 visitors present at the moment observation begins, 1400 is the *initial value*, that is, the value of b. Since visitors then begin *leaving* the museum, the number of visitors is *decreasing* at a rate of 9 visitors per minute. Hence, the rate of change, or slope, is –9, which is the value of m. The equation that models this situation is therefore, $y = -9x + 1400$. Since x represents the number of minutes since observation began, to find the number of visitors present after 80 minutes, we simply plug in 80 for x. The result is, $y = -9(80) + 1400 = -720 + 1400 = 680$. **The correct answer is 680.**

33. Once the florist receives the shipment of 30 white roses, he has $75 + 30 = 105$ white roses. Let $x =$ the number of red roses he should order. Once he places the order and receives the shipment, he will have $140 + x$ red roses. If he wishes for red roses to represent 5/8 of his rose inventory, he needs the expression (number of red roses) ÷ (total number of roses) to equal 5/8. Here is that condition represented as an equation, along with the steps required to solve the equation.

$$\frac{140 + x}{(140 + x) + 105} = \frac{5}{8} \Rightarrow \frac{140 + x}{245 + x} = \frac{5}{8} \quad \text{cross multiplication yields,}$$

$$8(140 + x) = 5(245 + x) \Rightarrow 1{,}120 + 8x = 1{,}225 + 5x \Rightarrow 3x = 105 \Rightarrow x = 35$$

The correct answer is 35.

34. This problem can be solved using the unit conversion technique most often taught in chemistry and physics classes.

$$105 \text{ pebbs} \cdot \frac{1 \text{ stum}}{11 \text{ pebbs}} \cdot \frac{8.43 \text{ ounces}}{1 \text{ stum}} \cdot \frac{1 \text{ pound}}{16 \text{ ounces}}$$

$$= \frac{105 \cdot 1 \cdot 8.43 \cdot 1}{1 \cdot 11 \cdot 1 \cdot 16} \text{ pounds} = \frac{885.15}{176} \text{ pounds} = 5.02926 \ldots \text{ pounds}$$

Rounding this result to the nearest hundredth yields the value 5.03. **The correct answer is 5.03.**

35. We use the formula for the length of an arc intercepted by a central angle of degree measure x, which is:

$$\text{Arc Length} = \frac{x}{360} \cdot (\text{circumference}) = \frac{x}{360} \cdot 2\pi r$$

Since the degree measure of the central angle is t, the radius is 15 cm, and the arc length is between 19 cm and 20 cm, we have,

$$19 < \frac{t}{360} 2\pi(15) < 20 \Rightarrow 19 < \frac{t}{360} 30\pi < 20$$

Multiplying all three parts of the second form of the inequality above by 360 gives us,
$19(360) < t(30\pi) < 20(360)$, or $6{,}840 < t(30\pi) < 7{,}200$. Dividing all three parts by 30π yields, $72.57 < t < 76.39$. Any integer between 72.57 and 76.39 is a correct answer. Therefore, **the correct answer is 73 or 74 or 75 or 76.**

eggheadprep.com

36. With the higher amount of pepper (2.5P) present, we have,

$$N = \frac{1}{3}k(2.5P)^2 = \frac{1}{3}k \cdot 6.25P^2.$$

With the lower amount of pepper (P) present, we have, $N = \frac{1}{3}kP^2$.

To find the ratio of the number of sneezes when the higher amount of pepper is present to the number when the lower amount of pepper is present, divide the two expressions found above.

$$\frac{\frac{1}{3}k \cdot 6.25P^2}{\frac{1}{3}kP^2} = \frac{6.25}{1} = 6.25$$

The correct answer is 6.25 or 25/4.

37. Since the value of the guitar will *increase* by 13% per year, the appropriate value for the growth factor r is 100% + 13% = 113% = 1.13. **The correct answer is 1.13.**

38. From the explanation for question #37 above, we know that $r = 1.13$, so the given formula may be rewritten with this value plugged in for r. The result is, $D = 3700(1.13)^t$, where t is the number of years. Therefore, the collector believes that the value of the guitar after 5 years will be, $D = 3700(1.13)^5 \approx$ $6,817.01. Rounding to the nearest whole dollar, $D \approx \$6,817$. **The correct answer is 6817.**

SCORING CONVERSION
RAW TO SCALED SCORE CONVERSION CHARTS

Sample Test 4:

A. SECTION 1: Conversion Chart for Reading Test:

RAW SCORE (# of correct answers)	READING TEST SCORE		RAW SCORE (# of correct answers)	READING TEST SCORE
0	10		27	26
1	10		28	26
2	10		29	27
3	11		30	27
4	12		31	28
5	13		32	28
6	14		33	28
7	15		34	29
8	16		35	29
9	16		36	30
10	17		37	30
11	18		38	31
12	18		39	31
13	19		40	32
14	20		41	32
15	20		42	33
16	21		43	33
17	21		44	34
18	22		45	35
19	22		46	35
20	23		47	36
21	23		48	37
22	23		49	38
23	24		50	39
24	24		51	39
25	25		52	40
26	25			

eggheadprep.com

B. SECTION 2: Conversion Chart for Writing and Language Test

RAW SCORE (# of correct answers)	WRITING AND LANGUAGE TEST SCORE		RAW SCORE (# of correct answers)	WRITING AND LANGUAGE TEST SCORE
0	10		23	26
1	10		24	26
2	10		25	27
3	10		26	27
4	11		27	28
5	12		28	29
6	13		29	29
7	14		30	30
8	15		31	31
9	16		32	31
10	16		33	32
11	17		34	32
12	18		35	33
13	19		36	33
14	19		37	34
15	20		38	35
16	21		39	36
17	22		40	37
18	23		41	37
19	23		42	38
20	24		43	39
21	24		44	40
22	25			

C. Evidence-Based Reading and Writing Section Score

To calculate the Evidence-Based Reading and Writing Section Score, add the Reading Test Score (10 – 40) to the Writing and Language Test Score (10 – 40), and then multiply that total by 10.

For example, if the Reading Test Score is 27 and the Writing and Language Test Score is 34, then the Evidence-Based Reading and Writing Section Score is,

$$27 + 34 = 61 \times 10 = 610.$$

SAMPLE TEST 4
Scoring Conversion

D. Sections 3 and 4: Math Test Score

The raw scores from Section 3 (Math—No Calculator) and Section 4 (Math—Calculator) should be added together to create the Math Raw Score. For example, if there were 18 correct answers in Section 3 (Math—No Calculator) and 24 in Section 4 (Math—Calculator), the Math Raw Score would be 18 + 24 = 42.

MATH RAW SCORE (Total # of correct answers, Sections 3 and 4 combined)	MATH SECTION SCORE		MATH RAW SCORE (Total # of correct answers, Sections 3 and 4 combined)	MATH SECTION SCORE
0	200		30	580
1	200		31	590
2	210		32	600
3	230		33	600
4	250		34	610
5	270		35	620
6	280		36	630
7	300		37	640
8	320		38	650
9	340		39	660
10	350		40	670
11	360		41	680
12	370		42	690
13	390		43	700
14	410		44	710
15	420		45	710
16	430		46	720
17	450		47	730
18	460		48	730
19	470		49	740
20	480		50	750
21	490		51	750
22	500		52	760
23	510		53	770
24	520		54	780
25	530		55	790
26	540		56	790
27	550		57	800
28	560		58	800
29	570			

eggheadprep.com

SAMPLE TEST 5

Including...

▶	SECTION 1: READING TEST	*414*
▶	ANSWERS, SECTION 1	*431*
▶	SECTION 2: WRITING & LANGUAGE TEST	*432*
▶	ANSWERS, SECTION 2	*447*
▶	SECTION 3: MATH TEST	*448*
▶	ANSWERS, SECTION 3	*454*
▶	SECTION 4: MATH TEST	*455*
▶	ANSWERS, SECTION 4	*466*
▶	ANSWER EXPLANATIONS	*467*
▶	SCORING CONVERSION	*501*

SECTION 1: READING TEST
65 MINUTES, 52 QUESTIONS

DIRECTIONS
Each group of questions below is based on a passage or pair of passages. Read each passage carefully, then choose the best answer to each question based on what is stated in or suggested by the passage(s). The questions may also refer to any graphical displays that accompany the passage(s), such as tables or graphs.

Questions 1-11 are based on the following passage.

This passage is adapted from Common Sense, *by Thomas Paine, written during the early stages of what would become the American Revolutionary War.*

By referring the matter from argument to arms, a new era for politics is struck; a new method of thinking has arisen. All plans and proposals prior to the commencement of hostilities are like the almanacs
[5] of last year, which, though proper then, are superseded and useless now. As much has been said of the advantages of reconciliation, it is right that we should examine the contrary side of the matter, and inquire into some of the material injuries which these
[10] colonies sustain, and always will sustain, by being connected with, and dependent on, Great Britain.

I have heard it asserted by some that, as America has flourished under its former connection with Great Britain, the same connection is necessary toward our
[15] future happiness, and will always have the same effect. Nothing can be more fallacious than this kind of argument. We may as well assert that because a child has thrived upon milk, the child should never have meat or vegetables. But even this is admitting
[20] more than is true, for I answer roundly that America would have flourished as much, and probably much more, had no European power had any thing to do with the colonies. The commerce by which the colonies have enriched themselves centers on the
[25] necessities of life, and will always have a market while eating is the custom of Europe.

But Great Britain has protected us, say some. That the British have defended this continent at our expense as well as their own is admitted, but they
[30] would have defended Turkey from the same motive, that is, for the sake of trade and dominion. We boast the protection of Great Britain without considering that the motive for such protection is *interest,* not *attachment*. The British do not protect us from *our*
[35] enemies on *our* account, but from *their* enemies on *their own* account—from those who had no quarrel with us on any *other* account. Let us throw off the dependence, and we should be at peace with France and Spain.

[40] But Britain is the parent country, say some. Then the more shame upon her conduct. Even brutes do not devour their young, nor savages make war upon their families; wherefore the assertion, if true, turns to her reproach. But it happens not to be true. For it is
[45] pleasant to observe by what regular gradations we surmount the force of local prejudice as we enlarge our acquaintance with the world. All Europeans who meet in America are *countrymen* to each other, be they from England, Holland, Germany, or Sweden.
[50] Not one third of the inhabitants of this continent are of English descent. I therefore reprobate the phrase of "parent" or "mother" country applied to England alone as being false, selfish, narrow, and ungenerous.

Much has been said of the united strength of
[55] Britain and the colonies, that in conjunction we might bid defiance to the world. But this is mere presumption, with respect to both the anticipated outcome and the legitimacy of the alliance. The fate of war is always uncertain, and this continent would
[60] never suffer itself to be drained of inhabitants to support the British arms in Asia, Africa, or Europe.

I challenge the warmest advocate for reconciliation to show a single advantage this continent can reap by being connected with Great

Britain. I repeat that not a single advantage is derived. Our corn will fetch its price in any market in Europe, and our imported goods must be paid for by us alone, buy them where we will. But the injuries and disadvantages we sustain by that connection are without number, and our duties to mankind at large, as well as to ourselves, instruct us to renounce the alliance, because any submission to, or dependence on, Great Britain tends directly to involve this continent in European wars and quarrels, and sets us at variance with nations who would otherwise seek our friendship, and against whom we have neither anger nor complaint. As Europe is our market for trade, we ought to form no partial connection with any part of it.

1. What is meant by the phrase, "referring the matter from argument to arms" in line 1?
   A) Those in disagreement over the cause of American independence should stop arguing and seek a referral to the appropriate arm of the continental government.
   B) The situation in the colonies has become more dangerous because power has shifted from the hands of those qualified to engage in intelligent debate over the matter of independence to the hands of those who possess the most powerful weaponry.
   C) If American colonists stop arguing over less important matters, they can stand together, arm in arm, and face the greater challenge of deciding whether to seek independence from Great Britain.
   D) The question of American independence is now being settled on the battlefield, rather than through parliamentary debate or political maneuvering.

2. As used in line 20, "roundly" is nearest in meaning to
   A) resoundingly.
   B) indirectly.
   C) eventually.
   D) uncertainly.

3. What specific reason does the author gives for the economic success of the American colonies?
   A) Representative government based on democratic elections
   B) Trade that is heavily based on exporting essential commodities, such as food
   C) Naval superiority over Great Britain and other European powers
   D) Trade agreements with Great Britain that create a market for American goods

4. Which option provides the strongest evidence in support of the answer to the previous question?
   A) Lines 12-16 ("I have … effect.")
   B) Line 19-23 ("But even … colonies.")
   C) Lines 23-26 ("The commerce … Europe.")
   D) Lines 41-43 ("Even brutes … families;")

5. The author implies that in addition to being motivated by self-interest, British protection of the American colonies actually

   A) creates enemies that the colonies would not otherwise have.
   B) yields many benefits that strengthen the connection between Great Britain and the colonies, a fact of which both the British and the colonists are rightly proud.
   C) is inferior to protection that could be provided by other European countries such as Spain.
   D) cannot be expected to continue, since Great Britain is distracted by conflicts in Europe and Asia.

6. Which option provides the strongest evidence in support of the answer to the previous question?

   A) Lines 27-31 ("That … dominion.")
   B) Lines 31-34 ("We boast … attachment.")
   C) Lines 34-39 ("The British … Spain.")
   D) Lines 54-56 ("Much … world.")

7. What is the meaning of the phrase, "the assertion, if true, turns to her reproach" (lines 43-44)?

   A) Viewing Great Britain as the "mother" country to the colonies may lead to a lessening of hostilities and the possibility of a peaceful resolution.
   B) Re-evaluating old conceptions about the relationship between the colonies and Great Britain may reveal that long-held beliefs are false, paving the way for a new era of cooperation.
   C) If it is true that Great Britain is the parent country to the colonies, then it is necessary to re-approach the question of American independence from a new perspective.
   D) If it is accurate to describe Great Britain as the parent country of the colonies, then that is all the more reason to view Great Britain unfavorably.

8. Apart from economic benefits, what specific benefit does the author claim the colonies have derived from associating with all of Europe, rather than with Great Britain alone?

   A) Greater protection from invasion by Asian or African powers
   B) Improved access to artistic centers in Paris, Florence, and other cities
   C) Reduction of regional prejudices and a growing sense of connectedness to people from many different countries
   D) The ability to engage in joint ventures in science and technology with experts from all over the world

9. Which of the following is a reason given by the author for doubting the validity of a military alliance between Great Britain and the colonies?

   A) Because British forces have been depleted by engagement in conflicts across multiple continents, Great Britain would be a weak and unreliable ally.
   B) Any such alliance is illusory, because American colonists would be unwilling to travel abroad to fight for British interests.
   C) Such an alliance would encourage war mongering, decreasing the likelihood of the "warmer" outcome of reconciliation.
   D) Great Britain would not be open to such an alliance because the colonies lack an organized military.

10. Which of the following could replace the phrase "at variance" in line 74 without any change of meaning?

    A) at odds
    B) of veracity
    C) in partnership
    D) in variants

11. As used in line 78, "partial" is nearest in meaning to

    A) incomplete.
    B) preferential.
    C) limited.
    D) deferential.

SAMPLE TEST 5
Section 1: Reading Test

Questions 12-22 are based on the following passage.

This passage is adapted from Agnes Grey, *by Anne Brontë.*

My sister Mary and I were brought up in the strictest seclusion. My mother, being at once highly accomplished, well informed, and fond of employment, took the whole charge of our education on herself, with
[5] the exception of Latin—which my father undertook to teach us—so that we never went to school. And, as there was no society in the neighborhood, our only intercourse with the world consisted in a stately tea party now and then with the principal farmers and tradespeople of the
[10] vicinity (just to avoid being stigmatized as too proud to consort with our neighbors), and our annual visit to our paternal grandparents. Sometimes our mother would amuse us with stories and anecdotes of her younger days, which, while they entertained us amazingly, frequently
[15] awoke—in me, at least—a secret wish to see a little more of the world.

I thought she must have been very happy in those days, but she never seemed to regret past times. My father, however, whose temper was neither tranquil nor
[20] cheerful by nature, often unduly vexed himself with thinking of the sacrifices his dear wife had made for him, and troubled his head with revolving endless schemes for the augmentation of his little fortune, for her sake and ours. In vain my mother assured him she was quite
[25] satisfied, and if he would but lay by a little for the children, we should all have plenty, both for time present and to come. But saving was not my father's forte. He would not run in debt (at least, my mother took good care he should not), but while he had money, he must spend it.
[30] He liked to see his house comfortable and his wife and daughters well clothed and well attended. He was charitably disposed, and liked to give to the poor, according to his means, or, as some might think, beyond them.

[35] At length, however, a kind friend suggested to him a means of doubling his private property at one stroke— and further increasing it, thereafter, to an untold amount. This friend was a merchant, a man of enterprising spirit and undoubted talent, who was somewhat straitened in
[40] his mercantile pursuits for want of capital. He generously proposed to give my father a fair share of his profits, if my father would only entrust him with what he could spare; and he thought he might safely promise that whatever sum my father chose to put into his hands, it
[45] should bring cent per cent in return. Thus it was that my family's small holdings were speedily sold, and the whole of their price deposited in the hands of the friendly merchant, who as promptly proceeded to arrange for the transport of his cargo and prepare for his voyage.

[50] My father was delighted, so were we all, with our brightening prospects. For the present, it was true, we were reduced to the narrow income of my father's humble work as a curate.* But my father seemed to think there was no necessity for scrupulously restricting our
[55] expenditures to that. So, with a standing bill at Mr. Jackson's, another at Smith's, and a third at Hobson's, we got along even more comfortably than before, though my mother affirmed we had better keep within bounds, for our prospects were but precarious, after all. If my
[60] father would only trust everything to her management, she offered, he should never feel himself stinted. Yet he, for once, was incorrigible.

What happy hours Mary and I passed while sitting at our work by the fire, or wandering the heath-clad hills, or
[65] idling under the weeping birch, talking of future happiness for ourselves and our parents, of what we would do, and see, and possess, with no firmer foundation for our goodly superstructure than the riches that were expected to flow in upon us from the success of
[70] the worthy merchant's speculations. Our father was nearly as bad as ourselves, only he affected not to be so much in earnest, expressing his bright hopes and sanguine expectations in jests and playful sallies that always struck me as exceedingly witty and pleasant. Our
[75] mother laughed with delight to see him so hopeful and happy, but still she feared he was setting his heart too much upon the matter. I once heard her whisper as she left the room, "God grant he be not disappointed!"

Disappointed he was, and bitterly, too. It came like a
[80] thunder clap on us all, news that the vessel that contained our fortune had wrecked and gone to the bottom with all its stores, together with several of the crew and the unfortunate merchant himself. I was grieved for him; I was grieved for the overthrow of all our air-built castles.
[85] But, with the elasticity of youth, I soon recovered from the shock.

Though riches had charms, poverty had no terrors for an inexperienced girl like me. Indeed, there was something exhilarating in the idea of being driven to
[90] straits and thrown upon our own resources. I only wished papa, mamma, and Mary were all of the same mind as myself. Mary did not lament, but she brooded continually over the misfortune, and sank into a state of dejection from which no effort of mine could rouse her. My mother
[95] thought only of consoling my father, and paying our debts by every available means. But my father was completely overwhelmed by the calamity: health, strength, and spirits sank beneath the blow, and he never wholly recovered them.

*An assistant to the vicar, or head, or the local church.

12. Which of the following is a specific cause mentioned by the narrator for the seclusion she and her sister experienced as children?

    A) Their family lived in a remote area, many miles from a town or village.
    B) They were not allowed to associated with children with different religious beliefs.
    C) Their family was stigmatized for being poor.
    D) They were home schooled.

13. What personal struggle does the narrator describe in the second paragraph (lines 17-34)?

    A) Her father's agonizing over his inability to provide for the family as he believed he should, in spite of many reassurances from his wife that his worries were unfounded
    B) Her mother's attempts to make peace with the contrast between past happiness and present discontentment
    C) Her father's fears that the success of his many financial schemes revolved around the misery of poor people, whom he did not have the means to help
    D) The narrator's own search for balance between opposites, such as tranquility versus cheerfulness, saving versus spending, and living for the present versus planning for the future.

14. As used in line 39, "straitened" means

    A) straightened.
    B) successful.
    C) constrained.
    D) greed-driven.

15. What was the narrator's opinion of her father's friend, the merchant?

    A) She found his tendency to keep secrets (to leave things "untold") to be suspicious.
    B) She believed he was overly miserly in his tendency to track every cent he invested or earned.
    C) She believed he was friendly and well meaning, but unskilled at his work.
    D) She believed he was an intelligent, determined man whom her father had good reason to trust.

16. What is the nature of the conflict between the narrator's mother and father described in the fourth paragraph (lines 50-62)?

    A) Her father was comfortable making friends with a number of people in the area, while her mother believed that the family should remain secluded within the boundaries of their own estate.
    B) Her mother believed that the family should live within the limitations of the family's current income, rather than counting on future wealth, while her father believed there was no reason to adhere to a strict budget.
    C) Her father believed that they should focus their expenditures on necessities, while her mother believed it would put them on precarious ground if they kept within those bounds and didn't give more consideration to their daughters' comfort.
    D) Her mother believed the family's affairs should be entrusted to someone with management experience, while her father was saddened by the idea, to the point of being inconsolable.

17. What is meant by the phrase, "with no firmer foundation for our goodly superstructure than the riches that were expected to flow in upon us from the success of the worthy merchant's speculations" (lines 67-70)?

    A) There could not be a more solid basis for making future plans than a partnership with the merchant, whose worth was established by past financial success as well as predictions of future wealth.
    B) The plans the narrator, her sister, and her father were making were not based on anything concrete, merely the presumption of future income from the merchant's venture.
    C) The merchant's wealth stemmed from shrewd investment in projects centered on the building of important infrastructure, such as bridges and canals.
    D) The narrator was inspired by the merchant's travels, and the way his business endeavors brought in a stream of wealth and goods from all over the world.

SAMPLE TEST 5
Section 1: Reading Test

18. How did the narrator's mother feel about the narrator's father's jokes about the family's future prospects?

    A) She did not find them funny and considered them inappropriate for the children to hear.

    B) She was afraid of disappointing him by not sharing in the laughter of her daughters.

    C) She found them very amusing and shared his optimistic outlook about the years ahead.

    D) She enjoyed them but was concerned that he was linking his happiness too exclusively to the possibility of increased wealth.

19. Which of the following best describes the outcome of the merchant's venture?

    A) All of the merchant's goods were lost when the ship on which he was traveling sank at sea; the merchant himself was killed in the disaster.

    B) The venture failed so utterly that the merchant lost everything and took his own life after killing several of his business partners.

    C) The venture was as successful as the merchant had projected, resulting in a steady flow of income for the family for many years, and the merchant receiving invitations to visit the castles of royalty.

    D) The venture was a great success, but the merchant did not keep his promises to the narrator's father, leaving the family at the bottom of the economic ladder.

20. Which option provides the strongest evidence in support of the answer to the previous question?

    A) Lines 40-45 ("He generously … return.")

    B) Lines 68-70 ("the riches … speculations.")

    C) Lines 80-83 ("news … himself.")

    D) Lines 84-85 ("I was … castles.")

21. As used in line 73, "sanguine" essentially means

    A) sorrowfully pessimistic.

    B) ancestrally related.

    C) unapologetically optimistic.

    D) sarcastic.

22. In what way does the narrator's attitude toward the events described in the passage differ from those of other members of her family?

    A) She is unable to bounce back like her sister and mother, becoming instead overwhelmed by feelings of grief and sadness that stay with her for years.

    B) She believes the rest of her family has given up on the possibility of increased wealth to easily, and encourages her father to continue pursuing joint ventures with merchants.

    C) Her lack of experience with economic hardship makes the situation much more terrifying for her than it is for her sister, mother, or father.

    D) Though saddened by the tragedy, she does not see any cause for despair, because she sees both wealth and financial struggle as opportunities for happiness.

Questions 23-32 are based on the following passage and supplemental information.

This passage summarizes a recently proposed hypothesis about the effects of Neaderthal DNA on modern human health. The species, homo neanderthalensis, *was an evolutionary "cousin," not a direct ancestor, of our own species,* homo sapiens. *The main facts presented in the passage are accurate, but some of the data have been fabricated to create figures appropriate for this test.*

Blaming the Caveman

High school biology students learn that organisms of different species cannot successfully interbreed—that is, they cannot mate and produce healthy offspring that can themselves reproduce. A donkey and a horse,
5 for example, can mate, resulting in the birth of a mule, but mules are sterile; they cannot have offspring of their own. Those who study biology in greater depth learn that this principle is oversimplified in high school textbooks: it is more accurate to say that creatures of
10 different species can interbreed *only with great difficulty*, but on rare occasions do succeed at it.

For proof of the possibility of such interbreeding, many modern humans (species *homo sapiens*) need only look as far as their own DNA. Today's advanced
15 genome mapping techniques have revealed that virtually all humans who have any ancestors from outside of sub-Saharan Africa (that is, from among the tribes that left Africa over 50,000 years ago) bear a small amount of non-*homo sapiens* DNA in their genes.
20 Specifically, the alien DNA came from Neanderthals, a separate hominid species (*homo neanderthalensis*) that dwelled in Europe and Asia, the descendants of ancient hominid ancestors who left Africa long before *homo sapiens* came into existence.

25   For the most part, this discovery has been viewed as just one of many curious cases of the occasionally successful intermingling of species during the long history of life on planet Earth. Some medical biologists are now suggesting, however, that modern humans'
30 absorption of traces of Neanderthal DNA was more detrimental than has been previously supposed. Statistics are showing with increasing clarity that humans of European or Asian descent have a significantly higher likelihood than those of solely sub-
35 Saharan African ancestry to suffer from immunological disorders such as allergies, antibody absence or deficiency, and autoimmune diseases like Crohn's disease, as well as from other health afflictions like depression and addiction. Evolutionary biologists point
40 out that the reason interbreeding of species usually fails is that the genes of the father and mother are too disparate to allow normal synthesizing of chromosomal pairs in offspring. Like all creatures, Neanderthals had immune systems based on unique
45 genetic coding that would create problematic mismatches when interlaced with the coding of another species. They also possessed brains that, though comparable in size to (actually slightly larger than) the brains of representatives of *homo*
50 *sapiens*, were organized differently than ours. It is possible, then, that many of the health woes of present-day humanity stem from genetic mismatches that put our bodily and mental systems at odds with themselves.

55   Possible, certainly, but no evidence presently available indicates clearly that such a conclusion is justified. The root cause of the proneness of European- and Asian-descended people to developing various ailments may in fact lie in what
60 their ancestors *lost* during the great migration out of Africa, not something they acquired. For it is well known that there is significantly greater genetic diversity among sub-Saharan Africans, especially those in East Africa (where species *homo sapiens*
65 arose) than among all other humans. In fact, if a randomly chosen person from the Americas were compared to a randomly chosen person from central Asia, it is rather likely that the two would be more genetically similar than two Ethiopians from
70 neighboring villages. We have long known that genetic homogeneity makes all animals vulnerable to health woes of all kinds and frequently causes immune system deficiencies. If indeed such homogeneity is the primary cause of many modern
75 human afflictions, then we may actually owe a debt of gratitude to *homo neanderthalensis* for adding a little variety to the human genetic stew.

SAMPLE TEST 5
Section 1: Reading Test

Figure 1

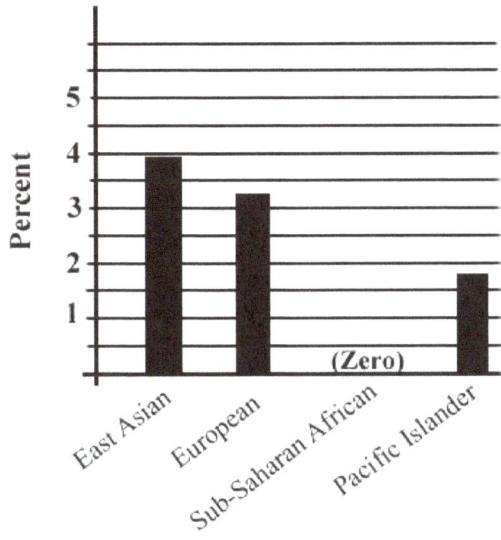

Average Percentage of Neanderthal DNA in Genes of Present-Day Humans of Various Groups

Figure 2

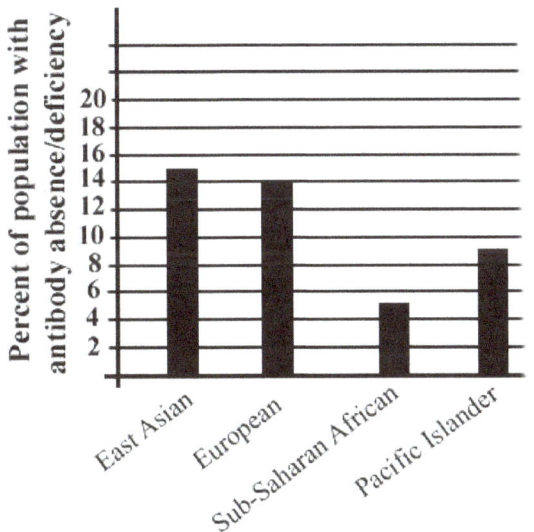

Prevalence of Antibody Absence or Deficiency Among Various Groups of Modern Humans

23. What is the primary purpose of the first paragraph of the passage (lines 1-11)?
    A) To explain a scientific principle and explain why it is frequently misunderstood
    B) To offer a critique of the teaching of science in schools
    C) To explain in detail the conditions under which different animals can successfully produce offspring
    D) To explain the differences between donkeys, horses, and mules

24. Which option best describes the passage as a whole?
    A) An enthusiastic description of a new discovery
    B) A skeptical analysis of a new scientific hypothesis, along with the presentation of an alternative hypothesis
    C) An aggressive rejection of a currently popular belief, along with a detailed presentation of evidence that contradicts that belief.
    D) An attempt to persuade the reader that current scientific practices cannot be trusted because hypotheses are constantly changing.

25. Which option best represents the meaning of "bear," as it is used in line 18?
    A) carry
    B) endure
    C) testify
    D) support

26. As used in line 20, "alien" is nearest in meaning to
    A) extra-terrestrial
    B) strange
    C) foreign
    D) non-citizen

27. According to the passage, which of the following is an accurate description of the history of *homo sapiens* and *homo neanderthalensis*, and of any interactions between the two species?

   A) Both species arose in Africa, then migrated together to Europe and Asia, interbreeding throughout their shared history.

   B) *Homo neanderthalensis* is a direct ancestor of *homo sapiens*. The two species did not exist simultaneously.

   C) *Homo sapiens* arrived in Europe and Asia several thousand years before *homo neanderthalensis* arrived there. It is unknown where the species *homo neanderthalensis* originated.

   D) The species *Homo neanderthalensis* evolved in Europe and Asia from African ancestors, but never existed in Africa. *Homo sapiens* encountered *homo neanderthalensis* after leaving Africa.

28. Which option provides the strongest evidence in support of the answer to the previous question?

   A) Lines 14-19 ("Today's … genes")

   B) Lines 19-24 ("Specifically, … existence.")

   C) Lines 43-47 ("Like all … species.")

   D) Lines 73-77 ("If indeed … stew.")

29. What is the main idea presented in the third paragraph (lines 25-54)?

   A) Regardless of a person's ancestry, living in sub-Saharan Africa reduces his or her risk of suffering from a variety of health problems, including mental health issues and immunological disorders.

   B) Neanderthals may have been more intelligent than modern humans because they possessed larger brains.

   C) Mismatches between *homo neanderthalensis* and *homo sapiens* DNA may be the cause of many health problems in present-day humans.

   D) The intermingling of *homo sapiens* and *homo neanderthalensis* may have been driven by the natural curiosity of one species about another; however, attempts by members of the two species to reproduce together largely failed.

30. The author proposes an explanation for the more frequent occurrence of certain health conditions in humans with European or Asian ancestry than in humans with only sub-Saharan African ancestry that does *not* involve Neanderthal DNA playing a role. Which option best summarizes that explanation?

   A) Humans with European or Asian ancestry display a relative lack of genetic variety.

   B) Sub-Saharan African peoples have not been exposed to many of the pathogens (bacteria and viruses) that are or were common in Asia and Europe.

   C) The root cause of the health conditions in question may be DNA from hominid species other than *homo neanderthalensis*.

   D) Conditions like immunological disorders and mental health challenges are not viewed negatively in sub-Saharan African cultures, so it is easier for those who suffer from such conditions to receive proper treatment.

31. Taken together, do Figure 1 and Figure 2 offer any support for the hypothesis presented in the third paragraph (lines 25-54)?

   A) Yes, because the graphs show that the percentage of Pacific Islanders who have Neanderthal DNA is roughly the same as the percentage of sub-Saharan Africans who suffer from certain health conditions.

   B) Yes, because the graphs show that one of the health conditions mentioned in the paragraph occurs more frequently among humans who have Neanderthal DNA than among those who do not.

   C) No, because the graphs show that even though sub-Saharan African people do not possess Neanderthal DNA, they still suffer from one of the health conditions mentioned in the paragraph.

   D) No, because the graphs do not provide any information about the percentage of people who suffer from depression or addiction.

32. What criticism of the data presented in the two figures would the author of the passage most likely offer?

   A) Several groups of humans are not represented, including humans living in the Americas.

   B) Only one of the health conditions discussed in the passage is represented in the data.

   C) Among all present-day human groups, Neanderthal DNA makes up less than 4 percent of genetic material. Therefore, such DNA could not affect the health of an individual.

   D) The graphs provide no information about the amount of genetic variation within each group of people studied.

Questions 33-42 are based on the following pair of passages. The authors named are fictitious.

Passage 1, by attorney Jerome P. Washington, esq.

    Few of our guaranteed protections as US citizens, few of the pillars upon which our society is built, do more to protect our most fundamental rights and freedoms as the assurance of a trial by jury for all those accused of
5 significant crimes. It was with great concern, therefore, that I learned recently of the comments of my friend and colleague, defense lawyer Kathleen Martin. That Ms. Martin is an exceptionally skilled attorney is beyond question, but when she speaks of abolishing the jury trial
10 system, she displays a recklessness with regard to safeguarding the liberty of all Americans that cannot go unanswered.
    Before evaluating any current practice within the justice system, it is prudent to review the history behind
15 the practice. Although the US legal system offers the option of a jury trial to more accused citizens than does any other legal system in the world, those who believe that Americans invented such trials have been poorly informed. The practice was common in England long
20 before the American colonies gained independence. The inclusion of the promise of trial by jury in the Bill of Rights, was, in fact, a direct response to the *denial* of jury trials to American colonists by British authorities in cases that, had they been tried in England, would have been
25 assigned a jury trial as a matter of course. Thus, although many aspects of the structure of the US Government have been described as a "grand experiment" undertaken by the founders, there was nothing experimental about the specification that accused persons shall be entitled to a
30 trial by a jury of their peers. The colonists were well acquainted with both trials by jury and trials by a judge alone. They did not dream up the idea of civilian juries; they expressed a clear preference for jury trials as the *superior* form of trial for the administering of justice
35 among all forms of trial that then existed.
    And it remains the superior form today. The implications of wresting power from the hands of ordinary citizens and concentrating it instead in the hands of single individuals should strike fear into all Americans'
40 hearts. A single, rogue judge could ruin the lives of thousands of innocent individuals over the course of his or her career. One should not be too quick to console oneself, either, with the thought that most judges are men and women of integrity who would never abuse their
45 power. Regardless of whether that characterization of judges is accurate in the present, it would not be so in the future. For under a system devoid of civilian juries, the power of judges would become absolute, and such unchecked power, by its very nature, will attract those
50 with the very worst of intentions.

Passage 2, by attorney Kathleen Martin, esq.

    I fully expected my recent remarks calling for major reforms of the jury trial system to spark an animated debate. Unfortunately, however, many of my esteemed
55 colleagues have, either deliberately or through ignorance, significantly misrepresented my arguments.
    I do not advocate, nor have I ever advocated, for the elimination of jury trials from the American justice system. Rather, it is my contention that the particulars of
60 the jury trial system, though they once represented the best practices available, are now woefully out of date, and that improvements can and should be made to bring us closer to what I trust is every American citizen's goal: creating the fairest, most just society Earth has ever seen.
65   A single example will demonstrate emphatically the need for reform. Several years ago, a jury in my home state struggled for a week in deliberations, ultimately agreeing that the prosecution's entire case rested on a single piece of witness testimony. Yet the jurors were
70 astonished to learn that under state law, they were not guaranteed access to a trial transcript, a reading of the transcript by a court reporter, or an audio or video recording of the testimony. Nor was such access granted to them. Why would we ever knowingly settle for a
75 system under which those determining guilt or innocence are denied access to evidence *that was ruled admissible by the court*? If we are to employ juries during trials, then surely the jurors must be granted every opportunity to evaluate every piece of evidence fully.
80   Consideration of how best to grant that opportunity necessarily forces one to re-evaluate the notion of juries composed entirely of civilians selected by random draw. Prior to the astounding scientific advances of the latter half of the twentieth century, it was reasonable to assume
85 that any citizen of sound mind was as qualified as any other to evaluate the evidence presented during a trial. Can such an assumption be defended in the year 2016? Forensic and demographic research alone—research with which even most college graduates have but a passing
90 familiarity—have radically altered the views of experts on the nature of criminal activity. To expect twelve people plucked from their everyday lives to have the knowledge required to evaluate the testimony of a witness described as a DNA "expert," for example, is simply unreasonable.
95   For these reasons and many others, I have proposed replacing traditional 12-person juries with juries comprised of nine ordinary citizens and three non-voting consultants with demonstrated expertise in fields relevant to the facts of the case (for example, an expert on
100 demographic patterns related to gun ownership). Jurors

should also have access *in the jury room* to a complete trial transcript and trusted digital reference guides. Thus, my goal is not to take power away from ordinary citizens, but to give them the resources they need to exercise the
105 power they are granted as responsibly as possible.

33. What is the primary argument put forth by the author of Passage 1 in the second paragraph (lines 13-35)?
   A) Although the idea of jury trials was new and untested at the time the Bill of Rights was written, such trials have been proven effective since then.
   B) The guarantee of jury trials in the Bill of Rights came about as the result of the colonists having the opportunity to compare the outcomes of jury and non-jury trials.
   C) Jury trials originated in England; therefore, since such trials are still employed there, it is logical to continue the practice in the US.
   D) The American colonists chose jury trials as the centerpiece of the US justice system primarily because that was the only form of trial with which they were familiar.

34. How does the author of Passage 1 believe the abolition of jury trials would affect the composition of the judiciary?
   A) He believes that a greater number of unscrupulous individuals would seek to become judges.
   B) He believes that more people of great integrity would wish to serve as judges.
   C) He believes that women would be discouraged from serving as judges.
   D) He believes that many individuals without sufficient legal experience would be elected as judges.

35. Which option provides the strongest evidence in support of the answer to the previous question?
   A) Lines 30-32 ("The colonists … alone.")
   B) Lines 32-35 ("They did … existed.")
   C) Lines 42-45 ("One should … power.")
   D) Lines 47-50 ("For under … intentions.")

36. As used in line 37, "wresting" is nearest in meaning to
   A) wreaking
   B) regenerating
   C) snatching
   D) accepting

37. Which statement in Passage 1 justifies the claim made by the author of Passage 2 that her opinions have been misrepresented?

    A) Lines 5-7 ('It was ... Martin.")
    B) Lines 7-12 ("That ... unanswered.")
    C) Lines 13-15 ("Before ... practice.")
    D) Lines 15-19 ("Although ... informed.")

38. How would the author of Passage 2 most likely respond to the assertion in Passage 1 that jury trials were the "*superior* form of trial for the administering of justice among all forms of trial that then existed" (lines 34-35)?

    A) She would deny that jury trials represent a superior form of trial, and point out the advantages of a trial conducted solely under the authority of a well-qualified judge.
    B) She would dispute the claim that at the time of the writing of the Bill of Rights, jury trials were the best form of trial available, but would agree that current jury trial practices are the best possible practices in the present day.
    C) She would acknowledge that jury trials are more in the spirit of the founding principles of the US, but would claim that trials by a judge alone are more practical in most cases.
    D) She would agree that jury trials, as currently practiced, are superior to any other form of trial that existed when the Bill of Rights was written, but would assert that they are not the best possible form of trial that could exist today.

39. What primary point is the author of Passage 2 making in the third paragraph of the passage (lines 65-79)?

    A) Simply guaranteeing defendants a trial by jury does not ensure that a just verdict will be reached, since jurors may not have sufficient access to, or understanding of, important evidence.
    B) Witness testimony is an unreliable basis for determining the guilt or innocence of a defendant, and therefore it is wise to limit jurors' access to such testimony.
    C) Many juries make unreasonable requests of the court, causing substantial delays and impairing the functioning of the entire US system of justice.
    D) The science of DNA is not well understood; therefore, it is not reasonable for DNA evidence to be admissible in court.

40. Which word or phrase could replace the word "comprised" in line 97 without any change of meaning?

    A) made up
    B) compromised
    C) conformed
    D) despoiled

41. Which of the following is NOT a specific reform of the current jury trial system proposed by the author of Passage 2?

    A) Changing the number of ordinary citizens who serve on a jury
    B) The addition of participants in jury deliberations who do not vote on the final verdict
    C) Alteration of rules regarding jurors' access to both trial evidence and supplementary infor- mation
    D) Revising jury selection procedures to ensure that all juries are diverse in their composition

42. A scholar who analyzed the two passage claims that the fundamental cause of conflict between the two authors is a difference in priorities. Which of the following options offers reasonable hypotheses about the first priority of each author?

    A) The first priority of the author of Passage 1 is remaining true to historical traditions; the first priority of the author of Passage 2 is increasing the power of authority figures such as judges.
    B) The first priority of the author of Passage 1 is experimentation and the exploration of new ideas; the first priority of the author of Passage 2 is preserving practices that have a proven record of success.
    C) The first priority of the author of Passage 1 is protection of individual freedoms and power; the first priority of the author of Passage 2 is improving the likelihood of an accurate verdict in criminal trials.
    D) The first priority of the author of Passage 1 is for trials to be conducted swiftly and efficiently; the first priority of Passage 2 is infusing trials with an appropriate tone of respect and seriousness.

Questions 43-52 are based on the following passage.

This passage is adapted from "In Stasis," my Karin E. Dahlin. ©2010 K. E. Dahlin and Coeval *literary journal. Reprinted by permission of the author.*

    Today, I took my tea and my notebook to the Mill Pond at Lincoln. My assigned task was to summon metaphors for memory. It rained a cold fall rain, the dampness filtering into my mind. Water, dense, taut at
5 its surface, carries all the years in stasis.
    Yesterday, I read a funny story by Albert Goldbarth. He invents intricate anecdotes of his own past lives; what he wants to show is that made-up stories do more than entertain. Stories make real memories: we can
10 actually be connected to our past selves, and to each other, through things that never happened. "It's not that we lie," he explains. "It's that we *make* the truth."
    My older brother, Joel, was my only steady playmate growing up. Between grades one and five, I
15 attended five separate schools. Amid all that changing of place, Joel was a constant.
    Joel is careful with his speech. He likes to *craft* each thought, he tells me. As a child, he said very little around strangers. In our exclusive kid domain, however,
20 he could relax into creativity. I was one of the lucky few admitted into his glimmering world of ingenuity.
    Whenever we were bored, Joel and I would step into stories. We would peer inside our skulls and unfold sagas of foreign lands, peril, and clever escape. We even
25 named this tapestry of adventures: we called it, "Lost Kids." Most often, we were kidnapped by strangers and dropped from an airplane into some unfamiliar wilderness, left to die. Conveniently, our kidnappers tended to overlook our smuggled survival gear: shovels,
30 pocketknives, and flint. Our own cleverness saved the day, as we fashioned a sturdy shelter from driftwood or cast an axe from scrap iron. Eventually, when the day grew long and our energy short, we swiftly found our way home.
35   I remember how, one lazy summer morning, Joel and I were pushed from a plane into the yawn of an empty sky…

    We drifted down slowly through the thick air,
40 settling into the wide mouth of the water, the sea slipping between my fingers and toes. I opened my eyes to gaze upward through the salt. A few feet to my left, Joel billowed in an oversized t-shirt and blue shorts, his pajamas. We crawled to the surface, clinging to frothy
45 foam. We floated sleepily on our backs, waves rumpling around us like bed sheets. The sea carried us forward until our shoulders settled into the soft sand of an island's shore. By the time our ankles left the water, we were already dry.
50   I remember all of this more vividly than I remember most of my birthdays. The disjointed fragments of narrative pull me inward to new way of seeing. At twenty, I am only a breath away from opening my eyes and gazing into an eight-year-old's
55 world. I inhabit the full breadth of this remembered expanse, but I do not inhabit it alone. I peer through scraps of detail, shards of image, squinting for clarity. And look, there is Joel, billowing in his pajamas.

60   My 11th grade chemistry teacher once told me everything is made up of mostly nothing. She said that in every atom, a vast expanse of emptiness, filled only by invisible magnetism, electrical energy, and unknowable nuclear forces, exists between the nucleus
65 and the electrons. I am, at this moment, resting my feet on a coffee table; even its dense wood is made up primarily of empty space.
    Yet I'm not quite sure I agree with my teacher's classification of that empty space as "nothing." Forces
70 and energies are certainly something. They carry the pieces together in a delicate balance through time and space. This balance determines the very identity of all matter. I would venture so far as to say that this "nothing" of unseen forces is even more real than the
75 "somethings" of electrons, protons, and neutrons.
    Maybe memory has building blocks like electrons and nuclei—what *really* happened. But maybe we give it shape and meaning, the delicate balance that holds it all together, with that nebulous
80 force field—what we *say* happened.

    Saint Augustine thought some funny things about memory. He believed we experience memories as impressions—in the physical sense—in our brains;
85 we can feel only one tiny piece of the impression at a time. I think he must have meant that it is like closing one's eyes and using just one finger to decipher an embossed word on a book cover. One can only touch one letter at a time, but the whole word is always
90 there, from the first letter to the last.

    As I sat this morning, light sparked from the raindrops as they met the pond, the water sizzling. The raindrops opened the surface of the pond and slipped
95 inside. Memory, like the water cycle, carries all the years at once.

43.
Which of the following is the best description of the passage as a whole?

A) The author recounts harrowing experiences from her own childhood to illustrate the dangers children face in today's world.

B) The author uses her own memories as a metaphor in order to provide a detailed explanation of complex scientific principles such as atomic theory and the water cycle.

C) The author uses her own recollections as the basis for speculating about the relationship between events, memories, and creative storytelling.

D) The author demonstrates the unreliability of human memory and advocates exploring the world using only scientific methods.

44.
What reason does the author imply for her brother, Joel, being her only long-term playmate during her childhood?

A) She had difficulty making friends due to social anxiety.

B) She grew up in a neighborhood where there were no other children present.

C) She held different values than other children who lived in the area.

D) Her family moved frequently.

45.
The author uses the phrase "peer inside our skulls" (line 23) to describe

A) medical X-rays.
B) imaginative play.
C) ear and sinus examinations.
D) examination of a collection of fossils.

46.
What is the author's primary purpose for including the story told in the seventh paragraph (lines 39-49)?

A) To illustrate her assertion that a memory of imagined events can be just as vivid as a memory of actual events To explain how lightweight, loose clothing can help a person float more easily in sea-water

B) To draw a contrast between the saltwater in her recollection and the freshwater of the pond described in the first paragraph (lines 1-5)

C) To make a connection between the water cycle, as exhibited in a rain shower, and the tidal motion of ocean water toward a shore

47.
Which option offers the strongest evidence in support of the answer to the previous question?

A) Lines 42-46 ("A few … sheets.")
B) Lines 46-48 ("The sea … shore.")
C) Lines 50-51 ("I … birthdays.")
D) Lines 92-95 ("At … inside.")

48.
In saying that she is only "a breath away … from gazing into an eight-year-old's world" (lines 53-55), the author means that

A) there are many children nearby at the pond, and she could readily join in their games.

B) her birthday memories include blowing out candles on a cake when she turned eight years old.

C) she is amazed at how quickly twelve years have passed.

D) she feels very little separation between her memories and the present moment.

49.
As used in line 79, "nebulous" is nearest in meaning to

A) unyielding.
B) formless.
C) nuclear.
D) fragile.

50. Which of the following is NOT a metaphor that the author employs in describing the nature of memory?

   A) The structure of an atom
   B) An intricately woven tapestry
   C) Earth's water cycle
   D) Reading raised lettering by feel

51. Which of the following words or phrases could replace the word "decipher" in line 87 without changing the meaning of the sentence?

   A) make sense of
   B) recite
   C) precisely define
   D) erase

52. Which of the following options best summarizes the author's view of the nature of memories, as expressed in the passage?

   A) They are a source of joy throughout one's life, so it is critically important to preserve them in words (such as journal entries) and images (such as videos).
   B) It is better to trust one's own memories of events than to rely on the reports of others, since people often describe their experiences dishonestly.
   C) Memories of real events have a very different nature from memories of events concocted in the mind; one can easily distinguish between the two.
   D) Either memories exist in our minds in fragmented form, or we can only access them in fragments; we use creativity to unite those pieces into a whole.

STOP

If you have finished this section before time expires, you may check your work. You cannot return to this section once you move on to the next section.

STOP!

If you have finished this section before time expires, you may check your work. You cannot return to this section once you move on to the next section.

www.eggheadprep.com

ANSWERS, SECTION 1
SAMPLE TEST 5 — READING

1. D
2. A
3. B
4. C
5. A
6. C
7. D
8. C
9. B
10. A
11. B
12. D
13. A
14. C
15. D
16. B
17. B
18. D
19. A
20. C
21. C
22. D
23. A
24. B
25. A
26. C
27. D
28. B
29. C
30. A
31. B
32. D
33. B
34. A
35. D
36. C
37. B
38. D
39. A
40. A
41. D
42. C
43. C
44. D
45. B
46. A
47. C
48. D
49. B
50. B
51. A
52. D

eggheadprep.com

SECTION 2:
WRITING & LANGUAGE TEST

35 MINUTES, 44 QUESTIONS

DIRECTIONS

Below you will find a number of reading passages. Each one is accompanied by a series of questions. A note before each passage will tell you which questions are related to that passage. Some questions will require you to consider possible revisions to the passage to help the writer express the ideas more clearly or effectively. Other questions will ask you to consider ways to edit the passage to correct errors in punctuation, word usage, or sentence structure. Some questions and passages include graphics, such as tables and graphs. As you make your decisions about possible changes, you should take the graphics into consideration along with the text.

Some questions will refer to a specific, underlined portion of the passage. Others will ask you to focus on a particular location within the passage. There will also be questions that ask you to think about the passage as a whole. Numbers enclosed in parentheses and written with a Q, such as (Q14) indicate the number of the question associated with that portion of the passage. Numbers bracketed in plain text, like [2], are used to identifying sentences within the passage, whereas a number surrounded by dashes, like –2– identifies a paragraph.

Read each passage and then choose the answer to each question that best improves the writing of the passage or brings the particular phrase or sentence into agreement with the conventions of standard written English. If you believe the best choice is to leave the indicated portion of the passage as it is, choose the option, "NO CHANGE."

SAMPLE TEST 5
Section 2: Writing & Language Test

Questions 1 – 11 are based on the following passage.

The dangers of motorcycle riding are well known to anyone who has ever witnessed the gut-wrenching scene of a shattered bike **(Q1)** construed across several lanes of a freeway. **(Q2)** Consequently, the allure of the open road continues to tug at the heart strings of men and women of all ages, drawing a whole new crop of riders into the two-wheel world every year. If you are considering joining their ranks, seek out the best safety training available in your area. While no amount of preparation can eliminate the risks associated with riding, receiving a thorough education in motorcycle handling techniques and defensive riding strategies **(Q3)** minimizes those risks.

1.
   A) *NO CHANGE
   B) *obstructed
   C) *strewn
   D) *conveyed

2.
   A) *NO CHANGE
   B) *Similarly,
   C) *In addition,
   D) *Nevertheless,

3.
   A) *NO CHANGE
   B) *is minimizing
   C) *minimize
   D) *have minimized

Outstanding motorcycle safety courses are offered in every major US **(Q4)** city, and also a surprising number of small towns have topnotch training centers as well. Finding the best educational program in your region will take some research, however. Some motorcycle safety courses offer **(Q5)** little more then a few rudimentary pointers on how to keep the bike upright. Well-designed training programs are challenging and intense, requiring aspiring riders to master precise evasive maneuvers and learn the safest ways to go down to the pavement when there is no other option. **(Q6)** After all, the majority of motorcycle accidents are caused by an automobile driver failing to see a cyclist, often a cyclist who is responsibly honoring the rules of the road. The best riders never assume

4.
- A) NO CHANGE
- B) city; a surprising number of small towns have
- C) city. Also, a surprising number of small towns have
- D) city, and also there are a surprising number of small towns with

5.
- A) NO CHANGE
- B) a little more then a few
- C) little more than a few
- D) few more than little

6.

At this point, the author is considering adding the following sentence.

> Safe riding does not come from physical techniques alone, however; rather, it arises from the blending of bike handling skills with constant awareness of everything happening on the road.

Should the author add this sentence here?

- A) Yes, because it creates a link between the previous sentences and the ideas presented in the rest of the paragraph.
- B) Yes, because it stresses the importance of bike handling skills, a point that is not made elsewhere within the paragraph.
- C) No, because it simply reformulates ideas expressed earlier in the paragraph.
- D) No, because it blurs the focus of the paragraph by introducing the concept of awareness, which is irrelevant to a discussion of training for motorcycle riders.

that they are visible to motorists. The best instructional programs, **(Q7)** though, will teach you how to develop a defensive riding strategy based on anticipating the actions of drivers who do not see you.

[1] Before you even sit on your new bike in your driveway and daydream of the adventures ahead of you, investing in a high-quality helmet is imperative. [2] **(Q8)** Traumatic Brain Injury (TBI); a classification that describes injuries ranging from temporary and mild to permanent and life changing, is a common and tragic outcome of motorcycle crashes. [3] Although helmets do not by any means eliminate the possibility of TBI, they do significantly reduce the risk of such an injury. [4] As important as rider safety programs are, receiving such training should actually be the second step of your preparation for years of safe and memorable experiences on the road. [5] Whether your state requires helmet use while riding is irrelevant. [6] Science and common sense both point to the same conclusion: you should never ride without a helmet. [7] **(Q9)** And while you're at the motorcycle shop picking out a helmet to match your personal style, purchase some sturdy, body-covering clothing as well. [8] Pavement and skin don't mix.

Approached sensibly and with diligent preparation, motorcycling can provides years of peaceful, soul-stirring adventures on the many scenic, winding country roads of North America. **(Q11)** Therefore, due to the excellent gas mileage motorcycles offer, making the switch to two wheels can be a money-saving and environmentally responsible choice for city dwellers, too.

7.
A) NO CHANGE
B) however,
C) because they
D) therefore,

8.
A) NO CHANGE
B) Traumatic Brain Injury (TBI), a classification that describes injuries ranging from temporary and mild to permanent and life changing, is
C) Traumatic Brain Injury (TBI): a classification that describes injuries ranging from temporary and mild to permanent and life changing, are
D) Traumatic Brain Injury (TBI), a classification that describes injuries ranging from temporary and mild to permanent and life changing is

9.
A) NO CHANGE
B) And while your at the motorcycle shop picking out a helmet to match your personal style,
C) And while you're at the motorcycle shop picking out a helmet to match you're personal style,
D) And while your at the motorcycle shop picking out a helmet to match you're personal style,

10.
In order for the paragraph to be as logical as possible, sentence 4 should be placed
A) Before sentence 1.
B) After sentence 2.
C) Where it is now.
D) After sentence 5.

11.
A) NO CHANGE
B) Nonetheless,
C) Furthermore,
D) As a result,

Questions 12-22 are based on the following passage.

NOTE: This passage is fictional; all quotations, events, and data described have been fabricated to create the passage. General statements made about forest fires and the regeneration of jack pines are accurate, however.

For Jack's Sake: Fire Management in Coniferous Forests

Messages about the dangers posed by human-caused wildfires are prevalent in the US today, and well they should be: a single act of human carelessness can adversely affect several million acres of forestland for decades. Many people are therefore surprised to learn that naturally occurring forest **(Q12)** fires, generally, those ignited by lightning strikes, although there are a few other rare phenomena that trigger them—are actually beneficial for many forest ecosystems. The US Forest Service has acknowledged that past management practices based on the principle of extinguishing every blaze as quickly as possible **(Q13)** was misguided, and has implemented new policies **(Q14)** where Forest Service personnel had allowed many natural fires to burn. Sensationalized coverage of the policy change by media outlets stimulated heated public debates, **(Q15)** actually calling for the arrest of Forest Service officials for destruction of public property. At least one US "resident" must be ecstatic to learn of the change, however: the northern jack pine.

12.
A) NO CHANGE
B) fires; generally, those ignited by lightning strikes, although there are a few other rare phenomena that trigger them, are
C) fires—generally, those ignited by lightning strikes, although there are a few other rare phenomena that trigger them—are
D) fires generally, those ignited by lightning strikes— although there are a few other rare phenomena that trigger them—are

13.
A) NO CHANGE
B) were
C) has been
D) as having been

14.
A) NO CHANGE
B) where Forest Service personnel allows
C) relating to Forest Service personnel having allowed
D) under which Forest Service personnel allow

15.
A) NO CHANGE
B) with some politicians actually calling
C) to actually call
D) DELETE the underlined portion

Jack pines are conifers, trees with needlelike leaves that store (Q16) it's seeds in cones. (Q17) <u>Mature jack pines are scraggly and asymmetrical. They wouldn't be likely to win a human-judged beauty pageant for evergreens.</u> Yet to many wildlife species, these iconic northern trees are very beautiful, indeed. (Q18) <u>In fact, northern US mixed coniferous forests in which jack pines make up more than 60 percent of all trees present have the highest wildlife diversity among all such forests.</u> Jack pine dominance of a forest tends to be short lived, however. Through the process known as forest succession, jack pines give way over time to their more

16.
- A) NO CHANGE
- B) its
- C) their
- D) they're

17. Which of the following options represents the most effective way to combine the two underlined sentences?

- A) Mature jack pines are scraggly and asymmetrical, resulting in their not being likely to have won a human-judged beauty pageant for evergreens.
- B) Mature jack pines wouldn't be likely to win a human-judged beauty pageant for evergreens, they are scraggly and asymmetrical.
- C) Mature jack pines are scraggly and wouldn't be likely to win a human-judged beauty pageant for evergreens, as they are also asymmetrical.
- D) Scraggly and asymmetrical, mature jack pines wouldn't be likely to win a human-judged beauty pageant for evergreens.

18. The author wants this sentence to reflect the data presented in Figure 1 below. Which option best accomplishes this goal?

- A) NO CHANGE
- B) In fact, the number of wildlife species present in northern mixed coniferous forests continuously increases as the percentage of jack pines present in the forest increases.
- C) In fact, northern US mixed coniferous forests in which jack pines account for about 30 percent of all trees present harbor fewer than half as many wildlife species as those in which jack pines account for over 40 percent of the trees present.
- D) In fact, northern US mixed coniferous forests in which jack pines make up between 45 and 60 percent of all trees present harbor at least twice the number of wildlife species as those in which less than 20 percent of trees are jack pines.

robust cousins, red and white pines, as well as to shallow-rooted spruces. (Q19) <u>Dr. Melanie Jackson, a plant biologist at the University of Minnesota-Bemidji, states that,</u> "In any northern forest of mixed conifers, jack pines will inevitably be squeezed out within the first century after their initial rise to dominance."

[1] Nevertheless, jack pines still exist in large numbers in many wild forests, seemingly against all odds. [2] The key to the survival of the species is what amounts to a secret evolutionary weapon. [3] Jack pine cones, however, do not open frequently or easily. [4] For a conifer to reproduce, the tree's cones must open, releasing the seeds to fall to the ground, where they either germinate in place or are consumed by browsing animals that expel them elsewhere in the forest. [5] In fact, only one catalyst can coax the cones of a mature jack pine tree to release the treasure they protect: extreme heat. [6] Naturally occurring forest fires thus result in a "blizzard" of jack pine seeds coating the forest floor, where they have immediate access to the nutrient-rich soil and ash left behind in the wake of the fire. [7] Those fortunate enough to come upon an expanse of northern conifer forest during the first three decades after a significant fire know that (Q20) <u>it's</u> an unforgettable sight, with thousands of jack pines of nearly identical height stretching out as far as the eye can see. [8] (Q21) <u>Northern coniferous forests that burned between 40 and 50 years ago have about half the percentage of jack pines as those that burned within the past 10 years.</u>

While it remains an important goal to eliminate wildfires

19.
A) NO CHANGE
B) Dr. Melanie Jackson, a plant biologist, at the University of Minnesota-Duluth states that
C) Dr. Melanie Jackson; a plant biologist at the University of Minnesota-Duluth states that,
D) Dr. Melanie Jackson—a plant biologist—at the University of Minnesota-Duluth states, that

20.
A) NO CHANGE
B) its
C) they're
D) it would have been

21. Which statement most accurately expresses information conveyed in Figure 2?
A) NO CHANGE
B) Northern coniferous forests that burned between about 17 and 37 years ago have at least twice the percentage of jack pines as those that have not burned in the last 75 years.
C) Northern coniferous forests in which jack pines account for 80 percent of all trees present are much more likely to burn than similar forests with a lower percentage of jack pines.
D) Northern coniferous forests that burned about 15 years ago have approximately the same percentage of jack pines as those that burned approximately 70 years ago.

22. The most logical position for sentence 3 would be
A) before sentence 2.
B) where it is now.
C) after sentence 4.
D) after sentence 5.

caused by human negligence, when it comes to naturally occurring fires in the North, the best policy is to let them burn as nature intended, for jack's sake.

Figure 1: *Relationship between wildlife diversity and jack pine prevalence in northern mixed conifer forests*

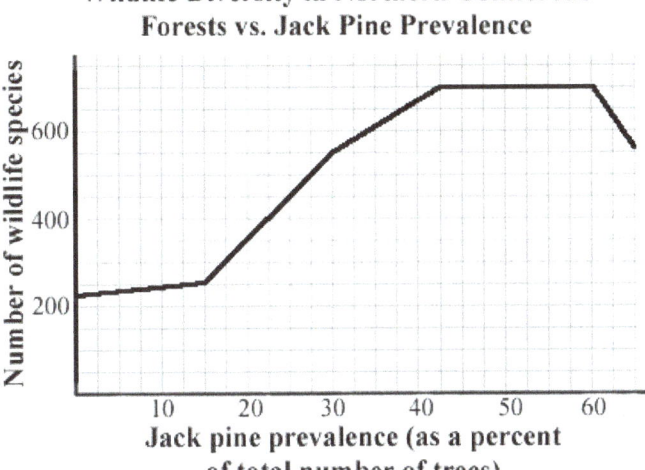

Figure 2: *Relationship between jack pine prevalence in northern mixed coniferous forests and time elapsed since last fire*

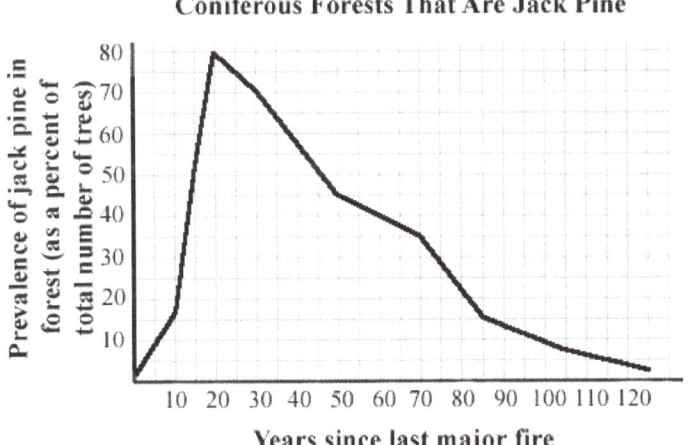

Questions 23-33 are based on the following passage.

Pajama Professionals: A Look at Modern Freelancing

During the twentieth century, those who **(Q23)** <u>espoused</u> traditional jobs and attempted to make a living through freelance work were often seen as **(Q24)** <u>they're being</u> slackers, people unwilling to make the sacrifices required to build a successful long-term career. Although **(Q25)** <u>most people now view freelancers with respect,</u> changing workplace realities have prompted many professionals to re-evaluate their feelings toward the freelancing lifestyle. In truth, the change is more a result of diminishing faith in the viability of traditional careers than of growing appreciation for the contributions freelance professionals make to society. For many years in the 1900s, signing on as an employee of a large company or nonprofit organization assured a worker of an excellent benefits package, long-term job **(Q26)** <u>security, and they were also promised a</u> comfortable pension. Few employers offer personnel more than one of those perks anymore; many offer none of them. In addition, many young people entering the workforce today fear that in this age of hyper-specialization, accepting any traditional job will lead to a lifetime of being pigeonholed.

23.
- A) NO CHANGE
- B) expounded
- C) esteemed
- D) eschewed

24.
- A) NO CHANGE
- B) they're having been
- C) their being like
- D) DELETE the underlined portion

25. Which option connects the sentence to the previous sentence while effectively setting up the rest of the passage?
- A) NO CHANGE
- B) some traditionalists still cling to that disparaging view of freelancers,
- C) freelance work is an undesirable option for many people due to the irregular hours,
- D) freelancers enjoy being their own bosses,

26.
- A) NO CHANGE
- B) security; also there was the promise of a
- C) security, and that they would receive a
- D) security, and a

(Q27) In response to that growing demand, numerous online freelancing websites have sprouted up in the US, Australia, and elsewhere. Work available through such websites includes not only quick turnaround projects for nominal **(Q28)** pay, there are also long-lasting, collaborative endeavors that can go a long way toward providing a professional with a comfortable and secure living. Those who enter the realm of online freelancing with the expectation of a leisurely routine of working in sweatpants without a financial care face a rude awakening, however. Competition is fierce, and it behooves any aspiring freelancer to thoroughly **(Q29)** research the pitfalls of online work. All freelancers should be especially wary of accepting "spec work" arrangements. "Spec" indicates **(Q30)** specific, meaning that there is no guarantee of payment for work completed. Often, spec work takes the form of a contest: numerous freelancers are asked to complete a project such as the design of a logo, and only the one creator designated as the contest winner receives any payment. Entering a few such competitions may be a useful way to gain some experience and build up a portfolio of completed work, but overall, spec work is a lopsided, exploitative arrangement that most freelancers should avoid.

27. At this point, the author is considering adding the following sentence.

    > Whatever the reason, the number of college graduates seeking to build a career out of freelance projects has more than tripled since 1996.

    Should the author make this addition?

    A) Yes, because it links the current paragraph to the previous paragraph's discussion of changing attitudes and sets up the next sentence.
    B) Yes, because it creates a distinction between workers with a college degree and those without one, which sets up the information that follows.
    C) No, because "more than tripled" is a vague description that would create confusion and blur the focus of the paragraph.
    D) No, because it introduces a statistic without showing the relevance of the statistic to the main ideas of the passage.

28.
    A) NO CHANGE
    B) pay but also long-lasting,
    C) pay, also including long-lasting,
    D) pay, they also have included long-lasting,

29.
    A) NO CHANGE
    B) research around the pitfalls
    C) research over the pitfalls
    D) be researching the pitfalls

30.
    A) NO CHANGE
    B) specialized
    C) speculative
    D) specified

Most importantly, "pajama professionals," as online freelancers are sometimes called, should negotiate as many of **(Q31)** his or her contracts as possible through reputable websites with strict regulations and sophisticated anti-fraud mechanisms. Yes, such websites do take a significant percentage of all money paid by employers to freelancers (generally 8-12 percent), but that is a small price to pay to be protected from the plethora of online employment scams in existence today. Even members of legitimate freelancing websites must remain vigilant. For example, they should be extremely wary of any prospective employer who pressures applicants to move all communications, including contract negotiations, offsite. In the vast majority of cases, **(Q32)** this is a telltale sign that the employer is a con artist, an intellectual property thief, or an identity thief. Legitimate hirers of online freelancers will be happy to execute contracts subject to third party review and to make an initial deposit of funds for the project into a secure reserve, thus guaranteeing that the freelancer will receive payment upon project completion.

It remains true that for most people, the simplicity and predictability of a traditional job is preferable to the somewhat chaotic life of a freelancer. For those who aspire above all else to work on their own terms, however, the proliferation of online freelancing platforms **(Q33)** is confusing and intimidating, so it is best to pursue other opportunities instead.

31.
   A) NO CHANGE
   B) their
   C) one's
   D) they're

32.
   A) NO CHANGE
   B) these are a
   C) such behavior is a
   D) this is representing a

33. The author wishes to end the passage on a positive note while stating a conclusion that is consistent with the rest of the passage. Which option best accomplishes the author's goals?

   A) NO CHANGE
   B) offers the opportunity to become wealthy over the course of just a few years, with a minimum of time invested.
   C) is likely to lead to the development of a whole new array of internet employment scams, costing hard-working people millions of dollars and robbing them of hope for a better future.
   D) has literally opened up a world of possibilities that, if approached with appropriate caution and intelligence, can help to make that dream a reality.

SAMPLE TEST 5
Section 2: Writing & Language Test

Questions 34-44 are based on the following passage

The following passage describes fictional events in a fictional country.

Far Below, Mysterious Knowledge of the Heavens Above

Although every significant archaeological discovery represents a major step forward in humanity's understanding of the world that surrounds us, **(Q34)** but only those that shed direct light on the history of the human lineage tend to create global sensations. **(Q35)** Nevertheless, the March 2016 discovery of the remains of a mysteriously advanced ancient human civilization in present-day Poutamonia has had the internet working overtime. The remains, which date to about 13,000 years ago, lie deep within prehistoric caves that collapsed during catastrophic earthquakes **(Q36)** that, apparently, were also wiping out the civilization itself. In 2014, strange moisture condensation patterns in present-day mines alerted scientists to the possibility that the seemingly solid rock beneath those mines might actually be composed of compressed debris that had tumbled into open spaces long ago. During the ensuing months, a few enterprising researchers made feeble attempts at breaking through the mine floors, but were unable to secure funding to support their work. Later, when highly sophisticated imaging instruments produced strong evidence in support of the hypothesis that the mines sat atop buried caves, the digging began in **(Q37)** honest. Even then, no one suspected that a previously unknown chapter in the history of *homo sapiens* was about to be revealed, to the bewilderment of scientists and anthropologists alike.

34.
 A) NO CHANGE
 B) also
 C) however
 D) DELETE the underlined word.

35.
 A) NO CHANGE
 B) For example,
 C) By contrast,
 D) Likewise,

36.
 A) NO CHANGE
 B) that were, apparently, also having wiped out
 C) that, apparently, also wiped out
 D) that also were apparently wiping out

37.
 A) NO CHANGE
 B) honesty
 C) urgent
 D) earnest

Many of the artifacts that the ancient inhabitants of the caves left behind, such as spear tips, stone tools, drawings on cave walls, and charred animal bones from cooking, are consistent with the era during which they lived. In one particular realm of human thought, however, these people were at least ten millennia ahead of **(Q38)** their time, they were scientists, and rather extraordinary scientists at that. Some of the drawings of groups of animals, for instance, take a form strongly reminiscent of a family tree, suggesting that the cave dwellers had at least some understanding of heredity. **(Q39) (Q40)** Other drawings seem to show that they hunted by throwing spears at animals. Intriguing though those possibilities are, however, they pale in comparison to the conclusion scientists are trying very hard to refrain from making based on figures etched into the stone floors of the caves. For there is tantalizing evidence that these hunter-gatherers were pondering a possibility that no human of that era had any business thinking about—namely, that planet Earth is in motion.

38.
A) NO CHANGE
B) their time: they were scientists,
C) they're time, they were scientists,
D) their time; they were scientists:

39.
At this point, the author is considering adding the following sentence.

> They drew pictures of animals in ways that imply that they understood something about the passing on of traits from parents to offspring.

Should the author make this addition here?

A) No, because it simply reformulates the ideas expressed in the previous sentence.
B) No, because the word "offspring" is not defined.
C) Yes, because it provides an additional example to support the claim that the cave dwellers understood science.
D) Yes, because it provides the important new information that the cave dwellers were interested in ancestry, just like present-day humans.

40.
Which of the following would best serve as another illustrative example in support of the author's point?

A) NO CHANGE
B) Other drawings show hunters appealing to various deities as they prepare to throw their spears.
C) Other drawings depicting hunting expeditions hint at an interest in the ways that design changes affected the trajectory of a thrown spear.
D) In other drawings depicting hunting expeditions, people shown throwing spears were adorned with crowns, showing that being a successful hunter elevated a person's status in the society.

The experts are quick to remind us that even a drawing produced by a living human would likely be misunderstood by many people who saw it, so any effort to discern the meaning of ancient etchings should be undertaken with the greatest of caution. Nevertheless, upon beholding the etchings, many of which depict a large circle **(Q41)** emanated rays of energy, surrounded by various objects arranged differently in each image, it is difficult to escape the inference that the artists believed that Earth was one of several bodies traveling around the sun. **(Q42)** **(Q43)** Admittedly, the cave dwellers imagined the motion of those bodies to be decidedly more chaotic than the orderly progression of orbits that can be seen in today's accurate models of the solar system. That fact does not diminish the brilliance of the ancient scientists' work in the slightest, however. To perceive the motion of our own planet simply by studying the apparent movement patterns of heavenly **(Q44)** bodies, it has so many precise observations that have to be made that for any group of people to undertake such a task before the dawn of agriculture would seem to be an impossibility.

Of course, further study may reveal that the etchings had nothing to do with the sun and planets, after all. For now, the wondrous notion that some of the greatest scientists of all time lived several thousand years before the first human use of metal has, appropriately enough, moved us all.

41.
A) NO CHANGE
B) emanating
C) which has emanated
D) is emanating

42.
At this point, the author is considering adding the following sentence.

> Johannes Kepler discovered the laws of planetary motion during the 17th century by completing an astounding number of complex calculations.

Should the author make this addition here?

A) Yes, because it shows that the cave dwellers' beliefs about the nature of planetary orbits were later confirmed.
B) Yes, because it explains the causes of the "orderly progression" mentioned in the next sentence.
C) No, because it interrupts the flow of the paragraph by introducing information only vaguely related to the main ideas of the passage.
D) No, because it does not explain how the cave dwellers successfully performed the same calculations as Johannes Kepler.

43.
A) NO CHANGE
B) Therefore,
C) Ironically,
D) Nonetheless,

44.
A) NO CHANGE
B) bodies, there have to be so many precise observations that are being made
C) bodies; so many precise observations have to be made
D) bodies requires the making of so many precise observations

STOP

If you have finished this section before time expires, you may check your work. You cannot return to this section once you move on to the next section.

STOP!

If you have finished this section before time expires, you may check your work. You cannot return to this section once you move on to the next section.

www.eggheadprep.com

ANSWERS, SECTION 2
SAMPLE TEST 5 — WRITING & LANGUAGE

1. C
2. D
3. A
4. B
5. C
6. A
7. D
8. B
9. A
10. A
11. C
12. C
13. B
14. D
15. B
16. C
17. D
18. D
19. A
20. A
21. B
22. C
23. D
24. D
25. B
26. D
27. A
28. B
29. A
30. C
31. B
32. C
33. D
34. D
35. B
36. C
37. D
38. B
39. A
40. C
41. B
42. C
43. A
44. D

eggheadprep.com

SECTION 3: MATH TEST
NO CALCULATOR, 25 MINUTES, 20 QUESTIONS

DIRECTIONS

For questions 1–15, solve the problem and choose the best answer from the options provided. For questions 16–20, solve the problem and type in your answer. Further instructions for typing in your answer are provided before question

NOTES

1. Calculator use is not permitted for this section. You will distort your score if you use one.
2. All variables and expressions represent real numbers unless stated otherwise.
3. Unless otherwise indicated, figures shown have been drawn to scale.
4. All figures lie in a plane unless stated otherwise.
5. The domain of a function f is the set of real numbers for which f(x) is a real number, unless stated otherwise.

REFERENCE

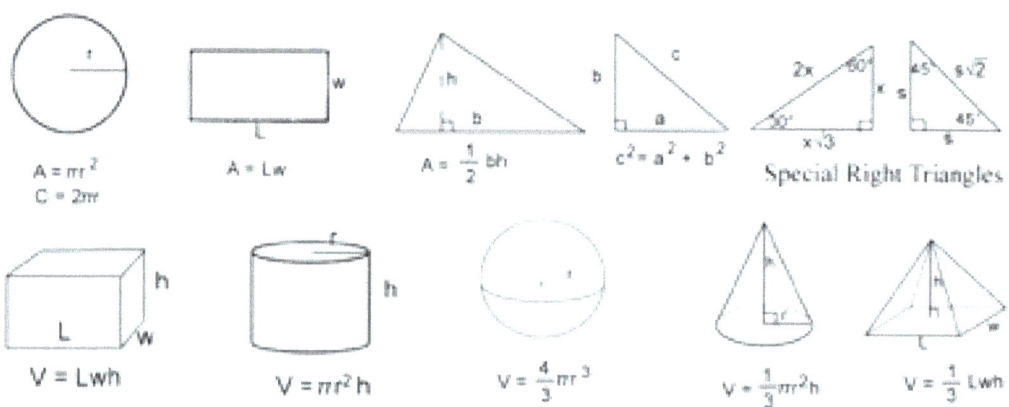

A full circle has 360 degrees of arc.
A full circle has 2π radians of arc.
The sum of the measures of the angles in a triangle is 180°.

EGGHEAD PREP

SAMPLE TEST 5
Section 3: Math, No Calculator

1. If $3x - 6 = 4$, then $9x - 2 = ?$

   A) 4
   B) 10
   C) 20
   D) 28

2. On Tuesday, Carla started work at 9 a.m. and worked until 5 p.m. Paul started work at 10 a.m. and worked until 4 p.m. Carla completes C projects per hour, and Paul completes P projects per hour. If both Carla and Paul took a one-hour break for lunch, during which they completed no projects, which expression represents the total number of projects completed by Carla and Paul on Tuesday?

   A) $7C + 5P$
   B) $9C + 10P$
   C) $5C + 4P$
   D) $8C + 6P$

3. The equation:
   $$H = 1.79 - 0.12d$$
   predicts the height of water H in a rain gauge, in inches, d days after the end of a major storm. What was the height of water in the gauge, in inches, immediately after the storm ended?

   A) 0
   B) 0.12
   C) 1.67
   D) 1.79

4. If $r \geq 0$, which expression below is equivalent to $\sqrt[5]{r^3}$?

   A) $\dfrac{1}{5r^3}$
   B) $\dfrac{3}{r^5}$
   C) $r^{3/5}$
   D) $r^{5/3}$

5.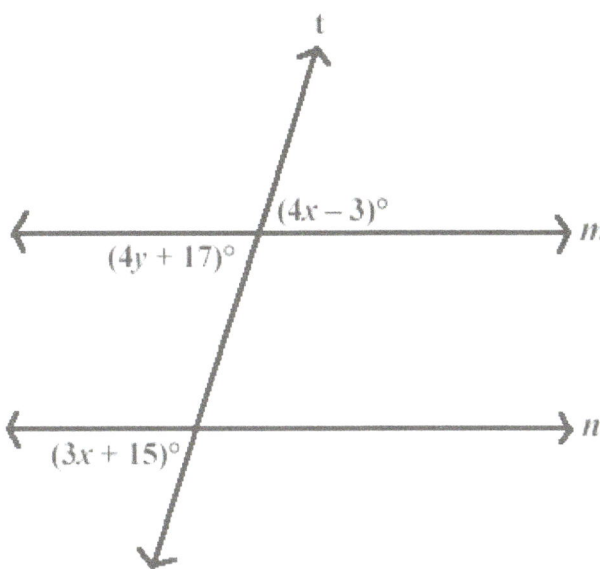

   NOTE: This figure is NOT drawn to scale.

   If $y = 15$ in the figure above, which of these statements MUST be true?
   I. Lines m and n are parallel.
   II. $x = 20$
   III. $x < 20$

   A) I only
   B) II only
   C) I and II only
   D) I and III only

6. $$4x - 2y = 14$$
   $$-3x + 6y = 3$$
   If the ordered pair (x, y) is a solution to the above system of equations, what is the value of $x - y$?

   A) 2
   B) 3
   C) 5
   D) 7

7. What is the solution to $\dfrac{4x}{2x + 5} = \dfrac{12}{7}$?

   A) $\dfrac{5}{4}$
   B) 3
   C) 15
   D) There is no solution.

8.

$$m^4 - 13m^2n^2 + 30n^4$$

Which of the following choices is equivalent to the expression shown above?

A) $(m - 13n)2 \, (m + 30n)2$

B) $(m2 - 10n2) \, (m2 - 3n2)$

C) $(m2 - 13n2) \, (m2 + 30n2)$

D) $(m - 10n)2 \, (m - 3n)2$

9. Let $f(= ax2 - 2ax + 5$. If $f(3) = -1$, what does $f(-1)$ equal?

A) -3

B) -1

C) 1

D) 3

Questions 10 and 11 refer to the following figure, which shows the graph of $y = x2 - 3x - 10$.

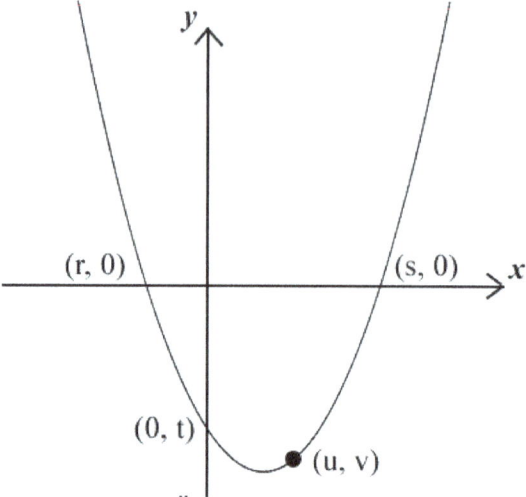

10. What is the value of r?

A) -10

B) -5

C) -3

D) -2

11. The point $(u,$ is on the curve and lies to the right of the vertex but to the left of the point $(s, 0)$, as shown. Which of the following statements CANNOT be true?

A) $|v| > |t| + 3$

B) $u > v$

C) $|u| < |v|$

D) $v \leq -12$

12. When an element in solid form is heated, it first turns to a liquid (the melting process) then, eventually, to a gas (the boiling process). During the periods when the element is melting and boiling, its temperature remains constant. The following graph shows the temperature of a sample of Liontinum, which is a solid at 100° Celsius, as it is heated.

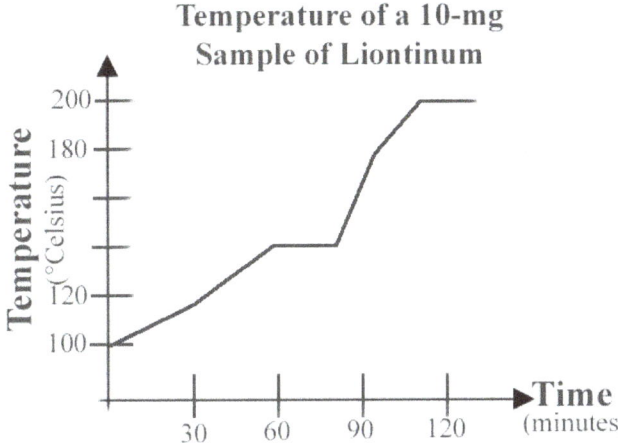

At which of the following times during the experiment did the sample of Liontinum begin melting?

A) After about 30 minutes
B) After about 60 minutes
C) After about 90 minutes
D) After about 110 minutes

13.
$$2x + ay = 4$$
$$-5x - by = 7$$

In the system of equations shown above, a and b are constants. If the system has no solutions, which of the following statements MUST be true?

A) $a = b$
B) $a = 2$
C) $a = \frac{2}{5}b$
D) $b = \frac{7}{4}a$

14. If $i = \sqrt{-1}$, which of the following expressions is equivalent to,
$$4i(-3 + 2i)(1 + 3i)?$$

A) $28 - 36i$
B) $-3 + 24i$
C) $-2 + 9i$
D) $-24i^3 + 28i^2 + 12i$

15. Consider the equation,
$$3x^2 - 4 = -2x$$

Which expression below is equal to 6 times the *positive* solution to the equation?

A) $-12 + \sqrt{52}$
B) $12\sqrt{\frac{2}{3}}$
C) $-2 + 2\sqrt{13}$
D) $\frac{48}{5}$

DIRECTIONS

For questions 16 – 20, solve the problem and type in your answer. Please follow these guidelines:

1. No questions have negative answers.
2. If a problem has more than one correct answer, any of those answers will be accepted as correct. Please enter only one answer.
3. Do not type in mixed numbers. A number such as 2 ¼ should be entered as 2.25 or 9/4. Mixed numbers will be misinterpreted by the computer.
4. If a decimal answer does not terminate after 3 decimal places, enter three decimal places only. You may either round or truncate the decimal. For example, 3/8 may be entered as 3/8 or .375, because the decimal ends there; 7/9 may be entered as 7/9, .777, or .778. Fractions should be reduced to simplest terms. For example, you should enter 1/2 instead of 2/4.

16.

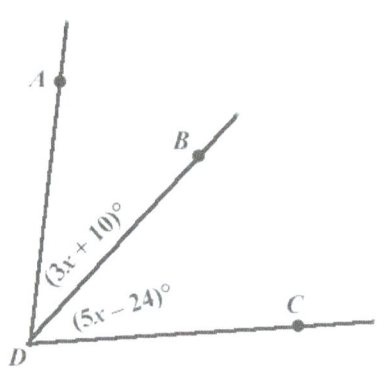

NOTE: This figure is NOT drawn to scale.

In the figure above, the measure of ∠ADC is less than or equal to 90°. What is the value of x if $\cos(\angle ABD) = \sin(\angle BDC)$?

17. The number of frogs at Larkin's Pond is 5 more than twice the number of turtles. If there are a total of 38 frogs and turtles at Larkin's Pond, how many turtles are there?

18. Given that $w = 2$, find a solution to the equation,

$$2\sqrt{x+7} + 3w = 2x - 4$$

19. The price P of a bracelet, in dollars, is directly proportional to the weight W of the bracelet, in ounces. If a 6-ounce bracelet costs 7 dollars more than a 4-ounce bracelet, what is the cost, in dollars of a 10-ounce bracelet? (Ignore the $ sign when typing in your answer.)

20.
$$y = x^2 - 4x$$
$$2x - y = -16$$

If (x, y) is a solution to the system of equations above and $x > 0$, what is the value of y?

STOP

If you have finished this section before time expires, you may check your work. You cannot return to this section once you move on to the next section.

STOP!

If you have finished this section before time expires, you may check your work. You cannot return to this section once you move on to the next section.

www.eggheadprep.com

ANSWERS, SECTION 3

SAMPLE TEST 5 — MATH, NO CALCULATOR

1. D
2. A
3. D
4. C
5. B
6. A
7. C
8. B
9. B
10. D
11. A
12. B
13. C
14. A
15. C

---

16. 13
17. 11
18. 9
19. 35
20. 32

EGGHEAD PREP

SECTION 4: MATH TEST
CALCULATOR, 55 MINUTES, 38 QUESTIONS

DIRECTIONS

For questions 1–30, solve the problem and choose the best answer from the options provided. For questions 31–38, solve the problem and type in your answer. Further instructions for typing in your answer are provided before question 31.

NOTES

1. Calculator use is permitted for this section.
2. All variables and expressions represent real numbers unless stated otherwise.
3. Unless otherwise indicated, figures shown have been drawn to scale.
4. All figures lie in a plane unless stated otherwise.
5. The domain of a function f is the set of real numbers for which f(x) is a real number, unless stated otherwise.

REFERENCE

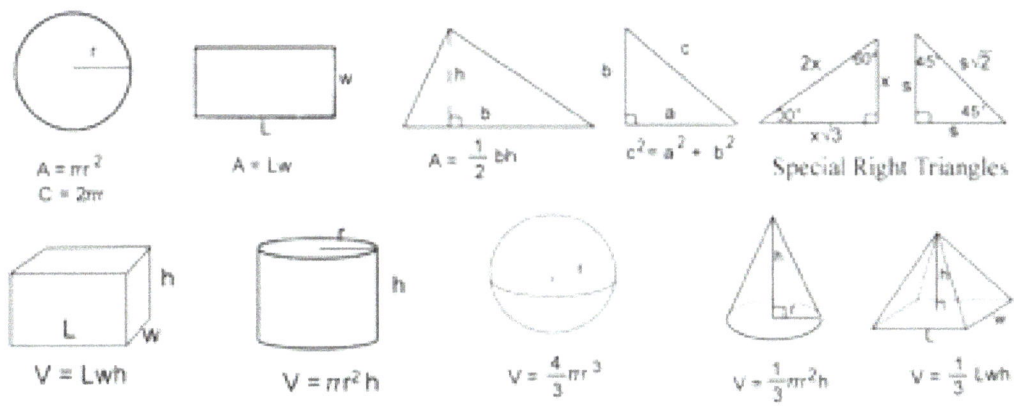

A full circle has 360 degrees of arc.
A full circle has 2π radians of arc.
The sum of the measures of the angles in a triangle is 180°.

eggheadprep.com

1. A public relations specialist asked 17 out of every 340 people who entered an amusement park on a certain day to complete a survey. If 2,800 people entered the amusement park that day, how many people were asked to complete the survey?

   A) 17
   B) 20
   C) 140
   D) 165

2. Renting lighting equipment from StageBright costs $85 plus $40 for each hour of use. Renting the same equipment from LightHouse costs $195 plus $30 for each hour of use. Let h equal the number of hours the rental lasts. Which of the following inequalities could be solved to find the values of h for which the cost of renting the equipment from LightHouse will be lower than the cost of renting the equipment from StageBright?

   A) 225h < 125h
      195 + 30h < 85 + 40h
   B) 195h + 30 < 85h + 40
   C) 195 − 30h < 85 − 40h

Questions 3 and 4 refer to the following graph, showing the budget of a school district over the years.

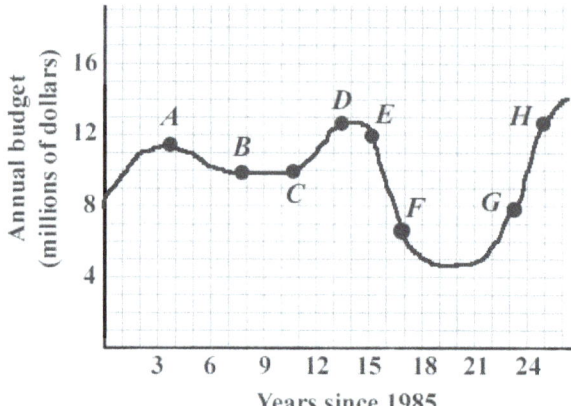

3. Between which two points indicated with letters did the average rate of change of the school district's budget, in units of millions of dollars per year, have its lowest value?

   A) A and B
   B) B and C
   C) E and F
   D) G and H

4. Which one of the following options is an accurate statement describing a relationship between the school district's budget in 2001 and its budget in 2010?

   A) The budget in 2010 was roughly 4% higher than the budget in 2001.
   B) The budget in 2010 was roughly 140% higher than the budget in 2001.
   C) The budget in 2001 was roughly 40% lower than the budget in 2010.
   D) The budget in 2010 was roughly 40% higher than the budget in 2001.

SAMPLE TEST 5
Section 4: Math, Calculator

5.

Students Participating in Regional High School Music Solo Competition

Gender	9th	10th	11th	12th	Total
Female	117	238	572	439	1,366
Male	98	281	514	487	1,380
Total	215	519	1,086	926	2,746

The table above shows the number of students who participated in a regional music solo competition, categorized by grade level and gender identification. If a student who participated in the competition is selected randomly, which percentage below is closest to the probability that the student identifies as female and is in 10th or 12th grade?

A) 25%
B) 47%
C) 50%
D) 53%

6. The equation, $f(x) = -2(x-3)^2 + 2$, defines a function f whose graph in the xy-plane is a parabola. Which of the following equivalent equations defining f displays the y-intercept of the parabola as a constant or coefficient?

A) $f(x) = -2(x-4)(x-2)$
B) $f(x) = -2x^2 + 12x - 16$
C) $f(x) = -2(x^2 - 6x + 9) + 2$
D) $f(x) = -2(x^2 - 6x + 8)$

7. A company estimates that 58% of the customer complaint calls it receives are related to billing issues; the rest pertain to deliveries and product performance. On a certain day, the company received 217 customer complaint calls at its Chicago call center, 182 at its Louisville call center, and 231 at its Wichita call center. Which option is closest to the total number of customer complaint calls related to deliveries and product performance received at the three call centers that day?

A) 265
B) 365
C) 630
D) 688

8. Pike Airlines cancels any flight for which there are fewer than 45 passengers, including children and adults. Airline experts estimate that the average adult passenger accounts for a total of 223 pounds of weight (including the passenger and any luggage), while the average child passenger accounts for a total of 136 pounds of weight. Any flight for which the total predicted weight of passengers and luggage (based on the averages specified) exceeds 33,000 pounds is canceled. If a represents the number of adult passengers and c represents the number of child passengers, which of the following systems of inequalities correctly represents the conditions under which a Pike Airlines flight will NOT be canceled?

A) $\begin{cases} a + c < 45 \\ 223a + 136c > 33,000 \end{cases}$

B) $\begin{cases} a + c \leq 45 \\ \dfrac{a}{223} + \dfrac{c}{136} \leq 33,000 \end{cases}$

C) $\begin{cases} ac \geq 45 \\ 359\,ac < 33,000 \end{cases}$

D) $\begin{cases} a + c \geq 45 \\ 223a + 136c \leq 33,000 \end{cases}$

9. The cost of printing 500 copies of a brochure at a certain print shop is $140. The cost of 1500 copies at the same shop is $180. The cost of 3,000 copies at the same shop is $240. If the relationship between the cost p and the number of copies N at this shop is linear, what would be the cost of printing 12,000 copies?

A) $320
B) $560
C) $600
D) $960

Questions 10 and 11 refer to the following information.

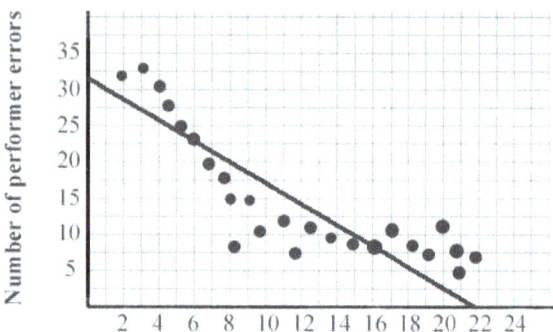

Performer Errors in Relation to Rehearsal Time

Time spent rehearsing for performance (hours)

A scientist wished to study how human memory of physical movements is affected by repetition of those movements. She divided a group of 250 randomly selected people into 10 groups of 25. Each group was given a 7-minute dance routine to learn, and instructed to practice the routine for a specific length of time, varying from 2 to 22 hours. Each group then performed the routine in front of a live audience. The scientist carefully kept track of the number of hours of practice time each group had and the total number of errors made by members of that group during the performance. Her results are displayed in the scatterplot above, along with the line of best fit.

10. Which of the following statements accurately describes the line of best fit?

A) The line of best fit would serve as an excellent model for the relationship between practice time and number of errors, since all but a few data points are very close to the line.

B) The line of best fit would have no value as a model for the relationship between practice time and number of errors, since only two of the data points actually lie on the line.

C) The line of best fit would have shortcomings as a model, because it consistently overestimates the number of errors made by groups that practiced for less than 6 hours or more than 16 hours, while underestimating the number of errors for groups that practiced for between 6 and 16 hours.

D) The line of best fit would have shortcomings as a model, because it consistently underestimates the number of errors made by groups that practiced for less than 6 hours or more than 16 hours, while overestimating the number of errors for groups that practiced for between 6 and 16 hours.

11. The group that practiced 6 hours made 23 errors; the group that practiced 16 hours made 8 errors. If x equals the number of hours of practice and y equals the number of errors, which of the following could be an equation for the line of best fit?

A) $y = -15x + 10$
B) $y = 32 - 1.5x$
C) $y = 32 + 1.5x$
D) $y = 32x - 1.5$

12.

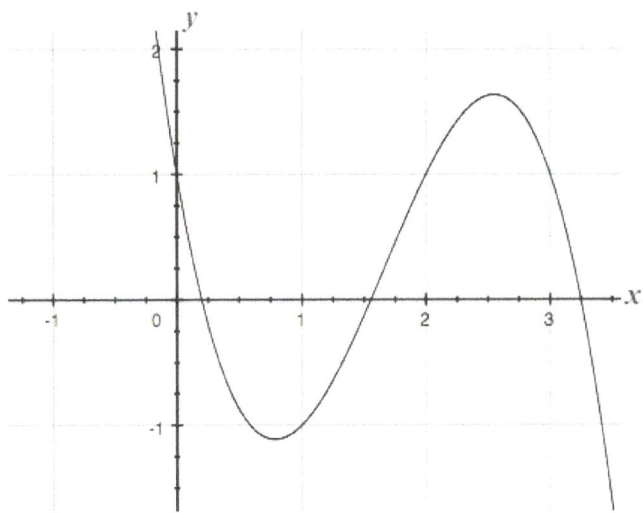

Shown above is a **partial** graph of $y = f(x)$, where f is a polynomial function. Which of the following CANNOT be the equation that defines f? (The letters a, b, c, d, and e all denote constants, none of which equal zero.)

A) $f(x) = ax^2 + bx + c$
B) $f(x) = ax^3 + bx^2 + cx + d$
C) $f(x) = ax^4 + bx^3 + cx^2 + dx + e$
D) $f(x) = ax^6 + bx^5 + cx^3 + dx^2 + e$

13. A certain machine can fabricate an average of 17.3 feet of pipe per hour. If the machine works nonstop (day and night), which equation represents the number of feet of pipe p that the machine will fabricate in w **weeks**?

A) $p = \dfrac{17.3(24)w}{7}$
B) $p = 17.3(24)(7w)$
C) $p = 17.3(7w) + 24$
D) $p = \dfrac{17.3(7)}{24w}$

14. If $f(x) = 3 - 4x$ and $g(x) = 5x + 1$, which of the following choices is equal to $g(f(2x))$?

A) $-4x^3 + 22x^2 + 6x$
B) $32x - 40x^2$
C) $16 - 40x$
D) $-1 - 40x$

15. A taste test was conducted to determine the marketability of a new soft drink. Participants in the study who had the opportunity to drink from a freshly opened can of the drink gave it an average rating of 8.37 out of 10 stars. Other participants were required to wait for a certain amount of time after the can was opened before tasting the beverage. It was found that for every five minutes participants had to wait after the opening of the can, their average rating of the beverage fell by 14.67%. Which of the following equations would correctly model the relationship between participants' average rating R and the number of minutes m that they had to wait after the can was opened before tasting the drink?

A) $R = 8.37(0.1467)^{5m}$
B) $R = 8.37(0.1467)^{m/5}$
C) $R = 8.37(0.8533)^{5m}$
D) $R = 8.37(0.8533)^{m/5}$

16. Researchers were interested in whether drinking coffee affects a person's ability to recover from a certain illness. An experiment was conducted in which 120 people with the illness were randomly selected, then divided into two groups of 60. The first group was instructed to drink coffee daily, while the second group was instructed to drink no coffee during the study. Researchers found that significantly fewer of the participants in the coffee drinking group recovered from the illness than participants in the group that drank no coffee. Which of the following conclusions is reasonable?

A) Drinking no coffee is the best of all possible treatments to increase the likelihood a person will recover from the illness.

B) Drinking coffee greatly decreases the likelihood a person will recover from the illness.

C) No one with the illness who drinks coffee will recover from the illness.

D) It is likely that people with the illness who drink coffee will have a lower probability of recovering from the illness than those who do not drink coffee.

Questions 17 and 18 refer to the following information.

An insurance specialist examined the driving records of 175 male and 175 female drivers, all 36 years of age. The specialist recorded the number of traffic citations (tickets) for non-parking violations each driver received between the ages of 18 and 35, inclusive, recording the results in the table shown below.

Number of Traffic Citations (Other Than Parking Violations) Received Between Ages 18 and 35

Number of Citations	Frequencies	
	Male	Female
0	15	37
1	39	58
2	51	39
3	44	27
4	14	9
5	8	3
6 or more	4	2

17. What was the median number of non-parking traffic citations received between the ages of 18 and 35, inclusive, by male drivers in the study?

   A) 2
   B) 3
   C) 4
   D) It cannot be determined because the exact number of citations received is not known for all drivers.

18. Suppose the specialist examines the records of four additional female drivers, age 36, and adds the results to the data. Two of the additional drivers received no citations between ages 18 and 35, inclusive; the other two each received 8 citations. Which of the following statements is/are true?

   I. The median of the number of citations for female drivers would change.

   II. The mean of the number of citations for female drivers would change

   III. The mode of the number of citations for female drivers would change.

   A) I only
   B) II only
   C) I and II only
   D) I, II, and III

19. The equation,
$$x^2 + y^2 - 8x + 9y = 6$$
represents a circle in the xy-plane. What is the y-coordinate of the center of the circle?

   A) –9
   B) 4
   C) –4.5
   D) 9

20. Which of the following scatterplots shows a relationship that could be reasonably modeled by an equation of the form $y = ax^b$, where $a > 0$ and $b \leq -1$?

A)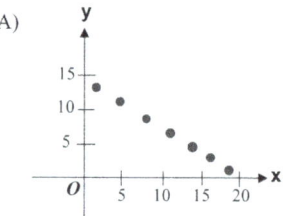

B)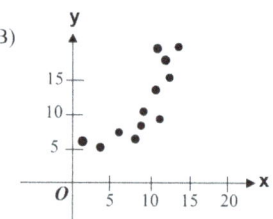

C)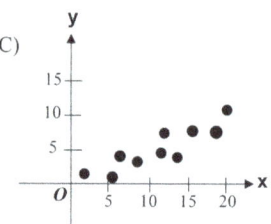

D)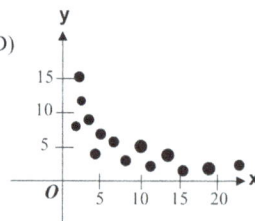

SAMPLE TEST 5
Section 4: Math, Calculator

21.
$$4x - \frac{3x+1}{x-5}$$

For $x \neq 5$, which of the following expressions is equivalent to the expression shown above?

A) $\dfrac{x+1}{x-5}$

B) $\dfrac{4x^2 - 23x - 1}{x-5}$

C) $\dfrac{4x^2 - 17x + 1}{x-5}$

D) $\dfrac{x-1}{x-5}$

22. If $7q - 15 > -6$ and q is an integer, what is the minimum possible value of $7q - 4$?

A) –6
B) –5
C) 5
D) 6

23.

Age at which person smoked first cigarette

Current smoking frequency	Age 11-14	Age 15-17	Age 18-20	Age 20 or older	Total
Fewer than 10 per week	4	11	24	41	80
11-30 per week	15	27	11	7	60
over 30 per week	36	50	3	1	90
Total	55	88	38	49	230

The table above shows the results of a recent survey of 230 cigarette smokers in the US over 20 years of age. "Current smoking frequency" indicates the number of cigarettes per week the smoker currently smokes. The column headings indicate how old the smoker was when he or she smoked his or her first cigarette. If a single smoker is selected at random from among all those who smoked their first cigarette at age 17 or younger, which option is closest to the probability that he or she currently smokes over 30 cigarettes per week?

A) 96%
B) 60%
C) 57%
D) 29%

24.
$$f(x) = 2x^3 - 5x^2 + cx + d$$

The graph of $y = f(x)$ in the xy-plane crosses the x-axis at $x = 1$ and $x = 3$. What is the value of d?

A) 9
B) 3
C) –1
D) –3

25. Scientists are studying the lakes in a remote area of Canada to determine how the depth of a lake affects its ability to absorb trace amounts of certain polluting chemicals without the aquatic ecosystem suffering any harm. For each lake, they use a sounding device to estimate the depth of the lake, H, in meters, where $H \geq 8$. Let D represent the exact depth of the lake, in meters. If the sounding device has a maximum error of 7 percent, which inequality below must be true?

A) $H + D \leq (1.07)8$
B) $H - 8 \leq .07D$
C) $-0.07D \leq H - D \leq 0.07D$
D) $-1.07H \leq D \leq 1.07H$

26. Xavier and Mahlia both have collections of jars in the shape of right circular cylinders. All of the jars in each person's collection are identical to each other, but not to the jars in the other person's collection. Mahlia's jars are five times as tall as Xavier's jars. The radius of Mahlia's jars is one half of the radius of Xavier's jars. Currently, 12 of Xavier's jars are full of brewed tea. If Xavier and Mahlia want to transfer all of the tea to Mahlia's jars, what is the minimum number of Mahlia's jars that they will need?

A) 5
B) 6
C) 10
D) 60

27. A linear function f is graphed in the xy-plane. The graph contains the points $(a, -3)$ and $(-4, -b)$. If $a + b = 0$ and $-2 \leq a \leq 2$, what must be true of the slope of the graph of f?

   A) It must be negative.
   B) It must be positive.
   C) It may be either positive or negative, but cannot be zero.
   D) It must be zero.

28. P and Q are endpoints of a diameter of a circle with center C. Points M and N lie on the circle, and point N divides arc PMQ into two arcs of equal length. If the sector bounded by $\angle PCN$ has area 16π square meters, what is the radius of the circle, in meters?

   A) 4
   B) 8
   C) 16
   D) 32

29. If $a + 2b - 2n = -18$ and n is 35% less than $a + 2b$, what does n equal?

   A) −27.7
   B) 39
   C) 60
   D) 65

30. During the Chicano art movement that began in the US in the 1960s, thousands of colorful murals were painted in California alone. The students at one particular California elementary school are fascinated by a mural painted on the wall of their school building. The mural, which covers a rectangular section of the wall measuring 45 feet by 21 feet, is a giant collage of faces. The students wondered how many faces are shown in the mural. A number of students volunteered to count the faces in a small section of the mural. Each student was assigned a section of the mural measuring 1 **square yard**. The table below shows the number of faces each student counted within her or his square.

Student	Number of faces counted
Ana Maria	17
Bethany	12
Diego	20
Elizabeth	15
Guillermo	16
Laticia	13
Mahmed	18
Michael	14
Vanessa	18

Which of the following is a reasonable estimate of the total number of faces shown in the mural?

   A) 15,000
   B) 5,000
   C) 1,100
   D) 150

SAMPLE TEST 5
Section 4: Math, Calculator

DIRECTIONS

For questions 31–38, solve the problem and type in your answer. Please follow these guidelines:

1. No questions have negative answers.

2. If a problem has more than one correct answer, any of those answers will be accepted as correct. Please enter only one answer.

3. Do not type in mixed numbers. A number such as 2 ¼ should be entered as 2.25 or 9/4. Mixed numbers will be misinterpreted by the computer.

4. If a decimal answer does not terminate after 3 decimal places, enter three decimal places unless otherwise instructed. You may either round or truncate the decimal. For example, 3/8 may be entered as 3/8 or .375, because the decimal ends there; 7/9 may be entered as 7/9, .777, or .778. Fractions should be reduced to simplest terms. In other words, you should enter 1/2 instead of 2/4.

5. Do not include a comma within any number. For example, for the number 3,750, simply enter 3750.

31.

$$f(x) = 20(x - 2.5)(x - 4.2)(x - k)^2$$

If the function f shown above has exactly two x-intercepts, what is one possible value of k?

32. Jordan and Campbell spent a summer collecting seashells. Together, they collected a total of 228 shells. If Campbell collected 46 more shells than Jordan, how many shells did Jordan collect?

33.

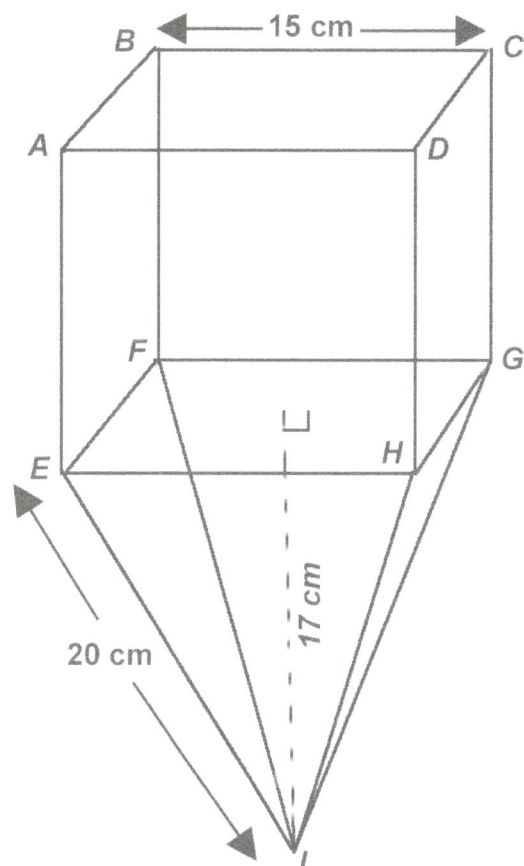

The figure above shows a three-dimensional solid with vertices A, B, C, D, E, F, G, H and I. The solid consists of a cube atop a regular square pyramid. Dimensions, in centimeters, are as shown. To the nearest whole number, what is the volume of the solid in cubic centimeters?

34. A dance marathon begins with 447 dancers participating. An average of 29 dancers drop out every 30 minutes. After how many **hours** will there be fewer than 50 dancers remaining? (Round your answer to the nearest whole number of hours.)

35.

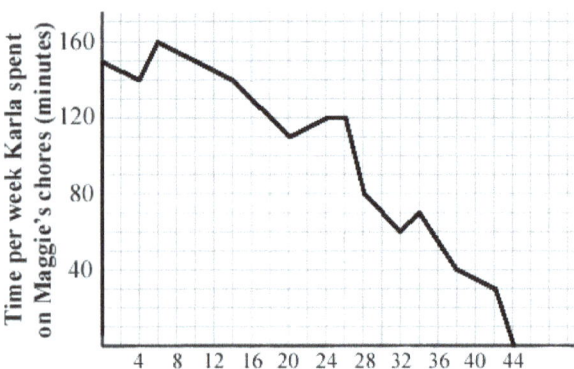

Karla's Time Spent Performing Maggie's Chores

Karla was frustrated that her roommate, Maggie, was not performing her assigned weekly cleaning chores, leaving Karla to do all the work. Karla decided to try to "train" Maggie to do her chores by leaving a reward, such as freshly cut mango slices or flowers, on the dining room table each time Maggie completed a chore. She did not explain to Maggie why the rewards were appearing on the table. The graph above shows the number of minutes Karla had to spend completing chores assigned to Maggie each week for about 10 months following the start of Karla's experiment.

According to the graph, the time Karla spent per week performing Maggie's chores 38 weeks after the start of the experiment was what fraction of the time Karla spent per week performing Maggie's chores 14 weeks after the start of the experiment?

36.

$$y \geq 250x - 4000$$
$$y \leq 8000 - 70x$$

If the point (a, b) lies in the solution set of the system of inequalities shown above, what is the largest possible value of a ?

37. A computer loses $\frac{1}{5}$ of its value every 18 months. If its original value was $2300, by how many dollars will its value decrease in 11 **years**? Round your answer to the nearest whole dollar. (Ignore the $ sign when typing in your answer.)

38.

$$g(x) = \frac{2x - 6}{(x - 2)^2 - 16}$$

Give a **positive** value of x for which the function g shown above is undefined.

STOP

If you have finished this section before time expires, you may check your work. You cannot return to this section once you move on to the next section.

STOP!

If you have finished this section before time expires, you may check your work. You cannot return to this section once you move on to the next section.

www.eggheadprep.com

ANSWERS, SECTION 4
SAMPLE TEST 5 — MATH, CALCULATOR

1. C
2. B
3. C
4. D
5. A
6. B
7. A
8. D
9. C
10. D
11. B
12. A
13. B
14. C
15. D
16. D
17. A
18. B
19. C
20. D
21. B
22. D
23. B
24. A
25. C
26. C
27. A
28. B
29. B
30. C

---

31. 2.5 or 5/2 or 4.2 or 21/5
32. 91
33. 4650
34. 7
35. 2/7
36. 37.5 or 75/2
37. 1850 or 1851 or 1852 or 1853 or 1854 or 1855
38. 6

ANSWER EXPLANATIONS
SAMPLE TEST 5 — SECTION 1, 2, 3, 4

NOTE: The SAT Reading Test emphasizes <u>evidence-based</u> analysis of the passages. While reading the passages, you will no doubt form opinions regarding whether the results of an experiment described should be trusted, or whether there are reasons beyond those presented in the passage for characters to act as they do. Those opinions may be perfectly valid, but when answering the questions, it is important to remember to draw conclusions based <u>solely</u> on evidence that is explicitly presented in the passage, not on your own personal feelings.

TEST SECTION 1: READING

1. Because all of the words in the phrase "referring the matter from arguments to arms" are familiar, the task here is to determine the author's meaning by studying the context in which the phrase is used. The second sentence of the passage (lines 3-6) provides an important clue, in the phrase, "All plans and proposals prior to the commencement of hostilities are like the almanacs of last year." "Commencement" means beginning, and "hostilities" most commonly refers to war, or at least skirmishes that might escalate to war. By associating ideas that were considered before hostilities began with "last year," Paine is making clear that the war is already in progress. The clear implication is that the progression of events has been from debate to warfare. Only choice (D) accurately summarizes this conclusion. **The correct answer is (D)**.

2. Immediately following his use of the word "roundly," Paine asserts that "America would have flourished as much, and probably much more, had no European power had any thing to do with the colonies." That is obviously a very strong statement, which suggests that the author is using the word "roundly" to mean something like "emphatically." The answer choice that best conveys this meaning is option (A), "resoundingly." **The correct answer is (A)**.

3. In lines 23-26, Paine states that, "The commerce by which the colonies have enriched themselves centers on the necessities of life, and will always have a market while eating is the custom of Europe." The last phrase is of course deliberately worded in a humorous way, since eating has always been the "custom" of every human society, given that humans cannot survive without food. The author is making clear that the trade in which the colonies have engaged centers on basic necessities of life, and therefore, he expects, will generate long-lasting prosperity. Answer choice (B) accurately summarizes this argument. **The correct answer is (B)**.

4. As noted in the explanation for question #3 above, lines 23-26 provide clear support for the correct answer to that question. **The correct answer is (C)**.

5. In lines 34-39, Paine argues that the "enemies" from which Great Britain has protected the colonies are not, in fact, enemies of the colonies ("those who had no quarrel with us"), but enemies of Great Britain itself. He further asserts that separation from Great Britain would result in the end of any hostilities between the colonies and the countries of France and Spain. He is thus implying that the colonies only have enemies in Europe because of their affiliation with Great Britain. Answer choice (A) makes this point clearly and simply. **The correct answer is (A)**.

eggheadprep.com

6. As noted in the explanation for question #5 above, lines 34-39 provide clear support for the correct answer to that question. **The correct answer is (C).**

7. Leading up to the phrase in question, Paine writes (lines 40-43), "But Britain is the parent country, say some. Then the more shame upon her conduct. Even brutes do not devour their young, nor savages make war upon their families …" The "assertion" he refers to in line 43, then, is the claim that Britain is the American colonies' "parent" country, and that therefore it is inappropriate to seek a separation from Britain. By immediately following an acknowledgement that such an assertion has been made with the statement, "the more shame upon her conduct," Paine makes the case that Great Britain's actions should be viewed even more harshly in light of the presumed "parental" relationship. He goes on to amplify this argument by comparing Britain's actions to devouring one's young or making war upon one's family, almost unimaginably grotesque acts. Answer choice (D) accurately summarizes Paine's argument. **The correct answer is (D).**

8. In lines 44-47, Paine claims that, "it is pleasant to observe by what regular gradations we surmount the force of local prejudice as we enlarge our acquaintance with the world. All Europeans who meet in America are *countrymen* to each other …" In other words, he believes that the colonies' association with many different countries is directly contributing to a reduction in the regional prejudices that have historically divided the people of Europe. Answer choice (C) accurately summarizes Paine's opinion on this matter. **The correct answer is (C).**

9. Clear evidence for the correct answer to this question can be found in lines 59-61, in which Paine claims that, "this continent would never suffer itself to be drained of inhabitants to support the British arms in Asia, Africa, or Europe." In other words, he believes the alliance between the American colonies and Great Britain is more imagined than real, because American colonists would never be willing to leave America to fight alongside Britain in other parts of the world. This statement is well summarized in answer choice (B). **The correct answer is (B).**

10. "Of veracity" means "of truth." The phrase, "sets us at truth with nations," would be very difficult to comprehend. Furthermore, that phrase would appear to have positive connotations, which is clearly not Paine's intent. Therefore, answer choice (B) may be eliminated. The phrase, "sets us in variants with nations," would seem to imply that Paine considers the American colonies to be essentially the same as other nations, with only minor differences, which is manifestly not his belief. Therefore, answer (D) may be ruled out as well. Now consider lines 74-76: "… sets us at variance with nations who would otherwise seek our friendship …" The use of "otherwise" strongly suggests that "at variance" implies the *opposite* of friendship, which rules out choice (C), "in partnership." The remaining option is answer (A). **The correct answer is (A).**

11. The most common meaning of "partial" is "incomplete," but that meaning would be inappropriate for the context in which Paine uses the word. Although the connections between countries vary in their depth, strength, and complexity, there really is no such thing as an "incomplete" connection between two countries; the countries are either connected or they are not. It is important to know that "partial" can also indicate bias or favoritism. (Hence, we want trial judges to be *impartial*.) This meaning of "partial" is clearly appropriate for line 78 of the passage, and is well expressed by the word "preferential." **The correct answer is (B).**

---

12. In lines 2-6, the narrator says, "My mother, being at once highly accomplished, well informed, and fond of employment, took the whole charge of our education on herself, with the exception of Latin—which my father undertook to teach us—so that we never went to school." This sentence makes it abundantly clear that the narrator and her sister were home schooled. **The correct answer is (D).**

SAMPLE TEST 5
Answer Explanations

13. In lines 20-24, the narrator states that her father "often unduly vexed himself with thinking of the sacrifices his dear wife had made for him, and troubled his head with revolving endless schemes for the augmentation of his little fortune, for her sake and ours." The similar meanings of "vexed himself" and "agonizing over" should immediately draw your attention to answer choice (A). The narrator goes on to say in lines 24-25 that "[i]n vain my mother assured him she was quite satisfied." This statement is also summarized well in answer choice (A), which mentions the "many reassurances" the narrator's mother gave to her father. **The correct answer is (A).**

14. Answer choice (A) is a decoy. Although "straitened" and straightened" look very much alike, they do not have the same meaning. You may be aware that a *strait* is a narrow water passage, such as the Bering Strait between Alaska and Russia. It is therefore reasonable to suppose that the verb "straiten" somehow refers to narrowing or restricting, and that is indeed the meaning of the word. (Do not feel bad if the word is new to you, by the way—it is seldom used in present-day English.) The only answer choice that suggests a meaning similar to "narrowed" or "restricted" is choice (C), "constrained." **The correct answer is (C).**

15. In lines 38-39, the narrator describes the merchant as "a man of enterprising spirit and undoubted talent." In line 40, she characterizes the merchant's offer to her father as "generous." The word "enterprising" is similar in meaning to "determined," and "undoubted talent" strongly suggests impressive intelligence. Furthermore, assuming that the offer made by the merchant was indeed generous (rather than merely seeming generous), it would be reasonable to believe that the merchant could be trusted. All of these clues point strongly toward answer choice (D). **The correct answer is (D).**

16. In lines 51-55, the narrator notes that in the wake of the transaction with the merchant, the family was temporarily "reduced to the narrow income" of her father's occupation as a curate, but states that her "father seemed to think there was no necessity for scrupulously restricting our expenditures to that." These observations are well summarized by the statement, "her father believed there was no reason to adhere to a strict budget," found at the end of answer choice (B). In lines 57-59, the narrator reveals that her mother believed that the family should "keep within bounds, for our prospects were but precarious." The opinion of the narrator's mother is summarized in answer choice (B) as well. ("[T]he family should live within the limitations of the family's current income, rather than counting on future wealth.") **The correct answer is (B).**

17. In the lines that immediately precede the text in question (lines 65-67), the narrator speaks of long conversations with her sister about all the wonderful things to come for their family. She reveals in lines 70-74 that her father engaged in similar speculation. It is clear from the previous three paragraphs, however, that their dreams would only be realized if the family's venture with the merchant proved successful. In other words, all of their speculation was based on the assumption that the partnership with the merchant would bring them significant income in the future. Answer choice (B) summarizes this idea clearly. **The correct answer is (B).**

18. In line 75, the narrator recalls her mother laughing "with delight" at her father's jokes, so answer choices (A) and (B) are clearly incorrect. In lines 76-77, however, the narrator states that her mother feared that her father was "setting his heart too much upon the matter." In other words, her mother was worried that her father saw the family's future happiness as entirely dependent on the success

of the venture with the merchant. The only answer choice that expresses this idea is choice (D). **The correct answer is (D).**

19. The basis for the answer to this question may be found in lines 80-83. The narrator recalls receiving the "news that the vessel that contained our fortune had wrecked and gone to the bottom with all its stores, together with several of the crew and the unfortunate merchant himself." In other words, the merchant's vessel was lost at sea, and he died in the accident. **The correct answer is (A).**

20. As noted in the explanation for question #19 above, lines 80-83 provide clear evidence for the correct answer to that question. **The correct answer is (C).**

21. Lines 72-73 contain the phrase, "high hopes and sanguine expectations," a phrase that strongly suggests optimism. Indeed, the most common meaning of the word sanguine is, "characterized by great optimism." Among the answer choices, only choice (C) suggests a meaning related to optimism. **The correct answer is (C).**

22. In lines 87-90, the narrator states that, "Though riches had charms, poverty had no terrors for an inexperienced girl like me. Indeed, there was something exhilarating in the idea of being driven to straits and thrown upon our own resources." It is reasonable to summarize these two sentences by saying that the narrator "sees both wealth and financial struggle as opportunities for happiness," a viewpoint not shared by others in her family. **The correct answer is (D).**

---

23. By focusing on the first sentence and the last sentence of the first paragraph, we can discern its purpose. In lines 1-2, we are told that, "High school biology students learn that organisms of different species cannot successfully interbreed." The paragraph ends (lines 9-11) with the statement, "[I]t is more accurate to say that creatures of different species can interbreed *only with great difficulty*, but on rare occasions do succeed at it." Hence, the author is demonstrating that an important principle of biology is not fully understood by those who only study biology briefly in high school. It is therefore accurate to say that the purpose of the paragraph is "to explain a scientific principle and explain why it is frequently misunderstood." **The correct answer is (A).**

24. In lines 28-39, the author explains the hypothesis put forth by some biologists that Neanderthal DNA is a cause of many modern human health problems. But at the beginning of the final paragraph of the passage (lines 55-57) the author states that although it is possible that the hypothesis is correct, "no evidence presently available indicates clearly that such a conclusion is justified." The author proceeds (lines 61-75) to propose that the actual cause of the various afflictions mentioned in the passage may be lack of genetic diversity among many modern humans. It is therefore accurate to say that the author presents a new scientific hypothesis, analyzes it skeptically, and then presents an alternative hypothesis. **The correct answer is (B).**

25. "Testify" is not an accepted meaning of the word "bear." (Do not be confused by the fact that testify *is* the meaning of the two-word phrase, "bear witness.") Therefore, answer (C) may be eliminated immediately. The remaining choices are all accepted meanings of the word bear, so it is necessary to analyze the context within which the word appears in the passage. Even if it were true that Neanderthal DNA caused health problems in modern humans, it would still be very strange to

SAMPLE TEST 5
Answer Explanations

say that a person "endures" DNA of any sort. Nor does a person "support" DNA; it would be far more accurate to say that DNA supports the person. However, all living creatures do *carry* DNA in their bodies. **The correct answer is (A).**

26. The word "alien" definitely can refer to an extra-terrestrial being (and it usually does in science fiction). However, the passage clearly identifies the source of the non-*homo sapiens* DNA that many modern humans carry as DNA from the species *homo neanderthalensis*. Neanderthals were not extra-terrestrials; they lived in Europe and Asia. The word "alien" can also mean non-citizen. For example, a person who is brought from the US to Guatemala by a company under a work contract is a *resident alien* of Guatemala. This meaning of "alien" would make no sense within the context of line 18, however, because a DNA molecule cannot be a citizen. We are therefore choosing between option (B), "strange" and option (C), "foreign." Arguably, a Neanderthal would indeed seem very strange to a modern human, but that is a non-scientific judgment, inappropriate for the passage. What is certain is that a strand of Neanderthal DNA would be *foreign* to (that is, would not belong to or with) a molecule of purely *homo sapiens* DNA. **The correct answer is (C).**

27. In lines 20-24, the passage explains that Neanderthals were "the descendants of ancient hominid ancestors who left Africa long before *homo sapiens* came into existence." From this statement alone, we know that:

    1. Neanderthals were *descendants* of hominids who left Africa but did not come from Africa themselves. We should therefore conclude that Neanderthals never existed in Africa (a conclusion consistent with the fossil record).

    2. The ancestors of Neanderthals left Africa long before any tribes of *homo sapiens* left that continent, because *homo sapiens* did not yet exist when the ancestors of Neanderthals migrated to Europe and Asia. Therefore, *homo sapiens* could only have encountered Neanderthals *after* leaving Africa.

These conclusions are summarized well in answer choice (D). **The correct answer is (D).**

28. As noted above in the explanation for question #27, lines 20-24 of the passage provide crucial information that enables the reader to understand the relationship between the species *homo sapiens* and *homo neanderthalensis*. Because these lines are included among the lines referenced in answer choice (B), **the correct answer is (B).**

29. The hypothesis proposed in answer choice (D) may well be correct (indeed, many scientists believe that it is), but that hypothesis is not an accurate summary of the information presented in the third paragraph. Rather, the third paragraph focuses on the possibility that the traces of Neanderthal DNA that many modern humans carry may cause various health problems. The paragraph concludes with the statement that, "It is possible, then, that many of the health woes of present-day humanity stem from genetic mismatches that put our bodily and mental systems at odds with themselves." These ideas are well summarized in answer choice (C). **The correct answer is (C).**

30. In lines 57-73, the author proposes that the fact that humans of European or Asian descent exhibit significantly less genetic diversity than those of purely sub-Saharan African ancestry may account

for the many health problems experienced by people in the former group. For example, the author points out that two randomly chosen people of European or Asian descent, even if they live halfway around the world from each other, are likely to be more genetically similar than two sub-Saharan Africans who live very close to each other. The author then notes that, "We have long known that genetic homogeneity [lack of genetic diversity] makes all animals vulnerable to health woes." The author's hypothesis is therefore well summarized in answer choice (A). **The correct answer is (A).**

31. Recall that the third paragraph presents the hypothesis that many modern human health problems are caused by Neanderthal DNA. Figure 1 shows clearly that present-day humans from East Asia, Europe, and the Pacific Islands usually possess Neanderthal DNA, whereas people from sub-Saharan Africa never do. Figure 2 shows that the groups of present-day humans with Neanderthal DNA more often suffer from antibody absence or deficiency, one of the health issues mentioned in the passage (lines 36-37), than humans without Neanderthal DNA. Answer choice (B) accurately summarizes these ideas. T**he correct answer is (B).**

32. The author has proposed that the actual cause of the human health problems discussed in the passage is lack of genetic diversity among humans with European and/or Asian ancestry (see the explanation for question #30 above). It is therefore reasonable to suppose that he or she would consider any information presented about DNA and human health issues to be incomplete if it did not contain data on genetic diversity. This likely objection from the author is mentioned only in answer choice (D). **The correct answer is (D).**

---

33. In lines 20-23, the author of Passage 1 states that, "The inclusion of the promise of trial by jury in the Bill of Rights, was, in fact, a direct response to the *denial* of jury trials to American colonists by British authorities." In lines 30-35, he adds, "The colonists were well acquainted with both trials by jury and trials by a judge alone. … [T]hey expressed a clear preference for jury trials as the *superior* form of trial." These ideas are summarized accurately in answer choice (B). **The correct answer is (B).**

34. The author of Passage 1 concludes the passage (lines 47-50) with the assertion that, "[U]nder a system devoid of civilian juries, the power of judges would become absolute, and such unchecked power, by its very nature, will attract those with the very worst of intentions." Unscrupulous individuals are people who do not exhibit morality or any sense of fairness, so it would be accurate to say that such individuals have very bad intentions. Answer choice (A) therefore accurately paraphrases the author's claim. **The correct answer is (A).**

35. As noted in the explanation for question #34 above, lines 47-50 provide strong evidence in support of the answer to that question. **The correct answer is (D).**

36. The most common meaning of "wrest" is to take away by force or intimidation. Within the context of line 37, this meaning is clearly appropriate. The sentence as a whole (lines 36-40) speaks of the danger of concentrating power in the hands of single individuals, which would only be possible if one were to first take power away from most people. The answer choice that best expresses the meaning of "wresting," then, is option (C), "snatching." **The correct answer is (C).**

SAMPLE TEST 5
Answer Explanations

37. In lines 57-59 of Passage 2, the author states, "I do not advocate, nor have I ever advocated, for the elimination of jury trials from the American justice system." Yet the author of Passage 1 asserts in lines 9-10 that the author of Passage 2 "speaks of abolishing the jury trial system." Clearly, the author of Passage 2 has every right to claim that her arguments have been misrepresented in lines 9-10 of Passage 1. Since these lines are among the lines referenced in answer choice (B), **the correct answer is (B)**.

38. In lines 59-61, the author of Passage 2 claims that, "the particulars of the jury trial system, though they once represented the best practices available, are now woefully out of date." She goes on to argue that the current jury trial system could be improved, proposing multiple specific ways of doing so. It is likely, then, that she would *agree* with the assertion made in Passage 1 that the founders of the US saw jury trials as the superior form of trial among those that existed at the time. But she would *not* agree that the current jury trial system remains the best possible way to conduct trials. Her likely response is thus well summarized in answer choice (D). **The correct answer is (D).**

39. In the third paragraph of Passage 2, the author describes a specific trial during which jurors wished to review one particular piece of testimony very carefully. They believed that the evidence provided by that testimony held the key to the entire case. She explains that the jurors were denied access to either a written transcript or an audio or video recording of the testimony in question, and so never had the opportunity to review it in detail as they desired. She is clearly implying that the trial verdict should be questioned because jurors did not have the degree of access to the evidence that they believed they needed in order to arrive at a fair and just decision. **The correct answer is (A).**

40. Even if you are not aware that the most common meaning of "comprised" or "comprised of" is "made up of," the context within which the word "comprised" appears should make very clear that the author of Passage 2 is describing a proposed composition, or makeup, of a jury. **The correct answer is (A).**

41. The author of Passage 2 proposes the reforms described in answer choices (A) and (B) in lines 95-100, and the reform described in answer choice (C) in lines 100-103. She does not at any point propose or discuss the reform described in answer choice (D). **The correct answer is (D).**

42. In the first sentence of Passage 1 (lines 1-5), the author asserts that the assurance of a jury trial for those accused of significant crimes does a great deal to protect our basic rights and freedoms as US citizens. In the final paragraph of the passage (lines 36-50), he warns of the dangers of "wresting power from the hands of ordinary citizens" by abolishing jury trials. It is therefore quite accurate to say that "[t]he first priority of the author of Passage 1 is protection of individual freedoms and power," a statement found in answer choice (C). Meanwhile, the author of Passage 2 frequently speaks of the challenges jurors face in attempting to fully evaluate evidence. (See, for example, lines 77-79 and lines 83-94.) She is clearly very concerned about the accuracy of verdicts in jury trials. Thus, her first priority is also accurately described in answer choice (C). **The correct answer is (C).**

---

43. In lines 9-11, the author writes, "Stories make real memories: we can actually be connected to our past selves, and to each other, through things that never happened." She later (lines 76-80) speculates that memory involves a delicate balance between the literal truth of what happened and the creatively generated truth of storytelling. In between those statements, in lines 39-58, she recalls a journey of imagination she shared with her brother during childhood, and describes how vivid the memory of that imagined adventure has remained to the present day. All of these ideas are well summarized in answer choice (C). **The correct answer is (C).**

44. In lines 14-16, the author states that she attended five different schools between first and fifth grade, and refers to "all that changing of place." The clear implication is that her family frequently moved. **The correct answer is (D).**

45. In order to answer this question correctly, it is necessary to read the entire sentence (lines 23-24) in which the phrase in question appears: "We would peer inside our skulls and unfold sagas of foreign lands, peril, and clever escape." Obviously, foreign lands cannot literally be seen inside a skull. The correct answer must therefore refer to metaphor or imagination. Only choice (B) makes such a reference. **The correct answer is (B).**

46. Immediately after recounting the imagined adventure, the author states (lines 50-51), "I remember all of this more vividly than I remember most of my birthdays." This evidence strongly points to answer choice (A). **The correct answer is (A).**

47. As noted in the explanation for question #46 above, lines 50-51 provide clear evidence in support of the correct answer to that question. **The correct answer is (C).**

48. As noted in the explanation for question #46 above, in lines 50-51, the author comments on the vividness of her memories of her childhood world of imagination. The phrase "only a breath away" implies extreme closeness. It is therefore most logical to conclude that the author means to suggest that she does not feel a significant separation between her present-day experiences and her memories of events of the past, both real and imagined. **The correct answer is (D).**

49. The word "nebulous" most often indicates that something is hazy or cloudlike. Clouds are not unyielding (they shift forms before our eyes), and certainly not nuclear, so answers (A) and (C) may be eliminated. The author's use of the word "delicate" in line 78 may well lead you to give serious consideration to choice (D), "fragile." It is important to note, however, that in lines 60-80, the author has set up a comparison between the composition of memories and the composition of atoms. You are probably aware that atoms are anything but fragile; they are, in fact, extremely difficult to break down. It is much more likely, then, that the author's intended meaning for the word "nebulous" is closer to "formless." **The correct answer is (B).**

50. As noted in the explanation for question #49 above, the author devotes lines 60-80 of the passage to setting up a comparison between the structure of memories and the structure of atoms. She compares memory to the water cycle in line 95. The reference to deciphering raised lettering by running a finger over it may be found in lines 86-88. Therefore, the metaphors described in answer choices (A), (C), and (D) are all employed by the author of the passage. **The correct answer is (B).**

51. To "decipher" literally means to decode. Obviously, one doesn't usually have to "decode" a book cover, since book titles are seldom written in code. We therefore need to choose a word or phrase that has a meaning similar to "decode" but does not in any way reference actual codes. Answer choices (A) and (C) both satisfy this criterion, and the distinction between them is subtle. To "precisely define" a word means to explain its exact meaning, using other words. One cannot explain anything in words by running one's finger over it. Therefore, though it comes very close to the desired meaning, answer choice (C) must be eliminated. **The correct answer is (A).**

52. In lines 56-57, the author describes the act of remembering as peering through "scraps of detail, shards of image." In lines 76-80, the author speculates that although actual events are the building blocks of memories, a memory only becomes whole through the creative act of describing those events. Through these two

statements and several others in the passage, the author suggests that memories are inherently fragmentary, and that it is the creative act of storytelling that gives them form and completeness. **The correct answer is (D).**

TEST SECTION 2: WRITING AND LANGUAGE

NOTE: As the instructions for this test section clearly state, the goal when answering questions is to bring each passage into compliance with the conventions of standard written English. Standard written English is a form of the English language specifically developed to facilitate clear communication in writing, even between people who speak very different forms of English. Therefore, many of the correct answers may seem different from the choices you would make in your everyday speech. That does not mean there is anything wrong with the version of spoken English you have learned. To perform well on this test section, you must learn to make distinctions between the English you speak on a daily basis and the guidelines governing word choices, punctuation, and sentence structure in standard written English.

1. The word "construe" refers to how a person interprets a statement, so "construed" is clearly an inappropriate word for the context. To "strew" things, however, is to scatter them in a disorganized manner. It would make sense to speak of the pieces of a shattered motorcycle being *scattered* across a highway. Therefore, "strewn" is the appropriate word choice. **The correct answer is (C).**

2. The word "consequently" implies that the sentence will describe a *consequence* (result) of the circumstances described in the previous sentence(s). In this case, the word would imply that men and women are drawn to motorcycle riding specifically because it is very dangerous. While that may be true for a few extreme thrill seekers, it certainly wouldn't be the case for the majority of riders. It would be better to begin the sentence with a word or phrase that suggests a contradiction or contrast, since the author's intention is to emphasize the fact that many people take up motorcycle riding every year *in spite of* the dangers. The only answer choice that suggests such a contrast or contradiction is choice (D), "Nevertheless." **The correct answer is (D).**

3. The subject to which the verb refers is the phrase, "receiving a thorough education." Since the phrase describes an act, it is considered singular in form. Therefore, the verb used should also be singular in form, which eliminates choices (C) and (D). The two-word phrase "is minimizing" has the same meaning as the single word "minimizes." Therefore, choice (B) adds clumsiness and wordiness for no reason. It is best to leave the underlined word alone. **The correct answer is (A).**

4. To include the word "Also" and the phrase "as well" in the same sentence is redundant, so answer choice (C) may be ruled out immediately. Answer choice (D) uses more words than the underlined portion of the sentence, but is no more informative or pleasing to read than the underlined portion, so it would be illogical to choose that answer. Note, however, that choice (B) conveys all the same information as the underlined portion in a more concise way. Notice also that in choice (B), a semicolon (;) is correctly employed. It separates the two phrases, "Outstanding motorcycle safety courses are offered in every major US city" and "a surprising number of small towns have topnotch training centers as well," either of which could stand on its own as a complete sentence. Therefore, choice (B) complies with the conventions of standard written English. **The correct answer is (B).**

5. The word "more" indicates that a comparison is being drawn. In this case, the comparison is between what the safety courses have to offer and "a few rudimentary pointers on how to keep the bike upright." The correct word to use in a comparison is **than**, not then. No other change needs to be made. **The correct answer is (C).**

SAMPLE TEST 5
Answer Explanations

6. The sentence immediately preceding the indicator for this question focuses on the physical aspects of riding a motorcycle—proper execution of evasive maneuvers and safe techniques for going to the ground if a crash cannot be avoided. The sentences that follow the indicator for this question focus more on the *mental* aspects of safe riding, such as the assumptions a rider should make and the importance of anticipating dangers. The logic of the paragraph would therefore be enhanced if a sentence that links these two topics were added at the indicated location. The proposed addition serves that purpose well, as indicated in answer choice (A). **The correct answer is (A).**

7. The word "though" suggests that the ideas to be presented in the sentence in question will contrast with or contradict the ideas presented in the previous sentence(s). In fact, the sentence in question describes a *consequence* (the manner in which the best rider safety training programs are designed) of the realities just described (the dangers posed by motorists' lack of awareness of motorcyclists). Among the answer choices, only option (D), "therefore," suggests that a consequence is about to be described. **The correct answer is (D).**

8. Notice that the entire phrase, "a classification that describes injuries ranging from temporary and mild to permanent and life changing," could be deleted, and the resulting sentence would still comply with the conventions of standard written English: "Traumatic Brain Injury (TBI) is a common and tragic outcome of motorcycle crashes." Therefore, the phrase, "a classification … changing," is a *supplemental phrase*. Remember that the standard punctuation of a supplemental phrase is to place a comma (NOT a colon or semicolon) both before AND after the phrase. Only answer choice (B) is correctly punctuated. **The correct answer is (B).**

9. Notice first that the intended meaning of the sentence is identical to the meaning of the sentence, "And while **you are** at the motorcycle shop picking out a helmet to match your personal style, purchase some sturdy, body-covering clothing as well." The word "you're" is a contraction of the two-word phrase "you are," and so its use in the underlined portion is entirely appropriate. The "personal style" mentioned *belongs to* you, and so the possessive form "your" is correctly used in the sentence as well. Hence, the underlined portion already complies with the conventions of standard written English, and is clear in meaning as well. **The correct answer is (A).**

10. Notice that by mentioning rider safety programs, sentence 4 refers back to the previous paragraph. It then sets up the discussion of the importance of wearing a helmet, the main topic of this paragraph. Therefore, sentence 4 would serve very well as a transitional sentence at the beginning of the paragraph. In other words, it should be placed before sentence 1. **The correct answer is (A).**

11. The word "Therefore" indicates that the statement about to be made is a conclusion based on, or a description of a consequence of, information presented in the previous sentence(s). But prior to this sentence, this passage has made no mention of the financial or environmental impact of riding a motorcycle. "Therefore" is thus an inappropriate word choice. The writer is actually introducing an added benefit of motorcycle ownership, so a word should be employed that suggests the sentence will present "bonus" information. "Furthermore" gives such an indication. **The correct answer is (C).**

12. Notice, first of all, that the sentence would be complete even if everything between the word "fires" and the word "are" were deleted: "Many people are surprised to learn that naturally occurring forest fires are actually beneficial for many forest ecosystems." Thus, the phrase, "generally, those … them," is a *supplemental phrase*. A supplemental phrase must be set off from the rest of the sentence. Most commonly, this setting off is accomplished through the placement of a comma at both the beginning and the end of the phrase. However, dashes (—) may also be used at the beginning and end of the phrase; in fact, dashes are preferred if the supplemental phrase is long and contains commas of its own. Most importantly, the *same* punctuation mark must be used at the beginning and end of the supplemental phrase. For instance, it is not acceptable to place a comma at the beginning of the supplemental phrase and a dash at its end. Therefore, only answer choice (C), in which a dash is used at the beginning and at the end of the supplemental phrase, complies with the conventions of standard written English. **The correct answer is (C).**

13. Answer choice (D), "as having been," would comply with the conventions of standard written English only if the author deleted the word "that" from earlier in the sentence. Even then, the sentence would be unnecessarily wordy. Therefore, option (D) must be eliminated. The subject of the sentence is "past management practices," which is plural in form. Therefore, a plural verb form is required. Of the remaining choices, only option (B), "were," satisfies this criterion. **The correct answer is (B).**

14. As written, the underlined portion has a verb tense issue: It makes no sense to speak of *new* policies where personnel *had allowed* fires to burn. The implication would be that new policies have been instituted regulating things that have already happened. Answer choice (C) has essentially the same problem, in that it also suggests that actions were taken by forest service personnel before the policies calling for those actions came into being. Choosing between answers (B) and (D) is a subtle matter, however. When used to refer to multiple employees of an organization, as is fairly clearly the case here, the word "personnel" usually takes a plural verb. That does not mean, however, that a singular verb would be unacceptable according to the conventions of standard written English. Much more importantly, the use of the word "where" in answer choice (B), though consistent with the conventions of many versions of spoken English, is considered very informal in written English, and therefore would be inappropriate for this article. By an admittedly narrow margin, then, answer (D) is the best option. **The correct answer is (D).**

15. The structure of the sentence indicates that the phrase "actually calling for" refers back to the subject, coverage. Although a reporter could call for a specific action to be taken, *coverage*, which is the act of reporting a story, could not call for anything. A person needs to do the calling. Only choice (B) answers the question, *Who is calling for that action?* **The correct answer is (B).**

16. Because the seeds "belong to" the trees, a possessive pronoun is required. Remember that the possessive form of "it" is "its" (no apostrophe), so a change is clearly required. However, as previously stated, the pronoun refers back to *trees*, a plural noun. Therefore, we need the possessive form of *they*, not of *it*. The possessive form of "they" is "their." **The correct answer is (C).**

17. Answer choice (B) does not comply with the conventions of standards written English. Either one of the phrases, "Mature jack … evergreens" and "they are … asymmetrical," could stand on its own as a complete sentence. Therefore, a semicolon (;), not a comma, would be required between the

phrases. Answers (A), (C), and (D) all technically comply with the conventions of standard written English. Notice, however, that all three options convey the exact same information. Choice (D) does so most clearly and with the fewest words, making it the best option. **The correct answer is (D).**

18. Figure 1 shows (horizontal segment of line graph) that the greatest diversity of wildlife species occurs in mixed coniferous forests in which jack pines represent between 42.5% and 60% of the trees in the forest. Giving a smaller range of percents, such as "between 45% and 60%," could still constitute an accurate statement, provided that the smaller percentage was not below 42.5% and the larger percentage was not above 60%. Figure 1 also shows that for forests in which between 42.5% and 60% of trees are jack pines, there are about 700 species present, whereas the number of species is less than 350 for forests in which jack pines account for less than 20% of the tree population. (Specifically, there are exactly 350 species when exactly 20% of trees are jack pines; the number of species declines as the percentage of jack pines decreases toward 0%). Since $350 \times 2 = 750$, it is accurate to say that forests in which between 42.5% and 60% (or between 45% and 60%) of trees are jack pines "harbor at least twice the number of wildlife species as those in which less than 20 percent of trees are jack pines." **The correct answer is (D).**

19. Note that the entire phrase, "a plant biologist … Minnesota-Bemidji," could be deleted without altering the meaning of the sentence: "Dr. Melanie Jackson states that, 'In any northern forest of mixed conifers, jack pines will inevitably be squeezed out within the first century after their initial rise to dominance.'" Hence, the phrase, "a plant biologist … Minnesota-Bemidji," is a *supplemental phrase*, and should be set off from the rest of the sentence by commas at *both* ends of the phrase. In other words, the underlined portion is correctly punctuated, and no change is required. **The correct answer is (A).**

20. The test to determine whether "it's" is an appropriate word choice is to replace it with the two words "it is." Here is the result of that replacement in this case: "Those fortunate enough to come upon an expanse of northern conifer forest during the first three decades after a significant fire know that it is an unforgettable sight, with thousands of jack pines of nearly identical height stretching out as far as the eye can see." The sentence is completely logical and complies with all conventions of standard written English. Therefore, "it's" is a correct word choice, and no change is needed. **The correct answer is (A).**

21. Here is a summary of the data displayed in Figure 2, organized by time since the last forest fire. (Time intervals and specific numbers of years have been chosen to match those mentioned in the underlined portion and answer choices.)

Years since last fire	Percent of trees that are jack pines
between 40 and 50	from 45% to about 57%
up to 10	from 0% to about 20%
between 17 and 37	at least 60%
75 or more	less than 30%
20	80%
about 15	about 47%
about 70	about 35%

Note that the percentage of jack pines in forests that burned between 17 and 37 years ago (at least 60%) is indeed at least twice the percentage of jack pines in forests that have not burned in the last 75 years (less than 30%). Therefore, answer choice (B) accurately expresses information conveyed in Figure 2. The underlined portion and the other answer choices do not accurately express information conveyed in the figure. **The correct answer is (B).**

22. Sentence 3 has been poorly placed by the author of the passage, because it discusses the opening of jack pine cones *before* the significance of a tree's cones opening has been explained. The explanation of that significance comes in sentence 4. It would therefore be most logical for sentence 3 to be place somewhere *after* sentence 4. Sentence 3 should also come *before* sentence 5, which discusses the opening of jack pine cones in greater detail. **The correct answer is (C).**

---

23. If a person attempts to make a living through freelance work, he or she is choosing *not* to pursue traditional jobs. Therefore, the underlined verb should have a meaning along the lines of "avoided" or "rejected." The word "espoused" means supported, which is clearly inappropriate for the context, so a change is required. Of the answer choices, only option (D), "eschewed," has the desired meaning. **The correct answer is (D).**

24. When one of the answer choices is to DELETE the underlined portion, it is always a good strategy to consider how the sentence would read if the underlined portion were, in fact, deleted. Here is the first sentence of the passage, with the correction from question #23 made and the underlined portion referenced in this question deleted: "During the twentieth century, those who eschewed traditional jobs and attempted to make a living through freelance work were often seen as slackers, people unwilling to make the sacrifices required to build a successful long-term career." Notice that the sentence is clear in meaning and complies with all conventions of standard written English. The underlined portion as written and answer choices (B) and (C) all add words without adding any meaning to the sentence. Therefore, deleting the underlined portion is the best option. **The correct answer is (D).**

25. The sentence as written has a logical flaw. The fact that most people now view freelancers with respect would imply that many people have, in fact, re-evaluated their feelings toward the freelancing lifestyle. Hence, the word "Although," which cues the reader to anticipate the presentation of contrasting ideas, has no place at the beginning of the sentence. A change is needed. Bear in mind that the previous sentence discussed the negative way in which many people viewed freelancers in the past. In order to connect the sentence to which this question refers with that previous sentence, it would be helpful to make some mention of that history, which answer choice (B) does, by referring to those who cling to a disparaging (that is, negative) view of freelancers. Answer choices (C) and (D) both introduce ideas that have no connection to either the previous sentence or the rest of the paragraph. **The correct answer is (B).**

26. This question tests your understanding of *parallel structure*. To help the reader process a list, all items in the list should be presented in the same style and grammatical format to the greatest extent possible. The previous two items in the list, "an excellent benefits package" and "long-term job security," are both noun phrases. Therefore, the third and final item in the list, "they were also promised a comfortable pension," should be rewritten as a noun phrase as well. The necessary

SAMPLE TEST 5
Answer Explanations

change can be made simply by deleting the words, "they were also promised," which leaves the noun phrase, "a comfortable pension." This revision is correctly made in answer choice (D). **The correct answer is (D).**

27. Whenever possible, an interior paragraph (that is, a paragraph other than the first or last paragraph) of an essay should begin with a *transitional sentence*. A transitional sentence refers back to the ideas presented in the previous paragraph, while introducing the topic to be discussed in the new paragraph. Here, the previous paragraph examined reasons a person might choose freelance work over a traditional career, such as the diminishing number of perks employers offer for employees and the risk of being pigeonholed. The simple phrase, "Whatever the reason," refers back to the topic of the previous paragraph, while alerting the reader that the discussion will now move on to other topics. The remainder of the proposed sentence nicely sets up the next sentence in the passage, by explaining the basis of the "growing demand" for freelance opportunities mentioned in that sentence. The proposed addition would therefore serve very well as a transitional sentence, linking the new paragraph to the previous one while shifting the reader's focus toward the new topic to be discussed. The addition *should* be made, which narrows our choices to answer choices (A) and (B). Since the remainder of the passage actually makes no distinction between freelancers with a college degree and those without one, choice (B) is incorrect. **The correct answer is (A).**

28. There are not many situations in which the conventions of standard written English dictate only one specific word choice. One of those rare situations is the "Not only …" construction. By convention, if a sentence begins with "Not only," the second half of the sentence should begin with some form of "but also." There is very little "wiggle room" with this construction. One should either use it in the standard manner or avoid it altogether. Only answer choice (B) correctly employs the expected phrase, "but also." **The correct answer is (B).**

29. It is critical to recognize that the word "research" is used as a *verb* in the sentence in question. The verb "research" does NOT require a preposition before the noun phrase to which it applies. For example, a person would *research Lou Gehrig's disease*; he or she would not *research on (or over or about) Lou Gehrig's disease*. Many people find this convention confusing, because they have often heard sentences like, "Jackie engaged in research on the history of cave exploration in St. Paul, Minnesota." The key distinction is that in the sentence just quoted, research is a *noun*, not a verb. Since the verb "research" should not be followed by a preposition, answers (B) and (C) are incorrect. Now notice that answer choice (D) communicates exactly and only the same information as the underlined portion, in a clumsier, wordier way. It is therefore best to make no change to the underlined portion. **The correct answer is (A).**

30. The word "specific" definitely does not mean that "there is no guarantee of payment for work completed." Rather, "specific" means precisely defined and clearly understood. Therefore, "specific" is an inappropriate word choice, and a change is necessary. Choice (D), "specified," has almost the same meaning as "specific," and so would not improve the writing of the passage. The word "specialized," which means related to very particular knowledge or training, also fails to convey the author's intended meaning, so answer (B) must also be eliminated. The remaining option is answer (C), "speculative," which does in fact imply that payment for work completed is not guaranteed. This meaning is consistent with the phrase that follows the underlined word. **The correct answer is (C).**

eggheadprep.com

31. The contracts "belong to" the online freelancers ("pajama professionals"), so the required word is the possessive form of the plural pronoun *they*. The possessive form of "they" is "their." **The correct answer is (B)**.

32. To avoid issues with lack of clarity, a writer should avoid using the word "this" in an essay to refer vaguely to information mentioned in the previous sentence(s). This guideline should, at a minimum, make you highly suspicious of leaving the underlined portion unchanged or choosing answer (D). The word "these" is simply the plural form of "this," so choice (B) does not improve the writing of the passage. In fact, it makes the writing worse, since the phrase "these are a telltale sign" has a plural/singular disagreement. Only answer choice (C) makes clear which specific information from the previous sentence(s) the author is referencing—suspicious behavior patterns exhibited by prospective employers. Therefore, answer (C) improves the writing of the passage. **The correct answer is (C)**.

33. The underlined portion as written is not particularly positive in tone or message, so a change is required in order to accomplish the author's goals. Option (C) is even more negative in its implications, so that answer may be eliminated. By contrast, choice (B) is undeniably positive in both tone and content. However, its unbridled optimism is inconsistent with the rest of the passage, in which many of the risks involved in pursuing an online freelancing career have been detailed. Answer choice (D) strikes the appropriate balance. The phrases "opened up a world of possibilities" and "make that dream a reality" both sound a positive note, while the phrase "appropriate caution" reminds the reader of the warnings offered earlier in the passage. **The correct answer is (D)**.

---

34. When one of the answer choices is to DELETE the underlined portion, it is always a good strategy to consider how the sentence would read if that portion of the passage were, in fact, deleted. Here is the first sentence of the passage, with the underlined word deleted: "Although every significant archaeological discovery represents a major step forward in humanity's understanding of the world that surrounds us, only those that shed direct light on the history of the human lineage tend to create global sensations." The sentence is clear in meaning and complies with all conventions of standard written English. There is no need for additional words. Therefore, deleting the underlined word would improve the writing of the passage. **The correct answer is (D)**.

35. The discovery described clearly sheds light on the history of the human lineage, since it pertains to a "mysteriously advanced ancient [human] civilization." Therefore, this sentence is introducing a specific *example* illustrating the general statement made in the first sentence of the paragraph. It would be best to begin the sentence with a word or phrase indicating to the reader that a specific example related to the general principle just outlined is about to be presented. The phrase "For example" clearly satisfies this criterion. **The correct answer is (B)**.

36. To an extent, this question deals with punctuation around an adverb that applies to an entire phrase. The conventions surrounding that issue are complicated and constantly evolving. Fortunately, we can work our way toward the correct answer without considering such complex matters. Notice that the phrase "also wiped out" conveys the exact same information as the longer constructions, "were also wiping out," "also having wiped out," and "also were … wiping out." In short, in comparison to answer choice (C), answers (A), (B), and (D) all involve adding words without adding

SAMPLE TEST 5
Answer Explanations

clarity or meaning, which, by definition, would not improve the writing of the passage. If in doubt, choose the simplest answer that accurately expresses the intended meaning. **The correct answer is (C).**

37. To say that the digging began "in honest" would imply that previous attempts to penetrate the mine floors were dishonest. The passage describes those attempts as "feeble," but that word certainly does not imply dishonesty. A change is required. The phase "in honesty" would comply with the conventions of standard written English more fully than the phrase "in honest," but the same issue of meaning would exist. The phrase "in urgent" would not be outlandish within the context of the sentence in question, since it is clear that the digging had taken on greater urgency, but it would need to be revised to "in urgency" in order to comply with the conventions of standard written English. In any case, choice (D) is a better option, because the phrase "in earnest" specifically means *with far greater intensity than before*. **The correct answer is (D).**

38. The phrase, "they were scientists, and rather extraordinary scientists at that," essentially answers a questions raised in the first part of the sentence. (*In which particular realm of human thought were these people ahead of their time?*) Therefore, the appropriate punctuation mark to set up this phrase is a colon (:). **The correct answer is (B).**

39. The phrase "the passing on of traits from parents to offspring" is essentially the definition of "heredity." Therefore, the proposed addition simply repeats the information already presented in the previous sentence in different words. Such repetition almost never constitutes good writing. **The correct answer is (A).**

40. The author's point is that the creators of the cave drawings were scientists. Throwing spears at animals is neither a rare human behavior nor an indication of impressive scientific awareness. However, to ponder the effects of design changes on the trajectory of a spear is certainly to think scientifically. Thus, only answer choice (C) suggests advanced scientific understanding. **The correct answer is (C).**

41. The phrase, "many of which depict a large circle emanated rays of energy," is not understandable as written. (It has, in effect, too many verbs and not enough subjects.) An acceptable rewrite would be, "many of which depict a large circle *that* emanated rays of energy," but that option does not appear among the answer choices. The problem with choice (C) is that it implies that the circle shown in the drawings emanated rays of energy at one time, but there is no sign of it doing so in the drawings themselves. This implication creates a logic problem. (How can someone looking at the picture tell that the circle once emanated rays of energy if there are no rays visible?) The best word choice will, as simply as possible, convey the idea that the emanation of energy from the large circle is apparent to any viewer of the etching, as if that emanation were occurring right now. The present progressive ("–ing") verb form, which appears in answer choices (B) and (D), clearly expresses this idea. Choice (D), however, would create the same sort of unacceptable "verb pileup" as already exists in the underlined portion. Only answer choice (B) improves the writing of the passage. **The correct answer is (B).**

42. The passage gives us no reason to believe that the cave dwellers performed the same calculations as Johannes Kepler, so answer choice (D) may be ruled out immediately. Remember that the passage

eggheadprep.com

as a whole focuses on the achievements of one particular ancient civilization, and the paragraph to which the proposed sentence would be added focuses on the civilization's achievements in the field of astronomy. Introducing information about other astronomers without showing that it is connected to the work of the cave dwellers would only obscure the author's main point. Therefore, the proposed sentence should NOT be added, and **the correct answer is (C).**

43. Although the passage as a whole portrays the people of the mysterious ancient civilization as extraordinary scientists, this particular sentence acknowledges something they got wrong. (They apparently believed that the motion of the planets is chaotic, when in fact it is quite orderly.) It would be appropriate to begin the sentence with a word indicating to the reader that the author is about to make such an acknowledgement. The word "Admittedly" provides such an indication far better than any of the other words suggested in choices (B), (C), and (D). Therefore, it is best to leave the underlined word alone. **The correct answer is (A).**

44. There are a number of grammatical considerations underlying this question, but we need only consider one of them to determine the correct answer. Hard though it may be to believe, the entire phrase, "To perceive the motion of our own planet simply by studying the apparent movement patterns of heavenly bodies," serves as the subject of the sentence. Therefore, that phrase should be followed by a verb or verb phrase. Only answer choice (D), in which the word "requires" immediately follows the word "bodies," fulfills this requirement. **The correct answer is (D).**

SAMPLE TEST 5
Answer Explanations

TEST SECTION 3: MATH—NO CALCULATOR

NOTE: Most problems in math can be solved using multiple different methods. In these explanations, the most standard methods taught in US middle school and high school mathematics are shown. You may have employed a different method that is equally valid.

1. Starting with the equation, $3x - 6 = 4$, add 6 to both sides to get $3x = 10$. Now multiply both sides by 3, yielding $9x = 30$. Subtract 2 from both sides to get the result, $9x - 2 = 30 - 2 = 28$. **The correct answer is (D).**

2. From 9 a.m. to 5 p.m. is 8 hours, as can be determined by simple counting. Therefore, since Carla took a one-hour break for lunch, she spent 7 hours completing projects. If she completes C projects per hour, she would complete $7C$ projects in 7 hours. Now, from 10 a.m. to 4 p.m. is 6 hours, so, taking away an hour for his lunch break, Paul spent 5 hours completing projects. Since he completes P projects per hour, Paul would complete $5P$ projects in 5 hours. Hence, the expression for the total number of projects completed by Carla and Paul on Tuesday is $7C + 5P$. **The correct answer is (A).**

3. The variable d represents the number of days *after* the end of the storm. Therefore, the value of d would be zero immediately after the storm ends, since no days have passed yet. At that moment, then, the height of water in the rain gauge, in inches, was $H = 1.79 - .12(0) = 1.79 - 0 = 1.79$. **The correct answer is (D).**

4. By definition,

$$r^{\frac{m}{n}} = \sqrt[n]{r^m}, \text{ where } n \neq 0.$$

Therefore, $\sqrt[5]{r^3} = r^{\frac{3}{5}}$.

The correct answer is (C).

5. The two angles with measures $(4x - 3)°$ and $(4y + 17)°$ are vertical angles, so their measures must be equal. We therefore know that $4x - 3 = 4y + 17$. Substituting the given value of 15 for y, we have, $4x - 3 = 4(15) + 17$. Simplifying the right side of the equation yields, $4x - 3 = 60 + 17$, or $4x - 3 = 77$. Now add 3 to both sides to get $4x = 80$. Dividing both sides by 4 yields the result, $x = 20$. We now know that statement II is true, while statement III is false. Now notice that the angles with measures $(4y + 17)°$ and $(3x + 15)°$ are *corresponding angles* created by the transversal, t. In order for lines m and n to be parallel, these angle measures must be equal. Using the given value of y and the value of x we just found, we see that $4y + 17 = 4(15) + 17 = 60 + 17 = 77$, whereas $3x + 15 = 3(20) + 15 = 60 + 15 = 75$. Since the angle measures are not equal, lines m and n are NOT parallel, and statement I is false. Only statement II is true. **The correct answer is (B).**

eggheadprep.com

6. There are many ways to solve the system of equations for x and y. Here is one method.

$$\begin{cases} 4x - 2y = 14 \\ -3x + 6y = 3 \end{cases}$$ multiply the first equation by 3 to get

$$\begin{cases} 12x - 6y = 42 \\ -3x + 6y = 3 \end{cases}$$ add these two equations to get

$9x = 45$ divide both sides by 9 to arrive at the solution,

$x = 5$

Now substitute this value for x in the second equation:

$-3(5) + 6y = 3 \Rightarrow -15 + 6y = 3$ add 15 to both sides to get

$6y = 18$ divide both sides by 6 to get the result,

$y = 3$

Therefore, the value of $x - y$ is $5 - 3 = 2$. **The correct answer is (A).**

7. The standard algebra technique of cross multiplication yields, $7(4x) = 12(2x + 5)$. Simplifying the left side and using the distributive property on the right side gives us, $28x = 24x + 60$. Subtract $24x$ from both sides to get, $4x = 60$. Divide both sides by 4 to obtain the result, $x = 15$.

Do not be too quick to dismiss answer choice (D), however. If the possible solution we have found were to create a denominator of zero in the original equation, there would in fact be no true solution to the equation. Whenever the possibility of "no solutions" is represented among the answer choices, check your answer:

$$\frac{4x}{2x+5} = \frac{4(15)}{2(15)+5} = \frac{60}{35} = \frac{12}{7}$$

Our solution is valid. **The correct answer is (C).**

8. Even though the exponents appear complicated, we may base our factoring method on the factoring of an expression of the form, $x^2 + bx + c$. Therefore, we look for two numbers with a sum of -13 and a product of 30. These two numbers are -10 and -3. As can be verified by expanding (FOILing), the correct factoring is thus $(m^2 - 10n^2)(m^2 - 3n^2)$. **The correct answer is (B).**

NOTE: Problem #8 may also be solved by expanding (FOILing) each expression given in the answer choices, and determining which result is equivalent to the given expression.

9. Using the given formula for $f(x)$, $f(3) = a(3)^2 - 2a(3) + 5 = a(9) - 6a + 5 = 9a - 6a + 5$, or $3a + 5$. Since we are also given that $f(3) = -1$, we now know that $3a + 5 = -1$. Subtracting 5 from both sides of this equation gives us, $3a = -6$. Now divide both sides by 3 to obtain the result, $a = -2$. We now use this value of a to rewrite the formula for $f(x)$:

$$f(x) = -2x^2 - 2(-2)x + 5 = -2x^2 + 4x + 5$$

SAMPLE TEST 5
Answer Explanations

Consequently, $f(-1) = -2(-1)^2 + 4(-1) + 5 = -2(1) - 4 + 5 = -2 - 4 + 5 = -1$. **The correct answer is (B).**

10. We can factor the right side of the given equation by finding two numbers with a sum of –3 and a product of –10. These two numbers are –5 and 2. Therefore, the given equation may be rewritten as, $y = (x - 5)(x + 2)$. We find the x-intercepts of the graph by setting each factor equal to zero. The equation, $x - 5 = 0$, yields $x = 5$. The equation, $x + 2 = 0$, yields $x = -2$. Therefore, the x-intercepts of the parabola are the points (–2, 0) and (5, 0), and these points are represented as (**r, 0**) and (**s, 0**) on the graph. Since the graph clearly shows that the value of r is negative, we conclude that $r = -2$. **The correct answer is (D).**

11. First notice that the description of the location of the point (**u, v**) ensures that the point is in quadrant IV of the xy-plane, so that $u > 0$ and $v < 0$. It is therefore certain that $u > v$, so answer choice (B) may be eliminated immediately. Second, observe that the x-coordinate of the point (**0, t**) is 0, so we may find the value of t simply by plugging in 0 for x in the given equation:

$$t = (0)^2 - 3(0) - 10 = 0 - 0 - 10 = -10.$$

We next determine the location of the vertex of the parabola. If a parabola has two x-intercepts, the x-coordinate of the vertex is the *average* of the x values at those intercepts. As shown in the explanation for question #10 above, the x-intercepts of this parabola are at the points (–2, 0) and (5, 0). Hence, the x-coordinate of the vertex is $\frac{-2 + 5}{2} = \frac{3}{2}$. The y-coordinate of the vertex is found by plugging this value in for x in the given equation.

$$y = \left(\frac{3}{2}\right)^2 - 3\left(\frac{3}{2}\right) - 10 = \frac{9}{4} - \frac{9}{2} - 10$$

Convert all terms to fractions with the common denominator, 4:

$$y = \frac{9}{4} - \frac{18}{4} - \frac{40}{4} = -\frac{49}{4} = -12\frac{1}{4}$$

The vertex of the parabola is thus the point $\left(\frac{3}{2}, -12\frac{1}{4}\right)$. The value $-12\frac{1}{4}$ is the *minimum* value of the function. Since v is the y-coordinate of a point on the parabola that is not the vertex, we know that $v > -12\frac{1}{4}$. Notice, however, that it would be possible for v to satisfy the condition, $v \leq -12$. This fact eliminates answer (D). Now recall that we determined previously that $v < 0$. We therefore know that $12\frac{1}{4} < v < 0$. As a result, $|v| < 12\frac{1}{4}$. Since the point (**u, v**) lies between the vertex and the x-intercept (5, 0), we know that $\frac{3}{2} < u < 5$, so it is clearly possible that $|u| < |v|$, which eliminates choice (C). We are left with only the statement given in answer choice (A), which indeed cannot be true, since $|t| + 3 = |-10| + 3 = 10 + 3 = 13$, and we previously observed that $|v| < 12\frac{1}{4}$. The **correct answer is (A)**.

12. Since we are told that the temperature of the sample will remain constant while the sample is melting, we look for a horizontal segment of the graph. Furthermore, since melting occurs *before* boiling, we should look for the *first* horizontal segment of the graph. The beginning of the first horizontal segment aligns roughly with the mark for 60 minutes on the horizontal access. Therefore, melting began after about 60 minutes. **The correct answer is (B).**

13. Here is one of many methods that can be used to solve this problem.

$\begin{cases} 2x + ay = 4 \\ -5x - by = 7 \end{cases}$ Multiply the first equation by 5 and the second by 2 to get

$\begin{cases} 10x + 5ay = 20 \\ -10x - 2by = 14 \end{cases}$ Add these two equations to get

$5ay - 2by = 34$ Factor out a y on the left side to arrive at,

$y(5a - 2b) = 34$ Divide both sides by $5a - 2b$ to obtain the result,

$y = \dfrac{34}{5a - 2b}$

The system will therefore have no solutions if $5a - 2b = 0$, since the expression for y would then have a zero denominator. Adding $2b$ to both sides of this equation yields, $5a = 2b$. Divide both sides by 5 to obtain the result, $a = \dfrac{2}{5}b$. **The correct answer is (C).**

14. Note first that since $i = \sqrt{-1}$, we know that $i^2 = -1$. Expand (FOIL) the expression, $(-3 + 2i)(1 + 3i)$, which yields, $-3 - 9i + 2i + 6i^2 = -3 - 7i + 6(-1) = -3 - 7i - 6 = -9 - 7i$. Now apply the distributive property to the expression, $4i(-9 - 7i)$, which yields $-36i - 28i^2 = -36i - 28(-1) = -36i + 28 = 28 - 36i$. **The correct answer is (A).**

15. Begin by adding $2x$ to both sides of the given equation to obtain, $3x^2 + 2x - 4 = 0$. Now use the quadratic formula to solve for x.

$$x = \dfrac{-2 \pm \sqrt{2^2 - 4(3)(-4)}}{2(3)} = \dfrac{-2 \pm \sqrt{4 + 48}}{6} = \dfrac{-2 \pm \sqrt{52}}{6}$$

$$= \dfrac{-2 \pm \sqrt{4} \cdot \sqrt{13}}{6} = \dfrac{-2 \pm 2\sqrt{13}}{6} = \dfrac{-2}{6} \pm \dfrac{2\sqrt{13}}{6} = -\dfrac{1}{3} \pm \dfrac{\sqrt{13}}{3}$$

Note that the "+" part of the "±" symbol must be used to obtain a positive solution, as required by the instructions for the problem. We now multiply this positive solution by 6:

SAMPLE TEST 5
Answer Explanations

$$6\left(-\frac{1}{3}+\frac{\sqrt{13}}{3}\right) = -\frac{6}{3}+\frac{6\sqrt{13}}{3} = -2+2\sqrt{13}$$

The correct answer is (C).

_____

16. A basic theorem of trigonometry states that $\cos(90° – z°) = \sin(z°)$. Therefore, since we know that the measure of $\angle ADC$ is at most 90°, we may conclude that the statement, $\cos(\angle ABD) = \sin(\angle BDC)$, implies that, in degrees, $m\angle ABD = 90 – m\angle BDC$. Substituting the given expressions for the angle measures, we have, $3x + 10 = 90 – (5x – 24)$. Distributing the (–) sign on the right side, we have, $3x + 10 = 90 – 5x + 24$, or $3x + 10 = 114 – 5x$. Subtracting 10 from both sides yields, $3x = 104 – 5x$. Now add $5x$ to both sides to obtain, $8x = 104$. Dividing both sides by 8 gives us the result, $x = 13$. **The correct answer is 13.**

17. Let F equal the number of frogs and T equal the number of turtles. The information in the first sentence may be expressed as the equation, $F = 2T + 5$. The second sentence corresponds to the equation, $F + T = 38$. Substituting the expression for F from the first equation into the second equation gives us, $(2T + 5) + T = 38$, or $3T + 5 = 38$. Subtracting 5 from both sides yields, $3T = 33$. Dividing both sides by 3, we obtain the result, $T = 11$. **The correct answer is 11.**

18. We begin by substituting the given value, 2, for w.

$$2\sqrt{x+7} + 3w = 2x – 4 \Rightarrow 2\sqrt{x+7} + 3(2) = 2x – 4 \Rightarrow 2\sqrt{x+7} + 6 = 2x – 4$$

Here is one method to solve the resulting equation.

Subtract 6 from both sides and then divide both sides by 2 :

$$2\sqrt{x+7} = 2x – 10 \Rightarrow \sqrt{x+7} = \frac{2x}{2} - \frac{10}{2} \Rightarrow \sqrt{x+7} = x – 5$$

Square both sides, expanding (FOILing) on the right :

$$x + 7 = (x – 5)^2 \Rightarrow x + 7 = x^2 – 10x + 25$$

Subtract x and 7 from both sides to get :

$$0 = x^2 – 11x + 18$$

Use the quadratic formula, or factor by finding two numbers with a sum of –11 and a product of 18. These numbers are –9 and –2.

$$0 = (x – 9)(x – 2)$$

We now set each factor equal to zero. The equation, $x – 9 = 0$, gives us $x = 9$, and $x – 2 = 0$ gives us $x = 2$. It may seem that either of these values of x would be a correct answer. However, whenever we square both sides of an equation in order to solve it, we must check for *extraneous solutions* by plugging each potential solution into the original equation. Here is the check, with the value 2 once again plugged in for *w*.

$$x = 2 \Rightarrow 2\sqrt{2+7} + 3(2) = 2(2) - 4 \Rightarrow 2\sqrt{9} + 6 = 4 - 4 \Rightarrow 2(3) + 6 = 0 \Rightarrow$$
$6 + 6 = 0$. This statement is false, so 2 is NOT a solution.

$$x = 9 \Rightarrow 2\sqrt{9+7} + 3(2) = 2(9) - 4 \Rightarrow 2\sqrt{16} + 6 = 18 - 4 \Rightarrow 2(4) + 6 = 14 \Rightarrow$$
$8 + 6 = 14$. This statement is true, so 9 IS a solution.

The correct answer is 9.

19. The information in the first sentence may be expressed as the equation, $P = kW$, where k is a constant. If the weight of the bracelet is 6 ounces, then, the price is given by, $P = k(6)$, or $P = 6k$. If the weight of the bracelet is 4 ounces, the price is, $P = k(4)$, or $P = 4k$. Since the cost of the 6-ounce bracelet is 7 dollars more than the cost of the 4-ounce bracelet, we have, $6k = 4k + 7$. Subtracting $4k$ from both sides gives us, $2k = 7$. Dividing both sides by 2 yields, $k = \frac{7}{2}$. Since k is a constant, its value cannot change, so we may now rewrite the formula for P as, $P = \frac{7}{2}W$. For a 10-ounce bracelet, then, $P = \frac{7}{2}(10) = \frac{70}{2} = 35$ dollars. **The correct answer is 35.**

20. Begin by substituting the expression for y from the first equation into the second equation, which gives us, $2x - (x^2 - 4x) = -16$. Distributing the (−) sign then yields, $2x - x^2 + 4x = -16$, or $-x^2 + 6x = -16$. Add 16 to both sides to get, $-x^2 + 6x + 16 = 0$. Multiply both sides by −1 to obtain the simpler form, $x^2 - 6x - 16 = 0$. We may factor this equation by finding two numbers with a sum of −6 and a product of −16. These two numbers are −8 and 2. Hence, the equation may be rewritten as, $(x - 8)(x + 2) = 0$. Setting each factor equal to zero gives us the equation, $x - 8 = 0$, from which we obtain the solution $x = 8$, and the equation, $x + 2 = 0$, from which we obtain the solution $x = -2$. Because we are told that $x > 0$, we conclude that $x = 8$. Now substitute this value for x in the first of the two given equations: $y = 8^2 - 4(8) = 64 - 32 = 32$. **The correct answer is 32.**

SAMPLE TEST 5
Answer Explanations

TEST SECTION 4: MATH—CALCULATOR

NOTE: Most problems in math can be solved using multiple different methods. In these explanations, the most standard methods taught in US middle school and high school mathematics are shown. You may have employed a different method that is equally valid.

1. The given information may be expressed as the proportion,

$$\frac{17}{340} = \frac{x}{2,800}$$

Cross multiplication yields, $17(2,800) = 340x$, or $47,600 = 340x$. Dividing both sides by 340, we obtain the result, $x = 140$. **The correct answer is (C).**

2. The cost of renting lighting equipment from each store may be modeled by an expression of the form, $mx + b$, or rather, $mh + b$, where h is the number of hours the rental lasts. For StageBright, 40 dollars per hour is the *rate of change*, or slope (as indicated by the key words "for each"), and is thus the value of m. The *initial value* (or, more appropriately in this case, initial cost) is $85, so 85 is the value of b. The cost of renting from StageBright for h hours is therefore $40h + 85$, or $85 + 40h$. Similarly, the cost of renting from LightHouse for h hours is $30h + 195$, or $195 + 30h$. The cost of renting from LightHouse will be lower than the cost of renting from StageBright if $195 + 30h < 85 + 40h$. **The correct answer is (B).**

3. *Average rate of change* is another term for slope. Recall that the slope of a line is positive if the line slants upward from left to right and negative if the line slants downward from left to right. Remember also that the absolute value of the slope of a line increases as the line becomes steeper. Therefore, to find the points between which the average rate of change is lowest (that is, most negative), we look for two points that determine a straight line that goes downward steeply as we read from left to right. The steepest decline toward the right between two labeled points on the graph occurs from point E to point F. **The correct answer is (C).**

4. Note first that 2001 was $2001 - 1985 = 16$ years after 1985. To estimate the 2001 budget, then, we look for the number 16 along the horizontal axis. Reading upward from that mark to the curve, we see that the 2001 budget was about 9 million dollars. The year 2010 was $2010 - 1985 = 25$ years after 1985, so we look for the number 25 on the horizontal axis, and conclude that the budget for that year was between 12 million and 13 million dollars; let's call it

12.6 million dollars. Therefore, the 2010 budget was about $12.6 - 9 = 3.6$ million dollars higher than the 2001 budget. We now express 3.6 million as a percentage of 9 million: $3.6 / 9 = 0.40$, or 40%. We conclude that the 2010 budget was 40% higher than the 2001 budget. **The correct answer is (D).**

5. We first find the number of participating students who were in 10th grade and identified as female, which is 238. The number of participating students who were in 12th grade and identified as female was 439. Hence, a total of $238 + 439 = 677$ participating students identified as female and were in 10th or 12th grade. Since the student is to be selected randomly from all those who participated in the contest, we find the desired probability by dividing 677 by the total number of participants,

eggheadprep.com

2,746. Performing the computation, 677 / 2,746 ≈ 0.2465, or 24.65%. Only answer (A), 25%, is close to this value. **The correct answer is (A).**

6. The y-intercept of a parabola is explicitly displayed as the constant c in the **standard form** of the equation of the parabola, $y = ax^2 + bx + c$. Only answer choice (B) is in standard form, so we know immediately that **the correct answer is (B).**

7. Since 58% of the complaint calls are related to billing issues, 100% – 58% = 42% must pertain to deliveries and product performance. The total number of complaint calls received on the day in question was 217 + 182 + 231 = 630. Therefore, we would expect the number of complaint calls that day pertaining to deliveries and product performance to be 42% of 630, or 0.42(630) = 264.6, which we round to the whole number 265. **The correct answer is (A).**

8. From the first sentence of the problem, we know that the total number of passengers, including children and adults, must be 45 or more in order for the flight not to be canceled. In symbols, then, we require $a + c \geq 45$. Notice that we already know that only answer choice (D) could be correct. To verify this conclusion, note that since one adult passenger accounts for an average weight of 223 pounds, a adult passengers would account for an expected weight of $223a$ pounds. Similarly, c child passengers would account for an expected weight of $136c$ pounds. Therefore, the total weight of a adult and c child passengers would be $223a + 136c$ pounds. The problem states that this total weight cannot exceed 33,000 pounds. That is, in order for a flight not to be canceled, it must be true that $223a + 136c \leq 33,000$. Note that this is the second inequality given in answer choice (D). **The correct answer is (D).**

9. Since the relationship between the printing cost and the number of copies is linear, we may express it with an equation of the form, $y = mx + b$, or in this case, $p = mN + b$. Note that we have identified the number of copies N as the "x" variable and the cost p as the "y" variable. We can therefore represent the given information as the three ordered pairs, (500, 140), (1500, 180), and (3000, 240). We could use any two of these three points to find the slope of the linear function. We will use the first two.

$$slope = m = \frac{y_2 - y_1}{x_2 - x_1} = \frac{180 - 140}{1500 - 500} = \frac{40}{1000} = \frac{4}{100} = \frac{1}{25}$$

We now choose any one of the three points to solve for the value of b. We will use the first point, so $N = 500$ and $p = 140$. Plugging the values of m, N, and p into the equation $p = mN + b$ yields,

$$140 = \frac{1}{25}(500) + b \Rightarrow 140 = 20 + b.$$

Subtracting 20 from both sides of the second equation immediately above, we obtain the result, 120 = b. Therefore, the linear relationship between p and N is expressed by the equation, $p = \frac{1}{25}N + 120$. The cost of printing 12,000 copies is $p = \frac{1}{25}(12000) + 120 = 480 + 120 = 600$ dollars. **The correct answer is (C).**

SAMPLE TEST 5
Answer Explanations

P. 493

10. Notice that the points in the scatterplot "snake" around the line of best fit according to a very clear pattern. Such a clear pattern always indicates that a linear model has shortcomings. To be specific, we see that for rehearsal times of 6 hours or less or 16 hours or more, all the points in the scatterplot are on or above the line of best fit. Therefore, the line of best fit consistently *underestimates* the number of errors for these amounts of rehearsal time. For rehearsal times of between 6 and 16 hours, all the points in the scatterplot are below the line of best fit, indicating that the line of best fit consistently *overestimates* the number of errors for these amounts of rehearsal time. These findings are summarized correctly in answer choice (D). **The correct answer is (D).**

11. The given information corresponds to the points (6, 23) and (16, 8) in the scatterplot, both of which fall on the line of best fit. We will use these two points to determine the equation of the line. We begin by finding the slope.

$$\text{slope} = m = \frac{y_2 - y_1}{x_2 - x_1} = \frac{8 - 23}{16 - 6} = \frac{-15}{10} = \frac{-3}{2} = -1.5$$

Now use either of the points identified above and the equation $y = mx + b$ to solve for b. We will use the point (6, 23), which gives us the equation, $23 = -1.5(6) + b$, or $23 = -9 + b$. Adding 9 to both sides yields, $32 = b$. Therefore, the line of best fit is $y = -1.5x + 32$, or $y = 32 - 1.5x$. **The correct answer is (B).**

12. The section of the graph visible in the image has three x-intercepts. Therefore, the polynomial function must be of degree 3 or greater. The polynomial given in answer choice (A) is second degree, and thus CANNOT represent the function graphed. If you are familiar with the end behavior of polynomial functions of various degrees, you may feel that the polynomials shown in answer choices (C) and (D) do not match the graph shown. Remember, however, that the image shows a **partial** graph of f, and therefore cannot be used to draw conclusions about the end behavior of f. **The correct answer is (A).**

13. We can solve this problem by using the unit conversion technique most commonly taught in chemistry and physics classes.

$$\text{Number of feet of pipe fabricated in 1 week} = \frac{17.3 \text{ feet}}{1 \text{ hour}} \cdot \frac{24 \text{ hours}}{1 \text{ day}} \cdot \frac{7 \text{ days}}{1 \text{ week}} w \text{ weeks} = \frac{17.3(24)(7)w \text{ feet}}{1} = 17.3(24)(7w)$$

The correct answer is (B).

14. We first find an expression for $f(2x)$ by substituting $2x$ for the x in the formula for $f(x)$. $f(2x) = 3 - 4(2x) = 3 - 8x$. We now generate the expression for $g(f(2x))$ by substituting the result just obtained for the x in the formula for $g(x)$. $g(f(2x)) = g(3 - 8x) = 5(3 - 8x) + 1 = 15 - 40x + 1 = 16 - 40x$. **The correct answer is (C).**

15. Because the average rating decreased by a consistent *percent* for each unit of time, the situation is modeled by an exponential function of the form, $y = ab^x$. The constant a represents the *initial*

value—in this case, the average rating assigned by participants who did not have to wait before tasting the beverage. Therefore, $a = 8.37$. To calculate the *decay factor*, *b*, it is critical to notice that the rating *decreases* by 14.67% for each interval of 5 minutes. The value of *b* is therefore 100% − 14.67% = 85.33%, or 0.8533. Notice that we have already narrowed the choices down to answer (C) or answer (D). The remaining analysis is subtle, however. Based on our work so far, we may model the situation using the equation, $R = 8.37(0.8533)^x$, where *R* is the average rating and *x* represents the *number of 5-minute intervals*. To express *R* in terms of *m*, note that because *x* is the number of 5-minute intervals and *m* is the number of minutes, when $x = 1$, $m = 5$. Similarly, when $x = 2$, $m = 10$. The emerging pattern may be expressed as $m = 5x$. Dividing both sides by 5 yields, $\frac{m}{5} = x$. Our equation may therefore be rewritten as, $R = 8.37(0.8533)^{\frac{m}{5}}$. **The correct answer is (D).**

16. We should rule out choice (A) immediately. We have been given no information about any treatment for the illness other than not drinking coffee, so comparing not drinking coffee to all other possible treatments is impossible. Answer choice (C) can also be eliminated quickly: the information given is that *significantly fewer* participants who drank coffee recovered, NOT that *none* of the participants who drank coffee recovered. The final important distinction we need to make is that a *significant* difference is not necessarily a *great* difference. In fact, a significant difference can be relatively small, as long as it is slightly greater than the differences one would expect to occur due to random variation. Therefore, choice (B) is also incorrect. **The correct answer is (D).**

17. Here is the table again, with a cumulative frequency column added for the male drivers.

Number of Citations	Freqency — Males	Cumulative Frequency — Males	Frequency — Females
0	15	15	37
1	39	15 + 39 = 54	58
2	51	54 + 51 = 105	39
3	44	105 + 44 = 149	27
4	14	149 + 14 = 163	9
5	8	163 + 8 = 171	3
6 or more	4	171 + 4 = 175	2

Since the total number of male drivers in the study was 175, the first cumulative frequency that exceeds 0.5(175) = 87.5 corresponds to the median number of citations for male drives. The first entry in the cumulative frequency column greater than 87.5 is 105, corresponding to 2 citations. Therefore, the median number of citations among male drivers was 2. **The correct answer is (A).**

18. Based on the method used to answer question #17, it should be quite apparent that the median number of citations for female drivers is neither 0 nor a value greater than or equal to 6. Therefore, two of the four additional female drivers had a citation total below the median for female drivers, while the other two had a citation total above the median for female drivers. Since these four additional drivers "balance each other out," with two on each side of the median (they need not precisely balance—it doesn't matter how far above or below the median the new data values are), the median does not change. Therefore, statement I is NOT true. Notice next that the mode for female drivers is 1 citation, with a frequency of 58. Adding 2 more drivers to the group with 0 citations

SAMPLE TEST 5
Answer Explanations

and 2 more to the group with 6 or more citations will only bring those frequencies up to 39 and 4, respectively. Therefore, the mode will not change, so statement III is NOT true. The mean, however, *always* changes when new values are added to a data set, unless all of the added values equal the existing mean, which is clearly impossible here since the new values are not even all equal to each other. Statement II, then, is TRUE. **The correct answer is (B).**

19. We must rewrite the equation of the circle using the method of completing the square. Here are the steps.

$$x^2 + y^2 - 8x + 9y = 6 \Rightarrow x^2 - 8x + y^2 + 9y = 6$$

We add $\left(\frac{1}{2}(-8)\right)^2 = (-4)^2 = 16$ to the "x" terms,

and $\left(\frac{1}{2}(9)\right)^2 = (4.5)^2 = 20.25$ to the "y" terms,

balancing the equation by adding the same values on the right side.

$$x^2 - 8x + 16 + y^2 + 9y + 20.25 = 6 + 16 + 20.25 \Rightarrow$$
$$(x - 4)^2 + (y + 4.5)^2 = 42.25$$

Comparing the final equation to the standard form of the equation of a circle with center (h, k) and radius r, $(x - h)^2 + (y - k)^2 = r^2$, we see that the center of the circle described by the given equation is (4, –4.5). The y-coordinate of the center is therefore –4.5. **The correct answer is (C).**

20. The first quadrant portion of the graph of an equation of the form, $y = ax^b$, where $a > 0$ and $b \leq -1$, decreases from left to right and has both the x-axis and the y-axis as asymptotes. Of the four answer choices, only choices (A) and (D) show a decreasing trend from left to right. The shape of the scatterplot shown in choice (D) is strongly suggestive of the required asymptotes; the shape of the scatterplot shown in choice (A) is linear and therefore does NOT suggest asymptotes. **The correct answer is (D).**

21. We need to express both terms as fractions with the same denominator and then subtract, **being careful to distribute the (–) sign across the numerator of the second fraction.** Here are the steps.

$$\frac{4x}{1} - \frac{3x+1}{x-5} = \frac{4x(x-5)}{x-5} - \frac{3x+1}{x-5} = \frac{4x^2 - 20x}{x-5} - \frac{3x+1}{x-5} =$$
$$\frac{4x^2 - 20x - (3x+1)}{x-5} = \frac{4x^2 - 20x - 3x - 1}{x-5} = \frac{4x^2 - 23x - 1}{x-5}$$

The correct answer is (B).

22. Starting with the inequality, $7q - 15 > -6$, add 15 to both sides to get, $7q > 9$. Now subtract 4 from both sides to get, $7q - 4 > 5$. Now, since q is an integer, the expression $7q - 4$ must also represent an integer. The minimum integer value greater than 5 is 6. **The correct answer is (D).**

23. Using the column totals for the columns representing age 11-14 and age 15-17, we determine that the total number of cigarette smokers in the study who smoked their first cigarette at age 17 or younger is 55 + 88 = 143. Focusing on the same two columns but now specifically on the row corresponding to a current smoking frequency of 30 or more cigarettes per week, we calculate a total of 36 + 50 = 86 smokers who smoked their first cigarette at age 17 or younger and currently smoke 30 or more cigarettes per week. Therefore, the requested probability is 86 / 143 ≈ .601, or about 60.1%. Answer choice (B), 60%, is closest to this value. **The correct answer is (B).**

24. Because the graph of $y = f(x)$ crosses the x-axis at $x = 1$ and $x = 3$, we know that $f(1)$ and $f(3)$ both equal zero. Using the given formula for $f(x)$, we have:
$f(1) = 2(1)^3 - 5(1)^2 + c(1) + d = 2(1) - 5(1) + c + d = 2 - 5 + c + d = -3 + c + d$
$f(3) = 2(3)^3 - 5(3)^2 + c(3) + d = 2(27) - 5(9) + 3c + d = 54 - 45 + 3c + d = 9 + 3c + d$
We therefore have the system of two equations, $-3 + c + d = 0$ and $9 + 3c + d = 0$. We can solve the system by multiplying the first equation by -1 and adding the resulting equation to the second equation:

$$\begin{cases} -1(-3+c+d) = 0(-1) \\ 9 + 3c + d = 0 \end{cases} \Rightarrow \begin{cases} 3 - c - d = 0 \\ 9 + 3c + d = 0 \end{cases} \Rightarrow 12 + 2c = 0$$

Subtracting 12 from both sides of the last equation yields, $2c = -12$. Dividing both sides by 2, we obtain the result, $c = -6$. Plugging this value of c into the second equation of the system gives us, $9 + 3(-6) + d = 0$, or $9 - 18 + d = 0$, or $-9 + d = 0$. Adding 9 to both sides, we obtain the result, $d = 9$. **The correct answer is (A).**

25. If the maximum measurement error is 7%, that means that the measured depth, H, must lie within the interval from 7% *below* the exact depth to 7% *above* the exact depth, where the exact depth is D. To find the value that is 7% below D, we must calculate a *percent decrease*, so we use the percent value, 100% – 7% = 93%, or 0.93. The value 7% below D is therefore 0.93D. To find the value that is 7% above D, we must calculate a *percent increase*, so we use the percent value, 100% + 7% = 107%, or 1.07. The value 7% above D is therefore 1.07D. Since we know that the value of H is between these two values, we have the inequality, $0.93D \leq H \leq 1.07D$. This conclusion, though correct, does not match any of the answer choices. Notice, however, that if we subtract D from all three parts of our inequality, we have, $0.93D - D \leq H - D \leq 1.07D - D$, which simplifies to, $-0.07D \leq H - D \leq 0.07D$. **The correct answer is (C).**

26. Because we are given no specific information about the exact dimensions of either Xavier's or Mahlia's jars, we may assume it is safe to simply assign dimensions to one person's jars. Since Mahlia's jars are compared to Xavier's jars in the problem, we will begin by assigning dimensions to Xavier's jars. Let's suppose Xavier's jars have a radius of 6 units and a height of 10 units. The radius of Mahlia's jars is half the radius of Xavier's jars, so her jars have a radius of 6 ÷ 2 = 3 units. Mahlia's jars are 5 times as tall as Xavier's jars, so her jars have a height of 5(10) = 50 units. We will now use the formula for the volume of a right cylinder provided in the test instructions to calculate the volume of one of Xavier's jars and one of Mahlia's jars.

SAMPLE TEST 5
Answer Explanations

$$\text{Xavier's jar}: \quad V = \pi r^2 h = \pi(6)^2(10) = 360\pi \text{ cubic units}$$

$$\text{Mahlia's jar}: \quad V = \pi r^2 h = \pi(3)^2(50) = 450\pi \text{ cubic units}$$

If 12 of Xavier's jars are full of brewed tea, the total volume of brewed tea is $12(360\pi) = 4{,}320\pi$ cubic units. To find the number of Mahlia's jars required to hold this much tea, divide $4{,}320\pi$ by 450π. $4{,}320\pi \div 450\pi = 4{,}320 \div 450 = 9.6$. The tea will completely fill 9 of Mahlia's jars, and part of a 10th jar, so at least 10 jars are required. **The correct answer is (C).**

27. Starting with the equation, $a + b = 0$, we subtract b from both sides to get, $a = -b$. Using this result, we may rewrite the coordinates of the given points as $(a, -3)$ and $(-4, a)$. The slope between these two points is given by the slope formula.

$$slope = \frac{y_2 - y_1}{x_2 - x_1} = \frac{a - (-3)}{-4 - a} = \frac{a + 3}{-4 - a}$$

Now, beginning with the inequality, $-2 \leq a \leq 2$, add 3 to all three parts to obtain, $1 \leq a + 3 \leq 5$. We therefore know the numerator of the slope expression is *positive*. Returning to the inequality, $-2 \leq a \leq 2$, multiply all three parts by -1, which reverses the inequalities, yielding, $2 \geq -a \geq -2$. Subtract 4 from all three parts to get, $-2 \geq -4-a \geq -6$. Hence, the denominator of the slope expression is *negative*. Because the slope is of the form, *negative ÷ positive*, it must be negative. **The correct answer is (A).**

28. The information given in this problem is presented in a (deliberately) confusing manner. We have to sort our way through it step by step. First, we must realize that because **P** and **Q** are endpoints of a diameter of the circle, the arc **PMQ** must measure 180°, regardless of where **M** lies on the circle. Since point **N** divides this arc into two equal arcs, each of the smaller arcs must measure 90°. Hence, arc **PN** and ∠**PCN** must both measure 90°. In the end, we have determined that the sector described represents 90 / 360, or 1 / 4 of the area of the circle. Using the formula for the area of a circle given in the test instructions, we may now set up and solve an equation.

$$\frac{1}{4}\pi r^2 = 16\pi \qquad \text{multiply both sides by 4 to get}$$

$$\pi r^2 = 64\pi \qquad \text{divide both sides by } \pi \text{ to get}$$

$$r^2 = 64$$

Taking the positive square root of both sides, we arrive at the result, $r = 8$. Therefore, the radius of the circle is 8 meters. **The correct answer is (B).**

29. If n is 35% *less than* the quantity $a + 2b$, n must equal 100% – 35% = 65% *of* the quantity $a + 2b$. That is, $n = 0.65(a + 2b)$. Substitute this expression for n in the given equation to get, $a + 2b - 2((0.65)(a + 2b)) = -18$, or $(a + 2b) - 1.3(a + 2b) = -18$. We have added the parentheses around the first two terms to emphasize that the "chunk" $a + 2b$ appears multiple times in the equation. Let x represent this "chunk." We can then rewrite the equation as, $x - 1.3x = -18$, or $-0.3x = -18$. Dividing both sides by -0.3, we obtain the result, $x = 60$. Since x

eggheadprep.com

represents the quantity $a + 2b$, we now know that $a + 2b = 60$. Therefore, $n = 0.65(60) = 39$. **The correct answer is (B).**

30. We must first notice that the dimensions of the mural are given in *feet*, while the sections the students examined had an area of 1 square *yard*. We therefore begin by converting the dimensions of the mural to yards. Since 3 feet = 1 yard, 45 feet = 45 ÷ 3 = 9 yards, and 21 feet = 21 ÷ 3 = 7 yards. We will use the dimensions 9 yards by 7 yards as the dimensions of the mural for the remainder of the problem. The area of the mural is thus 9 × 7 = 63 square yards. By counting rows in the table, it is easy to determine that there were 9 student volunteers who counted faces in sections of the mural. They counted a total of $17 + 12 + 20 + 15 + 16 + 13 + 18 + 14 + 18 = 143$ faces. Since each section studied by a student measured 1 square yard in area, they studied a total of 9 square yards of the mural. We may now produce an estimate for the total number of faces shown in the mural by setting up a proportion and solving it by cross multiplication.

$$\frac{143}{9} = \frac{x}{63} \Rightarrow 143(63) = 9x \Rightarrow 9,009 = 9x \Rightarrow 1,001 = x$$

Only answer choice (C) is close to our estimate. **The correct answer is (C).**

---

31. Setting the first two factors equal to zero, we obtain the equations $x - 2.5 = 0$, which yields the value $x = 2.5$, and $x - 4.2 = 0$, which yields the value $x = 4.2$. Therefore, we know that the function has x-intercepts with x-coordinates 2.5 and 4.2. If the function has *exactly* two x-intercepts, then the remaining factor, $(x - k)$, cannot yield any new x-intercepts. In other words, it must match one of the first two factors. Therefore, k must equal either 2.5 or 4.2. **The correct answer is 2.5 or 4.2 or 5 / 2 or 21 / 5.**

32. Let J equal the number of shells Jordan collected, and C equal the number of shells Campbell collected. The second sentence of the problem tells us that $J + C = 228$. The information in the third sentence of the problem may be expressed as the equation, $C = J + 46$. Substituting the expression for C from this equation into the first equation gives us, $J + (J + 46) = 228$, or $2J + 46 = 228$. Subtracting 46 from both sides yields, $2J = 182$. Dividing both sides by 2 gives us the result, $J = 91$. Jordan collected 91 shells. **The correct answer is 91.**

33. The volume of the cube is $15(15)(15) = 15^3 = 3,375$ cubic cm. Notice now that 20 cm is NOT the height of the pyramid. The height must be measured perpendicular to the base of the pyramid. Therefore, the height of the pyramid is 17 cm. We calculate the volume of the pyramid using the formula provided in the test instructions.

$$V = \frac{1}{3}Lwh = \frac{1}{3}15(15)(17) = 5(15)(17) = 75(17) = 1,275 \text{ cubic cm}$$

Therefore, the volume of the solid is $3,375 + 1,275 = 4,650$ cubic cm. **The correct answer is 4650. (Remember that you should not type in the comma when entering your answer.)**

SAMPLE TEST 5
Answer Explanations

34. Note that 30 minutes is a half hour. Therefore, if an average of 29 dancers drop out every 30 minutes, and average of 2(29) = 58 dancers drop out every hour. The *rate of change*, or slope, of the function representing the number of dancers still in the marathon at any given time is therefore –58, since the number of dancers is *decreasing*. The initial value for the number of dancers—that is, the number of dancers at the start of the marathon—is 447. Basing our work on the equation $y = mx + b$, then, we can model this situation with the equation, $y = -58x + 447$, where x equals the number of hours and y equals the number of dancers remaining. The condition "fewer than 50 dancers remaining" may therefore be represented by the inequality, $y < 50$, which is equivalent to, $-58x + 447 < 50$. Subtracting 447 from both sides yields, $-58x < -397$. Dividing both sides by –58, which reverses the inequality, gives us the result, $x > 6.844...$ hours. Rounded to the nearest whole number, the result is 7 hours. **The correct answer is 7.**

35. The graph indicates that 38 weeks after the start of the experiment, Karla spent 40 minutes per week completing chores assigned to Maggie. The graph also shows that 14 weeks after the start of the experiment, Karla spent 140 minutes per week completing chores assigned to Maggie. The requested fraction is therefore $\frac{40}{140} = \frac{4}{14} = \frac{2}{7}$. **The correct answer is 2 / 7.** (NOTE: This problem specifically asks for a *fraction*, so a decimal answer would not be accepted as correct.)

36. We begin by finding the intersection point of the two lines, $y = 250x - 4000$ and $y = 8000 - 70x$. This task may be accomplished by setting the two expressions for y equal to each other: $250x - 4000 = 8000 - 70x$. Adding 4000 to both sides yields, $250x = 12000 - 70x$. Adding $70x$ to both sides gives us, $320x = 12000$. Dividing both sides by 320, we obtain the result, $x = 37.5$. This value of x must be the "boundary value" of the solution set (also called a *vertex* of the *feasible region*). In other words, it is either the minimum or maximum possible value of x for all points in the solution set. Proving that it is, in fact, the *maximum x*-value in the solution set takes a considerable amount of time. But since the question would be unanswerable if 37.5 were the minimum *x*-value, it is completely logical to conclude that the desired largest possible value of the *x*-coordinate a is indeed 37.5. **The correct answer is 37.5 or 75 / 2.**

37. First note that if the computer *loses* $\frac{1}{5}$ of its value every 18 months, it *retains* $\frac{4}{5}$ of its value over that same time period. We can therefore model this situation with an exponential function of the form, $y = ab^x$, where a is the *initial value* of the computer, $2300, and the decay factor, b, is $\frac{4}{5}$. Our equation is, $y = (2300)\left(\frac{4}{5}\right)^N$, where N is the number of 18-month periods. Using the fact that 1 year = 12 months, we calculate that 11 years is 11(12) = 132 months. Therefore, 11 years equates to 132 ÷ 18 = $\frac{22}{3}$ eighteen-month periods. Hence, the value of the computer after 11 years is, $y = (2300)\left(\frac{4}{5}\right)^{\frac{22}{3}} \approx \$447.77$. This results shows that the value of the computer will *decrease* by

eggheadprep.com

$2300 − $447.77 = $1852.23 in 11 years. Rounding to the nearest whole dollar and ignoring the $ sign as instructed, we arrive at an answer of 1,852. **The correct answer is 1852.**

38. The function will be undefined if its denominator equals zero. We must therefore solve the equation, $(x-2)^2 - 16 = 0$. Adding 16 to both sides gives us, $(x-2)^2 = 16$. Taking positive and negative square roots of both sides yields, $x - 2 = \pm 4$. We next separately solve the two equations, $x - 2 = 4$ and $x - 2 = -4$. Adding 2 to both sides of both equations, we find the solutions $x = 6$ and $x = -2$. Since we are instructed to give a *positive* value of x, **the correct answer is 6.**

SCORING CONVERSION
RAW TO SCALED SCORE CONVERSION CHARTS

Sample Test 5:

A. SECTION 1: Conversion Chart for Reading Test:

RAW SCORE (# of correct answers)	READING TEST SCORE		RAW SCORE (# of correct answers)	READING TEST SCORE
0	10		27	26
1	10		28	26
2	10		29	27
3	11		30	28
4	12		31	28
5	13		32	29
6	14		33	29
7	15		34	30
8	15		35	30
9	16		36	31
10	17		37	31
11	18		38	32
12	18		39	32
13	19		40	33
14	19		41	33
15	20		42	34
16	21		43	34
17	21		44	35
18	22		45	36
19	22		46	36
20	23		47	37
21	23		48	38
22	23		49	38
23	24		50	39
24	24		51	40
25	25		52	40
26	25			

eggheadprep.com

B. SECTION 2: Conversion Chart for Writing and Language Test

RAW SCORE (# of correct answers)	WRITING AND LANGUAGE TEST SCORE		RAW SCORE (# of correct answers)	WRITING AND LANGUAGE TEST SCORE
0	10		23	26
1	10		24	26
2	10		25	27
3	11		26	27
4	12		27	28
5	13		28	28
6	14		29	29
7	14		30	30
8	15		31	30
9	16		32	31
10	17		33	32
11	17		34	32
12	18		35	33
13	19		36	33
14	19		37	34
15	20		38	35
16	21		39	35
17	22		40	36
18	22		41	37
19	23		42	38
20	24		43	39
21	24		44	40
22	25			

C. Evidence-Based Reading and Writing Section Score

To calculate the Evidence-Based Reading and Writing Section Score, add the Reading Test Score (10 – 40) to the Writing and Language Test Score (10 – 40), and then multiply that total by 10.

For example, if the Reading Test Score is 27 and the Writing and Language Test Score is 34, then the Evidence-Based Reading and Writing Section Score is,

$$27 + 34 = 61 \times 10 = 610.$$

SAMPLE TEST 5
Scoring Conversion

D. Sections 3 and 4: Math Test Score

The raw scores from Section 3 (Math—No Calculator) and Section 4 (Math—Calculator) should be added together to create the Math Raw Score. For example, if there were 18 correct answers in Section 3 (Math—No Calculator) and 24 in Section 4 (Math—Calculator), the Math Raw Score would be 18 + 24 = 42.

MATH RAW SCORE (Total # of correct answers, Sections 3 and 4 combined)	MATH SECTION SCORE		MATH RAW SCORE (Total # of correct answers, Sections 3 and 4 combined)	MATH SECTION SCORE
0	200		30	560
1	200		31	570
2	210		32	580
3	230		33	580
4	250		34	590
5	270		35	600
6	290		36	610
7	300		37	620
8	320		38	630
9	330		39	630
10	340		40	640
11	360		41	650
12	370		42	660
13	380		43	670
14	390		44	680
15	410		45	680
16	420		46	690
17	430		47	700
18	440		48	700
19	450		49	710
20	460		50	720
21	470		51	730
22	480		52	740
23	490		53	750
24	500		54	760
25	510		55	770
26	520		56	780
27	530		57	790
28	540		58	800
29	550			

eggheadprep.com

Preparing for Your ROAD TO College

Your Road to College: We'll Help You Map It Out!

Including...

► *Welcome to Our Guidance Center for College-Bound Students.*

► *What You'll Find Here: Answers, Information, and an Express Lane to the Experts*

► *Guide to Our Resource Pages*

Welcome to Our Guidance Center for College-Bound Students.

Every student's road to obtaining that beautiful document known as a college diploma is unique. Depending on your background, you may know a lot of people who have traveled such a road, or very few. But no matter what, you undoubtedly have many, many questions about how to chart a course from where you are now to your final pass through those campus gates, degree in hand. Whether you feel like you have nowhere to turn for answers, or have such a confusing barrage of contradictory answers raining down on you that you can't make sense of it all, we're here to help. We can't draw the whole map for you, but we can help you identify the most important landmarks along the way.

What You'll Find Here: Answers, Information, and an Express Lane to the Experts

In the following resource pages, we tackle some of the big questions almost every college-bound student ponders: *Where do I begin? What are college admissions officers looking for in a student? Which classes should I take in high school? How can I obtain financial assistance to pay for college?* We also take a look at some of the trending issues in college preparation, including the growing popularity of a "gap year" between high school and college.

We do not claim to have an answer to every question you may have, of course, but we do provide detailed, unbiased information that will, at the very least, help you formulate your questions as clearly as possible. That in itself is an enormous step toward connecting the dots to form a pathway. The more clearly you can express your concerns or describe the information you need, the more likely you will be to find signposts that guide you forward, rather than endless arrows that keep you traveling in circles.

Perhaps most importantly, every resource and link we provide for further information will take you to *highly respected, noncommercial, reliable guidance.* Nothing is more frustrating than trying to find objective guidance and receiving a sales pitch instead. Almost certainly, you have endured the frustration of searching the internet for college preparation advice, only to land on dozens of sites that are little more than cluttered messes of advertisements and links that lead you nowhere. It all adds up to a long, exasperating detour along your journey. We have thoroughly researched every resource to which we direct you to be certain it is a legitimate source of helpful, unbiased information. If your road to college has started to seem likely a giant, sprawling traffic jam, consider our resources your express lanes to the experts, to help you get moving again.

Preparing for Your Road to College

Guide to Our Resource Pages

Here is quick summary of our informational pages and what you can expect to find on each of them:

- **Resources for the College-Bound Student** If you are at the "Where do I begin?" stage of your process, this is the chapter for you. Here you will find great advice on utilizing the many resources within your school and community that you may not even realize are there and direction to some of the most trusted sources of information on preparation for college.

- **Preparing for College:** *Which Courses Should I Take?* As the title suggests, this chapter summarizes the high school classes that make up a standard college preparation curriculum. It will also help you discover how to merge what you "should" do with what you want to do, so that preparing for college becomes an opportunity rather than an obligation.

- **College Admissions Expectations:** *What Do They Want from Me?* Organized by school ranking and tier. No stage of your life, not even preparing for college, should ever be wholly driven by the question of what others expect from you. But all college-bound students should educate themselves about what college admissions officers are looking for when they review a student's application.

- **Financial Assistance for the College-Bound Student:** *It Costs HOW Much?!* For the majority of students with their eyes on the college diploma prize, no other issue is as daunting as the question of how to pay for college without spending a lifetime drowning in debt. We wish we had a magic wand to make college cost worries disappear. Sadly, we do not, but we can offer you the best possible information on how to explore every available option to obtain the assistance you need.

- **Preparing for the Gap Year** An interesting trend in the world of college preparation is the growing popularity of "gap" years. This page introduces you to the idea and describes some of the most common types of gap years in detail.

Resources for the COLLEGE-BOUND Student

Including...

▶ *Guidance office tips.*

▶ *How to research schools that interest you*

▶ *First-generation college student guidance*

▶ *Financial aid resources*

During the ancient period known as the second half of the twentieth century, just about every high school guidance office and public library in America had a copy of *Lovejoy's College Guide*, a massive book with information on the academic programs, tuition fees, and admission standards of almost every US college and university. Many college-bound students began and ended their research with that single book.

Today, you can hardly wave your finger at a touch screen without encountering a dozen cluttered and confusing "college prep" websites. There is no shortage of information available, but sifting through it to find what you need can be a daunting, even disheartening task.

We have included several additional chapters to address key issues every student preparing for college should consider, from financial aid to "gap year" possibilities. Each of these chapters will point you in the direction of some of the more reliable, user-friendly, and unbiased sources of information available on the web.

First, we will focus primarily on some of the best ways to utilize both key national resources and those available to you within your school and community.

Start at the Guidance Office ... and Possibly Leave Quickly

Almost every high school has a guidance office staffed by counselors tasked with helping students chart a course toward the college experiences of their dreams. Every college-bound student should make at least one appointment to speak with a school guidance counselor. You may find that you have the great fortune of attending a high school with dedicated, in-the-know counselors whose workload is kept reasonable enough that they actually have time to listen to your personal story and zero in on the best steps for you to take. If that is the case, then by all means, make regular visits to the guidance office throughout your college application and selection process. Then again, you may find, as I once did, that your designated guidance counselor is incapable of remembering your name for more than two minutes at a time. In that case, you should feel no guilt about beating a hasty retreat.

But on your way out to the door, take a look around the office. Even many understaffed, overloaded high school guidance offices have some very informative brochures about the college application process, strategies for securing the maximum possible amount of financial assistance, practice drills to help you hone your application essay crafting skills, and more. Some have dedicated computers available, set up to take you directly to only the most helpful college information websites, while steering you clear of all the clutter.

Resources for the College-Bound Student

Nearby Colleges and Universities

If you live within a short drive of a college or university, even if it is not a school you are considering attending, spend some time on the campus. Walk around and soak up the feeling of the place. Browse through the bookstore, grab a snack at the student union, and ask permission to see some parts of the library. (Most colleges have library sections that are off limits to non-students. Be respectful of any such rules!) If you are the outgoing type, strike up a few conversations with students and ask what they like and dislike about the school. Did you know that if you make appropriate arrangements with the school admission office and/or the relevant academic department, you might actually be allowed to sit in on some classes? It is absolutely true!

Spending time on a college campus, *any* college campus, is an excellent way to start identifying the characteristics of a postsecondary institution that appeal most, and matter most, to you personally. Even if your dream is to attend a school over a thousand miles away, do not underestimate the value of the resource just down the road.

Reliable News Sources for Information

There are three media outlets that have longstanding reputations for providing objective, accurate information about specific US colleges and about the college application process in general. A quick search of the websites of the New York *Times* (www.nytimes.com), the Washington *Post* (www.washingtonpost.com), and *U.S. News & World Report* (www.usnews.com) will turn up dozens of helpful articles on college rankings, admissions standards, helpful hints for college-bound students and their parents, and much more.

Key Resources for First-Generation College Students

Perhaps you are on the brink of becoming the first person in your family's history to attend college. If so, know that you are one of the most important applicants for the next collegiate academic year! Finding the information you need to prepare for yourself for college, however, can be extremely challenging if you don't have parents, siblings, or other relatives who have been through the process before. A very helpful website, titled, KnowHow2Go (knowhow2go.acenet.edu), is dedicated to helping students just like you, with great resources like workbooks on college preparation that you and your parent or guardian can complete together.

Financial Aid Resources

As you will see below, our website has a resource page dedicated to financial aid. Since financial support is such a critical issue for so many students with collegiate dreams, we want to also give you the option of jumping straight from this page to a couple of the most important national websites for students in need of financial aid. The first is a government website where you can download, read, and fill out the FAFSA (fafsa.ed.gov), or Free Application for Federal Student Aid, which the vast majority of American colleges and universities use as the basis for creating financial aid packages. If you need financial assistance, sooner or later, you will need to complete the FAFSA. No time like the present.

The National Association for College Admission Counseling (NACAC - www.nacacnet.org) provides comprehensive information on the cost of attending college and the vast, often confusing, array of scholarships and grants available for students in need of assistance.

Preparing for COLLEGE:
Which Courses Should I Take?

Including...

- *The Basics: Which Courses Will College Admissions Officers Expect to See on a High School Transcript?*

- *Humanities Classes for the College-Bound Student*

- *Mathematics Classes for the College-Bound Student*

- *Science Classes for the College-Bound Student*

- *Seek Additional Advice on Course Selections*

- *To STEM or Not to STEM, Or Is That Even the Question?*

- *What If I Cannot Complete All the Recommended Courses?*

Each stage of your educational journey, like every stage of your life generally, has value of its own. Preparation for college is just one of many benefits to be derived from a well-rounded high school education. To view secondary school solely as a four-year process of assembling the materials that make up an impressive college application would be to miss a great deal. Nevertheless, if college is your destination, it is critically important to make your high school course selections with that goal in mind.

The Basics: Which Courses Will College Admissions Officers Expect to See on a High School Transcript?

Colleges and universities vary widely in their admissions standards, so there is no one-size-fits-all answer to this question. Make sure to visit our page on **College Admissions Expectations by School Ranking and Tier** for some helpful hints on what the particular schools you are researching may be looking for in applicants. You may also wish to contact the admissions departments of schools that interest you to learn of any specific prerequisite courses they expect high school students to complete in preparation for particular majors.

Varying standards notwithstanding, there are certain courses that almost every North American college or university will expect to see on your high school transcript. A list of those courses follows.

Humanities Classes for the College-Bound Student

Make sure your high school classes include

- a year of US or American history.
- a year of European history or a semester each of European and world history.
- at least a semester (preferably a year) of social studies courses, which may include topics such as psychology, sociology, religious studies, and anthropology.
- at least one semester-long American literature course designed for college prep students.
- at least one semester-long course designed for college prep students that focuses on European or world literature (preferably one of each).
- at least one course or an equivalent amount of instruction focusing on writing technique. Your school may incorporate writing instruction into literature, history, and social studies classes, or offer a separate course on expository writing, generally with a title along the lines of "English Composition."
- at least one course with a focus on the humanities beyond literature and history—topics may include art history, philosophy, etc. Many high schools incorporate such instruction into English and history classes, but some schools offer separate courses with the specific word "Humanities" in the title.

PREPARING FOR COLLEGE
Which Courses Should I Take?

 ## *Mathematics Classes for the College-Bound Student*

At a minimum, your high school mathematics instruction should include

- two complete years of algebra, generally titled either Algebra I and Algebra II or Algebra and Advanced Algebra. If you take courses titled Algebra 1A and Algebra 1B, colleges will view that combination of two courses as **one** year of algebra.
- a full-year geometry course.
- at least six weeks of instruction in probability and statistics. Many schools will incorporate probability and statistics into their algebra or precalculus courses, but others offer a separate, usually elective, course titled Statistics.

NOTE: If your high school has an "integrated" mathematics curriculum, courses will not have titles like "Algebra" and "Geometry." More likely, course options will just have non-descriptive titles such as Mathematics 1, Mathematics 2, etc. Generally, completion of Mathematics 3 within such a curriculum would equate to completing the courses listed above. Make sure to check with your math teachers and the head of your school's math department, however.

As noted, the above list of courses represents the minimum level of mathematics experience colleges expect from applicants. Ideally, your high school mathematics transcript should also include

- a trimester or semester of study of trigonometry. Most schools include trigonometry in a precalculus course. Some include it in Algebra II / Advanced Algebra, while others offer a separate, semester- or trimester-long class simply titled, Trigonometry.
- a precalculus course (sometimes titled, Analysis).
- more extensive study in probability and statistics, preferably the equivalent of at least a full semester. Again, at most high schools, completion of both Algebra II / Advanced Algebra and a precalculus course will fulfill this requirement.

And of course, if at all possible, it is highly advantageous to complete a year of calculus in high school.

 ## *Science Classes for the College-Bound Student*

Colleges will expect to see, at a minimum, a general science class (sometimes titled, Earth Science, or something similar) and a yearlong biology course on your high school transcript. It is strongly recommended that you also take courses in chemistry and physics.

 ## *Seek Additional Advice on Course Selections*

eggheadprep.com

Depending on how creatively your high school titles courses, you may have difficulty sifting through course offerings to find the classes that best match the lists above. If so, do not be shy about speaking to your guidance counselor and as many other helpful adults as your school and community have to offer. Let them know that you are determined to take courses that will best prepare you to not only gain acceptance to a college but also succeed once you arrive there. For additional pointers, you may wish to pay a visit to KnowHow2Go, which offers a host of helpful tips on choosing classes and charting your path toward college.

To STEM or Not to STEM, Or Is That Even the Question?

If you've been researching preparation for college, you've almost certainly heard talk or seen articles about STEM, which stands for Science, Technology, Engineering, and Mathematics. Many organizations are advocating for a shift toward STEM as the focus of *all* education for US students. Just as many are pushing back, arguing that a traditional curriculum, centered on a well-rounded survey of all the arts and sciences, best prepares students for success in college and beyond.

Rather than trying to answer the "To STEM or not to STEM" question, it is perhaps best to examine how that question came to the forefront of debates about higher education in America. The reality is that many American high school students receive inadequate training in mathematics and the sciences, but the cause of the problem is not that students take an excess of courses in the humanities. Rather, the core issue is that students too often choose not to complete the foundational courses in mathematics and the sciences listed above (sometimes, sadly, acting on the advice of adults who should be looking out for their best interests), opting instead for less demanding courses that do not prepare them for higher-level learning.

If you complete all the classes listed above, including the upper-level math courses and chemistry and physics, you will have gained a very well-rounded and useful high school education, equally valued by advocates of a STEM-centered curriculum and proponents of a more traditional arts and sciences curriculum. Now that's a win-win!

For more information on the courses that constitute the STEM curriculum, visit the website of the National Education Association. For the "other side of the story," learn about Phi Beta Kappa, a prestigious academic honor society devoted to the arts and sciences curriculum. (You may be interested to know that the people who created most of the content on this website, including the practice tests, are Phi Beta Kappa members.)

What If I Cannot Complete All the Recommended Courses?

You may find yourself nicely on track to graduate from high school, but unable to take all the courses recommended here between now and graduation day due to scheduling limitations. If your transcript lacks only one or two of the above-listed courses, especially in the humanities, there is probably no great cause for concern. If, however, you see some significant holes on your transcript, you may wish to consider a "gap" year, which is an extra year of preparation for college that some students undertake after graduating from high school. For more information, read "Preparing for the Gap Year" (page 531).

College Admissions EXPECTATIONS:
What Do They Want from Me?

---

by School Ranking and Tier

Including...

- ▶ *Tiers and Rankings: What They Mean and What They Don't*
- ▶ *Admission Expectations for Tier One, Tier Two, and Tier Three Schools*
- ▶ *How Test Scores and Teacher Recommendations Fit In*
- ▶ *Research Tips and Resources*

Two central questions should drive every student's search for the right college:
- What am I looking for in a college or university?
- What are the schools that interest me looking for in students?

The first question is of course highly personal and we wouldn't presume to try to answer it for you. We can, however, provide some insights about the second question.

Tiers and Rankings: What They Mean and What They Don't

Each year, hundreds of lists appear ranking US colleges and universities. Many such lists are scarcely worth the pixels they are "printed" on, representing little more than the opinions of a bored, underpaid writer. For decades, the annual college rankings published by *U.S. News & World Report* have been considered the gold standard among surveys of excellence in higher education. Visit https://www.usnewsuniversitydirectory.com/us-news-rankings/best-colleges/national-universities to see the *U.S. News* list for the current year.

There are marked differences between the schools that consistently top the rankings and those that hover around the middle of the pack, differences in the credentials of admitted students, in the rate of on-time graduation among students who enroll, and in the number of honors accumulated by students and alumni on a yearly basis. It is therefore very helpful that the *U.S. News* list divides schools into three tiers. The big differences exist between the tiers.

Within each tier, differences between schools are minor, and the rankings can even be quite misleading. Keep in mind that the survey team determines the ranking of a school by averaging statistics gathered from all academic departments. For some majors, the university ranked #21 may well be the more prestigious institution than the one sitting at #8. The ranking of the school you attend will fluctuate throughout your time there, and you will never notice the difference. In short, focus much more on the tiers than on individual rankings.

What the rankings and tiers absolutely **DO NOT** indicate is whether students who attend the various schools will succeed in life. Yes, the top-ranked colleges have special attributes. But you would be amazed how many great American geniuses have attended schools you can't find anywhere in Tier 1 or Tier 2 of the rankings. Finding the right school for *you* is far, far more important than attending a college that has a small number next to its name on an internet list.

Some General Notes on Admissions Expectations Based on Tier

What follows is a summary of some of the known information about accepted students at schools ranked in Tier 1, Tier 2, and Tier 3. Bear in mind that these number represent *averages*. College admissions officers know what they are doing. If an applicant possesses rare talents and an obvious drive to succeed but performs poorly on standardized tests, he or she will be *more* likely to be accepted than one who has great test scores but doesn't otherwise stand out from the pack.

 ### *Tier One: What It Means to Be Elite*

Representatives of colleges and universities that consistently land in the top tier of the rankings will tell you that the defining word in their admissions process is *elite*. They want students who embody that word.

If you have your sights set on acceptance to a top tier institution, make sure that any time you have a choice between two courses in high school, you take the one regarded as more challenging. Do not take easier classes just to boost your grade point average (GPA); admissions officers will see through that trick in an instant. For although you will hear that your GPA is the most important factor in the college admissions process, experts will tell you that **it is your high school transcript as a whole that matters most**, with equal importance attached to your grades and the difficulty of the classes you completed. A student who has a GPA of 3.94 because he or she earned a B+ in AP Calculus is far more likely to be viewed as elite by an admissions officer than one who maintained a 4.0 GPA by taking a class called, Something Vaguely Calculus-ish But Not Really Calculus.

The overwhelming majority of students accepted at top-tier colleges rank in the top 10% of their high school classes, but since high schools vary in their methods of ranking students (and some do not rank students at all), that information may not be particularly relevant to your situation.

Students accepted to colleges in the top tier have, on average, test scores well above the 90th percentile, generally 700+ on both major sections of the SAT (Math and Reading/Writing) and over 30 (often 32+) on all sections of the ACT.

Tier Two: Schools That Seek Exceptional Students Who May Not Fit the Tier One Mold

Every school that appears in Tier 2 of the *U.S. News* rankings is a tremendous educational institution with an outstanding reputation. Many of the students who attend these schools have credentials that would qualify them for admission to a top-tier college, but for one reason or another, decided that a school positioned on the second tier better suited their needs. Expect to compete against some of the best when you apply to these colleges. Representatives of schools on this tier will tell you that they seek out students who are *exceptional*.

Ideally, if you are applying to a school on the second tier, you should be ranked in the top quarter (25%) of your high school class (if your school ranks students). Broadly speaking, exceptional students are generally considered to be those in the upper third (top 33%) of their high school classes who have demonstrated a highly level of commitment and accomplishment in other activities in their lives.

You will generally find that students admitted to Tier 2 schools scored 630+ on both major SAT sections (Math and Reading/Writing) and 27+ across the board on the ACT. **<u>It is important to remember, however, that the word "exceptional" contains the word "exception."</u>** Schools ranked on this tier pride themselves on finding students who can make unique contributions to campus intellectual life. Students whose transcripts have a few blemishes or whose test scores fall below expected levels, but who have accomplished extraordinary things, such as composing an orchestral work or building a computer out of scrap parts, have a real chance of catching the eye of an admissions officer at a second tier school.

Tier Three: Good Colleges, Good Students

Admissions officers at colleges ranked in Tier 3 seek *highly qualified* students. The standards upon which these schools base admissions are more flexible than those used by schools positioned on Tier 1 or Tier 2.

That does not mean, however, that you can just waltz into the admission office at one of these colleges and ask when you can expect to start classes. These are still highly respected institutions of higher learning. To be "highly qualified" means that your high school transcript shows courses with moderate and high levels of difficulty, and well above average performance in most of those courses.

Aim for a total SAT score above 1100 and ACT scores that *average* 26+ if you are seeking admission at a third tier institution.

Specific Information for Your Top Choice Schools

Generally, with a bit of savvy internet searching, you can find very detailed statistics for students recently admitted to the colleges that interest you most. Use a separate search phrase for each school, along the lines of, "admissions statistics X University." Avoid trying to do a general search for admissions data for a wide range of schools, which will likely land you on a site with more ads than information.

So, It's All About Test Scores, Right?

What Do They Want from Me?

If you've been reading this page carefully so far, you know that the answer to this question is **absolutely, positively, NO**. It is of course to your advantage to garner the highest scores you can on the SAT and ACT. Doing so can only help your chances of being accepted by the schools that interest you most. But in spite of all the hype about standardized tests, it remains true that *all* of the best schools consider test scores to be a secondary consideration, ranking well behind your transcript and teacher recommendations (see below) in importance. Some colleges do not even require applicants to submit test scores.

This is not an issue of educational philosophy or of the personal priorities of admissions officers. The reality is, the single greatest predictor of a student's success (or lack thereof) in college is, and always has been, his or her high school transcript.

In short, DO practice for the SAT and take reasonable steps to improve your performance on the test. **DO NOT under any circumstances prioritize standardized test preparation above your classwork.**

Teacher Recommendations

Okay, so let's say you have a "killer" high school transcript, with a top 3% GPA and a course list that includes almost all of your high school's toughest offerings, and elite SAT scores to boot. The first question an admissions officer will ask is, "Did you achieve these things by putting forth consistent, exceptional effort, or have you just coasted along on natural ability?" Given a choice between two students with the same credentials, an admissions pro will *always* choose the one with a clearer history of hard work. That is why teacher recommendations play such an important role in college admissions.

Choose the teachers who will write your recommendations very carefully. What they say is going to carry a lot of weight. Seek out at least one teacher who has known you for two years or more, because such a teacher can attest that your success is no fluke. Overall, focus on teachers from classes for which you went the extra mile, by writing a paper that the teacher shared with the entire class, by mentoring classmates, or by designing an original experiment. When writing recommendations, teachers are specifically (and rather awkwardly) asked to compare you to other students, so any teacher who has seen you do something unique and memorable is an outstanding choice as a letter writer, even if you didn't consider that teacher one of your favorites.

For Further Reading

The New York *Times* has run a number of excellent articles on the ins-and-outs of college admissions. You may find it very enlightening to search the paper's archives for pieces related to the expectations of a college admission office. One particularly helpful article centers on *Advice College*

Admissions Officers Give Their Own Kids (http://well.blogs.nytimes.com/2016/03/17/advice-college-admissions-officers-give-their-own-kids/?_r=1).

If you have an old-fashioned streak, you might want to pick up an old copy (well, all copies are old, since the book hasn't been around for quite a while) of *Lovejoy's College Guide*. Even though much of the specific information provided in the book will be out of date, many of the general observations about how to best present yourself on a college application still apply today.

Financial Assistance for the College-Bound STUDENT:
It Costs HOW Much?!

Including...

- ▶ *Guidance office tips.*
- ▶ *How to research schools that interest you*
- ▶ *First-generation college student guidance*
- ▶ *Financial aid resources*

If You Are Qualified to Go, You Deserve to Have a Way Get There!

Unless the thought of attending college just occurred to you within the last ten minutes, you are almost certainly (painfully) aware of the tremendous financial sacrifices necessary to attend college in the US. You have perhaps heard horror stories of highly qualified students who never even have a chance to set foot on a college campus due to financial obstacles, or college graduates who will spend their entire adult lives paying off student loan debt. It can be easy to feel like there is simply no hope.

A growing number of educators, university presidents, and public policymakers are realizing that the American higher education system cannot survive without sweeping changes. Change will come, probably painfully slowly. The financial realities of attending college will not always be as daunting as they are today.

Be that as it may, your primary concern, naturally, is not what the situation will be like in the future, but how to work within the circumstances that exist right now. Know, first, that you are not alone. There are more resources and more opportunities to receive financial assistance out there than you may realize. We hope this page will help you sift through all the information available and begin to develop an action plan that ensures you will not be denied the chance to pursue the educational opportunities you have earned.

Getting the Ball Rolling: What FAFSA Is and Why It's Important

If you need financial assistance to attend college—and the vast majority of American students do—you will eventually be required to complete the **FAFSA**, which stands for Free Application for Federal Student Aid. It is available at fafsa.ed.gov. Completing the FAFSA will be your family's first step toward qualifying for scholarships and grants (that is, *free* money for college that you never have to pay back!). In addition, most colleges use the FAFSA as the basis for putting together a financial aid package for every student who needs assistance, even those who do not qualify for federal aid. So by completing the FAFSA, you will take a giant step forward along the road to finding the financial support you need to pursue your college dreams.

Unfortunately, that step may be an uncomfortable one; filling out a FAFSA is not a particularly pleasant experience. Gathering all the necessary paperwork can be time consuming, and sharing your family's private financial information (annual income, assets in savings, current status of any loans, amount of credit card debt, stocks or bonds owned, monthly expenses, etc.) with complete strangers can feel humiliating. Allow plenty of time for the project and allow yourselves to take breaks whenever anxiety and other emotions start to swell to unmanageable levels. Once again, remember above all that you are not alone. All across America, families just like yours are going through the same process.

Financial Assistance for the College-Bound Student

Financial Aid Available Directly from the College You Attend

Some colleges have impressive endowments (essentially, the "nest egg" money that ensures the institution's long-term survival) that allow them to offer comprehensive financial aid packages directly to accepted students. If you are accepted to such a college and submit the FAFSA, you will receive a detailed aid offer within a few weeks after being notified of your acceptance.

Receiving such an offer does not mean that you cannot pursue additional aid from sources such as those listed below. Be advised, however, that most college financial aid offices will reduce the amount of aid you are offered directly from the school if you obtain financial support from other sources. In other words, if your chosen college offers you $29,000 in aid and you later obtain a corporate college scholarship of $7,500, your college will likely reduce your aid package to $21,500. Many students understandably find this practice extremely frustrating because it seems to all but punish those who go the extra mile to secure the funds they need to pursue a college education.

Those students have a point, but there is not a college on Earth that accepts frustration as a form of payment. Throughout the process of seeking financial assistance for college, do your best to keep your emotions in check and approach every issue pragmatically. With regard to the issue of whether it is worth the time and effort to pursue additional financial support if a college has offered you a direct aid package, focus on one simple question: is there a chance that through your efforts, you can secure "free" money (grants and scholarships) as a replacement for loans included in the school's assistance package? If so, then absolutely, the extra effort is more than worth it!

 Public (Government) Resources Available

The US Federal Government has multiple grant and scholarship programs to support college students, including Federal Pell Grants and Federal Supplemental Educational Opportunity Grants (FSEOG). Most US colleges and universities participate in both of these programs, and therefore will include federal government grant money in your direct financial aid package. In other words, if you attend a participating school, you will automatically receive any federal assistance for which you qualify, as long as you have submitted a FAFSA. However, if your chosen school does not participate in the Pell Grant and FSEOG programs, you may be eligible for assistance directly from the US Government. To learn more about federal student aid programs, visit the website of the Federal Student Aid (https://studentaid.ed.gov/sa/types/grants-scholarships) office of the US Department of Education.

Many state governments also offer various forms of financial assistance for college students who (a) are residents of the state and (b) attend college within the state. Scholarships and grants might be awarded to students who display unique academic talents, belong to a particular cultural group, have exceptional financial need, or choose to pursue a particular field of study. If you plan to attend college in your home state, it is well worth your time to research all grant and scholarship programs offered by your state government (try starting at http://www.collegescholarships.org/scholarships/states.htm).

 ## Resources Available from Private Sources

Every year, a great many students miss out on the opportunity to attend their favorite colleges simply because they are unaware of the financial assistance available to them. A number of private organizations, from the Boy Scouts and Girl Scouts of America to presenters of beauty pageants, offer college scholarships for members or participants. Your mother or father may work at one of the many companies and corporations that offer grant money for college tuition for children of employees.

Therefore, every parent of a college-bound student should inquire at his or her workplace about whether the company or organization offers grants or scholarships. And every student should ask the leaders of every club or society to which he or she belongs if any financial assistance is available through the organization. Leave no stone unturned.

Many websites, such as CollegeScholarships.org, provide summary information about the vast array of grants and scholarships available for college students. Be wary of sponsored links on such sites, however. They will sometimes send you along an endless chain of links that take you further and further away from trustworthy sites. Use summary sites to gather information only. Then carefully navigate directly to the websites of any programs for which you may qualify.

 ## Is It Safe to Accept Loans as Financial Aid?

The short answer is, yes, and it's a good thing it is safe, because almost all students who require financial assistance to attend college will need to accept some of that assistance in the form of loans. Take comfort in the fact that most of the creators of this very website received loan assistance to attend college and have paid off those debts and lived to tell about it.

What is unsafe is to accept an amount of debt that you will have no feasible way to pay off in the future. Be thoughtful in your research. If your chosen major will very likely pave the way to a future salary of over $200,000 per year, then almost no amount of college loan debt will harm you in the long run. If you are more likely to earn $55,000 a year at a job you love with all your heart, then be cautious about taking on too much loan debt. Nothing spoils a dream job faster than constantly fearing you won't have enough money to pay your bills.

If your chosen school's financial aid officer waves his or her hand at the idea of accumulating loan debt that will require you to pay $350 per month for 25 years, claiming that it's no big deal, seek a second opinion and a third. There is nothing inherently unsafe about loans. But acting solely on the advice of someone who has a great deal to gain by persuading you to follow one specific course of action can be very unsafe, indeed. Never let yourself believe that there are no other options.

You are not alone. You have worked hard and earned the right to pursue your dreams. Do not doubt that you can find agencies and people who will help you along the path if you don't give up on the search.

Preparing for the
GAP YEAR

Including...

- ▶ *What Is a "Gap" Year and Is It Right for Me?*
- ▶ *That Sounds Like Me!*
- ▶ *Advanced Study: The Academic Gap Year*
- ▶ *Travel and Study Abroad: Bridging the "Gaps" of Culture and Learning*
- ▶ *Internships and Volunteer Work: Hands-On Gap Years*
- ▶ *Design It Yourself: A Gap Year of Your Own Making*
- ▶ *Your Well-Being Matters: Emotional Health Gap Years*
- ▶ *If I Am Considering a Gap Year, Should I Even Apply to Colleges During My Senior Year of High School?*

What is a "Gap" Year and is it Right for Me?

The transition from high school to college represents one of the most dramatic changes in life circumstances that many people ever experience, especially for those who attend college far from home. There is a prevailing assumption in American society that a student who has completed high school and gained admission to an institution of higher learning must be ready for the college experience. But what does it even mean to be ready?

The best answer is, being ready means different things to different people. If you feel that you may not be prepared to make the transition to college life, know, first of all, that your feelings are legitimate and worthy of your and others' attention. Speak with friends and adults you trust and explain your concerns. You may learn that you are simply experiencing the jitters many people feel at the prospect of starting a new chapter in life, in which case, taking the challenge of starting college head on is probably the best thing you can do for yourself. But maybe there is more to it than that. Perhaps you feel a pull toward a non-academic interest that you have never really had a chance to explore. Maybe your studies of other cultures in your high school classes have awakened in you a desire to connect more deeply with the global community you will join as you pursue higher learning. Or perhaps you simply wish to take some additional classes to make up for a few shortcomings on your transcript and better prepare yourself for university-level study.

 ## That Sounds Like Me!

If you found yourself nodding your head in recognition as you read the previous paragraph, you may want to consider a "gap year." As the name suggests, a gap year is a year spent between high school and college pursuing non-academic endeavors or completing courses that do not count toward either a high school diploma or college degree. (That is, it is a year that creates a "gap" between a person's years of high school attendance and his or her years in college.) During a gap year, students explore their interests and address any issues that underlie their feelings of uncertainty about their readiness for the next phase of their educational journeys.

Below, we will look at some common gap year pursuits. You may also find it interesting to read Valerie Strauss's recent Washington Post article about the growing popularity of gap years in the US.

 ## Advanced Study: The Academic Gap Year

One of the most common (and best) reasons for a student to choose a gap year is that he or she either has not had the opportunity to take the high-level courses in math, the humanities, and the sciences that college admissions officers like to see on transcripts, or has not performed as well in such classes as he or she would like. For these students, a gap year is "all business." Nevertheless, many students who pursue academic gap years report that the year is liberating and fun, since they are able to experience classroom learning separated from the social pressures of high school life.

Many private college prep schools, including boarding schools, offer yearlong programs of study specifically created for students pursuing an academic gap year. The cost of attending a private school, even for a single year, is prohibitive for many families, but do not despair. A great many schools offer scholarship programs for gap year students with financial need.

Travel and Study Abroad: Bridging the "Gaps" of Culture and Learning

A great many programs for travel and study abroad exist for gap year students, and the number is growing almost daily. These programs are ideal for students who feel they have lived a "sheltered life," with very few opportunities to interact with people from other cultural, social, or experiential backgrounds.

- wish to advance their master of a foreign language to fluency or near-fluency.
- have found it difficult to grasp the vast cultural differences that exist among peoples of the world simply by reading about them in textbooks.
- have a taste for adventure or wish to significantly improve their independent living skills.

Because gap year abroad programs are abundant, a simple internet search using keywords like, "study abroad gap year" will unleash a veritable avalanche of information. Just be mindful that the majority of websites you find will be run or sponsored by for-profit companies providing gap year abroad experiences. They will indeed be trying to sell you something.

Internships and Volunteer Work: Hands-On Gap Years

If the primary purpose of your gap year is to develop greater maturity and strengthen your self-discipline, a "working" gap year may be the perfect choice for you. Gap year programs in which students are paid to work exist, but naturally, the application process for those opportunities is very competitive. Many unpaid internships do include food and housing, however. Try to find a program that offers at least those benefits. Depleting the family college fund while preparing to go to college wouldn't make a lot of sense.

The variety of work opportunities available to gap year students is dazzling. A good starting point might be a visit to usagapyearfairs.org. USA Gap Years sponsors informational fairs across the US to help students learn about gap year opportunities. Once again, however, bear in mind that many of the

eggheadprep.com

organizations offering the programs advertised on the website and at the fairs are making money by doing so.

Design It Yourself: A Gap Year of Your Own Making

It is important to remember that a gap year is a concept, not a specific program. You don't have to limit your gap year experiences to existing, ready-made opportunities. There may be employers right in your hometown offering paid or unpaid internships in fields that interest you. You may simply want to take some classes at your local community college to get a feel for college-level course expectations. Perhaps you have the opportunity to join a ballet company for a season, or play on a regional, semi-pro baseball team.

Ask yourself these questions. Will the endeavors you are considering for your gap year

- enhance your understanding of other cultures?
- help you to develop specific skills not taught at your high school?
- challenge you to think and act responsibly and independently, with less adult guidance than you are used to receiving?
- support your intellectual growth and thus better prepare you for the challenges of college?

If you answered "yes" even once, then you may be well on your way to a memorable, fulfilling gap year experience that will either help you to make the most of your time at the college you have committed to attend, or make you more attractive to admissions officers when you apply to schools.

Your Well-Being Matters: Emotional Health Gap Years

Attending school is stressful, even for the most naturally gifted, easygoing student. Some students put so much pressure on themselves to perform well in the most challenging courses offered at their high schools, to score in the upper echelons on standardized tests, and to write the best college application essays they can possibly produce, that by the time they are accepted to a school, they are too burned out to celebrate. Long-term anxiety can have devastating effects on a person's physical and emotional well- being. If you find yourself feeling exhausted all the time and struggling to muster enthusiasm for opportunities that once would have put you over the moon with excitement, do not be ashamed. Speak up and let your friends and trusted adults know of your struggles.

A gap year devoted solely to restoring mental and emotional balance can be absolutely transformative. Many students who take a year away from academics after high school to work with a counselor, study meditation techniques, or complete a course of training in stress management and reduction often report that it was the best decision they ever made. You are not a GPA, a transcript, a test score, a diploma, an acceptance letter, or a scholarship offer. You are a person. Never, ever be afraid to treat yourself as such.

If I Am Considering a Gap Year, Should I Even Apply to Colleges During My Senior Year of High School?

Surprisingly, the answer for most students is "YES." Many colleges allow accepted students to defer their admission for one calendar year. Therefore, there is usually no harm in applying to the colleges that interest you. You may even find that once you have been through the application and acceptance processes, you are more eager to jump right into college than you expected. But if not, odds are that you can make an arrangement with your chosen school to begin your studies there one year later. (In other words, if you were accepted for the fall of 2017, you could arrange to enroll in the fall of 2018.) Knowing that the college you have chosen to attend will be ready to greet you with open arms once your gap year is complete can provide you with a great deal of peace of mind.

If, however, you are considering a gap year specifically to shore up your high school transcript by taking upper level classes, then the answer is "NO," do NOT apply to colleges during your senior year. The academic work you do during the gap year will make you a more attractive applicant to all colleges, so it makes all the sense in the world to wait until that year is underway before filling out applications.

For additional information on learning programs designed specifically for students who choose to have a gap year, you may wish to visit the website of the National Association for College Admission Counseling.

eggheadprep.com

www.ingramcontent.com/pod-product-compliance
Lightning Source LLC
Chambersburg PA
CBHW080036100526
44584CB00023BA/3199